Lecture Notes in Computer Science   947

Springer

Berlin
Heidelberg
New York
Barcelona
Budapest
Hong Kong
London
Milan
Paris
Tokyo

Bernhard Möller (Ed.)

Mathematics of Program Construction

Third International Conference, MPC '95
Kloster Irsee, Germany, July 17-21, 1995
Proceedings

 Springer

Series Editors

Gerhard Goos
Universität Karlsruhe
Vincenz-Priessnitz-Straße 3, D-76128 Karlsruhe, Germany

Juris Hartmanis
Department of Computer Science, Cornell University
4130 Upson Hall, Ithaca, NY 14853, USA

Jan van Leeuwen
Department of Computer Science, Utrecht University
Padualaan 14, 3584 CH Utrecht, The Netherlands

Volume Editor

Bernhard Möller
Institut für Mathematik, Universität Augsburg
D-86135 Augsburg, Germany

CIP data applied for

Die Deutsche Bibliothek - CIP-Einheitsaufnahme

Mathematics of program construction : third international
conference ; proceedings / MPC '95, Kloster Irsee, Germany,
July 17 - 21, 1995. Bernhard Möller (ed.). - Berlin ; Heidelberg ;
New York : Springer, 1995
(Lecture notes in computer science ; 947)

ISBN 3-540-60117-1
NE: Möller, Bernhard [Hrsg.]; MPC <3, 1995, Irsee>; Kloster <Irsee>;
GT

CR Subject Classification (1991): D.1-2, F.2-4, G.2

ISBN 3-540-60117-1 Springer-Verlag Berlin Heidelberg New York

© Springer-Verlag Berlin Heidelberg 1995
Printed in Germany

Typesetting: Camera-ready by author
SPIN 10487107   06/3142 – 5 4 3 2 1 0   Printed on acid-free paper

Preface

The general theme of this series of conferences is the use of crisp, clear mathematics in the discovery and design of algorithms and in the development of corresponding software or hardware. The previous two conferences were held in 1989 at Twente, Netherlands, organised by the Rijksuniversiteit Groningen, and in 1992 at Oxford, United Kingdom. The conference theme reflects the growing interest in formal, mathematically based methods for the construction of software and hardware. The goal of the MPC conferences is to report on and significantly advance the state of the art in this area.

The emphasis is on the combination of *conciseness* and *precision* in *calculational techniques* for program construction. Typical areas are:

- formal specification of sequential and concurrent programs;
- constructing implementations to meet specifications;

in particular,

- program transformation;
- program analysis;
- program verification;
- convincing case studies.

The scientific programme for this third conference in the MPC series consisted of five invited lectures by distinguished international researchers and 19 contributed lectures selected by the programme committee out of 58 submissions. They were arranged into sessions with the following titles: Semantics and Verification, Refinement, Particular Calculi, Algebra of Data Structures, Applications, Programs and their Proofs, Verification and Construction of Parallel Programs and Support Systems. Overall, we witnessed significant progress in raising the level of abstraction, in simplifying the support calculi and in the treatment of the notoriously difficult subject of parallel programs.

The conference took place July 17–21, 1995 at Kloster Irsee, a former Baroque monastery located in the Southwest of Bavaria, Germany, close to the Alps. We gratefully acknowledge sponsorship by the Deutsche Forschungsgemeinschaft, the Society of the Friends of the University of Augsburg, Esprit Working Group 8533 NADA — New Hardware Design Methods, IBM Germany, sd&m (software design & management) Munich and Pandasoft Berlin. Finally, I would like to thank the programme committee members for their responsible and timely collaboration, Martin Russling for his assistance in preparing the final manuscript and Andrea Haupeltshofer for her help as Conference Secretary.

Augsburg, July 1995   Bernhard Möller

PROGRAMME COMMITTEE

Table of Contents

Invited Lectures

Contributed Lectures

Functional Algorithm Design

Richard S. Bird

Programming Research Group, Oxford University
Wolfson Building, Parks Road, Oxford, OX1 3QD, UK

Abstract. For an adequate account of a functional approach to Algorithm Design we need to find new translations of classical algorithms and data structures, translations that do not compromise efficiency. For an adequate formal account of a functional approach to the specification and design of algorithms we need to include relations in the underlying theory. These and other points are illustrated in the context of sorting.

1 Introduction

The title of this talk is intended to be slightly ambiguous, suggesting both the design of functional algorithms and also a functional approach to that particular subject – taught in the core curriculum of most undergraduate computing degrees – known generically as 'Algorithm Design'. You know the sort of thing: famous algorithms from the literature of computing science that serve as paradigms for basic design strategies, such as greedy algorithms and dynamic programming, together with clever data structures for various ADTs. A comprehensive treatment is given in the excellent text [5]. I recently gave a course on Algorithm Design to first year students whose only taught programming language was a purely functional one. I found the experience of trying to express old algorithms in functional form both exhilarating and challenging. It was exhilarating because of the amount of ground that could be covered with a functional approach, and challenging because many traditional algorithms needed to be completely rethought in a functional setting.

Some of the conclusions I came to, none of them particularly new, were:

- Unlike other formalisms, functional programming offers a unique opportunity to exploit a compositional approach to Algorithm Design, and to demonstrate the effectiveness of the mathematics of program construction in the presentation of many algorithms;
- But if we remain within a functional formalism, then we need to reformulate standard algorithms, and that involves finding new ways – especially new data structures – to achieve comparable efficiency;
- In order to calculate asymptotic running times, there is often no need to get embroiled in the consequences of a lazy evaluation strategy: where possible it is better to use a bit of judicious manipulation to eliminate the effect lazy evaluation may have on an algorithm;

Towards Automatic Parallelization of Logic Programs

Krzysztof R. Apt[1,2]

[1] CWI, P.O. Box 94079, 1090 GB Amsterdam, The Netherlands
[2] Department of Mathematics and Computer Science
University of Amsterdam, Plantage Muidergracht 24
1018 TV Amsterdam, The Netherlands

Abstract. One of the striking features of logic programs is that they can be easily parallelized. A particularly simple way of turning a logic program into a parallel program was proposed in Naish [Nai82, Nai88], by means of the so-called delay declarations.

The resulting programs exhibit a highly complex behaviour as during their executions dynamic networks of asynchronously communicating processes are created.

In our recent paper Apt and Luitjes [AL95] we studied verification of these programs. In particular, we showed how the methods originally developed for the analysis of Prolog programs can be naturally adapted to prove correctness of logic programs with delay declarations.

Here we discuss a reverse problem: how to parallelize a pure Prolog program by generating the appropriate delay declarations, so that correctness is maintained and deadlock avoided. To this end we identify the crucial properties that the original Prolog program should satisfy and analyze which aspects of the parallelization process and of the correctness proof could be automated.

References

[AL95] K. R. Apt and I. Luitjes. Verification of logic programs with delay declarations. In *Proceedings of the Fourth International Conference on Algebraic Methodology and Software Technology, (AMAST'95)*, Lecture Notes in Computer Science, Berlin, 1995. Springer-Verlag. Invited Lecture. In press.

[Nai82] L. Naish. An Introduction to MU-PROLOG. Technical Report TR 82/2, Dept. of Computer Science, Univ. of Melbourne, 1982.

[Nai88] L. Naish. Parallelizing NU-Prolog. In *Proceedings of the Fifth Annual Symposium on Logic in Computer Science*, pages 1546–1564. The MIT Press, 1988.

- For an adequate account of programming with functions we need to include *relations* in the underlying theory. Moreover, like the embedding of the real line in the complex plane, the extension to relations should be as seamless as possible, without altering the shape and simplicity of its functional subset.

As I said, most of these points have been appreciated long ago, though I continue to see textbooks and theses presenting functional programs as flat sequences of recursion equations with little attention to the structure that compositionality brings. On the second point, new algorithms for old are beginning to emerge. For example, one can cite David King's and John Launchbury's elegant treatment [12] of various graph algorithms, Oege de Moor's characterisation of dynamic programming [19], and a functional approach to pattern matching [2, 10]. But much remains to be done; for instance, I do not know of any effective treatment of the Union-Find problem in a functional setting, a point returned to below. It may be the case, as is suggested in [13], that some classes of algorithm are inherently inefficient in any formalism for programming that lacks updatable state. On the issue of laziness, Phil Wadler in his 1984 thesis "Listlessness is better than laziness"[24] discusses the elimination of lazy evaluation at compile-time (i.e. 'automatic' program manipulation), so that idea is not new either. On the need for relations in program development, many computing scientists ([1, 8, 11, 17, 19, 20], to cite just a few references) came to essentially the same conclusion around 1989, while I was persuaded of it only three years later. Not all of them would give prime importance to the preservation of the functional theory, however.

In the remainder of the talk I would like to amplify some of these points, partly in the hope of persuading colleagues to begin the university education of a computing scientist with the study of functional programming — that is, if their institutions do not do so already. In fact, I believe that such a study could profitably begin earlier, in secondary school; then the mathematics of functions on lists and trees could take its place alongside the mathematics of the trigonometric, logarithmic and exponential functions.

2   On Composition

Consider the following well-known functional version of Hoare's quicksort:

$$qsort\,[\,] = [\,]$$
$$qsort\,(a : x) = qsort\,(filter\,(\le a)\,x) \mathbin{+\!\!+} [a] \mathbin{+\!\!+} qsort\,(filter\,(> a)\,x).$$

It is an academic point (i.e. interesting, even intriguing, but probably not of practical consequence) whether this program can legitimately be called quicksort. After all, the heart of quicksort — the partition phase that burns the candle at both ends — is missing, and there is no notion of an *in situ* algorithm in functional programming. What is more, quicksort is a terrible algorithm in functional form: its expected running time is easily beaten by mergesort, among others, and it contains a space leak.

However, that is not the point at issue here. In most texts on Algorithm Design, sorting is quickly followed, in the same chapter or the following one, with a discussion of selection. The standard expected linear time selection algorithm is introduced by phrases such as "can be modelled on quicksort", or "follows the structure of quicksort". But if we define

$$select\ x\ k = (qsort\ x)!k,$$

where $x!k$ is the kth element of x (counting from 0), then we can calculate:

$$select\ (a : x)\ k$$
$$=\quad \{\text{definition of } select\}$$
$$(qsort\ (a : x))!k$$
$$=\quad \{\text{definition of } qsort,\ \text{writing } y = filter\ (\le a)\ x \text{ and } z = filter\ (> a)\ x\}$$
$$(qsort\ y \mathbin{+\!\!+} [a] \mathbin{+\!\!+} qsort\ z)!k$$
$$=\quad \{\text{since } (u \mathbin{+\!\!+} v)!k = (k < \#u \to u!k \parallel k \ge \#u \to v!(k - \#u))\}$$
$$(k < \#qsort\ y \to (qsort\ y)!k$$
$$\parallel k \ge \#qsort\ y \to ([a] \mathbin{+\!\!+} qsort\ z)!(k - \#qsort\ y))$$
$$=\quad \{\text{since } \#qsort\ y = \#y = n\ (\text{say})\}$$
$$(k < n \to (qsort\ y)!k \parallel k \ge n \to ([a] \mathbin{+\!\!+} qsort\ z)!(k - n))$$
$$=\quad \{\text{second step again and } [a]!0 = a\}$$
$$(k < n \to (qsort\ y)!k \parallel k = n \to a \parallel k > n \to (qsort\ z)!(k - n - 1))$$
$$=\quad \{\text{definition of } select\}$$
$$(k < n \to select\ y\ k \parallel k = n \to a \parallel k > n \to select\ z\ (k - n - 1)),$$

and we have derived the standard algorithm, namely

$$select\ (a : x)\ k = \begin{cases} select\ y\ k, & \text{if } k < n \\ a, & \text{if } k = n \\ select\ z\ (k - n - 1), & \text{if } k > n \\ \text{where } (y, z) = split\ a\ x \text{ and } n = \#y \end{cases}$$
$$split\ a\ x = (filter\ (\le a)\ x, filter\ (> a)\ x).$$

In my experience, this kind of calculation is not beyond the power of any first year student with a high school background in mathematics. It is also a very common one: a new function is expressed as the composition of earlier ones and then massaged to improve efficiency. I believe that teaching this kind of calculation is equally effective, perhaps more so, as teaching formal manipulations in propositional or predicate logic. Studying the ideas of equational reasoning in the setting of functional programming is simple, attractive, and has the not inconsiderable psychological benefit of showing why it is useful: just compare the running times of the two versions of the program.

The second version of *select* does not make use of laziness in any essential way, so it is straightforward to write down a recurrence for estimating its asymptotic worst (average, best) case running time. In the absence of a precise cost model, this analysis is a little crude, but the same criticism holds for algorithms expressed in 'pidgin' Pascal. It is a little more complicated to construct a recurrence relation for the running time of $(qsort\,x)!k$ that takes account of lazy evaluation, so another advantage of the calculation above is that it leads to a program with a more tractable asymptotic analysis. In this context, consider insertion sort:

$$isort\,[\,] = [\,]$$
$$isort\,(a:x) = insert\,(a,\,isort\,x)$$
$$insert\,(a,[\,]) = [a]$$
$$insert\,(a,b:x) = \begin{cases} a:b:x, & \text{if } a \le b \\ b:insert\,(a,x), & \text{otherwise} \end{cases}$$

It is well-known (see e.g. [3]) that under lazy evaluation *isort* turns out not to be sorting by insertion at all, but a version of selection sort. Consequently, defining $min = head \cdot isort$ gives a linear time method for computing the minimum of a list. Plugging in *qsort* instead of *isort* in the definition of *min* gives a quadratic time algorithm as one can easily check. In my view the consequences of a lazy evaluation strategy should be appreciated and understood, but the technique should be exploited only in well-defined situations, and certainly not in the definition of *min*.

Exercise By the way, while on the subject of sorting and selection, here is an attractive programming exercise: the function *merge* merges two ascending sequences into one; given x and y both of positive length n, and assuming that $x!k$ can be evaluated in constant time, find an $O(\log n)$ algorithm for computing $merge\,(x,y)!n$. As a variation, given two infinite sequences x and y compute $merge\,(x,y)!n$ in $O(\log n)$ steps.

3 On datatypes

Both quicksort and insertion sort were presented above as recursion equations, which seems to run contrary to the first point made in the introduction. So, what is the 'compositional' form of quicksort? The answer is tree sort, defined by

$$tsort = flatten \cdot mktree.$$

Here, $mktree : list\,A \to tree\,A$ and $flatten : tree\,A \to list\,A$, where A is the type of elements to be sorted, so trees are used as an intermediate datatype. The type $tree\,A$ is defined by a type equation

$$tree\,A ::= null \mid fork\,(tree\,A,\,A,\,tree\,A).$$

In a similar spirit, the datatype of (cons-) lists can be introduced by

$$list\,A ::= nil \mid cons\,(A,\,list\,A).$$

From now on we will use *nil* as an alternative to [] and *cons* (*a*, *x*) as an alternative to *a* : *x*.

The experienced functional programmer will have realised by now that in these and other definitions already given, some traditionally curried functions have been replaced by non-curried ones. In my view, currying — like lazy evaluation — should only be exploited in those situations that really need it. After all, a function space is a more complicated object than a cartesian product, a point universally appreciated by first year undergraduates as well as category theorists. If I were defining a programming language anew, I would at least make all binary arithmetic operations non-curried.

But, back to treesort. The function *flatten* is defined by

$$flatten\ null = []$$
$$flatten\ (fork\ (x, a, y)) = flatten\ x \mathbin{+\!\!+} [a] \mathbin{+\!\!+} flatten\ y.$$

This recursion is an instance of a fold operation on trees. More precisely, defining

$$foldtree\ (c, f)\ null = c$$
$$foldttree\ (c, f)\ (fork\ (x, a, y)) = f\ (foldtree\ (c, f)\ x, a, foldtree\ (c, f)\ y),$$

we have *flatten* = *foldtree* (*nil*, *join*), where *join* (*x*, *a*, *y*) = $x \mathbin{+\!\!+} [a] \mathbin{+\!\!+} y$. In the same spirit, the fold operator on the datatype of cons-lists is defined by

$$foldlist\ (c, f)\ nil = c$$
$$foldlist\ (c, f)\ (cons\ (a, x)) = f\ (a, foldlist\ (c, f)\ x).$$

In particular, the function *isort* of the previous section is now expressed by *isort* = *foldlist* (*nil*, *insert*). Fold operators are of fundamental importance in functional programming, not least because they provide one disciplined use of recursion, namely a recursive decomposition that follows the structure of the datatype. For this reason, Lambert Meertens called them *catamorphisms*, a term intended to mean "according to form". It was also Meertens (I think) who suggested using so-called "banana" brackets to denote fold operators, in which both *foldtree* (*c*, *f*) and *foldlist* (*c*, *f*) are written ⦇*c*, *f*⦈, the ambiguity being resolved by contextual type information. We will use this notation in what follows.

But, back to treesort. The function *mktree* produces an *ordered* tree *t* in the sense that for any subtree *fork* (*u*, *a*, *v*) of *t*, nodes in *u* have values which are no greater than *a*, and nodes in *v* have values which are no smaller than *a*. One way of defining *mktree* is

$$mktree\ [] = null$$
$$mktree\ (a : x) = fork\ (mktree\ (filter\ (\leq a)\ x), a, mktree\ (filter\ (> a)\ x)).$$

This recursion defines *mktree* as an instance of an unfold operation. The function *unfoldtree* : $B \to tree\ A$ is defined by

$$unfoldtree\ (p, f)\ x =$$
$$\begin{cases} null, & \text{if } p\ x \\ fork\ (unfoldtree\ (p, f)\ y, a, unfoldtree\ (p, f)\ z), & \text{otherwise} \\ \text{where } (y, a, z) = f\ x \end{cases}$$

The arguments to *unfoldtree* have types $p : B \rightarrow Bool$ and $f : B \rightarrow B \times A \times B$. There is a subtle point to make in connection with *unfoldtree* (p, f): in a formalism for functional programming in which elements of datatypes may be infinite, *unfoldtree* (p, f) is a well-defined function, though it may return an infinite tree. Under an interpretation that makes the constructor *fork* strict, the recursion is not well-defined unless f is 'well-founded' in a suitable sense that we will not make precise.

We can now write *mktree* = *unfoldtree* (*isnil*, *unjoin*), where *isnil* $x = (x = nil)$, and

$$unjoin\,(cons\,(a, x)) = (filter\,(\leq a)\,x, a, filter\,(> a)\,x).$$

Like folds, unfolds can be defined for arbitrary datatypes. For example, the operation *unfoldlist* : $B \rightarrow list\,A$ takes arguments $p : B \rightarrow Bool$ and $f : B \rightarrow A \times B$ and is defined by

$$unfoldlist\,(p, f)\,u = \begin{cases} nil, & \text{if } p\,u \\ cons\,(a, unfoldlist\,(p, f)\,v), & \text{otherwise} \\ \text{where } (a, v) = f\,u \end{cases}$$

The same remarks about *unfoldtree* apply here: under a strict interpretation of *cons* the function *unfoldlist* (p, f) will not be total unless f is well-founded.

The unfold operator on a datatype is also given a fancy name: *anamorphism*. We will use Meijer's concave lenses [16] to denote unfold operators, writing $[\![p, f]\!]$ in preference to *unfoldtree* (p, f) or *unfoldlist* (p, f), again leaving type information to disambiguate. We will see the relationship between folds and unfolds in Section 6.

Given these definitions, one can appreciate — and a short calculation of the kind seen earlier will justify — that *qsort* is simply that version of *tsort* in which the intermediate datatype has been eliminated. In fact the calculation is a standard one: any function expressed as the composition of an unfold over a datatype T followed by a fold can be recast as a recursion in which elements of T do not appear. This remark is formalised in Section 6.

4 On new algorithms for old

By changing the definitions of *flatten* and *mktree* one can arrive at a version of heapsort. Define

$$flatten = [\![nil, join]\!]$$
$$join\,(x, a, y) = cons\,(a, merge\,(x, y)),$$

where *merge* merges two sorted lists into one. Also, define

$$mktree = [\![isnil, unjoin]\!],$$

where *isnil* $x = (x = nil)$, and *unjoin* : $list\,A \rightarrow list\,A \times A \times list\,A$ is defined by

$$unjoin\,(cons\,(a, x)) = [\![base\,a, step]\!]\,x$$

$$base\ a = (nil, a, nil)$$

$$step\,(a, (x, b, y)) = \begin{cases} (cons\,(b, y), a, x), \text{ if } a \le b \\ (cons\,(a, y), b, x), \text{ otherwise} \end{cases}$$

The function *unjoin* takes a nonempty list and returns a triple in which the middle value is a minimum element of the list and the outer two values are lists of the remaining elements, chosen to be of as equal length as possible.

With the above definitions, *mktree* generates a balanced tree t that satisfies the condition that for any subtree *fork* (u, a, v) of t, no value in u or v is smaller than a. This is the condition that the tree forms a *min-heap*.

It is probable that J.W.J. Williams, the inventor of heapsort [23], would wince if he heard the above program described as heapsort. Translators of literary texts are allowed some degree of freedom, but the spirit of the original should be preserved, and it is arguable whether or not the two functions above do preserve the spirit of heapsort. For a start, *flatten* is usually expressed as an iterative algorithm, one that repeatedly removes the top element and combines the two subheaps into one until nothing remains. Calling this process *unheap* : *tree A* → *list A*, we have

$$unheap = [\![isnull, remove]\!],$$

where *isnull* $x = (x = null)$ and *remove* $(fork\,(x, a, y)) = (a, combine\,(x, y))$.

We will not spell out the definition of *combine*, except to say that it will satisfy the equation

$$unheap \cdot combine = merge \cdot (unheap \times unheap),$$

where $(f \times g)\,(a, b) = (f\,a, g\,b)$. This equation can be used in a short calculation to show *unheap* = *flatten*, so the two programs coincide.

The second, more telling, point is that *mktree* as defined above builds a heap in $O(n \log n)$ steps, where n is the length of the given list. The textbooks emphasise that one can build a heap in linear time. This is important in a number of applications, for example in Kruskal's algorithm for finding minimum cost spanning trees, where complete sorting may not be required.

So, let's try to translate the standard array-based linear time algorithm into purely functional form. The function *mkheap* : *list A* → *tree A* is defined by

$$mkheap = heapify \cdot mktree,$$

where *mktree* : *list A* → *tree A* builds a tree, not necessarily a heap, and *heapify* : *tree A* → *tree A* turns it into a valid heap. We can define *heapify* as a tree catamorphism. In the following definition, a fictitious element ∞_A is used to represent the largest element of type A; such a device can be avoided but it does make the algorithm simpler:

$$heapify = [\![null, sift]\!]$$

$$sift\,(u, a, v) = \begin{cases} fork\,(u, a, v), & \text{if } a \le min\,(b, c) \\ fork\,(sift\,(move\,(a, u)), b, v), & \text{if } b \le min\,(a, c) \\ fork\,(u, c, sift\,(move\,(a, v))), & \text{if } c \le min\,(a, b) \\ \text{where } b = root\ u \text{ and } c = root\ v \end{cases}$$

The functions *move* and *root* are given by

$$move\,(a, fork\,(x, b, y)) = (x, a, y)$$
$$root\,null = \infty_A$$
$$root\,(fork\,(x, a, y)) = a.$$

The value $min\,(a, b)$ is the smaller of a and b.

It remains to implement the function *mktree*. The standard algorithm takes a list $[a_0, a_1, \ldots]$ and builds a tree with a_0 at the top, a_1, a_2 at the next level, a_3, a_4, a_5, a_6 at the next level, and so on until the list is exhausted. The length of the list at the bottom level will not in general be a power of two. Of course, in the array based algorithm no building actually takes place; the array is just viewed as forming such a tree and everything is done by juggling subscripts.

We can build the tree from bottom to top by constructing a sequence of trees at each level; the trees at the next level higher up are formed by combining trees in pairs with appropriate elements of the list. At the end of this process we are left with a list containing a single tree. To implement the idea we define

$$mktree = head \cdot mktrees \cdot levels.$$

The function $levels : list\,A \to list\,(list\,A)$ applied to $[a_0, a_1, \ldots]$ produces the list

$$[[a_0], [a_1, a_2], [a_3, a_4, a_5, a_6], \ldots]$$

and is defined by an unfold:

$$levels = (\!|\,isrnil, level\,|\!) \cdot start,$$

where $start\,x = (1, x)$, and $isrnil\,(k, x) = (x = nil)$, and

$$level\,(k, x) = (take\,k\,x, (2 \times k, drop\,k\,x))).$$

The curried functions *take k* and *drop k* respectively take and drop the first k elements of a list.

The function $mktrees : list\,(list\,A) \to list\,(tree\,A)$ is defined by

$$mktrees = (\!|\,[null], layer\,|\!),$$

where $layer : list\,A \times list\,(tree\,A) \to list\,(tree\,A)$ is defined by an unfold; applied to the pair $([a_0, a_1, \ldots], [u_0, u_1, \ldots])$ this function produces the list

$$[fork\,(u_0, a_0, u_1), fork\,(u_2, a_1, u_3), \ldots].$$

If the list $[u_0, u_1, \ldots]$ of trees is not long enough, it is filled with a sufficient number of empty trees. The definition of *layer* is:

$$layer = (\!|\,islnil, step\,|\!),$$

where $islnil\,(x, ts) = (x = nil)$ and

$$step\,(cons\,(a, x), nil) = (fork\,(null, a, null), (x, nil))$$
$$step\,(cons\,(a, x), cons\,(u, nil)) = (fork\,(u, a, null), (x, nil))$$
$$step\,(cons\,(a, x), cons\,(u, cons\,(v, ts))) = (fork\,(u, a, v), (x, ts)).$$

This completes the new definition of *mkheap*. It is an instructive exercise, left to the reader, to show that *mkheap* takes linear time.

The new version of heapsort shows that some standard algorithms can be translated to functional form while preserving the spirit of the original. But there are other algorithms whose functional translations are not obvious. In particular, Kruskal's algorithm for minimum cost spanning trees uses, in addition to a heap, an algorithm for the Union-Find problem. The Union-Find problem concerns the efficient implementation of three operations on disjoint sets, specified as follows

$$units \ : \ set \ A \to set \ (set \ A)$$
$$units \ x = \{\{a\} \mid a \in x\}$$

$$find \ : \ set \ (set \ A) \to A \to set \ A$$
$$find \ xs \ a = \text{``the (unique) set } x \text{ in } xs \text{ that contains } a\text{''}$$

$$union \ : \ set \ (set \ A) \to set \ A \to set \ A \to set \ (set \ A)$$
$$union \ xs \ x \ y = (xs - \{x\} - \{y\}) \cup \{x \cup y\}.$$

Various schemes for maintaining partitions are known, but I do not know how to achieve comparable efficiency in a purely functional setting. This is an interesting research problem, and one I intend to set to an incoming research student. I discussed this briefly with Bob Tarjan, the inventor of the nearly linear path compression algorithm for disjoint sets [21, 22], and he seemed optimistic that a good functional solution might be found.

5 On relations

Relations have been knocking at the door, demanding entry for some time now, and it is time to let them in. One reason concerns the nature of the relationship between the fold and unfold operations, and another concerns program specification in general. In a purely functional framework one can model relations by set-valued functions, but the mathematics becomes fussy. It becomes even fussier if we have to model set-valued functions by list-valued ones. With relations things are significantly simpler. Moreover, unlike functions every relation has a converse, and the use of converse operations are important both in specification and program development.

Consider for instance the following functional specification of sorting:

$$sort = head \cdot filter \ ordered \cdot perms.$$

The function *perms* returns a list of all permutations of a sequence, and the boolean-valued function *ordered* is a suitable functional implementation of the predicate

$$ordered \ x = (\forall i, j : 0 \to \#x : i \leq j \Rightarrow x!i \leq x!j).$$

This is probably an acceptable specification of *sort*, but a better one is to define *sort* to be a function, capable of being implemented, satisfying the inclusion

$$sort \subseteq ordered? \cdot perm, \tag{1}$$

where *perm* and *ordered?* are now relations rather than functions. (If $\leq$ is a linear order, then *ordered?* · *perm* is itself a function, but the expression is not capable of being implemented directly in a standard functional language, so there is still work to do.)

Since we want to preserve compatibility with functions, we think of relations as taking arguments on the right and delivering results on the left, so our relational composition takes the same form as functional composition (we want an ordered permutation, not a permutation of an ordered list). To emphasise this convention, which is consistent with adjectival order in English, we reverse the usual order of writing the source and target types in type declarations, preferring $R : A \leftarrow B$ rather than $R : B \rightarrow A$. One consequence of this highly sensible notation (first suggested by Lambert Meertens, I think) is that the definition of composition now takes the smooth form: if $R : A \leftarrow B$ and $S : B \leftarrow C$, then $R \cdot S : A \leftarrow C$. If I'd have had the courage, I would have introduced this convention for writing function types right at the beginning.

As a relation, *ordered?* $\subseteq$ *id*, where *id* is the identity relation on lists, and holds for x just when *ordered* x is true. A relation R such that $R \subseteq id$ is called a *coreflexive* (because a relation R satisfying $id \subseteq R$ is a reflexive relation). More generally, p? is the coreflexive that holds for x just when the predicate $p\,x$ is true. One can define coreflexives by translating the corresponding predicate, but it is usually more satisfactory to define them directly. In particular, one can define *ordered?* as a *relational* catamorphism

$$ordered? = (\![nil, cons \cdot ok?]\!),$$

where

$$ok\,(a, x) = (\forall b : b\;inlist\;x : a \leq b).$$

The relation *inlist* : $A \leftarrow list\,A$ is the membership relation for lists. It is not immediately clear how to define the membership relation for an arbitrary datatype, but the matter was finally settled by Hoogendijk and de Moor in [9]. It would take too long to explain how to define *inlist* in the relational calculus, so we will just accept it. For the same reason, the following formal definition of *ok?* is given without explanation:

$$ok? = id \cap (outl^\circ \cdot (\leq /inlist^\circ) \cdot outr).$$

This 'point-free' style is typical in a number of presentations of the relational calculus (see [7]); at first sight it seems arcane, but one soon gets used to it and calculations without variables are significantly simpler.

To define the relation *perm* we need the fundamental operation of taking the converse R° of a relation R, defined by $x R^\circ y = y R x$. Then we can define

$$perm = bagify^\circ \cdot bagify,$$

where *bagify* turns a list into a bag of its elements. Thus *perm* is defined using bags as an intermediate type: turning a list into a bag and then turning it back into a list gives a permutation of the original. The function *bagify* can be defined as a catamorphism

$$bagify = ([\![nilbag, consbag]\!]),$$

where *nilbag* is the empty bag and *consbag* adds an element to a bag.

6 On fold and unfold

Now let us turn to the formal definitions of fold and unfold in a relational setting. What follows will be rather brief and incomplete in various ways, but I hope enough of the general idea comes across to stimulate further reading. Grant Malcolm's thesis [15] is a good starting point, as is [16] which was written for functional programmers. And, if you can wait long enough, a complete account will appear in the forthcoming text [4] to be published next year.

As we have seen in the case of lists and trees, whenever one declares a datatype a number of functions are brought into play. In part, declaring a datatype as an equation asserts the existence of an isomorphism between the types on the left and right. In the case of lists this takes the form

$$list\ A \cong 1 + (A \times list\ A).$$

The type 1 consists of just one member and serves as the source type for constants. The type constructor $\times$ is cartesian product, and $+$ is disjoint sum. The right-hand side can be rephrased as

$$list\ A \cong \mathsf{F}(A, list\ A),$$

where $\mathsf{F}(A, B) = 1 + (A \times B)$ is a mapping from types to types. We can also use F as a mapping from functions to functions by defining

$$\mathsf{F}(f, g) = id_1 + (f \times g).$$

A function having a dual role both as a mapping between types and a mapping between functions is, provided certain properties are satisfied, called a *functor*. The functor F defined above takes a pair of types or functions as argument and so is sometimes called a bifunctor. One property we require of a functor F is that if $f : A \leftarrow B$, then $\mathsf{F}f : \mathsf{F}A \leftarrow \mathsf{F}B$. The other properties are the identity and composition rules:

$$\mathsf{F}id = id$$
$$\mathsf{F}(f \cdot g) = \mathsf{F}f \cdot \mathsf{F}g.$$

In the case of bifunctors the rules are, firstly, that if $f : A \leftarrow C$ and $g : B \leftarrow D$, then $\mathsf{F}(f, g) : \mathsf{F}(A, B) \leftarrow \mathsf{F}(C, D)$; and, secondly, that

$$\mathsf{F}(id, id) = id$$
$$\mathsf{F}(f \cdot g, h \cdot k) = \mathsf{F}(f, h) \cdot \mathsf{F}(g, k).$$

The cartesian product constructor × can also be defined as a mapping between functions: if $f : A \leftarrow C$ and $g : B \leftarrow D$, then $f \times g : A \times B \leftarrow C \times D$ is defined by

$$(f \times g)(c, d) = (f\, c, g\, d).$$

This mapping satisfies the identity and composition rules for bifunctors, so × is a bifunctor. Similarly, the coproduct constructor + can be defined on functions: applied to a left component c, the function $f + g : A + B \leftarrow C + D$ returns $f\, c$ as a left component of the result; dually, applied to a right component d, the value of $(f + g)\, d$ is the right component $g\, d$. Again, the identity and composition rules are satisfied, so + is a bifunctor.

The declaration of *list A* also introduces two functions

$$nil : list\, A \leftarrow 1 \quad \text{and} \quad cons : list\, A \leftarrow A \times list\, A$$

that serve to construct lists. We can parcel these functions together as one function

$$[nil, cons] : list\, A \leftarrow \mathsf{F}(A, list\, A).$$

In general, if $f : A \leftarrow B$ and $g : A \leftarrow C$, then $[f, g] : A \leftarrow B + C$ applies f to left components and g to right components. The function $[nil, cons]$ has a special property, which captures the fact that we can define functions on lists by pattern-matching: given any function $[c, f] : B \leftarrow \mathsf{F}(A, B)$ there is a unique function $h : B \leftarrow list\, A$ such that

$$h \cdot [nil, cons] = [c, f] \cdot \mathsf{F}(id, h).$$

Unwrapping this compact equation, we get two equations

$$h \cdot nil = c$$
$$h \cdot cons = f \cdot (id \times h).$$

Thus, $h = (\!| c, f |\!)$.

In a general datatype declaration, which we will write in the form

$$data\, A \xleftarrow{\;\alpha\;} \mathsf{F}(A, data\, A),$$

the catamorphism $(\!| f |\!) : B \leftarrow data\, A$, taking an argument $f : B \leftarrow \mathsf{F}(A, B)$, is the unique function h satisfying

$$h \cdot \alpha = f \cdot \mathsf{F}(id, h).$$

As a consequence of the defining property of α we get that $(\!| \alpha |\!) = id$. For example, $(\!| nil, cons |\!)$ (which we should have written as $(\!| [nil, cons] |\!)$ but won't) is the identity function on lists. Less obviously, it also follows from its defining property that α is an isomorphism, meaning

$$\alpha \cdot \alpha^\circ = id \quad \text{and} \quad \alpha^\circ \cdot \alpha = id.$$

The first *id* is the identity relation on *data A*, and the second is the identity relation on $\mathsf{F}(A, data\, A)$.

Since α is an isomorphism, we can move it to the other side of the defining equation for $(\!|f|\!)$. Thus, $h = (\!|f|\!)$ is the unique solution of the equation

$$h = f \cdot \mathsf{F}(id, h) \cdot \alpha^\circ.$$

We will abbreviate this as $(\!|f|\!) = (\nu h : h = f \cdot \mathsf{F}(id, h) \cdot \alpha^\circ)$.

Finally, we also obtain the extremely useful fusion rule for combining two functions into one:

$$f \cdot (\!|g|\!) = (\!|h|\!) \Leftarrow f \cdot g = h \cdot \mathsf{F}f.$$

Now, let us extend all this stuff to relations. Everything we have said above goes through when functions are extended to relations, provided only that we restrict attention to functors that are monotonic; that is, if $R \subseteq S$ then $\mathsf{F}R \subseteq \mathsf{F}S$. It can be shown that monotonic functors preserve relational converse, that is, $(\mathsf{F}R)^\circ = \mathsf{F}(R^\circ)$. It follows that the expression $\mathsf{F}R^\circ$ is not ambiguous. In particular, since

$$(R \cdot S)^\circ = S^\circ \cdot R^\circ,$$

we get for a relation $R : data\ A \leftarrow \mathsf{F}(A, data\ A)$ that

$$(\!|R|\!) = (\nu X : X = R \cdot \mathsf{F}(id, X) \cdot \alpha^\circ)$$
$$(\!|R|\!)^\circ = (\nu X : X = \alpha \cdot \mathsf{F}(id, X) \cdot R^\circ).$$

Given a function $f : \mathsf{F}(A, B) \leftarrow B$ the unfold operator $[\![f]\!]$ is defined by

$$[\![f]\!] = (\!|f^\circ|\!)^\circ.$$

The (now) non-standard form $[\![p, f]\!]$ that we have used previously for unfold on lists stands more properly for $[\![g]\!]$, where $g = (p \rightarrow !\ [\!]\ \neg p \rightarrow f)$ and $! : 1 \leftarrow B$ and $f : A \times B \leftarrow B$.

With relations we also get two variants of the fusion rule:

$$R \cdot (\!|S|\!) \subseteq (\!|T|\!) \Leftarrow R \cdot S \subseteq T \cdot \mathsf{F}(id, R)$$
$$R \cdot (\!|S|\!) \supseteq (\!|T|\!) \Leftarrow R \cdot S \supseteq T \cdot \mathsf{F}(id, R).$$

Finally, writing $(\mu X : X = \phi X)$ for the least fixed point (under relational inclusion) of ϕ, we get the following formalisation of the remark made in Section 3 about the simplification of the composition of a fold over a parmaterised type $data\ A$ with an unfold:

$$(\!|R|\!) \cdot (\!|S|\!)^\circ = (\mu X : X = R \cdot \mathsf{F}(id, X) \cdot S^\circ). \tag{2}$$

7 On the derivation of sorting algorithms

The formal derivation and classification of sorting algorithms is not, of course, new (see e.g. [6, 18]), but let us end with a brief sampler of the kinds of derivations we can accomplish with the above material.

Our first sorting algorithm arises as a result of the following three-step development:

$ordered? \cdot perm$

$=$ {expressing $perm$ in the form $([nil, combine])$}

$ordered? \cdot ([nil, combine])$

$\supseteq$ {fusion}

$([nil, ordered? \cdot combine])$

$\supseteq$ {supposing $insert \subseteq ordered? \cdot combine$}

$([nil, insert])$.

In outline, we can express $perm$ as a relational catamorphism, use fusion with $ordered?$ to obtain a second catamorphism, and finally refine the result to a functional catamorphism.

The relation $combine$ that makes $perm = ([nil, combine])$ can be defined recursively by

$$combine = cons \ \cup \ cons \cdot (id \times combine) \cdot swap \cdot (id \times cons^\circ), \qquad (3)$$

where $swap\,(a, (b, x)) = (b, (a, x))$. We omit the proof of this fact, as well as most others in this section. The function $insert$ that refines $ordered? \cdot combine$ can be defined by

$$insert = (ok' \to cons \ [\!] \ \neg ok' \to cons \cdot (id \times insert) \cdot swap \cdot (id \times cons^\circ)),$$

where

$$ok'\,(a, nil) = true$$
$$ok'\,(a, cons\,(b, x)) = (a \leq b).$$

The remaining step of the development requiring justification is the appeal to fusion, whose proviso is

$$ordered? \cdot [nil, combine] \supseteq [nil, ordered? \cdot combine] \cdot \mathsf{F}(ordered?).$$

But this follows quickly from the monotonicity of the functor F and the fact that $ordered?$ is a coreflexive. The resulting sorting algorithm, namely $sort = ([nil, insert])$, is of course insertion sort.

Our second sorting algorithm comes from the following development:

$ordered? \cdot perm$

$=$ {since $perm = perm^\circ$ and $ordered? = ordered?^\circ$}

$(perm \cdot ordered?)^\circ$

$=$ {fusion}

$([nil, perm \cdot cons \cdot ok?])^\circ$

$\supseteq$ {supposing $select \subseteq ok? \cdot cons^\circ \cdot perm$}

$([nil, select^\circ])^\circ$

$=$ {definition of unfold}

$[\![isnil \to ! \ [\!] \ \neg isnil \to select]\!]$.

The result is selection sort.

To derive quicksort, we need the fact that if f is a function, then $f \cdot f^\circ \subseteq id$. This inclusion captures the fact that functions map to at most one result. We also need the coreflexive *ordtree?* defined by

$$ordtree? = (\!(null, fork \cdot okt?)\!),$$

where

$$okt\,(x, a, y) = (\forall b : b\ intree\ x : b \leq a) \wedge (\forall b : b\ intree\ y : a \leq b).$$

Then we can argue along the same lines as in selection sort:

> $ordered? \cdot perm$
>
> $\supseteq$ {since $flatten : list\ A \leftarrow tree\ A$ is a function}
>
> $ordered? \cdot flatten \cdot flatten^\circ \cdot perm$
>
> $=$ {claim: $ordered? \cdot flatten = flatten \cdot ordtree?$}
>
> $flatten \cdot ordtree? \cdot flatten^\circ \cdot perm$
>
> $=$ {since $perm = perm^\circ$ and $ordtree? = ordtree?^\circ$}
>
> $flatten \cdot (perm \cdot flatten \cdot ordtree?)^\circ$
>
> $=$ {fusion}
>
> $flatten \cdot (\!(null, perm \cdot join \cdot okt?)\!)^\circ$
>
> $\supseteq$ {supposing $split \subseteq okt? \cdot join^\circ \cdot perm$}
>
> $flatten \cdot (\!(null, split^\circ)\!)^\circ$
>
> $=$ {definition of unfold}
>
> $flatten \cdot [\![isnull \rightarrow !\ [\!]\ \neg isnull \rightarrow split]\!].$
>
> $=$ {introducing $mktree$}
>
> $flatten \cdot mktree.$

We will omit the proof of the claim, and the detailed justification of the fusion step.

References

1. R.C. Backhouse, P.J de Bruin, G. Malcolm, E. Voermans, and J.C.S.P. van der Woude. Relational Catamorphisms. In B. Möller, editor *Proceedings of the IFIP TC2/WG2.1 Working Conference on Constructing Programs from Specifications*, 287–318, 1991.
2. R.S. Bird, J. Gibbons, G. Jones. Formal derivation of a pattern matching algorithm. *Science of Computer Programming*, 12, 93–104, 1989.
3. Richard Bird and Philip Wadler. *Introduction to Functional Programming* Prentice Hall International, 1988.
4. Richard Bird and Oege de Moor. *The Algebra of Programming*. To be published by Prentice Hall International, 1996.

5. Thomas H. Cormen, Charles E. Leiserson, and Ronald L. Rivest. *Introduction to Algorithms*. MIT Press, Cambridge, Mass. USA, 1990.

6. John Darlington. A synthesis of several sorting algorithms. *Acta Informatica* 11, 1–30, 1978.

7. P.J. Freyd and A. Ščedrov. *Categories, Allegories*, volume 39 of *Mathematical Library*. North–Holland, 1990.

8. A.M. Haeberer and P.A.S. Veloso. Partial relations for program development. in B. Möller (ed.) *Constructing Programs from Specifications*. Proc. IFIP TC2/WG2.1 Conference, Pacific Grove, CA, USA (1991), North-Holland, Amsterdam (1991), 373–397.

9. Paul Hoogendijk and Oege de Moor. Membership of datatypes. Unpublished Draft, 1993.

10. Rob Hoogerwoord. *The design of functional programs: a calculational approach*. Ph.D thesis, University of Eindhoven 1989.

11. Geraint Jones and Mary Sheeran. *Circuit design in Ruby*, in Jørgen Staunstrup (ed.), *Formal methods for VLSI design*, North-Holland, 1990. pp. 13–70.

12. David King and John Launchbury. Structuring Depth-First Search Algorithms in Haskell. *Proc. ACM Principles of Programming Languages*, San Francisco, 1995.

13. John Launchbury and Simon Peyton Jones. State in Haskell. University of Glasgow, preprint, 1995.

14. Grant Malcolm. Homomorphisms and promotability. In J. Snepscheut, editor *1989 Groningen Mathematics of Program Construction Conference*. Springer–Verlag LNCS 375, 335-347, 1989.

15. Grant Malcolm. *Algebraic Types and Program Transformation*. Ph.D thesis, University of Groningen, The Netherlands, 1990.

16. Erik Meijer, Maarten Fokkinga, and Ross Paterson. Functional programming with bananas, lenses, envelopes and barbed wire. in John Hughes, (ed.) *Proceedings of the 1991 ACM Conference on Functional Programming and Computer Architecture*. Springer–Verlag LNCS 523, 1991.

17. B. Möller. Relations as a program development language. in B. Möller (ed.) *Constructing Programs from Specifications*. Proc. IFIP TC2/WG2.1 Conference, Pacific Grove, CA, USA (1991), North-Holland, Amsterdam (1991), 373–397.

18. B. Möller. Algebraic calculation of graph and sorting algorithms. In D. Bjorner, M. Broy, I.V. Pottosin (eds) *Formal methods in Programming and their Applications*. Springer-Verlag LNCS 735, 394–413, 1993.

19. O. de Moor. Categories, relations and dynamic programming. D.Phil. thesis. Technical Monograph PRG-98, Computing Laboratory, Oxford, 1992. Also in *Mathematical Structures in Computer Science*, vol 4 (1), 1994, 33–70.

20. Gunther Schmidt and Thomas Ströhlein. *Relations and Graphs*. EATCS Monographs on Theoretical Computer Scince. Springer-Verlag, 1991.

21. Robert E. Tarjan. Efficiency of a good but not linear set union algorithm. *Journal of the ACM*. vol 22 (2), 1975, 215–225.

22. Robert E. Tarjan and Jan van Leeuwen. Worst-case analysis of set union algorithms. *Journal of the ACM*. vol 31 (2), 1984, 245–281.

23. J.W.J. Williams. Algorithm 232 (heapsort). *Communications of the ACM*, vol 7, 1964, 347–348.

24. Philip L. Wadler *Listlessness is better than Laziness*. Ph.D. thesis, Carnegie–Mellon University, USA, 1984.

Mathematics of Software Engineering[1]

Manfred Broy

SysLab, Institut für Informatik, Technische Universität München
D-80290 München, Germany

Abstract. Software engineering incorporates technical and organizational aspects. Technically, in software engineering we work with a development method and with description techniques, with modeling and implementation techniques. Mathematical techniques can provide a scientific basis for software engineering. They lead to a deeper understanding of the development process and a more powerful tool support. For finding the best mathematical foundation, we need a clear recognition of the economical and technical benefits of mathematical concepts in software engineering. This requires a careful analysis of the role of mathematics and logic in software engineering. We show, how software engineering methods can be backed up by mathematical techniques. We discuss the benefits that go far beyond so called formal methods for the formal specification and verification of software.

1. Introduction

It is extremely unsatisfactory that in spite of the large amount of in many cases excellent theoretic work in programming and system development methods a consequent practical application is mainly missing so far. In this paper, we try to outline the reasons for this situation and to sketch perspectives for its improvement.

It is widely accepted by now that the development of software is to be considered as an engineering discipline and called software engineering. When doing so, we have to keep in mind that all engineering disciplines are based on theoretical foundations. By the engineering discipline these theoretical foundations are used as a basis to form a body of rules, procedures and engineering processes. There cannot be any doubts that software engineering has and needs its own theoretical foundation like all other disciplines. A lot has been achieved by research in the mathematical foundations of programming during the last three decades. Still a lot is to be done, however. Moreover, our foundational work needs focus and reflection to avoid dead end streets and unrealistic conceptions of the use and benefits of foundations in practical program development.

There is a remarkable discrepancy between the practice of software engineering and the more theoretical and basic research carried out over the last 40 years. In spite of the impressive number of deep and exciting results including techniques for describing, structuring, specifying, and verifying programs, the amount of the application of these results in practice so far is not very encouraging. This paper is an appeal for an improvement of the software engineering discipline by combining pragmatic software engineering methods with and basing them on mathematical techniques.

Software engineering in practice deals with the development of large and often complex information processing systems. It includes techniques for the description of requirements and systems in the disparate development phases. Its main goals are a good quality and economy of the engineering process and its results leading to high productivity. In this paper we sketch how a mathematical basis of software engineering may look like and discuss where its practical benefits are.

---

[1]This work was carried out within the project SysLab sponsored by Siemens-Nixdorf and partially supported by the Deutsche Forschungsgemeinschaft under the Leibniz program.

1.1 The Role of Formal Methods

Starting with the pioneering work of Petri, Strachey, Scott, Floyd, Hoare, deBakker, Reynolds, the VDM group and many others formal methods in software development have been investigated over the last 25 years. Nowadays formal methods are a well-established subject in academia. Special circles have been formed, investigating sometimes bizarre aspects that do not have any connections to practical applications. Still the consequent application of many of the results of the research in formal methods in practice is missing.

There are many explanations for this fact. Often it is claimed that the software engineers in practice do not have the appropriate skills to recognize and exploit the potentials of formal methods. These claims range from doubts about the appropriate education of the software engineers in practice to doubts about the qualification of the management personnel. Although many of these arguments certainly are correct, they cannot be the only reason for the lack of the application of advanced and mathematically based techniques.

Certainly, the software industry is extremely conservative. The reason is obvious. The investment into old software is so high that it seems very risky and costly to change to new techniques. It is intrinsic that old hardware is replaced every 3 to 5 years. For software this is not done, in general. Old software systems based on bygone software engineering techniques or ancient languages often are kept in operation.

Therefore, in our scientific work we must not only concentrate on an idealized practical environment. We have to recognize the shortcomings in practice not only in isolated technical fields but to understand what progress is realistic and how evolutionary changes can be envisaged. Revolutionary changes are not very likely.

To support an evolutionary change to more advanced methods with better laid foundations we have to improve the educational standards. Today, the lack of a proper terminological and mathematical basis makes software engineering into a soft discipline that is rather determined by opinions and beliefs instead of scientific foundation.

We have to be aware that time has progressed. Thirty years ago any understanding of a mathematical foundation of software engineering was missing. After we have seen denotational semantics, axiomatic specifications and numerous logical calculi, many of the theoretical problems for modeling software engineering concepts by mathematical and logical techniques are solved (see also [Abrial 92]). More work is needed along the lines of [Jones 86] and [Guttag, Horning 93]. That theoretical foundations are sufficient nowadays is demonstrated, for instance, by [Hußmann 95] which provides a complete formalization by translating SSADM into SPECTRUM. SSADM is a pragmatic requirement engineering method used as the UK government's standard method for carrying out systems analysis and design stages of information technology development projects. SPECTRUM is an axiomatic specification language.

How many problems still have to be studied and how much work is needed and can be stimulated by practical problems can be seen, for instance, by the concept of state charts (see [Beeck 94] for a long list of open problems).

1.2 Bringing Theory to Practice

The time has changed. Thirty years ago, for many practical concepts in computing science the theoretical foundation was completely missing. This is no longer true nowadays. A solid body of foundational work is available by now giving principle answers to many of the demanding questions of theoretical foundations of software engineering.

The next step must be to increase the experimentation and the transfer of these theoretical results to engineering. Yes, this needs the good will of both the practical software engineers and theoreticians. This means that also the theoreticians are requested to undertake serious efforts to get a better understanding of the needs of nowadays software engineers and of advanced engineering concepts.

1.3 Prerequisites for the Transfer

To bring theory to practice, we need well-understood application scenarios for proposed formal methods, clearly stating their application area and their technical, social and economic contexts. Formal methods and mathematical foundations can only be successful, if they guarantee a return of investment. For being attractive to people in practice, they are required to be cost effective like any other development technique.

One should keep in mind that of course many results achieved by research in formal methods have found their way from theory to practice by now. Many of the today's programming concepts have been developed on theoretical grounds. Nevertheless, it is sometimes discouraging to see how slowly good ideas in theory find their way into practice. We should carefully analyze the reason for that to improve the situation.

Clearly, especially in Europe, much research is carried out in academia without much thought how its results could be transferred to practice. Also convincing sample transfer concepts and success stories are missing.

Often formal methods concentrate too much on the formal aspects of the engaged calculi. However, applicability, tractability, and understanding are often more important than logical completeness. Engineering principles are more important than formalisms, however, if applicability is our goal. We have to understand the difference of logic as a discipline for analyzing and studying calculi and their properties and *logic as an engineering tool*.

In software engineering the different aspects of technical and management issues are so closely intertwined that it is dangerous, misleading or simply impossible to study them in isolation if practical applicability is envisaged. Many of the isolated problems in the foundation of software engineering have been treated and at least partly solved over the last years. Now much more integration of the various technical aspects and of the management aspects has to be envisaged. Nowadays, many of the theoretical problems seem to be solved, in principle. Scaling up, however, and practical wage are maybe the most critical issue.

If we want to bring formal methods closer to practice we have to have a clear understanding of the software production nowadays. In addition, we need competent partners in industrial applications. Our goal must be simplicity, scaling up, and understanding of our proposed techniques. We have to be ready for experimentation. We have to understand the differences between development in the small versus development in the large. We have to provide clear and honest measures of the advantages of introducing formal methods concerning cost, quality and software process organization.

We need realistic experimentation scenarios. These consist in well thought out small or medium size experiments in applying advanced mathematical based software engineering techniques in case studies or in real life application. This experimentation needs clear measures of success.

The adequate modeling of applications is an important task. We need more research in modeling and design techniques studying architectures and concepts for description. It was one of the striking experiences of a recent workshop at Dagstuhl presenting solutions to a specification problem posed in [Broy, Lamport 93] to see that for most of the proposed solutions not so much the used specification approach and the calculi were decisive for the specification task, but the modeling ideas that were used.

Development needs methodological guidance. We cannot expect that we just provide specification notation and logical calculi and maybe a few small, hopefully illustrative case studies and then everyone in practice develops his own ideas how to use the methods in a systematic manner. Industrial applications need well-defined development processes.

We also have to keep in mind which type of engineer with which educational profile should apply the more advanced, mathematically based methods. When proposing methods, we need a clear idea of the skills of the people that are supposed to apply those methods.

Certainly, we as theoreticians were too much obsessed by formal specification and verification. Correctness is an important, but by far not the only issue in software engineering. As a result, most of the work on formal methods is concentrated on formal specification and verification calculi, but not enough work is devoted to the mathematical foundation of more advanced software development concepts.

Software engineering has developed a rich and often confusing plenty of proposals for overcoming the difficulties of organizing large development processes. These include among others

- team organization and management,
- cost prediction,
- development process organization and integration (phases, mile stones, documentation),
- integration with existing software components,
- tool support.

It is naive to assume that managers responsible for large projects would switch to methods for which these questions are not positively answered.

Of course, it is a long way to provide a complete development method, but only when we start to work in this direction there might be a chance to transfer theoretical results more effectively into practice. When working towards such a method, we will discover many challenging theoretical problems. Examples are the mathematical capture of the concepts of software architectures, design patterns, and the normalization of existing description methods.

1.4 What is Not Needed - Avoiding the Esoteric

The study of the history of mathematics shows that this discipline always had its best times when it was in a feedback process with applications. For computing science this applies even more. So more foundational work should be devoted to concentrate on today's real life problems. From such practical experiments we should develop more advanced proposals for software engineering techniques.

We have to be much more thoughtful and critical with our work concerning its long term scientific and practical goals. I do not say that speculative long term oriented theoretical work should be stopped. What we should avoid, however, is inbreeding, the development of irrelevant schools that lose their contact with engineering issues by confusing their calculi with reality.

We should be critical with the amount of formality in our notation. It is not clear why we should use a strictly formal notation, if we are interested in the first place in a mathematical foundation of software engineering techniques and not in machine supported formal verification calculi.

We have to increase the discussion between theory and practice to improve the transfer process in both directions. More experimentation is needed in trying out new methods. A method that can help to solve a toy problem need not necessarily help to solve a large scale real life problem. A method that cannot even deal with a toy problem is not worth to be studied any more.

We often concentrate too much on academic and theoretical issues. It is not the logical completeness what makes a mathematical software engineering method valuable in practice. It is cost effectiveness and utility.

Finally, we should never forget how much effort is needed to make a method pertinent in practice. It is a long and cost-intensive process to turn a theoretical idea into a method that works in practice. So no one is ready to go that way without clear perspectives about the advantages of a new approach. Software engineering, like all engineering disciplines, has to take economical issues as seriously as technical issues.

1.5 Elements of Software Engineering

Software engineering is a discipline that involves organizational and management aspects as well as technical aspects. The organizational and management aspects include

- team organization and management,
- productivity,
- quality management,
- reusability,
- cost prediction and cost break down,
- prediction of time and deadlines,
- planning, contracting, marketing.

The more technical aspects comprise:

- development process organization (phases, mile stones, documentation),
- formulation of strategic goals and of constraints,
- modeling, description, specification,
- quality guarantee,
- integration with existing software components,
- documentation,
- tool support.

We will concentrate in the following on the technical aspects, mainly. However, we want to keep in mind that there is a close relationship between technical and management aspects. Whenever it is necessary to assess the role of technical aspects with respect to management aspects, we will refer to them. We find the closest connection between management and technical issues in the organization of the development process, often called *process model*.

A central notion in software engineering is method. We distinguish between method and methodology. Methodology is the systematic study of methods. A method in software engineering comprises description techniques in its syntax, semantics and pragmatics, rules for working with these techniques, development techniques and general principles.

1.6 Overall Organization of the Paper

The paper is organized as follows. In section 2 on models we introduce the notions of data model, process, component and system and give mathematical denotations for them. On this basis, we discuss description techniques in section 3. We devote section 4 to modeling techniques. In section 5 we deal with development methods and development process models. We conclude after a short section on implementation issues and tools.

2. Models

A software system is given by a description, a textual or graphical document, and at the same time is a product that can be brought to life and then show a complex dynamic behavior. Like no other discipline, software engineering deals with models, description and modeling. In the following we want to carefully distinguish between

- *models*: the mathematical structures forming the semantical conceptual model associated with a description technique,
- *description*: the description technique, given by the syntax, graphics, or tables used in the documentation of a software system,
- *modeling*: the mapping representing and relating real life aspects of the application to software description techniques.

Of course, these three aspects are closely related. Nevertheless, we want to carefully perceive these distinctions in the following, since these distinctions are of major relevance for the understanding and foundation of software engineering. It is, in particular, important to distinguish between the description techniques and the modeling idea for systems. We start with models.

2.1 Data Models

Data models are needed to give computing science structures for representing the data of information processing systems. From a mathematical point of view, a data model consists of a heterogeneous algebra that is given by a family of carrier sets and a family of functions. More technically, we assume a set of sorts (often also called types or modes) S and a set F of function symbols with a fixed functionality

$$\textbf{fct} : F \rightarrow (S^* \times S)$$

The function **fct** associates with every function symbol in F its domain sorts and its range sort. Both the sets S and F provide names. The pair (S, F) is often called the *signature* of the algebra. In every algebra of signature (S, F) we associate with every sort a carrier set and with every function symbol a function of the requested functionality. It is typical for mathematical structures modeling information processing concepts that they include syntactic parts such as name spaces (in the algebraic case the signature) and semantical parts (in the algebraic case sets and functions).

Algebras are a very general mathematical concept. All kinds of mathematical structures and mathematical models can be understood as heterogeneous algebras. Nevertheless, we will use algebras for data models only and in the following give specific mathematical structures for other system aspects.

2.2 Component Models: State Machines and Stream Functions

State machines are a well-known concept of a system model. We consider only a specific version of a state machine that corresponds well to our notion of a system component. For us, a component is an information processing unit that communicates with its environment through input and output channels.

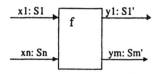

Fig. 1 Graphical representation of a component
with input channels x1, ..., xn and output channels y1, ... , ym and their respective sorts

In software engineering, it is helpful to work with a *black box view* and a *glass box view* of a specification. In a black box view we only are interested in the interface of a component with its environment. In a glass box view we are interested in the internal structure of a component, be it its local state space or its distribution into subcomponents.

Let I be the set of input channels and O be the set of output channels. Then by (I, O) the *syntactic interface* of a system component is given. With every channel in I ∪ O in a syntactic interface we associate a data sort indicating the sort of messages sent on that channel. For simplicity, we use just one set M of data sorts for messages on the channels in the sequel to keep the mathematics more readable. A graphical representation of a component with its syntactic interface is shown in Fig. 1.

A *glass box view* of a component with the syntactic interface (I, O) can be given by a state machine. A state machine (δ, σ_0) is given (for a state set Σ and the syntactic interface (I, O)) by a transition function

$$\delta : \Sigma \times (I \rightarrow M^*) \rightarrow \wp(\Sigma \times (O \rightarrow M^*))$$

and an initial state $\sigma_0 \in \Sigma$. A state machine models the behavior of an information processing unit with input channels from the set I and output channels from the set O in a time frame as follows. If the family of finite sequences $x \in (I \to M^*)$ represents the sequence of input message $x(c)$ received in time interval i on the channel $c \in I$ of the component in state $\sigma \in \Sigma$, then every pair (σ', y) in the set $\delta(\sigma, x)$ represents a possible successor state and the sequence of output messages $y(c)$ produced on channel $c \in O$ at time point i+1.

As a basic model for the behavior of system components we can also use relations on timed streams that are streams of data messages and time ticks (see [Broy 95b]). A timed stream is a sequence of messages and time ticks that contains an infinite number of time ticks. Apart from the time ticks the stream may contain a finite or an infinite number of messages. The basic idea is that the time ticks indicate the time bounds in which the messages are sent on a channel. On the basis of this simple model we can introduce a quite flexible notation that we will use throughout the paper in specifications.

We model the time flow by a special time signal called a time tick that indicates the end of a time interval. By

$$\sqrt{}$$

we denote the time tick signal. Let M be a set of messages that does not contain the time signal $\sqrt{}$. By M^ω we denote streams of messages of set M which are finite or infinite sequences of elements from M and by

$$M^{\overline{\omega}}$$

we denote the set of infinite streams of elements of set $M \cup \{\sqrt{}\}$ which contain an infinite number of ticks. Every element in the set $M^{\overline{\omega}}$ denotes a complete communication history over an unbounded time period. Mathematically, such a stream in $M^{\overline{\omega}}$ can also be understood as a function $N \to M \cup \{\sqrt{}\}$.

We describe the *black box behavior* of a component by a *behavior relation*. A behavior relation is a relation between the input streams and the output streams of a component that fulfills certain conditions with respect to their timing.

A black box model of a component representing its behavior is given by a relation that is represented by a set-valued function on the timed streams of input and output messages.

$$f : (I \to M^{\overline{\omega}}) \to \wp(O \to M^{\overline{\omega}})$$

For a behavior relation we assume the following timing property:

$$x{\downarrow}i = z{\downarrow}i \Rightarrow \{y{\downarrow}i+1: y \in f(x)\} = \{y{\downarrow}i+1: y \in f(z)\}$$

Here $x{\downarrow}i$ denotes the family of streams that are the largest prefixes of x that contain i time ticks. The timing property expresses that the set of possible output histories for the first i+1 time intervals only depends on the input histories for the first i time histories. In other words, the processing of messages in a component takes at least one tick of time. We could work with more liberal conditions. However, this timing condition is very convenient for us.

By C we denote the set of data flow components. By C[I, O] we denote the set of data flow components with input channels I and output channels O.

Stream relations provide a black box view of the behavior of a component. Only the relationship between the data flowing into the component and out of the component is represented. State machines provide a glass box view. By a state machine an internal detail of the system in terms of the states is provided. In the following section we provide another type of a glass box view by distributed systems.

With a glass box view of a component given by a state machine (δ, σ_0) we may associate a black box view for every state $\sigma \in \Sigma$ as follows: the behavior function

$$f_\sigma : (I \to M^{\overline{\omega}}) \to \wp(O \to M^{\overline{\omega}})$$

for the state σ is specified by the following formula:

$$f_\sigma(x) = \{y_0\hat{}\langle\sqrt{}\rangle\hat{}y: \exists \sigma': (\sigma', y_0) \in \delta(\sigma, x{\downarrow}0) \wedge y \in f_{\sigma'}(x{\uparrow}0)\}$$

By x^y we denote the concatenation of the streams x and y and by x↑i we denote the family of streams obtained from the streams in x by deleting the largest prefix of x containing i time ticks.

We have chosen a particular model of system components with a concurrent timed interface that we find especially useful for engineering purposes. A more explicit justification is given in [Broy 95b].

2.3 System Models

An interactive distributed system consists of a family of interacting components often also called *agents* or *objects*. These components interact by exchanging messages. A structural system view consists of a network of communicating components. Its nodes model components and its arcs communication lines (channels) on which streams of messages are sent. A glass box view of a system component can be represented by a distributed system or by a state machine. In the first case we speak of a *composed distributed system* and in the later case we speak of a *nondistributed system*. Fig. 4 shows the data flow representation of a simple example of a distributed system.

We model distributed systems by data flow nets. A data flow net (v, O) with syntactic interface (I, O) is given by a set N of nodes and a mapping

$$v: N \to C$$

that associates with every node a component behavior where N is a set of identifiers for data flow nodes (for components) and a set of output channels O. As a well-formedness condition we require that for all identifiers $i, j \in N$ (with $i \neq j$) the sets of output channels of the components $v(i)$ and $v(j)$ are disjoint:

$$Out(v(i)) \cap Out(v(j)) = \emptyset$$

We denote the set of nodes of the net by

$$Nodes((v, O)) = N$$

We denote the set of channels of the net by

$$Chan((v, O)) = O \cup \{In(v(i)): i \in N\} \cup \{Out(v(i)): i \in N\}$$

The set

$$I = \{In(v(i)): i \in N\} \setminus \{Out(v(i)): i \in N\}$$

denotes the set of input channels of the net. The channels in

$$\{Out(v(i)): i \in N\} \setminus O$$

are called *internal*.

For a function $g: D \to R$ and a set $T \subseteq D$ we denote by $g|_T: T \to R$ the restriction of g to the domain T. Every data flow net defines a black box view by a component behavior $f \in C[I, O]$ via the following specification:

$$f(x) = \{y|_O: y|_I = x \wedge \forall i \in N: y|_{Out(v(i))} \in v(i)(y|_{In(v(i))}) \}$$

This formula essentially says that the output is the restriction of a fixpoint for all the net equations.

In recent years the theoretical and practical interest in distributed dynamic systems increased, also called systems with mobile communication. In a dynamic system the set of components changes over its lifetime. Such systems can also be described by the type of system models introduced above. However, then more refined models are needed where either the net is used as a state of the system that changes over time or possibly infinite nets are considered that comprise all components that may be created over the lifetime of the system. In the case of dynamic channel creation similar ideas can be used (see [Grosu 94], [Broy 95a], [Grosu et al. 95]).

2.4 Processes

A process is a family of actions that are in some causal relationship. In the case of interacting systems an action is triggered by a number of messages received and carried out by sending a number of messages that may cause further actions. If an action a1 is directly causal for an action a2 in a process there must exist a message from a1 to a2.

Each instance of sending or receiving of a message is called an *event*. Each event is caused by the sender of the respective message. Events that are caused by the environment are called *external* events. All other events are called *internal* events. An internal event the receiver of which is the environment is called an *output* event. Special events are *time* events. They can be understood also as messages that are sent by a timer.

The notion of a process is crucial in software engineering, as we can see by the term information *processing*. Pioneering work on the notion of a process was done by Carl Adam Petri who suggested by the so-called Petri nets a fundamental technique for the description of processes. Strictly speaking Petri nets are a kind of automata that implicitly describe concurrent processes. An explicit description of processes is obtained by the so-called occurrence nets (see [Reisig 86]) which are basically Petri nets without cycles and conflicts.

In our model of a distributed system a process is represented by an acyclic data flow net (v_p, O_p) and a valuation function

$$\eta: Chan((v_p, O_p)) \rightarrow M$$

that associates with all of its arcs exactly one message. So a process is a special case of a data flow net. In contrast to general data flow diagrams, however, through each of its channels exactly one message is sent. So channels correspond to communication events and nodes correspond to action events.

There are many variations of mathematical models for processes including trace sets and action structures (see [Broy 91b]). We do not introduce a more explicit mathematical model of a process here but consider processes as a special form of a distributed systems. The relationship of our notion of process to data flow nets is explained in detail in section 5.4.

2.5 Application Domain Models

System models are needed that support both requirement specification and design. In particular applications we need, in addition, specific models of the applications. We speak of *domain specific models*. We just want to mention this here as an important issue of the mathematics of software engineering, but do not go deeper into this subject.

3. Description Techniques in Software Engineering

In software engineering it is necessary to describe large information processing systems. Of course, this cannot be done by just providing one description technique or one single document. Therefore software engineering uses several conjoint description techniques and documents. Each of these documents describes particular views on the system.

Integration of description techniques and mathematics is an indispensable requisite for more advanced software development methods. In this section we discuss the description techniques in software engineering and their mathematics.

3.1 Description by Text, Formulas and Graphics

Description techniques are used to represent models like programming languages are used to represent algorithms. It is not obvious to distinguish between description and modeling techniques. For us a description technique is a textual or graphical formalism, also a diagram or a table, for describing systems, system views and system aspects. A model is a mathematical image of a system. Description techniques allow us to represent models and their properties.

Practical software engineers tend to overemphasize the importance of description techniques in terms of syntax while theoreticians underestimate often the significance of notation. In the engineering process, notation, be it graphics, tables, or texts, serves as a vehicle for expressing ideas, for analysis, communication, and documentation. To provide optimal support for these purposes both the presentation of the descriptions and the mathematical models behind them have to be appropriate. Since, depending on the purpose and the education of the user, the effectiveness of the presentations may be quite different, it is often wise to have several presentations for the same description, for instance text, diagrams, and tables.

When describing systems, we distinguish between static and dynamic aspects. Static aspects of an information processing system are those that do not change over the life time of a system. Dynamic aspects have to do with behavior. We can use the same description techniques for static and for dynamic aspects.

Especially dynamic aspects of components can be described either axiomatically, property-oriented, or in more operational terms. Property-oriented descriptions are mostly based on logic, of course.

Throughout the rest of this paper we use as a running example a simple business application to illustrate the introduced concepts. The example is an order, sales and delivery system. It serves only one business task namely to provide a service for the ordering of products and to organize their production and delivery.

3.2 Description of Data Models

In the data view we fix the relevant sorts and their characteristic functions for the system we want to describe or implement. In addition, we may describe the system states. This can be done by sort declarations, by axiomatic data structure specifications, and/or by an E/R-diagram, especially when our system processes mass data.

In our example we use a sort Bestellung and fix the data attributes of it that also can be used as selector functions by a sort declaration. The sort Bestellung is described by the following sort declaration:

    Sort Bestellung = M_Bestellung(Ware,
                             Status,
                             Kunde)

Here, we assume the convention that we use the sort identifiers as selectors, if no selectors are mentioned explicitly. Each element of the sort Bestellung represents an order that has a status:

    Sort Status = {Ware_bestellt, Rechnung_offen, Done}

Data models can also be used to describe the state space of components. In our ordering system we may use a component Verwalter. The component Verwalter then has the data view given in Fig. 2. The data view is described by an E/R-model. See Fig. 2 as a simple example of a data structure diagram and an E/R-diagram.

With this data view the behavior of the component Verwalter can be made more precise later. Each action of a component may change certain of its attributes.

Graphical representations and diagrams can be used as an illustrative, but nevertheless fully formal description technique, if a formal syntax and a mathematical semantics is provided. A useful form to do this is a translation into axiomatic specifications. This allows us to integrate formal axiomatic data description techniques and pragmatic graphical description techniques in software engineering. A careful translation of E/R-concepts into axiomatic specifications is given by [Hettler 94]. Hettler distinguishes between E/R-techniques for modeling static aspects and dynamic aspects of systems.

28

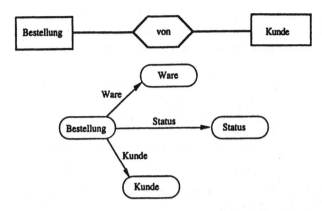

Fig. 2 Data sort diagram for the sort Bestellung and data view of the component Verwalter illustrated by an E/R-diagram

Often data models are used to describe the state of systems and components. For software engineering techniques, it is extremely important to have a proper concept of the names and attributes of such a data store. Formal techniques can provide a mathematical concept of such an organized store. An example is the specification of an organized store given in following by a polymorphic algebraic specification in the style of the specification language SPECTRUM:

ORGANIZED_STORE = {

    sort   Store, **Ref** α, **var** α,

emptyStore :	Store,	*empty store*
nil :	**Ref** α,	*reference to undefined*
update :	Store, **var** α, $\alpha \to$ Store,	*selective update of a variable*
newvar :	Store, $\alpha \to$ **var** α,	*variable creation*
newvarstore :	Store, $\alpha \to$ Store,	*storage allocation for a new variable*
declared :	Store, **var** $\alpha \to$ Bool,	*test, if a variable is declared*
value :	Store, **var** $\alpha \to \alpha$,	*value of a variable*
newref :	Store, $\alpha \to$ **Ref** α,	*creation of a reference*
newrefstore :	Store, $\alpha \to$ Store,	*allocation of storage for a new reference*
valid :	Store, **Ref** $\alpha \to$ Bool,	*test, if a reference is declared*
deref :	Store, **Ref** $\alpha \to \alpha$,	*dereferencing*

Axioms:

For nil: (δ[t] is true, iff the term t is defined):

    $\neg\delta[\mathrm{deref}(\sigma, \mathrm{nil})]$

For the empty store:

    declared(emptyStore, v) = false,
    valid(emptyStore, r) = (r = nil),

For variable declaration:

    declared(σ, newvar(σ, a)) = false,
    declared(newvarstore(σ, a), v) = (declared(σ, v) $\vee$ v = newvar(σ, a)),
    valid(newvarstore(σ, a), r) = valid(σ, r),

declared(newvarstore(σ, a), w) $\Rightarrow$
    value(newvarstore(σ, a), w) = **if** w = newvar(σ, a) **then** a **else** value(σ, w) **fi**,
valid(σ, r) $\Rightarrow$ deref(newvarstore(σ, a), r) = deref(σ, r),

For selective update:
declared(σ, v) $\Rightarrow$ declared(update(σ, v, a), w) = declared(σ, w) $\wedge$
                valid(update(σ, v, a), r) = valid(σ, r) $\wedge$
                deref(update(σ, v, a), r) = deref(σ , r) $\wedge$
                declared(σ, w) $\Rightarrow$
                    value(update(σ, v, a), w) = **if** w = v **then** a **else** value(σ, w) **fi**

For reference storage allocation:

declared(newrefstore(σ, a), w) = declared(σ, w),
valid(σ, newref(σ, a)) = false,
valid(newrefstore(σ, a), r) = (valid(σ, r) $\vee$ r = newref(σ, a)),
declared(σ, w) $\Rightarrow$ value(newrefstore(σ, a), w) = value(σ, w),
valid(newrefstore(σ, a), r) $\Rightarrow$
    deref(newrefstore(σ, a), r) = **if** r = newref(σ, a) **then** a **else** deref(σ, r) **fi**}

This gives a very powerful and general specification of an organized store that can be adapted to particular applications.

3.3 Description of the Behavior

As well-known an I/O-state machine can be described by a state transition diagram or equivalently by state transition table. Such descriptions receive much more acceptance in practice than purely logical representations of state transition systems. However, without any problems we may describe state transition systems by tables or diagram and translate these into logic.

Tab. 1 State transition table

State	Input message	Successor state	Output message
	Bestellung	Ware_bestellt	Produktionsauftrag
Ware_bestellt	Produktionsbestätigung	Rechnung_offen	Rechnung
Rechnung_offen	Zahlung		Lieferbon/Lieferauftrag

More research is needed, however, to work out concepts that show how more powerful logical descriptions can be encoded into tables and diagrams in a readable way (see [Parnas, Madley 91]).

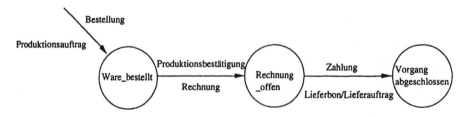

Fig. 3 State transition view of the component Verwalter

The behavior of the Verwalter can be easily described by a state transition table defining an input/output state machine. We show such a table in Tab. 1. It is rather informal, it can, nevertheless, be completed to a fully formal description. This table gives only a very rough description of the behavior of the component Verwalter. This table can be generated from the business case shown in Fig. 5 if we add the appropriate names for the states. A state transition diagram providing exactly the same information as the table is given in Fig. 3.

Of course we get much more complicated tables and diagrams if we add all the exceptional cases. Such exceptional cases can be gathered quite systematically from the description of the business process showing the nonexceptional process (see Fig. 6). Often diagrams are helpful to provide only a rough, incomplete (sometimes even incorrect) first idea, while more formal descriptions provide a rigorous description.

3.4 Description of Interactive Systems

An interactive system as we defined it in the previous section can be described by a data flow network (CD in GRAPES, see [Grapes 90], block diagram in SDL, see [SDL 88]) which is a directed graph. This way the structure of interactive systems can be represented.

Data flow nets can be shown by illustrative diagrams (see Fig. 4) that give a structural view on information processing systems. They are very suggestive as long as the set of the components of a system is static. As soon as the sets of components get dynamic, it is impossible to provide a static view of systems by data flow nets. Nevertheless, even for object oriented techniques that include the dynamic creation and deletion of objects, data flow models are useful. We can represent a complete class of objects in object oriented programming by a data flow node. Each such node represents the set of objects of that class operating in parallel. It is not very helpful, of course, to represent the structure of a class by a data flow diagram, in general.

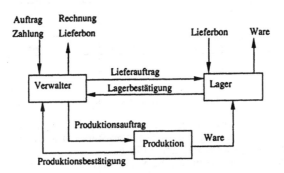

Fig. 4 Structural System View

A data flow net shows the components of a system and their communication inter-connections. A data flow net provides a static view on a set of components and their connections. For systems with a more dynamic structure as mentioned above, where the set of components as well as their interconnection by communication links do change over the lifetime of a system, a classical data flow net can only provide a snapshot. However, we can also use data flow models that incorporate all components (or classes of components) that may exist over the lifetime of the system.

The exact meaning of data flow models is not always described precisely for the software engineering methods used in practice, although most of these methods advocate versions of data flow diagrams as part of their description techniques. Nevertheless, as well known we can formalize the meaning of data flow nets by stream processing functions (see [Broy 95b]).

The weak side of data flow nets are their limited possibilities to describe the behavior of systems. They indicate which components exist and may exchange messages, however, this does not say much about the causality of the exchanged messages.

Of course, we can annotate data flow diagrams by information about the sorts and structure of the messages exchange on a data link. This provides a description of the syntactic interfaces of the components of a system.

The mathematics of data flow nets can be based directly on the mathematical system models introduced above. We use stream processing functions to represent the meaning of a data flow node. Since we used timed streams, we can also model timing events.

3.5 Processes

A system behavior (also called a run of a system) can be described by the set of events (exchanged messages) and their causal relationship. It is represented by a process. In software engineering the concept of process is found for instance in SDL (see [SDL 88]) called *sequence charts* or in objectory (see [Booch 91]) called *use cases*.

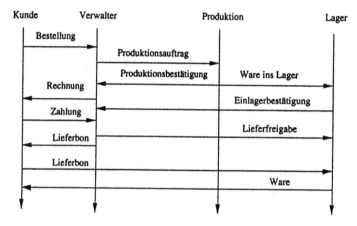

Fig. 5 Sequence Chart

Technically, a sequence chart defines a trace of communication events for the system and for each of the components. Fig. 5 provides an example of a sequence chart giving the same information as the process diagram of Fig. 6.

Processes of interactive systems can be nicely represented by acyclic data flow graphs where each node stands for exactly one action in the business case and each arc stands for one event of a message or a signal transfer from one action to another. So each action in the business case is represented by exactly one node and each event is represented by exactly one arc.

Graphically each event can be represented by an arc and by the two involved agents (sender and receiver). Since causality between events is always realized through the agents, an event e1 can only be directly causal (triggering) for an event e2, if the sender of e2 is the receiver of e1.

We get component-based process views. Such processes are obtained as specific subprocesses of the behaviors of structural system views. Of course, in a structural view several business processes and several business tasks may be carried out in an interleaved manner.

In the processes we do not include the data flow between the different activities of one component. This may, however, be necessary if the process view is to be refined into a structural system view during the system development. Similarly, the access to a common data base may not be modeled explicitly in a first development step. However, later such a modeling is necessary to obtain a correct representation of the data dependencies between the involved actions. Fig. 6 gives a process view of a standard business case.

32

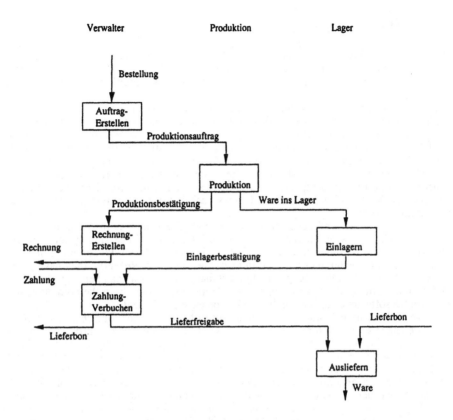

Fig. 6 Process Description of a Business Case

The behavior of a component mentioned in a process view can be described again by a data flow network or by a state machine (PD in [Grapes 90]). A formal definition of the interpretation of processes as runs of systems described by data flow graphs is given in section 5.4.

3.6 The Role of Description Techniques

Description techniques and the underlying semantic models form the heart of the documentation of the development process. We may understand the development process as the working out of documents describing the requirements and the system in more and more details, adding implementation aspects until an implementation level is reached.

In the development process description techniques serve mainly the following purposes:

- means for the analysis and requirement capture for the developer,
- basis for the validation of development results,
- communication between the engineers and the application experts,
- documentation of development results and input for further development steps.

Software engineering has provided many different description techniques for the various aspects. A proper relationship between these description techniques and a foundation of them are the task of the mathematics of software engineering.

4. Modeling Techniques

Description techniques give - similar to programming languages for describing algorithms - a solid basis for representing models. There is as much freedom in how to use a description technique as there is freedom to provide an algorithm for a problem in a programming language.

For the development of information processing systems we have to develop an adequate model of the information process task. Since it is difficult or even impossible to describe a complex system in full detail in one document, we structure the description by providing models and abstractions. An abstraction is a simplification of the problem. A useful abstraction allows us to concentrate on significant aspects of the problem reducing the overall complexity. A view shows us the system under a specific perspective also concentrating on specific aspects. So a view is also an abstraction. However, since we generally work with a fixed collection of views, each of the views provides a more uniform type of abstraction.

Certain views are well accepted in software engineering. For instance, data views, which provide a view on the data aspects of an information processing system, are well received and can be found in terms of E/R-models in nearly all development methods. Process modeling techniques are used in many methods, too. Recently, they have gained more attention. It is widely recognized by now that process views can help significantly in understanding the problem and properties of solutions, especially in the communication between the software engineer and the application expert and client.

Nevertheless, how to make a systematic use of process modeling techniques in the software and system development cause is still not fully understood. A process represents the history of the run of a system in terms of the actions performed by a system and their causal relationship. Since often the processes of a system are too large to show them in toto the behavior of a system is illustrated by sample subprocesses handling individual business cases. There is a general agreement that besides data views and structural views the modeling of processes is essential for the development of interactive systems. Process modeling techniques can be used in many application areas. In telecommunication, for instance, SDL provides sequence charts (see [SDL 88]). Object oriented techniques provide use cases. In business applications this leads to business process views.

We believe that process modeling is a helpful concept in most application areas of information processing. We believe, too, that a systematic use of process modeling techniques can be helpful, in principle, both in technical and in business applications.

In the early phases of system development often called systems analysis or requirements engineering we work out the following five complementary system views:

- data views (also called information model),
- process views (dynamic view),
- structural views (also called organizational or architectural model),
- behavior views (interface model, behavior history model),
- state view (state transition model).

Software engineering has provided many different description techniques for all these modeling aspects (see above). What is lacking in many methods is the integration of these views (see below). In particular, it is not always clear what the role of process views is in system and software engineering from a methodological point of view.

In the following we sketch the role of business process views in the development process of a system. We concentrate on business applications, but most of what we outline can be carried over to technical applications as well.

Structuring descriptions is one of the most important goals. This leads to levels of abstractions. The question, how levels of abstractions are connected by refinement notions is discussed in the section 5 on the development method.

4.1 Modeling the Data View

Data views can be used for modeling dynamic and static aspects of a system. There are strictly object-oriented approaches that suggest to mix static and dynamic aspects into one E/R-diagram. They suggest also to model each business case by an object. This object includes all the attributes needed to represent the state of the individual business case and all the methods needed to change the business case attributes. This is suggestive as long as such an object is modeled as passive. It becomes questionable as soon as such an object gets active and calls methods of other objects. This contradicts the principle of object orientation that has the goal to represent reality as "naturally" as possible.

A more formal and more detailed state machine description can be obtained by giving a precise description of the state of the object Verwalter. We have done this by giving a data view for the component Verwalter.

We can give a data view of the state of a distributed system (v, O) by an E/R-diagram that defines a number of components in terms of the set of entities N and provides a state space for each of these components by a number of attributes with their sorts. Mathematically we obtain a function

$$\rho: N \to \Sigma$$

that associate with every entity a component and its state. Since we consider asynchronous communication in our distributed system models, we need a buffer for every input channel. Then the state of the distributed system is defined by the function:

$$\rho: N \to B \times \Sigma$$

where B is the set of all functions $I \to M^*$ where I is a set of input channels. This way a state space is obtained for a distributed system and the distributed system can be understood as a distributed state machine by providing a state transition function that includes message transmission and local state changes.

4.2 Behavior Views of Components

A structural system view does only provide a description of the overall system behavior if for each data flow node a behavior is fixed. We distinguish between a black box view and a glass box view of components. In a black box view the behavior of a component of an interactive system can be represented either by a trace set or by a stream processing function. In a glass box view the behavior can either be represented by a state machine or by an interactive distributed system.

Often, it is advisable first to take into consideration only the regular aspects of behavior and in a second step to consider exceptional cases. We distinguish the following classes of exceptional cases concerning external input events:

• external input events that are expected, but do not occur (within certain time bounds),
• external input events that occur unexpectedly,
• external output events that cannot be generated by the system.

The same distinctions can be made for the internal events.

Of course, a component like the Verwalter does not control exactly one business case at a time but many. This has to be taken into account when implementing it.

4.3 Process Modeling

In this section we show how to use process modeling in system development. We concentrate on business applications, which are more unusual as a target for formal methods. We model actions in a process by a data flow node that formally represents an component. However, a component representing an action has a very special simple structure. On each of its input arcs it receives exactly one message and on each of its output arcs it issues exactly one message. In a complete modeling of an action all the information an action needs is provided by its input messages. Since an action is represented formally by a data flow component we can describe it by the same techniques as we describe components.

Currently there is much interest in business process engineering and reengineering. We study business processes for representing business cases.

Business cases are processes of activities. By a *business task* we understand all activities of an enterprise that serve a specific purpose. An example for such a business task is the task car rental in a car rental company; it comprises all activities that serve the rental of cars. Of course, for an application there are several possibilities to collect and structure the actions of a system into business tasks. An appropriate structuring of the actions is depending on the skills of the application and systems engineers.

Typically, we can decompose the activities of a business task hierarchically into (disjoint families of) activities that belong to one particular instance of the task. In the example of the car rental these instances are all activities that serve the purpose of one particular instance of a car rental. We call each instance of a business task a *business case*.

We distinguish between the following three different approaches to the description of business tasks by business processes:

(1) instances of business processes: only one sample of a business case is described,

(2) partial business process view: a representative set of samples of business processes is described,

(3) complete business process view: the set of all possible business processes is described.

The first case is easy: a sample of a business process view can easily be described (if it is not too large and too complex) by a directed, acyclic data flow graph. Fig. 6 gives an instance of a business case description by a graphical representation of a business process. Formally the diagram is understood as a data flow net. However, in contrast to general data flow nets, the data flow nets representing processes are acyclic. Each arc corresponds to exactly one event in the process and represents exactly one message sent, while, in general, in data flow graphs an arc corresponds to a stream of messages. This way the arcs in the diagram express causality and the boxes represent actions.

The role of business case views in the analysis phase is simple: representative instances of processes are used to illustrate the cooperation of the components. Often only the nonexceptional cases of business cases are modeled. Exceptional cases with all the details of exception handling are not considered explicitly. This way implicitly exceptional business cases are distinguished from standard cases.

A simple way of identifying all actions and events associated with a business case uniquely is given by introducing keys for business cases. Such keys need not occur explicitly in the real life system, but are often useful as pure description means.

The second approach to business process description is more difficult both from the descriptional and the methodological point of view. A set of processes (a set of directed graphs) cannot be described very easily by directed graphs. The description of a set of quite different processes in a graphical way is difficult and may not be very helpful, if the causal structure of the process cannot be recognized from the graphical description easily. Only in cases where the individual processes show much similarity, a graphical description visualizing the causality flow may be readable. From a rigorous methodological point of view its usefulness is also not clear. What does it mean to give a representative subset of samples of the processes that are possible for a task? This way unwanted behaviors cannot be excluded. Only a subset of the set of possible behaviors that are allowed (or even required) is given. Only an informal interpretation and usage of such description makes sense.

The third case is as difficult from the descriptional point of view as approach (2). However, from a methodological point of view it is rather suggestive. If we give the complete set of all allowed processes we clearly indicate which behaviors are allowed and which are not allowed. Since we can distinguish between events caused by the environment and events caused by the system, of course, the existence of processes without certain patterns of events leads to different implications for the systems involved depending on the question whether the events are external or internal.

Given all business views for the nonexceptional cases we can generate the tables listing all exceptional events possible in particular situations. Here we can distinguish the following situations:

(a) unexpected events,
(b) missing expected events within a defined time interval.

An example of an unexpected event is the arrival of a payment before an invoice was sent. An example of a missing expected event is the nonarrival of a payment within a particular time interval after the invoice has been sent.

There is a rich body of research on the topic (Petri nets, process algebras like CCS and CSP, event structures, etc.) how to describe sets of processes. However, most of this work can only be used as a theoretical foundation and does not help in concrete description tasks. So more needs to be done to make these theoretical approaches practically useful.

Also methodological questions still need to be answered. In many practical applications the description of the complete set of processes would not lead to a comprehensible document.

4.4 Structural System Views

In a structural system view the structural decomposition of a system into a family of components is shown. A complete description of a structural system view by a data flow net where for each of its data flow nodes black box behaviors are given contains enough information to simulate system behaviors, provided the behavior of all components is described by means for which an operational interpretation is given. Structural system views are easily provided by data flow diagrams as shown in Fig. 4.

In a system development there may be several structural views, for instance, indicating the logical structure and the physical structure of a system.

4.5 The Step to Information Processing

The techniques described so far work for all kinds of systems, independently of the fact whether the actions are executed by human beings, hardware devices or information processing systems. Aiming at software development we are interested to identify those parts of the system (those actions of a system) that are to be carried out by computer-based information processing system (CIPS).

This identification is the basis for the description of the interface (the functionality) of the CIPS given by the requirement specification.

An important question concerns the relation and interaction between the CIPS and the actions and processes of its environment. This is, in particular, the basis for specifying and realizing the user interface. Formally, this modeling step can be understood again as a structural decomposition of a system into components modeling the environment and the information processing machinery. This brings the notion of software into the discussion. This can be done by modeling a software architecture. In addition, hardware constraints may be given.

4.6 Software Architecture

The modeling of *software architectures* is an important application of mathematical techniques in software engineering. A first interesting question is what a software architecture is. We need appropriate mathematical models of the notion of a software architecture.

The notion of software architecture is treated systematically but informally in the stimulating paper [Garlan, Shaw 93]. However, there only diagram descriptions of the different types of architectures are used and therefore their classification suffers from the missing precision of their descriptions.

Intuitively, a software architecture is given by a family of components and their connections/relationships. Depending on the concept of components used we get quite different forms of architectures. Basic types of components of architectures are:

- statements and procedures leading to *remote procedure call architectures,*
- functions leading to function call *hierarchical architectures,*
- data flow nodes, state machines, objects leading to *interactive system architectures* (also called pipes and filters),
- abstract data types leading to *hierarchical data type architectures,*
- modules leading to *layered architectures.*

For a better foundation of software engineering we need not only formal models for all these types of components and architectures, which are more or less available by now, but also concepts for translating one into the other. This would provide interfaces between the various modeling techniques and architectural concepts that are of high importance for practical applications, where often different concepts are used side by side.

A *homogeneous architecture* is one that is built out of components of one type. A *heterogeneous architecture* is built out of components of different types. For all these notions we need more mathematics as a solid foundation. We distinguish between static and dynamic aspects of components and architectures. Also this structuring has to be reflected more explicitly in mathematical models.

Software architectures typically deal with questions of programming and development in the large. In this area many questions are still open. Design patterns and application frames are examples for promising ideas in architectures that need more mathematical foundation.

5. Development Method

A development method gives hints and suggestions, how to use description and modeling techniques in a systematic way to develop a computer-based information processing system. In software engineering the development is carried out in phases. We speak of a *development process model.*

5.1 Development Process Model

In pragmatic software engineering the discussion of the development process model plays a central role. This has clear reasons. The development process model determines the whole development process and is therefore decisive for the economy and the quality of the development.

Often religious fights are fought in software engineering whether the waterfall model, the spiral model, the experimental or evolutionary prototyping model, or object oriented development methods provide the best development process models. Not much theoretical work has been invested to discuss, characterize, relate, or formally specify these different development models.

Mathematical techniques can help to relate the various views and documents in a development process. They help to understand whether a particular proceeding is appropriate and how the interaction between the various documents and views can be formalized and supported by methods and tools.

A more rigorous formalization of the development process is suggestive. Development processes are instances of processes as they are discussed in theoretical computer science. So we can apply all our notions from process theory here, too. In the discussions on development process models it is often not recognized that we have to distinguish between the overall structure of the development documents and how they are related and the temporal order in which they are produced. So we can talk about the statics and the dynamics of the development method.

5.2 Refinement

In software engineering, systems are described by different complementing views and on different levels of abstraction. Of course, we need clear mathematical relations between the different levels of abstraction. This is closely related to refinement notions.

Much theoretical work has been devoted towards the refinement notion. After the more pragmatic and informal ideas of stepwise refinement developed by Dahl, Wirth and many others in the seventies, much formalization has taken place converging essentially into the following two concepts:

- *property refinement*: In property refinement a system is developed by adding additional properties (requirements) and further system parts (enriching the signature). The basic mathematical notion of property refinement is logical implication (with respect to the logical properties) or set inclusion (with respect to the set of models). This allows us also to replace component specifications by logically equivalent component implementations.
- *representation refinement*: In representation refinement we change the representation of a data model or of the states and messages of a system model. This can be done by a function associating the two models.

For data models representation refinement was studied extensively over the last 25 years after stimulating papers by Hoare. For system components such studies have emerged only more recently.

For our concept of system model property refinement is very simple. A component

$$\hat{f}: (I \rightarrow M^{\omega}) \rightarrow \wp(O \rightarrow M^{\omega})$$

is called a refinement of a component:

$$f: (I \rightarrow M^{\omega}) \rightarrow \wp(O \rightarrow M^{\omega})$$

if for all $x \in (I \rightarrow M^{\omega})$ we have:

$$\hat{f}(x) \subseteq f(x)$$

For a systematic use of refinement concepts compositionality of refinement is essential. Compositionality means that if we replace a component of a system by its refinement we obtain a refinement of the overall system. Of course, refinement notions can be carried over to state machines.

An interface refinement changes the syntactic interface of a component, but provides a precise interpretation of the behavior of the refined component as behaviors of the given one. We introduce what is called an *upwards simulation* in the literature. We consider two components:

$$f: (I \rightarrow M^{\omega}) \rightarrow \wp(O \rightarrow M^{\omega}),$$
$$\hat{f}: (\hat{I} \rightarrow M^{\omega}) \rightarrow \wp(\hat{O} \rightarrow M^{\omega}).$$

If we want to consider the behavior $\hat{f}$ as an interface refinement of the behavior f we have to interpret all computations of $\hat{f}$ as behaviors of f. However, in general, not all computations

$$s: (\hat{I} \cup \hat{O}) \rightarrow M^{\omega}$$

may be needed as representations of computations of the component f. Therefore we introduce a subset S that contains all the computations in $(\hat{I} \cup \hat{O}) \rightarrow M^{\omega}$ that represent computations in $I \cup O \rightarrow M^{\omega}$:

$$S \subseteq (\hat{I} \cup \hat{O}) \to M^{\varpi}$$

and a surjective function

$$\alpha: S \to ((I \cup O) \to M^{\varpi}) \qquad \textit{(the abstraction function)}$$

that allows us to interpret every computation in S as a computation in $(I \cup O) \to M^{\varpi}$. The function α is called an *upward simulation* or *abstraction function*, if

(0) α is consistent on input streams

$$\forall \ s, s' \in S: \ s|_{\hat{I}} = s'|_{\hat{I}} \Rightarrow \alpha(s)|_I = \alpha(s')|_I$$

(1) every output of the component $\hat{f}$ for an input in S is in S, too:

$$\forall \ s \in S, t \in (\hat{I} \cup \hat{O}) \to M^{\varpi}: \ s|_{\hat{I}} = t|_{\hat{I}} \wedge t|_{\hat{O}} \in \hat{f}(t|_{\hat{I}}) \Rightarrow t \in S$$

(2) every computation of $\hat{f}$ is a computation in $(I \cup O) \to M^{\varpi}$ of f:

$$\forall \ s \in S: \ s|_{\hat{O}} \in \hat{f}(s)|_{\hat{I}}) \Rightarrow \alpha(s)|_O \in f(\alpha(s)|_I)$$

Since α is surjective, for every computation $r \in (I \cup O) \to M^{\varpi}$ there exists a computation $s \in S$ such that

$$r|_I = \alpha(s)|_I$$

By condition (1) and assuming $\hat{f}(x) \neq \emptyset$ for all $x \in (\hat{I} \cup \hat{O}) \to M^{\varpi}$ there exists a computation $t \in S$ such that

$$s|_{\hat{I}} = t|_{\hat{I}} \wedge t|_{\hat{O}} \in \hat{f}(t|_{\hat{I}})$$

Then by condition (2) we obtain:

$$\alpha(t)|_O \in f(\alpha(t)|_I)$$

So for every input of the component f a computation of f is represented by a computation of $\hat{f}$. The development of systems can be understood as a joint development of the process, the data, the behavior and the structural model. Each of these views is only worked out to a level of detail regarded appropriate.

5.3 The Modeling Universe

In the development of a system, we fix the five views and work out respective models:

- structure (organization, distribution),
- information (data),
- process (business cases),
- interface,
- subsystem behavior by state change (state transitions).

These views have to be consistent. They include a number of formal concepts, in our case the notions of

- actors,
- communication links,
- action,
- state,
- event,
- message.

For all application details to be described the corresponding modeling notions have to be agreed on and to be fixed during the development process.

A central notion of refinement is decomposition. We can use static or dynamic notions of decomposition.

5.4 View Integration, Relating Processes to Structural System Views

Given a complete system description, say by a structural system view (a hierarchical data flow graph), and a state transition description for each atomic component (a data flow node) the overall behavior of a system is fixed. Now we can associate processes with such a system by unraveling the cycles. This leads, in general, to infinite acyclic data flow graphs corresponding to a run of the system.

In this unrolling of the data flow nodes the information flow between the actions of one component by the states of the components has to be made explicit.

A process is represented by an acyclic data flow net (v_p, O_p) and a valuation function

$$\eta: \text{Chan}((v_p, O_p)) \to M$$

that associates with all of its input arcs exactly one message.

In the view integration we have to associate the process view with the structural view. This means that we have to define when a process is a view of a system. Now we define when we call a process a *run* of a data flow net (v, O) with input x. We require that there is a function

$$\kappa: \text{Nodes}((v_p, O_p)) \to \text{Nodes}((v, O))$$

that associates with every action of the process a component of the data flow net. Moreover, we require that there exists a function

$$\chi: \text{Chan}((v_p, O_p)) \to \text{Chan}((v, O))$$

that associates with every arc in the process a channel such that for every node $i \in \text{Nodes}((v_p, O_p))$ each channel in its set of input channels is mapped onto an input channel of the node onto which the node i is mapped:

$$\{\chi(c): c \in \text{In}(i)\} \subseteq \text{In}(\kappa(i))$$

$$\{\chi(c): c \in \text{Out}(i)\} \subseteq \text{Out}(\kappa(i))$$

We assume that for each channel $c \in \text{Chan}((v, O))$ we have a linear order on the sets of channels (arcs)

$$\{c': \chi(c') = c\}$$

in the process. This fixes in which order the messages are sent in the process. Of course, this order has to be consistent with the causality in the process. This way we can associate a finite stream $\upsilon(c)$ with each channel $c \in \text{Chan}((v, O))$ of the data flow net. The process (v_p, O_p) is called a run for input x if there exists a valuation $y : \text{Chan}((v, O)) \to M^\omega$ such that

$$y|_I = x \wedge \forall i \in N: y|_{\text{Out}(v(i))} = v(i)(y|_{\text{In}(v(i))})$$

and

$$\upsilon(c)|_{\text{In}(v(i))} \sqsubseteq y(c)$$

In words, the process is a prefix of a computation of the net. In many cases, processes are not used to model initial segments of system computations. Then a process may consist of all messages of a particular subset M' of the set messages M. Then we require

$$\upsilon(c)|_{\text{In}(v(i))} \sqsubseteq M' \copyright y(c)$$

where M'©y denotes the family of streams obtained from y by filtering out all messages in M'.

Another possibility to visualize the interaction between the components of a net by processes are sequence charts (see Fig. 5). They can be associated with processes in an analogous way.

5.5 The Role of Business Process Views in the Development

In the development process business process views are used for the following purposes:

- In the early development phases instances of business processes and business process views can help in the requirement capture. They can be a valuable means for communication between an application expert and the system analysis expert.

- As soon as a complete structural system view is provided, process views and business process views can be used to illustrate the system behavior by simulations. One may also think of a model checking tool that checks whether only the required business processes are possible behaviors of the structural system view.

We can associate a set of states with every business case. Formally, the set of states can be represented by the set of prefixes that, in fact, represents all partial executions (snapshots) of a business case. Of course such a representation of the states of a business process is much too abstract and therefore not very helpful. However, by introducing appropriate names and representations for the states we can gain additional views on a business case.

As we have seen, a component can be described by a state machine. The state machine can be systematically derived from the business process view. For every component we can construct a local view onto the business case and represent this by a set of states. It can be understood as the projection of the state view of a business case onto a component. Then we can describe the behavior of the component concerning the business case by a state machine.

5.6 View Integration by Axiomatic Specifications

The different views developed in systems modeling finally have to be integrated into a consistent system description. Here axiomatic specification techniques are extremely helpful that allow to see all views as providing axioms about a system. This technique was successfully applied in [Hußmann 95].

View integration can be made on a purely mathematical level by joining together all the mathematical structures given by the various description methods. Another possibility is to understand every description method as a logical statement about the system. Then all the logical statements provided by the description can be composed into one big axiomatic specification. Then consistency of a description coincides with logical consistency.

5.7 Dialog Modeling

The modeling of the input and output to systems by dialogs is an important part in system development which is of special interest in transaction systems and in business application. For modeling the dialog by several levels of abstractions these refinement notions are especially helpful.

There are a number of pragmatic description techniques for dialog modeling. We do not mean the GUI (graphical user interface) tools here, which provide an extremely helpful technique to implement user interfaces, but rather mean the logical design of user interfaces. This is of high relevance for instance in telecommunication. There the system mainly has to provide services between SAPs (service access points).

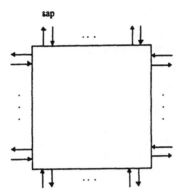

Fig. 7 Telecommunication system with its saps

For the description of these services pragmatic techniques are used for describing following views:

- *Interaction view*, described by time sequence diagrams or sequence charts,

- *Service access point view*, described by an I/O-state machine.

In the interaction view the causality between the actions at different SAPs is described. This corresponds closely to the process view we have discussed in detail.

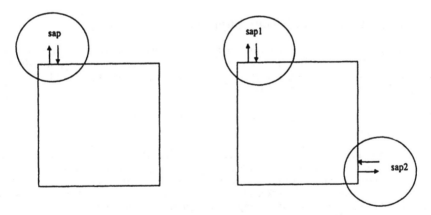

Fig. 8 Service access view and interaction view on the SAPs of a telecom system

The service access point view describes the local view of a SAP. It describes which actions are possible for a user at a SAP. The description of a system this way needs the integration of these views and the formal modeling of the views (see [Facchi 95]).

In a mathematical model a telecom system as show in Fig. 7 is a component with a behavior in C[I, O] where I contains one input channel for each SAP and O also contains one output channel for each SAP. The behavior is given by a function:

$$f : (I \to M^{\omega}) \to \wp(O \to M^{\omega})$$

The interaction view then corresponds to the concentration of the view on two SAPs with input channels i_k and output channels o_k where $k = 1, 2$. The function

$$h: (\{i_1, i_2\} \to M^{\omega}) \to \wp(\{o_1, o_2\} \to M^{\omega})$$

models the interaction view:

$$h(x) = \{ f(z)|_{\{o_1, o_2\}} : x = z|_{\{i_1, i_2\}} \}$$

The service access view then corresponds to the concentration of the view on one SAP with input channel i and output channels o. The function

$$g: (\{i\} \to M^{\overline{\omega}}) \to \wp(\{o\} \to M^{\overline{\omega}})$$

models the service access point view:

$$g(x) = \{ f(z)|_{\{o\}} : x = z|_{\{i\}} \}$$

Often, the families of communications z used in the definitions above have to be further restricted to well-formed computations.

In dialog modeling often we have to use interaction refinement to be able to break up one logical interaction (communication of one message) into a number of dialog interactions.

5.8 Task Modeling

In modern software engineering techniques application oriented modeling techniques are considered as extremely helpful. This comprises the modeling of goals and tasks. Of course, the description of abstract "strategic" goals by mathematical techniques is hardly possible. However, a formal task modeling is thinkable. One may use "logical" components that are responsible for certain tasks. This again leads to two complementing views: the task and the actor view.

6. Implementation and Tool Support

There are many arguments that formal methods can only be applied effectively, if the appropriate tools are available. However, looking at the commercial and experimental case tools around it soon gets clear that tooling is not the only and certainly not the decisive issue for the usage of formal methods.

6.1 Tool Support

Tool support is an important field in software engineering. It is exciting, of course, to think about an advanced tool support of software engineering, where much of the subordinate work is taken over by the tool while the engineer concentrates on the real design issues. A closer look at the tools in the market shows how far away we are from these dreams. For an advanced tool support we need a deeper understanding of the integration of the various views worked out in the development process.

No one in engineering can do with a tool what he or she does not understand to do without a tool. Nevertheless, large development tasks can hardly be done without tool support. Moreover, it is the strength of formal methods that, thanks to their formality, more consequent tool support is possible.

As also observable in the pragmatic tooling for supporting the software engineering so far, we do not have an integrated tool supporting the basic activities such as documentation, version control, specification, engineering support, validation, verification by deduction and model checking, implementation support by code generation. To build such a tool is a costly activity. The area of application and the technical context (implementation platforms, target code) have to be chosen carefully including the economical and technical constraints and perspectives.

6.2 Implementation Vision

Our implementation vision is that a running system implementation (at least a prototype both for the CIPS and its environments) can be generated directly from the result of the system modeling process. What do we need to be able to do this? We need the definition of the state changes for each action and in addition a concept for controlling the state of a business process.

Rapid prototyping is regarded of high importance in practice. Therefore formal methods should always keep prototyping and production system generation as a goal, since only this way the overhead of applying formal methods will pay in the long run.

6.3 Testing

Testing is obviously considered not be within the range of political correctness by most computer scientists working in formal methods. From a historical view this is understandable, since in the early days of computing there was no systematic software development and testing was seen as the only way to assure quality. This is a poor approach. However, in combination with other quality assurance techniques, testing is a vital part of development and has to be integrated into a well-founded method of software development.

7. Conclusions

What we have achieved in theory is impressive, what we have accomplished in practice is not enough, however. We have to rethink the way we carry out research in the mathematics of software engineering to make sure that the feedback process between theory and practice is improved.

We are at an exciting stage in software engineering and formal methods. Most of the theoretical work required for the foundations has been done. What is needed is an experimental integration and application.

In the SysLab-project at the Technical University of Munich we try to follow this line and make a significant effort to gain a closer relationship between formal methods and pragmatic software engineering.

Acknowledgment

The thoughts presented above have benefited greatly from discussions within the SysLab team, the IFIP working group 2.3, with software engineers from Siemens, Siemens Nixdorf, Digital and many others.

References

[Abrial 92]
J.R. Abrial: On Constructing Large Software Systems. In: J. van Leeuwen (ed.): Algorithms, Software, Architecture, Information Processing 92, Vol. I, 103-119

[Bauer, Wössner 82]
F.L. Bauer, H. Wössner: Algorithmic language and program development, Berlin: Springer, 1982

[Beeck 95]
M. v. d. Beeck: A Comparison of State Charts Variants. In: H. Langmaack, W.-P. de Roever, J. Vytopil (eds): Formal Techniques in Real Time and Fault-Tolereant Systems. Lecture Notes in Computer Science 863, 1994, 128-148

[Booch 91]
G. Booch: Object Oriented Design with Applications. Benjamin Cummings, Redwood City, CA, 1991

[Boyer, Moore 89]
R.S. Boyer, J.S. Moore: The Addition of Bounded Quantification and Partial Functions to a Computational Logic and Its Theorem Prover. In: M. Broy (Hrsg.): Constructive Methods in Computing Science. Springer NATO ASI Series, Series F: Computer and System Sciences, Vol. 55, 1989, 95-145

[Broy 88]
M. Broy: Nondeterministic data flow programs: how to avoid the merge anomaly. Science of Computer Programming 10 (1988), 65-85

[Broy 91a]
M. Broy: Towards a Formal Foundation of the Specification and Description Language SDL. Formal Aspects of Computing 3, 21-57 (1991)

[Broy 91b]
M. Broy: Formalisation of distributed, concurrent, reactive systems. In: E.J. Neuhold, M. Paul (eds.): Formal Description of Programming Concepts. IFIP W.G. 2.2 advanced seminar, Rio de Janeiro 1989. Berlin: Springer, 1991, 319-361

[Broy 92]
M. Broy: Experiences with Software Specification and Verification Using LP, the Larch Proof Assistent. DIGITAL Systems Research Center, SRC 93, 1992

[Broy 93]
M. Broy: (Inter-)Action Refinement: The Easy Way. In: Broy, M. (ed.): Program Design Calculi. Springer NATO ASI Series, Series F: Computer and System Sciences, Vol. 118, pp. 121-158, Berlin, Heidelberg, New York: Springer 1993

[Broy 94a]
M. Broy: Specification and Refinement of a Buffer of Length One. Marktoberdorf Summer School 1994

[Broy 94b]
M. Broy: A Functional Rephrasing of the Assumption/Commitment Specification Style. Technische Universität München, Institut für Informatik, TUM-I9417, June 1994

[Broy 95a]
M. Broy: Equations for Describing Dynamic Nets of Communicating Systems. In: E. Astesiano, G. Reggio, A. Tarlecki (eds): Recent Trends in Data Types Specification, 10th Workshop on Specification of Abstract Data Types joint with the 5th COMPASS Workshop, S.Margherita, Italy, May/June 1994 Lecture Notes in Computer Science 906, Springer 1995

[Broy 95b]
M. Broy: Advanced Component Interface Specification. In: Takayasu Ito, Akinori Yonezawa (Eds.). Theory and Practice of Parallel Programming, International Workshop TPPP'94, Sendai, Japan, November 7-9, 1994, Proceedings, Lecture Notes in Computer Science 907, Springer 1995

[Broy, Dendorfer, Stølen 93]
M. Broy, C. Dendorfer. K. Stølen: HOPSA - High Level Programming Language for Parallel Computations. P.P. Spies (ed): EuroArch 93, Springer 1993, 636-646

[Broy, Lamport 93]
M. Broy, L. Lamport: Specification Problem. http://www.research.digital.com/SRC/personal/Leslie_Lamport/dagstuhl/all.html

[Broy, Stølen 94]
M. Broy, K. Stølen: Specification and Refinement of Finite Dataflow Networks – a Relational Approach. In: Langmaack, H. and de Roever, W.-P. and Vytopil, J. (eds): Proc. FTRTFT'94, Lecture Notes in Computer Science 863, 1994, 247-267

[CIP 84]
M. Broy: Algebraic methods for program construction: The project CIP. SOFSEM 82, also in: P. Pepper (ed.): Program Transformation and Programming Environments. NATO ASI Series. Series F: 8. Berlin-Heidelberg-New York-Tokyo: Springer 1984, 199-222

[Coad, Yourdan 91]
P. Coad, E. Yourdon: Object-oriented Analysis. Prentice Hall International Editions 1991

[DeMarco 79]
T. DeMarco: Structured Analysis and System Specification. Yourdan Press, New York, NY, 1979

[Denert 91]
E. Denert: Software-Engineering. Springer 1991

[Dijkstra 76]
E.W. Dijkstra: A Discipline of Programming. Englewood Cliffs: Prentice-Hall 1976

[Facchi 95]
Ch. Facchi: Methodik zur formalen Spezifikation des ISO/OSI-Schichtenmodells. Dissertation, Fakultät für Informatik, Technische Universität München, to appear

[Floyd 67]
R.W. Floyd: Assigning Meanings to Programs. Proc. of Symposia in Applied Mathematics of the Amer. Math. Soc. 19, 1967, 19-32

[FOCUS 92]
M. Broy, F. Dederichs, C. Dendorfer, M. Fuchs, T.F. Gritzner, R. Weber: The Design of Distributed Systems - an Introduction to FOCUS. Technical University Munich, Institute of Computer Science, TUM-I9203, Januar 1992, see also: Summary of Case Studies in FOCUS - a Design Method for Distributed Systems. Technical University of Munich, Institute for Computer Science, TUM-I9203, Januar 1992

[Garlan, Shaw 93]
D. Garlan, M. Shaw: An Introduction To Software Architecture. In: Advances in Software Engineering and Knowledge Engineering. 1993

[Grapes 90]
GRAPES-Referenzmanual, DOMINO, Integrierte Verfahrenstechnik. Siemens AG, Bereich Daten-und Informationstechnik 1990

[Grosu 94]
R. Grosu: A formal foundation for concurrent object-oriented programming. Dissertation, Fakultät für Informatik, Technische Universität München, December 94

[Grosu et al. 95]
R. Grosu, K. Stølen, M. Broy: A Denotational Model for Mobile Data Flow Networks. To appear

[Guttag, Horning 93]
J.V. Guttag, J.J. Horning: A Larch Shared Language Handbook. Springer 1993

[Hettler 94]
R. Hettler: Zur Übersetzung von E/R-Schemata nach Spectrum. Technischer Bericht TUM-I9409, TU München, 1994

[Hoare 69]
C.A.R. Hoare: An Axiomatic Approach to Computer Programming. Comm. ACM 12, October 1969, 576-580, 583

[Hußmann 94]
H. Hußmann: Formal foundation of pragmatic software engineering methods. In: B. Wolfinger(ed.): Innovationen bei Rechen- und Kommunikationssystemen, Informatik aktuell, Berlin: Springer, 1994, 27-34

[Hußmann 95]
H. Hußmann: Formal Foundations for SSADM. Technische Universität München, Fakultät für Informatik, Habilitationsschrift 1995

[Jones 86]
C.B. Jones: Systematic Program Development Using VDM. Prentice Hall 1986

[KORSO 93]
M. Broy, S. Jähnichen (Hrsg.): Korrekte Software durch formale Methoden. GMD Karlsruhe 1993

[MacKenzie 91]
D. MacKenzie: The Fangs of the VIPER. Nature Vol. 352, 1991, 467-468

[Nickl 94]
F. Nickl: Ablaufspezifikation durch Datenflußdiagramme und Axiome. In: B. Wolfinger (ed.): Innovationen bei Rechen- und Kommunikationssystemen, Informatik aktuell, Berlin: Springer, 1994, 10-18

[Nipkow 89]
T. Nipkow: Term Rewriting and Beyond - Theorem Proving in Isabelle. Formal Aspects of Computing 1, 1989, 320-338

[Parnas, Madrey 91]
D. L. Parnas, J. Madrey: Functional Documentation for Computer Systems Engineering (Version 2). CRL Report 237. McMaster University, Hamilton Ontario, Canada 1991

[Pepper, Wirsing 95]
P. Pepper, M. Wirsing: KORSO: a method for the development of correct software. To appear

[Procos 92]
D. Björner, H. Langmaack, C.A.R. Hoare: Provably Correct Systems. ProCoS I Final Delivery, März 1992

[Reisig 86]
W. Reisig: Petrinetze - Eine Einführung. Studienreihe Informatik; 2. Überarbeitete Auflage (1986).

[Rumpe et al. 95]
B. Rumpe, C. Klein, M. Broy: Ein strombasiertes mathematisches Modell verteilter informationsverarbeitender Systeme - Syslab-Systemmodell. Technische Universität München, Institut für Informatik, 1995, TUM-I9510

[SDL 88]
Specification and Description Language (SDL), Recommendation Z.100. Technical report, CCITT, 1988

[Stølen et al. 93]
K. Stølen, F. Dederichs, R. Weber: Assumption/Commitment Rules for Networks of Agents. Technische Universität München, Institut für Informatik, TUM-I9302

Program Construction in Intuitionistic Type Theory

Thierry Coquand

Computer Science Department, Chalmers Technical University and University of
Göteborg, S-41296 Göteborg, Sweden
e-mail: coquand@cs.chalmers.se

Abstract. This talk is an introduction to the Type Theoretical approach to the
Mathematics of Program Construction.

The basic idea of this approach can be summarized briefly. It was realised by
Bishop (1967) that a constructive proof of an existential statement is an algorithm for
computing a witness of this statement. Furthermore, a specification of a functional
program can be thought of as an existential proposition which may have parameters.
The potential of these remarks for the problem of Program Construction is the
following: to constructively prove such a proposition can be seen as a systematic
and elegant way to achieve a "hand-in-hand" development of programs together
with a proof that they satisfy their specification.

Type Theory is a particular formal language designed by P. Martin-Löf to express
proofs in constructive mathematics. Type Theory has strong connections with functional programming and it is thus a natural candidate for actualizing this approach
of Program Construction on computers.

We survey the recent development in this field and base the presentation on a
particular implementation of Type Theory that emphasizes these connections. Type
Theory is there seen as a functional programming language with dependent types,
and proofs are functional programs.

We present some implemented examples where this type theoretical approach is
particularly elegant, among others a representation of constructive geometry due to
J. von Plato (Helsinki). We also compare it on one example with constructive (or
transformational) programming.

Computer-Aided Computing*

Natarajan Shankar

Computer Science Laboratory
SRI International
Menlo Park CA 94025 USA
shankar@csl.sri.com
URL: http://www.csl.sri.com/shankar.html
Phone: +1 (415) 859-5272 Fax: +1 (415) 859-2844

Abstract. Formal program design methods are most useful when supported with suitable mechanization. This need for mechanization has long been apparent, but there have been doubts whether verification technology could cope with the problems of scale and complexity. Though there is very little compelling evidence either way at this point, several powerful mechanical verification systems are now available for experimentation. Using SRI's PVS as one representative example, we argue that the technology of mechanical verification is already quite effective. PVS derives its power from an integration of theorem proving with type-checking, decision procedures with interactive proof construction, and more recently, model checking with theorem proving. We discuss these individual aspects of PVS using examples, and motivate some of the challenges that lie ahead.

1 Introduction

Should hardware and software designs be formally verified, and if so, should the verification process be mechanized? The answer to these questions depends crucially on whether it is feasible to formally verify large and complex systems with demonstrable benefits and without an immoderate amount of effort. The basic thesis defended in this paper is that powerful and sophisticated mechanization is needed to facilitate the productive use of formal methods.

Formality and mechanization go hand-in-hand. Formal syntax and proof theory provide the foundation for building mechanized tools. Mechanization supplies the speed, accuracy, and repeatability needed for formal manipulations. Even so, mechanization is widely regarded as more of a hindrance than an aid. We argue that mechanization is not inherently unwieldy, and that through careful engineering, mechanization can be made responsive and flexible.

Several excellent mechanized verification tools have been developed in the recent past. A few of these have even been put to serious industrial use, and

* Supported by by NSF Grant CCR-930044.

the indications are that through these tools, formal methods are slowly gaining acceptance at least for the design of safety-critical systems.

We focus here on one such verification system, PVS, merely out of familiarity [23].[2] We describe the key facets of the design of PVS and illustrate their role in effective verification by means of examples. Our main observation is that general-purpose tools like PVS must be integrated with domain-specific tools, notations, methodologies in order to achieve truly effective mechanization.

We first give a brief introduction to PVS in Section 2. We then discuss three important features of PVS in some detail in Sections 3, 4, and 5. In Section 6, conclusions are drawn from this discussion about the challenges that lie ahead.

2   A Brief Introduction to PVS

PVS (Prototype Verification System) is intended as an environment for constructing clear and precise specifications and for developing readable proofs that have been mechanically verified. While many of the individual ideas in the system pre-date PVS, what is new is the coherent realization of these ideas in a single system. The key elements of the PVS design are captured by the following combinations:

- *An expressive language with powerful deductive capabilities.* The PVS specification language is based on classical, simply typed, higher-order logic with type constructors for functions, records, tuples, predicate subtypes, dependent types, and abstract datatypes. Typechecking is undecidable for PVS. The PVS typechecker checks for simple type correctness and generates proof obligations corresponding to predicate subtypes. PVS also has parametric theories so that it is possible to capture, say, the notion of sorting with respect to arbitrary sizes, types, and ordering relations. By exploiting these features, researchers at NASA Langley Research Center and SRI have developed a very general bit-vector library. Paul Miner at NASA has developed a specification of portions of the IEEE 854 floating-point standard in PVS [22].
- *Powerful decision procedures with user interaction.* PVS proofs are constructed interactively. The primitive inference steps for constructing proofs are quite powerful. They make extensive use of efficient decision procedures for equality and linear arithmetic. They also exploit the tight integration between rewriting, the decision procedures, and the use of type information.

---

[2] The design and development of PVS was a collaborative effort involving several people, primarily Sam Owre. Other contributors include David Cyrluk, Patrick Lincoln, Steven Phillips, Sree Rajan, John Rushby, Mandayam Srivas, Friedrich von Henke, and Carl Witty. Ricky Butler (NASA), Damir Jamsek (ORA), and Paul Miner (NASA) provided valuable support in testing and validating PVS. The development of PVS was funded by SRI International.

PVS also uses BDD-based propositional simplification so that it can combine the capability of simplifying very large propositional expressions with equality, arithmetic, induction, and rewriting.

Higher-level inference steps can be defined by means of strategies (akin to LCF tactics [16]) written in a simple strategy language. Typical strategies include heuristic instantiation of quantifiers, propositional and arithmetic simplification, and induction and rewriting. The PVS proof checker strives to strike a careful balance between an automatic theorem prover and a low-level proof checker. Through the use of BDD-based simplification, simple PVS proof strategies can be defined for efficiently and automatically verifying simple processor designs and N-bit arithmetic circuits [9].

- *Model checking with theorem proving.* Many forms of finite-state verification, such as linear temporal logic model checking, language containment, and bisimulation checking, can be expressed in the mu-calculus [3, 13]. The higher-order logic of PVS is used to define the least and greatest fixpoint operators of the mu-calculus. When the state type is finite, the mu-calculus expressions are translated into the propositional mu-calculus and a propositional mu-calculus model checker can be used as a decision procedure. The finite types are those built from booleans and scalars using records, tuples, or arrays over subranges. Fairness cannot be expressed in CTL, but it can be defined using the mu-calculus.

  With this integration, PVS includes a useful model checker that is complemented with the theorem proving capabilities of PVS. In particular, PVS can be used to define property-preserving abstractions from an unbounded-state system to a finite-state one [5, 11]. The induction and rewriting capabilities of PVS can also be used in conjunction with model checking. We have in fact verified two illustrative examples with a combination of theorem proving and model checking: a processor-memory combination and an N-process mutual exclusion algorithm [27].

A variety of examples have been verified using PVS. It has been used to verify fault-tolerant agreement protocols under Byzantine and hybrid fault models, and real-time protocols such as Fischer's mutual exclusion algorithm and a generalized railroad crossing [10, 18]. The most substantial use of PVS has been in the verification of the microcode for selected instructions of a commercial-scale microprocessor called AAMP5 designed by Rockwell-Collins and containing about 500,000 transistors [21].

We now discuss each of the above facets of PVS in greater detail.

3 Combining Theorem Proving and Typechecking

The PVS specification language is based on classical, simply typed higher-order logic, but the type system has been augmented with subtypes and dependent types.

Subtypes and Proof Obligations.   Early in the design of PVS, it was decided that a simply typed language in which all types were distinct would be too restrictive and would disallow types such as the even numbers and the prime numbers which could be seen as subtypes of the integers. Once this kind of subtyping was permitted, it was quite clear that the language should permit subtype definitions with respect to arbitrary predicates. This kind of *naive comprehension* is acceptable in a typed language since the type classification rules out any Russellian inconsistencies. With arbitrary *predicate subtypes* in a higher-order logic, not only can we define the various useful subsets of the numbers but also such subtypes as the injective and surjective functions between two types. In PVS, the injective function space injection can be defined as a predicate subtype using the higher-order predicate injective? as shown below. The notation (injective?) is an abbreviation for {f | injective?(f)} which is the subtype of functions from D to R for which the predicate injective? holds.

```
functions [D, R: TYPE]: THEORY
 BEGIN
 f, g: VAR [D -> R]
 x, x1, x2: VAR D

 injective?(f): bool = (FORALL x1, x2: (f(x1) = f(x2) => (x1 = x2)))

 injection: TYPE = (injective?)


END functions
```

Once we define such a subtype, we can define the type even of even numbers and declare a function double as an injective function from the type of natural numbers nat to the subtype even. Note that bound variables can also have their types *locally* declared in the binding as in (j : nat) below.

```
even: TYPE = {i : nat | EXISTS (j : nat): i = 2 * j}

double : injection[nat, even] = (LAMBDA (i : nat): 2 * i)
```

When the declaration of double is typechecked, the typechecker generates two proof obligations or type correctness conditions (TCCS):

```
double_TCC1: OBLIGATION (FORALL (i: nat): EXISTS (j: nat): 2 * i = 2 * j)

double_TCC2: OBLIGATION injective?[nat, even]((LAMBDA (i: nat): 2 * i))
```

The first TCC checks that the result computed by double is an even number. The second TCC checks that the definition of double is injective. Both TCCs

are proved quickly and automatically using the default TCC strategy employed
by the PVS proof checker. Proofs of more complicated TCCs can be constructed
interactively. The PVS decision procedures are very handy for discharging typical TCC proof obligations. These decision procedures automate the theories
of equality and linear arithmetic with uninterpreted function symbols and are
discussed further in Section 4.

Dependent Types. The next example illustrates the use of dependent types
where the dependencies are expressed using predicate subtypes. The theory
newstacks introduces an implementation of stacks using a record consisting
of a size field indicating the number of elements in the stack, and an elements
field which is an array of size elements. The newstacks theory is parametric in
the element type. The type below(size) is just $\{i|i < size\}$. The empty stack
empty has size zero and an empty array of elements. The push operation yields
a nonempty stack. The pop operation is only defined for nonempty stacks.

```
newstacks[T: TYPE]: THEORY
  BEGIN

  i, j: VAR nat
  stack: TYPE = [# size: nat, elements: ARRAY[below(size) -> T] #]
  u, s: VAR stack
  x, y: VAR T
  e: T
  nonemptystack?(s): bool = (size(s) > 0)

  empty: stack = (# size := 0, elements := (LAMBDA (j | j < 0): e) #)

  push(x, s): (nonemptystack?) =
        (# size := size(s) + 1,
           elements := elements(s) WITH [(size(s)) := x] #)

  ns: VAR (nonemptystack?)
  pop(ns): stack  =
        (# size := size(ns) - 1,
           elements := (LAMBDA (j | j < size(ns) - 1):
                           elements(ns)(j)) #)

  top(ns): T = (elements(ns)(size(ns) - 1))

  END newstacks
```

Typechecking the above theory yields seven TCCS, all of which are proved automatically by the TCC proof strategy. Note that the pop operation updates
the stack by decrementing the size field by one, and simultaneously domain-
restricting the elements field to track the dependency. It is interesting to see
what happens when this domain-restriction is omitted by redefining pop as shown
below.

```
pop(ns): stack =
      ns WITH [ (size) := size(ns) - 1]
```

In this case, the typechecker successfully typechecks the theory but we are left with one TCC that the proof checker does not prove.

```
pop_TCC2: OBLIGATION
      (FORALL (ns: (nonemptystack?), x1:
                  below(size(ns)), y1: below(size(ns) - 1)):
          y1 < size(ns) AND x1 < size(ns) - 1);
```

It is easy to see that this is an unprovable TCC since it requires showing that if x1 is a natural number less than size(ns), then it is also less than size(ns) − 1. Thus there can be two kinds of type errors: one, where the typechecker finds a blatant syntactic violation at the level of arities or simple types, and the second, a more subtle, semantic class of errors where the typechecker generates TCCs that are unprovable.

The PVS specification language has a number of other features that exploit the interaction between theorem proving and typechecking. These include *assumptions* on theory parameters that must be discharged when a theory is imported with actual parameters, user-specified *type conversions* that are automatically inserted when the corresponding type mismatch is detected, *typing judgements* which can be used to assert a more refined type for an existing operation. PVS also has a facility for automatically generating abstract datatype theories with induction and recursion schemes.

Type information is used heavily within a PVS proof. The predicate subtype constraints are automatically asserted to the contextual database of assertions maintained by the decision procedures. Most of the abstract datatype simplifications are also carried out automatically. The typepred command of the PVS proof checker makes the type constraints of a given expression explicit in a proof subgoal. The extensionality command introduces extensionality axiom schemes corresponding to abstract datatypes or function, record, or tuple tuple types into a proof subgoal. Quantifier instantiations are typechecked and can generate TCC subgoals during a proof attempt. We do not describe these features in further detail here.

The main point of the above discussion is that PVS takes an expansive view of types and automated typechecking to encompass both syntactic and semantic restrictions. The crucial design decision in PVS is the strict separation between automatic typechecking for the simply typed fragment and proof obligation generation for subtyping and other extensions. The practical experience with PVS has been that the type system does rapidly detect a lot of common specification errors.

4 Combining Decision Procedures with Interactive Proof

Decision Procedures. The use of decision procedures is essential for effective proof construction, as we have already seen above, but it is by no means sufficient. Decision procedures can automatically carry out simplifications that may otherwise require tedious amounts of manipulation. They can make use of highly efficient data structures as for example with congruence closure graphs for equality, and binary decision diagrams for boolean simplification. However, most decision procedures operate as black boxes and do not give much insight into why they have succeeded or failed. PVS therefore employs decision procedures for the low-level manipulations used to support user-directed inferences at the higher levels of the proof.

Integrating decision procedures with interactive proof is a delicate exercise. The brute-force nature of decision procedures has to be balanced against the requirement that in an interactive proof, the individual proof steps must be easy to comprehend. In PVS, decision procedures are used very aggressively, but they operate mostly in the background by recording and propagating equality, inequality, and type information. The simplifications wrought by the decision procedures are not always immediately comprehensible but they are typically ones that would be quite tedious to carry out manually.

The basic PVS decision procedures were originally developed by Shostak in the context of the STP theorem prover [29, 30]. These decision procedures use the congruence closure algorithm for equality reasoning to combine decision procedures for various theories such as linear arithmetic, arrays, and tuples, in the presence of function symbols that are uninterpreted by any of the function symbols. As an example, the decision procedures can prove the assertion arith by linear arithmetic, the assertion eq1 by congruence closure, and eq2 using a combination of the two.

```
x,y,v: VAR real

arith: THEOREM
  x < 2*y AND y < 3*v IMPLIES 3*x < 18*v

f: [real -> real]

eq1: THEOREM x = f(x) IMPLIES f(f(f(x))) = x

g : [real, real -> real]

eq2: THEOREM x = f(y) IMPLIES g(f(y + 2 - 2), x + 2) = g(x, f(y) + 2)
```

Note that the functions symbols f and g are uninterpreted.

PVS does not merely make use of decision procedures to prove theorems but also to record type constraints and to simplify subterms in a formula using any assumptions that *govern* the occurrence of the subterm. These governing assumptions can either be the test parts of surrounding conditional (IF-THEN-ELSE) expressions or type constraints on governing bound variables. Such simplifications typically ensure that formulas do not become too large in the course of a proof. Also important, is the fact that automatic rewriting is closely coupled with the use of decision procedures, since many of the conditions and type correctness conditions that must be discharged in applying a rewrite rule succumb rather easily to the decision procedures.

Strategies. The PVS proof checker provides powerful primitive inference steps that make heavy use of decision procedures, but proof construction solely in terms of even these inference steps can be quite tedious. PVS therefore provides a language for defining high-level inference strategies (which are similar to *tactics* in LCF [16, 24]). This language includes recursion, a let binding construct, a backtracking try strategy construction, and a conditional if strategy construction. For example, one can use recursion and backtracking to repeatedly apply the disjunctive simplification step flatten, and the conjunctive splitting step split, to define a simple propositional simplification strategy as shown below.

```
(defstep prop ()
  (try (flatten) (prop) (try (split)(prop) (skip))))
```

The above strategy applies the flatten step, and if it succeeds and generates a subgoal, then it recursively applies prop to that subgoal. If flatten has no effect because there are no available disjunctive simplifications in the goal, then prop tries to apply the split step in a similar manner. The strategy terminates with the do-nothing step skip when there are no disjunctive or conjunctive simplifications available in the goal.

Typical strategies include:

- inst? for the heuristic instantiation of quantifiers
- grind for repeatedly applying rewriting, skolemization, heuristic instantiation, and if-lifting.
- induct-and-simplify for applying induction followed by simplifications similar to those given by grind.

An Example: The Binomial Theorem. We now examine a somewhat nontrivial example, namely, the proof of the binomial theorem in PVS. First, the number of ways of selecting k distinct elements from a set of n distinct elements, namely $\binom{n}{k}$, was defined as the function chooses. The lemma chooses_step isolates a simple case of the definition.

```
i, j, k, l, m, n: VAR nat

chooses(n, k):
    RECURSIVE
      nat = (IF k = 0 THEN 1
             ELSIF n < k THEN 0
             ELSE chooses(n - 1, k) + chooses(n - 1, k - 1)
             ENDIF)
      MEASURE (n + k)

chooses_step: LEMMA
      k <= n
        IMPLIES chooses(n + 1, k + 1) =
                chooses(n, k) + chooses(n, k + 1)
```

The exponentiation and summation operations are defined recursively as shown below. The definition of exponentiation holds no surprises, but the summation operation sigma is defined on domain that is a dependent tuple type $[n : nat, rat\_array(n)]$, which is not unlike the type used above to define stack. This refined typing of sigma helps to streamline the inductive proof of the binomial theorem.

```
x, y, z: VAR rational

exp(x, k):
    RECURSIVE rational =
    (IF k > 0 THEN exp(x, k - 1) * x ELSE 1 ENDIF)
     MEASURE k

rat_array(n): TYPE = [below[n] -> rational]

sigma(n, (f: rat_array(n))):
    RECURSIVE
      rational =
      (IF n = 0
       THEN 0
       ELSE f(n - 1)
            + sigma(n - 1, (LAMBDA (i: below[n - 1]): f(i)))
       ENDIF)
      MEASURE (LAMBDA n, (f: rat_array(n)): n)
```

Three lemmas about the summation operation sigma are needed in the main proof of the binomial theorem. All three lemmas are proved using a simple variant of the induct-and-simplify strategy. The first one requires two additional steps, but the other two lemmas are proved automatically by the strategy.

```
sigma_split0: LEMMA
    (FORALL n, (f: rat_array(n + 1)):
        sigma(n + 1, f) =
        f(0) + sigma(n, (LAMBDA (i: below[n]): f(i + 1)))))

sigma_times: LEMMA
    (FORALL n, (f: rat_array(n)):
        sigma(n, f) * x =
        sigma(n, (LAMBDA (i: below[n]): f(i) * x)))

sigma_plus: LEMMA
    (FORALL n, (f, g: rat_array(n)):
        sigma(n, (LAMBDA (i: below[n]): f(i) + g(i)))
          = sigma(n, f) + sigma(n, g))
```

The binomial theorem was then stated in the form shown below.

```
bin_thm: THEOREM
    exp(x + y, n)
    =
    sigma(n + 1,
          (LAMBDA (k: below[n + 1]):
                chooses(n, k) * exp(x, k) * exp(y, n - k)))
```

The proof of bin_thm is by induction and requires about eighteen interactions in order to apply the lemmas and expand the definitions in an orderly manner. This number of interactions could be reduced through further experimentation. The main point is, however, that with the use of refined typing, decision procedures, and strategies, the number of interactions roughly corresponds to the number of suggestive hints in a textbook proof. The level of detail is also roughly similar to that of a textbook proof. The entire verification occupied less than a day.

5 Integrating Model Checking and Theorem Proving

In the theorem proving approach to program verification, one verifies a property P of a program M by proving $M \supset P$. The model checking approach verifies the same program by showing that the state machine for M is a satisfying model of P, namely $M \models P$. For control-intensive approaches over small finite states, model checking is very effective since a more traditional Hoare logic style proof involves discovering a sufficiently strong invariant. These two approaches have traditionally been seen as incompatible ways of viewing the verification problem. In recent work [27], we were able to unify the two views and incorporate a model checker as decision procedure for a well-defined fragment of PVS.

This integration uses the mu-calculus as a medium for communicating between PVS and a model checker for the propositional mu-calculus. The advantage of this integration can be illustrated by means of an inductive proof of an N-process mutual exclusion protocol where the induction step used the correctness of the 2-process version of the protocol as verified by the model checker. This example is described very briefly below.

The Mu-Calculus. The general mu-calculus over a given *state* type essentially provides operators for defining least and greatest fixpoints of monotone predicate transformers. The propositional mu-calculus is a restriction of the general mu-calculus where the state type is an n-tuple of booleans. The propositional mu-calculus thus extends quantified boolean formulas (i.e., propositional logic with boolean quantification) to include the application of n-ary relational terms to n argument formulas [20]. The relational terms can constructed by means of lambda-abstraction, or by taking the least fixpoint $\mu Q.F[Q]$ where Q is an n-ary predicate variable and F is a monotone predicate transformer. The greatest fixpoint operation can be written as $\nu Q.F[Q]$ and defined as $\neg \mu Q.\neg F[\neg Q]$. The mu-calculus can be easily defined in PVS as shown in the theory mu_calculus below.

```
mucalculus[T:TYPE]: THEORY
  BEGIN

  s: VAR T
  p,p1,p2: VAR pred[T]
  predtt: TYPE = [pred[T]->pred[T]]
  pp: VAR predtt
  setofpred: VAR pred[pred[T]]

  IMPORTING orders[pred[T]]
  <=(p1,p2):bool = FORALL s: p1(s) IMPLIES p2(s)

  ismono(pp):bool =
    FORALL p1,p2: p1 <= p2 IMPLIES pp(p1) <= pp(p2)

  glb (setofpred):pred[T] =
    LAMBDA s: (FORALL p: member(p,setofpred) IMPLIES  p(s))

  % least fixpoint
  lfp (pp):pred[T] = glb(p | pp(p) <= p)

  mu(pp): pred[T] = lfp(pp)

END mucalculus
```

We omit the detailed explanation of the above specification except to note that pred[T] is an abbreviation for the type [T -> bool] which consists of the predicates over T. When a predicate transformer pp is monotonic (given by ismono), the least fixpoint operator lfp yields a fixpoint. The usual Tarski-Knaster argument for this can be easily verified in PVS.

More usefully, the temporal operators of the branching time logic CTL can be defined using the mu-calculus. A sampling of these definitions is shown below. Given a next-state relation N, EX(N, f) holds of a state if there exists a next state where f holds. The assertion EG(N, f) holds at a state if there is an infinite path along which f always holds. The assertion AG(N, f) holds at a state if f holds along all outgoing paths.

```
ctlops[state : TYPE]: THEORY
  BEGIN
  IMPORTING mucalculus[state], connectives[state]

  u,v,w: VAR state
  f,g,Q,P,p1,p2: VAR pred[state]
  Z: VAR pred[[state, state]]

  N: VAR [state, state->bool]

  EX(N,f)(u):bool =  (EXISTS v: (f(v) AND N(u, v)))

  EG(N,f):pred[state] = nu (LAMBDA Q: (f AND EX(N,Q)))

  EU(N,f,g):pred[state] = mu (LAMBDA Q: (g OR (f AND EX(N,Q))))

  EF(N,f):pred[state] = EU(N,(LAMBDA u: TRUE),f)

  AG(N,f):pred[state] = NOT EF(N, NOT f)

END ctlops
```

Fairness is not definable in CTL but fair variants of the CTL operators can be defined in the mu-calculus.

When the state type is finite, i.e., constructed inductively from the booleans and scalar types using records, tuples, or arrays over subranges, the mu-calculus over such finite types (and the corresponding CTL) can be translated into the propositional mu-calculus and model checking can be used as a decision procedure for this fragment. We do not discuss the details of this encoding here (see [27]).

An efficient model checking algorithm for the propositional mu-calculus was presented by Emerson and Lei [13], and the symbolic variant employing BDDs was presented by Burch, et al [4]. The above embedding of the mu-calculus and CTL owes much to these seminal papers.

Compositionality. We now digress from our main point to describe a technique for compositional verification of concurrent systems [28]. We say that the parallel composition $P_1 \| P_2$ of two specifications P_1 and P_2 is *compositional* if every local property, that is, a property of one of the P_i, is also a global property of the composition $P_1 \| P_2$. A system component P is specified as a triple $\langle I, G, R \rangle$ consisting of an initialization predicate I on the state type, and two *actions* or binary predicates on the state type, G and R. The action G represents the *guarantee* action performed by P, and the action R is a constraint on actions performed by the environment. A trace satisfying a specification P is sequence of states where the initial state satisfies I and the adjacent states are related by G or R actions, indicating an interleaving between system and environment actions.

The composition of two specifications P_1 given by $\langle I_1, G_1, R_1 \rangle$ and P_2 given by $\langle I_2, G_2, R_2 \rangle$ is the system

$$\langle I_1 \wedge I_2, \qquad (G_1 \wedge R_2) \vee (G_2 \wedge R_1), \qquad R_1 \wedge R_2 \rangle.$$

Here, conjunction (disjunction) of predicates on state is the pointwise conjunction (disjunction) of the predicate applied to individual states. The main point is that there is no attempt here to discharge any rely-guarantee proof obligations since we are dealing with specifications (where I, G and R are only partially specified) and not programs. The main outcome of the above form of composition is that any trace of $P_1 \| P_2$ is also a trace of P_1 and of P_2. If a property is simply a subset of traces, then any property of P_1 or P_2 is also a property of $P_1 \| P_2$.

Two Process Mutual Exclusion. Peterson's mutual exclusion algorithm [26] is a easy exercise for a model checker, and is somewhat less easily verified by means of theorem proving. We merely sketch the details of the PVS verification of this algorithm. Compositionality is not necessary for specifying this algorithm, but it is used here to properly abstract the N-process version where compositionality is need.

Given processes P and Q, the global system state consists of five boolean variables which can be represented as a record with five fields in PVS. The state component tryp (tryq) indicates whether P (Q) is trying to get into or is already in its critical section. The state component CSP (CSQ) indicates whether P (Q) is in its critical section. The state component turn is used to arbitrate between P and Q. The initialization predicate for P asserts that tryp (tryq) and CSP (CSQ) are both FALSE. In its G or guarantee action, the process P can either stutter, enter its trying phase by setting tryp to TRUE and turn to TRUE, or enter its critical section by first checking whether TURN or trypq is FALSE, and then setting CSP to TRUE. The R or rely part of P requires tryp and CSP to be left unchanged. The specification of the Q process is similar except that turn is set to FALSE on entering the trying phase and checked to be TRUE before entry into the critical section. The main safety property of the protocol can be stated as an **AG** property in the CTL fragment shown above. In the statement below, abs_pet is the composition of P and Q. The I componenent is given by init(abs_pet).

63

```
correct: LEMMA
      init(abs_pet)(s) IMPLIES
        AG((LAMBDA s0, s1: G(abs_pet)(s0, s1) OR R(abs_pet)(s0, s1)),
           (LAMBDA s0: NOT (CSP(s0) AND CSQ(s0)))))(s)
```

The proof of correct using model checking takes only about fifteen seconds of machine time, most of which is spent outside the model checker.

N-process mutual exclusion. The algorithm we use here is a simple recursive variant of the two-process Peterson algorithm. The N processes are numbered from 0 to N − 1. A process i can be at a critical section level between i and N given by the variable cs(i). The object of the algorithm is to ensure that at most one process is at critical section level N. Each process i has a turn component turn(i) for coordinating with its predecessor. Each process also as boolean component try(i) to indicate whether it is trying to enter the critical section or is already in its critical section. Each process i starts a critical section level i and with try(i) set to FALSE. It executes a two-process Peterson protocol with the one preceding process j, if any, such that cs(j) is i. The "winner" reaches critical section level i + 1 and gets to compete with the i + 1st process. The rely conditions ensure that the turn variables are modified in a constrained manner, since otherwise the algorithm might violate the mutual exclusion property.

The protocol for n processes is given by Pet(n). The correctness assertion is stated as safety below.

```
AG_C(Cprog, Cprop) : bool =
  (FORALL s: init(Cprog)(s)
    IMPLIES AG((LAMBDA s0, s1: G(Cprog)(s0, s1) OR
                                R(Cprog)(s0, s1)),
              Cprop)(s))

safety: LEMMA AG_C(Pet(n),
              (LAMBDA s: (FORALL (j, k: below[n]):
                          cs(s)(j) >= n AND  cs(s)(k) >= n
                        IMPLIES j = k)))
```

The informal proof of the protocol is by induction. If there is exactly one process, the proof is trivial. This base case of the proof could also have been verified by means of abstraction and model checking. At the induction step, we know that there is at most one process below i that is at critical section level i. We can use this induction hypothesis to abstract the first i processes to the process P in the two-process algorithm, and to abstract process i to the process Q. If we have ensured that the abstraction preserves the correctness property, then the correctness of the N-process algorithm follows. Such abstractions have been studied by Clarke, Grumberg, and Long [5], and by Dams, Grumberg, and Gerth [11].

The above example is of course purely illustrative since the algorithm is a somewhat naive and contrived one. It shows how theorem proving and model checking can be combined to simplify an argument by using compositionality, induction, and abstraction.

6 Observations and Conclusion

Despite all our claims above, mechanical verification is not easy but the main difficulty is in constructing a correct proof. Mechanization is the only reasonable technique for keeping the verification process honest. Furthermore, mechanization delivers extremely valuable feedback by catching even subtle errors that might have otherwise gone unnoticed. There are several examples of published proofs of important results where the errors have gone unnoticed until they were revealed by mechanical verification. Mechanical verification is not a substitute for the social process [12] but is merely a tool that aids the social process. There is nothing inherently inhuman about mechanized verification. A mechanical verifier plays the role of an implacable skeptic that highlights weaknesses in an argument such as misapplied lemmas, missing cases, and inappropriate inductions or instantiations.

We have argued that computer-aided computing can be realized by carefully designing language features for mechanized syntactic and semantic checks, and by integrating powerful and efficient decision procedures and model checking within an interactive proof checking framework.

There still are certain inflexibilities with mechanical verification since the technology is still in its infancy. For example, it is not yet easy to introduce new notation or switch formalisms. Computing is rife with such formalisms. It is typically not easy to introduce derived inference rules as is frequently done in informal mathematics. Informal mathematics also often mixes mathematical and metamathematical argumentation, and this too is not easily mechanized.

The case for mechanized verification is very strong. We now know that it is feasible to verify large systems. Bevier, Hunt, Moore, and Young [1] present a proof of a system consisting of a microprocessor, an assembler for this microprocessor, a compiler for a Pascal-like language with the assembler as its target language, and an operating system kernel. This verification used the Boyer-Moore theorem prover [2]. There are many other impressive verification examples carried out on a variety of systems including Coq [7], EVES [8], IMPS [14], HOL [17], Isabelle [25], LP [15], Nuprl [6], and RRL [19], to name a few.

The main challenge is to make mechanical verification less arduous and more perspicuous. Specific challenges are in

- the design of expressive specification languages that interact synergistically with mechanization
- the integration of decision procedures with interactive proof development
- support for multiple formalisms
- the design of customized domain-specific verification methodologies.

References

1. William R. Bevier, Warren A. Hunt, Jr., J Strother Moore, and William D. Young. An approach to systems verification. *Journal of Automated Reasoning*, 5(4):411–428, December 1989.

2. R. S. Boyer and J S. Moore. *A Computational Logic Handbook*. Academic Press, New York, NY, 1988.

3. J. R. Burch, E. M. Clarke, K. L McMillan, D. L. Dill, and L. J. Hwang. Symbolic model checking: 10^{20} states and beyond. In *5th Annual IEEE Symposium on Logic in Computer Science*, pages 428–439, Philadelphia, PA, June 1990. IEEE Computer Society.

4. J. R. Burch, E. M. Clarke, K. L. McMillan, D. L. Dill, and L. J. Hwang. Symbolic model checking: 10^{20} states and beyond. *Information and Computation*, 98(2):142–170, June 1992.

5. Edmund M. Clarke, Orna Grumberg, and David E. Long. Model checking and abstraction. *ACM Transactions on Programming Languages and Systems*, 16(5):1512–1542, September 1994.

6. R. L. Constable, S. F. Allen, H. M. Bromley, W. R. Cleaveland, J. F. Cremer, R. W. Harper, D. J. Howe, T. B. Knoblock, N. P. Mendler, P. Panangaden, J. T. Sasaki, and S. F. Smith. *Implementing Mathematics with the Nuprl Proof Development System*. Prentice-Hall, Englewood Cliffs, NJ, 1986.

7. T. Coquand and G. P. Huet. Constructions: A higher order proof system for mechanizing mathematics. In *Proceedings of EUROCAL 85, Linz (Austria)*, Berlin, 1985. Springer-Verlag.

8. Dan Craigen, Sentot Kromodimoeljo, Irwin Meisels, Bill Pase, and Mark Saaltink. EVES: An overview. In S. Prehn and W. J. Toetenel, editors, *VDM '91: Formal Software Development Methods*, volume 551 of *Lecture Notes in Computer Science*, pages 389–405, Noordwijkerhout, The Netherlands, October 1991. Springer-Verlag. Volume 1: Conference Contributions.

9. D. Cyrluk, S. Rajan, N. Shankar, and M. K. Srivas. Effective theorem proving for hardware verification. In Ramayya Kumar and Thomas Kropf, editors, *Preliminary Proceedings of the Second Conference on Theorem Provers in Circuit Design*, pages 287–305, Bad Herrenalb (Blackforest), Germany, September 1994. Forschungszentrum Informatik an der Universität Karlsruhe, FZI Publication 4/94.

10. David Cyrluk, Patrick Lincoln, Paliath Narendran, Sam Owre, Sreeranga Ragan, John Rushby, Natarajan Shankar, Jens Ulrik Skakkebæk, Mandayam Srivas, and Friedrich von Henke. Seven papers on mechanized formal verification. Technical Report SRI-CSL-95-3, Computer Science Laboratory, SRI International, Menlo Park, CA, January 1995.

11. Dennis Dams, Orna Grumberg, and Rob Gerth. Abstract interpretation of reactive systems: Abstractions preserving ∀CTL*, ∃CTL* and CTL*. In Ernst-Rüdiger Olderog, editor, *Programming Concepts, Methods and Calculi (PROCOMET '94)*, pages 561–581, 1994.

12. Richard A. De Millo, Richard J. Lipton, and Alan J. Perlis. Social processes and proofs of theorems and programs. *Communications of the ACM*, 22(5):271–280, May 1979.

13. E.A. Emerson and C.L Lei. Efficient model checking in fragments of the propositional mu-calculus. In *Proceedings of the 10th Symposium on Principles of Programming Languages*, pages 84–96, New Orleans, LA, January 1985. Association for Computing Machinery.

14. William M. Farmer, Joshua D. Guttman, and F. Javier Thayer. IMPS: An interactive mathematical proof system. *Journal of Automated Reasoning*, 11(2):213–248, October 1993.

15. Stephen J. Garland and John V. Guttag. LP: The Larch prover. In E. Lusk and R. Overbeek, editors, *9th International Conference on Automated Deduction (CADE)*, volume 310 of *Lecture Notes in Computer Science*, pages 748–749, Argonne, IL, May 1988. Springer-Verlag.

16. M. Gordon, R. Milner, and C. Wadsworth. *Edinburgh LCF: A Mechanized Logic of Computation*, volume 78 of *Lecture Notes in Computer Science*. Springer-Verlag, 1979.

17. M. J. C. Gordon and T. F. Melham, editors. *Introduction to HOL: A Theorem Proving Environment for Higher-Order Logic*. Cambridge University Press, Cambridge, UK, 1993.

18. Constance Heitmeyer and Nancy Lynch. The generalized railroad crossing: A case study in formal verification of real-time systems. In *Real Time Systems Symposium*, pages 120–131, San Juan, Puerto Rico, December 1994. IEEE Computer Society.

19. D. Kapur and H. Zhang. *RRL: A User's Manual*. General Electric Corporate Research and Development, Schenectady, NY, March 1986. Unpublished Manuscript.

20. D. Kozen. Results on the propositional mu-calculus. *Theoretical Computer Science*, pages 333–354, December 1983.

21. Steven P. Miller and Mandayam Srivas. Formal verification of the AAMP5 microprocessor: A case study in the industrial use of formal methods. In *WIFT '95: Workshop on Industrial-Strength Formal specification Techniques*, Boca Raton, FL, 1995. IEEE Computer Society. To appear.

22. Paul S. Miner. Defining the IEEE-854 floating-point standard in PVS. Technical Memorandum 110167, NASA Langley Research Center, 1995.

23. S. Owre, N. Shankar, and J. M. Rushby. *User Guide for the PVS Specification and Verification System (Beta Release)*. Computer Science Laboratory, SRI International, Menlo Park, CA, February 1993. Three volumes: Language, System, and Prover Reference Manuals.

24. L. C. Paulson. *Logic and Computation: Interactive Proof with Cambridge LCF*. Cambridge University Press, Cambridge, England, 1987.

25. Lawrence C. Paulson. *Isabelle: A generic Theorem Prover*, volume 828 of *Lecture Notes in Computer Science*. Springer-Verlag, 1994.

26. G. L. Peterson. Myths about the mutual exclusion problem. *Information Processing Letters*, 12(3):115–116, 1981.

27. S. Rajan, N. Shankar, and M.K. Srivas. An integration of model-checking with automated proof checking. In Pierre Wolper, editor, *Computer-Aided Verification, CAV '95*, Lecture Notes in Computer Science, Liege, Belgium, June 1995. Springer-Verlag. To appear.

28. N. Shankar. A lazy approach to compositional verification. Technical Report SRI-CSL-93-8, Computer Science Laboratory, SRI International, Menlo Park, CA, December 1993.

29. R. E. Shostak, R. Schwartz, and P. M. Melliar-Smith. STP: A mechanized logic for specification and verification. In D. Loveland, editor, *6th International Conference on Automated Deduction (CADE)*, volume 138 of *Lecture Notes in Computer Science*, New York, NY, 1982. Springer-Verlag.

30. Robert E. Shostak. Deciding combinations of theories. *Journal of the ACM*, 31(1):1–12, January 1984.

Derivation of Parallel Algorithms from Functional Specifications to CSP Processes

Ali E. Abdallah

The University of Reading
Department of Computer Science
Reading, RG6 6AY, U.K.

Abstract. A transformational programming approach is proposed as a means for developing a class of parallel algorithms from clear functional specifications to efficient networks of communicating sequential processes (CSP). A foundation for the systematic refinement of functional specifications into CSP processes is established. Techniques for exhibiting implicit parallelism in functional specification are developed. Their use is illustrated by deriving new efficient parallel algorithms to several problems. Derivation and reasoning are conducted in an equational style using the calculus for program synthesis developed by Bird and Meertens.

1 Introduction

Many algorithms are best abstracted as the input-output functions that they represent. For such algorithms, the functional programming style (FP) seems to offer an ideal framework for formulating their specifications, proving their properties and presenting their developments. However, at present, it may not be adequate for expressing their efficient parallel implementations. The latter task seems to be better achieved in a CSP-like framework since, through its communication primitives and parallel composition operators, CSP offers opportunities for expressing any desirable parallelism and therefore, by exploiting parallel machines, a potential for efficient implementations.

Since it is our intention to use the FP notation for specification but the CSP notation for implementation, the fundamental questions which we have to address are: what does it mean for a given FP specification to be correctly *implemented* as a CSP process and how can an implementation be derived from its specification? Therefore, the first objective of this paper is to establish a foundation for the systematic refinement of functional specifications into CSP processes.

Clear functional specifications of applications such as sorting, graph searching algorithms, text processing, database manipulations and optimisation problems [BrW88, Brd84, Drl78] tend to be straightforward. Concurrency is not a part of the starting specifications of these problems. The main motivation for using concurrency is to achieve *speed*. Typically, parallelism and communications are introduced at a later stage in the development of these algorithms for the sole purpose of capturing the precise behaviour of a functionally equivalent but more efficient parallel algorithm.

Since parallelism is not a part of the starting functional specification of a system, the central problem which we address is how to develop strategies and techniques for *exhibiting* implicit parallelism in the system at an abstract specification level. By exhibiting parallelism we mean *decomposing* the specification of a system into a collection of simpler specifications of parallel processes with an appropriate interface between them. A significant challenge is how to obtain the specifications of the local processes and their corresponding interface from the specification of the whole system. A much more important challenge, however, is how to ensure that the decomposition of the specification leads to an *efficient* parallel implementation.

Unlike other operational approaches for exhibiting *fine* parallelism at a low level (for example: parallelising sequential programs [Mtr85, LnH82], Data-flow approaches [Dnn85] and parallel graph reductions GRIP [PCS87]) the approach adopted in this paper aims at exhibiting *coarse* and modular parallelism at a more abstract level. Another important difference is that control is distributed throughout the network. Efficiency is achieved by establishing direct communication between processes.

The remainder of this paper is organised as follows: section 2 contains a brief summary of the notation, in section 3 we establish the concept of refinement from functional specification to CSP processes, section 4 contains useful refinement rules that relates parameterised functional templates to parameterised processes and section 5 contains compositional refinement rules that facilitate the refinement of a combination of functional values into an appropriate combination of processes. A decomposition strategy for exhibiting parallelism in functional specifications is introduced in section 6, its usefulness is illustrated on two case stuies in section 7. In section 8, we show how the decomposition strategy could be combined with other strategies such as partitions and divide and conquer in order to derive new efficient parallel algorithms.

2 Notation

Throughout this paper, we will use the functional notation and calculus developed by Bird and Meertens [Brd86, BrM86, Brd88, BrW88] for specifying algorithmics and reasoning about them and will use the CSP notation and its calculus developed by Hoare [Hor85] for specifying processes and reasoning about them. We give a brief summary of the notation and conventions used in this paper. The reader is advised to consult the above references for details.

Lists are finite sequences of values of the same type. The list concatenation operator is denoted by ++ and the list construction operator is denoted by :. The elements of a list are displayed between square brackets and separated by comas. Functional application is denoted by a space and functional composition is denoted by $\circ$. Functions are usually defined using higher order functions or by sets of recursive equations. The operator $*$ (pronounced "map") takes a function on its left and a list on its right and maps the function to each element of the list. Informally, we have:

$$f * [a_1, a_2, \cdots, a_2] = [f(a_1), f(a_2), \cdots, f(a_n)]$$

The operator $/$ (pronounced "reduce") takes a binary operator on its left and a list on its right. It can be informally described as follows

$$(\oplus)/[a_1, a_2, \cdots, a_n] = a_1 \oplus a_2 \oplus \cdots \oplus a_n$$

Another useful operator $\lhd$ (pronounced "filter") takes a predicate p and a list s and returns the sublist of s consisting, in order, of all those elements of s that satisfy p.

We use identifiers with lower case letters to name functional values and with upper case letters to name processes. The noptation $v :: A$ stands for the value v is drawn from the type A.

We will use $PROC$ to denote the space of CSP processes including vectors of processes (that is the space of functions which return processes). In order to concisely describe structured networks of processes we find it very convenient to use, in addition to the CSP notation, functions which return processes, such as $PROD$, MAP, $FILTER$, $INSERT$, and $MERGE$ (see section 4) and FP operators such as map ($*$) and reduce ($/$). Functions which return processes are treated as ordinary functions which can be, in particular, applied to values, composed with other functions and supplied as arguments to other higher order functions. In particular, if F is a function which returns processes, that is $F ::$ $T \to PROC$, $\oplus$ is an associative CSP operator and $[a_1, a_2, \cdots, a_n]$ is a list of values drawn from T, we have

$$F * [a_1, a_2, \cdots, a_2] = [F(a_1), F(a_2), \cdots, F(a_n)]$$
$$(\oplus)/F * [a_1, a_2, \cdots, a_n] = F(a_1) \oplus F(a_2) \oplus \cdots \oplus F(a_n)$$

For examples, we have

$$(\gg)/[COPY, COPY, COPY] = COPY \gg COPY \gg COPY$$
$$(;)/PROD * [[1], [2], [3]] = PROD([1]) ; PROD([2]) ; PROD([3])$$
$$(\|)/F * [a_1, a_2, \cdots, a_n] = F(a_1) \| F(a_2) \| \cdots \| F(a_n)$$

The network of chaining n copies of the process $COPY$ can be described by

$$(\gg)/F * [1 \cdots n] \quad \text{WHERE } F :: \text{NAT} \to PROC; \ F(i) = COPY$$

Occasionally, we will underline a symbol, such as $\underline{F}$, in order to emphasize the fact that it is a function which returns processes. We will also use the notation $\underline{F}(x)$ instead of $(\underline{F} \ x)$ to denote the process obtained by applying the function $\underline{F}$ to the value x. When parsing expressions, we assume that functional application has the highest precedence and associates to the left but all other FP operators have equal precedence and associate to the right. For example, the expression $PROD * s + \!\!+ t$ means $PROD * (s + \!\!+ t)$ and not $(PROD * s) + \!\!+ t$. By using this extended notation we hope to avoid subscripts, enhance readability, and facilitate further algebraic manipulations.

3 Refinement from FP to CSP

3.1 The basic idea

We can view a function as a system which takes values as input and returns values as output. For example, the factorial function defined by the equations:

$$\begin{aligned}
&factorial \ :: \mathrm{NAT} \to \mathrm{NAT} \\
&factorial \ 0 \qquad = 1 \\
&factorial \ (n+1) = (n+1) \times (factorial \ n)
\end{aligned}$$

can be viewed as a specification of a process $FACTORIAL$ with one input channel, say $left$, and one output channel, say $right$. Observations on these channels should agree with the functionality of $factorial$. For example, if the value 5 is communicated on the input channel, the value communicated on the output channel should be the same as that of the expression $(factorial \ 5)$. In CSP we are only interested in the external behaviour of the process $FACTORIAL$ which, in this case, can be captured as follows:

$$FACTORIAL = left?n \ \to \ right!(factorial \ n) \ \to \ SKIP$$

The most useful functions for designing algorithms as networks of communicating processes are those which manipulate lists. A function which manipulates lists of values can be viewed as a specification of a process that consumes a stream of input values and produces a stream of output values. For example, the function $doubles$, which maps the the function $double$ to each number in a list, can be viewed as a specification of a process that inputs a finite stream of numbers (ending with a special message eot) and outputs the double of each number in the input stream. A definition of $doubles$ is:

$$\begin{aligned}
&doubles \ \ :: [\mathrm{NUM}] \to [\mathrm{NUM}] \\
&doubles \ s = map \ (\times 2) \ s
\end{aligned}$$

A particular CSP definition of a process $DOUBLES$ which satisfies this specification is:

$$DOUBLES = ?x \ \to \ (!eot \ \to \ SKIP \ \{x = eot\} \ !2 \times x \ \to \ DOUBLES \ )$$

After receiving an input, this process immediately outputs its double. A semantically different CSP process $DOUBLES2$ which also refines the function $doubles$ but accepts up to two inputs before producing any output is:

$$\begin{aligned}
&DOUBLES2 = ?x \ \to \ (!eot \ \to \ SKIP \ \{x = eot\} \ D(x) \ ) \\
&D(x) \qquad = ?y \to !2 \times x \ \to \ (!eot \ \to \ SKIP \ \{y = eot\} \ D(y) \ )
\end{aligned}$$

Yet another process DS which *refines* the function *doubles* but insists on consuming all the input messages before producing any output is:

$$DS \; = ?x \; \rightarrow \; (\,!eot \; \rightarrow \; SKIP \;\; \langle\!\langle x = eot \rangle\!\rangle \;\; D([x])\,)$$
$$D(s) = ?y \; \rightarrow \; (\,Prd(doubles\; s) \;\; \langle\!\langle y = eot \rangle\!\rangle \;\; D(s + \!\!+ [y])\,)$$

The main advantage of using functions as specifications of processes is that there could be several (possibly infinite) semantically different processes that intuitively implement a function. Some of these processes may be more suitable than others in the construction of specific applications (especially in the context of parallel algorithms constuctions).

Now let's consider functions which take more than one argument. Such a function can be viewed as a specification of a function which returns processes. For example, the following function:

$$times :: \textsc{Num} \rightarrow [\textsc{Num}] \rightarrow [\textsc{Num}]$$
$$times\; n \; s = map \; (n\times) \; s$$

can be seen as a specification which, for each number i, specifies a process $TIMES(i)$ that refines the function (with one argument) (*times i*). A possible CSP process which satisfies this specification is:

$$TIMES(n) = ?x \; \rightarrow \; (\,!eot \; \rightarrow \; SKIP \;\; \langle\!\langle x = eot \rangle\!\rangle \;\; !n \times x \; \rightarrow \; TIMES(n)\,)$$

Observe that since *doubles* = (*times 2*), the process $TIMES(2)$ is a refinement of the specification given by the function *doubles* .

3.2   Classes of FP Values

The *type* of an FP value serves two purposes. Firstly, it determines whether the value is to be refined into a single CSP process (such as *doubles*) or into a funtion which returns processes (such as *times*). Secondly, it determines the *alphabet* of the corresponding CSP process. Let $FPVS$ be the space of denotable values which can be expressed in our functional notation and Σ be the set of values which can be communicated over channels in CSP networks of processes. We assume that Σ is a subset of $FPVS$. We will distinguish three kinds of values: *data* values denoted by $\mathcal{D}$, *simple functions* values denoted by $\mathcal{F}$ and *higher order functions* values denoted by $\mathcal{H}$. We will give a brief description of values in each of these classes.

– **Data Values $\mathcal{D}$**

$\mathcal{D}$ contains non-function values. A value v in this class is either a *basic* value ($v :: A$ and $A \subseteq \Sigma$) or a finite list of basic values ($v :: [A]$ and $A \subseteq \Sigma$). Basic values will be used as contents of messages which can be communicated on channels in CSP networks of processes.

- **First Order Functions** $\mathcal{F}$:

  $\mathcal{F}$ contains simple functions whose source and target are types containing *data* values. A typical function f in this class has type $(A \to B)$ where A and B are types containing *data* values. Examples of functions in this class:

$$plus \qquad :: \text{NUM} \times \text{NUM} \to \text{NUM}$$
$$map \ (+2) :: [\text{NUM}] \to [\text{NUM}]$$

- **Higher Order Functions** $\mathcal{H}$

  This class contains functions which return simple functions (in $\mathcal{F}$) as results. The type of a typical function h in this class is of the form $(T \to (A \to B))$ where A and B are types containing *data* values but T can be a much more complex type. In particular, T can be a function space or a space containing lists of functions. Examples of functions in this class: *map*, *filter*, *take*, *drop*, *foldl* and *accumulate*.

$$take :: \text{NAT} \to (A \to B)$$
$$map :: (A \to B) \to ([A] \to [B])$$

This completes our characterisation of classes of FP values. The next stage is to define a refinement relation $(\prec) \subset FPVS \times PROC$ which captures the refinement between FP values and CSP processes. Since $\mathcal{D}$, $\mathcal{F}$ and $\mathcal{H}$ are pairwise disjoint, the refinement relation $\prec$ is uniquely determined by its restrictions, say $\prec_D$, $\prec_F$, $\prec_H$ over $\mathcal{D}$, $\mathcal{F}$ and $\mathcal{H}$ respectively.

3.3 Transformation of Data Values

We can view a *data* value v as a producer process which generates, according to a specific protocol, the value v on its output channel. We will define a mapping Prd that transforms any *data* value $v \in \mathcal{D}$ into a unique CSP producer process $Prd(v)$. For any value v which is drawn from a basic type A $(A \subseteq \Sigma)$, the process $Prd(v)$ outputs the value of v and then successfully terminates. Formally, we have

$$\alpha \ Prd(e) = !A \cup \{\sqrt{}\}$$
$$Prd(e) \quad = !e \to SKIP$$

The notation $!A$ stands for the set of events $\{!x \mid x \in A\}$ and the event $\sqrt{}$ indicates successful termination.

A list of basic values will be modelled as a producer which outputs a stream of messages ending with a specific symbol. We first define the process EOT which outputs a single message eot, indicating the end of transmission, and then successfully terminates. That is

$$EOT = !eot \to SKIP$$

We also define the function $PROD$ that takes a list of values and returns a process that outputs the elements of the list (in the same order) on its output channel. $PROD$ is defined as follows:

$$PROD([]) \quad = SKIP$$
$$PROD(a : s) = !a \rightarrow PROD(s)$$

Finally, for any list $s \in [A]$ such that $A \subseteq \Sigma$, we define the producer process $Prd(s)$ as follows:

$$\alpha \; Prd(s) = !(A \cup \{eot\}) \cup \{\sqrt{}\}$$
$$Prd(s) \quad = PROD(s) \, ; \, EOT$$

Informally, we have

$$Prd([a_1, a_2, \cdots, a_n]) = !a_1 \rightarrow !a_2 \rightarrow \cdots \rightarrow !a_n \rightarrow !eot \rightarrow SKIP$$

Definition 1. Given a CSP process P and a value $v \in T$, where T is a type containing *data* values, P is said to *refine* (or correctly *implement*) v iff P is identical to $Prd(v)$. That is:

$$\boxed{\text{DR}} \quad v \prec P \Longleftrightarrow Prd(v) = P$$

3.4 Refinement of Simple Functions

A very special aspect of computable functions is that they can be defined by *application*. This style is adopted as a definition mechanism in many functional programming languages such as MIRANDA^{TM} [Trn85]. Hence, in any semantic model for FP, the "meaning" of functions may be inferred from the "meaning" of the function application operator. Therefore, in order to model functions as CSP processes we only need to answer the following question: what CSP operator should correspond to function application?

Function Application as a Parallel Composition It is usual when designing interactive functional programs to view the function application operator as a kind of parallel composition. The application of a function f to a vlaue v can be viewed as the result of interaction between two processes: a producer P, representing the argument, and a consumer Q, representing the function. A typical behaviour of the producer P is such as that described by the process $Prd(v)$. The consumer Q, on the other hand, consumes part of the argument v (by communicating with P), produces part of the result $(f \; v)$ (by communicating with an external environment) and either terminates or repeats the same pattern of behaviour. To illustrate this idea consider applying the function *doubles*, which doubles the elements of a list, to the list $[a_1, a_2, .., a_k]$. In this case, the producer $Prd([a_1, a_2, .., a_k])$ generates the elements of the list, in the given order and ending with the message *eot*, and passes them to the consumer Q. A typical behaviour of the consumer is to repeatedly input some messages from the producer and output their doubles to the outside world such as:

$$DOUBLES = ?x \rightarrow (\,!eot \rightarrow SKIP \ \{x = eot\} \ !2 \times x \rightarrow DOUBLES\,)$$

This process repeatedly consumes one element of the argument and produces one element of the result. The question now is: how can we model the interactions between the producer and the consumer in CSP ?

The Feeding Operator We will model the producer/consumer interactions in CSP by a new parallel operator ($\triangleright$) called *feeding* or *injecting*. To define this operator, observe that the producer P is only capable of outputting messages but the consumer Q can input as well. The processes P and Q can be pictured as in Figure 1.

Producer   Consumer

Fig. 1. A producer and a consumer processes

The combination $(P \triangleright Q)$ is a form of parallel composition in which the output channel of P is connected to the input channel of Q. Communications between P and Q are synchronous. Furthermore, the common connecting channel is concealed from the environment. This definition ensures that messages which are output by P are simultaneously input to Q. Observe that the process $(P \triangleright Q)$ is also a producer and can be composed with another consumer. The process $(P \triangleright Q)$ can be pictured as in Figure 2.

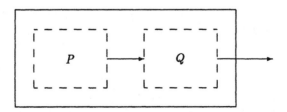

Fig. 2. The process $(P \triangleright Q)$

The feeding operator $\triangleright$ is very similar to the CSP piping operator, $\gg$, in that all messages output by the left operand are simultaneously input to the right operand. These two operators differ, however, in two aspects. Firstly, the left operand of $\triangleright$ has no input channels. Secondly, the concurrent termination of the compound $(P \triangleright Q)$ is not synchronized. In order to give an algebraic definition of the operator $\triangleright$, observe that its left operand takes one of five possible forms: $CHAOS, STOP, !x \rightarrow P, P \sqcap Q$ and $SKIP$ but its right operand can take two additional forms: $?y \rightarrow Q(y)$ and $(!y \rightarrow Q \,|?z \rightarrow R(z))$. The algebraic definition of the operator $\triangleright$ is given by a number of algebraic equations which show how $\triangleright$ deals with each form of the operands. The equations are stated in such a way that any call to $\triangleright$ can be eliminated from any expression describing a process by pushing it inwards until it reaches the occurence of either $STOP$ or $CHAOS$. These equations also allow the behaviour of an infinite or recursively defined process to be explored as deeply as desired [Hor90]. The *feedind* operator $\triangleright$ can be algebraically defined by the following equations:

Distributivity Laws: All CSP operators are carefully defined so that they distribute through non-determinism. The operator $\triangleright$ is no exception.

D1	$P \triangleright (Q \sqcap R) = (P \triangleright Q) \sqcap (P \triangleright R)$	$\{ \triangleright$ DISTRIBUTIVITY $\}$
D2	$(P_1 \sqcap P_2) \triangleright Q = (P_1 \triangleright Q) \sqcap (P_2 \triangleright Q)$	$\{ \triangleright$ DISTRIBUTIVITY $\}$

Strictness: The operator $\triangleright$ is strict.

S1	$CHAOS \triangleright Q = CHAOS$	$\{ \triangleright$ STRICTNESS $\}$
S2	$P \triangleright CHAOS = CHAOS$	$\{ \triangleright$ STRICTNESS $\}$

Communications: The following laws capture the interactions between the producer and the consumer.

C1.0	$STOP \triangleright STOP$	$= STOP$
C1.1	$STOP \triangleright (?y \rightarrow Q(y))$	$= STOP$
C1.2	$STOP \triangleright (!y \rightarrow Q)$	$= !y \rightarrow (STOP \triangleright Q)$
C1.3	$STOP \triangleright (!y \rightarrow Q \,|?z \rightarrow R(z))$	$= !y \rightarrow (STOP \triangleright Q)$

C2.0	$(!x \rightarrow P) \triangleright STOP$	$= STOP$
C2.1	$(!x \rightarrow P) \triangleright (?y \rightarrow Q(y))$	$= P \triangleright Q(x)$
C2.2	$(!x \rightarrow P) \triangleright (!y \rightarrow Q)$	$= !y \rightarrow ((!x \rightarrow P) \triangleright Q)$
C2.3	$(!x \rightarrow P) \triangleright (!y \rightarrow Q \,|?z \rightarrow R(z)) = (!y \rightarrow ((!x \rightarrow P) \triangleright Q))$	
	$\square \,(STOP \sqcap (P \triangleright R(x)))$	

Termination:
Special care has to be taken when dealing with termination of the combination $(P \triangleright Q)$. Synchronized termination is undesirable because this means all internal communications must happen even if they are not relevant to the external

behaviour of the process $(P \rhd Q)$. In the functional setting, this corresponds to imposing an unreasonable restriction that function application does not terminate unless the argument is completely consumed, even though it may not be needed. Therefore, it is necessary to insist that the termination of $(P \rhd Q)$ should be solely controlled by the right operand Q. In other words, for a non-diverging process P, we would like to have

$$P \rhd SKIP = SKIP$$

Hence, the termination laws are as follows:

T1	$SKIP \rhd Q = STOP \rhd Q$	
T2	$P \rhd SKIP = SKIP$	where $P \neq CHAOS$

The above laws defining $\rhd$ can be used to calculate, for instance, the process $Prd([4]) \rhd DOUBLES$ as follows:

$$DOUBLES = ?x \rightarrow (!eot \rightarrow SKIP \ \{\!\!\{ x = eot \}\!\!\} \ !2 \times x \rightarrow DOUBLES)$$

$Prd([4]) \rhd DOUBLES$
$= (!4 \rightarrow Prd([])) \rhd DOUBLES$ { Unfolding }
$= Prd([]) \rhd (!2 \times 4 \rightarrow DOUBLES)$ { C2.1 }
$= (!eot \rightarrow SKIP) \rhd (!2 \times 4 \rightarrow DOUBLES)$ { Unfolding }
$= !8 \rightarrow ((!eot \rightarrow SKIP) \rhd DOUBLES)$ { C2.2 }
$= !8 \rightarrow (SKIP \rhd !eot \rightarrow SKIP)$ { C2.1 }
$= !8 \rightarrow (STOP \rhd !eot \rightarrow SKIP)$ { T1 }
$= !8 \rightarrow !eot \rightarrow (STOP \rhd SKIP)$ { C1.2 }
$= !8 \rightarrow !eot \rightarrow SKIP$ { T2 }
$= Prd([8])$ { Folding }

Finally, the feeding and the piping operators are related by the following law:

P	$(P \rhd Q) \rhd R = P \rhd (Q \gg R)$	{ $\rhd$ Pipe Law }

3.5   Processes Refining Functions

Given a simple function $f :: A \rightarrow B$ and a CSP process Q, What are the criteria for formally establishing whether Q is a refinement of f?. For any value x in the domain of the function f, $dom(f)$, the behaviour of applying the function f to the value x can be perceived in two different ways. On the one hand, it is the result of interactions between the producer $Prd(x)$ and the consumer Q, that is, $Prd(x) \rhd Q$. On the other hand, it is the process modeling the value $(f\ x)$, that is, $Prd(f\ x)$. If Q is a valid implementation of f, we should expect that the processes $Prd(x) \triangleright Q$ and $Prd(f\ x)$ to be identical. Therefore, the condition for establishing whether Q is a refinement of f is

$$(C)\ \forall x \in \mathrm{dom}(f) \bullet\ Prd(x) \triangleright Q\ =\ Prd(f\ x)$$

Definition 2. Given a CSP process Q and a function $f :: A \to B$, where A and B are types containing *data* values, Q is said to *refine* (or correctly *implement*) f if the following condition holds:

$$\boxed{\textbf{FR}}\quad f \prec Q \iff \forall x \in \mathrm{dom}(f) \bullet\ Prd(x) \triangleright Q\ =\ Prd(f\ x)$$

This formulation allows a concise algebraic specification style and an easy proof method for establishing the correctness of refinement. For example, by a simple inductive argument we can prove that the process $DOUBLES$ is a correct implementation of the function *doubles*. Section 4 contains several applications and proofs in this style.

Example: id_B
There is only one process $COPYONE$ which refines the identity function over basic values id_B:

$$
\begin{aligned}
id_B &\quad :: A \to A, \text{ where } A \subseteq \varSigma \\
id_B\ x &\quad = x
\end{aligned}
$$

$$COPYONE = ?x \to !x \to SKIP$$

Example: id_L
There are many CSP processes, however, which correctly implement the identity function id_L over lists of values. A typical CSP process which refines id_L is $COPY$.

$$
\begin{aligned}
id_L &\quad :: [A] \to [A] \\
id_L\ x &\quad = x
\end{aligned}
$$

$$COPY = \mu X \bullet ?x \to !x \to (SKIP \ {\triangleleft}\, x = eot \,{\triangleright}\ X)$$

Furthermore, any bounded CSP buffer process is a correct refinement of the function id_L.

3.6 Refinement of Higher Order Functions

The refinement relation $(\prec)$ can be extended to higher order functions in $\mathcal{H}$. Recall that a typical function in $\mathcal{H}$ has the following type:

$$h :: T \to (A \to B)$$

That is, h associates with each value m in T a function $(h\ m)$ in $\mathcal{F}$. We will view h as a specification of a vector of processes $\underline{H} :: T \to PROC$ that associates with each value m in T a process $\underline{H}(m)$.

Definition 3. Given the functions $h :: T \to (A \to B)$ and $\underline{H} :: T \to PROC$, $\underline{H}$ is said to refine h ($h \prec \underline{H}$) if the following condition holds:

$$\boxed{\text{HC}} \quad \forall m \in T \bullet (h\ m) \prec \underline{H}(m)$$

By substituting the definition of $\prec$ over simple functions, we can obtain from the above refinement condition the proof obligations for establishing whether $\underline{H}$ is a refinement of h as follows:

$$h \prec \underline{H} \iff \forall m \in T;\ \forall s \in \text{dom}\ (h\ m) \bullet prd(s) \triangleright \underline{H}(m) = prd(h\ m\ s)$$

Note that the refinement of a function with more than two arguments such as: $h :: T_1 \to T_2 \cdots \to T_n \to A \to B$ is the same as if h takes the first n arguments as a tuple: $h :: (T_1 \times T_2 \cdots \times T_n) \to A \to B$. This completes the definition of the refinement relation $\prec$. In the next section we will investigate its properties.

4 Parametrised Refinement Rules

We will now concentrate on establishing some general transformation rules which will directly refine parameterised functional templates into parameterised CSP processes. This will allow any instance of the functional template to be directly refined into the corresponding instance of the CSP template. The functional templates are generalizations of many useful functions which form the basic building blocks for the construction of more complex programs. We find it convenient to describe these rules using the notation (based on [CIP84]):

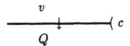

which means that the process Q is a refinement of the functional value v provided that the condition c holds.

The correctness proof of these rules is based on structural induction over lists. The proofs also make use of algebraic properties of some CSP operators such as sequential composition, prefixing and parallel composition in addition to several algebraic identities concerning $PROD$ and Prd.

$PROD$ Laws

$\boxed{\text{L1}}$	$PROD(s \mathbin{+\!\!+} t) = PROD(s)\,;\,PROD(t)$
$\boxed{\text{L2}}$	$PROD = (\oplus \not\vdash SKIP), \quad \text{WHERE } a \oplus P =! a \to P$
$\boxed{\text{L3}}$	$PROD(\text{if } b \text{ then } s \text{ else } t\,) = PROD(s) \mathbin{\{\!b\!\}} PROD(t)$
$\boxed{\text{L4}}$	$P \triangleright (PROD(s)\,;\,Q) = PROD(s)\,;\,(P \triangleright Q)$
$\boxed{\text{L5}}$	$PROD(s) \triangleright COPY = PROD(s)$

The notation $(\oplus \not\leftarrow e)$ stands for the right reduce operator (also known as "foldr"). Informally, we have:

$$(\oplus \not\leftarrow e)[a_1, a_2, \cdots, a_n] = a_1 \oplus (a_2 \oplus \cdots \oplus (a_n \oplus e) \cdots)$$

Prd Laws

L1	$Prd(s) \;=\; PROD(s)\,;\,EOT$
L2	$Prd \;=\; (\oplus \not\leftarrow EOT), \quad \text{WHERE} \quad a \oplus P =!a \rightarrow P$
L3	$Prd(s +\!\!+ t) \;=\; PROD(s)\,;\,Prd(t)$
L4	$Prd(\,\text{if } b \text{ then } s \text{ else } t\,) \;=\; Prd(s) \; \langle\!\langle p \rangle\!\rangle \; Prd(t)$
L5	$Prd(s) \rhd COPY \;=\; Prd(s)$

Sequential Composition (;) Laws

We will make use of the following laws concerning the sequential composition operator (;):

L1	$SKIP\,;\,P \;=\; P$
L2	$P\,;\,(Q\,;\,R) \;=\; (P\,;\,Q)\,;\,R$
L3	$(!a \rightarrow P)\,;\,Q \;=\, !a \rightarrow (P\,;\,Q)$
L4	$(P \; \langle\!\langle p \rangle\!\rangle \; Q)\,;\,R \;=\; (P\,;\,R) \; \langle\!\langle p \rangle\!\rangle \; (Q\,;\,R)$
L5	$(PROD(s)\,;\,P) \; \langle\!\langle p \rangle\!\rangle \; (PROD(s)\,;\,Q) = PROD(s)\,;\,(P \; \langle\!\langle p \rangle\!\rangle \; Q)$

4.1 Refinement Rule 1

The first rule $\boxed{\text{RR1}}$ deals with a class of functions which can compute any list in a single pass. We have

$\boxed{\text{RR1}}$
$f :: [\alpha] \rightarrow [\beta]; \; l :: \alpha \rightarrow [\beta]; \; e :: [\beta]$
$f \,[\,] \quad = e$
$f\,(x : s) = (l\;x) +\!\!+ (f\;s)$

$$F \;=\; \mu X \bullet \; ?x \rightarrow (PROD(e)\,;\; EOT \; \langle\!\langle x = eot \rangle\!\rangle \; PROD(l\;x)\,;\,X)$$

Note that in these refinement rules, type variables such as α, β and γ can only be substituted for types containning basic values so that values communicated by the corresponding CSP process are indeed drawn from σ.

Proof. We need to prove that $f \prec F$, that is

$$\forall s \in dom(f) \bullet \; Prd(s) \rhd F \;=\; Prd(f\;s)$$

We will establish this by induction as follows

Case []

$$
\begin{array}{ll}
LHS = Prd([]) \rhd F & \{ \text{ Definition } \} \\
\quad = (!eot \rightarrow SKIP) \rhd F & \{ \text{ Unfolding } Prd \} \\
\quad = SKIP \rhd (PROD(e)\,;\,EOT) & \{ \text{ Unfolding } F, \rhd \; \boxed{\text{C2.2}} \} \\
\quad = PROD(e)\,;\,(SKIP \rhd EOT) & \{ PROD \text{ Law4 } \} \\
\quad = PROD(e)\,;\,EOT & \{ \rhd \text{ Laws } \} \\
\quad = Prd(e) & \{ \text{ Folding } Prd \} \\
\quad = Prd(f\,[]) & \{ \text{ Folding } f \} \\
\quad = RHS & \{ \text{ Definition } \}
\end{array}
$$

Case $(a:s)$ Assume that $Prd(s) \rhd F = Prd(f\ s)$, we have to prove

$$Prd(a:s) \rhd F = Prd(f(a:s))$$

$$
\begin{array}{ll}
LHS = Prd(a:s) \rhd F & \{ \text{ Definition } \} \\
\quad = (!a \rightarrow Prd(s)) \rhd F & \{ \text{ Unfolding } Prd \} \\
\quad = Prd(s) \rhd (PROD(l\ a)\,;\,F) & \{ \text{ Unfolding } F, \rhd \; \boxed{\text{C2.2}} \} \\
\quad = PROD(l\ a)\,;\,(Prd(s) \rhd F) & \{ PROD \text{ Law } 4 \} \\
\quad = PROD(l\ a)\,;\,Prd(f\ s) & \{ \text{ Induction Hyp. } \} \\
\quad = Prd((l\ a) \mathbin{+\!\!+} f\ s) & \{ Prd \text{ Law } 3 \} \\
\quad = Prd(f(a:s)) & \{ \text{ Folding } f \} \\
\quad = RHS & \{ \text{ Definition } \}
\end{array}
$$

Example *List Homomorphisms:* A list homomorphism $h :: [\alpha] \rightarrow [\beta]$, is a function which distributes through the concatenation operator $+\!\!+$ (this is a simplified version of Bird's definition [Brd86]). That is, h satisfies the following condition:

$$h\,(s \mathbin{+\!\!+} t) = (h\ s) \mathbin{+\!\!+} (h\ t)$$

From this condition it follows that $h\ [] = []$. Hence, h can be defined as follows:

$$
\begin{array}{ll}
h\ [] & = [] \\
h\ (x:s) & = (h\ [x]) \mathbin{+\!\!+} (h\ s)
\end{array}
$$

This definition matches the template in rule $\boxed{\text{RR1}}$ therefore, its corresponding CSP refinement is the process:

$$H = \mu X \bullet ?x \rightarrow (\,EOT \mathbin{\not\!\Leftarrow} x = eot \mathbin{\not\!\Rightarrow} PROD(h\ [x])\,;\,X\,)$$

Example *map*: Given a function $f :: \alpha \to \beta$, the function $f* :: [\alpha] \to [\beta]$, is a list homomorphism. Therefore, $f*$ can be refined into the following process $MAP(f)$:

$$MAP(f) = \mu X \bullet ?x \to (\, EOT \,\{x = eot\}\, PROD(f*[x])\,;\, X\,)$$

by expanding $PROD(f*[x])$, the above process can be rewritten as:

$$MAP(f) = \mu X \bullet ?x \to (\, EOT \,\{x = eot\}\, !(f\ x) \to X\,)$$

Since this refinement is valid for any function f, that is $\forall f \bullet (f*) \prec MAP(f)$, we infer that the process MAP refines the higher order function *map* i.e. $map \prec MAP$.

Example *filter*: Given a predicate $p :: \alpha \to Bool$, the filter function $(p \triangleleft) :: [\alpha] \to [\alpha]$ takes a list of values s and returns the sublist of s whose elements satisfy p. Since the function $p\triangleleft$ is a list homomorphism, it can be directly refined into the following process $FILTER(p)$:

$$FILTER(p) = \mu X \bullet ?x \to (\, EOT \,\{x = eot\}\, PROD(p \triangleleft [x])\,;\, X\,)$$

By simple algebraic manipulations, unfolding $p \triangleleft [x]$, the above process can be transformed to:

$$FILTER(p) = \mu X \bullet ?x \to (\, EOT \,\{x = eot\}\, !x \to X \,\{p\ x\}\, X\,)$$

Since the refinement *filter* $p \prec FILTER(p)$ holds for any predicate p, we have: *filter* $\prec FILTER$.

4.2 Refinement Rule 2

This rule is very similar to RR1 except that the definition of f involves case analysis. In this rule, the case analysis is simply shifted into the CSP template.

RR2

$f,\ g :: [\alpha] \to [\beta];\ l_1,\ l_2 :: \alpha \to [\beta];\ e :: [\beta];\ p :: \alpha \to Bool$

$f\ [] \quad = e$
$f\ (x : s) = (l_1\ x) + (f\ s), \quad \text{IF } p\ x$
$\qquad\quad = (l_2\ x) + (g\ s), \quad \text{OTHERWISE}$

$\rule{10cm}{0.4pt}\ \{g \prec G$

$F = \mu X \bullet ?x \to (\, PROD(e)\,;\, EOT \quad \{x = eot\}$
$\qquad\qquad\qquad PROD(l_1\ x)\,;\, X \quad \{p\ x\}$
$\qquad\qquad\qquad PROD(l_2\ x)\,;\, G\,)$

The proof of this rule is straightforward by induction and case analysis.

Example *insert*: The function (*insert a*) takes a list *s* and produces a list (*u* ++ [*a*] ++ *v*) in which all the elements of *u* are less than or equal to *a*, the list *v* is either empty or its first element is greater than *a* and finally, *s* is the concatenation of *u* and *v*. *insert* can be defined as follows:

$$
\begin{aligned}
insert\ a\ [] \quad &= [a] \\
insert\ a\ (x:s) &= [x] +\!\!+ (insert\ a\ s), \quad \text{IF } x \le a \\
&= [a, x] +\!\!+ (id_L\ s), \quad\ \text{OTHERWISE}
\end{aligned}
$$

We have already established that the identity function over lists id_L can be refined into the process *COPY*. Therefore, by applying $\boxed{RR2}$, the function (*insert a*) can be refined into the following CSP process $INSERT(a)$:

$$
INSERT(a) = \mu X \bullet ?x \rightarrow \begin{array}{ll} (\ PROD([a]) \,;\, EOT & \langle\!\langle\ x = eot\ \rangle\!\rangle \\ PROD([x]) \,;\, X & \langle\!\langle x \le a \rangle\!\rangle \\ PROD([a, x]) \,;\, COPY\ ) \end{array}
$$

By expanding *PROD* and *EOT*, the above definition can be written as

$$
INSERT(a) = \mu X \bullet ?x \rightarrow \begin{array}{ll} (\ !a \rightarrow !eot \rightarrow SKIP & \langle\!\langle x = eot \rangle\!\rangle \\ !x \rightarrow X & \langle\!\langle x \le a \rangle\!\rangle \\ !a \rightarrow !x \rightarrow COPY\ ) \end{array}
$$

5 Compositional Refinement Rules

What can we do with functions? apply them to values, compose them, and refine them into various implementations. The refinement rules below map operations on functions to operations on processes so that if *v* is a combination of two values v_1 and v_2 using an *FP* operation, say *combine*:

$$
v\ =\ combine(v_1, v_2)
$$

then *v* can be refined into a process which is obtained from P_1, a refinement of v_1, and P_2, a refinement of v_1, using a CSP operation, say *compose*, as follows:

$$
v \prec compose(P_1, P_2)
$$

These rules will facilitate the modular and systematic refinement of functional specifications into CSP processes. In what follows, we will use the type variables T, T_1 and T_2 to stand for any type but the variables α, β, and γ to stand for types containing data values only.

5.1 Simple Function Application

The first rule associates the application of simple functions with the feeding operator $\triangleright$ (see section 3.5):

$$\frac{\begin{array}{l} f :: \alpha \to \beta \\ f\ a \end{array}}{Prd(a) \triangleright F} \quad\!\!\!-\!\!\!\!\!\bigdoubleplus\!\!\!\!\!-\!\!\!\langle\, f \prec F \wedge a \in \mathrm{dom}(f)$$

5.2 Higher Order Function Application

The second rule associates the application of higher order functions with parameter instantiation:

$$\frac{\begin{array}{l} h :: T \to (\alpha \to \beta);\ \underline{H} :: T \to PROC \\ (h\ x) \end{array}}{\underline{H}(x)} \quad\!\!\!-\!\!\!\!\!\bigdoubleplus\!\!\!\!\!-\!\!\!\langle\, h \prec \underline{H}$$

The correctness of this rule follows from the definition of $h \prec \underline{H}$.

5.3 Simple Function Composition

The composition of simple functions can be refined by the CSP piping operator.

$$\frac{\begin{array}{l} f :: \alpha \to \beta;\ g :: \beta \to \gamma \\ g \circ f \end{array}}{F \gg G} \quad\!\!\!-\!\!\!\!\!\bigdoubleplus\!\!\!\!\!-\!\!\!\langle\, f \prec F \wedge g \prec G$$

5.4 Higher Order Function Composition

The following rule allows a trivial refinement of $(h \circ g)$ from the refinement of $h :: T_2 \to (\alpha \to \beta)$.

$$\frac{\begin{array}{l} g :: T_1 \to T_2;\ h :: T_2 \to (\alpha \to \beta) \\ h \circ g \end{array}}{\underline{H} \circ g} \quad\!\!\!-\!\!\!\!\!\bigdoubleplus\!\!\!\!\!-\!\!\!\langle\, h \prec \underline{H}$$

The correctness of this rule directly follows from the definition of $h \prec \underline{H}$.

5.5 Conditional

This rule associates case analysis in FP with case analysis in CSP:

$$\frac{\text{if } b \text{ then } f \text{ else } g}{F \,\lessdot b \rgroup\, G} \Big\langle\, f \prec F \wedge g \prec G$$

The proof of this rule immediately follows from case analysis on whether the predicate b holds.

5.6 Non-Determinism Refinement

In development, non-determinism refinement can be applied after functional refinement and this will result in functional refinement. In other words, if a functional value v is refined (using $\prec$) into a process Q, and Q is refined, using non-determinism refinement ($\sqsubseteq$), into a process R, then R is a refinement (under $\prec$) of v. This result can be shown by case analysis on whether the value v is in $\mathcal{D}$, $\mathcal{F}$ or $\mathcal{H}$.

$$\frac{v}{Q} \Big\langle\, v \prec (Q \sqcap R)$$

The correctness of this rule directly follows from the facts that $v \prec (Q \sqcap R)$ and $(Q \sqcap R) \sqsubseteq Q$.

6 Function Decomposition Strategies

The fundamental objective of the *function decomposition* strategy is to transform a given algorithmic expression into a new form in which the dominant term is expressed as a composition of an appropriate collection of functions. The decomposition of a function h can be concisely captured by expressing it, for some list of functions fs, in the following form:

$$(\circ)/\,fs$$

Another form which will often be used to succinctly capture the decomposition of h is

$$(\circ)/\,f * s$$

where f is a higher order function and s is a list of values, say $[a_1, a_2, \cdots, a_k]$. In this case, we have

$$\begin{aligned}
h &= (\circ)/\,f * [a_1, a_2, \cdots, a_k] \\
&= (\circ)/\,[f\ a_1, f\ a_2, \cdots, f\ a_k] \\
&= (f\ a_1) \circ (f\ a_2) \circ \ldots \circ (f\ a_k)
\end{aligned}$$

6.1 Refinement to CSP

The main motivation for the function decomposition strategy is the result, shown in section 5.3, that the composition of simple functions can be naturally refined by the CSP piping operator as follows

$$
\boxed{\text{RL1}}
$$
$$
f :: \alpha \to \beta;\ g :: \beta \to \gamma
$$
$$
g \circ f
$$
$$
\rule{5cm}{0.4pt}\ \langle\ f \prec F \wedge g \prec G
$$
$$
F \gg G
$$

By an inductive argument, using the associativity of $\gg$, this result can be generalised so that the composition of any finite list function fs, say $[f_1,\ f_2,..,\ f_{n-1},\ f_n]$, can be refined into the piping of the list of processes $[F_n,\ F_{n-1},..,\ F_2,\ F_1]$ provided that for each index i, $1 \le i \le n$, the process F_i refines the function f_i.

$$
\boxed{\text{RL2}}
$$
$$
f_i :: \alpha \to \alpha
$$
$$
(\circ)/[f_1,\ f_2,..,\ f_{n-1},\ f_n]
$$
$$
\rule{5cm}{0.4pt}\ \langle\ \forall i \in \{1..n\} \bullet f_i \prec F_i
$$
$$
(\gg)/[F_n,\ F_{n-1},..,\ F_2,\ F_1]
$$

Another general refinement law which will be frequently used is:

$$
\boxed{\text{RL3}}
$$
$$
h :: T \to (\alpha \to \alpha);\ \underline{H} :: T \to PROC;\ s :: [T]
$$
$$
(\circ)/\ h * s
$$
$$
\rule{5cm}{0.4pt}\ \langle\ h \prec \underline{H}
$$
$$
(\gg)/\ \underline{H} * (reverse\ s)
$$

The refinement laws $\boxed{\text{RL2}}$ and $\boxed{\text{RL3}}$ show clearly that the functional forms resulting from the function decomposition strategy can be systematically transformed into pipes of processes. For completeness, we note that the refinement of higher order function composition (shown in section 5.4) is defined as

$$
g :: T_1 \to T_2;\ h :: T_2 \to (\alpha \to \alpha)
$$
$$
(\circ)/\ h \circ g
$$
$$
\rule{5cm}{0.4pt}\ \langle\ h \prec \underline{H}
$$
$$
(\gg)/\ \underline{H} \circ g
$$

By combining this refinement rule with $\boxed{\text{RL3}}$, we can derive the following refinement rule:

$$
\boxed{\text{RL4}}
$$
$$
g :: T_1 \to T_2;\ h :: T_2 \to (\alpha \to \alpha);\ s :: [T_1]
$$
$$
(\circ)/\ (h \circ g) * s
$$
$$
\rule{5cm}{0.4pt}\ \langle\ h \prec \underline{H}
$$
$$
(\gg)/\ (\underline{H} \circ g) * (reverse\ s)
$$

6.2 Pipe Patterns

We consider a number of general recursive functional patterns, we call *pipe patterns*, that can be systematically transformed into pipes of linearly connected CSP processes. Theses patterns encapsulate algorithmic definitions which are frequently encountered in functional specifications. Parallelism is exhibited by using the function decomposition strategy. The underlying technique for achieving decomposition is called *"recursion unrolling"*.

Pipe patterns are generally suitable for efficient large scale parallel implementations. Processes in the pipe are usually instantiations of a single CSP process. Therefore, in development we only need to transform a single function into an appropriate CSP process. This aspect greatly facilitates the design of the underlying algorithm, the argument for its correctness, its presentation and its efficient implementation. The pipe pattern which will be used most frequently is

$$spec :: [T] \to \beta; \ f :: T \to (\beta \to \beta); \ e :: \beta$$
$$spec \ [] \quad = e$$
$$spec \ (a : s) = f \ a \ (spec \ s)$$

An alternative formulation of this pattern can be captured by the higher order function $foldr$ as ($spec \ s = foldr \ f \ e \ s$). This pattern has a high degree of implicit parallelism. The parallelism can be clearly exhibited by using the function decomposition strategy. All we need is to transform ($spec \ s$) into an expression in which the dominant term is of the form $(\circ)/ fs$, for some list of functions fs. This is achieved by using the following recursion unrolling rule:

Recursion Unrolling (RU1)

$$spec :: [T] \to \beta; \ f :: T \to (\beta \to \beta); \ e :: \beta$$
$$spec \ [] = e$$
$$spec \ (a : s) = f \ a \ (spec \ s)$$

$$spec \ s = ((\circ)/ f * s) \ e$$

Proof. The proof of this rule is by induction as follows:

Case []

$$\begin{aligned} spec \ [] &= e && \{ \text{ Definition of } spec \} \\ &= ((\circ)/ f * []) \ e && \{ \text{ Definitions } \} \end{aligned}$$

Case $(a : s)$ Assume that $spec \ s = ((\circ)/ f * s) \ e$. We have

$$\begin{aligned} spec(a : s) &= f \ a \ (spec \ s) && \{ \text{ Unfolding } spec \} \\ &= f \ a \ (((\circ)/ f * s) \ e) && \{ \text{ Induction Hyp. } \} \\ &= ((f \ a) \circ ((\circ)/ f * s)) \ e && \{ \text{ Definition of } (\circ) \} \\ &= ((\circ)/ [f \ a] \mathbin{+\!\!+} f * s) \ e && \{ (\circ)/ \text{ Law } \} \\ &= ((\circ)/ f * [a] \mathbin{+\!\!+} s) \ e && \{ \text{ Distributivity of } (*) \} \\ &= ((\circ)/ f * (a : s)) \ e && \{ \text{ Definition of } (\mathbin{+\!\!+}) \} \end{aligned}$$

Now provided that $f \prec \underline{F}$, $spec(s)$ can be refined into the following network of communicating processes

$$SPEC(s) = Prd(e) \triangleright (\gg)/\underline{F} * (reverse\ s)$$

The proof of this result directly follows from $\boxed{RL3}$ and the refinement of function application. If the list s contains n values, that is $s = [a_1, a_2, \cdots, a_n]$, then $spec\ s$ can be implemented as a pipe of $(n + 1)$ processes. Processes in the pipe are mainly instantiations of a single process $\underline{F}$. The network $SPEC([a_1, a_2, \cdots, a_n])$, can be pictured as follows:

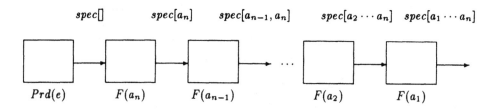

Fig. 3. $SPEC([a_1, a_2, \cdots, a_n])$

In order to ensure efficiency of the resulting parallel implementation $SPEC([a_1, a_2, \cdots, a_n])$, the function f must satisfy some additional requirements [Abd94].

Another recursion unrolling rule $\boxed{RU2}$ which is similar to $\boxed{RU1}$ except that $spec$ is inductively defined over the natural numbers is:

$$\boxed{\textbf{Recursion Unrolling (RU2)}}$$

$spec :: \text{NAT} \to \beta;\ f :: \text{NAT} \to (\beta \to \beta);\ e :: \beta$
$spec\ 0 = e$
$spec\ (n + 1) = f\ (n + 1)\ (spec\ n)$

$\updownarrow$

$spec\ n = ((\circ)/f * (reverse[1 \cdots n]))\ e$

If $\underline{F}$ is a refinement of f, that is $f \prec \underline{F}$, $spec\ n$ can be implemented as a network of $(n + 1)$ similar CSP processes as follows

$$SPEC(n) = Prd(e) \triangleright (\gg)/\underline{F} * [1 \cdots n]$$

7 Applications

7.1 Parallel Insert Sort

A functional specification of a sorting (by insertion) algorithm is

88

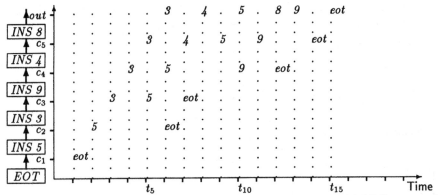

Fig. 5. Time diagram depicting the parallel computation of $SORT\ [8,4,9,3,5]$

7.2 Parallel Generation of Prime Numbers

Consider constructing a pipe of processes to generate, in increasing order, all prime numbers which are less than a given bound, say k. A functional specification of the algorithm can be stated as follows:

$$
\begin{aligned}
primesto\ k &= sift\ [2 \cdots k] \\
sift\ [] &= [] \\
sift\ (n:s) &= n:(n\ notdiv) \lhd (sift\ s) \\
n\ notdiv\ x &= (x \bmod n \neq 0)
\end{aligned}
$$

By matching this with the *pipe pattern* general form, we get

$$
\begin{aligned}
sift\ (n:s) &= f\ n\ (sift\ s) \\
f\ n\ t &= n:(n\ notdiv) \lhd t
\end{aligned}
$$

Therefore, provided $f \prec F$, $(sift\ s)$ can be implemented as the following network $SIFT(s)$ of communicating CSP processes

$$
SIFT(s) = EOT \rhd ((\gg)/\underline{F}*(reverse\ s))
$$

Hence, we have

$$
\begin{aligned}
PRIMESTO(k) &= EOT \rhd ((\gg)/\underline{F}*(reverse\ [2 \cdots k])) \\
F(n) &= !n \rightarrow FILTER(n\ notdiv) \\
FILTER(p) &= \mu X \bullet ?x \rightarrow (\ EOT \qquad \langle\!\langle x = eot \rangle\!\rangle \\
&\qquad\qquad\qquad\quad !x \rightarrow X \quad \langle\!\langle p\ x \rangle\!\rangle \\
&\qquad\qquad\qquad\ X\ )
\end{aligned}
$$

Which corresponds to the following network

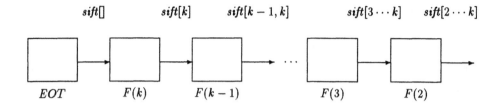

Fig. 6. Prime number generation.

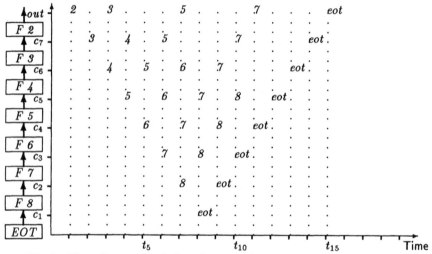

Fig. 7. Time diagram depicting the parallel computation of $PRIMESTO(8)$

The timed behaviour of the network PRIMESTO(8) can be depicted as in figure 7. This diagram shows how the behaviour of each process in the network might evolve with time.

The time complexity of a sequential implementation of $primesto(n)$ is $O(n^2)$ but the time complexity of its parallel implementation as a network of n communicating processes $PRIMESTO(n)$ is $O(n)$.

8   Combining Divide and Conquer Strategies and Decompositions

A well known programming paradigm for the construction of efficient algorithms is the *divide and conquer* strategy. The essence of the strategy is to divide the problem into parts and construct a solution to the problem by combining the

$$sort :: [\alpha] \rightarrow [\alpha]; \; insert :: \alpha \rightarrow [\alpha] \rightarrow [\alpha]$$
$$sort \; [] \qquad = []$$
$$sort \; (a:s) \qquad = insert \; a \; (sort \; s)$$
$$insert \; a \; [] \qquad = [a]$$
$$insert \; a \; (x:s) = x : insert \; a \; s, \qquad \text{IF } x < a$$
$$\qquad\qquad\qquad = a : x : s, \qquad\qquad \text{OTHERWISE}$$

Clearly *sort* is expressed as a *pipe pattern*. In a previous section we have shown how the function *insert* can be refined into the following process $\underline{INSERT}$:

$$INSERT(a) = \mu X \bullet ?x \rightarrow \quad (\, !a \rightarrow !eot \rightarrow SKIP \quad \{x = eot\}$$
$$!x \rightarrow X \qquad\qquad \{x < a\}$$
$$!a \rightarrow !x \rightarrow COPY \,)$$

Hence, *sort(s)* can be implemented as the following network $SORT(s)$ of communicating processes:

$$SORT(s) = EOT \rhd ((\gg)/\,\underline{INSERT} * (reverse \; s))$$

The network $SORT([a_1 \cdots a_n])$ can be pictured as in figure 4.

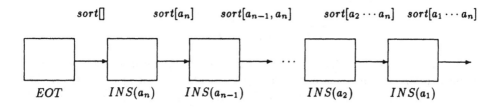

Fig. 4. Pipe sort.

The diagram in figure 5 depicts how the network $SORT([9, 4, 8, 3, 5])$ might evolve with time by illustrating the timed behaviour of the individual processes in the network.

To analyse the time complexity of the network for a list of n elements $T(SORT, n)$, observe that the first element of the result is output on the external channel after n steps, after which the remaining elements of the sorted list will be repeatedly output after two steps interval (one communication and one comparaison). Hence, $T(SORT, n) = O(n)$. Therefore, using n parallel processes, the parallel implementation of *sort* shows an $O(n)$ speed up over its sequential implementation.

solutions to the parts. Typically, the solution has the following form

$$solve :: [\alpha] \to [\beta]; \quad l :: \alpha \to [\beta]; \quad combine :: [\alpha] \to [\alpha] \to [\beta]$$

D1

$$solve \; [] \qquad = []$$
$$solve \; [a] \qquad = l \; a$$
$$solve \; (s \mathbin{+\!\!+} t) = combine(solve \; s) \; (solve \; t)$$

This strategy is very useful for tackling problems which operate on large sets of data. It is also particularly useful for exhibiting parallelism in these problems. The underlying techniques for achieving this is to partition the data into parts, compute in parallel the solutions to all the parts, and combine in parallel these intermediate solutions to form a solution to the whole.

The *divide and conquer* paradigm has been used in transformational programming as a strategy for deriving efficient sequential algorithms from high level specifications [Drl78, BrM93]. We will show how this strategy can be smoothly combined with the decomposition strategy in order to derive efficient parallel algorithms from their specifications.

8.1 Partition

Our main aim is to derive a pipe pattern version of *solve*, say *pisolve*, which exploits the partitioning of the underlying data in order to exhibit parallelism and achieve efficiency. To formulate this, we start by specifying a function called *parts* that splits a list into a collection of consecutive segments. The specification of *parts* is captured by the following condition:

$$parts :: [\alpha] \to [[\alpha]]$$

C1

$$(\mathbin{+\!\!+})/ \circ parts = id$$

The above equation $\boxed{C1}$ states that *parts* is a right inverse of the function *concat*, $(\mathbin{+\!\!+})/$, which concatenates all the elements of a list of lists. Obviously, there are many different functions which satisfy $\boxed{C1}$. Nevertheless, additional details for the specification of *parts* are not required. This means that the final result of the derivation will be applicable for any partition function which satisfies $\boxed{C1}$.

Our objective is to derive a new function *solve'*, that operates on a list partition, which is related to *solve* by the commutativity of diagram in figure 8.

That is, the specification of *solve'* can be captured by the following condition:

$$solve' :: [[\alpha]] \to [\beta]$$

C2

$$solve = solve' \circ parts$$

In order to synthesize a proper definition of *solve'*, we massage the right hand side of $\boxed{C2}$ as follows:

$$
\begin{array}{lll}
solve' \circ parts & = solve & \{ \text{ By } \boxed{C2} \} \\
 & = solve \circ id & \{ \; id \text{ UNIT FOR } (\circ) \; \} \\
 & = solve \circ (concat \circ parts) & \{ \text{ By } \boxed{C1} \} \\
 & = (solve \circ concat) \circ parts & \{ \text{ ASSOCIATIVITY OF } (\circ) \}
\end{array}
$$

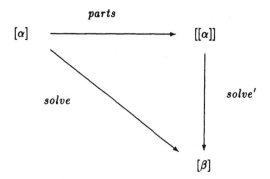

Fig. 8. Partitioning.

By stripping off *parts*, we get

$$\boxed{\textbf{D2}} \quad solve' = solve \circ concat$$

8.2 Applying the Decomposition Strategy

The main task now is to transform the above definition of *solve'* into a pipe pattern. That is, our goal is to find a function f such that

$$solve' \; (v \colon vs) = f \; v \; (solve' \; vs)$$

We have

$$
\begin{aligned}
solve' \; (v \colon vs) & \\
= (solve \circ concat) \; (v \colon vs) &\qquad \{ \; \boxed{\text{D2}} \; \} \\
= solve \; (concat \; (v \colon vs)) &\qquad \{ \; \text{DEFINITION OF } (\circ) \; \} \\
= solve \; (v \mathbin{+\!\!+} concat \; vs) &\qquad \{ \; \text{UNFOLDING} \; \} \\
= combine \; (solve \; v) \; (solve \; (concat \; vs)) &\qquad \{ \; \boxed{\text{D1}} \; \} \\
= combine \; (solve \; v) \; (solve' \; vs) &\qquad \{ \; \text{FOLDING } \boxed{\text{D2}} \; \}
\end{aligned}
$$

Therefore, by matching both of the above forms of *solve'*, the required definition of f is synthesized as follows

$$f = combine \circ solve$$

The remaining task is to define *solve'* for the empty list. We have

$$
\begin{aligned}
solve' \; [] &= (solve \circ concat) \; [] \\
&= []
\end{aligned}
$$

Therefore the complete definition of the new version, say *pisolve*, of *solve* is

$$
\begin{aligned}
pisolve \; s \quad &= solve' \; (parts \; s) \\
solve' \; [] \quad &= [] \\
solve' \; (v \colon vs) &= f \; v \; (solve' \; vs) \\
f \quad\quad &= combine \circ solve
\end{aligned}
$$

8.3   Transformation to CSP

Since *solve'* is expressed as a pipe pattern, by unrolling recursion, we get

$$
\begin{aligned}
solve'\ vs &= ((\circ)/\,f * vs)\ (solve'\ []) \\
&= ((\circ)/\,f * vs)\ []
\end{aligned}
$$

Hence, *pisolve* can be expressed as follows

$$
\begin{aligned}
pisolve\ s &= solve'\ (parts\ s) \\
&= ((\circ)/\,f * (parts\ s))\ []
\end{aligned}
$$

Finally, we have shown that, provided $f \prec \underline{F}$, the above pipe pattern can be implemented as a network of communicating CSP processes as follows.

$$
PISOLVE(s) = EOT \rhd ((\gg)/\,\underline{F} * (parts\ s))
$$

Assuming that we have *combine* $\prec \underline{C}$, and since $f = combine \circ solve$, we get

$$
\begin{aligned}
f = combine \circ solve \quad &\{\ \text{Definition}\ \} \\
\prec \underline{C} \circ solve \quad &\{\ \text{Refinement of } (\circ)\ \text{section } 5.4\ \}
\end{aligned}
$$

Therefore, we can choose $\underline{F}$ to be $\underline{C} \circ solve$. That is we have

$$
\underline{F}(v) = \underline{C}(solve\ v)
$$

Given a list s, and assuming that $parts\ s = [v_1, v_2, \cdots, v_p]$, the network $PISOLVE(s)$ can be pictured as in figure 9.

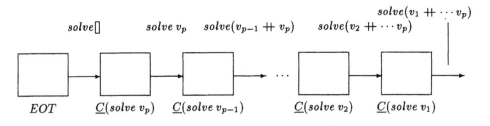

Fig. 9. $PISOLVE(s)$, where $parts\ s = [v_1, v_2, \cdots, v_p]$

8.4 Parallel Pipe Merge Sort

A well known divide and conquer algorithm for sorting is the following $mergesort$ [Drl78, BrW88] algorithm:

$$sort :: [\alpha] \rightarrow [\alpha]; \ merge :: [\alpha] \rightarrow [\alpha] \rightarrow [\alpha]$$
$$sort \ [a] \qquad = [a]$$
$$sort \ (s + t) = merge \ (sort \ s) \ (sort \ t)$$

where the function $merge$ is defined as follows

$$merge \ t \ [] \qquad = t$$
$$merge \ [] \ (a : s) \qquad = (a : s)$$
$$merge \ (b : t) \ (a : s) = [b] + merge \ t \ (a : s), \qquad \text{IF } b < a$$
$$\qquad\qquad\qquad = [a] + merge \ (b : t) \ s, \qquad \text{OTHERWISE}$$

Provided that $merge \prec MERGE$, $(sort \ s)$ can be refined into the following network $PISORT(s)$ of CSP processes.

$$PISORT(s) = EOT \rhd ((\gg)/ \ F * (parts \ s))$$
$$F(v) \qquad = MERGE(sort \ v)$$

For any list t, the function $merge(t)$ can be refined into the process $MERGE(t)$ as follows:

$$MERGE(t) = ?x \rightarrow MRG(x,t)$$
$$MRG(x,t) \ = (\ PROD(t) ; EOT \qquad\quad \{x = eot\}$$
$$!x \rightarrow COPY \qquad\qquad\quad \{t = []\}$$
$$!(hd \ t) \rightarrow MRG(x, tl \ t) \quad \{(hd \ t) < x\}$$
$$!x \rightarrow ?x \rightarrow MRG(x,t) \ )$$

This completes the derivation of the network $PISORT(s)$.

8.5 An Optimal-Work Parallel Sorting Algorithm

To analyse the time complexity of the pipe network, we assume that the length of the sequence to be sorted is n, the number of processors available is $(p + 1)$ and the list is partitioned into p segments of equal size, say k. That is, we have

$$n = p \times k$$

To determine the time required for the first message to appear on the external channel, τ_{FO}, observe that each process initially needs to (internally) sort a sequence of length k. This task can be achieved by all the processes, in parallel, in $O(k \log k)$ steps. Then after p comparisons the first message can be output on the external channel of the pipe. Hence, we have:

$$\tau_{FO} = T(sort, k) + p$$
$$= O(k \log k) + p$$

Thereafter, the elements of the sorted sequence successively appear on the external output channel within two time units (one comparison and one communication) each. Thus, the time complexity of the algorithm is

$$
\begin{aligned}
T(PISORT, n) &= \tau_{FO} + 2 \times n \\
&= O(k \log k) + p + 2 \times n \\
&= O(k \log k) + O(n)
\end{aligned}
$$

For $p = \log n$, we have $k = n \operatorname{div} \log n$. We also have

$$
k \times \log k \ \leq \ k \times \log n \ \leq \ (n \operatorname{div} \log n) \times \log n \ \leq \ n
$$

Hence,

$$
\begin{aligned}
T(PISORT, n) &= O(k \log k) + O(n) \\
&= O(n) + O(n) \\
&= O(n)
\end{aligned}
$$

Thus with only $\log n$ processors $PISORT$ sorts a sequence of length n in linear time. It also uses linear space. Hence, $PISORT$ is an optimal-work parallel algorithm which is suitable for $VLSI$ implementation.

9 Conclusion

We have proposed a transformational programming approach for the development of parallel algorithms from lucid functional specifications to networks of CSP processes. We have given several illustrative examples where, by applying this approach, a substantial gain in efficiency is achieved and the time complexity of the problem under consideration is reduced. Among these solutions is a new optimal parallel sorting algorithm which was discovered by systematically applying this approach.

We have established a mathematical foundation for the refinement of FP specifications to CSP processes and we have given a number of compositional laws which greatly facilitate this refinement. We have developed techniques and strategies for exhibiting parallelism in functional specifications and showed how this parallelism can be efficiently realized in CSP. We have shown that by relating the Functional Programming and the CSP fields we were able to exploit a well established body of FP programming paradigms and transformation techniques in order to develop efficient CSP processes. It is interesting to note the simplicity with which the refinement is done and the conciseness of the resulting CSP programs.

Acknowledgments

This work has been inspired by the work of C. A. R. Hoare on CSP and the work of R. S. Bird and L. Meertens on transformational programming. This article has been enriched by comments from Jeff Sanders, Mark Joseph, James Anderson and three anonymous referees.

References

[Abd94] Abdallah, A. E. "An Algebraic Approach for the Refinement of Functional Specifications to CSP Processes". *Internal Report*. The University of Reading, 1994.

[Brd84] Bird, R. S. "The Promotion and Accumulation Strategies in Transformational Programming". *ACM TOPLAS*, Vol. 6, No. 4, 1984.

[Brd86] Bird, R. S. "An Introduction to the Theory of Lists". *PRG-56*, Oxford University, Programming Research Group, 1986.

[Brd88] Bird, R. S. "Constructive functional programming". In *Constructive Methods in Computer Science*, Springer-Verlag, 1988.

[BrM86] Bird, R. S. and Meertens, L. G. L. T. Two Exercices Found in a Book on Algorithmics. In *Program Specification and Transformation*. North Holland, 1986

[BrM93] Bird, R. S. and Moor, O. de "List Partitions" *Formal Aspects of Computing*, Vol 5, No 1, 1993.

[BrW88] Bird, R. S. and Wadler, P. *Introduction to Functional Programming*. Prentice-Hall, 1988.

[Bry88] Broy, M. "Towards a design methodology for distributed systems". In *Constructive Methods in Computer Science*. Springer-Verlag, 1988.

[CIP84] CIP language group. *The Munich project CIP*, LNCS Vol. 1, Springer-Verlag, 1984.

[Dnn85] Dennis, J. B. "Data Flow Computations". In *Control Flow and Data Flow: Concepts of Distributed Porgramming*. Springer-Verlag, 1985.

[Drl78] Darlington, J. "A Synthesis of Several Sorting Algorithms". *Acta Informatica*, Vol. 11, No. 1, 1978.

[Hor85] Hoare, C. A. R. *Communicating Sequential Processes*. Prentice-Hall, 1985.

[Hor90] Hoare, C. A. R. "Algebraic Specifications and Proofs for Communicating Sequential Processes". In *Development in Concurrency and Communication*. Addison Wesley, 1990.

[LnH82] Lengauer, C. and Hehner, E. C. R. "A methodology for programming with concurrency: an informal presentation". *Sci. Comput. Programming*, Vol. 2, 1982.

[LkJ88] Luk, W. and Jones, G. "The derivation of regular synchronous circuits". *Proc. International Conference on Systolic Arrays*, San Diego, May, 1988.

[Mrt86] Meertens L. G. L. T. (Ed) *Program Specification and Transformation*. North Holland. 1986

[Mtr85] Moitra, A. "Automatic construction of CSP programs from sequential non-deterministic programs". *Science of Computer Programming*, Vol. 5, No 3, 1985.

[PCS87] Peyton-Jones, S., Clack, C. Salkid, J., and Hardie, M. "GRIP: a high-performance architecture for parallel graph reduction". In *Proc. ACM Conference on Functional Programming and Computer Architechture*, Portland, USA, Sep. 1987.

[Shr83] Sheeran, M. "μFP – An Algebraic VLSI Design Language". *D.Phil Thesis*, (also *PRG-39*), Oxford University, Programming Research Group, 1983.

[Trn85] Turner, D. A. "Miranda: a non-strict functional language with polymorphic types". In *Proc. Functional Programming Languages and Computer Architecture*, Nancy, 1985 (*Lecture Notes in Computer Science* 201, Springer-Verlag).

Architecture Independent
Massive Parallelization of
Divide-and-Conquer Algorithms

Klaus Achatz and Wolfram Schulte

Fakultät für Informatik, Universität Ulm
E-mail: {achatz,wolfram}@informatik.uni-ulm.de

Abstract. We present a strategy to develop, in a functional setting, correct, efficient and portable Divide-and-Conquer (DC) programs for massively parallel architectures. Starting from an operational DC program, mapping sequences to sequences, we apply a set of semantics preserving transformation rules, which transform the parallel control structure of DC into a sequential control flow, thereby making the implicit data parallelism in a DC scheme explicit. In the next phase of our strategy, the parallel architecture is fully expressed, where 'architecture dependent' higher-order functions are introduced. Then – due to the rising communication complexities on particular architectures – topology dependent communication patterns are optimized in order to reduce the overall communication costs. The advantages of this approach are manifold and are demonstrated with a set of non-trivial examples.

1 Introduction

It is well-known that the main problems in exploiting the power of modern parallel systems are the development of correct, efficient and portable programs [Pep93, Fox89]. The most promising way to treat these problems in common seems to be a systematic, formal, top-down development of parallel software.

In this paper we choose *transformational programming* to develop parallel programs where transformational programming summarizes a methodology for constructing correct and efficient programs from formal specifications by applying meaning-preserving rules [Par90]. Starting with a functional specification, we derive programs for the *massively data parallel model*, which assumes a large data collection that needs to be processed and that there is a single processor element (PE) for each member in the collection. The same set of instructions is concurrently applied to all data elements, i.e., there is a single control flow which guides the computation on all PEs.

The main characteristics of our strategy, using transformational programming to develop data parallel software, are the following ones: as a *problem adequate structure* we restrict ourselves to *sequences*, which are fully satisfactory in the vast majority of situations. The usual data parallel operations, like *apply-to-all* or *reduce*, are provided. In addition, certain high level operations are introduced, which can be interpreted as communication operations on the machine level (cf. Sect. 2).

As the starting point of our strategy, we choose a very popular tactic for designing parallel algorithms: *Divide-and-Conquer* (DC). Batcher's bitonic sort is a well-known example. DC algorithms are particularly suited for parallel implementation because the sub-problems can be solved independently and thus in parallel. Obviously DC algorithms have explicit control parallelism, i.e., there are separate independent parts that can be processed simultaneously by distinct CPUs. However, our model of computation does not allow several control flows. Therefore we aim at exploiting the inherent data parallelism. Hence, we present a set of semantic preserving *transformation rules*, which make the implicit data parallelism in a DC scheme on sequences explicit, thereby introducing architecture independent communication operations on sequences (cf. Sect. 3).

The architecture is fully expressed in the next step of our strategy, where *skeletons* are introduced. Skeletons are higher-order functions to express data parallel operations on specific architectures. The aforementioned sequence operations each have a straightforward implementation in terms of skeletons. In particular it turns out that even the communication oriented sequence operations can be implemented on arrays, meshes and hypercubes equally well. Due to the rising communication complexity on particular architectures, *topology dependent optimizations* become more and more important. We calculate two architecture dependent optimizations (for arrays and meshes) using only the skeleton definitions, where correspondent communications followed by broadcasts can be realized using less communication operations (cf. Sect. 4)

However, aside from answering theoretical questions concerning the correctness of our approach, we want to stress the advantages of our work from a practical and methodological point of view:

- The identification of a transformation rule to exploit the implicit data parallelism of DC and its necessary applicability condition makes the transformation process target directed.
- The developed DC algorithms are efficient and can be ported across several architectures. If, in addition, topology dependent optimizations are applied very efficient algorithms can be derived.
- The presented transformations can be automated using an extended compilation approach, where the user may give hints in the form of laws to the compiler [Fea87].
- Architecture independent data parallelism is distinguished from architecture dependent one. Correspondingly we operate on different levels of abstraction (sequences vs. skeletons) and supply different transformation rules (data parallelization vs. communication transformation).

These aspects are demonstrated with three examples: the parallel prefix computation, Batcher's bitonic sort, and computing the convex hull of a set of points in the plane.

The rest of this paper is organized as follows. Section 2 briefly presents our sequence model, and its relation to the massively data parallel model.

The new DC transformation rules are introduced in Sect. 3. Section 4 defines skeletons, their use and optimizations. We follow in Sect. 5 with two examples, demonstrating the applicability of our approach. Section 6 compares our approach with others. Finally, Sect. 7 draws conclusions and raises issues for further research. Proofs and more examples are given in an accompanying technical report [AS95].

Notation. In notation we follow the standard of lazy functional programming languages, like Haskell or Miranda. For example, we write function application in curried form, as in $f \, x \, y$ which is equivalent to $(f \, x) \, y$, and define functions – whenever possible – using pattern matching. If, in addition, assertions on parameters are used, they are given in the surrounding text.

2 The Balanced Sequence Model

Sequences in general can be used to express data parallelism in an abstract way, where parallelism is achieved exclusively through operations on sequences [Ble92]. In this section we explore this approach, present the traditional operations on sequences and its data parallel view (Sect. 2.1), introduce communication oriented operations (Sect. 2.2), and define some properties (Sect. 2.3) that will be of value in the following exposition.

2.1 Basic Sequence Operations

Our so called *balanced sequence model* is motivated by the underlying parallel program development strategy, viz. divide-and-conquer (see Sect. 3), and by the need to perform the same computation on all data elements of the sequence in parallel. The term "balanced sequence" stems from the fact that our DC scheme always results in balanced computation trees.

The constructors of our balanced sequence model are the following ones: $[]$ is the empty sequence, $[e]$ is the sequence which contains the single element e, and $x \mathbin{+\!\!+} y$ is the sequence formed by concatenating sequences x and y, but only if both have *equal* length. This always results in sequences of lengths powers of 2, which is appropriate, since all known massively parallel machines work with 2^n PEs.

The following auxiliary functions are used to specify programs. They will be removed during program development: the operator ($\#$) returns the length of a sequence. The first-order functions *first* and *last* extract the first or last element from a nonempty sequence, respectively. The function *copy* creates a sequence of n copies of identical elements.

It is perfectly well to assume every sequence element corresponds to a data element resting on a particular processor element. Two sequences can be seen as two different storage levels on the parallel machine.

We now start to introduce the set of balanced sequence functions, most of them are commonly used functions [BW88, AJ93]:

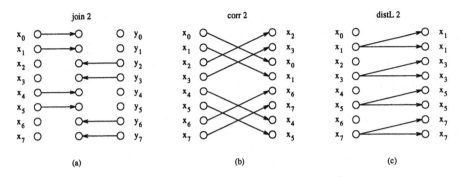

Fig. 1. Sequence operations: (a) *join* 2 *x y*, (b) *corr* 2 *x*, (c) *distL* 2 *x*

- *map.* Applies a function to every element of a sequence independently, and therefore reflects the massively data parallel programming paradigm in the most obvious way.
- *zip With/zip With3.* Takes a pair/triple of sequences, having equal length, into a new sequence in which corresponding elements are combined using any given binary/ternary operator. The family of *zip With* functions correspond to the *map* functional working on two or more storage levels.
- *reduce.* Reduces a nonempty sequence using any binary operator. This function can be implemented on a parallel machine in logarithmic time using a 'tree' [Ski93].

In a data parallel environment conditionals are somewhat different to their sequential counterparts. The action of a parallel **if** can be summarized this way: on every PE the condition is evaluated; in components where the condition is true, the *then*-branch is executed, otherwise the *else*-branch.

A specialization of a *parallel conditional* is the operation *join*. It takes a pair of sequences *x, y*, having equal length, into a new sequence, which consists of alternate slices of *x* and *y* each of length *n*, *n* > 0 (see Fig. 1(a)). We can define *join* by:

$$
\begin{aligned}
& join\ n\ (x1 + x2)\ (y1 + y2) = x1 + y2, && \text{if } n = \#x1 \\
& join\ n\ (x1 + x2)\ (y1 + y2) = join\ n\ x1\ y1 + \\
& \qquad\qquad\qquad\qquad join\ n\ x2\ y2, && \text{if } n < \#x1
\end{aligned}
\tag{1}
$$

Like the functions defined in the next subsection, *join* is a partial operation. Since these functions are introduced during program development, definedness of the resulting programs must be guaranteed by the appropriate transformation rules (cf. Sect. 3).

2.2 Communication Oriented Sequence Operations

A very wide range of scientific problems can be computed under the DC scheme using a regular communication pattern. Naturally, some communication patterns are better than others for developing parallel algorithms. Essentially, they have structural properties that make it easier to describe the data movement operations necessary for parallel computations. In the case of our particular DC scheme (see Sect. 3), the following communication operations seem to be the most suitable ones:

Correspondent communication – modeled by function *corr* n x – exhibits a butterfly-like communication pattern: for a particular value of n, each PE communicates with each PE whose index differs in the nth bit from the left. An example is depicted in Fig. 1(b). Its definition is straightforward:

$$
\begin{array}{lll}
corr\ n\ (x \mathbin{+\!\!+} y) = (y \mathbin{+\!\!+} x), & \text{if } n = \#x \\
corr\ n\ (x \mathbin{+\!\!+} y) = corr\ n\ x \mathbin{+\!\!+} corr\ n\ y, & \text{if } n < \#x
\end{array} \tag{2}
$$

First or last communication can be realized using a correspondent communication followed by a *directed broadcast*. A directed broadcast operates from right to left, where the value of the rightmost element is distributed to the left (*distL*), e.g., *distL* n x copies the value of the last element of each slice of length n to its left neighbors (see Fig. 1(c)). The function *distR* operates from left to right. Directed broadcast is related to *copy* by the following definition:

$$
\begin{array}{lll}
distL\ n\ x & = copy\ n\ (last\ x), & \text{if } n = \#x \\
distL\ n\ (x \mathbin{+\!\!+} y) & = distL\ n\ x \mathbin{+\!\!+} distL\ n\ y, & \text{if } n \leq \#x
\end{array} \tag{3}
$$

The introduced sequence operations *corr*, *distL/distR* and *join*, mirror the necessity of our DC scheme to exchange data between PEs and to select different data elements on each PE, respectively.

2.3 Properties: Distributivity and Length Preservation

Our balanced sequence model fulfills a number of properties, where especially the following two are needed in our transformation rules given below (cf. Sect. 3). Let f denote a function, which maps sequences to sequences. The function is said to be *distributive*, if it distributes through concatenation of sequences:

$$f\ (x \mathbin{+\!\!+} y) = f\ x \mathbin{+\!\!+} f\ y$$

It is said to be *length preserving*, if the length of the output sequence is equal to the length of the input sequence:

$$\#(f\ x) = \#x$$

The generalization to functions taking a tuple of sequences yielding a single sequence is straightforward.

Another generalization concerns the distributivity of functions like *corr* or *distL*, which work on slices of length n. This time, let f n denote a function, which maps sequences to sequences. If it distributes through a sequence $x \mathbin{+\!\!+} y$, where $n \leq \#x$, then the function is said to be *distributive modulo n*, or – more general spoken – *slice-distributive*.

All (slice-)distributive functions that either map the empty sequence to the empty sequence, or are undefined for empty sequences, are uniquely defined by specifying their effect on 'elementary' sequences (having length n).

It can be shown that functions *map* and *zipWith* are distributive, *corr*, *distL* and *join* are slice-distributive, and *map*, *zipWith*, *corr*, *distL* and *join* are length preserving.

3 Divide and Conquer

First, the idea and assumption of our DC tactic is discussed (Sect. 3.1) followed by its formal account (Sect. 3.2) that aims at transforming the parallel control-structure of DC into a sequential control flow with a parallel data-structure.

3.1 The DC Scheme

DC is a well-known tactic for designing parallel algorithms. It consists of three steps:

1. If the input is not primitive, partition the input.
2. Solve recursively the subproblems, defined by each partition of the input.
3. Compose the solutions of the different subproblems into a solution for the overall problem.

A general DC tactic can be defined as the following higher-order function:

$$
\begin{aligned}
&DC\ q\ t\ g\ h\ k\ j = f \\
&\textbf{where } f\ x\qquad = t\ x, &&\textbf{if } q = \#x \\
&\qquad\ f(x + y) = (k\ v\ w) + (j\ v\ w), &&\textbf{otherwise} \\
&\qquad\qquad \textbf{where } (v, w) = (f(g\ x\ y), f(h\ x\ y))
\end{aligned}
$$

In DC, when the input has length q, the problem is solved trivially by t, otherwise the input is split (by pattern matching), the subinputs are preadjusted by g and h, solved in a recursive manner, postadjusted by k and j and then concatenated. Thus the decompose and compose operations consist of two steps: $(g, h) \circ +^{-1}$ and $+ \circ (k, j)$, respectively. This leads to a computation, where the control flow, expressed by the sequence primitives, is separated from the computation, expressed by the adjust functions. In addition, it is assumed that the trivial, the pre- and the postadjust functions are length preserving.

This DC scheme is perfectly appropriate for data parallelization, since the sequence primitives are independent of the elements in the sequence and hence can be performed in constant time.

The power of this scheme stems from the fact that the pre- and postadjust functions receive the complete input and output sequence, respectively. However, since the adjust functions must be length preserving only "balanced" algorithms can be derived.

These assumptions rule out certain important non-balanced algorithms, as for instance Quicksort. But algorithms that either are not balanced or depend on values are not suitable for massively data parallel computation. They require – in contrast to our adjust functions – irregular communication patterns to get things in the right place, which normally causes high communication costs. Therefore such algorithms are not considered relevant for our current study.

Note. The restrictions in the DC scheme are not intrinsic to the presented constructor set. Other patterns, as for instance odd-even composition and division can be used instead (cf. [AS95]).

3.2 The Rules

The presented DC scheme exhibits cascading recursion and explicit data decomposition. In order to transform this scheme into a corresponding data parallel program, we have to introduce a sequential control flow, i.e., we must transform the cascading recursion into linear, or – even better – tail recursion, and we have to make the explicit data decomposition implicit.

First, we concentrate on simplifying the recursion. The computation proceeds in two phases: in a decompose or 'top-down' phase the preadjust functions g and h are applied to the subsequences, whereas in the compose or 'bottom-up' phase the postadjust functions k and j are applied. For a sequential flow of control, we have to decouple the phases of f, i.e., we introduce two functions one for the top-down computation $f{\downarrow}$ and one for the bottom-up computation $f{\uparrow}$.

Theorem 1 (Generalized divide-and-conquer rule). *Assume $g, h, j, k, t{\uparrow}$, $t{\downarrow}$ and t are length preserving functions and $t = t{\uparrow} \circ t{\downarrow}$. Let f be a general DC algorithm of the form:*

$$
\begin{aligned}
f\ x &= t\ x, &&\textbf{if } q = \#x \\
f\ (x \mathbin{+\!\!+} y) &= (k\ v\ w) \mathbin{+\!\!+} (j\ v\ w), &&\textbf{otherwise} \\
&\quad \textbf{where } (v, w) = (f\ (g\ x\ y), f\ (h\ x\ y))
\end{aligned}
$$

Then, f can be decomposed into an equivalent function $f{\uparrow} \circ f{\downarrow}$:

$$
\begin{aligned}
f\ x = f{\uparrow}\ (f{\downarrow}\ x) \\
\textbf{where } f{\downarrow}\ x &= t{\downarrow}\ x, &&\textbf{if } q = \#x \\
f{\downarrow}(x \mathbin{+\!\!+} y) &= f{\downarrow}(g\ x\ y) \mathbin{+\!\!+} f{\downarrow}(h\ x\ y), &&\textbf{otherwise} \\
f{\uparrow}\ x &= t{\uparrow}\ x, &&\textbf{if } q = \#x \\
f{\uparrow}(x \mathbin{+\!\!+} y) &= (k\ v\ w) \mathbin{+\!\!+} (j\ v\ w), &&\textbf{otherwise} \\
&\quad \textbf{where } (v, w) = (f{\uparrow}\ x, f{\uparrow}\ y)
\end{aligned}
$$

Proof. By induction on the length of the argument, see [AS95]. □

The resulting functions $f{\uparrow}$ and $f{\downarrow}$ still have cascading recursion. But now pre- and postadjust functions are decoupled. Additionally, we know the number of iterations 'beforehand', since the recursive computation only uses split and concatenation on balanced sequences.

We rewrite the functions $f{\downarrow}$ and $f{\uparrow}$ to include an additional parameter, which determines the recursion depth. Thus, it is not necessary anymore to use the sequence to determine the recursion depth – its length becomes constant. On the other hand, the trivial, pre- and postadjust functions have to be performed on the appropriate slices. This is possible, if they are length preserving. Then it is easy to define their slice-distributive generalizations, which work on the whole sequence and not only on the subsequences as in the case of cascading recursion. In order to supply the appropriate slices to the pre- and postadjust functions, we must explicitly introduce correspondent communication followed by a join of the different solutions of the subproblems.

The following two transformation rules enable us to derive tail-recursive and therefore data parallel versions of $f{\downarrow}$ and $f{\uparrow}$.

Theorem 2 (Top-down with pre-adjustment). *Assume functions g, h and t are length preserving. Let $f{\downarrow}$ be a cascading top-down algorithm of the form:*

$$
\begin{aligned}
f{\downarrow}\, x &= t\, x, && \text{if } q = \#x \\
f{\downarrow}(x \mathbin{+\!\!+} y) &= f{\downarrow}\,(g\, x\, y) \mathbin{+\!\!+} f{\downarrow}(h\, x\, y), && \textbf{otherwise}
\end{aligned}
$$

Then, $f{\downarrow}$ is transformed into an equivalent function $f{\Downarrow}$, which is a tail-recursive top-down computation with pre-adjustment. As an assertion on the parameters of $f{\Downarrow}$ we require $\#x \geq n$:

$$f{\downarrow}\, x = f{\Downarrow}\,(\#x)\, x$$
where
$$
\begin{aligned}
f{\Downarrow}\, n\, x &= t'\, q\, x, && \text{if } q = n \\
f{\Downarrow}\, n\, x &= f{\Downarrow}\, \tfrac{n}{2}\,(join\, \tfrac{n}{2}\,(g'\, \tfrac{n}{2}\, x\, x')\,(h'\, \tfrac{n}{2}\, x'\, x)), && \textbf{otherwise}
\end{aligned}
$$
where
$$
\begin{aligned}
x' &= corr\, \tfrac{n}{2}\, x \\
t'\, n\, x &= t\, x, && \text{if } n = \#x \\
t'\, n\, (x \mathbin{+\!\!+} y) &= (t'\, n\, x) \mathbin{+\!\!+} (t'\, n\, y), && \text{if } n \leq \#x \\
g'\, n\, x\, y &= g\, x\, y, && \text{if } n = \#x \\
g'\, n\, (x1 \mathbin{+\!\!+} x2)(y1 \mathbin{+\!\!+} y2) &= (g'\, n\, x1\, y1) \mathbin{+\!\!+} (g'\, n\, x2\, y2), && \text{if } n \leq \#x1 \\
h'\, n\, x\, y &= h\, x\, y, && \text{if } n = \#x \\
h'\, n\, (x1 \mathbin{+\!\!+} x2)(y1 \mathbin{+\!\!+} y2) &= (h'\, n\, x1\, y1) \mathbin{+\!\!+} (h'\, n\, x2\, y2), && \text{if } n \leq \#x1
\end{aligned}
$$

Proof. By computational induction, see [AS95]. □

Theorem 3 (Bottom-up with post-adjustment). *Assume functions k, j and t are length preserving. Let $f{\uparrow}$ be a cascading bottom-up algorithm of the form:*

$$
\begin{aligned}
f{\uparrow}\, x &= t\, x, && \text{if } q = \#x \\
f{\uparrow}\,(x \mathbin{+\!\!+} y) &= (k\, v\, w) \mathbin{+\!\!+} (j\, v\, w), && \textbf{otherwise} \\
&\quad \textbf{where } (v, w) = (f{\uparrow}\, x, f{\uparrow}\, y)
\end{aligned}
$$

Then $f{\uparrow}$ is transformed into an equivalent function $f{\Uparrow}$, which is a tail-recursive bottom-up computation with post-adjustment. As an assertion on the parameters of $f{\Uparrow}$ we require $\#x \geq n$:

$f{\uparrow}\ x = f{\Uparrow}\ (\#x)\ q\ (t'\ q\ x)$
where

$\quad f{\Uparrow}\ m\ n\ x = x, \hfill \text{if } n = m$

$\quad f{\Uparrow}\ m\ n\ x = f{\Uparrow}\ m\ (2n)\ (join\ n\ (k'\ n\ x\ x')\ (j'\ n\ x'\ x)), \hfill \textbf{otherwise}$

$\quad$ **where**

$\qquad x' = corr\ n\ x$

$\qquad t'$ as defined in Theorem 2

$\qquad k', j'$ are renamings of g' and h' of Theorem 2

Proof. By computational induction. $\hfill \square$

Example Parallel prefix. One of the simplest and most useful building blocks for parallel algorithms is the *parallel prefix* function [Ble93, Bir89], which takes a binary operator $\oplus$, a sequence of 2^i elements

$$[e_1, e_2, \ldots, e_{2^i}]$$

and returns

$$[e_1, (e_1 \oplus e_2), \ldots, (e_1 \oplus e_2 \ldots \oplus e_{2^i})]$$

If $\oplus$ denotes addition, then a possible initial specification for this function (shortly coined *psum*) is:

$psum_0\ x \quad\quad\quad = x, \hfill \text{if } \#x = 1$

$psum_0\ (x \mathbin{+\!\!+} y) = v \mathbin{+\!\!+} (map\ ((+)\ (last\ v))\ w), \hfill \textbf{otherwise}$

$\quad\quad\quad\quad \textbf{where } (v, w) = (psum_0\ x, psum_0\ y)$

This specification immediately leads to a DC computation, which can be done in $\mathcal{O}(\log n)$ time on n PEs – ignoring the communication costs – since each addition can be computed in one timestep, and the depth of the computation is $\mathcal{O}(\log n)$.

Applying our strategy, first, we derive a data parallel version for *psum*. Obviously, $psum_0$ matches the input pattern of the bottom-up computation rule. An appropriate instantiation is:

$t\ x \quad = x$

$k\ x\ y = x$

$j\ x\ y = map\ ((+)(last\ x))\ y$

We immediately obtain an iterative data parallel version of $psum_0$. The new functions t', k' and j', however, are still recursive. Although they can be implemented using DC too, it is much better to circumvent the recursion. Therefore, we carry out some precomputations to determine their closed forms:

Derivation. Let $n = (\#x1)$ and $x = x1 \mathbin{+\mkern-8mu+} x2$ and $x' = x2 \mathbin{+\mkern-8mu+} x1$:

$k'\ n\ x\ x'$
$\quad = [\ \text{def. of } x \text{ and } x', \text{ slice-distrib. of } k', \text{ unfold } k']$
$\qquad (k\ x1\ x2) \mathbin{+\mkern-8mu+} (k\ x2\ x1)$
$\quad = [\ \text{unfold } k]$
$\qquad x1 \mathbin{+\mkern-8mu+} x2$
$\quad = [\ \text{assumption: } x = x1 \mathbin{+\mkern-8mu+} x2\ ]$
$\qquad x$

$j'\ n\ x\ x'$
$\quad = [\ \text{def. } x \text{ and } x', \text{ slice-distrib. } j', \text{ unfold } j'\ ]$
$\qquad (j\ x1\ x2) \mathbin{+\mkern-8mu+} (j\ x2\ x1)$
$\quad = [\ \text{unfold } j]$
$\qquad (map\ ((+)\ (last\ x1))\ x2) \mathbin{+\mkern-8mu+} (map\ ((+)\ (last\ x2))\ x1)$
$\quad = [\ \text{property of } map \text{ wrt. } zipWith\ ]$
$\qquad (zipWith\ (+)\ (copy\ n\ (last\ x1))\ x2) \mathbin{+\mkern-8mu+}$
$\qquad (zipWith\ (+)\ (copy\ n\ (last\ x2))\ x1)$
$\quad = [\ \text{fold } distL\ ]$
$\qquad zipWith\ (+)\ (distL\ n\ x1)\ x2 \mathbin{+\mkern-8mu+} zipWith\ (+)\ (distL\ n\ x2)\ x1$
$\quad = [\ \text{distrib. of } zipWith\ ]$
$\qquad zipWith\ (+)\ ((distL\ n\ x1) \mathbin{+\mkern-8mu+} (distL\ n\ x2))\ (x2 \mathbin{+\mkern-8mu+} x1)$
$\quad = [\ \text{slice-distrib. of } distL, \text{ assumption on } x \text{ and } x']$
$\qquad zipWith\ (+)\ (distL\ n\ x)\ x'$

Due to the slice-distributivity of k' and j', definitions of k' and j' hold for all $n \leq \#x1$. In a similar way, t' can be shown to be equivalent to the identity function.

By means of these definitions, we apply Theorem 3 to $psum_0$ and result in:

$psum_0\ x = psum_1\ \#x\ 1\ x$
where
$\quad psum_1\ m\ n\ x \qquad\qquad = x, \qquad \text{if } n = m$
$\quad psum_1\ m\ n\ (x1 \mathbin{+\mkern-8mu+} x2) = p, \qquad \textbf{otherwise}$
$\quad \textbf{where } x' = corr\ n\ x$
$\qquad\qquad p\ = psum_1\ m\ (2n)\ (join\ n\ x\ (zipWith\ (+)\ (distL\ n\ x')\ x))$

In the following section, we will pick up $psum_1$, and will systematically derive architecture specific array, mesh and hypercube algorithms, respectively. $\qquad \square$

4 Skeletons and Skeleton Transformations

In this section, the basis for the derivation of architecture specific programs is given, i.e., topology independent skeletons are introduced (Sect. 4.1), followed by topology dependent ones (Sect. 4.2), then the derived sequence skeletons are calculated (Sect. 4.3), and finally communication transformations are presented (Sect. 4.4).

4.1 Basic Skeletons

The skeleton idea is fairly simple. The *data components on all processors are modeled as a data field* [YC92], i.e., as a function over some index domain D, which describes the PE's indices, into some codomain V of problem related values. Then, *data parallel operations can be defined as higher-order functions* (called *skeletons*), which are either abstractions of

- elementary communication-independent computations on all PEs or
- communication operations, which pass values along the network connections.

For instance, the most typical elementary operation on data parallel architectures is a single function operating on multiple PEs. This computation is expressed by the *MAP* skeleton:

$$MAP \ f \ a = \lambda i.f(a \ i) \tag{4}$$

The higher-order function *MAP* takes an operator f and a data field a, and returns a data field in which each element is the result of operation f applied to the corresponding element of a.

The skeleton *ZIPWITH* generalizes the *MAP* skeleton in the sense that *ZIPWITH* takes a pair of data fields a and b, and combines them using a dyadic operator $\oplus$.

$$ZIPWITH \ \oplus \ a \ b = \lambda i.(a \ i) \oplus (b \ i) \tag{5}$$

The introduced skeletons can be applied to every data parallel architecture, because no data exchange between two processors takes place. All data parallel architectures share these *topology independent skeletons*.

Individual types of architectures differ in their topology and thus, in their possible patterns of communication. Communication patterns for linear arrays, meshes and hypercubes will be given in the next subsection.

4.2 Communication Skeletons

This section formally defines three important static processor organizations: linear arrays, meshes and hypercubes.

Linear arrays. Linear arrays have a very simple interconnection network. Every PE is linked to its left and right neighbor, if they exist. An abstraction of a linear array with N PEs, where N in general is a power of 2, will be written as a parameterized type:

$$array(\alpha) = index \to \alpha$$
where $index = \{\, i \mid 0 \leq i < N \,\}$

Arrays can have wrap-around connections (then called rings), i.e., PE 0 is connected to PE $N - 1$. Here, we only consider arrays without wrap-around connections.*

We identify two basic data parallel exchange operations: shifting all elements one position to the left or to the right. The next two skeletons allow communication of k steps at a time, although only one step at a time is an elementary computation on these architectures:

$$
\begin{aligned}
SHL_A \; k \; a = \lambda i. \;\; &a(N-1), &&\text{if } i \geq N - k \\
&a(i+k), &&\text{otherwise} \\
SHR_A \; k \; a = \lambda i. \;\; &a(0), &&\text{if } i < k \\
&a(i-k), &&\text{otherwise}
\end{aligned}
$$

Note. The above communication skeletons are modeled in such a way that PEs, which do not receive a valid data element, yield the appropriate value of a boundary PE. Other patterns could be chosen too.

Meshes. In a mesh network, the nodes are arranged in a q-dimensional lattice. Communication is allowed only between neighboring nodes. Two-dimensional meshes, for instance, have $N \times N$ identical PEs, which are positioned according to an $N \times N$ matrix. Each PE $P(i,j)$ is connected to its neighbor PEs $P(i + 1, j), P(i-1, j), P(i, j+1)$, and $P(i, j-1)$, if they exist. The abstraction of two-dimensional meshes reads:

$$mesh(\alpha) = index \to \alpha$$
where $index = \{\, (i,j) \mid 0 \leq i,j < N \,\}$

Meshes also can have wrap-around connections, where each column and each row of the mesh is connected like a ring. Again, we only consider meshes without wrap-around connections.

According to these interconnections, we distinguish four different exchange operations: data is sent to its left(SHL), to its right (SHR) to its upper (SHU) or lower neighbors (SHD). The skeletons have the form:

---

* Wrap-around connections do not add further functionality to the system, but make communication patterns more efficiently implementable.

$$\begin{aligned}
SHL_M \ k \ m &= \lambda(i,j).\ \begin{array}{ll} m(i, N-1), & \textbf{if } j \geq N-k \\ m(i, j+k), & \textbf{otherwise} \end{array} \\
SHR_M \ k \ m &= \lambda(i,j).\ \begin{array}{ll} m(i, 0), & \textbf{if } j < k \\ m(i, j-k), & \textbf{otherwise} \end{array} \\
SHU_M \ k \ m &= \lambda(i,j).\ \begin{array}{ll} m(N-1, j), & \textbf{if } i \geq N-k \\ m(i+k, j), & \textbf{otherwise} \end{array} \\
SHD_M \ k \ m &= \lambda(i,j).\ \begin{array}{ll} m(0, j), & \textbf{if } i < k \\ m(i-k, j), & \textbf{otherwise} \end{array}
\end{aligned} \tag{6}$$

Hypercubes. In an n-dimensional hypercube, which has 2^n nodes, each PE has n neighbors, which it can reach in one time step. Its abstraction looks like the one for arrays, i.e., we have:

$$hyper(\alpha) = index \rightarrow \alpha$$
$$\textbf{where } index = \{\ i \mid 0 \leq i < 2^n\ \}$$

A PE in an n-dimensional hypercube can communicate with n of its neighbors, where nodes are adjacent to each other when their indices differ in exactly one bit position. This bit can be set on or off – correspondingly, we can communicate 'up' or 'down'. Once again we generalize this communication, by specifying communication in dimension d, which has to be a power of 2:

$$\begin{aligned}
COMMU \ d \ h &= \lambda i.\ \begin{array}{ll} h(i-d), & \textbf{if } i \geq (i \text{ div } (2d)) \cdot 2d + d \\ h(i), & \textbf{otherwise} \end{array} \\
COMMD \ d \ h &= \lambda i.\ \begin{array}{ll} h(i+d), & \textbf{if } i < (i \text{ div } (2d)) \cdot 2d + d \\ h(i), & \textbf{otherwise} \end{array}
\end{aligned} \tag{7}$$

Note. The integer parameter for shifting elements on the array or mesh describes *the number of elementary communication steps*, whereas the first parameter of *COMMU* and *COMMD* specifies the dimension in which a communication takes place – thus the elementary hypercube communication is performed in *a single step*.

4.3 Derived Skeletons

Now that on the one side, we have derived data parallel functions on sequences, and on the other have specified architecture specific skeletons, it remains to close the gap, i.e., to implement the sequence primitives in terms of skeletons.

We state without proof the correspondence of *map* with *MAP* and *zipWith* with *ZIPWITH*. This can easily be seen, if we recognize that each operation (by means of *map* or *MAP* and *zipWith* or *ZIPWITH*, respectively) is applied *independently* to each data element. Therefore, it makes no difference whether the data component is an element of a sequence or an element of a data field. The communication oriented sequence operations, however, have to be defined in the context of the architecture the algorithm is aimed at.

Arrays. Sequences of length N and linear arrays defined as data fields have a one-to-one correspondence:

$$g : \begin{cases} [\alpha] \rightarrow array(\alpha) \\ x \mapsto \lambda i.x_i \end{cases}$$

where x_i is the selection of the ith element of the sequence. The inverse of g is:

$$g^{-1} : \begin{cases} array(\alpha) \rightarrow [\alpha] \\ x \mapsto [x(0), \ldots, x(N-1)] \end{cases}$$

We derive the skeleton functions, operating on a linear array from the communication oriented sequence operations. We start with the following definition:

$$\begin{aligned}
g(join\ n\ x\ y) &= JOIN_A\ n\ (g\ x)\ (g\ y) \\
g(corr\ n\ x) &= CORR_A\ n\ (g\ x) \\
g(distL\ n\ x) &= DISTL_A\ n\ (g\ x) \\
g(distR\ n\ x) &= DISTR_A\ n\ (g\ x)
\end{aligned} \tag{8}$$

After eliminating the bijection g, we get the following direct definitions:

Corollary 4.

$$\begin{aligned}
JOIN_A\ n\ a\ b &= \lambda i.a\ i, \quad \text{if } even(i \text{ div } n) \\
&\qquad\quad b\ i, \quad \text{otherwise} \\
CORR_A\ n\ a &= JOIN_A\ n\ (SHL_A\ n\ a)\ (SHR_A\ n\ a) \\
DISTR_A\ n\ a &= \lambda\ i.\ a(l \cdot n) \quad \text{where } l = i \text{ div } n \\
DISTL_A\ n\ a &= \lambda\ i.\ a((l+1) \cdot n - 1) \quad \text{where } l = i \text{ div } n
\end{aligned} \tag{9}$$

Proof. By induction on n, see [AS95]. □

In order to obtain an array specific program, we replace the sequence operations by operations on data fields.

Example Parallel prefix cont'd. Unfolding the skeleton operations for arrays in $psum_1$, results in the following architecture specific $psum_2$ program:

$psum_0\ x = psum_2\ \#x\ 1\ x$
where
$\quad psum_2\ m\ n\ x = x, \qquad\qquad\qquad\qquad \text{if } m = n$
$\quad psum_2\ m\ n\ x = psum_2\ m\ (2n)\ (JOIN_A\ n\ x\ x'), \text{ otherwise}$
$\quad\textbf{where } x' = (ZIPWITH(+)\ (DISTL_A\ n\ (CORR_A\ n\ x))\ x)$

Note that the resulting program suffers from a lot of redundant communication operations. Due to our architecture independent transformation rules 2 and 3, we always introduce a correspondent communication. But in the particular case of the above example, we only have to distribute data in one direction, which leads to many superfluous shifts. Below, we will present communication transformations to remove redundant communication operations. □

Index Translations. In order to define the derived skeletons for meshes and hypercubes, we could proceed as already done for arrays. However, having defined arrays as data fields, it is much simpler to map only the index domain of the array to the hypercube or mesh domain instead of mapping the whole data structure.

Let D and E be two index domains. A bijective mapping $g : D \to E$, with inverse $g^{-1} : E \to D$ is called an *index translation*.

In fact, the application of an index translation results in a change of the underlying coordinate system, given by the source index domain D.

Meshes. Linear arrays of length N^2 are mapped onto a mesh with N columns and N rows, using the following index translation:

$$g : \begin{cases} \{0, \ldots, N^2 - 1\} \to \{0, \ldots, N - 1\} \times \{0, \ldots, N - 1\} \\ k \mapsto (k \text{ div } N, k \text{ mod } N) \end{cases}$$

where it is assumed that the indices are in row-major-order. The inverse mapping reads:

$$g^{-1} : \begin{cases} \{0, \ldots, N - 1\} \times \{0, \ldots, N - 1\} \to \{0, \ldots, N^2 - 1\} \\ (i, j) \mapsto i \cdot N + j \end{cases}$$

The mesh oriented skeletons $JOIN_M, CORR_M, DISTR_M$ and $DISTL_M$ can be derived starting from the corresponding array skeletons, this time using index translations:

$$\begin{aligned} JOIN_M \; n \; x \; y &= (JOIN_A \; n (x \circ g)(y \circ g)) \circ g^{-1} \\ CORR_M \; n \; x &= (CORR_A \; n(x \circ g)) \circ g^{-1} \\ DISTL_M \; n \; x &= (DISTL_A \; n(x \circ g)) \circ g^{-1} \\ DISTR_M \; n \; x &= (DISTR_A \; n(x \circ g)) \circ g^{-1} \end{aligned} \tag{10}$$

Eliminating the index mapping, we obtain the following direct definitions:

Corollary 5.

$$\begin{aligned} JOIN_M \; n \; x \; y = {} & \lambda(i,j). \, x(i,j), \; \textbf{if } \; even((i \cdot N + j) \text{ div } n) \\ & \quad y(i,j), \; \textbf{otherwise} \\ CORR_M \; n \; x = {} & \lambda(i,j). JOIN_M \; n \; x1 \; x2 \\ & \quad \textbf{where } x1 = SHL_M \; (n \text{ mod } N) \; (SHU_M \; (n \text{ div } N) \; x) \\ & \qquad\qquad x2 = SHR_M \; (n \text{ mod } N) \; (SHD_M \; (n \text{ div } N) \; x) \\ DISTL_M \; n \; x = {} & \lambda(i,j).x(((l+1)n - 1) \text{ div } N, ((l+1)n - 1) \text{ mod } N) \\ & \quad \textbf{where } l = (i \cdot N + j) \text{ div } N \\ DISTR_M \; n \; x = {} & \lambda(i,j).x((l \cdot n) \text{ div } N, (l \cdot n) \text{ mod } N) \\ & \quad \textbf{where } l = (i \cdot N + j) \text{ div } n \end{aligned}$$

Proof. By induction on n, see [AS95]. $\qquad\qquad\qquad\qquad\qquad\qquad\qquad\qquad\quad$ □

Hypercubes. Derived skeletons for the hypercube architecture are defined by choosing the identity function as an index translation ($g = id$). From (10) by replacing the subscript M with H, we obtain:

Corollary 6.

$$JOIN_H \ n \ x \ y = \lambda i . x \ i, \ \textbf{if} \ even(i \ \text{div} \ n)$$
$$y \ i, \ \textbf{otherwise}$$
$$CORR_H \ n \ x \ = \lambda i .JOIN_H \ n \ (COMMD_H \ n \ x) \ (COMMU_H \ n \ x)$$
$$DISTL_H \ n \ x \ = \lambda i .x((l+1) \cdot n - 1) \quad \textbf{where} \ \ l = i \ \text{div} \ n$$
$$DISTR_H \ n \ x \ = \lambda i .x(l \cdot n) \quad \textbf{where} \ \ l = i \ \text{div} \ n$$

Proof. By equational reasoning, see [AS95]. □

4.4 Communication Transformations for Array and Mesh

The result of our derivation leads to communication patterns, which probably are not the most efficient ones on a particular architecture. This is caused by the fact that for reasons of architecture independence, we always introduce correspondent communication. Sometimes first or last communication would be perfectly sufficient. Whereas correspondent communication is cheap on the hypercube – it can be performed in one step – it is more expensive on the mesh and rather expensive on the array. Thus it is obvious to specialize first or last communications on these architectures by eliminating correspondent communication. This can be achieved by *partial evaluation of the communication pattern*. As an example, we give two lemmas for arrays and meshes:

Lemma 7 (Communication transformation for linear arrays). *Let the following compound communication pattern for linear arrays be given:*

$$JOIN_A \ n \ x \ (ZIPWITH \oplus (DISTL_A \ n \ (CORR_A \ n \ x)) \ x)$$

This pattern is partially evaluated into:

$$JOIN_A \ n \ x \ (ZIPWITH \oplus (DISTR_A \ n \ (SHR_A \ 1 \ x)) \ x)$$

Proof. By equational reasoning, see [AS95]. □

Note. The expression $DISTL_A \ n \ (CORR_A \ n \ x)$ is slice-distributive, whereas the substituted expression $DISTR_A \ n \ (SHR_A \ 1 \ x)$ is not. However both expressions are at least equal on every second slice of length n. Therefore the expression must be embedded as the second parameter in a $JOIN_A \ n$. The use of $ZIPWITH$ generalizes the communication transformation.

While the communication pattern with the correspondent communication needs $3n - 1$ elementary shifts, the improved pattern can do with n shifts.

In a similar way, we can derive a communication improvement for mesh connected computers.

Lemma 8 (Communication transformation for meshes). *Let the following compound communication pattern for meshes be given:*

$$JOIN_M \; n \; x \; (ZIPWITH \oplus (DISTL_M \; n \; (CORR_M \; n \; x)) \; x)$$

This pattern is partially evaluated into:

$$JOIN_M \; n \; x \; (ZIPWITH \oplus x \; x')$$
$$\textbf{where} \;\; x' = DISTR_M \; n \; (SHR_M \; 1 \; x), \quad \textbf{if} \;\; n < N$$
$$DISTL_M \; n \; (SHD_M \; \tfrac{n}{N} \; x), \; \textbf{otherwise}$$

Proof. By equational reasoning. □

In the worst case $(n > N)$, the improved pattern requires $N + \frac{n}{N} - 1$ elementary shifts on meshes, while the original communication with correspondent shifts needs $N + 3\frac{n}{N} - 2$. Since communication costs are crucial for the efficiency of real parallel programs, a reduction of elementary shifts by a factor of about 3 seems worth the work.

Example Parallel prefix cont'd. Applying the communication transformation for arrays to $psum_2$ results in:

$$psum_0 \; x = psum_3 \; \#x \; 1 \; x$$
$$\textbf{where}$$
$$psum_3 \; m \; n \; x = x, \qquad\qquad\qquad\qquad \textbf{if} \; m = n$$
$$psum_3 \; m \; n \; x = psum_3 \; m \; (2n) \; (JOIN_A \; n \; x \; x'), \; \textbf{otherwise}$$
$$\textbf{where} \; x' = ZIPWITH \; (+) \; (DISTR_A \; n \; (SHR_A \; 1 \; x) \; x)$$

An implementation of $psum_3$ in a real data parallel language is now straightforward and presented in [AS95]. □

5 Applications

In order to demonstrate the usefulness of the presented approach, we work out two somewhat more complex examples. In Sect. 5.1, we treat one of the most popular sorting algorithms for data parallel computers viz. Batcher's bitonic sort. Section 5.2 deals with a problem in computational geometry, namely the construction of a convex hull.

5.1 Bitonic Sort

The well-known bitonic sort algorithm was proposed by K. E. Batcher in 1968 for so called sorting networks [Bat68] and later adapted to parallel computers [NS79].

114

Preliminaries and Operational Specifications

The bitonic sort algorithm is based on the central notion of the *bitonic sequence*. A sequence s is said to be bitonic if it either monotonically increases and then monotonically decreases, or else monotonically decreases and then monotonically increases. For example, the sequences $[1, 4, 6, 8, 3, 2]$ and $[9, 8, 3, 2, 4, 6]$ are both bitonic.

The fundamental idea behind the bitonic sort algorithm rests on the following observation: let $s = x \, \text{+\!\!+} \, y$ be a bitonic sequence and let $d = zip \, With \, min \, x \, y$ and $e = zip \, With \, max \, x \, y$, where *min* computes the minimum and *max* the maximum of two ordered values. Then we have:

(i) d and e are each bitonic and
(ii) *reduce max d $\leq$ reduce min e*.

The proof of this proposition can be found in [Bat68].

Bitonic Sorter. This fact, merging two bitonic sequences gives an ascending sequence, immediately gives us an operational specification according to the DC paradigm. As a precondition, we require the input sequence to be nonempty and bitonic.

$$bimerge \, [e] \quad = [e]$$
$$bimerge(x \, \text{+\!\!+} \, y) = bimerge(zip \, With \, min \, x \, y) \, \text{+\!\!+} \, bimerge(zip \, With \, max \, x \, y)$$

Arbitrary Sorter. A sorter for arbitrary sequences (implemented by function *bisort*) can be constructed from bitonic sorters using a sorting-by-merging scheme: decompose a sequence of length n into separate intervals of length 2. Trivially, these intervals are bitonic so that we can use the algorithm for bitonic sequences. In this way, we obtain $\frac{n}{2}$ pairs of sorted elements.

Unfortunately, two adjacent subsequences in ascending order cannot be put together to form a single bitonic sequence. To achieve this, the intervals have to be sorted alternately in ascending and descending order, or every second interval has to be reversed. Doing so, we get $\frac{n}{4}$ intervals of length 4, all of them are bitonic so that again the above algorithm for bitonic sequences can be applied. This process is repeated until we get a single bitonic interval, which eventually will be sorted by function *bimerge*.

Again, we can summarize this informal description into an operational specification using the DC strategy:

$$sort \, s = bimerge(bisort \, s)$$
where
$$bisort \, [e] \quad = [e]$$
$$bisort(x \, \text{+\!\!+} \, y) = bimerge \, (bisort \, x) \, \text{+\!\!+} \, reverse \, (bimerge \, (bisort \, y))$$

Note. Algorithm *bisort* explicitly reverses every second interval, putting an ascending sequence into a descending one by means of the auxiliary function *reverse*. The same effect can be achieved by inverting the comparisons, i.e., instead of *min* in function *bimerge* we use *max* and vice versa. Function $bimerge' = reverse \circ bimerge$ uses inverted comparisons in order to return sequences in descending order.

We redefine function *sort* by explicitly using function *bimerge'*:

$sort\ s = bimerge(bisort'\ s)$
where
$\qquad bisort'\ [e] \qquad = [e]$
$\qquad bisort'(x \mathbin{+\!\!+} y) = bimerge\ (bisort'\ x) \mathbin{+\!\!+} bimerge'\ (bisort'\ y)$

Parallelization

A closer inspection of the operational specifications shows that they both fit the patterns provided by the transformation rules given in Sect. 3.

Transformation of function *bimerge*. In order to apply the rule *Top-down with pre-adjustment* to function *bimerge*, we have to instantiate the input scheme given by Theorem 2:

$t\ x = x$
$g\ x\ y = zipWith\ min\ x\ y$
$h\ x\ y = zipWith\ max\ x\ y$

In the next step, we want to rewrite the cascading recursive definitions of t', g' and h' given in Theorem 2. Remember that we aim at a data-parallel computation scheme, where we can apply a single instruction to multiple data elements.

Derivation. Let $n = \#x1$ and $x = x1 \mathbin{+\!\!+} x2$ and $x' = x2 \mathbin{+\!\!+} x1$:

$g'\ n\ x\ x'$
$= $ [definition of x and x', slice-distributivity of g', unfold g', unfold g]
$\qquad (zipWith\ min\ x1\ x2) \mathbin{+\!\!+} (zipWith\ min\ x2\ x1)$
$= $ [distributivity of $zipWith$, assumption: $x = x1 \mathbin{+\!\!+} x2$ and $x' = x2 \mathbin{+\!\!+} x1$]
$\qquad zipWith\ min\ x\ x'$

In a similar way, we derive simplified definitions for functions t' and h':

$t'\ n\ x \qquad = x$
$h'\ n\ x\ x' = zipWith\ max\ x\ x'$

Due to the slice-distributivity of t', g' and h', their definitions hold for all $n \leq \#x1$. $\qquad\qquad\qquad\qquad\qquad\qquad\qquad\qquad\qquad\qquad\qquad\qquad\qquad$ $\square$

Under the assumption $\#x \geq 1$, application of the transformation rule (see Theorem 2) results in:

$bimerge\ x = bimerge{\Downarrow}\ (\#x)\ x$
where
  $bimerge{\Downarrow}\ n\ x = x,$ **if** $n = 1$
  $bimerge{\Downarrow}\ n\ x = bimerge{\Downarrow}\ \frac{n}{2}\ (join\ \frac{n}{2}\ v\ w),$ **otherwise**
  where $x' = corr\ \frac{n}{2}\ x$
    $(v, w) = (zipWith\ min\ x\ x',\ zipWith\ max\ x'\ x)$

Analogously, we can develop a top-down version of function $bimerge'$:

  $bimerge'{\Downarrow}\ n\ x = x,$ **if** $n = 1$
  $bimerge'{\Downarrow}\ n\ x = bimerge'{\Downarrow}\ \frac{n}{2}\ (join\ \frac{n}{2}\ v\ w),$ **otherwise**
  where $x' = corr\ \frac{n}{2}\ x$
    $(v, w) = (zipWith\ max\ x\ x',\ zipWith\ min\ x'\ x)$

Transformation of function $bisort'$. We start with an instantiation of the transformation rule *Bottom-up with post-adjustment* (see Theorem 3):

$t\ x = x$
$k\ x\ y = bimerge\ x$
$j\ x\ y = bimerge'\ x$

Again, we replace the (recursive) definitions of t', k' and j' by appropriate data parallel (non-recursive) versions:

Derivation. Let $n = \#x1$ and $x = x1 + x2$ and $y = y1 + y2$:

$k'\ n\ x\ y$
$= $ [definition of x and y, slice-distributivity of k', unfold k', unfold k]
  $(bimerge\ x1) + (bimerge\ x2)$
$= $ [property of $bimerge{\Downarrow}$, assumption: $n = \#x1$ and $x = x1 + x2$]
  $bimerge{\Downarrow}\ n\ x$

In exactly the same way, we compute instantiations for t' and j':

$t'\ n\ x\ \ = x$
$j'\ n\ x\ y = bimerge'{\Downarrow}\ n\ x$

Due to the slice-distributivity of t', k' and j', their definitions hold for all $n \leq \#x1$.   □

Under the assumption $\#x \geq 1$, the application of the transformation rule *Bottom-up with post-adjustment* yields:

$bisort'\ x = bisort\mathord{\Uparrow}\ (\#x)\ 1\ x$
where
$\quad bisort\mathord{\Uparrow}\ m\ n\ x = x,$ if $m = n$
$\quad bisort\mathord{\Uparrow}\ m\ n\ x = bisort\mathord{\Uparrow}\ m\ (2n)\ (join\ n\ v\ w),$ **otherwise**
$\quad$ **where** $x' = corr\ n\ x$
$\qquad\qquad (v, w) = (bimerge\mathord{\Downarrow}\ n\ x, bimerge'\mathord{\Downarrow}\ n\ x)$

An obvious simplification (since x' does not occur in the body of $bisort\mathord{\Uparrow}$) results in:

$bisort'\ x = bisort\mathord{\Uparrow}\ (\#x)\ 1\ x$
where
$\quad bisort\mathord{\Uparrow}\ m\ n\ x = x,$ if $m = n$
$\quad bisort\mathord{\Uparrow}\ m\ n\ x = bisort\mathord{\Uparrow}\ m\ (2n)\ (join\ n\ v\ w),$ **otherwise**
$\quad$ **where** $(v, w) = (bimerge\mathord{\Downarrow}\ n\ x, bimerge'\mathord{\Downarrow}\ n\ x)$

The final result of our transformational derivation of bitonic sort

$sort\ s = bimerge\mathord{\Downarrow}\ (\#x)\ (bisort\mathord{\Uparrow}\ (\#x)\ 1\ x)$

can be efficiently executed on massively parallel computers with such diverse topologies as linear array, mesh connected computer or hypercube.

5.2 Convex Hull

This section considers the problem of constructing the convex hull from a finite set S of points in the two-dimensional real space $\mathbb{R} \times \mathbb{R}$. The algorithm given here is mainly an adaptation of a sequential one presented in [PH77] with major changes to fit the massively parallel paradigm.

Preliminaries and Operational Specifications

Given a set $S = \{s_1, s_2, \ldots, s_{2n}\}$ of points in the plane, the convex hull of S is the smallest convex polygon P, for which each point in S is either on the boundary of P or in its interior. The following analogy given in [Akl89] might be useful: Assume that the points of S are nails driven halfway into a wooden board. A rubber band is now stretched around the set of nails and then released. When the band settles, it has the shape of a polygon. Those nails touching the band at the corners of that polygon are the vertices of the convex hull.

It simplifies the exposition, if we divide the problem into two sub-problems. First, we calculate the upper hull $UH(S)$ of set S. This is that part of its boundary traced by a clockwise path from the leftmost to rightmost points in S. In a second phase, we compute the according lower hull $LH(S)$. Since the computation of $UH(S)$ is analogous to the computation of $LH(S)$, we omit the latter. In a preprocessing step, a sequence is created containing the elements of S sorted by x-coordinate (e.g., by applying the bitonic sort algorithm given above).

To start with, we consider an algebraic type that defines the points in the plane in addition with suitable operations on it. Suppose *Point* denotes a pair of real numbers on which the following operations are defined:

$$.x, .y \qquad\qquad\qquad :: Point \rightarrow Real$$
$$. = . \qquad\qquad\qquad :: Point \rightarrow Point \rightarrow Bool$$
$$max_x, max_y, min_x, min_y :: Point \rightarrow Point \rightarrow Point$$

The interpretation of these operations is as follows:

$$(a, b).x = a \qquad\qquad\qquad (a, b).y = b$$
$$max_x\ p\ q = q, \text{ if } p.x < q.x \qquad max_y\ p\ q = q, \text{ if } p.y < q.y$$
$$\qquad\qquad p, \text{ otherwise} \qquad\qquad\qquad\quad p, \text{ otherwise}$$
$$min_x\ p\ q = p, \text{ if } p.x < q.x \qquad min_y\ p\ q = p, \text{ if } p.y < q.y$$
$$\qquad\qquad q, \text{ otherwise} \qquad\qquad\qquad\quad q, \text{ otherwise}$$
$$(p = q) = (p.x = q.x) \wedge (p.y = q.y)$$

The DC method of constructing $UH(S)$ given in [PH77] is as follows: Let S be a sequence of $2n$ points in the plane such that $s_1.x \leq s_2.x \leq \ldots \leq s_{2n}.x$ where n is a power of 2. If $n \leq 1$, then S itself is an upper hull of S (primitive case). Otherwise, we subdivide S into two subsequences $S_1 = [s_1, s_2, \ldots, s_n]$ and $S_2 = [s_{n+1}, \ldots, s_{2n}]$. Then, we recursively compute $UH(S_1)$ and $UH(S_2)$ in parallel. As the final step, we must find the upper common tangent between $UH(S_1)$ and $UH(S_2)$, and deduce the upper hull of S.

The informal description given above can immediately be formulated as an operational specification on non-empty sequences of points:

$$UH :: [Point] \rightarrow [Point]$$
$$UH\ s \qquad\quad = s, \qquad\qquad\qquad \text{if } \#s \leq 2$$
$$UH\ (s1 \mathbin{+\!\!+} s2) = UCT\ (UH\ s1)\ (UH\ s2), \qquad \textbf{otherwise}$$

Function *UCT* combines two nonintersecting upper hulls $UH(S_1)$ and $UH(S_2)$ by means of the *upper common tangent*, which is the unique line touching both $UH(S_1) = [p_1, \ldots, p_M]$ and $UH(S_2) = [q_1, \ldots, q_N]$ at unique corners p and q (see Fig. 2(b)).

The upper common tangent can be computed by first determining those points p_y and q_y of $UH(S_1)$ and $UH(S_2)$, respectively, with the maximal y-coordinates. To compute a point s_y with the maximal y-coordinate in a sequence of points s, we use the reduce operation: $s_y =_{def} reduce\ max_y\ s$.

Then, p is defined as the rightmost point in $UH(S_1)$ with the minimal slope wrt. q_y. Its formal definition is: $p =_{def} p_i$, $i \in \{1, \ldots, M\}$ such that

1. $g\ q_y\ p_i < g\ q_y\ p_j$, for all $j \in \{i+1, \ldots, M\}$ and
2. $g\ q_y\ p_i \leq g\ q_y\ p_j$ for all $j \in \{1, \ldots, i-1\}$

where g determines the slope of the line passing through the points a and b:

$$g :: Point \rightarrow Point \rightarrow Real$$
$$g\ a\ b = \perp, \qquad\qquad\qquad\qquad \text{if } (a = \perp) \vee (b = \perp)$$
$$\qquad\quad (b.y - a.y)/(b.x - a.x), \qquad \textbf{otherwise}$$

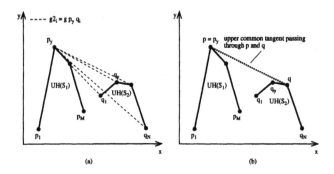

Fig. 2. Upper common tangent of $UH(S_1)$ and $UH(S_2)$

Henceforth, $\perp$ denotes an undefined value, which remains unchanged during computation.

The second corner q in $UH(S_2)$ is specified in a similar way, where only the signs of the slopes are inverted.

Figure 2(a) depicts two upper hulls $UH(S_1)$ and $UH(S_2)$. The dashed lines are the tangents passing through p_y. The tangent with the minimal slope (modulo sign) determines the right corner q. Figure 2(b) pictures the result of computing the upper common tangent. The new upper hull now consists of points $[p_1, p, q, q_N]$.

An operational specification of the above description reads as follows:

$$UCT :: [Point] \rightarrow [Point] \rightarrow [Point]$$
$$UCT\ s1\ s2 = s1' +\!\!+ s2'$$
$$\textbf{where}\quad (p_y, q_y)\quad = (reduce\ max_y\ s1, reduce\ max_y\ s2)$$
$$(g1, g2)\quad = (map\ (g\ q_y)\ s1, map\ (neg \circ (g\ p_y))\ s2)$$
$$(m1, m2) = (reduce\ min\ g1, reduce\ min\ g2)$$
$$(f1, f2)\quad = (find\ m1\ g1\ s1, find\ m2\ g2\ s2)$$
$$(p, q)\quad\ = (reduce\ max_x\ f1, reduce\ min_x\ f2)$$
$$(s1', s2') = (map\ (upd\ (<)\ p)\ s1, map\ (upd\ (>)\ q)\ s2)$$

In UCT, first the maximal points in $s1$ and $s2$ wrt. the y-coordinate are determined, resulting in the pair (p_y, q_y). Then, in every subsequence $s1$ and $s2$, respectively, the slopes are computed by means of the auxiliary function g. In $s2$, function neg additionally negates the slopes, where

$$neg\ x = \perp, \quad \textbf{if}\ x = \perp$$
$$-x, \quad \textbf{otherwise}$$

The pair $(m1, m2)$ denotes the minimal slope in each subsequence $s1$ and $s2$. Points, whose tangents wrt. p_y and q_y have a slope equal to $m1$ and $m2$ are assembled in the pair of sequences $(f1, f2)$ by means of function *find*:

$$find :: Real \to [Real] \to [Point] \to [Point]$$
$$find\ m\ gs\ s = zipWith\ (is_m\ m)\ gs\ s$$
$$\textbf{where}\ is_m\ m\ m'\ x = x, \quad \textbf{if}\ m = m'$$
$$\bot, \quad \textbf{otherwise}$$

Then, the unique corners p and q of $s1$ and $s2$ are the rightmost and leftmost points in the according subsequences. Finally those elements in $s1$ and $s2$, resp., which do not belong to the upper hull, are replaced by dummy elements, according to the definition of function *upd*:

$$upd :: (Point \to Point \to Bool) \to Point \to Point \to Point$$
$$upd\ \oplus\ a\ b = \bot, \quad \textbf{if}\ a.x\ \oplus\ b.x$$
$$b, \quad \textbf{otherwise}$$

Unfolding function *UCT* in the body of *UH* leads to a version, which fits the input scheme of transformation rule *Bottom-up with post-adjustment*:

$$UH\ s \qquad\qquad = s, \qquad\qquad\quad \textbf{if}\ \#s \leq 2$$
$$UH\ (s1 \mathbin{+\!\!+} s2) = k\ v\ w \mathbin{+\!\!+} j\ v\ w, \quad \textbf{otherwise}$$
$$\textbf{where}$$
$$(v, w) = (UH\ s1,\ UH\ s2)$$

$k\ v\ w\ \ = map\ (upd\ (<)\ (p\ v\ w))\ v$	$j\ v\ w\ \ = map\ (upd\ (>)\ (q\ v\ w))\ w$
$p\ v\ w\ \ = reduce\ max_x\ (f1\ v\ w)$	$q\ v\ w\ \ = reduce\ min_x\ (f2\ v\ w)$
$f1\ v\ w\ = find\ (m1\ v\ w)\ (g1\ v\ w)\ v$	$f2\ v\ w\ = find\ (m2\ v\ w)\ (g2\ v\ w)\ w$
$m1\ v\ w = reduce\ min\ (g1\ v\ w)$	$m2\ v\ w = reduce\ min\ (g2\ v\ w)$
$g1\ v\ w\ = map\ (g\ (q_y\ v\ w))\ v$	$g2\ v\ w\ = map\ (neg \circ (g\ (p_y\ v\ w)))\ w$
$p_y\ v\ w\ = reduce\ max_y\ v$	$q_y\ v\ w\ = reduce\ max_y\ w$

Note. In order to ease the following parallelization we lifted the object declarations of *UCT* to functions in *UH*.

Parallelization

As in the previous subsection, we carry out some precomputations in order to derive instantiations of t', k' and j' without using recursion:

Derivation. Let $n = \#s1$ and $s = s1 \mathbin{+\!\!+} s2$ and $s' = s2 \mathbin{+\!\!+} s1$.

$$k'\ n\ s\ s'$$
$$= [\ \text{definition of}\ s\ \text{and}\ s',\ \text{slice-distributivity of}\ k'\ \text{unfold}\ k',\ \text{unfold}\ k\ ]$$
$$\qquad map\ (upd\ (<)\ (p\ s1\ s2))\ s1 \mathbin{+\!\!+} map\ (upd\ (<)\ (p\ s2\ s1))\ s2$$
$$= [\ \text{property of}\ map\ \text{wrt.}\ zipWith,\ \text{distributivity of}\ zipWith\ ]$$
$$\qquad zipWith\ (upd\ (<))\ (copy\ n\ (p\ s1\ s2) \mathbin{+\!\!+} copy\ n\ (p\ s2\ s1))\ (s1 \mathbin{+\!\!+} s2)$$
$$= [\ s = s1 \mathbin{+\!\!+} s2,\ p'\ n\ s\ s' =_{def} copy\ n\ (p\ s1\ s2) \mathbin{+\!\!+} copy\ n\ (p\ s2\ s1)\ ]$$
$$\qquad zipWith\ (upd\ (<))\ (p'\ n\ s\ s')\ s$$

$p'\ n\ s\ s' =_{def}\ copy\ n\ (p\ s1\ s2)\ +\!\!+\ copy\ n\ (p\ s2\ s1)$

$= [\ \text{unfold}\ p\ ]$

 $copy\ n\ (reduce\ max_x\ (f1\ s1\ s2))\ +\!\!+\ copy\ n\ (reduce\ max_x\ (f1\ s2\ s1))$

$= [\ reduce{\uparrow}\ \oplus\ s =_{def}\ copy\ (\#s)(reduce\ \oplus\ s)\ ]$

 $reduce{\uparrow}\ max_x\ (f1\ s1\ s2)\ +\!\!+\ reduce{\uparrow}\ max_x\ (f1\ s2\ s1)$

$= [reduce{\Uparrow}^{**}\ \oplus\ (\#s1)\ 1\ (s1\ +\!\!+\ s2) = reduce{\uparrow}\ \oplus\ s1\ +\!\!+\ reduce{\uparrow}\ \oplus\ s2]$

 $reduce{\Uparrow}\ max_x\ n\ 1\ (f1\ s1\ s2\ +\!\!+\ f1\ s2\ s1)$

$= [\ f1'\ n\ s\ s' =_{def}\ f1\ s1\ s2\ +\!\!+\ f1\ s2\ s1\ ]$

 $reduce{\Uparrow}\ max_x\ n\ 1\ (f1'\ n\ s\ s')$

In an analogous way, we can find generalizations for $f1, m1, g1$ and q_y:

$f1'\ n\ s\ s'\ = zipWith3\ is_m\ (m1'\ n\ s\ s')\ (g1'\ n\ s\ s')\ s$
$m1'\ n\ s\ s' = reduce{\Uparrow}\ min\ n\ 1\ (g1'\ n\ s\ s')$
$g1'\ n\ s\ s'\ = zipWith\ g\ (q'_y\ n\ s\ s')\ s$
$q'_y\ n\ s\ s'\ = reduce{\Uparrow}\ max_y\ n\ 1\ s'$

Due to the slice-distributivity of k', definition of k' holds for all $n \leq \#s1$. Analogously, we can derive:

$t'\ n\ s = s$
$j'\ n\ s\ s' = zipWith\ (upd\ (>))\ (q'\ n\ s\ s')\ s'$
where
 $q'\ n\ s\ s'\ \ = reduce{\Uparrow}\ min_x\ n\ 1\ (f2'\ n\ s\ s')$
 $f2'\ n\ s\ s'\ = zipWith3\ is_m\ (m2'\ n\ s\ s')\ (g2'\ n\ s\ s')\ s'$
 $m2'\ n\ s\ s'\ = reduce{\Uparrow}\ min\ n\ 1\ (g2'\ n\ s\ s')$
 $g2'\ n\ s\ s'\ = map\ neg\ (zipWith\ g\ (p'_y\ n\ s\ s')\ s')$
 $p'_y\ n\ s\ s'\ = reduce{\Uparrow}\ max_y\ n\ 1\ s$

                         $\square$

The application of Theorem 3 results in:

$UH\ s = UH'\ (\#s)\ 2\ s$
where
 $UH'\ m\ n\ s = s,$ **if** $m = n$
     $UH'\ m\ (2n)\ (join\ n\ (k'\ n\ s\ s')\ (j'\ n\ s'\ s)),$ **otherwise**
 where
   $s' = corr\ n\ s$
   k' and j' as defined above

[**] The function $reduce{\Uparrow}$ is a parallel version of $reduce{\uparrow}$. Its derivation is analogous to the given ones.

which, after several unfolding steps and consistent renaming, leads to a data parallel version of UH':

$$UH' \; m \; n \; s = s, \qquad\qquad\qquad \textbf{if } m = n$$
$$\qquad\qquad UH' \; m \; (2n) \; (join \; n \; \overline{k} \; \overline{j}), \quad \textbf{otherwise}$$

where

$$s' = corr \; n \; s$$

$\overline{k} \;\; = zip With \; (upd \; (<)) \; \overline{p} \; s$	$\overline{j} \;\;\; = zip With \; (upd \; (>)) \; \overline{q} \; s$
$\overline{p} \;\; = reduce{\Uparrow} \; max_x \; n \; 1 \; \overline{f1}$	$\overline{q} \;\;\; = reduce{\Uparrow} \; min_x \; n \; 1 \; \overline{f2}$
$\overline{f1} = zip With3 \; is_m \; \overline{m1} \; \overline{g1} \; s$	$\overline{f2} \;\; = zip With3 \; is_m \; \overline{m2} \; \overline{g2} \; s$
$\overline{m1} = reduce{\Uparrow} \; min \; n \; 1 \; \overline{g1}$	$\overline{m2} = reduce{\Uparrow} \; min \; n \; 1 \; \overline{g2}$
$\overline{g1} = zip With \; g \; \overline{p_y} \; s$	$\overline{g2} \;\; = map \; neg \; (zip With \; g \; \overline{q_y} \; s)$
$\overline{q_y} = reduce{\Uparrow} \; max_y \; n \; 1 \; s'$	$\overline{p_y} \;\; = reduce{\Uparrow} \; max_y \; n \; 1 \; s'$

A closer inspection of this version of UH' shows that due to the generality of our transformation rules we wasted a lot of parallelism. Since *join* only takes half of the elements of its argument sequences, we compute some data values sequentially instead of parallel. Thus, we continue our derivation by applying an adapted horizontal fusion strategy [Par90], which amounts to "merging" different computations into a single one.

Derivation. Without loss of generality, we assume $n = \frac{\#s}{2}$. The auxiliary functions *left* and *right* take the first and the second half of a sequence, respectively: *left* $(s1 +\!\!+ s2) = s1$ and *right* $(s1 +\!\!+ s2) = s2$.

$join \; n \; \overline{k} \; \overline{j}$
$= [\, \text{unfold } \overline{k} \text{ and } \overline{j} \,]$
$\qquad join \; n \; (zip With \; (upd \; (<)) \; \overline{p} \; s) \; (zip With \; (upd \; (>)) \; \overline{q} \; s)$
$= [\, \text{distributivity of } zip With, \text{ unfold } join \,]$
$\qquad zip With \; (upd \; (<)) \; (left \; \overline{p}) \; s1 +\!\!+ zip With \; (upd \; (>)) \; (right \; \overline{q}) \; s2$
$= [\, \overline{pq} =_{def} left \; \overline{p} +\!\!+ right \; \overline{q} \,]$
$\qquad join \; n \; (zip With \; (upd \; (<)) \; \overline{pq} \; s) \; (zip With \; (upd \; (>)) \; \overline{pq} \; s)$

$\overline{pq} =_{def} left \; \overline{p} +\!\!+ right \; \overline{q}$
$= [\, \text{unfold } \overline{p} \text{ and } \overline{q} \,]$
$\qquad left \; (reduce{\Uparrow} \; max_x \; n \; 1 \; \overline{f1}) +\!\!+ right \; (reduce{\Uparrow} \; min_x \; n \; 1 \; \overline{f2})$
$= [\, \text{property of } reduce{\Uparrow} \text{ under the assumption } n = \#\overline{f1} = \#\overline{f2} \,]$
$\qquad reduce{\Uparrow} \; max_x \; n \; 1 \; (left \; \overline{f1}) +\!\!+ reduce{\Uparrow} \; min_x \; n \; 1 \; (right \; \overline{f2})$
$= [\, \overline{f} =_{def} left \; \overline{f1} +\!\!+ right \; \overline{f2} \,]$
$\qquad join \; n \; (reduce{\Uparrow} \; max_x \; n \; 1 \; \overline{f}) \; (reduce{\Uparrow} \; min_x \; n \; 1 \; \overline{f})$

Similar derivations lead to appropriate equations for $\overline{f}, \overline{m}, \overline{g}, \overline{a}$ and $\overline{pq_y}$ (see below). $\qquad\qquad\qquad\qquad\qquad\qquad\qquad\qquad\qquad\qquad\qquad\qquad\qquad\qquad$ □

Our final version of the convex hull algorithm is summarized in the following program:

$UH\ s = UH'\ (\#s)\ 2\ s$
where
$\quad UH'\ m\ n\ s = s,$ **if** $m = n$
$\qquad\qquad\qquad UH'\ m\ (2n)\ (join\ n\ \overline{k}\ \overline{j}),$ **otherwise**
$\qquad$**where** $s' = corr\ n\ s$
$\qquad\qquad\quad \overline{k} = zipWith\ (upd\ (<))\ \overline{pq}\ s$
$\qquad\qquad\quad \overline{j} = zipWith\ (upd\ (>))\ \overline{pq}\ s$
$\qquad\qquad\quad \overline{pq} = join\ n\ (reduce\!\Uparrow\ max_x\ n\ 1\ \overline{f})\ (reduce\!\Uparrow\ min_x\ n\ 1\ \overline{f})$
$\qquad\qquad\quad \overline{f} = zipWith3\ is_m\ \overline{m}\ \overline{g}\ s$
$\qquad\qquad\quad \overline{m} = reduce\!\Uparrow\ min\ n\ 1\ \overline{g}$
$\qquad\qquad\quad \overline{g} = join\ n\ \overline{a}\ (map\ neg\ \overline{a})$
$\qquad\qquad\quad \overline{a} = zipWith\ g\ \overline{pq_y}\ s$
$\qquad\qquad\quad \overline{pq_y} = reduce\!\Uparrow\ max_y\ n\ 1\ s'$

This algorithm uses all those higher order functions on sequences, which can immediately be rewritten as skeletons for a particular massively parallel architecture.

The algorithm we have derived here differs from those in the parallel literature (cf. [JáJ92, Akl89]). Especially, it does not need unrealistic assumptions like a concurrent read access to shared memory variables as e.g. given by the PRAM model, but is well suited for massively parallel computation on distributed memory architectures by making efficiently use of the underlying interconnection network to exchange data.

6 Related Work

Much attention has been paid to the formal parallelization of DC algorithms. Smith develops a DC theory [Smi85, Smi93], e.g., DC can be treated as a morphism from a decomposition algebra on the input domain to a composition algebra on its output domain. His emphasis is on the development of a DC algorithm, whereas we are interested in its data parallelization on a particular architecture. Thus, our work can be seen as a completion of Smith's work towards data parallel execution.

Mou and Houdak describe DC in a algebraic model called Divacon [MH88]. They recognize that the original DC model is too restrictive with respect to decomposition and communication. For the latter, they introduce so called pre- and postmorphims, which correspond with our 'adjustment' functions g, h, k and j. They illustrate the expressive power of this generalized DC, with a broad range of examples. However, they only sketch the mapping of the model on parallel computers.

This algebraic model was later picked up by Carpentiery and Mou, who study communication issues in the model [CM91]. They present hypercube specific rules to optimize communication by introducing new storage levels. These rules are expressed in Divacon, whereas our approach takes the architecture explicitly into account. They replace shuffle and unshuffle operations by split and concatenation. This works in our model too, and is adopted in [AS95]. However, their approach is neither calculated nor transparent.

Axford and Joy [Axf92, AJ93] have proposed to use DC as a fundamental design principle, and have either proposed arrays or sequences as suitable data structures. In fact, the balanced sequence primitives that we use, were proposed by Axford and Joy. Aside from this, no calculation nor interesting distributed implementation is presented.

Among the first, who used the skeleton approach in a functional setting, initiated by Cole [Col89], was a group at Imperial College [DFH+93]. Their skeletons are rather highlevel, e.g., they distinguish farming, pipelining, DC and other high level skeletons, but do not tackle massive parallelism, as it is understood by us.

Still more abstract is the work on investigating parallelism within the Bird-Meertens formalism, which recently has gained much attention (cf. e.g. [Col93]). However, all these different approaches have in common that they stop on the level of DC algorithms or homomorphisms, whereas our approach proceeds down to an architecture specific target program.

An exception to these works is presented by Gorlatch and Lengauer [GL93]. They develop a DC function, using mainly the control parallelism. In particular, they do not require that there is a single PE for each member in the sequence, but assume that there is a single PE for a group of members in the sequence. As before, the step to a working imperative implementation is still left open.

Work that is closely related to ours is done at the University of Nijmegen [Gee92, Gee93, Par93, BGP93, Gee94]. In fact, the skeletons which we propose were adapted from their work. Opposite to our goals, their research aims at introducing data parallelism out of a parallel control structure, which can be achieved by means of partial inversion. Recently, Geerling also considers data type transformations in order to adapt algorithms to different hardware. We start, however, with a problem dependent data structure, which enables right from the start implicit data parallelism.

In contrast to our approach, a group in Yale introduces data fields right from the beginning of the derivation process [CC90, YC92]. They make extensive use of so called domain morphisms in order to specify parallel-program optimizations. Their approach seems to work well for numerical problems, where the problem domain is given by matrices. The main problems lie in the absence of a strategy for deriving programs and in difficulties to find appropriate index domain morphisms, which lead to optimizations.

The important problem of how to cope with the usual situation that the number of processors is smaller than the size of the input domain is ignored in our work. We believe that this is perfectly reasonable, since either the hardware of massively parallel computers (e.g. Connection Machine CM-2), or the software (e.g. Fortran on the MASPAR) abstracts from the number of real processors. However, not all massively parallel machines support virtual processors. The-

125

refore, data distribution is still a major problem, which is tackled by a group around Pepper [PES93].

7 Conclusion and Future Research

In this paper, we have presented a transformation strategy to develop correct, efficient, data parallel DC algorithms, and showed how such derivation is guided. The main advantage of making the strategy explicit lies in its reuseability. A similar problem can be solved in a similar fashion, which is demonstrated by the examples.

We distinguish data parallelism in the problem domain (here: sequences) from data parallelism on the level of the architecture (here: skeletons). This distinction gives rise to develop portable parallel programs, since data parallelism on the problem domain must be mapped differently on existing hardware, if the diversity in architectures is exploited in full.

In addition, we claim that the transformational approach taken here is rather crucial to the presented development: The calculational properties of functional programs, in particular skeletons, give a basis for a solid understanding and a formal treatment for the derivation of massive parallel algorithms from a high-level specification down to the low-level hardware.

More research is necessary for the development of further strategies. In this context, our ultimate goal is the development of a methodology for transformational data parallel program development.

Acknowledgements. We would like to thank Helmuth A. Partsch and Ton Vullinghs for their helpful comments.

References

[AJ93]   T. Axford and M. Joy. List processing primitives for parallel computation. *Computer Languages*, 19(1):1–12, 1993.

[Akl89]   S. G. Akl. *The Design and Analysis of Parallel Algorithms*. Prentice-Hall, 1989.

[AS95]   K. Achatz and W. Schulte. Architecture independent massive parallelization of devide-and-conquer algorithms. Technical Report 05-95, Universität Ulm, Fakultät für Informatik, April 1995.

[Axf92]   T. Axford. Crystal: The divide-and conquer paradigm as a basis for parallel language design. In L. Kronsjo and D. Shumsheruddin, editors, *Advances in Parallel Algorithms*, chapter 2. Blackwell, 1992.

[Bat68]   K. E. Batcher. Sorting networks and their applications. *AFIPS Spring Joint Computer Conference*, pages 307–314, 1968.

[BGP93]   E. A. Boiten, A. M. Geerling, and H. A. Partsch. Transformational derivation of (parallel) programs using skeletons. Technical Report 93-20, Katholieke Universiteit Nijmegen, September 1993. Also: Proceedings of Computer Science in the Netherlands 1993, Utrecht.

[Bir89]   R. Bird. Lectures on constructive functional programming. In M. Broy, editor, *Constructive methods in computing science. NATO ASI Series. Series F: Computer and systems sciences 55*, pages 151–216, Berlin, 1989. Springer-Verlag.

[Ble92]   G. E. Blelloch. NESL: A nested data-parallel language (version 2.0). Technical Report CMU-CS-93-129, School of Computer Science, Carnegie Mellon University, April 1992.

[Ble93]   G. E. Blelloch. Prefix sums and their applications. In J Reif, editor, *Synthesis of Parallel Algorithms*, chapter 1, pages 35–60. Morgan Kaufmann Publishers, 1993.

[BW88]   R. Bird and Ph. Wadler. *An Introduction to Functional Programming*. Prentice-Hall, 1988.

[CC90]   M. Chen and Y. Choo. Domain morphisms: A new construct for parallel programming and formalizing program optimization. Technical Report DCS/TR-817, Department of Computer Science, Yale University, August 1990.

[CM91]   B. Carpentieri and G. Mou. Compile-time transformations and optimizations of parallel divide-and conquer algorithms. *ACM SIGPLAN Notices*, 20(10):19–28, 1991.

[Col89]   M. Cole. *Algorithmic Skeletons: Structured Management of Parallel Computation*. MIT Press, 1989.

[Col93]   M. Cole. List homomorphic parallel algorithms for bracket matching. Technical Report CSR-29-93, Department of Computer Science, University of Edinburgh, August 1993.

[DFH+93] J. Darlington, A. Field, P. Harrison, P. Kelly, D. Sharp, Q. Wu, and R. White. Parallel programming using skeleton functions. In A. Bode, M. Reeve, and G. Wolf, editors, *PARLE'93 Parallel Architectures and Languages Europe*, volume 694 of *Lecture Notes in Computer Science*, pages 146–160, 1993.

[Fea87]   M. S. Feather. A survey and classification of some program transformation approaches and techniques. In L.G.L.T. Meertens, editor, *Program Specification and Transformation*. North-Holland, 1987.

[Fox89]   G.C. Fox. Parallel computing comes of age: Supercomputer level parallel computations at caltech. *Concurrency: Practice and Experience*, 1(1):63–103, 1989.

[Gee92]   A. M. Geerling. Two examples of parallel-program derivation: Parallel-prefix and matrix multiplication. Technical Report DoC 92/33, Imperial College London, November 1992.

[Gee93]   A. M. Geerling. Formal derivation of SIMD parallelism from non-linear recursive specifications. Technical Report CSI-R9324, Katholieke Universiteit Nijmegen, September 1993.

[Gee94]   A.M. Geerling. Formal derivation of SIMD parallelism from non-linear recursive specifications. In B. Buchberger and J. Volkert, editors, *CONPAR'94 VAPP VI International Conference on Parallel and Vector Processing*, pages 136–147. Springer-Verlag, 1994.

[GL93]   S. Gorlatch and C. Lengauer. Parallelization of divide-and conquer in the Bird- Meertens formalism. Technical Report 12/93, Fakultät für Mathematik und Informatik, Universität Passau, Dezember 1993.

[JáJ92]   J. JáJá. *An introduction to parallel algorithms*. Addison-Wesley, 1992.

[MH88]   Z.G. Mou and M. Hudak. An algebraic model for divide-and-conquer algorithms and its parallelism. *Journal of Supercomputing*, 2(3):257–278, 1988.

[NS79]   D. Nassimi and S. Sahni. Bitonic sort on a mesh-connected parallel computer. *IEEE Transactions on Computers*, 27(1):2–7, 1979.

[Par90]   H. A. Partsch. *Specification and Transformation of Programs*. Springer-Verlag, 1990.

[Par93]   H. Partsch. Some experiments in transforming towards parallel executability. In R. Paige, J. Reif, and R. Wachter, editors, *Parallel Algorithm Derivation and Program Transformation*. Kluwer Academic Publisher, 1993.

[Pep93]   P. Pepper. Deductive derivation of parallel programs. In R. Paige, J. Reif, and R. Wachter, editors, *Parallel Algorithm Derivation and Program Transformation*. Kluwer Academic Publishers, 1993. Also: Technical Report 92-23, Technische Universität Berlin, July 1992.

[PES93]   P. Pepper, J. Exner, and M. Südholt. Functional development of massively parallel programs. In D. Bjorner, M. Broy, and I.V. Pottosin, editors, *Formal Methods in Programming and Their Applications. Proceedings International Conference Novosibirsk, June/July 1993.*, volume 735 of *Lecture Notes in Computer Science*, pages 217–238, Berlin, 1993. Springer-Verlag.

[PH77]   F. P. Preparata and S. J. Hong. Convex hulls of finite sets of points in two and three dimensions. *Communications of The ACM*, 20:88–93, 1977.

[Ski93]   D.B. Skillicorn. A cost calculus for parallel functional programming. Technical Report ISSN-0836-0227-93-348, Department of Computing and Information Science, Queen's University, March 1993.

[Smi85]   D.R. Smith. The design of divide-and-conquer algorithms. *Science of Computer Programming*, 5:37–58, 1985.

[Smi93]   D. R. Smith. Derivation of paralel sorting algorithms. In R. Paige, J. Reif, and R. Wachter, editors, *Parallel Algorithm Derivation and Program Transformation*. Kluwer Academic Publisher, 1993.

[YC92]   J. A. Yang and Y. Choo. Data fields as parallel programs. Technical Report CT 06520-2158, Department of Computer Science, Yale University, March 1992.

Exploring Summation and Product Operators in the Refinement Calculus

Ralph-Johan Back and Michael Butler

Department of Computer Science, Åbo Akademi, Finland

Abstract. Product and summation operators for predicate transformers were introduced by Naumann [23] and by Martin [18] using category theoretic considerations. In this paper, we formalise these operators in the higher order logic approach to the refinement calculus of [5], prove various algebraic properties of these operators, and look at several of their applications. We look at how the product operator provides a model of simultaneous execution of statements, while the summation operator provides a simple model of late binding. We also generalise the product operator slightly to form an operator that corresponds to conjunction of specifications. We show how the product operator may be used to model extension and modification operators for programs, and how a combination of the product and summation operators may be used to model inheritance in an object-oriented programming language.

1 Introduction

Dijkstra introduced weakest-precondition predicate transformers as a means of verifying total correctness properties of sequential programs [9]. In the *refinement calculus* of Back, Morgan, and Morris [2, 19, 21], specifications and programs are regarded uniformly as predicate transformers, and refinement laws are derived from properties of predicate transformers.

The refinement calculus provides various choice and assignment operators that are generalisations of Dijkstra's operators, and the applications of these operators are well-known. However, the applications of an operator representing simultaneous execution of program statements are less well developed in the refinement calculus. Such an operator was introduced by Naumann [23] and by Martin [18] using category theoretic considerations. This *product* operator combines predicate transformers by forming the cartesian product of their state spaces. In this paper, we examine the product operator using the higher-order logic formalisation of the refinement calculus of Back and von Wright [5]. We examine various distributivity and refinement preserving properties of the operator and show that it can be used to model simultaneous execution and to extend the state spaces of statements so they can be more easily matched with other statements. We also generalise the definition of the product operator slightly to form what we call a *fusion* operator and show that the product operator is a special case of the fusion operator. The fusion operator can also be applied to conjoining or amalgamating program specifications.

The *summation* (or *co-product*[1]) operator, which is the categorical dual of the product operator and combines statements by forming the disjoint union of their state spaces, is also described in [23] and [18]. The summation operator is a form of choice operator and we show that it is a special case of the existing choice operators of the refinement calculus. We show that this operator provides a simple yet powerful model of late binding, and that when combined with the product operator, provides a model of inheritance in an object-oriented programming language.

The paper is organised as follows. First the refinement calculus basics are described. Then Section 3 examines properties of the summation operator, while Section 4 examines properties of the product and fusion operators. In Section 5 we look briefly at the categorical properties of the summation and product operators. Section 6 looks at various applications of the operators including simultaneous execution, extending state spaces, late binding, and inheritance.

2 Refinement Calculus Basics

A *predicate* over a set of states Σ is a boolean function $p : \Sigma \rightarrow \mathbf{Bool}$ which assigns a truth value to each state. The set of predicates on Σ is denoted $\mathcal{P}\,\Sigma$:

$$\mathcal{P}\,\Sigma \;\hat{=}\; \Sigma \rightarrow \mathbf{Bool}.$$

We define the *entailment ordering* on predicates by pointwise extension: for $p, q : \mathcal{P}\,\Sigma$,

$$p \le q \;\hat{=}\; (\forall \sigma : \Sigma \cdot p\,\sigma \;\Rightarrow\; q\,\sigma).$$

The identically false predicate is denoted $\bot$, and the identically true predicate is denoted $\top$. Negation, conjunction, and disjunction of (similarly-typed) predicates are defined by pointwise extension, so that, e.g.,

$$(p \wedge q)\,\sigma \;\hat{=}\; (p\,\sigma \,\wedge\, q\,\sigma).$$

For state space Σ, the set of predicates $\mathcal{P}\,\Sigma$ is a complete lattice under the entailment ordering. Conjunction and disjunction represent meet and join respectively, while $\top$ and $\bot$ represent top and bottom respectively.

A *relation* from Σ to Γ is a function $P : \Sigma \rightarrow \mathcal{P}\,\Gamma$ that maps each state σ to a predicate on Γ. We write

$$\Sigma \leftrightarrow \Gamma \;\hat{=}\; \Sigma \rightarrow \mathcal{P}\,\Gamma.$$

This view of relations is isomorphic to viewing them as predicates on the cartesian space $\Sigma \times \Gamma$. The domain and range of relation P, are denoted *dom P* and *ran P* respectively. Conjunction and disjunction of relations are defined pointwise, so that, e.g., $(P \wedge Q)\,\sigma\,\gamma \;=\; (P\,\sigma\,\gamma) \wedge (Q\,\sigma\,\gamma)$. The *inclusion ordering* on relations is defined by pointwise extension: for $P, Q : \Sigma \leftrightarrow \Gamma$,

$$P \le Q \;\hat{=}\; (\forall \sigma : \Sigma \cdot P\,\sigma \;\le\; Q\,\sigma).$$

For state spaces Σ and Γ, the set of relations $\Sigma \leftrightarrow \Gamma$ is a complete lattice under the inclusion ordering. We write $P;Q$ for the relational composition of $P : \Sigma \leftrightarrow$

---

[1] The direction of arrows in [23] and [18] are the reverse of what we use, so our product operator corresponds to their co-product operator, and vice versa.

Γ and $Q : \Gamma \leftrightarrow \Lambda$, and P^{-1} for the inverse relation. For function $f : \Sigma \to \Gamma$, we write f^{-1} for the relation $(\lambda \gamma \cdot \lambda \sigma \cdot \gamma = f\sigma) : \Gamma \leftrightarrow \Sigma$. A partial function $g : \Sigma \to_p \Gamma$ is a relation from Σ to Γ such that $g \, \sigma \, \gamma \wedge g \, \sigma \, \gamma' \Rightarrow \gamma = \gamma'$.

A *predicate transformer* is a function $S : \mathcal{P}\,\Gamma \to \mathcal{P}\,\Sigma$ from predicates to predicates. We write,

$$\Sigma \longmapsto \Gamma \; \hat{=} \; \mathcal{P}\,\Gamma \to \mathcal{P}\,\Sigma.$$

Note the reversal of Γ and Σ: program statements in the refinement calculus are identified with weakest-precondition predicate transformers that map a post-condition $q : \mathcal{P}\,\Gamma$ to the weakest precondition $p : \mathcal{P}\,\Sigma$ such that the program is guaranteed to terminate in a final state satisfying q whenever the initial state satisfies p. For program statement $S : \Sigma \longmapsto \Gamma$, we say that S has *source* Σ (the initial state space) and *target* Γ (the final state space). Programs need not have identical initial and final state spaces, though if they do, we write $S : \Delta(\Sigma)$ instead of $S : \Sigma \longmapsto \Sigma$. Note that, in order to aid intuition, we sometimes discuss commands from an operational viewpoint, though our formal reasoning is always in terms of predicate transformers.

The *refinement ordering* on predicate transformers is defined by pointwise extension: for $S, T : \Sigma \longmapsto \Gamma$,

$$S \leq T \; \hat{=} \; (\forall q : \mathcal{P}\,\Gamma \cdot S \, q \leq T \, q).$$

The refinement ordering on predicate transformers models the notion of total-correctness preserving program refinement. A total-correctness specification is typically given as a precondition-postcondition pair $(pre, post)$, and program (i.e., predicate transformer) S satisfies $(pre, post)$ if $pre \leq (S \, post)$. Now, for programs S and T, $S \leq T$ holds if and only if T satisfies any specification satisfied by S.

For state spaces Σ and Γ, the set of predicate transformers $\Sigma \longmapsto \Gamma$ is a complete lattice under the refinement ordering. The bottom element is the predicate transformer *abort* that maps each postcondition to $\perp$, and the top element is the predicate transformer *magic* that maps each postcondition to $\top$. The *abort* statement is never guaranteed to terminate, while the *magic* statement is *miraculous* since it is always guaranteed to establish any postcondition. A miraculous statement cannot be implemented. For statement S, *halt* $S \; \hat{=} \; S \top$ describes those initial states under which S is guaranteed to terminate, while $gd \, S \; \hat{=} \; \neg (S \perp)$ (called *guard* of S) describes those initial states under which S behaves non-miraculously.

Conjunction and disjunction of (similarly-typed) predicate transformers are defined pointwise, so that, e.g., $(S \wedge T) \, q = (S \, q) \wedge (T \, q)$. Conjunction of statements models *demonic nondeterministic choice* between executing S and T (i.e., each alternative must establish the postcondition), whereas disjunction models *angelic nondeterministic choice* (i.e., some alternative must establish the post-condition). If *halt* $S = \neg$ *halt* T, then $S \vee T$ becomes a deterministic choice, while if $gd \, S = \neg gd \, T$, then $S \wedge T$ becomes a deterministic choice.

Sequential composition of program statements is modelled by functional composition of predicate transformers, i.e., for $S : \Sigma \longmapsto \Gamma, T : \Gamma \longmapsto \Lambda, p : \mathcal{P}\,\Lambda$, $S;T \, p \; \hat{=} \; S \, (T \, p)$. The program statement $skip_\Sigma$ is modelled by the identity predicate transformer on $\mathcal{P}\,\Sigma$.

Given a relation $P : \Sigma \leftrightarrow \Gamma$, the *angelic update statement* $\{P\} : \Sigma \longmapsto \Gamma$ and *demonic update statement* $[P] : \Sigma \longmapsto \Gamma$ are defined by

$$\{P\}\,q\,\sigma \;\hat{=}\; (\exists \gamma : \Gamma \cdot (P\,\sigma\,\gamma) \wedge (q\,\gamma))$$

$$[P]\,q\,\sigma \;\hat{=}\; (\forall \gamma : \Gamma \cdot (P\,\sigma\,\gamma) \Rightarrow (q\,\gamma)).$$

When started in a state σ, $\{P\}$ angelically chooses a new state γ such that $P\sigma\gamma$ holds, while $[P]$ demonically chooses a new state γ such that $P\sigma\gamma$ holds. If no such new state exists then $\{P\}$ aborts, while $[P]$ behaves as *magic*. Angelic update is monotonic w.r.t. relational inclusion, while demonic update is antimonotonic:

$$P \leq Q \quad \Rightarrow \quad \{P\} \leq \{Q\} \;\wedge\; [P] \geq [Q].$$

For predicate $p : \mathcal{P}\,\Sigma$, let $\bar{p} : \Sigma \leftrightarrow \Sigma$ be the corresponding test relation for p, i.e., $(\lambda\sigma \cdot \lambda\sigma' \cdot p\,\sigma \wedge \sigma = \sigma')$. Then we write $\{p\}$ for $\{\bar{p}\}$ and $[p]$ for $[\bar{p}]$. $\{p\}$ models the *assert* statement that behaves as *skip* if p holds, otherwise it aborts. $[p]$ models the *guard* statement that behaves as *skip* if p holds, otherwise it behaves as *magic*.

Given a function $f : \Sigma \to \Gamma$, the *deterministic update statement* $\langle f \rangle :$ $\Sigma \longmapsto \Gamma$ is defined by

$$\langle f \rangle\,q\,\sigma \;\hat{=}\; q\,(f\,\sigma).$$

Let $\tilde{f}$ be the the deterministic relation corresponding to function f, i.e., $(\lambda\sigma \cdot \lambda\gamma \cdot f\,\sigma = \gamma)$. Then we have $\{\tilde{f}\} = \langle f \rangle = [\tilde{f}]$.

Ordinary program constructs such conditionals, recursions, and assignments may be modelled using the basic operators presented above. For example, the statement **if** g **then** S **else** T **fi** may be modelled by $[g]; S \wedge [\neg\,g]; T$ or alternatively by $\{g\}; S \vee \{\neg\,g\}; T$. Program variables may be modelled as cartesian components of the state space, and a multiple assignment $x, y := e, f$ in a state space with three components, representing program variables (x, y, z), may be modelled by the deterministic update:

$$\langle \lambda x, y, z \cdot (e, f, z) \rangle.$$

It is easy to show, for predicates *pre* and *post*, that $\{pre\}; [post]$ is the least statement satisfying the specification pair $(pre, post)$. Thus, implementing the specification $(pre, post)$ involves constructing a statement S such that $\{pre\}; [post] \leq S$. If *post* is a relation rather than a predicate, we can model postconditions on the before and after states in the manner of VDM [17] and Z [26]. Rules for the stepwise refinement of program specifications of the form $\{p\}; [P]$ into more familiar program constructs may be found in [2, 19, 21].

All predicate transformers S constructed using the operators described above will be *monotonic*, i.e., $p \leq q \Rightarrow S\,p \leq S\,q$. A predicate transformer S is *bottom homomorphic* if $S \perp = \perp$, and *top homomorphic* if $S \top = \top$. *Conjunctive* predicate transformers form a subset of the monotonic predicate transformers satisfying $S\,(\forall i \in I \cdot q_i) = (\forall i \in I \cdot S\,q_i)$, for non-empty I. S is *universally conjunctive* if it is conjunctive and top homomorphic. *Disjunctive* and *universally disjunctive* predicate transformers are defined dually. A predicate transformer is *continuous* if it is disjunctive over non-empty chains of predicates. Demonic update statements are universally conjunctive, angelic update statements are universally disjunctive, and deterministic update statements are both. The operators $\wedge$ and ; preserve the conjunctivity of their operands, while $\vee$ and ; preserve the disjunctivity of their operands. Also, each of $\wedge$, $\vee$, and ; preserve refinement of monotonic predicate transformers, e.g., $S \leq S' \Rightarrow S; T \leq S'; T$.

In Dijkstra's original calculus, all statements were conjunctive and non-miraculous. Also, for conjunctive statements, disjunctivity corresponds to determinism, while continuity corresponds to bounded nondeterminism [9].

In the rest of this paper, we use identifiers p, q for predicates, P, Q for relations, and S, T for predicate transformers.

3 Summation Operators

In this section, we describe two summation operators for predicate transformers: the first only sums the operand sources, while the second sums both the operand sources and the operand targets.

The sum (or disjoint union) of two state spaces Σ_1 and Σ_2 is written $\Sigma_1 + \Sigma_2$. Associated with the summation are two *injections* ϕ_1 and ϕ_2 which map elements of the base type to elements of the summation ($A \to_\iota B$ represents the set of injective functions from A to B):

$$\phi_1 : \Sigma_1 \to_\iota \Sigma_1 + \Sigma_2 \tag{1}$$

$$\phi_2 : \Sigma_2 \to_\iota \Sigma_1 + \Sigma_2. \tag{2}$$

Since any element of $\Sigma_1 + \Sigma_2$ must either come from Σ_1 or Σ_2, but not both, the injections also satisfy:

$$(ran\,\phi_1, ran\,\phi_2)\text{ partition }\Sigma_1 + \Sigma_2. \tag{3}$$

We refer to such injections, ϕ_1, ϕ_2, as *inclusions*.

Since ϕ_1 and ϕ_2 are injective, their inverses ϕ_1^{-1} and ϕ_2^{-1} are partial functions:

$$\phi_1^{-1} : \Sigma_1 + \Sigma_2 \to_p \Sigma_1 \quad \phi_2^{-1} : \Sigma_1 + \Sigma_2 \to_p \Sigma_2.$$

For $\sigma \in \Sigma_1 + \Sigma_2$, $(\phi_1^{-1}\sigma)$ is only defined if $\sigma \in (dom\,\phi_1^{-1})$ and similarly for $(\phi_2^{-1}\sigma)$.

Summation of predicates is given by:

Definition 1. For $p_1 : \mathcal{P}\,\Sigma_1$, $p_2 : \mathcal{P}\,\Sigma_2$, $p_1 + p_2$ is of type $\mathcal{P}\,(\Sigma_1 + \Sigma_2)$, where for $\sigma : \Sigma_1 + \Sigma_2$,

$$(p_1 + p_2)\,\sigma \;\hat{=}\; \sigma \in (dom\,\phi_1^{-1}) \wedge p_1(\phi_1^{-1}\sigma) \;\vee\; \sigma \in (dom\,\phi_2^{-1}) \wedge p_2(\phi_2^{-1}\sigma).$$

Given an injection $\phi_1 : \Sigma_1 \to_\iota \Sigma_1 + \Sigma_2$, the deterministic update

$$\langle \phi_1 \rangle : \Sigma_1 \longmapsto \Sigma_1 + \Sigma_2 \quad (\,=\, \mathcal{P}\,(\Sigma_1 + \Sigma_2) \to \mathcal{P}\,\Sigma_1)$$

maps predicates in the summation type to predicates in the first base type. The updates can be used to select the components of a summation of predicates:

Theorem 2. For $p_1 : \mathcal{P}\,\Sigma_1$, $p_2 : \mathcal{P}\,\Sigma_2$,

$$\langle \phi_1 \rangle\,(p_1 + p_2) \;=\; p_1 \quad and \quad \langle \phi_2 \rangle\,(p_1 + p_2) \;=\; p_2.$$

The following theorem shows that a predicate in the summation type can always be separated into a summation of predicates:

Theorem 3. *For* $p : \mathcal{P}(\Sigma_1 + \Sigma_2)$, $\quad p = \langle\phi_1\rangle\, p \,+\, \langle\phi_2\rangle\, p$.

Proof. for $\sigma : \Sigma_1 + \Sigma_2$,

$\qquad (\langle\phi_1\rangle\, p \,+\, \langle\phi_2\rangle\, p)\, \sigma$

$= \sigma \in (dom\,\phi_1^{-1}) \,\wedge\, (\langle\phi_1\rangle\, p)\, (\phi_1^{-1}\sigma) \quad \vee \quad \sigma \in (dom\,\phi_2^{-1}) \,\wedge\, (\langle\phi_2\rangle\, p)\, (\phi_2^{-1}\sigma)$

$= \sigma \in (dom\,\phi_1^{-1}) \,\wedge\, p\, (\phi_1\, (\phi_1^{-1}\sigma)) \quad \vee \quad \sigma \in (dom\,\phi_2^{-1}) \,\wedge\, p\, (\phi_2\, (\phi_2^{-1}\sigma))$

$= \sigma \in (dom\,\phi_1^{-1}) \,\wedge\, p\,\sigma \quad \vee \quad \sigma \in (dom\,\phi_2^{-1}) \,\wedge\, p\,\sigma$

$= \qquad \{\text{Partition property (3)}\}$

$\qquad p\,\sigma$.

$\hfill \square$

3.1 Summation of Predicate Transformers

The summation of predicate transformers S_1 and S_2 is written $S_1 \oplus S_2$, where S_1 and S_2 have the same target, but possibly distinct sources:

Definition 4. *For* $S_1 : \Sigma_1 \longmapsto \Gamma$, $S_2 : \Sigma_2 \longmapsto \Gamma$, $S_1 \oplus S_2$ *is of type* $\Sigma_1 + \Sigma_2 \longmapsto \Gamma$, *where for* $q : \mathcal{P}\,\Gamma$:

$$(S_1 \oplus S_2)\, q \,\,\widehat{=}\,\, (S_1\, q) \,+\, (S_2\, q).$$

The selection and separation properties of the summation operator follow directly from Theorems 2 and 3:

Theorem 5. *For* $S_1 : \Sigma_1 \longmapsto \Gamma$, $S_2 : \Sigma_2 \longmapsto \Gamma$, $S : \Sigma_1 + \Sigma_2 \longmapsto \Gamma$,

$$\langle\phi_1\rangle; (S_1 \oplus S_2) \,=\, S_1 \quad and \quad \langle\phi_2\rangle; (S_1 \oplus S_2) \,=\, S_2$$

$$S \,=\, \langle\phi_1\rangle; S \,\oplus\, \langle\phi_2\rangle; S.$$

Summation of predicate transformers is a form of choice operator since the effect of executing $S_1 \oplus S_2$ in some initial state σ depends on the base type of σ: if it is of type Σ_1, then S_1 is executed, while if it is of type Σ_2, then S_2 is executed. This may be seen more clearly in the following theorem where the summation operator is characterised purely in terms of the existing choice operators. The theorem uses the following angelic and demonic updates formed from the inverse injections:

$$\{\phi_1^{-1}\} : \Sigma_1 + \Sigma_2 \longmapsto \Sigma_1 \qquad [\phi_1^{-1}] : \Sigma_1 + \Sigma_2 \longmapsto \Sigma_1.$$

Theorem 6. *For* $S_1 : \Sigma_1 \longmapsto \Gamma$, $S_2 : \Sigma_2 \longmapsto \Gamma$,

$$S_1 \oplus S_2 \,=\, \{\phi_1^{-1}\}; S_1 \vee \{\phi_2^{-1}\}; S_2 \,=\, [\phi_1^{-1}]; S_1 \wedge [\phi_2^{-1}]; S_2.$$

It is also clear from Theorem 6 that the choice between S_1 and S_2 is deterministic since ϕ_1^{-1} and ϕ_2^{-1} have disjoint domains, so that

$$halt\, \{\phi_1^{-1}\} = \neg\, halt\, \{\phi_2^{-1}\} \text{ and } gd\, [\phi_1^{-1}] = \neg\, gd\, [\phi_2^{-1}].$$

Before proving Theorem 6 we note the following, easily-proven lemmas:

Lemma 7. *For injective function* $f : \Sigma \rightarrow_\iota \Gamma$,

$$\langle f\rangle; \{f^{-1}\} \,=\, \langle f\rangle; [f^{-1}] \,=\, skip.$$

Lemma 8. *For function* $f : \Sigma \to \Gamma$, *and relation* $P : \Gamma \leftrightarrow \Lambda$, *such that* $ran\, f \cap dom\, P = \emptyset$,

$$\langle f\rangle; \{P\} \,=\, abort \quad and \quad \langle f\rangle; [P] \,=\, magic.$$

Proof. (Of Theorem 6)

$$\{\phi_1^{-1}\}; S_1 \ \vee \ \{\phi_2^{-1}\}; S_2$$

$=$ {Theorem 5 (separation)}

$$\langle\phi_1\rangle; (\{\phi_1^{-1}\}; S_1 \ \vee \ \{\phi_2^{-1}\}; S_2) \ \oplus \ \langle\phi_2\rangle; (\{\phi_1^{-1}\}; S_1 \ \vee \ \{\phi_2^{-1}\}; S_2)$$

$=$ { $\langle\phi_1\rangle, \langle\phi_2\rangle$ disjunctive}

$$(\langle\phi_1\rangle; \{\phi_1^{-1}\}; S_1 \ \vee \ \langle\phi_1\rangle; \{\phi_2^{-1}\}; S_2) \ \oplus \ (\langle\phi_2\rangle; \{\phi_1^{-1}\}; S_1 \ \vee \ \langle\phi_2\rangle; \{\phi_2^{-1}\}; S_2)$$

$=$ {partition property of ϕ_1, ϕ_2 and Lemmas 7 and 8}

$$(skip; S_1 \ \vee \ abort; S_2) \ \oplus \ (abort; S_1 \ \vee \ skip; S_2)$$

$=$ { $abort; S = abort$, $S \vee abort = S$ }

$$S_1 \oplus S_2.$$

$$[\phi_1^{-1}]; S_1 \ \wedge \ [\phi_2^{-1}]; S_2$$

$$= \langle\phi_1\rangle; ([\phi_1^{-1}]; S_1 \ \wedge \ [\phi_2^{-1}]; S_2) \ \oplus \ \langle\phi_2\rangle; ([\phi_1^{-1}]; S_1 \ \wedge \ [\phi_2^{-1}]; S_2)$$

$=$ { $\langle\phi_1\rangle, \langle\phi_2\rangle$ conjunctive}

$$(\langle\phi_1\rangle; [\phi_1^{-1}]; S_1 \ \wedge \ \langle\phi_1\rangle; [\phi_2^{-1}]; S_2) \ \oplus \ (\langle\phi_2\rangle; [\phi_1^{-1}]; S_1 \ \wedge \ \langle\phi_2\rangle; [\phi_2^{-1}]; S_2)$$

$$= (skip; S_1 \ \wedge \ magic; S_2) \ \oplus \ (magic; S_1 \ \vee \ skip; S_2)$$

$=$ { $magic; S = magic$, $S \wedge magic = S$ }

$$S_1 \oplus S_2.$$

□

Theorem 6 allows us to derive properties of the summation operator from properties of angelic choice and demonic choice:

Theorem 9. *The summation operator preserves monotonicity and bottom and top homomorphism, as well as conjunctivity, disjunctivity, and continuity.*

Proof. Preservation of monotonicity follows from Theorem 6 and the fact that the choice and sequencing constructs preserve monotonicity. Preservation of bottom homomorphism, disjunctivity, and continuity follows from Theorem 6 and the fact that they are preserved by angelic choice and sequential composition. Preservation of top homomorphism and conjunctivity follows from Theorem 6 and the fact that they are preserved by demonic choice and sequential composition. □

Summation with *abort* and *magic* gives the following:

Theorem 10. $S_1 \oplus abort = \{\phi_1^{-1}\}; S_1$ *and* $S_1 \oplus magic = [\phi_1^{-1}]; S_1$.

Summation distributes through disjunction and conjunction as follows:

Theorem 11. *For* $S_1, S_1' : \Sigma_1 \longmapsto \Gamma$, $S_2, S_2' : \Sigma_2 \longmapsto \Gamma$,

(i) $(S_1 \vee S_1') \oplus S_2 = (S_1 \oplus S_2) \vee (S_1' \oplus S_2)$ *and*

$\qquad S_1 \oplus (S_2 \vee S_2') = (S_1 \oplus S_2) \vee (S_1 \oplus S_2')$.

(ii) $(S_1 \wedge S_1') \oplus S_2 = (S_1 \oplus S_2) \wedge (S_1' \oplus S_2)$ *and*

$$S_1 \oplus (S_2 \wedge S_2') = (S_1 \oplus S_2) \wedge (S_1 \oplus S_2').$$

(iii) $(S_1 \vee S_1') \oplus (S_2 \vee S_2') = (S_1 \oplus S_2) \vee (S_1' \oplus S_2').$

(iv) $(S_1 \wedge S_1') \oplus (S_2 \wedge S_2') = (S_1 \oplus S_2) \wedge (S_1' \oplus S_2').$

Proof. We prove **(iii)**; **(i)**, **(ii)** and **(iv)** are similar:

$$
\begin{aligned}
(S_1 \vee S_1') \oplus (S_2 \vee S_2') &= \{\phi_1^{-1}\}; (S_1 \vee S_1') \ \vee\ \{\phi_2^{-1}\}; (S_2 \vee S_2') \\
&= \quad \{\ \{\phi_1^{-1}\}\ \text{disjunctive}\} \\
&\quad \{\phi_1^{-1}\}; S_1 \ \vee\ \{\phi_1^{-1}\}; S_1' \ \vee\ \{\phi_2^{-1}\}; S_2 \ \vee\ \{\phi_2^{-1}\}; S_2' \\
&= \{\phi_1^{-1}\}; S_1 \ \vee\ \{\phi_2^{-1}\}; S_2 \ \vee\ \{\phi_1^{-1}\}; S_1' \ \vee\ \{\phi_2^{-1}\}; S_2' \\
&= (S_1 \oplus S_2) \vee (S_1' \oplus S_2').
\end{aligned}
$$

$\square$

Part **(iii)** of Theorem 11 is interesting. By applying **(i)** twice, we get

$$(S_1 \vee S_1') \oplus (S_2 \vee S_2') = (S_1 \oplus S_2) \vee (S_1 \oplus S_2') \vee (S_1' \oplus S_2) \vee (S_1' \oplus S_2'),$$

which is more complicated than **(iii)**. But, because of the type discrimination between Σ_1 and Σ_2, if the initial state is from Σ_1 then the effect of the first and second disjuncts of the right-hand side will be the same, and likewise if the initial state is in Σ_2. A similar observation may be made about part **(iv)**.

In order to consider the summation of angelic and demonic updates, we require the following definition of summation of relations:

Definition 12. For $P_1 : \Sigma_1 \leftrightarrow \Gamma$, $P_2 : \Sigma_2 \leftrightarrow \Gamma$, $\sigma : \Sigma_1 + \Sigma_2$, $\gamma : \Gamma$,

$$
\begin{aligned}
(P_1 \oplus P_2)\, \sigma\, \gamma \ \hat{=}\ & \sigma \in (dom\, \phi_1^{-1}) \ \wedge\ P_1\, (\phi_1^{-1}\sigma)\, \gamma \ \vee \\
& \sigma \in (dom\, \phi_2^{-1}) \ \wedge\ P_2\, (\phi_2^{-1}\sigma)\, \gamma.
\end{aligned}
$$

We have the following lemma for this operator on relations:

Lemma 13. $P_1 \oplus P_2 \ =\ \phi_1^{-1}; P_1 \ \vee\ \phi_2^{-1}; P_1.$

Now we see that summation distributes through angelic and demonic update:

Theorem 14. $\{P_1\} \oplus \{P_2\} = \{P_1 \oplus P_2\}$ *and* $[P_1] \oplus [P_2] = [P_1 \oplus P_2].$

Proof. We show the demonic case here. Proof of the angelic case is similar:

$$
\begin{aligned}
[P_1] \oplus [P_2] =\ & \quad \{\text{Theorem 6}\} \\
& [\phi_1^{-1}]; [P_1] \ \wedge\ [\phi_2^{-1}]; [P_2] \\
=\ & \quad \{\text{Properties of demonic choice and update}\} \\
& [\phi_1^{-1}; P_1 \ \vee\ \phi_2^{-1}; P_2] \\
=\ & \quad \{\text{Lemma 13}\} \\
& [P_1 \oplus P_2].
\end{aligned}
$$

$\square$

3.2 Derived Summation Operator

Next we define a summation operator on predicate transformers with distinct sources and distinct targets. Let ψ_1 and ψ_2 be the inclusions for the summation $\Gamma_1 + \Gamma_2$ (thus, e.g., $\langle \psi_1 \rangle$ has type $\Gamma_1 \longmapsto \Gamma_1 + \Gamma_2$).

Definition 15. For $S_1 : \Sigma_1 \longmapsto \Gamma_1$, $S_2 : \Sigma_2 \longmapsto \Gamma_2$, $S_1 + S_2$ is of type $\Sigma_1 + \Sigma_2 \longmapsto \Gamma_1 + \Gamma_2$, where
$$S_1 + S_2 \triangleq S_1; \langle \psi_1 \rangle \oplus S_2; \langle \psi_2 \rangle.$$

Theorem 16. *The derived summation operator (Definition 15) preserves monotonicity and bottom and top homomorphism, as well as conjunctivity, disjunctivity, and continuity.*

Proof. Preservation of these properties follows from Theorem 9 and the fact that they are preserved by deterministic update and sequential composition. □

The components of $S_1 + S_2$ may be selected as follows:

Theorem 17. *For $S_1 : \Sigma_1 \longmapsto \Gamma_1$, $S_2 : \Sigma_2 \longmapsto \Gamma_2$,*
$$\langle \phi_1 \rangle; (S_1 + S_2); \{\psi_1^{-1}\} = \langle \phi_1 \rangle; (S_1 + S_2); [\psi_1^{-1}] = S_1$$
$$\langle \phi_2 \rangle; (S_1 + S_2); \{\psi_2^{-1}\} = \langle \phi_2 \rangle; (S_1 + S_2); [\psi_2^{-1}] = S_2.$$

Proof.
$$\langle \phi_1 \rangle; (S_1 + S_2); \{\psi_1^{-1}\} = \quad \{\text{Definition 15}\}$$
$$\langle \phi_1 \rangle; (S_1; \langle \psi_1 \rangle \oplus S_2; \langle \psi_1 \rangle); \{\psi_1^{-1}\}$$
$$= \quad \{\text{Theorem 5}\}$$
$$S_1; \langle \psi_1 \rangle; \{\psi_1^{-1}\}$$
$$= \quad \{\text{Lemma 7}\}$$
$$S_1.$$

Similarly for the other equalities. □

The derived summation operator does not, in general, satisfy a separation property, i.e., for $S : \Sigma_1 + \Sigma_2 \longmapsto \Gamma_1 + \Gamma_2$,
$$S \neq \langle \phi_1 \rangle; S; \{\psi_1^{-1}\} + \langle \phi_2 \rangle; S; \{\psi_2^{-1}\}.$$
For example, consider the following constant update statement (let $c : \Gamma_1$ be some constant value):
$$\langle \lambda \sigma : \Sigma_1 + \Sigma_2 \cdot \psi_1 \ c \rangle : \Sigma_1 + \Sigma_2 \longmapsto \Gamma_1 + \Gamma_2.$$
We have
$$\langle \phi_1 \rangle; \langle \lambda \sigma : \Sigma_1 + \Sigma_2 \cdot \psi_1 \ c \rangle; \{\psi_1^{-1}\} + \langle \phi_2 \rangle; \langle \lambda \sigma : \Sigma_1 + \Sigma_2 \cdot \psi_1 \ c \rangle; \{\psi_2^{-1}\}$$
$$= \quad \{\text{calculation}\}$$
$$\langle \lambda \sigma_1 : \Sigma_1 \cdot c \rangle; \langle \psi_1 \rangle; \{\psi_1^{-1}\} + \langle \lambda \sigma_2 : \Sigma_2 \cdot c \rangle; \langle \psi_1 \rangle; \{\psi_2^{-1}\}$$
$$= \quad \{\text{Lemmas 7 and 8}\}$$
$$\langle \lambda \sigma_1 : \Sigma_1 \cdot c \rangle + abort$$
$$\neq \langle \lambda \sigma : \Sigma_1 + \Sigma_2 \cdot \psi_1 \ c \rangle.$$
The reason that $\langle \lambda x : \Sigma_1 + \Sigma_2 \cdot \psi_1 \ c \rangle$ cannot be separated is that it always ends in a state in Γ_1 even if the initial state is in Σ_2.

The following properties follow from the corresponding properties of the $\oplus$ operator:

Theorem 18.
$$\text{(i)} \quad S_1 + abort = \{\phi_1^{-1}\}; S_1; \langle \psi_1 \rangle.$$

(ii) $S_1 + magic = [\phi_1^{-1}]; S_1; \langle \psi_1 \rangle.$

(iii) $(S_1 \vee S_1') + S_2 = (S_1 + S_2) \vee (S_1' + S_2)$ *and*
$S_1 + (S_2 \vee S_2') = (S_1 + S_2) \vee (S_1 + S_2').$

(iv) $(S_1 \wedge S_1') + S_2 = (S_1 + S_2) \wedge (S_1' + S_2)$ *and*
$S_1 + (S_2 \wedge S_2') = (S_1 + S_2) \wedge (S_1 + S_2').$

(v) $(S_1 \vee S_1') + (S_2 \vee S_2') = (S_1 + S_2) \vee (S_1' + S_2').$

(vi) $(S_1 \wedge S_1') + (S_2 \wedge S_2') = (S_1 + S_2) \wedge (S_1' + S_2').$

Summation distributes through sequential composition as follows:

Theorem 19.

(i) $(S_1 + S_2) ; (T_1 \oplus T_2) = (S_1; T_1) \oplus (S_2; T_2).$

(ii) $(S_1 + S_2) ; (T_1 + T_2) = (S_1; T_1) + (S_2; T_2).$

Proof. Firstly (i):

$(S_1 + S_2) ; (T_1 \oplus T_2) = \quad$ {Theorem 6 and Definition 15}

$\qquad ([\phi_1^{-1}]; S_1; \langle \psi_1 \rangle \wedge [\phi_2^{-1}]; S_2; \langle \psi_2 \rangle) ; (T_1 \oplus T_2)$

$= \quad$ {Distribution of $\wedge$ and ;}

$\qquad [\phi_1^{-1}]; S_1; \langle \psi_1 \rangle; (T_1 \oplus T_2) \wedge [\phi_2^{-1}]; S_2; \langle \psi_2 \rangle; (T_1 \oplus T_2)$

$= \quad$ {Theorem 5}

$\qquad [\phi_1^{-1}]; S_1; T_1 \wedge [\phi_2^{-1}]; S_2; T_2$

$= \quad$ {Theorem 6}

$\qquad S_1; T_1 \oplus S_2; T_2.$

(ii) then follows from (i). $\qquad\qquad\qquad\qquad\qquad\qquad\qquad\qquad\qquad$ □

The derived summation operator also distributes through update statements:

Definition 20. For relations $Q_1 : \Sigma_1 \leftrightarrow \Gamma_1$, $Q_2 : \Sigma_2 \leftrightarrow \Gamma_2$,
$$Q_1 + Q_2 \,\hat{=}\, Q_1; \tilde{\psi}_1 \oplus Q_2; \tilde{\psi}_2.$$

Theorem 21. $\{Q_1\} + \{Q_2\} = \{Q_1 + Q_2\}$ *and* $[Q_1] + [Q_2] = [Q_1 + Q_2].$

We have the following lemma about the summation of test relations:

Lemma 22. *For predicates* $p_1 : \mathcal{P} \Sigma_1$, $p_2 : \mathcal{P} \Sigma_2$, $\quad \overline{p_1} + \overline{p_2} = \overline{p_1 + p_2}.$

Thus we have that summation distributes through assert and guard statements:

Theorem 23. $\{p_1\} + \{p_2\} = \{p_1 + p_2\}$ *and* $[p_1] + [p_2] = [p_1 + p_2].$

The above theorems allow us to show that summation distributes through program specifications, i.e.,

$$\{p_1\}; [P_1] \oplus \{p_2\}; [P_2] = \{p_1 + p_2\}; [P_1 \oplus P_2]$$
$$\{p_1\}; [Q_1] + \{p_2\}; [Q_2] = \{p_1 + p_2\}; [Q_1 + Q_2].$$

3.3 Refinement

Both the summation operators preserve refinement allowing us to refine summands separately:

138

Theorem 24.
$$S_1 \leq S_1' \land S_2 \leq S_2' \Rightarrow (S_1 \oplus S_2) \leq (S_1' \oplus S_2')$$
$$T_1 \leq T_1' \land T_2 \leq T_2' \Rightarrow (T_1 + T_2) \leq (T_1' + T_2').$$

Proof of this follows directly from Theorem 6 and the fact that sequential composition and the choice operators preserve refinement.

The well-known technique of data refinement involves replacing abstract program variables with concrete program variables using an abstraction relation [13]. In the refinement calculus, the abstraction relation is modelled by an abstraction command, and we say that $S : \Delta(\Sigma)$ is data refined by $S' : \Delta(\Sigma')$ under abstraction command $\alpha : \Sigma' \longmapsto \Sigma$ if $\alpha; S \leq S'; \alpha$ [11, 28]. We can easily show that summation preserves data refinement:

Theorem 25. *Let* $S_1 : \Delta(\Sigma_1)$, $S_1' : \Delta(\Sigma_1')$, $S_2 : \Delta(\Sigma_2)$, $S_2' : \Delta(\Sigma_2')$, *be predicate transformers. Let* $\alpha_1 : \Sigma_1' \longmapsto \Sigma_1$, $\alpha_2 : \Sigma_2' \longmapsto \Sigma_2$ *be abstraction commands. Then*
$$\alpha_1; S_1 \leq S_1'; \alpha_1 \land \alpha_2; S_2 \leq S_2'; \alpha_2 \Rightarrow$$
$$(\alpha_1 + \alpha_2); (S_1 + S_2) \leq (S_1' + S_2'); (\alpha_1 + \alpha_2).$$

Proof.

$$
\begin{aligned}
(\alpha_1 + \alpha_2); (S_1 + S_2) = & \quad \{\text{Distribution of} + \text{and} ;\} \\
& (\alpha_1; S_1) + (\alpha_2; S_2) \\
\leq & \quad \{\text{Theorem 24 and assumptions}\} \\
& (S_1'; \alpha_1) + (S_2'; \alpha_2) \\
= & (S_1' + S_2'); (\alpha_1 + \alpha_2).
\end{aligned}
$$

□

3.4 Recursion

A recursive command has the form $(\mu X \cdot F\ X)$ (least fixed-point of F) where X ranges over $\Delta(\Sigma)$ and F is a function from $\Delta(\Sigma)$ to $\Delta(\Sigma)$, i.e., from predicate transformers to predicate transformers. For example, the DO-loop **do** S **od** is defined as the least fixed point of the function D, where
$$D\ X\ =\ S; X\ \land\ [\neg\, gd\ S].$$

F should be monotonic (w.r.t. refinement) for its least fixed-point to exist, and this is guaranteed if $F\ X$ is constructed from X using refinement preserving operators, as is the case with D above.

Summation distributes through recursion as follows:

Theorem 26. *Given* $F_1 : \Delta(\Sigma_1) \to \Delta(\Sigma_1)$, $F_2 : \Delta(\Sigma_2) \to \Delta(\Sigma_2)$, *let*
$$F\ Y\ \hat{=}\ F_1(\langle\phi_1\rangle; Y; \{\phi_1^{-1}\})\ +\ F_2(\langle\phi_2\rangle; Y; \{\phi_2^{-1}\}).$$
Then
$$(\mu X \cdot F_1 X)\ +\ (\mu X \cdot F_2 X) = (\mu Y \cdot F\ Y).$$

This theorem may be proven using ordinal induction which does not depend on F being continuous.

We shall attempt to show that summation distributes through DO-loops using Theorem 26:

$$\textbf{do } S_1 \textbf{ od } + \textbf{ do } S_2 \textbf{ od}$$

$$= (\mu X \cdot S_1; X \ \wedge \ [\neg \, gd \, S_1] \,) \ + \ (\mu X \cdot S_2; X \ \wedge \ [\neg \, gd \, S_2] \,)$$

$$= \quad \{\text{distribution of } + \text{ through recursion}\}$$

$$(\mu Y \cdot (S_1; \langle \phi_1 \rangle; Y; \{\phi_1^{-1}\} \ \wedge \ [\neg \, gd \, S_1] \,) \ +$$
$$(S_2; \langle \phi_2 \rangle; Y; \{\phi_2^{-1}\} \ \wedge \ [\neg \, gd \, S_2] \,) \,)$$

$$= \quad \{\text{distribution of } + \text{ and } \wedge\}$$

$$(\mu Y \cdot (S_1; \langle \phi_1 \rangle; Y; \{\phi_1^{-1}\} \ + \ S_2; \langle \phi_2 \rangle; Y; \{\phi_2^{-1}\}) \ \wedge$$
$$(\, [\neg \, gd \, S_1] + [\neg \, gd \, S_2] \,) \,)$$

$$= \quad \{\text{distribution of } + \text{ and } ;\}$$

$$(\mu Y \cdot ((S_1 + S_2); (\langle \phi_1 \rangle; Y; \{\phi_1^{-1}\} + \langle \phi_2 \rangle; Y; \{\phi_2^{-1}\})) \ \wedge$$
$$(\, [\neg \, gd \, S_1] + [\neg \, gd \, S_2] \,) \,)$$

$$= \quad \{ \ [\neg \, gd \, S_1] + [\neg \, gd \, S_2] \ = \ [\neg \, gd \, (S_1 + S_2)] \ \}$$

$$(\mu Y \cdot (S_1 + S_2); (\langle \phi_1 \rangle; Y; \{\phi_1^{-1}\} + \langle \phi_2 \rangle; Y; \{\phi_2^{-1}\})) \ \wedge \ [\neg \, gd \, (S_1 + S_2)] \,).$$

We would like to be able to continue as follows:

$$= (\mu Y \cdot (S_1 + S_2); Y \ \wedge \ [\neg \, gd \, (S_1 + S_2)] \,)$$

$$= \textbf{do } S_1 + S_2 \textbf{ od}.$$

But it is not always the case that

$$Y = \langle \phi_1 \rangle; Y; \{\phi_1^{-1}\} \ + \ \langle \phi_2 \rangle; Y; \{\phi_2^{-1}\},$$

as the counterexample after Theorem 17 shows. However, we do have the following theorem:

Theorem 27. *Let F be as defined in Theorem 26.*
If $F \, Y \ = \ G(\langle \phi_1 \rangle; Y; \{\phi_1^{-1}\} + \langle \phi_2 \rangle; Y; \{\phi_2^{-1}\})$, then
$$(\mu Y \cdot F \, Y) = (\mu Y \cdot G \, Y).$$

This theorem may be proven by inductively showing that the ordinal limits of F and G are equal.

Now, by taking

$$F \, Y = (S_1; \langle \phi_1 \rangle; Y; \{\phi_1^{-1}\} \ \wedge \ [\neg \, gd \, S_1]) \ + \ (S_2; \langle \phi_2 \rangle; Y; \{\phi_2^{-1}\} \ \wedge \ [\neg \, gd \, S_2]),$$
$$G \, Y = (S_1 + S_2); Y \ \wedge \ [\neg \, gd \, (S_1 + S_2)],$$

the step in the above derivation of **do** $S_1 + S_2$ **od** where
$\langle \phi_1 \rangle; Y; \{\phi_1^{-1}\} \ + \ \langle \phi_2 \rangle; Y; \{\phi_2^{-1}\}$ is replaced by Y is justified, giving:

Theorem 28. do S_1 **od** $+$ **do** S_2 **od** $=$ **do** $S_1 + S_2$ **od**.

4 Product Operators

The cartesian product of state spaces Σ_1 and Σ_2 is denoted $\Sigma_1 \times \Sigma_2$. Given two predicates q_1 and q_2 their product is denoted $q_1 \times q_2$ and is defined as follows:

Definition 29. For $q_1 : \mathcal{P} \Sigma_1$, $q_2 : \mathcal{P} \Sigma_2$, $q_1 \times q_2$ is of type $\mathcal{P}(\Sigma_1 \times \Sigma_2)$ where for $\sigma_1 : \Sigma_1$, $\sigma_2 : \Sigma_2$,

$$(q_1 \times q_2)(\sigma_1, \sigma_2) = (q_1 \, \sigma_1) \wedge (q_2 \, \sigma_2).$$

Note that, in contrast to summation of predicates where any predicate of type $\mathcal{P}(\Sigma_1 + \Sigma_2)$ may be represented by the summation of two predicates of types $\mathcal{P} \Sigma_1$ and $\mathcal{P} \Sigma_2$ respectively, predicates of the form $q_1 \times q_2$ only form rectangular subsets of $\mathcal{P}(\Sigma_1 \times \Sigma_2)$. Also, the components of a product of predicates cannot always be selected, e.g., p_1 cannot be retrieved from $p_1 \times \perp$. As we shall see, these facts mean that the product operators for predicate transformers do not satisfy as many properties as the summation operator.

Consider the following two predicate transformers which have a common source but distinct targets:

$$S_1 : \Sigma \longmapsto \Gamma_1, \qquad S_2 : \Sigma \longmapsto \Gamma_2.$$

The product operator combines these two commands to form a command with target $\Gamma_1 \times \Gamma_2$ as follows [23]:

Definition 30. For $S_1 : \Sigma \longmapsto \Gamma_1$, $S_2 : \Sigma \longmapsto \Gamma_2$, $S_1 \otimes S_2$ is of type $\Sigma \longmapsto \Gamma_1 \times \Gamma_2$, where for $q : \mathcal{P}(\Gamma_1 \times \Gamma_2)$:

$$(S_1 \otimes S_2) \, q \; \hat{=} \; (\exists q_1 : \mathcal{P} \Gamma_1; \; q_2 : \mathcal{P} \Gamma_2 \,|\, q_1 \times q_2 \leq q \cdot S_1 q_1 \wedge S_2 q_2).$$

We shall see later that execution of $S_1 \otimes S_2$ has the same effect as simultaneous execution of S_1 and S_2.

Before investigating properties of the product operator further, we first look at two related operators. The first is derived from the product operator. Let π_1 and π_2 be the projections from $\Sigma_1 \times \Sigma_2$ to Σ_1 and Σ_2 respectively:

$$\pi_1 : \Sigma_1 \times \Sigma_2 \to \Sigma_1, \qquad \pi_2 : \Sigma_1 \times \Sigma_2 \to \Sigma_2,$$
$$\pi_1(\sigma_1, \sigma_2) = \sigma_1, \qquad \pi_2(\sigma_1, \sigma_2) = \sigma_2.$$

The projections give the following deterministic updates:

$$\langle \pi_1 \rangle : \Sigma_1 \times \Sigma_2 \longmapsto \Sigma_1 \quad \text{and} \quad \langle \pi_2 \rangle : \Sigma_1 \times \Sigma_2 \longmapsto \Sigma_2.$$

The statement $\langle \pi_1 \rangle$ starts in a state (σ_1, σ_2) and ends in the state σ_1 simply discarding the second component. The derived product operator combines commands with distinct sources and distinct targets, and is defined as follows:

Definition 31. For $S_1 : \Sigma_1 \longmapsto \Gamma_1$, $S_2 : \Sigma_2 \longmapsto \Gamma_2$, $S_1 \times S_2$ is of type $\Sigma_1 \times \Sigma_2 \longmapsto \Gamma_1 \times \Gamma_2$, where

$$S_1 \times S_2 \; \hat{=} \; \langle \pi_1 \rangle; S_1 \otimes \langle \pi_2 \rangle; S_2.$$

We shall see later that the derived product operator models simultaneous execution of two commands with distinct initial states and distinct final states.

Definition 30 may be generalised to define what we term a *fusion* operator that combines commands with common sources and common targets as follows:

Definition 32. For $S_1, S_2 : \Sigma \longmapsto \Gamma$, $S_1 \odot S_2$ is of type $\Sigma \longmapsto \Gamma$, where for $q : \mathcal{P}\,\Gamma$:

$$(S_1 \odot S_2)\, q \;\hat{=}\; (\exists q_1, q_2 : \mathcal{P}\,\Gamma \mid q_1 \wedge q_2 \leq q \cdot S_1 q_1 \wedge S_2 q_2).$$

Neither product operator is commutative, since $\Sigma_1 \times \Sigma_2$ is different to $\Sigma_2 \times \Sigma_1$ when Σ_1 and Σ_2 are different. However, it is clear from Definition 32 that the fusion operator is commutative. We proceed by investigating further properties of the fusion operator and showing that the product operators are special cases of the fusion operator.

4.1 Properties of Fusion Operator

Theorem 33. *The fusion operator preserves monotonicity, top homomorphism, and conjunctivity. Also, if either S_1 or S_2 is disjunctive then $S_1 \odot S_2$ is disjunctive; similarly for continuity.*

The second part of this theorem tells us that if either S_1 or S_2 is deterministic, then the fusion of S_1 and S_2 is deterministic, and if either S_1 or S_2 is boundedly nondeterministic, then the fusion of S_1 and S_2 is boundedly nondeterministic. Note that the fusion operator does not preserve bottom homomorphism. For example, although both the deterministic updates $\langle \lambda x \cdot 0 \rangle$ and $\langle \lambda x \cdot 1 \rangle$ are bottom homomorphic, we can easily show that

$$\langle \lambda x \cdot 0 \rangle \odot \langle \lambda x \cdot 1 \rangle = magic,$$

which is certainly not bottom homomorphic.

The fusion operator combines with *abort* and *magic* as follows:

Theorem 34. $S \odot abort = abort$ *and* $S \odot magic = \{halt\ S\}; magic$.

The *havoc* statement, where $havoc = [\lambda \sigma, \gamma \cdot true]$, is the most (demonically) nondeterministic statement that is guaranteed to terminate; *havoc* acts as a unit for the fusion operator, i.e., $S \odot havoc = S$.

The fusion operator distributes through disjunction and conjunction and preserves refinement:

Theorem 35.

(i) $(S_1 \vee S_1') \odot S_2 = (S_1 \odot S_2) \vee (S_1' \odot S_2)$.

(i) *for conjunctive S_2,* $(S_1 \wedge S_1') \odot S_2 = (S_1 \odot S_2) \wedge (S_1' \odot S_2)$.

Theorem 36. $S_1 \leq S_1' \wedge S_2 \leq S_2' \Rightarrow (S_1 \odot S_2) \leq (S_1' \odot S_2')$.

The fusion operator acts as a form of 'co-refinement' operator:

Theorem 37. *For predicate transformers S_1 and S_2, $S_1 \odot S_2$ solves:*

$$\{halt\ S_2\}; S_1 \leq X \tag{4}$$

$$\{halt\ S_1\}; S_2 \leq X, \tag{5}$$

and furthermore, for any conjunctive Y that solves (4) and (5),

$$S_1 \odot S_2 \leq Y. \tag{6}$$

Proof. Firstly, $S_1 \odot S_2$ solves (4):

$$(S_1 \odot S_2)\, q = (\exists q_1, q_2 : \mathcal{P}\, \Gamma \mid q_1 \wedge q_2 \leq q \cdot S_1 q_1 \wedge S_2 q_2)$$
$$\geq S_1 q \wedge S_2 \mathsf{T}$$
$$= \{S_2 \mathsf{T}\}; S_1\, q.$$

Similarly, $S_1 \odot S_2$ solves (5). Finally, $S_1 \odot S_2$ satisfies (6):

$$(S_1 \odot S_2)\, q = (\exists q_1, q_2 : \mathcal{P}\, \Gamma \mid q_1 \wedge q_2 \leq q \cdot S_1 q_1 \wedge S_2 q_2)$$
$$\leq \quad \{Y \text{ satisfies (4) and (5)}\}$$
$$(\exists q_1, q_2 : \mathcal{P}\, \Gamma \mid q_1 \wedge q_2 \leq q \cdot Y q_1 \wedge Y q_2)$$
$$= \quad \{Y \text{ conjunctive}\}$$
$$(\exists q_1, q_2 : \mathcal{P}\, \Gamma \mid q_1 \wedge q_2 \leq q \cdot Y(q_1 \wedge q_2))$$
$$\leq \quad \{Y \text{ monotonic}\}$$
$$Y\, q.$$

□

Thus for conjunctive S_1 and S_2, $S_1 \odot S_2$ is the least conjunctive predicate transformer satisfying (4) and (5). Note that $S_1 \odot S_2$ is not a true refinement of S_1 since it cannot replace S_1, but rather it can replace $\{halt\, S_2\}; S_1$. Theorem 37 allows us to prove the following absorption rule:

Theorem 38. *For conjunctive S_1, S_2,* $\quad S_1 \leq S_2 \Rightarrow S_1 \odot S_2 = S_2$.

Proof. S_2 is the least conjunctive predicate transformer satisfying (4) and (5).

□

Morgan [20] has developed an operator □ on predicate transformers such that $\square S$ is the least-refined predicate transformer that is both universally conjunctive and refines S. By these properties, it is easy to show for universally conjunctive S_1 and S_2, that $\square(S_1 \vee S_2)$ is the least conjunctive predicate transformer satisfying (4) and (5). Thus by Theorem 37 we have, for universally conjunctive S_1 and S_2,

$$\square(S_1 \vee S_2) = S_1 \odot S_2.$$

The following theorem provides a simple way of calculating the fusion of two program specifications:

Theorem 39. *For relations $P, Q : \Sigma \leftrightarrow \Gamma$, and predicates $p, q : \mathcal{P}\, \Sigma$,*

$$\{p\}; [P] \odot \{q\}; [Q] = \{p \wedge q\}; [P \wedge Q].$$

Proof. It is easy to show that $\{p \wedge q\}; [P \wedge Q]$ solves (4) and (5), thus by Theorem 37 $(\{p\}; [P] \odot \{q\}; [Q]) \leq \{p \wedge q\}; [P \wedge Q]$. To show the reverse, we have for $r : \mathcal{P}\, \Gamma, \sigma : \Sigma$,

$$\{p \wedge q\}; [P \wedge Q]\, r\, \sigma$$
$$= \quad \{\text{by definition}\}$$
$$p\, \sigma \wedge q\, \sigma \wedge (\forall \sigma' : \Gamma \cdot (P\, \sigma\, \sigma') \wedge (Q\, \sigma\, \sigma') \Rightarrow r\, \sigma')$$
$$= \quad \{\text{pointwise extension}\}$$
$$p\, \sigma \wedge q\, \sigma \wedge ((\lambda \sigma' : \Gamma \cdot P\, \sigma\, \sigma') \wedge (\lambda \sigma' : \Gamma \cdot Q\, \sigma\, \sigma') \leq r)$$

$$
\begin{aligned}
= \quad \{ \quad &\{p\}; [P] \, (\lambda\sigma' : \Gamma \cdot P \, \sigma \, \sigma') \, \sigma \\
&= p \, \sigma \wedge (\forall \sigma' : \Gamma \cdot (P \, \sigma \, \sigma') \Rightarrow (\lambda\sigma' : \Gamma \cdot P \, \sigma \, \sigma') \, \sigma') \\
&= p \, \sigma \wedge (\forall \sigma' : \Gamma \cdot (P \, \sigma \, \sigma') \Rightarrow (P \, \sigma \, \sigma')) \\
&= p \, \sigma \qquad\qquad\qquad\qquad\qquad\qquad\qquad\qquad\qquad\qquad\qquad \}
\end{aligned}
$$

$$
\begin{aligned}
&\{p\}; [P] \, (\lambda\sigma' : \Gamma \cdot P \, \sigma \, \sigma') \, \sigma \; \wedge \\
&\{q\}; [Q] \, (\lambda\sigma' : \Gamma \cdot Q \, \sigma \, \sigma') \, \sigma \; \wedge \\
&((\lambda\sigma' : \Gamma \cdot P \, \sigma \, \sigma') \wedge (\lambda\sigma' : \Gamma \cdot Q \, \sigma \, \sigma') \; \leq \; r) \\
\Rightarrow \quad &\{ \text{take } q_1 = (\lambda\sigma' : \Gamma \cdot P \, \sigma \, \sigma'), \, q_2 = (\lambda\sigma' : \Gamma \cdot Q \, \sigma \, \sigma') \} \\
&(\exists q_1, q_1 : \mathcal{P} \, \Gamma \cdot (q_1 \wedge q_2 \; \leq \; r) \; \wedge \; \{p\}; [P] \, q_1 \, \sigma \; \wedge \; \{q\}; [Q] \, q_2 \, \sigma) \\
= \quad &(\, \{p\}; [P] \odot \{q\}; [Q] \,) \, r \, \sigma.
\end{aligned}
$$

$\qquad\qquad\qquad\qquad\qquad\qquad\qquad\qquad\qquad\qquad\qquad\qquad\qquad\qquad\qquad\quad\square$

The theorem illustrates that the effect of the fusion operator is to reduce the (demonic) nondeterminism of the terminating behaviour of both commands. The theorem also illustrates that the fusion operator can be used as a (refinement preserving) way of combining program specifications.

Given a predicate transformer $S : \Sigma \longmapsto \Gamma$, we derive a relation, called $rel \, S$, of type $\Sigma \leftrightarrow \Gamma$ as follows:

$$
(rel \, S) \, \sigma \, \gamma \; \hat{=} \; \neg \, S(\lambda\gamma' \cdot \gamma \neq \gamma') \, \sigma.
$$

This definition is from [10]. It can be shown that any conjunctive predicate transformer may be characterised as a specification involving $halt \, S$ and $rel \, S$:

Lemma 40. *For conjunctive predicate transformer S,* $\quad S \, = \, \{halt \, S\}; [rel \, S]$.

Using this lemma and Theorem 39, we arrive at the following theorem:

Theorem 41. *For conjunctive predicate transformers S and T,*

$$
S \odot T = \{ \, (halt \, S) \wedge (halt \, T) \, \} ; [\, (rel \, S) \wedge (rel \, T) \,].
$$

Abrial [1] describes a parallel operator for statements whose definition is similar to the right-hand side of Theorem 41. Thus our fusion of statements is the same as Abrial's parallel composition, for conjunctive statements.

We say that two specifications $\{p\}; [P]$ and $\{q\}; [Q]$ are *contradictory* in some initial state σ if σ has a successful outcome in each specification, but does not have a successful outcome in their fusion, i.e., σ holds in p, q, $dom \, P$, and $dom \, Q$, but not in $dom \, (P \wedge Q)$. For those contradictory initial states, the fusion of both specifications behaves miraculously. Ward [29] has defined a slight variant of Abrial's parallel combinator where the combination behaves as *abort* when both specifications are contradictory. Thus, in Ward's case, a contradictory combination may be refined by any statement whereas, in our case, it is unimplementable. Furthermore, Ward's combinator is not refinement preserving.

4.2 Properties of Product Operator

Now we show that the product operator is a special case of the fusion operator. Let ϖ_1 and ϖ_2 be the projections from $\Gamma_1 \times \Gamma_2$ to Γ_1 and Γ_2 respectively:

$$
\varpi_1 : \Gamma_1 \times \Gamma_2 \to \Gamma_1, \qquad \varpi_2 : \Gamma_1 \times \Gamma_2 \to \Gamma_2.
$$

Lemma 42. *For* $p_1 : \mathcal{P}\,\Gamma_1$, $p_2 : \mathcal{P}\,\Gamma_2$, $\quad \langle\varpi_1\rangle p_1 \,\wedge\, \langle\varpi_2\rangle p_2 \;=\; p_1 \times p_2$.

The inverses of ϖ_1 and ϖ_2 are relations:

$$\varpi_1^{-1} : \Gamma_1 \leftrightarrow \Gamma_1 \times \Gamma_2, \qquad \varpi_2^{-1} : \Gamma_2 \leftrightarrow \Gamma_1 \times \Gamma_2,$$

so that the demonic update $[\varpi_1^{-1}]$ transforms predicates in $\Gamma_1 \times \Gamma_2$ to predicates in Γ_1:

$$[\varpi_1^{-1}] : \Gamma_1 \longmapsto \Gamma_1 \times \Gamma_2, \qquad (= \mathcal{P}\,(\Gamma_1 \times \Gamma_2) \to \mathcal{P}\,\Gamma_1),$$

and similarly for $[\varpi_2^{-1}]$. The command $[\varpi_1^{-1}]$ starts in a state $\gamma_1 : \Gamma_1$ and ends in a state $(\gamma_1', \gamma_2') : \Gamma_1 \times \Gamma_2$ such that $\gamma_1 = \gamma_1'$ and γ_2' is chosen nondeterministically. We then have the following lemmas:

Lemma 43. *For projections* ϖ_1, ϖ_2,

$$[\varpi_1^{-1}];\langle\varpi_1\rangle \;=\; skip, \qquad \langle\varpi_1\rangle;[\varpi_1^{-1}] \;\leq\; skip,$$
$$[\varpi_2^{-1}];\langle\varpi_2\rangle \;=\; skip, \qquad \langle\varpi_2\rangle;[\varpi_2^{-1}] \;\leq\; skip.$$

Lemma 44. *For* $q_1, q_2 : \mathcal{P}\,\Sigma_1 \times \Sigma_2$, $\quad [\varpi_1^{-1}]\,q_1 \;\times\; [\varpi_2^{-1}]\,q_2 \;\leq\; q_1 \wedge q_2$.

Given $S_1 : \Sigma \longmapsto \Gamma_1$, the predicate transformer $S_1;[\varpi_1^{-1}] : \Sigma \longmapsto \Gamma_1 \times \Gamma_2$ is a 'lifted' version of S_1 that behaves as S_1 on the first component of the final state, and nondeterministically writes any value to the second component. Similarly for $S_2;[\varpi_2^{-1}]$. Now we have:

Theorem 45. *For* $S_1 : \Sigma \longmapsto \Gamma_1$, $S_2 : \Sigma \longmapsto \Gamma_2$,

$$S_1 \otimes S_2 = S_1;[\varpi_1^{-1}] \;\odot\; S_2;[\varpi_2^{-1}].$$

Proof. For $q : \mathcal{P}\,(\Gamma_1 \times \Gamma_2)$,

$\qquad (S_1;[\varpi_1^{-1}] \;\odot\; S_2;[\varpi_2^{-1}])\,q$

$= (\exists q_1, q_2 : \mathcal{P}\,(\Gamma_1 \times \Gamma_2) \,|\, q_1 \wedge q_2 \leq q \cdot (S_1;[\varpi_1^{-1}]\,q_1) \wedge (S_2;[\varpi_2^{-1}]\,q_2))$

$\leq \qquad \{\text{Lemma 44}\}$

$\qquad (\exists q_1, q_2 : \mathcal{P}\,(\Gamma_1 \times \Gamma_2) \,|\, [\varpi_1^{-1}]q_1 \times [\varpi_2^{-1}]q_2 \leq q \cdot (S_1;[\varpi_1^{-1}]\,q_1) \wedge (S_2;[\varpi_2^{-1}]\,q_2))$

$\leq \qquad \{\text{take } q_1' = [\varpi_1^{-1}]q_1, \;\; q_2' = [\varpi_2^{-1}]q_2\}$

$\qquad (\exists q_1' : \mathcal{P}\,\Gamma_1; \; q_2' : \mathcal{P}\,\Gamma_2 \,|\, q_1' \times q_2' \leq q \cdot S_1 q_1' \,\wedge\, S_2 q_2')$

$= (S_1 \otimes S_2)\,q.$

$\qquad (S_1 \otimes S_2)\,q$

$= (\exists q_1 : \mathcal{P}\,\Gamma_1; \; q_2 : \mathcal{P}\,\Gamma_2 \,|\, q_1 \times q_2 \leq q \cdot S_1 q_1 \,\wedge\, S_2 q_2)$

$= \qquad \{\text{Lemma 42}\}$

$\qquad (\exists q_1 : \mathcal{P}\,\Gamma_1; \; q_2 : \mathcal{P}\,\Gamma_2 \,|\, \langle\varpi_1\rangle q_1 \wedge \langle\varpi_2\rangle q_2 \leq q \cdot S_1 q_1 \,\wedge\, S_2 q_2)$

$= \qquad \{\text{Lemma 43}\}$

$\qquad (\exists q_1 : \mathcal{P}\,\Gamma_1; \; q_2 : \mathcal{P}\,\Gamma_2 \,|\, \langle\varpi_1\rangle q_1 \wedge \langle\varpi_2\rangle q_2 \leq q \;\cdot$

$\qquad\qquad (S_1;[\varpi_1^{-1}];\langle\varpi_1\rangle\, q_1) \wedge (S_2;[\varpi_2^{-1}];\langle\varpi_2\rangle\, q_2))$

$\leq \qquad \{\text{take } q_1' = \langle\varpi_1\rangle q_1, \;\; q_2' = \langle\varpi_2\rangle q_2\}$

$\qquad (\exists q_1', q_2' : \mathcal{P}\,(\Gamma_1 \times \Gamma_2) \,|\, q_1' \wedge q_2' \leq q \cdot (S_1;[\varpi_1^{-1}]\, q_1') \wedge (S_2;[\varpi_2^{-1}]\, q_2'))$

$= (S_1;[\varpi_1^{-1}] \;\odot\; S_2;[\varpi_2^{-1}])\,q.$

$\hfill\square$

Preservation of monotonicity, top homomorphism and conjunctivity then follow from the fact that they are preserved by the fusion, sequential composition, and demonic update operators. Preservation of disjunctivity does hold but requires a separate proof (given in [23]). Unlike the fusion operator, the product operator does preserve bottom homomorphism: assume $S_1 \perp = \perp$ and $S_2 \perp = \perp$, then

$$
\begin{aligned}
(S_1 \otimes S_2) \perp &= (\exists q_1 : \mathcal{P}\, \Gamma_1;\ q_2 : \mathcal{P}\, \Gamma_2 \,|\, q_1 \times q_2 \leq \perp \cdot S_1 q_1 \wedge S_2 q_2) \\
&= (\exists q_1 : \mathcal{P}\, \Gamma_1;\ q_2 : \mathcal{P}\, \Gamma_2 \,|\, q_1 = \perp \vee q_2 = \perp \cdot S_1 q_1 \wedge S_2 q_2) \qquad (*) \\
&= (\exists q_2 : \mathcal{P}\, \Gamma_2 \cdot S_1 \perp \wedge S_2 q_2) \vee (\exists q_1 : \mathcal{P}\, \Gamma_1 \cdot S_1 q_1 \wedge S_2 \perp) \\
&= \perp .
\end{aligned}
$$

The step marked * holds for $q_1 \times q_2$ but not $q_1 \wedge q_2$.

Theorem 46. *The product operator preserves monotonicity and top and bottom homomorphism, as well as conjunctivity and disjunctivity.*

We have not been able to find a proof that the product operator preserves continuity, though neither can we find a counterexample. Naumann [23] describes a continuous product operator in which the quantification is over finitary predicates. He also shows that this corresponds to the product operator for countable state spaces when the operands are continuous, i.e., the product operator preserves continuity for countable state spaces.

Distribution of the product operator through disjunction and conjunction follows from Theorems 35 and 45. Preservation of refinement follows from Theorems 36 and 45.

The following refinement theorem follows from Theorem 45 and Theorem 37:

Theorem 47.
$$
\{halt\ S_2\}; S_1; [\varpi_1^{-1}] \leq S_1 \otimes S_2 \qquad \{halt\ S_1\}; S_2; [\varpi_2^{-1}] \leq S_1 \otimes S_2 .
$$

In order to consider the product of deterministic updates and specification statements, we require product operators for functions and relations:

Definition 48. For functions $f_1 : \Sigma \to \Gamma_1$, $f_2 : \Sigma \to \Gamma_2$, $f_1 \otimes f_2$ is a function of type $\Sigma \to (\Gamma_1 \times \Gamma_2)$, where for $\sigma : \Sigma$,
$$
(f_1 \otimes f_2)\, \sigma \ \widehat{=}\ (f_1\, \sigma, f_2\, \sigma).
$$

Definition 49. For relations $P_1 : \Sigma \leftrightarrow \Gamma_1$, $P_2 : \Sigma \leftrightarrow \Gamma_2$, $P_1 \otimes P_2$ is a relation of type $\Sigma \leftrightarrow (\Gamma_1 \times \Gamma_2)$, where for $\sigma : \Sigma$, $\gamma_1 : \Gamma_1$, $\gamma_2 : \Gamma_2$,
$$
(P_1 \otimes P_2)\, \sigma\, (\gamma_1, \gamma_2) \ \widehat{=}\ P_1\, \sigma\, \gamma_1 \ \wedge\ P_2\, \sigma\, \gamma_2.
$$

Lemma 50. $P_1 \otimes P_2 \ =\ P_1; \varpi_1^{-1} \ \wedge\ P_2; \varpi_2^{-1}.$

From Theorem 39 (fusion of specification statements) we can then show that the product operator combines with specification statements and deterministic updates in the following manner:

Theorem 51. For $p_1, p_2 : \mathcal{P}\, \Sigma$, and $P_1 : \Sigma \leftrightarrow \Gamma_1$, $P_2 : \Sigma \leftrightarrow \Gamma_2$,
$$
\{p_1\}; [P_1] \ \otimes\ \{p_2\}; [P_2] = \{p_1 \wedge p_2\}; [P_1 \otimes P_2].
$$

Theorem 52. For $f_1 : \Sigma \to \Gamma_1$, $f_2 : \Sigma \to \Gamma_2$,
$$
\langle f_1 \rangle \otimes \langle f_2 \rangle \ =\ \langle f_1 \otimes f_2 \rangle.
$$

4.3 Properties of the Derived Product Operator

Theorem 45 shows that the derived product operator is also a special case of the fusion operator:

Theorem 53. *For* $S_1 : \Sigma_1 \longmapsto \Gamma_1$, $S_2 : \Sigma_2 \longmapsto \Gamma_2$,
$$S_1 \times S_2 = \langle \pi_1 \rangle; S_1; [\varpi_1^{-1}] \odot \langle \pi_2 \rangle; S_2; [\varpi_2^{-1}].$$

Here, the command $\langle \pi_1 \rangle$ starts in a state $(\sigma_1, \sigma_2) : \Sigma_1 \times \Sigma_2$ and ends simply in the state σ_1. Given $S_1 : \Sigma_1 \longmapsto \Gamma_1$, the predicate transformer $\langle \pi_1 \rangle; S_1; [\varpi_1^{-1}] :$ $\Sigma_1 \times \Sigma_2 \longmapsto \Gamma_1 \times \Gamma_2$ is a 'lifted' version of S_1 that behaves as S_1 on the first components of the before and after state, and behaves nondeterministically on the second components. Similarly for $\langle \pi_2 \rangle; S_1; [\varpi_1^{-1}]$.

Preservation of monotonicity and homomorphic properties follows directly from Theorems 53 and 46:

Theorem 54. *The derived product operator (Definition 31) preserves monotonicity, bottom and top homomorphism, and conjunctivity and disjunctivity.*

The derived product operator may also be characterised in disjunctive form:

Theorem 55. *For* $S_1 : \Sigma_1 \longmapsto \Gamma_1$, $S_2 : \Sigma_2 \longmapsto \Gamma_2$, $q : \mathcal{P}\,(\Gamma_1 \times \Gamma_2)$:
$$(S_1 \times S_2)\, q = (\exists q_1 : \mathcal{P}\,\Gamma_1; \ q_2 : \mathcal{P}\,\Gamma_2 \,|\, q_1 \times q_2 \leq q \cdot S_1 q_1 \times S_2 q_2).$$

Proof.
$$
\begin{aligned}
(S_1 \times S_2)\, q &= (\langle \pi_1 \rangle; S_1 \otimes \langle \pi_2 \rangle; S_2)\, q \\
&= (\exists q_1 : \mathcal{P}\,\Gamma_1; \ q_2 : \mathcal{P}\,\Gamma_2 \,|\, q_1 \times q_2 \leq q \cdot (\langle \pi_1 \rangle; S_1\, q_1) \wedge (\langle \pi_2 \rangle; S_2\, q_2)) \\
&= \quad \{\text{Lemma 42}\} \\
&\ (\exists q_1 : \mathcal{P}\,\Gamma_1; \ q_2 : \mathcal{P}\,\Gamma_2 \,|\, q_1 \times q_2 \leq q \cdot S_1 q_1 \times S_2 q_2).
\end{aligned}
$$
$\square$

The following results, showing how the derived product operator combines with specification statements and deterministic updates, follow directly from Theorems 51 and 52:

Definition 56. *For functions* $g_1 : \Sigma_1 \to \Gamma_1$, $g_2 : \Sigma_2 \to \Gamma_2$, $g_1 \times g_2$ *is a function of type* $(\Sigma_1 \times \Sigma_2) \to (\Gamma_1 \times \Gamma_2)$, *where*
$$g_1 \times g_2 \ \hat{=} \ g_1; \varpi_1 \otimes g_2; \varpi_2.$$

Definition 57. *For relations* $Q_1 : \Sigma_1 \leftrightarrow \Gamma_1$, $Q_2 : \Sigma_2 \leftrightarrow \Gamma_2$, $Q_1 \times Q_2$ *is a relation of type* $(\Sigma_1 \times \Sigma_2) \leftrightarrow (\Gamma_1 \times \Gamma_2)$, *where*
$$Q_1 \times Q_2 \ \hat{=} \ Q_1; \tilde{\varpi}_1 \otimes Q_2; \tilde{\varpi}_2.$$

Theorem 58. *For functions* $g_1 : \Sigma_1 \to \Gamma_1$, $g_2 : \Sigma_2 \to \Gamma_2$,
$$\langle g_1 \rangle \times \langle g_2 \rangle = \langle g_1 \times g_2 \rangle.$$

Theorem 59. *For predicates* $p_1 : \mathcal{P}\,\Sigma_1$, $p_2 : \mathcal{P}\,\Sigma_2$, *and relations* $Q_1 : \Sigma_1 \leftrightarrow \Gamma_1$, $Q_2 : \Sigma_2 \leftrightarrow \Gamma_2$,
$$\{p_1\}; [Q_1] \ \times \ \{p_2\}; [Q_2] = \{p_1 \times p_2\}; [Q_1 \times Q_2].$$

Distribution of the derived product operator through disjunction and conjunction follows from Theorems 35 and 53. Preservation of refinement follows from Theorems 36 and 53.

Unlike the derived summation operator, the derived product operator does not distribute through recursion. For example, we have that

$$\textbf{do } skip \textbf{ od} \times \textbf{do } magic \textbf{ od} \quad = \quad abort \times skip \quad = \quad abort,$$

while,

$$\textbf{do } skip \times magic \textbf{ od} \quad = \quad \textbf{do } magic \textbf{ od} \quad = \quad skip.$$

The product operators distribute through sequential composition as follows:

Theorem 60. *For* $R_1 : \Sigma \longmapsto \Gamma_1$, $R_2 : \Sigma \longmapsto \Gamma_2$, $S_1 : \Sigma_1 \longmapsto \Gamma_1$, $S_2 : \Sigma_2 \longmapsto \Gamma_2$, $T_1 : \Gamma_1 \longmapsto \Lambda_1$, $T_2 : \Gamma_2 \longmapsto \Lambda_2$,

$$(R_1; T_1) \otimes (R_2; T_2) \leq (R_1 \otimes R_2); (T_1 \times T_2)$$
$$(S_1; T_1) \times (S_2; T_2) \leq (S_1 \times S_2); (T_1 \times T_2).$$

In the case that T_1 *and* T_2 *are universally conjunctive, then the inequalities become equalities.*

Proof: See [6].

This result allows us to show how the derived product operator preserve data-refinement. First we note the following from [28]: for predicate transformer S, the *right adjoint* of S, denoted S^r, satisfies

$$S; S^r \leq skip \qquad skip \leq S^r; S.$$

S has a right adjoint if and only if S is universally disjunctive. In this case, S^r is universally conjunctive. For example, for relation P, $\{P\}^r = [P^{-1}]$. In the case that abstraction command α is universally disjunctive, we have:

$$\alpha; S \leq S'; \alpha \Leftrightarrow S; \alpha^r \leq \alpha^r; S'.$$

Now, we have the following theorem for universally disjunctive[2] abstraction commands[3]:

Theorem 61. *Let* $S_1 : \Delta(\Sigma_1)$, $S_1' : \Delta(\Sigma_1')$, $S_2 : \Delta(\Sigma_2)$, $S_2' : \Delta(\Sigma_2')$, *be predicate transformers. Let* $\alpha_1 : \Sigma_1' \longmapsto \Sigma_1$, $\alpha_2 : \Sigma_2' \longmapsto \Sigma_2$ *be abstraction commands. If* α_1 *and* α_2 *are universally disjunctive, then*

$$S_1; \alpha_1^r \leq \alpha_1^r; S_1' \ \wedge \ S_1; \alpha_1^r \leq \alpha_1^r; S_1' \ \Rightarrow$$
$$(S_1 \times S_2); (\alpha_1^r \times \alpha_2^r) \ \leq \ (\alpha_1^r \times \alpha_2^r); (S_1' \times S_2').$$

Proof.

$$(S_1 \times S_2); (\alpha_1^r \times \alpha_2^r) = \qquad \{\text{Theorem 60, } \alpha_1^r \text{ and } \alpha_2^r \text{ universally conjunctive}\}$$
$$(S_1; \alpha_1^r) \times (S_2; \alpha_2^r)$$
$$\leq \qquad \{\times \text{ preserves refinement}\}$$
$$(\alpha_1^r; S_1') \times (\alpha_2^r; S_2')$$
$$\leq \qquad \{\text{Theorem 60}\}$$
$$(\alpha_1^r \times \alpha_2^r); (S_1' \times S_2').$$

$\square$

---

[2] The case where α is univ. disj. corresponds to downwards data refinement [28].

[3] For a direct proof that $(\alpha_1 \times \alpha_2); (S_1 \times S_2) \leq (S_1' \times S_2'); (\alpha_1 \times \alpha_2)$, for univ. disj. α_1, α_2, see [25].

5 Categorical Properties

In this section, we briefly consider some categorical properties of the summation and product operators. A *category* C is a pair (O, A) of objects O and arrows A. Associated with each arrow f in A is a source object, $source(f) \in O$, and a target object, $target(f) \in O$. For $a, b \in O$, we write $f : a \to b$ if f is an arrow of A with source a and target b. Associated with each object $a \in O$, there is an identity arrow $i_a : a \to a$, and with each pair of arrows $f : a \to b$ and $g : b \to c$ there is the composition of f and g, denoted $f; g : a \to c$. For objects a, b, c, d, and arrows $f : a \to b$, $g : b \to c$ and $h : c \to d$, the following holds:

$$i_a; f = f = f; i_b, \tag{7}$$
$$f; (g; h) = (f; g); h. \tag{8}$$

Predicate transformers form a category: the category $PTran$ has state spaces as objects and predicate transformers as arrows. If Σ, Γ are state spaces, then each predicate transformer $S : \Sigma \longmapsto \Gamma$ is an arrow with source Σ and target Γ. For composition of arrows we use sequential composition, and as the identity arrow of object Σ we use $skip_\Sigma$.

Let a and b be objects in a category C. Then a (categorical) *product* of a and b is an object $a \times b$, together with a pair of projection arrows $proj_1 : a \times b \to a$ and $proj_2 : a \times b \to b$, such that for all objects c and arrows $f : c \to a$ and $g : c \to b$, there is a unique arrow $f \otimes g^4$ satisfying

$$(f \otimes g); proj_1 = f \ \wedge \ (f \otimes g); proj_2 = g. \tag{9}$$

A *coproduct* is the dual of a product: a (categorical) coproduct of a and b is an object $a + b$, together with a pair of injection arrows $inj_1 : a \to a + b$ and $inj_2 : b \to a + b$, such that for all objects c and arrows $f : a \to c$ and $g : b \to c$, there is a unique arrow $f \oplus g$ satisfying

$$inj_1; (f \oplus g) = f \ \wedge \ inj_2; (f \oplus g) = g. \tag{10}$$

It is easy to see that the summation operator for predicate transformers yields a categorical coproduct: Let ϕ_1 and ϕ_2 be the injections for $\Sigma_1 + \Sigma_2$. By using the updates $\langle \phi_1 \rangle$ and $\langle \phi_2 \rangle$ as injection arrows, we have, by the selection property of the summation operator (Theorem 5), that for predicate transformers $S_1 : \Gamma \longmapsto \Sigma_1$ and $S_2 : \Gamma \longmapsto \Sigma_2$, the summation $S_1 \oplus S_1$ satisfies (10). Furthermore, the separation property of the summation operator shows that $S_1 \oplus S_1$ is the unique predicate transformer satisfying (10): assume X satisfies (10), i.e., $\langle \phi_1 \rangle; X = S_1$ and $\langle \phi_2 \rangle; X = S_2$, then

$$X = \quad \{\text{Separation property}\}$$
$$\langle \phi_1 \rangle; X \ \oplus \ \langle \phi_2 \rangle; X$$
$$= \quad \{\text{assumption}\}$$
$$S_1 \oplus S_2.$$

Thus, for objects Σ_1 and Σ_2, the summation $\Sigma_1 + \Sigma_2$, together with the injections $\langle \phi_1 \rangle$ and $\langle \phi_2 \rangle$, is a coproduct in $PTran$.

---

[4] In category theory literature, this is usually written $\langle f, g \rangle$ while the coproduct arrow is written $[f, g]$.

The product operator for predicate transformers does not yield a proper categorical product. To see this, we examine its selection and separation properties. The operator satisfies a weak form of the selection property:

Theorem 62. *For monotonic* $S_1 : \Sigma \longmapsto \Gamma_1$, $S_2 : \Sigma \longmapsto \Gamma_2$, $q : \mathcal{P}\, \Gamma_1$,
$$(S_1 \otimes S_2); \langle \varpi_1 \rangle \, q = (S_1 q \,\wedge\, S_2 \mathsf{T}) \,\vee\, (S_1 \mathsf{T} \,\wedge\, S_2 \perp).$$

Proof. Firstly, we have for $q_1 : \mathcal{P}\, \Gamma_1, q_2 : \mathcal{P}\, \Gamma_2$,

$$
\begin{aligned}
q_1 \times q_2 \;\leq\; \langle \varpi_1 \rangle q \;&=\; (\forall \gamma_1 : \Gamma_1;\ \gamma_2 : \Gamma_2 \cdot q_1 \times q_2 \,(\gamma_1, \gamma_2) \;\Rightarrow\; \langle \varpi_1 \rangle q \,(\gamma_1, \gamma_2)) \\
&=\; (\forall \gamma_1 : \Gamma_1;\ \gamma_2 : \Gamma_2 \cdot q_1 \gamma_1 \,\wedge\, q_2 \gamma_2 \;\Rightarrow\; q\, \gamma_1) \\
&=\; (\forall \gamma_1 : \Gamma_1 \cdot q_1 \gamma_1 \;\Rightarrow\; q\, \gamma_1) \;\vee\; (\forall \gamma_2 : \Gamma_2 \cdot \neg \, q_2 \gamma_2) \\
&=\; q_1 \leq q \;\vee\; q_2 = \perp .
\end{aligned}
$$

Then,

$$
\begin{aligned}
&(S_1 \otimes S_2); \langle \varpi_1 \rangle \, q \\
=\; &(\exists q_1 : \mathcal{P}\, \Gamma_1;\ q_2 : \mathcal{P}\, \Gamma_2 \,|\, q_1 \times q_2 \leq \langle \varpi_1 \rangle q \cdot S_1 q_1 \,\wedge\, S_2 q_2) \\
=\; &(\exists q_1 : \mathcal{P}\, \Gamma_1;\ q_2 : \mathcal{P}\, \Gamma_2 \,|\, q_1 \leq q \cdot S_1 q_1 \,\wedge\, S_2 q_2) \;\vee\; \\
&\quad (\exists q_1 : \mathcal{P}\, \Gamma_1;\ q_2 : \mathcal{P}\, \Gamma_2 \,|\, q_2 = \perp \cdot S_1 q_1 \,\wedge\, S_2 q_2) \\
=\; &\quad \{S_2 \text{ monotonic}\} \\
&(\exists q_1 : \mathcal{P}\, \Gamma_1 \,|\, q_1 \leq q \cdot S_1 q_1) \,\wedge\, S_2 \mathsf{T} \;\vee\; (\exists q_1 : \mathcal{P}\, \Gamma_1 \cdot S_1 q_1) \,\wedge\, S_2 \perp \\
=\; &\quad \{S_1 \text{ monotonic}\} \\
&S_1 q \,\wedge\, S_2 \mathsf{T} \;\vee\; S_1 \mathsf{T} \,\wedge\, S_2 \perp .
\end{aligned}
$$

$\square$

If S_2 is $\perp$-homomorphic, we get
$$(S_1 \otimes S_2); \langle \varpi_1 \rangle \leq S_1.$$
If S_2 is both $\perp$- and T-homomorphic, this becomes an equality. A similar result holds for $(S_1 \otimes S_2); \langle \varpi_2 \rangle$.

The separation property does not hold for the product operator, though we do have the following inequality for conjunctive S:

Theorem 63. *For conjunctive* $S : \Sigma \longmapsto \Gamma_1 \times \Gamma_2$, $\quad S; \langle \varpi_1 \rangle \otimes S; \langle \varpi_2 \rangle \;\leq\; S$.

Proof. For $q : \mathcal{P}\,(\Gamma_1 \times \Gamma_2)$,

$$
\begin{aligned}
&(S; \langle \varpi_1 \rangle \otimes S; \langle \varpi_2 \rangle)\, q \\
=\; &(\exists q_1 : \mathcal{P}\, \Gamma_1;\ q_2 : \mathcal{P}\, \Gamma_2 \,|\, q_1 \times q_2 \leq q \cdot S; \langle \varpi_1 \rangle \, q_1 \,\wedge\, S; \langle \varpi_2 \rangle \, q_2) \\
=\; &\quad \{S \text{ conjunctive}\} \\
&(\exists q_1 : \mathcal{P}\, \Gamma_1;\ q_2 : \mathcal{P}\, \Gamma_2 \,|\, q_1 \times q_2 \leq q \cdot S(\langle \varpi_1 \rangle \, q_1 \,\wedge\, \langle \varpi_2 \rangle \, q_2)) \\
=\; &\quad \{\text{Lemma 42}\} \\
&(\exists q_1 : \mathcal{P}\, \Gamma_1;\ q_2 : \mathcal{P}\, \Gamma_2 \,|\, q_1 \times q_2 \leq q \cdot S(q_1 \times q_2)) \\
\leq\; &\quad \{S \text{ monotonic}\} \\
&S\, q.
\end{aligned}
$$

$\square$

The reverse inequality does not hold for a command that chooses nondetermin-

istically from some non-rectangular subset of $\Gamma_1 \times \Gamma_2$. For example, take
$$C = [\lambda\sigma \cdot \lambda\gamma_1, \gamma_2 \cdot \gamma_1 = \gamma_2].$$
We have that $C; \langle \varpi_1 \rangle \otimes C; \langle \varpi_1 \rangle = havoc$, but $C \not\leq havoc$.

Thus Theorems 62 and 63 tell us that the product operator does satisfy weaker selection and separation inequalities on predicate transformers that are $\bot$-homomorphic and conjunctive. This is called a *weak* product in [18]. Let $PTran_{\bot,\wedge}$ be the category of $\bot$-homomorphic and conjunctive predicate transformers, i.e., Dijkstra's original command language. For objects S_1 and S_2 of $PTran_{\bot,\wedge}$, $S_1 \otimes S_2$ is also an object of $PTran_{\bot,\wedge}$. Thus the product operator for predicate transformers yields a weak categorical product in $PTran_{\bot,\wedge}$ (a result that is known from [18]).

Like the product operator, the derived product operator only satisfies the selection inequality for $\bot$-homomorphic predicate transformers:
$$[\pi_1^{-1}]; (S_1 \times S_2); \langle \varpi_1 \rangle \leq S_1 \qquad [\pi_2^{-1}]; (S_1 \times S_2); \langle \varpi_2 \rangle \leq S_2.$$
The inequalities become equalities if S_1 and S_2 are also $\top$-homomorphic.

The derived product operator does not satisfy a separation property. For example, the command
$$\langle \lambda(x, y) : \Sigma \times \Sigma \cdot (y, x) \rangle : \Delta(\Sigma \times \Sigma)$$
that simply swaps the values of two state components, cannot be separated into two commands of type $\Delta(\Sigma)$. Recall that the same was true of the derived summation operator.

6 Applications

In Section 4.1 (c.f. Theorem 39), we saw that the fusion operator corresponds to a form of conjunction operator for specifications. Here we look more closely at applications of the other operators.

6.1 Simultaneous Assignment

As mentioned in Section 2, variables may be modelled as cartesian components of the state space. We take the view that the predicate transformer $S_1 : \Sigma_1 \times \Sigma_2 \longmapsto \Sigma_1$ models a statement that reads from program variables x and y, and assigns a value to program variable x, while $S_2 : \Sigma_1 \times \Sigma_2 \longmapsto \Sigma_2$ reads from the same variables and assigns a value to y. The product $S_1 \otimes S_2$ has type $\Delta(\Sigma_1 \times \Sigma_2)$ and models simultaneous assignment to x and y. For example, we have
$$
\begin{aligned}
x := f(x, y) \otimes y := g(x, y) &= \langle \lambda x, y \cdot f(x, y) \rangle \otimes \langle \lambda x, y \cdot g(x, y) \rangle \\
&= \quad \{\text{Theorem 52}\} \\
&\quad \langle \lambda x, y \cdot f(x, y), g(x, y) \rangle \\
&= x, y := f(x, y), g(x, y).
\end{aligned}
$$
If S_1 and S_2 read from distinct state components, i.e., S_1 has type $\Delta(\Sigma_1)$ and S_2 has type $\Delta(\Sigma_2)$, then their simultaneous execution is modelled by the

derived product $S_1 \times S_2$. With both product operators we know that if either assignment is nonterminating, then the combined assignment is nonterminating, e.g., $S_1 \otimes abort = abort$.

The *action system* formalism of Back and Kurki-Suonio [3] uses predicate transformers to model parallel programs. An action system consists of an initialisation predicate transformer and a set of action predicate transformers. Execution of an action system proceeds by firstly executing the initialisation, then, repeatedly, executing an enabled action (an action A is enabled when $gd\ A$ holds). Two action systems are composed in parallel by composing their initialisations such that they are executed simultaneously and forming the union of their actions. Conventionally, the initialisations are demonic updates $[I_1]$, $[I_2]$, and their composition is simply $[I_1 \wedge I_2]$. The product operator provides a way of composing more general initialisations achieving the same effect.

In [8], the actions of an action system are given labels and a correspondence with Hoare's CSP [14] is established. A version of parallel composition of action systems is described in which commonly labelled actions from the respective action systems are composed such that they are executed simultaneously. In [7], this composition is defined by the properties that it should satisfy. One such property is that the composition should only be enabled when both actions are enabled. The product operator almost satisfies all the required properties: it fails if one of the actions can abort. However, by guarding the product of the actions as follows, we get an operator that satisfies the required properties:

$$A_1 \| A_2 \ \hat{=} \ [(gd\ A_1) \times (gd\ A_2)] \ ; \ (A_1 \times A_2).$$

6.2 Superposition

Consider the following two predicate transformers:
$$S_1 : \Delta(\Sigma_1), \qquad S_2 : \Sigma_1 \times \Sigma_2 \longmapsto \Sigma_2.$$
S_1 only operates on Σ_1, while S_2 reads from $\Sigma_1 \times \Sigma_2$ and writes to Σ_2. Superposition of S_2 on to S_1 allows S_2 to add extra program variables which it writes to, as well as allowing S_2 to read the program variables of S_1. Such an operation may be defined as a special case of the product operator:

Definition 64. $S_1 \sup S_2 \ \hat{=} \ \langle \pi_1 \rangle; S_1 \otimes S_2.$

Here, $\langle \pi_1 \rangle$ reads from $\Sigma_1 \times \Sigma_2$ though it discards the Σ_2 component. For example, we have:

$$x := f(x) \quad \sup \quad y := g(x,y) \quad = \quad x, y := f(x), g(x,y).$$

Superposition preserves refinement:

Theorem 65. $S_1 \leq S_1' \ \wedge \ S_2 \leq S_2' \ \Rightarrow \ (S_1 \sup S_2) \leq (S_1' \sup S_2').$

Superposition also satisfies the following refinement rule:

Theorem 66. $\{halt\ S_2\}; \langle \pi_1 \rangle; S_1 \ \leq \ (S_1 \sup S_2); \langle \pi_1 \rangle.$

Proof.

$$
\begin{aligned}
\{halt\ S_2\}; \langle \pi_1 \rangle; S_1 = \quad & \{\ [\pi_1^{-1}]; \langle \pi_1 \rangle = skip \ \text{(Lemma 43)}\ \} \\
& \{halt\ S_2\}; (\langle \pi_1 \rangle; S_1); [\pi_1^{-1}]; \langle \pi_1 \rangle \\
\leq \quad & \{\text{Theorem 47}\} \\
& (\langle \pi_1 \rangle; S_1 \otimes S_2); \langle \pi_1 \rangle \\
= \quad & (S_1\ \mathbf{sup}\ S_2); \langle \pi_1 \rangle.
\end{aligned}
$$

$\square$

In the case that $halt\ S_2 = \top$, then this theorem shows that superposition is a form of data refinement with $\langle \pi_1 \rangle$ as the abstraction statement.

Superposition refinement of action systems is described in [4], where superposition on individual actions is described in terms of sequential composition. Our superposition operator could be used instead.

6.3 Modification

Consider the following two predicate transformers:
$$
S_1 : \Delta(\Sigma_1 \times \Sigma_2), \qquad S_2 : \Sigma_1 \times \Sigma_2 \longmapsto \Sigma_2.
$$
S_1 operates on $\Sigma_1 \times \Sigma_2$, while S_2 reads from $\Sigma_1 \times \Sigma_2$ and writes to Σ_2. For example, we could have
$$
S_1 = x, y := f(x, y), g(x, y), \qquad S_2 = y := h(x, y).
$$
We wish to modify S_1 with S_2 so that S_1 writes to Σ_1 as before, but the value written to Σ_2 is determined instead by S_2. Again, such an operation may be defined as a special case of the product operator:

Definition 67. $S_1\ \mathbf{mod}\ S_2 \ \hat{=}\ S_1; \langle \pi_1 \rangle \otimes S_2.$

Here, $\langle \pi_1 \rangle$ discards the Σ_2 component written to by S_1 preserving only the Σ_1 component. For example,
$$
x, y := f(x, y), g(x, y) \quad \mathbf{mod} \quad y := h(x, y) \quad = \quad x, y := f(x, y), h(x, y).
$$
Modification preserves refinement:

Theorem 68. $S_1 \leq S_1' \wedge S_2 \leq S_2' \ \Rightarrow\ (S_1\ \mathbf{mod}\ S_2) \leq (S_1'\ \mathbf{mod}\ S_2').$

6.4 Rearranging and Extending State Components

Sometimes when combining statements, their state components may not match in the required way. For example, the statements $S_1 : \Delta(\Sigma_1 \times \Sigma_2 \times \Sigma_3)$ and $S_2 : \Delta(\Sigma_2 \times \Sigma_3 \times \Sigma_1)$ may not be combined directly as $S_1; S_2$, (even if Σ_1, Σ_2, and Σ_3 are the same sets, constructing $S_1; S_2$ directly will result in the state components being mismatched). Instead, the state components may be rearranged using an update statement before combining the statements:
$$
S_1; \langle \delta \rangle; S_2,
$$
where $\delta(\sigma_1, \sigma_2, \sigma_3) = (\sigma_2, \sigma_3, \sigma_1)$.

The same technique can be used to match statements modulo associativity. For example, although
$$(S_1 \times S_2) \times S_3 \neq S_1 \times (S_2 \times S_3),$$
we do have (let $\kappa((\sigma_1, \sigma_2), \sigma_2) = (\sigma_1, (\sigma_2, \sigma_2))$):
$$(S_1 \times S_2) \times S_3 = \langle \kappa \rangle; (S_1 \times (S_2 \times S_3)); \langle \kappa^{-1} \rangle.$$

Sometimes the state components of a statement need to be extended in order to combine it with another statement. For example, suppose we wish to combine $S_1 : \Delta(\Sigma_1 \times \Sigma_2)$ and $S_2 : \Delta(\Sigma_2)$. Here, S_2 is independent of Σ_1, so when combining it with S_1 we would most likely expect it to leave the Σ_1 component unchanged. To achieve this, we first combine S_2 with $skip$:
$$S_1; (skip_{\Sigma_1} \times S_2).$$
Extension of the state space is required, for example, when composing action systems: the state space of all actions must be extended to the state space of the combined action system.

6.5   Shared Variable Assignment

The fusion operator may be viewed as a way of combining statements such as that they both assign a value that they agree on to the same state component. In the case that two statements have only partially overlapping state components, then they need to be extended firstly with the *havoc* statement, before being combined using the fusion operator. For example, $S_1 : \Delta(\Sigma_1 \times \Sigma_2)$ and $S_2 : \Delta(\Sigma_2 \times \Sigma_3)$ may be combined as follows:
$$(S_1 \times havoc_{\Sigma_3}) \odot (havoc_{\Sigma_1} \times S_2).$$
Since *havoc* acts as a unit for the fusion operator, the effect of this statement on the Σ_1 component will be determined purely by S_1, and the effect on the Σ_3 component will be determined by Σ_3. The effect on the Σ_2 component will be the intersection of the nondeterministic possibilities allowed by S_1 and S_2. If that intersection is empty, then, provided S_1 and S_2 terminate, the combination behaves as magic.

Note that the above operands of the fusion operator, do not match exactly: the first operand is of type $\Delta((\Sigma_1 \times \Sigma_2) \times \Sigma_3)$, while the second is of type $\Delta(\Sigma_1 \times (\Sigma_2 \times \Sigma_3))$. However, these can easily be made to match using the function $(\lambda((\sigma_1, \sigma_2), \sigma_3) \cdot (\sigma_1, (\sigma_2, \sigma_3)))$ as described in Subsection 6.4.

6.6   Late Binding of Procedures

We model a procedure by simply associating a statement with a procedure name. Calling a procedure then involves executing the statement associated with the procedure name. The following example shows the concrete syntax used to describe procedures:

proc *Increment*

var x : **Int**

$x := x + 1$

The concept of *late binding* of procedures is important in object-oriented programming. Late binding means that the effect of executing a procedure depends on the value of the state on which it is to be executed. For example, Utting and Robinson [27] model late binding in the refinement calculus by regarding a procedure as being a function from values to statements:

$$proc \; : \; \Sigma \to \Delta(\Sigma).$$

The effect of executing procedure *proc* in state σ is then determined by the statement $(proc \; \sigma)$. This is sometimes referred to as *instance-centered* late binding [12].[5]

A simpler notion of late binding uses types rather than values to determine which statement is selected when a procedure is called (so-called *class-centered* late binding [12]). Here we show how the summation operator may be used to model this form of late binding.

Firstly, the following operator lifts predicate transformers in either base type of a summation to the summation type:

Definition 69. Let $S_1 : \Sigma_1 \longmapsto \Gamma_1$ and $S_2 : \Sigma_2 \longmapsto \Gamma_2$ be predicate transformers. Then,

$$S_1^+ \; \hat{=} \; S_1 + abort \qquad S_2^+ \; \hat{=} \; abort + S_2.$$

Now, given predicate transformers

$$S_1 : \Sigma_1 \longmapsto \Gamma_1 \qquad S_2 : \Sigma_2 \longmapsto \Gamma_2$$
$$T_1 : \Gamma_1 \longmapsto \Lambda_1 \qquad T_2 : \Gamma_2 \longmapsto \Lambda_2,$$

we have the following result:

Theorem 70.

$$S_1^+ ; (T_1 + T_2) \; = \; (S_1; T_1)^+ \qquad S_2^+ ; (T_1 + T_2) \; = \; (S_2; T_2)^+.$$

That is, the effect of $(T_1 + T_2)$ depends on whether S_1 or S_2 is executed beforehand.

Proof.

$$S_1^+ ; (T_1 + T_2) = (S_1 + abort); (T_1 + T_2)$$
$$= \qquad \{\text{Distribution of } + \text{ and } ;\}$$
$$(S_1; T_1) + (abort; T_2)$$
$$= (S_1; T_1) + abort$$
$$= (S_1; T_1)^+$$

Similarly for $S_2^+ ; (T_1 + T_2)$. □

---

[5] Sometimes the terms "late binding" and "dynamic binding" are used interchangeably in the literature. We prefer to reserve the term "dynamic binding" for the case where the procedure associated with an instance/class may change during execution. Such an effect may be achieved, for example, by using stored procedures as provided in Oberon [22] where procedures are themselves values. A predicate transformer model of stored procedures may be found in [24].

Consider the following two procedures:

$$\textbf{proc } Invert_1 \qquad \textbf{proc } Invert_2$$
$$\textbf{var } x : \textbf{Int} \qquad \textbf{var } x : \textbf{Bool}$$
$$x := -x \qquad x := \neg \, x$$

Let $Invert \,\hat{=}\, Invert_1 + Invert_2$. Then

$$(x := 10)^+; Invert = (x := 10)^+; (Invert_1 + Invert_2)$$
$$= (x := 10; Invert_1)^+$$
$$= (x := -10)^+,$$

while

$$(x := true)^+; Invert = (x := true)^+; (Invert_1 + Invert_2)$$
$$= (x := true; Invert_2)^+$$
$$= (x := false)^+.$$

Thus the effect of $Invert$ depends on whether an integer or boolean value has been assigned to x beforehand.

The following refinement rule for summation follows trivially from Theorem 24:

Theorem 71. *For any S_2,* $\quad S_1^+ \leq S_1 + S_2$.

6.7 Inheritance

Consider the following object-oriented definition of a procedure:

$$\textbf{proc } R$$
$$\textbf{inherits } S$$
$$\textbf{extended by } E$$
$$\textbf{modified by } M$$

Here, R inherits the behaviour of S, extends the behaviour of S by E and modifies the behaviour of S by M.

Suppose S, E and M have the following types:

$$S : \Delta(\Sigma_1 \times \Sigma_2)$$
$$E : \Sigma_1 \times \Sigma_2 \times \Sigma_3 \longmapsto \Sigma_3$$
$$M : \Sigma_1 \times \Sigma_2 \times \Sigma_3 \longmapsto \Sigma_2.$$

That is, E introduces a new component of type Σ_3, while M modifies how S behaves on the Σ_2 component. One way to define R would be as follows:

$$R \,\hat{=}\, (S \textbf{ sup } E) \bmod M.$$

However, in object-oriented programming, as well as performing the extended and modified behaviour on the extended type of R, we would expect R to behave as S on values of the type of S. But some of the behaviour of S has been discarded in $(S \textbf{ sup } E) \bmod M$. So instead we define R as follows:

$$R \,\hat{=}\, S + ((S \textbf{ sup } E) \bmod M).$$

Now, R uses late binding when choosing whether to perform the inherited behaviour or the extended/modified behaviour.

From Theorem 71, we have that $S^+ \leq R$.

Also, this form of inheritance preserves refinement:

Theorem 72.

$$S \leq S' \ \wedge\ M \leq M' \ \wedge\ E \leq E' \ \Rightarrow$$
$$S + ((S \sup E) \bmod M) \ \leq \ S' + ((S' \sup E') \bmod M').$$

It should also be possible to define multiple inheritance in a similar way, with the fusion operator being used in the case where two inherited procedures act on the same state component.

7 Conclusions

We have investigated summation and product operators for predicate transformers and shown that they satisfy a rich set of algebraic laws. These are mostly distributivity laws that experience with other operators in the refinement calculus has shown to be useful. For example, in showing that summation preserves data refinement (Theorem 25), we made use of the fact that summation distributes through sequential composition.

Since the summation operator may be characterised in terms of existing choice operators (Theorem 6), it is not a true extension of the refinement calculus. However, it does satisfy properties not satisfied by the existing choice operators, in particular, the late-binding effect.

The fusion operator is a true extension of the refinement calculus since it cannot be modelled by existing choice operators[6]. Both product operators were shown to be special cases of the fusion operator. The operands of the fusion operator may write to the same final state while those of the product operators write to separate final states; this means that the fusion operator may introduce miraculousness while the product operators never do, i.e., $\otimes$ and $\times$ preserve $\perp$-homomorphism, while $\odot$ does not.

Although some of the results presented here may be found in [23] and [18], we do have several new results: the fusion operator and it's relationship to the product operator and Abrial's parallel operator, the relationship between the summation operator and existing refinement calculus constructs, and the distribution of summation through recursion. Also our approach is different: We develop product and summation operators for predicates and use properties of these operators when reasoning about predicate transformers, whereas Martin [18] uses a categorical construction that promotes products and coproducts in the category of functions to the category of relations and then to the category of predicate transformers, and Naumann [23] takes a more direct approach working within the category of predicate transformers.

Hoogendijk and Backhouse [15] have investigated summations and products of relations. Their summation and product operators for relations are the same as our Lemmas 13 and 50 respectively, and satisfy similar distributivity properties as our operators on predicate trasnsformers. However, with a relation one has

---

[6] Theorem 41 shows how fusion can be modelled using $rel\ S$ and demonic update, but this only holds for conjunctive predicate transformers.

to choose between whether its domain represents termination or guardedness, and whether nondeterminism should be demonic or angelic, whereas all of these possibilities may be modelled with predicate transformers, i.e., relation P can be embedded into the appropriate predicate transformer lattice in at least four different ways:

$$[P], \quad \{dom\ P\}; [P], \quad \{P\}, \quad [dom\ P]; \{P\}.$$

Thus, for example, summation of relations is characterised only as a disjunction of relations (c.f. Lemmas 13), whereas summation of predicate transformers is characterised in both conjunctive and disjunctive form (c.f. Theorem 6).

We examined possible applications of these operators such as simultaneous execution, conjunction of specifications, late binding and inheritance. Of course, the use of products and summations as models of simultaneous execution and choice respectively in programming languages is not new (see, for example, [16]). Simultaneous execution is important, for example, for various forms of action system parallel composition. The fusion operator provides a refinement-preserving way of composing requirements (specifications) which could also be viewed as a form of multiple inheritance. Late binding and inheritance are important features of object-oriented programming languages, and although our approach is limited in that we only model class-centered late binding, we believe it to be sufficiently powerful and find the rich set of associated laws encouraging.

Acknowledgements

The work reported here was carried out within the IRENE-project supported by the Academy of Finland. We are grateful to David Naumann, Xu Qiwen, and the anonymous MPC referees for useful comments.

References

1. J.R. Abrial. *The B-Book.* To be published by Cambridge University Press, 1995.

2. R.J.R. Back. *Correctness Preserving Program Refinements: Proof Theory and Applications.* Tract 131, Mathematisch Centrum, Amsterdam, 1980.

3. R.J.R. Back and R. Kurki-Suonio. Decentralisation of process nets with centralised control. In *2nd ACM SIGACT-SIGOPS Symp. on Principles of Distributed Computing,* pages 131–142, 1983.

4. R.J.R. Back and K. Sere. Superposition refinement of parallel algorithms. In K.A. Parker and G.A. Rose, editors, *FORTE'91.* North–Holland, 1992.

5. R.J.R. Back and J. von Wright. Refinement concepts formalised in higher order logic. *Formal Aspects of Computing,* 5:247–272, 1990.

6. R.J.R. Back and J. von Wright. *Refinement Calculus.* Book in preparation, Åbo Akademi, 1994.

7. M.J. Butler. *A CSP Approach To Action Systems.* D.Phil. Thesis, Programming Research Group, Oxford University, 1992.

8. M.J. Butler. *Refinement and Decomposition of Value-Passing Action Systems.* In E. Best, editor, *CONCUR'93,* volume LNCS 715. Springer–Verlag, 1993.

9. E.W. Dijkstra. *A Discipline of Programming*. Prentice-Hall, 1976.

10. E.W. Dijkstra. *From Predicate Transformers to Predicates*. Manuscript EWD821, April 1982.

11. P.H.B. Gardiner and C.C. Morgan. Data refinement of predicate transformers. *Theoretical Computer Science*, 87:143–162, 1991.

12. J. Gutknecht. *Object-Oriented Programming with Oberon*. Lecture Notes from Eastern Finland Universities International Summer School on Novel Computing, Lapeenranta University of Technology, Finland, 1994.

13. J. He, C.A.R. Hoare, and J.W. Sanders. Data refinement refined. In *European Symposium on Programming*, volume LNCS 213. Springer–Verlag, 1986.

14. C.A.R. Hoare. *Communicating Sequential Processes*. Prentice-Hall, 1985.

15. P.F. Hoogendijk and R.C. Backhouse. Relational programming laws in the tree, list, bag, set hierarchy. *Science of Computer Programming*, 22(1-2):67–105, 1994.

16. He Jifeng and C.A.R. Hoare. *Categorical Semantics of Programming Languages*. In *Mathematical Foundations of Programming Semantics*, volume LNCS 442. Springer–Verlag, 1990.

17. C.B. Jones. *Systematic Software Development using VDM – Second Edition*. Prentice-Hall, 1990.

18. C.E. Martin. *Preordered Categories and Predicate Transformers*. D.Phil. Thesis, Programming Research Group, Oxford University, 1991.

19. C.C. Morgan. *Programming from Specifications*. Prentice-Hall, 1990.

20. C.C. Morgan. The cuppest capjunctive capping, and Galois. In A.W. Roscoe, editor, *A Classical Mind: Essays in Honour of C.A.R. Hoare*. Prentice-Hall, 1994.

21. J.M. Morris. A theoretical basis for stepwise refinement and the programming calculus. *Science of Computer Programming*, 9(3):298–306, 1987.

22. H.P. Mossenboeck. *Object-Oriented Programming in Oberon-2*. Springer-Verlag, 1994.

23. D.A. Naumann. *Two-Categories and Program Structure: Data Types, Refinement Calculi, and Predicate Transformers*. Ph.D. Thesis, University of Texas at Austin, 1992.

24. D.A. Naumann. *On the Essence of Oberon*. In J. Gutknecht, editor, *Conference on Programming Languages and System Architectures*, volume LNCS 782. Springer–Verlag, 1994.

25. D.A. Naumann. *Data Refinement, Call by Value, and Higher Order Programs*. Accepted for publication in Formal Aspects of Computing, 1995.

26. J.M. Spivey. *The Z Notation - A Reference Manual*. Prentice-Hall, 1989.

27. B.M. Utting and K. Robinson. Modular reasoning in an object-oriented refinement calculus. In *Mathematics of Program Construction, 1992*, volume LNCS 669. Springer–Verlag, 1993.

28. J. von Wright. The lattice of data refinement. *Acta Informatica*, 31(2):105–135, 1994.

29. N. Ward. Adding specification constructs to the refinement calculus. In *FME'93*, volume LNCS 670. Springer–Verlag, 1993.

An Action System Specification of the Caltech Asynchronous Microprocessor

R.J.R. Back[1], A.J. Martin[2], K. Sere[3]

[1] Åbo Akademi University, Department of Computer Science,
FIN-20520 Turku, Finland
[2] California Institute of Technology, Department of Computer Science,
Pasadena CA 91125, USA
[3] University of Kuopio, Department of Computer Science and Applied Mathematics,
FIN-70211 Kuopio, Finland, email: Kaisa.Sere@uku.fi, fax: +358-71-162595

Abstract. The action system framework for modelling parallel programs is used to formally *specify* a microprocessor. First the microprocessor is specified as a sequential program. The sequential specification is then *decomposed* and *refined* into a concurrent program using correctness-preserving program transformations. Previously this microprocessor has been specified in a semi-formal manner at Caltech, where an asynchronous circuit for the microprocessor was derived from the specification. We propose a specification strategy that is based on the idea of *spatial decomposition* of the program variable space. Applying this strategy we give a completely formal derivation of a high level specification for the Caltech microprocessor. We also demonstrate the suitability of action systems and the stepwise refinement paradigm for *formal VLSI circuit design*.

1 Introduction

An *action system* is a parallel or distributed program where parallel activity is described in terms of events, so called actions. The actions are *atomic*: if an action is chosen for execution, it is executed to completion without any interference from the other actions in the system. Several actions can be executed in parallel, as long as the actions do not share any variables. Atomicity guarantees that a parallel execution of an action system gives the same results as a sequential and nondeterministic execution.

A recent extension of the action system framework, adding procedure declarations to action systems [7], gives us a very general mechanism for synchronized communication between action systems. When an action in one action system calls a procedure in another action system, the effect is that of a remote procedure call. The calling action and the procedure body involved in the call are executed as a single atomic entity.

The use of action systems permits the design of the logical behaviour of a system to be separated from the issue of how the system is to be implemented. The decision whether the action system is to be executed in a sequential or parallel fashion can be postponed to a later stage, when the logical behaviour of the action system has been designed. The construction of the program is thus done within a single unifying framework.

The action systems formalism was proposed by Back and Kurki-Suonio [4]. Later similar event-based formalisms have been put forward by several other researcher, see for example the work of Chandy and Misra [10], who describe their UNITY framework and Francez [12], who develops his IP-language.

The *refinement calculus* is a formalization of the stepwise refinement method of program construction. It was originally proposed by Back [1] and it has been later studied and extended by several researchers, see [15, 17] among others.

Originally, the refinement calculus was designed as a framework for systematic derivation of sequential programs only. Back and Sere [6, 18] extended the refinement calculus for the design of action systems and hence, it was possible to handle *parallel algorithms* within the calculus. Back [3] made yet another extension to the calculus showing how *reactive programs* could be derived in a stepwise manner within it relying heavily on the work done in data refinement. In both cases parallel and concurrent activity is modelled within a purely sequential framework. In [7] Back and Sere show how action systems with remote procedure calls can be derived within the refinement calculus for reactive systems. We will here show how this extention of the refinement calculus/action system framework is applied to a non-trivial case study, the formal derivation of an asynchronous microprocessor.

The initial specification of the microprocessor will be given as a sequential program that has the syntactic form of an action system. Our goal is to isolate the different functional components of the microprocessor, like instruction memory, data memory, ALU, registers etc., into action systems of their own. The component action systems are joined together in a parallel composition, where they interact with each other using shared variables and remote procedure calls. The parallel composition of action systems is derived from the sequential specification using correctness-preserving program transformations within the refinement calculus.

The derivation is based on the idea of *spatial decomposition* of the program variables. At each step we identify one functional component of the microprocessor and gather the program variables and their associated code relevant to this component into a separate module, i.e., an action system. Back and Sere [8] show how this idea is reflected in a specification language based on action systems and the refinement calculus.

Martin [14] has developed a methodology for designing asynchronous VLSI circuits that is based on methods familiar from parallel program design. Using this method he has specified the same microprocessor within the CSP-framework, but without a completely formal calculus. A delay-insensitive, asynchronous circuit for the microprocessor was derived from the concurrent program that is more or less equivalent to the parallel composition of action systems that we derive here.

Our purpose here is to demonstrate that, in addition with software design, action systems and the refinement calculus provide us with a uniform framework for *formal VLSI circuit design*. In this paper we concentrate on the initial steps of circuit design focusing on a high level specification of the microprocessor as a collection of parallel processes. In an accompanying paper [13] we develop these ideas close to the architectureal level by e.g. taking into account the delay-insensitive features of the target circuit.

A somewhat related method and formalism is developed in [19], but the emphasis is put on the verification of and formal models for delay-insensitive circuits. The work of the ProCoS-project [9] is also related to ours, as their goal is to develop uniform methods for constructing both software and hardware that is correct.

Overview of the Paper. In Sect. 2, we describe the action systems formalism. In Sect.3, we describe how action systems are composed into parallel systems. We also briefly describe the refinement calculus. In Sect. 4, we give an initial specification for the microprocessor as a sequential program. In Sect. 5, this specification is stepwise turned into a parallel composition of action systems, where each action system represents one functional component of the target microprocessor. Finally in Sect. 6, we conclude with some remarks on the proposed method.

2 Action Systems

An *action system* (with procedures) is a statement of the form

$$
\begin{aligned}
\mathcal{A} :: \quad &\textbf{var } v; \textbf{proc } w \bullet \\
&\quad |[\textbf{ var } x_1, \ldots, x_h := x_1 0, \ldots, x_h 0; \textbf{proc } p_1 = P_1; \ \ldots; p_n = P_n; \\
&\quad\quad \textbf{do } A_1 \ [\!] \ \ldots \ [\!] \ A_m \textbf{ od} \\
&\quad]| : z
\end{aligned}
$$

The identifiers $x_1, \ldots, x_h$ are the variables declared in $\mathcal{A}$ and initialized to $x_1 0, \ldots, x_h 0$, $p_1, \ldots, p_n$ are the *procedure headers*, and P_i is the *procedure body* of p_i, $i = 1, \ldots, n$. Within the loop, $A_1, \ldots, A_m$ are the *actions* of $\mathcal{A}$. Finally, z, v and w are pairwise distinct lists of identifiers. The list z is the *import list*, indicating which variables and procedures are referenced, but not declared in $\mathcal{A}$. The lists v and w are the *export lists*, indicating which variables and procedures declared in $\mathcal{A}$ are accessible from other action systems. Procedure bodies and actions can be arbitrary statements, and may contain procedure calls.

The *guard* of a program statement S is the condition gS, defined by

$$
gS \ = \ \neg \text{wp}(S, \textit{false})
$$

where wp is the *weakest precondition* predicate transformer of Dijkstra [11]. The statement S is said to be *enabled* in a given state when the guard is true in that state. The statement S is said to be *always enabled*, if $\text{wp}(S, \textit{false}) = \textit{false}$ (i.e., $gS = \textit{true}$).

Both procedure bodies and actions will in general be *guarded commands*, i.e., statements of the form

$$C = g \rightarrow S,$$

where g is a boolean condition and S is a program statement. In this case, the guard of C is $g \wedge \neg wp(S, false)$. The *body* sC of C is defined by

$$sC = \textbf{if } gC \rightarrow C \parallel \neg gC \rightarrow abort \textbf{ fi}$$

If the body of each action of an arbitrary action system is always enabled, action systems coincide with the language of guarded commands.

The *local* variables (procedures) of $\mathcal{A}$ are those variables x_i (procedures p_i) that are not listed in the export list. The *global* variables (procedures) of $\mathcal{A}$ are the variables (procedures) listed in the import and export lists. The local and global variables (procedures) are assumed to be distinct. Hence, $x \cap z = \emptyset$, where x denotes the list of variables declared in $\mathcal{A}$ (no redeclaration of variables is thus permitted). Each variable may be associated with an explicit type. The *state variables* of $\mathcal{A}$ consist of the local variables and the global variables. A statement or an action is said to be *local* to an action system if it only refers to local variables of the action system. The procedures and actions are allowed to refer to all the state variables of an action system. Furthermore, each procedure and action may have local variables of its own.

We consider two different parameter passing mechanisms for procedures, *call-by-value* and *call-by-result*. Call-by-value is denoted with $p(f)$, where f stands for the formal parameters, and call-by-result with $p(\textbf{var } f)$. For simplicity, we will here assume that the procedures are not recursive.

Definition of Procedures. The meaning of a call on a parameterless procedure $p = P$ in a statement S is determined by the *substitution principle*:

$$S = S[P/p],$$

i.e., the body P of procedure p is substituted for each call on this procedure in statement S.

Procedures with parameters can be handled in a similar way by substitution. Let $p(x, \textbf{var } y) = P$ be a procedure declaration, where x denotes the formal call-by-value parameters and y the formal call-by-result parameters. Then a call on p with the actual parameters a, b is removed by the substitution

$$S = S[P'/p(a, b)],$$

where P' is the statement

$$\lvert [\textbf{ var } x, y; x := a; P; b := y] \rvert.$$

The definition of procedures is studied in more detail in [2, 7, 16].

Enabledness of an Action. Let $p = (b \rightarrow T)$ be a procedure and let $a \rightarrow S; p$ be an action that calls on p. Then the enabledness of this action is determined by the value of the action guard

$$g(a \rightarrow S; p) = a \wedge g(S; p)$$

where $g(S; p)$ is calculated as follows:

$$
\begin{aligned}
& g(S; p) \\
&= g(S; (b \rightarrow T)) \\
&= \neg wp(S; (b \rightarrow T), \mathit{false}) \\
&= \neg wp(S, wp((b \rightarrow T), \mathit{false})) \\
&= \neg wp(S, b \Rightarrow wp(T, \mathit{false})) \\
&= \neg wp(S, b \Rightarrow \neg gT) \\
&= \{\text{assuming } T \text{ always enabled}\} \\
& \quad \neg wp(S, \neg b)
\end{aligned}
$$

If a procedure or action contains a call to a procedure that is not declared in the action system, then the behavior of the action system will depend on the way in which the procedures are declared in some other action system, which constitutes the environment of the action system as will be described below.

3 Composing and Refining Action Systems

Consider two action systems,

$\mathcal{A} ::$ **var** v; **proc** r •
   $|[$ **var** $x := x0$; **proc** $p_1 = P_1$; $\ldots$; $p_n = P_n$;
      do $A_1 \| \ldots \| A_m$ **od**
   $]|: z$

and

$\mathcal{B} ::$ **var** w; **proc** s •
   $|[$ **var** $y := y0$; **proc** $q_1 = Q_1$; $\ldots$; $q_l = Q_l$;
      do $B_1 \| \ldots \| B_k$ **od**
   $]|: u$

where $x \cap y = \emptyset$, $v \cap w = \emptyset$, and $r \cap s = \emptyset$. Furthermore, the local procedures declared in the two action systems are required to be distinct.

We define the *parallel composition* $\mathcal{A} \| \mathcal{B}$ of $\mathcal{A}$ and $\mathcal{B}$ to be the action system $\mathcal{C}$

$\mathcal{C} ::$ **var** b; **proc** c •
   $|[$ **var** $x, y := x0, y0$;
      proc $p_1 = P_1$; $\ldots$; $p_n = P_n$; $q_1 = Q_1$; $\ldots$; $q_l = Q_l$;
      do $A_1 \| \ldots \| A_m \| B_1 \| \ldots \| B_k$ **od**
   $]|: a$

where $a = z \cup u - (v \cup r \cup w \cup s), b = v \cup w, c = r \cup s$.

Thus, parallel composition will combine the state spaces of the two constituent action systems, merging the global variables and global procedures and keeping the local variables distinct. The imported identifiers denote those global variables and/or procedures that are not declared in either $\mathcal{A}$ or $\mathcal{B}$. The exported identifiers are the variables and/or procedures declared global in $\mathcal{A}$ or $\mathcal{B}$. The procedure declarations and the actions in the parallel composition consists of the procedure declarations and actions in the original systems.

Parallel composition is a way of associating a meaning to procedures that are called in an action system but which are not declared there, i.e., they are part of the import list. The meaning can be given by a procedure declared in another action system, provided the procedure has been declared global, i.e., it is included in the action systems export list.

The behaviour of a parallel composition of action systems is dependent on how the individual action systems, the *reactive components*, interact with each other. We have for instance that a reactive component does not terminate by itself: termination is a global property of the composed action system. More on these topics can be found in [3].

Enabledness. We permit procedure bodies to have guards that are not identically true. Hence, it is possible that an action which guard is true, calls a procedure in another action system, which then turns out to have its guard false in the state in which it is called. This situation is then the same as if the calling action had never initiated the call. In other words, the enabledness of an action is determined by the enabledness of the whole statement that is invoked when the action is executed, including enabledness of all procedures that might be invoked.

Decomposing Action Systems. Given an action system

$$
\begin{aligned}
&\mathcal{C} :: \; \textbf{var } u; \, \textbf{proc } s \; \bullet \\
&\quad |[\; \textbf{var } v := v0; \\
&\qquad \textbf{do } C_1 \; [\!] \; \ldots \; [\!] \; C_n \; \textbf{od} \\
&\quad]|: z
\end{aligned}
$$

we can *decompose* it into smaller action systems by parallel composition. This means that we split the variables, actions and procedures of $\mathcal{C}$ into disjoint sets so that

$$
\begin{aligned}
&\mathcal{C} = \; \textbf{var } u; \, \textbf{proc } s \; \bullet \\
&\quad |[\; \textbf{var } w := w0; \, \textbf{proc } r = R; \\
&\qquad \mathcal{A} \parallel \mathcal{B} \\
&\quad]|: z
\end{aligned}
$$

where

$$
\begin{aligned}
&\mathcal{A} :: \; \textbf{var } a_2; \, \textbf{proc } a_3 \; \bullet \\
&\quad |[\; \textbf{var } x := x0; \, \textbf{proc } p = P; \\
&\qquad \textbf{do } A_1 \; [\!] \; \ldots \; [\!] \; A_m \; \textbf{od} \\
&\quad]|: a_1
\end{aligned}
$$

$\mathcal{B} ::$ **var** b_2; **proc** b_3 •
   $[\![$ **var** $y := y0$; **proc** $q = Q$;
      do $B_1 \ [\!]\ \ldots\ [\!]\ B_k$ **od**
   $]\!]$: b_1

The reactive components $\mathcal{A}$ and $\mathcal{B}$ interact with each other via the global variables and procedures included in the lists a_2, a_3, b_2, b_3.

In the process of decomposing the action system C into parallel reactive components, it may also be necessary to introduce some new procedures r, to handle situations where an action affects program variables in both x and y. As these variables are local in the decomposed action system, no procedure or action can access both. Hence, one needs to introduce auxiliary procedures that have access to the local variables, and in terms of which the original procedure/action can be expressed.

Hiding and Revealing. Let

$$\textbf{var } v_1, v_2; \textbf{ proc } v_3, v_4 \bullet \mathcal{A} : z$$

be an action system of the form above, where z denotes the import list and v_1, v_2, v_3, v_4 denote the export lists. We can *hide* some of the exported global variables (v_2) and procedure names (v_4) by removing them from the export list,

$$\mathcal{A}' = \textbf{var } v_1; \textbf{ proc } v_3 \bullet \mathcal{A} : z.$$

Hiding the variables v_2 and procedure names v_4 makes them inaccessible from other actions outside $\mathcal{A}'$ in a parallel composition. Hiding thus has an effect only on the variables and procedures in the export list. The opposite operation, *revealing*, is also useful.

In connection with the parallel composition below we will follow the following convention. Let **var** a_1; **proc** $a_2 \bullet \mathcal{A} : a_3$ and **var** b_1; **proc** $b_2 \bullet \mathcal{B} : b_3$ be two action systems. Then their parallel composition is the action system

$$\textbf{var } a_1 \cup b_1; \textbf{ proc } a_2 \cup b_2 \bullet \mathcal{A} \parallel \mathcal{B} : c$$

where $c = a_3 \cup b_3 - (a_1 \cup a_2 \cup b_1 \cup b_2)$ according to the definition above. Hence, the parallel composition exports all the variables and procedures exported by either $\mathcal{A}$ or $\mathcal{B}$. Sometimes there is no need to export all these identifiers, i.e., when they are exclusively accessed by the two component action systems $\mathcal{A}$ and $\mathcal{B}$. This effect is achieved with the following construct that turns out to be extremely useful later:

$$\textbf{var } v; \textbf{ proc } p \bullet [\![\ \mathcal{A} \parallel \mathcal{B}\ ]\!] : c$$

Here the identifiers v and p are as follows: $v \subseteq a_1 \cup b_1$ and $p \subseteq a_2 \cup b_2$.

Refining Action Systems. Most of the steps we will carry out within the micro-processor derivation are purely syntactic decomposition steps. There are, how-ever, a couple of steps where a higher level action system is refined into an other action system. These steps are formally carried out within the refinement calcu-lus, where we consider action systems as ordinary statements, i.e., as initialized iteration statements.

The refinement calculus is based on the following definition. Let S and S' be two statements. Then S is correctly *refined* by S', denoted $S \leq S'$, if for any postcondition Q

$$\text{wp}(S, Q) \Rightarrow \text{wp}(S', Q).$$

We will not go into details of this calculus here. The interested reader should consult [1, 6, 18, 3, 7].

4 Initial Specification of the Caltech Microprocessor

The microprocessor we want to specify has a conventional 16-bit-word instruc-tion set of *load-store* type. The processor uses two separate memories for in-structions and data. There are three types of instructions: ALU, memory and program-counter (*pc*). The ALU instructions operate on the 16 registers. The memory instructions involve a register and a data word. Some instructions use the following word as *offset*.

The action system $\mathcal{M}_0$ below describes the processor:

$\mathcal{M}_0 ::$ **var** *imem, dmem* •
$\quad |[$ **var** $i \in record, pc, offset, imem[ilow..ihigh], dmem[dlow..dhigh],$
$\qquad\qquad reg[0..15], f$
$\quad pc := pc0;$
$\quad$ **do** $true \rightarrow$
$\qquad i, pc := imem[pc], pc + 1;$
$\qquad$ **if** $offset(i.op) \rightarrow offset, pc := imem[pc], pc + 1$
$\qquad [\![\neg offset(i.op) \rightarrow skip$
$\qquad$ **fi**;
$\qquad$ **if** $alu(i.op) \rightarrow < reg[i.z], f >:= aluf(reg[i.x], reg[i.y], i.op, f)$
$\qquad [\![ld(i.op) \rightarrow reg[i.z] := dmem[reg[i.x] + reg[i.y]]$
$\qquad [\![st(i.op) \rightarrow dmem[reg[i.x] + reg[i.y]] := reg[i.z]$
$\qquad [\![ldx(i.op) \rightarrow reg[i.z] := dmem[offset + reg[i.y]]$
$\qquad [\![stx(i.op) \rightarrow dmem[offset + reg[i.y]] := reg[i.z]$
$\qquad [\![lda(i.op) \rightarrow reg[i.z] := offset + reg[i.y]$
$\qquad [\![stpc(i.op) \rightarrow reg[i.z] := pc + reg[i.y]$
$\qquad [\![jmp(i.op) \rightarrow pc := reg[i.y]$
$\qquad [\![brch(i.op) \rightarrow$
$\qquad\qquad$ **if** $cond(f, i.cc) \rightarrow pc := pc + offset [\![\neg cond(f, i.cc) \rightarrow skip$ **fi**
$\qquad$ **fi**
$\quad$ **od**
$\quad]\!]:<>$

The initial action system is a sequential non-terminating loop. The variable i holds the instruction under execution. It is of record type containing several fields. Each instruction has an *op* field for the *opcode*, the other fields depend on the instruction.

The two memories are represented by the globally visible arrays *imem* and *dmem*. The index to *imem* is the program-counter variable *pc*. The registers are described as the array $reg[0..15]$.

5 Decomposition into Parallel Action Systems

Let us decompose the action system $\mathcal{M}_0$ into a parallel composition of action systems so that each system models one functional component of the microprocessor. At each step one component is identified and its program variables and associated code is gathered into a module of its own. The components in the order of their introduction and their associated variables are as follows:

(1) Instruction memory: $imem[ilow..ihigh]$
(2) Program counter and offset: pc, *offset*
(3) Register array: $reg[0..15]$
(4) Arithmetic-logical unit: f
(5) Data memory: $dmem[dlow..dhigh]$
(6) Instruction execution: i

The main lines of the derivation will follow the presentation of Martin [14] rather closely. We describe the first three steps more carefully, the other steps follow a similar pattern.

5.1 Instruction Memory

We start by making the instruction memory an action system of its own. We assign the variable *imem* to this action system and hence, references to *imem* must be done via a procedure call. There are two such references in the specification, one that writes $imem[pc]$ into the variable i and the other that writes $imem[pc]$ to *offset*.

Let us create a procedure *IMEM* that reads the instruction denoted by pc, $imem[pc]$, into a variable k (k will be later instantiated to i and *offset* respective):

$$
\begin{aligned}
&k, pc := imem[pc], pc + 1 \\
\leq\ &k := imem[pc];\ pc := pc + 1 \\
\leq\ &|[\ \mathbf{var}\ j;\ j := imem[pc];\ k := j\ ]|;\ pc := pc + 1 \\
=\ &|[\ \mathbf{proc}\ IMEM\,(\mathbf{var}\ j) = (j := imem[pc]);\ IMEM\,(k);\ pc := pc + 1\ ]|
\end{aligned}
$$

Hence, the action system $\mathcal{M}_0$ is refined by the following action system:

$\mathcal{M}_1 ::$ **var** *imem, dmem* •
    |[**var** $i \in$ *record, pc, offset, imem*[*ilow..ihigh*], *dmem*[*dlow..dhigh*],
          $reg[0..15], f$
    proc *IMEM*(**var** j) = ($j := imem[pc]$);
    $pc := pc0$;
    do   *true* →
        IMEM(i); $pc := pc + 1$;
        if *offset*($i.op$) → *IMEM*(*offset*); $pc := pc + 1$
        [¬*offset*($i.op$) → *skip*
        fi;
        if ... as before ... **fi**
    od
    ]|:<>

Separate FETCH and IMEM. The next step is to separate the instruction memory into an action system of its own. We therefore decompose the initial specification of the microprocessor as follows

$$\mathcal{M}_1 = \mathbf{var} \ imem, dmem \ • \ |[\ \mathcal{M}_2 \ || \ \mathcal{I} \ ]| :<>$$

where

$\mathcal{M}_2 ::$ **var** *pc, dmem* •
    |[**var** $i \in$ *record, pc, offset, dmem*[*dlow..dhigh*], $reg[0..15], f$
    $pc := pc0$;
    do   *true* →
        IMEM(i); $pc := pc + 1$;
        if *offset*($i.op$) → *IMEM*(*offset*); $pc := pc + 1$
        [¬*offset*($i.op$) → *skip*
        fi;
        if ... as before ... **fi**
    od
    ]|: *IMEM*

$\mathcal{I} ::$ **var** *imem*; **proc** *IMEM* •
    |[**var** *imem*[*ilow..ihigh*]
    proc *IMEM*(**var** j) = ($j := imem[pc]$)
    ]|: *pc*

The instruction memory *imem* is now located in the module $\mathcal{I}$. The program counter, *pc*, is a shared variable between the two component modules. It is located in the module $\mathcal{M}_2$. Also the procedure *IMEM* has become global as it is accessed from $\mathcal{M}_2$. The instruction memory *imem* is not directly accessed in $\mathcal{M}_2$. However, both *pc* and *IMEM* are local to the parallel composition. Therefore this exports only the two memories, *imem* and *dmem*.

5.2 Program Counter

Our next step is to isolate the program counter and offset administration from the rest of the processor. The program counter pc is referenced at instruction and offset fetch and during the execution of the $stpc$, jmp, and $brch$ instructions.

Let us start by refining the pc updates at instruction fetch time as follows:

$$IMEM(k); pc := pc + 1$$
$$\leq \,|[\ \textbf{var}\ y;\ IMEM(k);\ y := pc + 1;\ pc := y\ ]|$$
$$\leq \,|[\ \textbf{var}\ y;\ y := pc + 1;\ IMEM(k);\ pc := y\ ]|$$
$$= \,|[\ \textbf{var}\ y;\ \textbf{proc}\ PCI1 = (y := pc + 1);\ \textbf{proc}\ PCI2 = (pc := y)\ ]|;$$
$$PCI1;\ IMEM(k);\ PCI2$$

where y is a fresh variable. We have refined the pc access into a separate read-access and a write-access. This will allow us a parallel pc update and instruction fetch as will become clear below. The pc update at the $brch$ instruction can be treated similarly:

$$pc := pc + \mathit{offset}$$
$$\leq \,|[\ \textbf{var}\ z;\ z := pc + \mathit{offset};\ pc := z\ ]|$$
$$= \,|[\ \textbf{var}\ z;\ \textbf{proc}\ PCA1 = (z := pc + \mathit{offset});\ \textbf{proc}\ PCA2 = (pc := z)\ ]|$$
$$PCA1;\ PCA2$$

The other two pc accesses are read-accesses and hence, correspond to procedure calls.

Now it is a straightforward task to make the pc accesses via procedures:

$\mathcal{P}_0 ::$ **var** $pc;$ **proc** $PCI1, PCI2, PCA1, PCA2, PCST, PCJMP \bullet$

    $|[\ \textbf{var}\ pc;$

      $|[\ \textbf{var}\ y, z$

        proc $PCI1 = (y := pc + 1);$

        proc $PCI2 = (pc := y);$

        proc $PCA1 = (z := pc + \mathit{offset});$

        proc $PCA2 = (pc := z);$

        proc $PCST(\textbf{var}\ o) = (o := pc);$

        proc $PCJMP(o) = (pc := o);$

      $]|;$

      $pc := pc0;$

    $]|:\ \mathit{offset}$

Every access to pc is now done via these procedures. For instance, the instruction fetch and the subsequent pc-update $IMEM(i); pc := pc + 1$ is transformed to

$$PCI1;\ IMEM(i);\ PCI2.$$

Furthermore, the pc update $pc := pc + \mathit{offset}$ in the branch instruction $brch$ is transformed to a pair of procedure calls

$$PCA1;\ PCA2.$$

The offset is read during the execution of the *ldx*, *stx*, and *lda* instructions. Furthermore, it is referenced at instruction fetch and during the program counter update at *brch* execution.

The *offset* value in the load and store instructions is received via a call to a procedure *XOFF* as follows:

$$reg[i.z] := dmem[offset + reg[i.y]]$$
$$\leq \;|[\; \textbf{var } off;\; off := offset;\; reg[i.z] := dmem[off + reg[i.y]]\;]|$$
$$= \;|[\; \textbf{proc } XOFF(\textbf{var } o) = (o := offset);$$
$$|[\; \textbf{var } off;\; XOFF(off);\; reg[i.z] := dmem[off + reg[i.y]]\;]|\;]|$$

The module for offset administration is defined next:

$\mathcal{X} ::$ **var** *offset*; **proc** *XOFF* •
   $|[\;$ **var** *offset*
      proc $XOFF(\textbf{var } o) = (o := offset)$
   $]|$:<>

We now have that

$$\mathcal{M}_2 = \textbf{var } dmem, pc \; \bullet \; |[\; \mathcal{M}_3 \;||\; \mathcal{P}_0 \;||\; \mathcal{X} \;]| : IMEM$$

where $\mathcal{M}_3$ is as follows:

$\mathcal{M}_3 ::$ **var** *dmem* •
  $|[\;$ **var** $i \in record,\; dmem[dlow..dhigh],\; reg[0..15], f$
    do $\;true \rightarrow$
       $PCI1;\; IMEM(i);\; PCI2;$
       if $offset(i.op) \rightarrow PCI1;\; IMEM(offset);\; PCI2$
       $[\!]\; \neg offset(i.op) \rightarrow skip$
       fi;
       if $alu(i.op) \rightarrow\; < reg[i.z], f >:= aluf(reg[i.x], reg[i.y], i.op, f)$
       $[\!]\; ld(i.op) \rightarrow reg[i.z] := dmem[reg[i.x] + reg[i.y]]$
       $[\!]\; st(i.op) \rightarrow dmem[reg[i.x] + reg[i.y]] := reg[i.z]$
       $[\!]\; ldx(i.op) \rightarrow$
         $|[\; \textbf{var } off;\; XOFF(off);\; reg[i.z] := dmem[off + reg[i.y]]\;]|$
       $[\!]\; stx(i.op) \rightarrow$
         $|[\; \textbf{var } off;\; XOFF(off);\; dmem[off + reg[i.y]] := reg[i.z]\;]|$
       $[\!]\; lda(i.op) \rightarrow$
         $|[\; \textbf{var } off;\; XOFF(off);\; reg[i.z] := off + reg[i.y]\;]|$
       $[\!]\; stpc(i.op) \rightarrow |[\; \textbf{var } r;\; PCST(r);\; reg[i.z] := r + reg[i.y]\;]|$
       $[\!]\; jmp(i.op) \rightarrow |[\; \textbf{var } y;\; y := reg[i.y];\; PCJMP(y)\;]|$
       $[\!]\; brch(i.op) \rightarrow$
         if $cond(f, i.cc) \rightarrow PCA1;\; PCA2\; [\!]\; \neg cond(f, i.cc) \rightarrow skip$ **fi**
       fi
    od
  $]|$: $IMEM, PCI1, PCI2, PCA1, PCA2, PCST, PCJMP, XOFF, offset$

Observe that *offset* is shared between $\mathcal{M}_3$, $\mathcal{P}_0$ and $\mathcal{X}$, whereas *pc* is shared between $\mathcal{M}_3$, $\mathcal{P}_0$ and $\mathcal{I}$. Therefore *offset* is a hidden variable. The variable *pc* is revealed from this parallel composition, because it is needed in the module $\mathcal{I}$.

Parallelize $\mathcal{P}_0$. Finally, $\mathcal{P}_0$ should allow parallel *pc* update and instruction fetch in $\mathcal{I}$. In the action systems framework this means that we have to relax the atomicity requirements of actions, i.e., we have to carry out an atomicity refinement. This is realized by the refinement $\mathcal{P}_0 \leq \mathcal{P}_1$ where

$\mathcal{P}_1 ::$ **var** *pc*; **proc** *PCI*1, *PCI*2, *PCA*1, *PCA*2, *PCST*, *PCJMP* •
$\quad$ |[**var** *pc*;
$\quad\quad$ |[**var** $y, z, b, ba \in$ *boolean*
$\quad\quad\quad$ **proc** $PCI1 = (\neg(b \vee ba) \rightarrow b := true)$;
$\quad\quad\quad$ **proc** $PCI2 = (\neg(b \vee ba) \rightarrow pc := y)$;
$\quad\quad\quad$ **proc** $PCA1 = (\neg(b \vee ba) \rightarrow ba := true)$;
$\quad\quad\quad$ **proc** $PCA2 = (\neg(b \vee ba) \rightarrow pc := z)$;
$\quad\quad\quad$ **proc** $PCST(\textbf{var } o) = (\neg(b \vee ba) \rightarrow o := pc)$;
$\quad\quad\quad$ **proc** $PCJMP(o) = (\neg(b \vee ba) \rightarrow pc := o)$;
$\quad\quad\quad$ $pc := pc0$;
$\quad\quad\quad$ $b, ba := false, false$;
$\quad\quad\quad$ **do**
$\quad\quad\quad\quad$ [] $b \rightarrow y := pc + 1$; $b := false$
$\quad\quad\quad\quad$ [] $ba \rightarrow z := pc + offset$; $ba := false$
$\quad\quad\quad$ **od**
$\quad\quad$]|
$\quad$]| : *offset*

Now both procedures *PCI*1 and *PCA*1 consist of two parts, the first part receives the request for *pc*-update as a result of a call from $\mathcal{M}_3$, after which the control returns to the caller. The program counter is updated in separate, autonomous actions in module $\mathcal{P}_1$ simultaneously with the fetch of the next statement in $\mathcal{M}_3$, i.e., the execution of $y := pc + 1$ and $IMEM(i)$ can overlap in time as well as the exection of $y := pc + 1$ and $IMEM(offset)$. Also the update $pc := pc + offset$ is now carried out by two separate atomic actions instead of one.

Observe that the effect of carrying out the above refinement is that of adding an explicit **return** statement into the procedures *PC*1 and *PCA*1, which is here considered as syntactic sugering for the procedures. We therefore write the following for short:

$\mathcal{P}_1 = $ **var** pc; **proc** $PCI1, PCI2, PCA1, PCA2, PCST, PCJMP \bullet$
  $|[$ **var** pc;
    $|[$ **var** y, z
      proc $PCI1 = (\textbf{return}; y := pc + 1)$;
      proc $PCI2 = (pc := y)$;
      proc $PCA1 = (\textbf{return}; z := pc + \mathit{offset})$;
      proc $PCA2 = (pc := z)$;
      proc $PCST(\textbf{var } o) = (o := pc)$;
      proc $PCJMP(o) = (pc := o)$;
    $]|$;
    $pc := pc0$;
  $]|: \mathit{offset}$

5.3 Other Components

Let us now briefly consider the registers, arithmetic-logical unit, data memory and the intruction execution. These modules are specified using similar argumentation as above.

Registers. First we isolate the register array from the rest of the program. The 16 registers are accessed through four busses in [14]. The busses are used by the ALU and the memory unit to concurrently access the registers. With this in mind we decompose our system further.

We define three procedures $REGRX$, $REGRY$, and $REGRZ$ to read the value stored in a register, corresponding to the x, y and z fields of an instruction i. Furthermore, the ALU and the memory unit will use different procedures (busses), $REGWA$ and $REGWM$ respectively, to write on the registers. The instruction under consideration is kept in a shared variable j which is imported to the register modules from $\mathcal{M}_3$.

Let $\mathcal{R}$ be the action system

$\mathcal{R} :: $ **proc** $REGRX, REGRY, REGRZ, REGWA, REGWM \bullet$
  $|[$ **var** $reg[0..15]$
    proc $REGRX(\textbf{var } v) = (v := reg[j.x])$
    proc $REGRY(\textbf{var } v) = (v := reg[j.y])$
    proc $REGRZ(\textbf{var } v) = (v := reg[j.z])$
    proc $REGWA(v) = (reg[j.z] := v)$
    proc $REGWM(v) = (reg[j.z] := v)$
  $]|: j$

This module represents the register array and also the four busses as will become clear later when we derive modules for the memory unit, the ALU and the instruction execution.

We now have that

$\mathcal{M}_3 = $ **var** $dmem \bullet |[\mathcal{M}_4 \| \mathcal{R}]| :$
    $IMEM, PCI1, PCI2, PCA1, PCA2, PCST, PCJMP, XOFF, \mathit{offset}$

where $\mathcal{M}_4$ is derived from $\mathcal{M}_3$ by the following changes. Each read-access to $reg[i.x]$ in $\mathcal{M}_3$ is replaced with a call to $REGRX$ in $\mathcal{M}_4$, every read-access to $reg[i.y]$ is replaced with $REGRY$ and every read-access to $reg[i.z]$ is replaced with $REGRZ$. A write-access to $reg[i.z]$ is replaced with a call to $REGWA$ when the ALU writes this register and with a call to $REGWM$ when the access is made from the memory unit as will be seen below. The register array $reg[0..15]$ is missing from $\mathcal{M}_4$.

The register module $\mathcal{R}$ and $\mathcal{M}_4$ communicate via a shared variable j which is exported from $\mathcal{M}_4$. The variable j is assigned the value i immediatly prior the execution of the instruction kept in i. This effect is achieved in $\mathcal{M}_4$ by refining $\mathcal{M}_3$ as follows:

$$
\begin{aligned}
&\textbf{if } \textit{offset}(i.op) \rightarrow \ldots \text{ as before } \ldots \textbf{ fi}; \\
&\textbf{if } \textit{alu}(i.op) \rightarrow \ldots \text{ as before } \ldots \textbf{ fi} \\
\leq \;&\textbf{if } \textit{offset}(i.op) \rightarrow \ldots \text{ as before } \ldots \textbf{ fi}; \\
&j := i; \\
&\textbf{if } \textit{alu}(i.op) \rightarrow \ldots \text{ as before } \ldots \textbf{ fi}
\end{aligned}
$$

In the full paper [5] we refine the registers further in order to allow more parallelism. In the final confifuration each of the 16 registers constitutes a module of its own.

Arithmetic-Logical Unit. Our following task is to isolate the arithmetic-logical unit. This unit is accessed in the *alu* instruction execution. As mentioned above, it has its own buss to access the register array, modelled by the procedure $REGWA$. Hence, this piece of code is refined as follows:

$$
\begin{aligned}
&< reg[i.z], f >:= aluf(reg[i.x], reg[i.y], i.op, f) \\
\leq \;&\{ \text{ introducing register procedures, from above } \} \\
&|[\textbf{ var } x, y;\ REGRX(x),\ REGRY(y); \\
&\quad |[\textbf{ var } v;\ < v, f >:= aluf(x, y, i.op, f);\ REGWA(v) \;]|\;]|
\end{aligned}
$$

from where it is a straightforward task to generate the module for the arithmetic-logical unit:

$$
\begin{aligned}
\mathcal{A} ::\;& \textbf{proc } ALU, ALUF \bullet \\
&|[\textbf{ var } f \\
&\quad \textbf{proc } ALU(u, w, op) = \\
&\qquad (|[\textbf{ var } v;\ < v, f >:= aluf(u, w, op, f);\ REGWA(v) \;]|); \\
&\quad \textbf{proc } ALUF(\textbf{var } e) = (e := f) \\
&]|:\ REGWA
\end{aligned}
$$

The $ALUF$ procedure is used during the *brch* execution to read the value of the flag f.

We now have that

$$\mathcal{M}_4 = \textbf{var } dmem \ \bullet \|[\ \mathcal{M}_5 \ \| \ \mathcal{A} \ ]\| :$$
$$IMEM, PCI1, PCI2, PCA1, PCA2, PCST, PCJMP, XOFF, \textit{offset}$$

where for instance the above ALU reference in $\mathcal{M}_4$ is transformed to a call to the ALU unit as follows

$$\|[\ \textbf{var } x, y; \ REGRX(x); \ REGRY(y); \ ALU(x, y, i.op) \ ]\|$$

Data Memory. Let us now consider the data memory, *dmem*. It also has its own buss to access the registers, modelled by the procedures $REGRZ$ and $REGWM$. The data memory is read during the execution of the *ld* and *ldx* instructions and it is written during the store instructions *st* and *stx*. In the final implementation, the execution of the *lda* instruction is also carried out via the data memory unit. Let us look at the *ld* and *st* instructions more carefully.

We have for the load instruction that

$$reg[i.z] := dmem[reg[i.x] + reg[i.y]]$$
$$\leq \{ \text{ introducing register procedures, from above } \}$$
$$\|[\ \textbf{var } x, y; \ REGRX(x); \ REGRY(y);$$
$$\|[\ \textbf{var } v; \ v := dmem[x + y]; \ REGWM(v) \ ]\| \ ]\|$$

and for the store instruction that

$$dmem[reg[i.x] + reg[i.y]] := reg[i.z]$$
$$\leq \{ \text{ introducing register procedures, from above } \}$$
$$\|[\ \textbf{var } x, y; \ REGRX(x); \ REGRY(y);$$
$$\|[\ \textbf{var } v; \ REGRZ(v); \ dmem[x + y] := v \ ]\| \ ]\|$$

We now define

$\mathcal{D} ::$ $\textbf{var } dmem; \textbf{ proc } MADD, MSTO, MLDA \ \bullet$
     $\|[\ \textbf{var } dmem[dlow..dhigh]$
        $\textbf{proc } MADD(u, w) = (\|[\ \textbf{var } v; \ v := dmem[u + w]; \ REGWM(v) \ ]\|);$
        $\textbf{proc } MSTO(u, w) =$
                 $(\textbf{return}; \|[\ \textbf{var } v; \ REGRZ(v); \ dmem[u + w] := v \ ]\|);$
        $\textbf{proc } MLDA(u, w) = (\|[\ \textbf{var } ma; \ ma := u + w; \ REGWM(ma) \ ]\|);$
     $]\|: REGWM, REGRZ$

The memory is now represented by the following module:

$$\textbf{var } dmem; \textbf{ proc } MADD, MSTO, MLDA \ \bullet \mathcal{D} : REGWM, REGRZ$$

which exports the three memory access procedures $MADD$, $MSTO$, and $MLDA$ and imports the buss, i.e., the procedures $REGWM$ and $REGRZ$.

The memory unit is taken apart from the module $\mathcal{M}_5$. Therefore, we have that

$\mathcal{M}_5 = \mathbf{var}\ dmem\ \bullet |[\ \mathcal{M}_6\ ||\ \mathcal{D}\ ]|$:

$\quad\quad IMEM, PCI1, PCI2, PCA1, PCA2, PCST, PCJMP, XOFF, offset,$

$\quad\quad REGWM, REGRZ$

In $\mathcal{M}_6$ we have replaced the direct memory accesses with the appropriate procedure calls, for instance the above refined load and store instructions are transformed to

$$|[\ \mathbf{var}\ x, y;\ REGRX(x);\ REGRY(y);\ MADD(x, y)\ ]|$$

and

$$|[\ \mathbf{var}\ x, y;\ REGRX(x);\ REGRY(y);\ MSTO(x, y)\ ]|$$

in $\mathcal{M}_6$ respectively.

A slightly more optimised version of the memory unit is derived in the full paper [5].

Instruction Execution. We next isolate the instruction execution into a separate module:

$\mathcal{E} ::\ \mathbf{var}\ j;\ \mathbf{proc}\ EXEC\ \bullet$

$\quad |[\ \mathbf{var}\ j \in record$

$\quad\quad \mathbf{proc}\ EXEC(k) =$

$\quad\quad\quad (j := k;$

$\quad\quad\quad \mathbf{if}\ alu(k.op) \rightarrow \mathbf{return};$

$\quad\quad\quad\quad |[\ \mathbf{var}\ x, y;\ REGRX(x);\ REGRY(y);\ ALU(x, y, k.op)\ ]|$

$\quad\quad\quad \llbracket\ ld(k.op) \rightarrow \mathbf{return};$

$\quad\quad\quad\quad |[\ \mathbf{var}\ x, y;\ REGRX(x);\ REGRY(y);\ MADD(x, y)\ ]|$

$\quad\quad\quad \llbracket\ st(k.op) \rightarrow \mathbf{return};$

$\quad\quad\quad\quad |[\ \mathbf{var}\ x, y;\ REGRX(x);\ REGRY(y);\ MSTO(x, y)\ ]|$

$\quad\quad\quad \llbracket\ ldx(k.op) \rightarrow$

$\quad\quad\quad\quad |[\ \mathbf{var}\ off, y;\ XOFF(off);\ REGRY(y);\ MADD(off, y)\ ]|$

$\quad\quad\quad \llbracket\ stx(k.op) \rightarrow$

$\quad\quad\quad\quad |[\ \mathbf{var}\ off, y;\ XOFF(off);\ REGRY(y);\ MSTO(off, y)\ ]|$

$\quad\quad\quad \llbracket\ lda(k.op) \rightarrow$

$\quad\quad\quad\quad |[\ \mathbf{var}\ off, y;\ XOFF(off);\ REGRY(y);\ MLDA(off, y)\ ]|$

$\quad\quad\quad \llbracket\ stpc(k.op) \rightarrow$

$\quad\quad\quad\quad |[\ \mathbf{var}\ r, y;\ PCST(r);\ REGRY(y);\ ALU(r, y, add)\ ]|$

$\quad\quad\quad \llbracket\ jmp(k.op) \rightarrow |[\ \mathbf{var}\ y;\ REGRY(y);\ PCJMP(y)\ ]|$

$\quad\quad\quad \llbracket\ brch(k.op) \rightarrow |[\ \mathbf{var}\ ff;\ ALUF(ff);$

$\quad\quad\quad\quad\quad\quad\quad\quad \mathbf{if}\ cond(ff, k.cc) \rightarrow PCA1;\ PCA2$

$\quad\quad\quad\quad\quad\quad\quad\quad \llbracket\ \neg cond(ff, k.cc) \rightarrow skip$

$\quad\quad\quad\quad\quad\quad\quad\quad \mathbf{fi}\ ]|$

$\quad\quad\quad \mathbf{fi})$

$\quad]|{:}PCA1, PCA2, PCST, PCJMP, XOFF, REGRX, REGRY,$

$\quad\quad ALU, ALUF, MADD, MSTO, MLDA$

The instruction under execution is in this module represented by the variable j, which is shared with the register array. The module uses two busses, modelled by the procedures $REGRX$ and $REGRY$ respective, for additional communication with the registers. We have replaced all the register, pc, $offset$, memory, and ALU references with appropriate procedure calls. Observe that the pc update during $stpc$ execution is carred out via a call to ALU.

This gives us the system

$$\mathcal{M}_6 = \textbf{var } j \bullet |[\, \mathcal{M}_7 \,\|\, \mathcal{E} \,]| :$$
$$IMEM, PCI1, PCI2, PCA1, PCA2, PCST, PCJMP, XOFF,$$
$$REGRX, REGRY, ALU, ALUF, MADD, MSTO, MLDA$$

where the execution of an instruction in the variable i in $\mathcal{M}_7$ is now initiated via a procedure call

$$EXEC(i).$$

5.4 Refine the Fetch-and-Execute Cycle

Finally, we refine the fetch and execute cycle to make parallel instruction fetch and execution possible. In our framework, as mentioned earlier, we have to create independent actions in order to make parallel activity possible. This calls for atomicity refinement.

Create FETCH. Let us first collect all the transformations above, and see what is left of the action system $\mathcal{M}_3$, i.e., the system $\mathcal{M}_7$ above. The procedures $EXEC$ and its related ALU together with the instruction and data memories, register array, and pc and $offset$ administration were all isolated into action systems of their own, separate from $\mathcal{M}_3$ leaving only the appropriate procedure calls behind. The result is the system $\mathcal{M}_7$ that will be from here on called $\mathcal{F}_0$ where

$$\mathcal{F}_0 :: \quad |[\quad \textbf{var } i \in record$$

$$\textbf{do} \quad true \rightarrow$$
$$PCI1; IMEM(i); PCI2;$$
$$\textbf{if } offset(i.op) \rightarrow PCI1; IMEM(offset); PCI2$$
$$[\!] \neg offset(i.op) \rightarrow skip$$
$$\textbf{fi};$$
$$EXEC(i)$$
$$\textbf{od}$$
$$]|: offset, IMEM, PCI1, PCI2, EXEC$$

In this system there is only one atomic action and no parallelism is possible. Hence, we split the action into two distinct parts so that $\mathcal{F}_0 \leq \mathcal{F}_1$ where

$\mathcal{F}_1 ::$ $\lVert$ **var** $i \in record;$
    $\lVert$ **var** $be \in boolean;$
      $be := false;$
      do $\neg be \to$
          $PCI1; IMEM(i); PCI2;$
          if $offset(i.op) \to PCI1; IMEM(offset); PCI2$
          $\rVert \neg offset(i.op) \to skip$
          fi;
          $be := true$
      $\rVert$ $be \to$
          $be := false;$
          $EXEC(i)$
      od
    $\rVert$
  $\rVert: offset, IMEM, PCI1, PCI2, EXEC$

We have that $\mathcal{F}_1$ and $\mathcal{E}$ share no variables. They communicate through the global procedure $EXEC$ only. When looking into the specification of the procedure $EXEC$ we notice, that when we are executing an ALU, load or store instruction, the control returns to $\mathcal{F}_1$ immediatly after the call of $EXEC$ due to the **return** statements. At this point the next instruction is fetched from the instruction memory. Hence, the execution of these three instructions in $\mathcal{E}$ can proceed in parallel with the fetch of the next instruction in $\mathcal{F}_1$.

Sequential Notation. We can use sequential notation for $\mathcal{F}_1$ by removing the boolean be and denoting the atomicity explicitly with brackets:

$\mathcal{F}_1 =$ $\lVert$ **var** $i \in record$
    do
    $< PCI1; IMEM(i); PCI2;$
    if $offset(i.op) \to PCI1; IMEM(offset); PCI2$
    $\rVert \neg offset(i.op) \to skip$
    fi $> ;$
    $< EXEC(i) >$
    od
  $\rVert: offset, IMEM, PCI1, PCI2, EXEC$

6 Concluding Remarks

We have created the action system $\mathcal{M}_8$

$$\mathcal{M}_8 :: \textbf{var } imem, dmem \; \bullet \lVert[\, \mathcal{I} \parallel \mathcal{F}_1 \parallel \mathcal{P}_1 \parallel \mathcal{X} \parallel \mathcal{E} \parallel \mathcal{A} \parallel \mathcal{D} \parallel \mathcal{R} \,]\rVert :<>$$

that is by construction a correct refinement of the initial high level microprocessor specification $\mathcal{M}_0$, i.e.,

$$\mathcal{M}_0 \leq \mathcal{M}_8.$$

At Caltech, a delay-insensitive circuit is derived from a concurrent program that is essentialy the same as our resulting action system [14]. The main advantage of our method is that it is based on a completely formal calculus for reasoning about programs, the refinement calculus.

The main method used throughout our derivation was the spatial decomposition of an action system into a parallel compostion of action systems that mainly communicate via (remote) procedure calls. Hence, most of the steps we carried out are correct by construction. Only a couple of steps required more tedious proofs, i.e., those where the atomicity of the system was refined and **return** from a procedure was propagated backwards.

When we compare our system to that in [14] there are a couple of notions that are implicit in an action system. The bullet-operator used in [14] corresponds to an action in the sense that when an action is chosen for execution, it is jointly executed to completion by the involved modules without interference from other actions. The point of termination for an action need not the coincide for every module involved in it as long as atomicity is guaranteed. The probes in [14] are here modelled by the interplay between the caller and the callee while making procedure calls.

Acknowledgements

The work reported here was supported by the Academy of Finland.

References

1. R. J. R. Back. *On the Correctness of Refinement Steps in Program Development.* PhD thesis, Department of Computer Science, University of Helsinki, Helsinki, Finland, 1978. Report A–1978–4.
2. R. J. R. Back. *Procedural abstraction in the refinement calculus.* Technical Report, Åbo Akademi University, Department of Computer Science. Turku, Finland 1987.
3. R. J. R. Back. Refinement calculus, part II: Parallel and reactive programs. In J. W. de Bakker, W.–P. de Roever, and G. Rozenberg, editors, *Stepwise Refinement of Distributed Systems: Models, Formalisms, Correctness. Proceedings. 1989*, volume 430 of *Lecture Notes in Computer Science.* Springer–Verlag, 1990.
4. R. J. R. Back and R. Kurki-Suonio. Decentralization of process nets with centralized control. In *Proc. of the 2nd ACM SIGACT-SIGOPS Symp. on Principles of Distributed Computing*, pages 131–142, 1983.
5. R. J. R. Back, A. J. Martin, and K. Sere. *Specification of a Microprocessor.* Technical Report, Åbo Akademi University, Department of Computer Science. Ser. A, No 148, Turku, Finland 1992.
6. R. J. R. Back and K. Sere. Stepwise refinement of parallel algorithms. *Science of Computer Programming* 13, pages 133–180, 1989.
7. R. J. R. Back and K. Sere. Action systems with synchronous communication. Proc. of *PROCOMET'94*, San Miniato, Italy, June 1994. E.-R. Olderog, editor, *Programming Concepts, Methods and Calculi*, IFIP Transactions A-56, pages 107–126, North–Holland 1994.

8. R. J. R. Back and K. Sere. From modular systems to action systems. Proc. of *Formal Methods Europe'94*, Spain, October 1994. *Lecture Notes in Computer Science.* Springer–Verlag, 1994.

9. J. Bowen et al.. A ProCoS II Project Description: ESPRIT Basic Research project 7071. In *Bulletin of the EATCS*, volume 50, pages 128–137, June 1993.

10. K. Chandy and J. Misra. *Parallel Program Design: A Foundation.* Addison–Wesley, 1988.

11. E. W. Dijkstra. *A Discipline of Programming.* Prentice–Hall International, 1976.

12. N. Francez. Cooperating proofs for distributed programs with multiparty interactions. *Information Processing Letters*, 32:235–242, 1989.

13. T. Kuusela, J. Plosila, R. Ruksenas, K. Sere, and Zhao Yi. Designing delay-insensitive circuits within the action systems framework. Manuscript, 1995.

14. A. J. Martin. Synthesis of Asynchronous VLSI Circuits. *CalTech*, Technical Report, 1993.

15. C. C. Morgan. The specification statement. *ACM Transactions on Programming Languages and Systems*, 10(3):403–419, July 1988.

16. C. C. Morgan, K. A. Robinson, and P. H. B. Gardiner. *On the Refinement Calculus.* Technical Monograph PRG-70, Programming Research Group, Oxford University, October 1988.

17. J. M. Morris. A theoretical basis for stepwise refinement and the programming calculus. *Science of Computer Programming*, 9:287–306, 1987.

18. K. Sere *Stepwise Refinement of Parallel Algorithms.* PhD thesis, Department of Computer Science, Åbo Akademi University, Turku, Finland, 1990.

19. J. Staunstrup and M. R. Greenstreet. *Synchronized Transitions.* IFIP WG 10.5, Summer school on Formal Methods for VLSI Design, Lecture Notes 1990.

Formal Derivation of CSP Programs From Temporal Specifications

Rudolf Berghammer and Burghard von Karger*

Institut für Informatik und Praktische Mathematik
Christian-Albrechts-Universität Kiel
Preusserstraße 1–9
D–24105 Kiel, Germany

Abstract. The algebra of relations has been very successful for reasoning about possibly non-deterministic programs, provided their behaviour can be fully characterized by just their initial and final states. We use a slight generalization, called *sequential algebra*, to extend the scope of relation-algebraic methods to reactive systems, where the behaviour between initiation and termination is also important. To illustrate this approach, we integrate Communicating Sequential Processes and linear temporal logic in sequential algebra and show that the associated calculus permits the formal derivation of CSP programs from temporal specifications.

1 Introduction

CSP is a process language for describing concurrent agents that cooperate via synchronous communication [12]. It is the conceptual core of the occam programming language. The theory of CSP and occam is anchored in denotational semantics [3, 21, 11], which has been used to establish algebraic identities between processes [14]. The collection of these laws constitutes a mechanizable calculus for process transformations [10]. We aim at an extension to a *design calculus* which allows the derivation of processes from abstract descriptions of their desired behaviour. The calculational approach to program derivation is by now traditional (see, for example, [6, 20, 4, 18]).

Since most errors in software engineering result from erroneous descriptions of the intended behaviour, it is vital that these specifications be as clear and concise as possible. The language CSP is oriented towards implementability, and less suitable for expressing specifications. Some desirable specification operations, especially the temporal connectives, are not even definable in the standard models of CSP given in [3, 21]. We build a new model, which is based on sequential algebra and blends the relational calculus with interval logic.

---

* The second author has been funded by the Deutsche Forschungsgemeinschaft under grant KA 1052/1-1.

A system (reactive or otherwise) may be described as a set whose elements represent single observations of a single experiment on it. This allows modelling non-deterministic choice as set union, refinement as set inclusion and, cum grano salis, parallel composition as set intersection. The set of all such system descriptions has the structure of a complete Boolean algebra. Besides the purely set-theoretic operations we also need to express time-wise composition of systems. The addition of an associative sequence operation leads from Boolean algebra to sequential algebra [15, 17]. It is distinguished from the algebra of relations[2] by the absence of a converse operation $R \mapsto R^\mathsf{T}$. This is justified by the irreversible nature of observations on reactive systems: Once an event (a communication) has happened, it cannot be cancelled or undone by what comes after. The lack of a converse operation is somewhat compensated by the existence of quotient operations which allow a style of reasoning very similar to that of the relational calculus.

By abandoning the converse operation we accept the irreversibility of time and enable temporal reasoning. In [17] a fragment of interval temporal logic is developed within sequential algebra. The operations of linear temporal logic are also definable in sequential algebra; see [16], where it is also shown that the axioms of the complete proof system given in [19] for this logic are in fact theorems of the sequential calculus. This allows us to integrate CSP with temporal logic, a well-understood tool for specifying reactive systems. Mixed terms may be constructed using arbitrary combinations of temporal operators and CSP constructs. In this framework executable programs can be derived from, or verified against, temporal specifications.

A full design calculus for the CSP language is a very ambitious objective, and a first approach must make some simplifying assumptions. The transformation calculus of CSP started from the trace model; only when that was well-understood, it was extended to capture deadlock, livelock, timing, probability, etc. Similarly, a design calculus for CSP must start from a trace model; more sophisticated observables may be added later. To avoid unnecessary duplication, however, we will endeavour to develop the theory as model-independent as possible.

In Section 2 we develop the algebra of sequence (composition) and quotients on which the sequential calculus is founded, and we demonstrate how it may be used as an algebraic foundation of temporal logic. Then, in Section 3, we move from a single sort to the many-sorted case; this gives us operations for hiding, concurrency, and synchronization. Altogether, in these two sections we integrate both CSP and temporal operators in sequential algebra. The power of the calculus to express specifications is illustrated by some examples in Section 4. In this section we show also how they may be transformed into programs. In the concluding section, we indicate further applications of the ideas underlying this paper.

---

[2] The axiomatic version of the relational calculus was developed by Tarski and his co-workers (see, for example, [25, 7]). Some applications to computer science can be found in [2, 22, 5, 13, 1].

2 Boolean Operations, Sequence and Quotients

The hardest task in modelling reactive systems is in choosing the right set of possible observations. Rather than fix a particular domain of observations, such as set of pairs as in the relational calculus, as set of words as in the case of regular expressions, or as set of functions from time intervals to states as in temporal logic, a general reactive system theory should only rely on their properties, thereby retaining flexibility. In Section 2.1 we discuss the algebraic properties of individual observations. Both as an example and in preparation for later sections we introduce an observation space for describing CSP processes and giving meaning to temporal formulae. The operations on single observations can be lifted to operations on system descriptions (sets of observations). These are the objects of our calculus. Its theorems can be proved from the properties of the observations. However, such proofs are considered undesirable, because they are not calculational. Instead we will single out a small number of theorems and call them *axioms* of sequential algebra. The sequential calculus is the body of algebraic laws provable from the axioms.

2.1 Observation Spaces

We are mainly interested in properties shared by many different kinds of observations. The most basic property is the existence of a *composition operation* which makes a possibly longer observation $x; y$ from sub-observations x and y. We require the associative law

$$(x; y); z = x; (y; z). \tag{O_1}$$

The composition operation need not be total. For example, if R_1 and R_2 are relations then the composition of $(r_1, s_1) \in R_1$ and $(r_2, s_2) \in R_2$ is only defined if $s_1 = r_2$, and when this equality holds then $(r_1, s_1); (r_2, s_2) =_{def} (r_1, s_2)$. To help reasoning about the definedness of composition, we introduce two functions between observations. Each observation has a *left unit* $\overleftarrow{x}$ and a *right unit* $\overrightarrow{x}$, which satisfy the unit properties for composition:

$$\overleftarrow{x}; x = x \qquad\qquad x; \overrightarrow{x} = x \tag{O_2}$$

For example, in the relational case the left unit of (r, s) is (r, r) and the right unit of the same pair is (s, s). Now definedness of composition is described by the law

$$x; y \text{ is defined} \iff \overrightarrow{x} = \overleftarrow{y}. \tag{O_3}$$

In the following it is understood that $\overrightarrow{x} = \overleftarrow{y}$ whenever we write $x; y$. The unit functions have some additional properties. They map units to themselves,

$$\overleftarrow{\overleftarrow{x}} = \overrightarrow{\overleftarrow{x}} = \overleftarrow{x} \qquad\qquad \overrightarrow{\overrightarrow{x}} = \overleftarrow{\overrightarrow{x}} = \overrightarrow{x}, \tag{O_4}$$

and they depend only on the left or right operands of composition:

$$\overleftarrow{x; y} = \overleftarrow{x} \qquad\qquad \overrightarrow{x; y} = \overrightarrow{y}. \tag{O_5}$$

Two observations that have identical first parts are equal if and only if they also have identical second parts (and vice versa). This is expressed by the rules of cancellation

$$x_1; y = x_2; y \implies x_1 = x_2 \qquad\qquad x; y_1 = x; y_2 \implies y_1 = y_2. \qquad (O_6)$$

To formalize the idea that time can only progress in a single dimension, we introduce a prefix preorder on observations. We call x a *prefix* of y (and write $x \preceq y$) if there is some z with $x; z = y$. The following postulate is known as the *local linearity*, or *antilattice* property:

$$(x \preceq z) \wedge (y \preceq z) \implies (x \preceq y) \vee (y \preceq x). \qquad (O_7)$$

To summarize, an *observation space* $\mathcal{O}$ is a non-empty set equipped with a (partially defined) composition operation ; and two total unary functions $\overleftarrow{}$ and $\overrightarrow{}$ such that (O_1) through (O_7) hold.

2.2   Observations of Communicating Sequential Processes

A simple observation space that already is useful for reasoning about "classical" CSP is the set A^* of all *finite sequences* of events drawn from a set A. Here composition equals concatenation and the empty sequence ϵ is the left and right unit of every $t \in A^*$. Adding special observations representing deadlocks and divergences, one arrives at the standard models for CSP [3, 21].

We need a sequential algebra in which not only the CSP operations but also the temporal connectives can be defined. Temporal formulas can describe what happens in the future (or the past), so observations will carry information about the history and the continuation of the present experiment.

Let A^∞ denote the set of all *finite or infinite sequences* over A. We define

$$\mathcal{O}_A =_{def} \{ (t, i, j) \in A^\infty \times \mathbf{N}_\infty \times \mathbf{N}_\infty \mid 0 \le i \le j \le |t| \}, \qquad (C_1)$$

where $\mathbf{N}_\infty =_{def} \mathbf{N} \cup \{\infty\}$ and $|t| \in \mathbf{N}_\infty$ denotes the length of a trace $t \in A^\infty$. An observation (t, i, j) may be pictured as a window with contents t and currently visible part $t_{i+1} \dots t_j$ (where t_n denotes the nth element of t). It is convenient to think of the sub-trace $t_1 \dots t_i$ as the past and the sub-trace $t_{j+1} t_{j+2} \dots$ as the future, respectively. Two windows may be composed when they are adjacent and have the same contents. Thus, we define on $\mathcal{O}_A$ a partial composition operation by

$$(t, i, j); (t, j, k) =_{def} (t, i, k). \qquad (C_2)$$

For all other patterns, composition is not defined. The left and right units of a window (t, i, j) have no width; they just mark a division of a trace into a past and a future part:

$$\overleftarrow{(t, i, j)} =_{def} (t, i, i) \qquad\qquad \overrightarrow{(t, i, j)} =_{def} (t, j, j). \qquad (C_3)$$

We invite the reader to check that the observation space defined by (C_1) through (C_3) satisfies the postulates (O_1) through (O_7). But $\mathcal{O}_A$ has interesting additional properties. For example, the only observations that have an inverse are the unit observations. In other words, unit observations cannot be decomposed, except trivially:

$$x; y \text{ is a unit} \implies x \text{ is a unit and } y \text{ is a unit}. \tag{O_8}$$

Another distinguishing feature of $\mathcal{O}_A$ is that each observation carries within it a knowledge of the entire past and future. Two windows that have the same left or right unit must have the same contents and can differ only in size. In the case of left units this is expressed by

$$\overleftarrow{x} = \overleftarrow{y} \implies (x \preceq y) \vee (y \preceq x), \tag{O_9}$$

which is an immediate consequence of (C_2) and (C_3). An observation space satisfying (O_9) and its time-wise dual (saying that observations with identical right units are comparable in the postfix preorder) is called *deterministic*, because from every observation the entire past and future can be inferred – in other words: from each state there is only one way to continue.

2.3 Sequential Calculus

Let $\mathcal{O}$ be an observation space. The objective of sequential algebra is to formalize a calculus of the subsets of $\mathcal{O}$. The powerset $2^{\mathcal{O}}$ obviously forms a complete Boolean algebra with union $\cup$, intersection $\cap$, complement $^-$, ordering $\subseteq$, least element $0 =_{def} \emptyset$ and greatest element $L =_{def} \mathcal{O}$. Just as relational composition is a lifted form of the composition of pairs (cf. Section 2.1), our more general sequential composition is obtained by lifting the composition defined for single observations to sets by

$$PQ =_{def} \{z \mid \exists x \in P, y \in Q : x; y = z\}. \tag{S_1}$$

The identity element of composition is the set of all units:

$$I =_{def} \{x \mid \overleftarrow{x} = x = \overrightarrow{x}\}. \tag{S_2}$$

The absence of a converse operation forces us to define the *right quotient* $P \overset{\top}{;} Q$ to play the same role that $PQ^{\top}$ plays in the relational calculus. Each observation of $P \overset{\top}{;} Q$ is obtained from an observation of P by cutting from the end something that is an observation of Q. Formally,

$$P \overset{\top}{;} Q =_{def} \{x \mid \exists z \in P, y \in Q : x; y = z\}. \tag{S_3}$$

Its symmetric counterpart is the *left quotient* operation defined by

$$Q \overset{\top}{;} P =_{def} \{y \mid \exists z \in P, x \in Q : x; y = z\}. \tag{S_4}$$

We rule that composition binds more strongly than the quotient operations, and, in turn, these bind more strongly than $\cup$ and $\cap$.

Now we perform a classical abstraction step by selecting a set of theorems valid in the above setup and taking these as the axioms of a new algebraic structure.

1 Definition. A *sequential algebra* S is a complete Boolean algebra equipped with three binary operations $\cdot$ (denoted by juxtaposition), $\overset{\scriptscriptstyle\top}{;}$ and $;^{\scriptscriptstyle\top}$ and a constant I such that $(S, \cdot, I)$ is a monoid and the axioms

$$PQ \subseteq \overline{R} \iff P\,\overset{\scriptscriptstyle\top}{;}R \subseteq \overline{Q} \iff R\,;^{\scriptscriptstyle\top}Q \subseteq \overline{P}$$
$$PQ\,;^{\scriptscriptstyle\top}R = P(Q\,;^{\scriptscriptstyle\top}R) \cup P\,\overset{\scriptscriptstyle\top}{;}(R\,;^{\scriptscriptstyle\top}Q)$$

(called *Schröder law* resp. *split axiom*) hold. $\square$

The Schröder law corresponds to the same law from the relational calculus (see [23]), except that PQ^{T} and $P^{\mathsf{T}}Q$ are replaced by $P\,\overset{\scriptscriptstyle\top}{;}Q$ and $P\,\overset{\scriptscriptstyle\top}{;}Q$. With the definitions (S_1) through (S_4) we obtain a sequential algebra, which we call the *sequential set algebra* (over the observation space $\mathcal{O}$). In such a model, the set $PQ\,;^{\scriptscriptstyle\top}R$ describes all observations obtained from PQ by cutting off the right something in R. The split axiom then requires the cut to be placed after (described by $P(Q\,;^{\scriptscriptstyle\top}R)$) or before (described by $P\,\overset{\scriptscriptstyle\top}{;}(R\,;^{\scriptscriptstyle\top}Q)$) the transition from P to Q. We need not postulate its symmetric counterpart, because it can be proved as a theorem. The sequential calculus enjoys a perfect symmetry between past and future and with every theorem we prove we get for free its time-wise dual.

We note that every relation algebra can be made into a sequential algebra by *defining* the quotient operations by $P\,;^{\scriptscriptstyle\top}Q =_{def} PQ^{\mathsf{T}}$ and $P\,\overset{\scriptscriptstyle\top}{;}Q =_{def} P^{\mathsf{T}}Q$.

2 Additional Postulates. Assume S to be a sequential set algebra over an observation space $\mathcal{O}$. Then the *atomicity axiom*

$$\mathsf{L}\bar{\mathsf{I}}\mathsf{L} = \bar{\mathsf{I}}$$

holds in S just when $\mathcal{O}$ satisfies postulate (O_8), the indivisibility of units. Similarly, the *determinacy axioms*

$$(P\,;^{\scriptscriptstyle\top}\mathsf{L})\mathsf{L} = (P\mathsf{L})\,;^{\scriptscriptstyle\top}\mathsf{L} \qquad \mathsf{L}(\mathsf{L}\,\overset{\scriptscriptstyle\top}{;}P) = \mathsf{L}\,\overset{\scriptscriptstyle\top}{;}(\mathsf{L}P).$$

hold in S if and only if the underlying observation space satisfies (O_9) and its time-wise dual, i.e., is deterministic. In the remainder of the paper we assume the axioms of determinacy and atomicity because they are needed to prove certain properties of the temporal operations defined below (e.g., the conjunctivity of the 'next' operation). See [16] for details. $\square$

Now we introduce a number of concepts and operations for reasoning about programs and specifications. Their definitions refer only to the operations of sequential algebra, and we shall use only properties that can be proved from its axioms.

3 Transitions. The smallest measurements of progress are non-unit observations that cannot be further decomposed into non-unit sub-observations. Such observations correspond to single transitions of the observed system. A formal algebraic definition of the *set of all transitions* is

$$\text{step} =_{def} \bar{\mathsf{I}} \cap \bar{\bar{\mathsf{II}}}.$$

Besides **step**, we need also **step***, where *reflexive-transitive closure* of an element $P \in \mathcal{S}$ is defined as usual as union of all powers P^n. In the case of a sequential set algebra over the specific observation space $\mathcal{O}_A$ of Section 2.2, the set **step** contains exactly the triples $(t, i, i+1)$ with $i \in \mathbf{N}$ and, hence, **step*** consists of the elements $(t, i, j) \in \mathcal{O}_A$ with $i, j \in \mathbf{N}$ or $i = j = \infty$. □

4 Representing Sets by Predicates. In the relational calculus, a state s can be represented by the observation (s, s). This leads to a description of sets of states, or predicates on states, by sub-relations of the identity relation. In the sequential calculus, *states are represented by units* and so we call P a *predicate* if $P \subseteq \mathsf{I}$.

By convention, in the following, B and C always denote predicates. With negation, conjunction, and disjunction defined as

$$\neg B =_{def} \overline{B} \cap \mathsf{I} \qquad B \vee C =_{def} B \cup C \qquad B \wedge C =_{def} B \cap C$$

the set of all predicates forms a Boolean algebra with least element $\mathsf{F} =_{def} \mathsf{O}$ and greatest element $\mathsf{T} =_{def} \mathsf{I}$. As usual, we define implication by

$$B \rightarrow C =_{def} \neg B \vee C.$$ □

5 Domain and Co-Domain. As in the relational calculus, every element P from a sequential algebra can be projected to its *domain* $\overleftarrow{P}$ or *co-domain* $\overrightarrow{P}$. These predicates are defined by

$$\overleftarrow{P} =_{def} \mathsf{I} \cap (P \mathbin{;}^{\mathsf{T}} P) \qquad \overrightarrow{P} =_{def} \mathsf{I} \cap (P^{\mathsf{T}} \mathbin{;} P).$$

A more elegant definition consists of the following Galois connections:

$$P \subseteq B\mathsf{L} \iff \overleftarrow{P} \subseteq B \qquad P \subseteq \mathsf{L}B \iff \overrightarrow{P} \subseteq B. \tag{D}$$

In a sequential set algebra, $\overleftarrow{P} = \{\overleftarrow{x} \mid x \in P\}$ and $\overrightarrow{P} = \{\overrightarrow{x} \mid x \in P\}$. □

6 Temporal Operations. In a sequential set algebra, the predicate $\bigcirc B$ ('next B') holds at some state s if there is an observation $x \in \text{step}$ with $\overrightarrow{x} \in B$, and $\overleftarrow{x} = s$. Taking as an example the observation space $\mathcal{O}_A$ of Section 2.2, we have $\bigcirc B$ at a state (t, i, i) just when B holds at $(t, i+1, i+1)$. Using the operations of 3 and 5, we are able to define $\bigcirc$ and its time-wise dual, the 'previous' operator $\ominus$, without reference to states by

$$\bigcirc B =_{def} \overleftarrow{\text{step } B} \qquad \ominus B =_{def} \overrightarrow{B \text{ step}}.$$

The operations 'eventually', 'henceforth', 'until', 'first' and their time-wise duals 'once', 'always has been', 'since', 'last' are defined by

$$\Diamond B =_{def} \overleftarrow{\text{step}^* B} \qquad\qquad \diamondsuit B =_{def} \overrightarrow{B \, \text{step}^*}$$

$$\Box B =_{def} \neg \Diamond \neg B \qquad\qquad \boxminus B =_{def} \neg \diamondsuit \neg B$$

$$B \, \mathcal{U} \, C =_{def} \overleftarrow{(B \, \text{step})^* C} \qquad B \, \mathcal{S} \, C =_{def} \overrightarrow{C(\text{step} \, B)^*}$$

$$\text{first} =_{def} \neg \ominus \mathsf{T} \qquad\qquad \text{last} =_{def} \neg \bigcirc \mathsf{T}.$$

In our model space we obtain for example that $(t, \infty, \infty) \in \Diamond B$ if and only if $(t, \infty, \infty) \in B$ and for $i \in \mathbf{N}$ we have $(t, i, i) \in \Diamond B$ if and only if there exists $j \in \mathbf{N}$ with $i \leq j$ and $(t, j, j) \in B$.

All the temporal operators defined above map predicates to predicates. In contrast, the 'all-the-time' operator, which we borrow from temporal logic, maps predicates to sets of arbitrary observations. In a sequential set algebra, $[B]$ specifies the set of all observations that satisfy the predicate B at every finitely reachable state. In other words, $[B]$ excludes all observations of the form $u; v; w$, where $u \in \text{step}^*$, v is a state but not in B, and w is arbitrary. This leads to the definition

$$[B] =_{def} \overline{\text{step}^*(\neg B)\mathsf{L}} \, .$$

In the case of our model space $\mathcal{O}_A$, the set $[B]$ consists of the triples (t, i, j) for which $(t, k, k) \in B$ for all $k \in \mathbf{N}$ with $i \leq k \leq j$.

Many valid formulae of temporal logic are established as algebraic laws of sequential calculus in [16], including the axioms of the proof system given in [19]. In Section 4 we will use the laws

$$\overleftarrow{\text{step} \, P} = \bigcirc \overleftarrow{P} \qquad\qquad [B] \cap [C] = [B \wedge C] \qquad\qquad (\Box B)\mathsf{L} \subseteq [B] \qquad (\text{T}_1)$$

and, furthermore, we will apply the induction rule

$$(\nu X . B \wedge \bigcirc X) \subseteq \Box B \qquad\qquad\qquad (\text{T}_2)$$

for the 'henceforth' operation, where νf denotes the $\subseteq$-greatest fixed point of a monotone function f. The existence of νf follows from the well-known Tarski fixed point theorem [26]. $\qquad\qquad\qquad\qquad\qquad\qquad\qquad\qquad\qquad\qquad\qquad\qquad\Box$

3 Concurrency

In this section, we shall explore the use of sequential algebra for modelling concurrent processes. In CSP each process is associated with a specific set of events it can engage in, called its alphabet; see [12]. In general, concurrent agents operate on different sets of events, whereas a single sequential algebra can only model processes with the same alphabet.

For the following, assume a universe $\mathcal{E}$ of events. Then, for each set $A \in 2^{\mathcal{E}}$ let $\mathcal{S}_A$ denote the sequential set algebra over the specific observation space $\mathcal{O}_A$ given in Section 2.2. We call an element of a sequential algebra a *process*. For convenience, we shall pretend that $S_A \cap S_B = \emptyset$ for $A \neq B$ since this allows the *alphabet* $\alpha.P$ of a process P to be defined by

$$\alpha.P = A \iff P \in S_A.$$

All operations defined so far operate on processes with a fixed alphabet. In contrast, parallel composition and hiding relate processes with different alphabets. In Section 3.1, we introduce the hiding operator as a new primitive that relates sequential algebras over different alphabets. Subsequently, parallel composition and synchronization are defined in terms of hiding and its adjoint, the lifting operation.

3.1 Hiding and Lifting

Assume sets $A, B \in 2^{\mathcal{E}}$ such that $A \subseteq B$. First, we define the hiding operation $\downarrow_A : \mathcal{O}_B \to \mathcal{O}_{B-A}$ as a function between observation spaces by

$$(t, i, j)\downarrow_A =_{def} (t\downarrow_A, i', j'),$$

where $t\downarrow_A$ results from t by deleting all occurrences of elements in A, i' is the number of indices $n \leq i$ with $t_n \notin A$, and, similarly, j' is the number of indices $n \leq j$ with $t_n \notin A$. Note that $t\downarrow_A$ may be finite even when t is infinite. This corresponds exactly to the fact that in CSP hiding can transform an infinite trace of visible events into a divergent run.

Now we lift the function $\downarrow_A$ on observations to a function on sets of observations in the obvious way and obtain the *hiding operation* $\downarrow_A : S_B \to S_{B-A}$ on processes as

$$P\downarrow_A =_{def} \{x\downarrow_A \mid x \in P\}.$$

Obviously, this operation is universally disjunctive, i.e., distributes over all unions including the empty one, but for intersections only subdistributivity holds:

$$(\bigcup_{k \in I} P_k)\downarrow_A = \bigcup_{k \in I} P_k\downarrow_A \qquad (\bigcap_{k \in I} P_k)\downarrow_A \subseteq \bigcap_{k \in I} P_k\downarrow_A.$$

Due to $\cup$-distributivity of hiding, we can define a uniquely determined adjoint $\uparrow^A : S_{B-A} \to S_B$ to hiding, called *lifting operation*, by the Galois connection

$$P \subseteq Q\uparrow^A \iff P\downarrow_A \subseteq Q.$$

Using set-theoretic notation and the above hiding operation on observations, the lifting operation can also be stated directly by

$$Q\uparrow^A = \{x \in \mathcal{O}_B \mid x\downarrow_A \in Q\}.$$

Unlike hiding, lifting is universally disjunctive *and* universally conjunctive:

$$(\bigcup_{k \in I} Q_k)\uparrow^A = \bigcup_{k \in I} Q_k\uparrow^A \qquad (\bigcap_{k \in I} Q_k)\uparrow^A = \bigcap_{k \in I} Q_k\uparrow^A.$$

Together, the hiding and lifting operations endow the $\supseteq$-ordered family $(\mathcal{S}_A)_{A \in 2^{\mathcal{E}}}$ of sequential set algebras with the structure of what is sometimes called an inverse system of order type $(2^{\mathcal{E}}, \subseteq)$. In particular, we have

$$P\downarrow_A\uparrow^A \supseteq P \qquad\qquad Q\uparrow^A\downarrow_A = Q .$$

We abbreviate $\downarrow_{\{a\}}$ and $\uparrow^{\{a\}}$ to $\downarrow_a$ and $\uparrow^a$, respectively.

3.2 Parallel Composition and Communication

If two processes P and Q have the same alphabet, their *parallel composition* $P \parallel Q$ is simply their intersection. In other words, any given observation can be made on $P \parallel Q$ only when neither P nor Q prevents it. In the general case, the intersection can only be formed after lifting P and Q to their least common alphabet. We define

$$P \parallel Q =_{def} P\uparrow^A \cap Q\uparrow^B ,$$

where $A = \alpha.Q - \alpha.P$ and $B = \alpha.P - \alpha.Q$. Thus, the two processes P and Q must synchronize on events that are in the intersection $\alpha.P \cap \alpha.Q$, but neither needs the green light from its partner to proced with an event that belongs only to its own alphabet.

Let $a \in A$. We want to define a process $\mathbf{a} \in \mathcal{S}_A$ that performs a single a event and then terminates. We need an auxiliary definition. The process $only(a)$ can perform an arbitrary (even infinite) number of a events. Let I denote the identity of $\mathcal{S}_A$. We define

$$only(a) =_{def} \mathrm{I}_{A-\{a\}}\uparrow^a = \mathrm{I}\downarrow_a\uparrow^a ,$$

with $\mathrm{I}_{A-\{a\}}$ as identity of $\mathcal{S}_{A-\{a\}}$. Strictly speaking, we should write $only(a)_A$ instead of $only(a)$. We will not, however, burden ourselves with such heavy notation, since usually A can be reconstructed from the context. Now a process that will produce exactly one a event is given by

$$\mathbf{a} =_{def} \mathbf{step} \cap only(a) .$$

When $a \in \alpha.P$ we may *prefix* P with the *communication* $\mathbf{a}$. The resulting process $\mathbf{a}\,P$ starts with the event a and then behaves like P.

4 Examples

This section is devoted to some examples that illustrate the power of the calculus to express specifications and its use in the formal derivation of programs from specifications.

4.1 Specifications

Traditionally, descriptions of CSP processes yet to be written have been set down directly in the semantic domain using arbitrary mathematics rather than the restricted notation of some calculus [12, 21, 8]. Such specifications have the advantage of simplicity and clarity, but they cannot be transformed into programs by algebraic calculation and there are hard to mechanize. The purpose of this section is to show how to write specifications inside the many-sorted sequential calculus.

7 Oscillator. An oscillator has two states. In one state it always sends a, and in the other it always sends b. It cannot stay in one state forever. A temporal specification can be given by the alphabet $\alpha.oscillator =_{def} \{a, b\}$ and the inclusion

$$oscillator \subseteq [\Diamond \overleftarrow{a} \wedge \Diamond \overleftarrow{b}].$$

Note that this is a liveness condition, which cannot be stated in the classical models of CSP. □

8 Fire Alarm. Next, we consider the specification of a fire alarm. Once a fire signal has been received (e.g., from a sensor), a fire alarm has to ring the bell continuously, until it is reset. Using events *fire*, *bell*, and *reset* for a fire signal, ringing a bell, and the reset procedure, this leads to the specification

$$fire\text{-}alarm \subseteq [\overrightarrow{\text{fire}} \rightarrow \overleftarrow{\text{bell}}\, \mathcal{U}\, \overleftarrow{\text{reset}}]$$

with alphabet $\alpha.fire\text{-}alarm =_{def} \{fire, bell, reset\}$. In words: Whenever we reach a state such that the *previous* action was a fire alarm, then, until a reset occurs, the *next* action must be the bell signal. □

9 Buffer. This example is taken from [21]. A buffer has an input channel a and an output channel b. Whenever it has received an input, it has to perform an output before it can accept another input; and it can only output if it has not done so since the last input. In our approach, this is described by $\alpha.buffer =_{def} \{a, b\}$ and the inclusion

$$buffer \subseteq [(\overrightarrow{a} \rightarrow (\neg \overleftarrow{a})\, \mathcal{U}\, \overleftarrow{b}) \wedge (\overleftarrow{b} \rightarrow (\neg \overrightarrow{b})\, \mathcal{S}\, \overrightarrow{a})].$$

From a practical point of view, this specification is silly. It is much harder to understand than the natural implementation of a buffer, and it does not generalize to buffers of capacity greater than one. A much more desirable specification of an n-place-buffer (n-buffer for short) can be written by constraining its history. At any time, the number of inputs received so far must at least equal, but not exceed by more than n, the number of outputs produced so far. This is expressed by

$$buffer(n) \subseteq [0 \le \#a - \#b \le n].$$

We have yet to explain the meaning of the *interval predicate* $0 \le \#a - \#b \le n$ within the 'all-the-time' operation. In our model, the sequential set algebra over the observation space of Section 2.2, this is easy. The predicate contains exactly those observations $(t, i, i) \in \mathcal{O}_{\{a,b\}}$ with $i \in \mathbf{N}$ such that in the sub-trace $t_1 \ldots t_i$ there are at least as many as as bs, but at most n more as than bs.

Instead of the interval predicate we can also use two simpler *counting predicates* $\#a = n$ and $\#b = m$ expressing that exactly n events a and m events b have occurred in the past. Thereby, we can define a *difference predicate* as

$$(\#a - \#b = k) =_{def} \bigvee_{r \in \mathbf{N}} (\#a = r + k) \wedge (\#b = r) \qquad (\text{DP}_1)$$

which in turn yields the interval predicate as finite disjunction

$$(0 \leq \#a - \#b \leq n) = \bigvee_{0 \leq k \leq n} (\#a - \#b = k). \qquad (\text{DP}_2)$$

However, we can do yet better and describe the two simple counting predicates completely in the abstract calculus, i.e., without reference to the specific observation space $\mathcal{O}_{\{a,b\}}$. This is the subject of the next example. $\square$

10 Counting Predicates. Let $A \in 2^{\mathcal{E}}$ and assume an event $a \in A$. We define a process with alphabet A that may do anything, except produce any a events by

$$never(a) =_{def} \mathrm{I}_{\{a\}} \uparrow^{A - \{a\}}. \qquad (\text{CP}_1)$$

Strictly speaking, we should write again $never(a)_A$ instead of $never(a)$. Using $never(a)$ in combination with the temporal operation first of 6, we can already express that no a event has occurred in the past by

$$(\#a = 0) = \overrightarrow{\text{first } never(a)}. \qquad (\text{CP}_2)$$

In the case of the space $\mathcal{O}_A$, this predicate selects all final points of observations $(t, 0, j)$ – i.e., all triples (t, j, j) – with $j \in \mathbf{N}$ and $a \notin \{t_1, \ldots, t_j\}$. We extend this definition inductively by

$$(\#a = n + 1) =_{def} \overrightarrow{(\#a = n)(a \, never(a))}. \qquad (\text{CP}_3)$$

By (DP_1) through (CP_3) we have a characterization of the interval predicate $0 \leq \#a - \#b \leq n$ using only the operations of sequential algebra. $\square$

4.2 Deriving Programs

Next, we demonstrate how non-algorithmic problem specifications may be transformed into programs. We consider again buffers. Compared with the approach taken in [21], the new feature of our treatment is the free mixing of specification constructs with implementable operations and the formal program derivation within a single algebraic framework.

Assume three different events a, b, and c. Then, for the difference predicates of 9 we have the laws

$$(\#a - \#b = n)a = a(\#a - \#b \overset{\cdot}{=} n + 1) \tag{1}$$

$$(\#a - \#b = n)b = b(\#a - \#b \overset{\cdot}{=} n - 1) \tag{2}$$

$$\text{first} \subseteq (\#a - \#b = 0) \tag{3}$$

$$(\#a - \#b = n){\downarrow}_B = (\#a - \#b = n) \qquad \text{if } a, b \notin B \tag{4}$$

$$(\#a - \#b = n){\uparrow}^B \cap I = (\#a - \#b = n) \qquad \text{if } a, b \notin B \tag{5}$$

$$(\#a - \#b = n) \wedge (\#b - \#c = m) \subseteq (\#a - \#c = n + m). \tag{6}$$

Using the set-theoretic definitions of the predicates as subsets of a sequential set algebra over our model space $\mathcal{O}_A$, proofs are rather trivial. Remarkably, (1) through (6) may also be derived using only the equations (DP_1) through (CP_3) of 9 and 10. In doing so, one needs also for hiding and lifting that

1. the two laws of an inverse system hold,
2. lifting distributes over composition, quotients, and all unions,
3. hiding is cumulative in the sense that $P{\downarrow}_A{\downarrow}_B = P{\downarrow}_{A \cup B}$,
4. commutativity $P{\downarrow}_A{\uparrow}^B = P{\uparrow}^B{\downarrow}_A$ holds for disjoint sets A and B,
5. for the identity one has $I{\downarrow}_A = I$, $I_{\emptyset}{\uparrow}^A = L_A$, and $I_A \parallel I_B = I_{A \cup B}$.

However, these purely algebraic proofs are a little bit harder than the model-oriented ones.

11 Composing Buffers. Assume that the two processes P and Q with alphabets $\alpha.P = \{a, b\}$ and $\alpha.Q = \{b, c\}$ are buffers with n and m places, respectively. Then P and Q satisfy the inclusions

$$P \subseteq [0 \le \#a - \#b \le n] \qquad\qquad Q \subseteq [0 \le \#b - \#c \le m].$$

We want to show that an $(n + m)$-buffer with input a and output c can be implemented by combining the n-buffer P in parallel with the m-buffer Q and hiding the connecting wire b. We start with an auxiliary calculation:

$$
\begin{aligned}
&[0 \le \#a - \#b \le n]{\uparrow}^c \\
&= [I \cap (0 \le \#a - \#b \le n){\uparrow}^c] && [B]{\uparrow}^A = [I \cap B{\uparrow}^A] \\
&= [I \cap \textstyle\bigcup_{0 \le k \le n}(\#a - \#b = k){\uparrow}^c] && (DP_2) \text{ and distributivity } {\uparrow} \\
&= [\textstyle\bigvee_{0 \le k \le n} I \cap (\#a - \#b = k){\uparrow}^c] && \text{distributivity } \cap \\
&= [\textstyle\bigvee_{0 \le k \le n}(\#a - \#b = k)] && (5) \\
&= [0 \le \#a - \#b \le n]. && (DP_2)
\end{aligned}
$$

Similarly, one obtains the equation $[0 \le \#b - \#c \le m]{\uparrow}^a = [0 \le \#b - \#c \le m]$.

Now we can prove the desired result:

$$(P \parallel Q)\downarrow_b$$
$$\subseteq ([0 \le \#a - \#b \le n] \parallel [0 \le \#b - \#c \le m])\downarrow_b \qquad \text{assumptions on } P, Q$$
$$= ([0 \le \#a - \#b \le n]\uparrow^c \cap [0 \le \#b - \#c \le m]\uparrow^a)\downarrow_b \qquad \text{parallel composition}$$
$$= ([0 \le \#a - \#b \le n] \cap [0 \le \#b - \#c \le m])\downarrow_b \qquad \text{see above}$$
$$\subseteq [0 \le \#a - \#c \le n + m]\downarrow_b \qquad (\text{T}_1) \text{ and } (6)$$
$$\subseteq [(0 \le \#a - \#c \le n + m)\downarrow_b] \qquad [B]\downarrow_b \subseteq [B\downarrow_b]$$
$$\subseteq [\bigvee_{0 \le k \le n+m}(\#a - \#c = k)\downarrow_b] \qquad (\text{DP}_2) \text{ and distributivity } \downarrow$$
$$= [\bigvee_{0 \le k \le n+m}(\#a - \#c = k)] \qquad (4)$$
$$= [0 \le \#a - \#c \le n + m] \qquad (\text{DP}_2)$$

We tacitly used monotonicity of various operations, which in all cases is obvious from the definitions. $\qquad\qquad\Box$

12 Implementing Buffers. As larger buffers can be built from smaller ones due to 11, we need only implement a 1-buffer. For this we use recursion. Suppose f to be a monotonic function on processes (over a fixed alphabet A). Then the $\subseteq$-greatest fixed point of f fulfills (cf. [26])

$$\nu f = f(\nu f) \qquad P \subseteq f(P)) \implies (P \subseteq \nu f.$$

Now we can implement a 1-buffer as

$$P =_{def} \nu X . \mathbf{a}\,\mathbf{b}\,X.$$

Process P does not quite satisfy the specification of $buffer(1)$ given in 9 because it has no control on its sequential predecessor, which may have upset the balance between a and b events before P is activated. But a buffer typically starts up together with its clients, so we shall simply assume that it has no sequential predecessor. This is expressed formally by replacing P with first P. Effectively we are requiring first as a precondition for the correct working of the buffer, and it is the responsibility of the environment not to use a buffer in the wrong context.

For convenience let $B_k =_{def} (\#a - \#b = k)$. Then, we can derive

$$\text{first } P \subseteq [0 \le \#a - \#b \le 1]$$
$$\Longleftrightarrow \text{ first } P \subseteq [B_0 \vee B_1] \qquad (\text{DP}_2)$$
$$\Longleftarrow B_0 P \subseteq (\Box(B_0 \vee B_1))\mathsf{L} \qquad (\text{T}_1) \text{ and first} \subseteq B_0 \text{ by } (3)$$
$$\Longleftrightarrow \overleftarrow{B_0 P} \subseteq \Box(B_0 \vee B_1) \qquad (\text{D})$$
$$\Longleftarrow \overleftarrow{B_0 P} \subseteq \nu X . (B_0 \vee B_1) \wedge \bigcirc((B_0 \vee B_1) \wedge \bigcirc X) \qquad \text{induction rule } (\text{T}_2)$$
$$\Longleftarrow \overleftarrow{B_0 P} \subseteq (B_0 \vee B_1) \wedge \bigcirc((B_0 \vee B_1) \wedge \bigcirc\overleftarrow{B_0 P}). \qquad \text{fixed point property}$$

Note that this derivation uses in the fifth line the induction rule for the 'henceforth' operation in the expanded form $(\nu X . B \wedge \bigcirc(B \wedge \bigcirc X)) \subseteq \Box B$, which is correct since for a monotone function f the greatest fixed points νf and νf^2 coincide. Now we prove

$$\overleftarrow{B_0 P}$$

$$= B_0 \wedge \overleftarrow{B_0 \mathsf{ab} P} \qquad\qquad \overleftarrow{B_0 P} \subseteq B_0 \text{ by (D) and } P = \mathsf{ab}P$$

$$= B_0 \wedge \overleftarrow{\mathsf{a}B_1 \mathsf{b} P} \qquad\qquad B_k \mathsf{a} = \mathsf{a}B_{k+1} \text{ by (1)}$$

$$\subseteq B_0 \wedge \bigcirc \overleftarrow{B_1 \mathsf{b} P} \qquad\qquad \mathsf{a} \subseteq \text{step and (D)}$$

$$= B_0 \wedge \bigcirc(B_1 \wedge \overleftarrow{\mathsf{b}B_0 P}) \qquad \overleftarrow{B_1 \mathsf{b} P} \subseteq B_1 \text{ by (T}_1\text{) and } B_k \mathsf{b} = \mathsf{b}B_{k-1} \text{ by (2)}$$

$$\subseteq B_0 \wedge \bigcirc(B_1 \wedge \bigcirc \overleftarrow{B_0 P}), \qquad\qquad \mathsf{b} \subseteq \text{step and (T}_1\text{)}$$

which implies the last member of the preceding calculation. Thus, we have proved that first P indeed satisfies the specification of a 1-buffer. □

5 Concluding Remarks

We have exploited two new ideas in this paper. Firstly, temporal operations may be reduced to composition and quotients. This allowed us to integrate temporal logic into an imperative framework. Secondly, we moved from a single-sorted sequential algebra to a many-sorted family and appropriate hiding and lifting operations, in order to define the basic operations of CSP in an algebraic and model-independent way.

Both ideas are much more general than the scope in which they were applied here. In a companion paper [16] it is shown that it is possible to obtain various forms of temporal logic from sequential algebra by selecting a few additional axioms from a pool of alternatives. In particular, linear temporal logic and its complete proof system [19] have been worked out entirely within the calculus.

C.A.R. Hoare and L. Lamport have argued that parallel composition means intersection. Others believe it should be modelled as direct product. We believe that both parties are right – some of the time. $P \parallel Q = P \cap Q$ holds when P and Q have the same alphabet and $P \parallel Q$ may be seen as a direct product when the alphabets are disjoint. Using many sorts and the lifting operations, we covered both extremes, and all positions in-between. This technique applies not just to the sequential calculus. In the predicate calculus, hiding is just existential quantification. In fact, our definition of parallel composition has already been used in that context. It is precisely the conjunction of schemas in the Z specification language; see [24]. Unlike in the usual notation, the adjoint of existential quantification (lifting) can be expressed, which is very useful in the calculational style of reasoning. Other obvious candidates are the relational calculus, interval temporal logic, and Dijkstra's regularity calculus [9], all of which may be enriched with hiding, lifting, and parallel composition. To make this idea really useful, we must achieve model independence by axiomatizing the theory of hiding and lifting. We found that all theorems concerning hiding and lifting considered up to now, in particular all the rules presented in this paper, may be reduced to the algebraic laws 1. through 5. of hiding and lifting given at the beginning of Section 4.2. Further research must show if they are complete, or at least sufficient for practical purposes.

Acknowledgement: We are indebted to Tony Hoare who encouraged the emergence of sequential algebra, and suggested its application to CSP. Furthermore, we thank Jules Desharnais, Bernhard Möller, Martin Russling and Walter Vogler for valuable remarks.

References

1. Backhouse R.C., de Bruin P., Malcolm G., Voermans T.S., van der Woude J.: Relational catamorphisms. In: Möller B. (ed.): Constructing programs from specifications. Proceedings IFIP TC2 / WG 2.1 Working Conference on Constructing Programs, Elsevier Science Publishers, 287-318 (1991)
2. de Bakker J.W., de Roever W.P.: A calculus for recursive program schemes. In: Nivat M. (ed.): Proceedings ICALP 73, North-Holland, 167-196 (1973)
3. Brookes S.D., Roscoe A.W.: An improved failure model for communicating sequential processes. In: Brookes S.D. et al. (eds.): Proceedings NSF-SERC Seminar on Concurrency, LNCS 197, Springer Verlag, 285-305 (1985)
4. Bauer F.L., Möller B., Partsch H., Pepper P.: Formal program construction by transformations – Computer-aided intuition guided programming. IEEE Transactions on Software Engineering 15, 165-180 (1989)
5. Berghammer R., Zierer H.: Relational algebraic semantics of deterministic and nondeterministic programs. Theoretical Computer Science 43, 123-147 (1986)
6. Burstall R.M., Darlington J.: A transformation system for developing recursive programs. Journal of the ACM 24, 44-67 (1977)
7. Chin L.H., Tarski A.: Distributive and modular laws in the arithmetic of relation algebras. University of California Publications in Mathematics (new series) 1, 341-384 (1951)
8. Davies J.: Specification and Proof in Real Time Systems. D. Phil. Thesis, Oxford University (1991)
9. Dijkstra E.W.: The unification of three calculi. In: Broy M. (ed.): Program Design Calculi. Springer Verlag, 197-231 (1993)
10. Goldsmith M.H.: The Oxford occam transformation system (draft user documentation). Oxford University (1994)
11. Goldsmith M.H., Roscoe A.W., Scott B.G.O.: Denotational Semantics for occam 2, parts I & II. Transputer Communications 1(2), 65-91 (1993) and 2(1), 25-67 (1994)
12. Hoare C.A.R.: Communicating Sequential Processes. Prentice-Hall International (1985)
13. Hoare C.A.R., He Jifeng: The weakest prespecification, parts I & II. Fundamenta Informaticae IX, 51-84 & 217-252 (1986)
14. Hoare C.A.R., Roscoe A.W.: The laws of occam programming. Technical Report PRG-53, Oxford University (1986)
15. von Karger B.: Sequential calculus. ProCoS II Report Kiel BvK 15/4, Institut für Informatik und Praktische Mathematik, Christian-Albrechts-Universität Kiel (1994)

16. von Karger B.: An algebraic foundation of temporal logic. In: Peter D. Mosses et al. (eds.): Proceedings TAPSOFT '95, LNCS 915, Springer Verlag, 232-246 (1995) Also available as: ProCoS II Report Kiel BvK 17/1, Institut für Informatik und Praktische Mathematik, Christian-Albrechts-Universität Kiel (1994)

17. von Karger B., Hoare C.A.R.: Sequential calculus. Information Processing Letters 53, 123-130 (1995)

18. Lamport L., Merz S.: Specifying and verifying fault-tolerant systems. In: Langmaack H. et al. (eds.): Formal techniques in real-time and fault-tolerant systems. LNCS 863, Springer Verlag, 41-76 (1994)

19. Manna Z., Pnueli A.: The temporal logic of reactive and concurrent systems-specification. Springer Verlag (1991)

20. Meertens L.G.L.T: Algorithmics – Towards programming as a mathematically activity. In: de Bakker J.W. et al. (eds.): Proceedings CWI Symposium on Mathematics and Computer Science, CWI Monographs Vol. 1, North Holland, 289-334 (1986)

21. Olderog E.-R., Hoare C.A.R.: Specification-oriented semantics for communicating processes. Acta Informatica 33, 9-66 (1986)

22. Schmidt G.: Programs as partial graphs, parts I & II. Theoretical Computer Science 15, 1-25 & 159-179 (1981)

23. Schmidt G., Ströhlein T.: Relations and graphs. Discrete Mathematics for Computer Scientists, EATCS Monographs on Theoretical Computer Science, Springer Verlag (1993)

24. Spivey J.M.: The Z notation: A reference manual. 2nd ed., Prentice Hall (1992)

25. Tarski A.: On the calculus of relations. Journal of Symbolic Logic 6, 73-89 (1941)

26. Tarski A.: A lattice-theoretical fixpoint theorem and its applications. Pacific J. Math. 5, 285-309 (1955)

A Compositional Proof System for Asynchronously Communicating Processes

F.S. de Boer and M. van Hulst

Utrecht University
Dept. of Comp. Sc.
P.O. Box 80089
3508 TB Utrecht, The Netherlands
email: {frankb,marten}@cs.ruu.nl

Abstract. We present a Hoare logic for distributed systems composed of processes which communicate asynchronously via (unbounded) FIFO buffers. The calculus is based on an assertion language which allows the specification of the communication interface of a process at a high level of abstraction. As such our formalism serves well as a basis for refinement and top-down development of distributed systems composed of asynchronously communicating processes. Moreover, we show that the first-order logic underlying the interface-specification language is decidable, which makes (semi-) automated verification more feasible.

1 Introduction

Hoare logics have been used successfully for reasoning about correctness of a variety of distributed systems [AdB94, AFdR80, HdR86, OG76, Pan88, Zwi88]. In general, proof systems for distributed systems based on some kind of Hoare logic formalize reasoning about communication and synchronization in terms of sequences of communication events called *histories*.

Distributed systems based on synchronous communication allow an elegant compositional proof theory [Zwi88] essentially because there exists a simple logical formulation of the *compatibility* of the local histories of the processes of a system: The local histories are compatible, that is, they can be combined into a global history of the entire system, if they can be obtained as the projection of some sequence of communication events.

On the other hand distributed systems based on asynchronous communication do not allow such a simple criterion: to check the compatibility of the local histories one has in general to consider all possible interleavings [Pan88]. As such its logical formulation involves quantification over histories, and this will obviously complicate the reasoning process.

The recent book on program correctness by Francez [Fra92] contains a section on *non-deterministic* processes which communicate asynchronously via FIFO buffers, featuring a proof system that uses a logic based on *input/output variables* instead of histories. A buffer is logically represented by an input variable which records the sequence of values read from the buffer and by an output variable which records the sequence of values sent to the buffer. The difference between input/output variables and histories is that in the former information of the relative ordering of communication events on different buffers is lost. However, it can be shown that this logic is incomplete for non-deterministic processes; in general, the information expressible by input/output variables only is insufficient to obtain a complete specification of an entire system by composing the local specifications of its constituent processes. As a consequence not all valid correctness formulas are derivable.

In [dBvH94] however, we showed that, provided the programming language is restricted to deterministic processes, a complete compositional proof system can be based on input/output variables only.

So naturally the question arises what is the minimal information we need to add to the input/output variables to obtain a compositional proof system for asynchronously communicating non-deterministic processes. Here the notion of minimal information is defined with respect to the semantic interpretation of a program as a state-transformation, a state being an assignment of values to the program variables.

From a semantical point of view the determination of the minimal information needed to characterize a notion of observables compositionally gives rise to a fully abstract semantics. For asynchronously communicating processes it is well-known that histories are not fully abstract ([Jon89]); for example, the order between inputs (outputs) on different channels is irrelevant with respect to observing the final values of the program variables. Thus the abstraction level of a proof system for asynchronously communicating processes based on histories does not coincide with the appropriate abstraction level of the programming language. With respect to program refinement and top-down program development however it is crucial to be able to specify a program at the right level of abstraction, such that the specification itself does not give rise to irrelevant design choices.

In this paper we introduce a Hoare logic based on an assertion language which allows the specification of the communication interface of a process at the right level of abstraction in the sense that no irrelevant information is included. An interface specification will consist of two separate parts; a *data* component and a *control* component. The data component specifies the FIFO buffers, that is, the sequences of values read from a channel and sent to a channel, respectively. These FIFO buffers are described in terms of input/output variables, as explained above. The control component specifies the relevant order of the communication events in terms of a *abstract history*. An abstract history describes the reactive behavior of a process in terms of the number of inputs (for each channel) it needs in order to be able to produce a certain number of outputs, abstracting from the values communicated. Mathematically, such an abstract history can be formalized by a function which takes as input a *multiset* of channel names and outputs again a multiset of channel names. The number of occurrences of a channel name in the argument then corresponds to the number of required input actions on that channel, whereas the number of occurrences of a channel name in the resulting multiset corresponds to the number of outputs generated on that channel. The distinction between the data and control component of an interface specification introduces a nice separation of concerns which will in general simplify the reasoning process. Moreover, we show that the logic underlying the control component can be formalized in a first-order logic of multisets, and we show that this logic is decidable, which makes (semi-) automated verification more feasible.

This paper is organized as follows: In the following section we introduce the programming language. The proof system is discussed in section 3, and in section 4 we discuss the first-order logic underlying the control component of an interface, and show its decidability. Finally, section 5 contains some conclusions and perspectives.

2 The programming language

In this section, we define the syntax of the programming language. The language describes the behaviour of asynchronously communicating processes. Processes interact only via communication channels which are implemented by (unbounded) FIFO-buffers. A process can send a value along a channel or it can input a value from a channel. The value sent will be appended to the buffer, whereas reading a value from a buffer consists of retrieving its first element. Thus the values will be read in the order in which they have been sent. A process will be suspended when it tries to read a value from an empty buffer. Since buffers are assumed to be unbounded sending values can always take place.

We assume given a set of program variables *Var*, with typical elements $x, y, \ldots$. Channels are denoted by $c, c_1, c_2, \ldots$; the set of channels is denoted C.

Definition 1. The syntax of a statement S which describes the behaviour of a sequential process, is defined by

$$S ::= x := e$$

$$|\quad c!!e$$

$$|\quad S_1; S_2$$

$$|\quad \|_i[b_i; c_i??x_i \rightarrow S_i]$$

$$|\quad \star\|_i[b_i; c_i??x_i \rightarrow S_i]$$

In the assignment statement $x := e$ we restrict for technical convenience to arithmetical expressions e. Sending a value of an (arithmetical) expression e along channel c is described by $c!!e$, whereas storing a value read from a channel c in a variable x is described by $c??x$. Sequential composition is denoted by $;$. The execution of a guarded command $\|_i[b_i; c_i??x_i \rightarrow S_i]$ consists of the selection of a non-empty buffer c_i for which the corresponding boolean guard b_i is true, subsequently a value is read from the buffer and stored in x_i, and control is passed on to the statement S_i. If there exists no non-empty buffer c_i for which the corresponding boolean b_i is true the execution of the guarded command suspends; in case all the boolean guards are false the execution fails. The iterative construct $\star\|_i[b_i; c_i??x_i \rightarrow S_i]$ consists of repeatedly executing the guarded command $\|_i[b_i; c_i??x_i \rightarrow S_i]$ until all the boolean guards b_i are false. In the following some examples will be given using boolean guards $b \rightarrow S$; it is easy to extend the syntax and the semantics of the programming language to include such boolean guards.

Definition 2. A parallel program P is of the form $[S_1 \parallel ... \parallel S_n]$, where we assume the following restrictions: The statements S_i do not share program variables, channels are unidirectional and connect exactly one sender and one receiver.

3 The proof system

3.1 Assertion Language

A compositional proof system for asynchronously communicating processes can be obtained by specifying the interface of a process in terms of a local history which consists of a sequence of communication records. A communication record $c!!v$ indicates that the value v has been sent along channel c, and $c??v$, on the other hand, indicates that the value v has been read from channel c. The local history of a process itself can be described as the projection of a global history which satisfies the requirement that at any point the number of inputs on a channel does not exceed the number of preceding outputs on the same channel and that the values are read in the order in which they are sent.

Let us illustrate the above informally described proof methodology.

Example 1. Consider the sequential processes

$$S_1 = [c??x \to c??y \| true \to c??y]; d!!0$$

and

$$S_2 = c!!0; [d??z \to c!!1].$$

After termination of $[S_1 \| S_2]$ we have that $y = 0$, since the selection of the branch $c??x \to c??y$ leads to deadlock. This can be proved by deriving locally the postcondition

$$p_1 = \forall u, v[s_1 = \langle c??u, c??v, d!!0 \rangle \to y = v] \lor \forall u[s_1 = \langle c??u, d!!0 \rangle \to y = u]$$

for S_1 and the postcondition

$$p_2 = \exists u[s_2 = \langle c!!0, d??u, c!!1 \rangle]$$

for S_2. Here s_1 and s_2 are history variables which denote sequences of communication events. Let $compat(s_1, s_2)$ be the compatibility predicate which expresses that there exists an interleaving of s_1 and s_2 such that at any point the number of inputs on a channel does not exceed the number of preceding outputs on the same channel and that the values are read in the order in which they are sent. Then we have that $p_1 \land p_2 \land compat(s_1, s_2)$ implies $y = 0$. This follows from the fact that there exists no compatible interleaving of the sequences $\langle c??u, c??v, d!!0 \rangle$ and $\langle c!!0, d??u, c!!1 \rangle$.

Note that a history as defined above records the order of the communications on different channels. But we are primarily interested in observing the final values of the program variables, and it can be shown that history variables encode too detailed information about the flow of control of a process. For example, with respect to the final values of the program variables, the order between outputs on different channels is irrelevant. This can be formalized by a fully abstract semantics, which introduces certain abstractions from the order of communications (see also [Jon89, Jos92]): inputs and outputs on different channels can be swapped, and the order between an output followed by an input can be reversed.

A necessary requirement of top-down program development is a specification language which allows the description of a program at the right level of abstraction, such that the specification itself does not give rise to irrelevant design choices. Therefore the above proof methodology, since it is based on the description of the communication interface in terms of sequences of communication records, is not appropriate as a basis for program refinement.

As an example of this observation, consider an implementation of S_1 satisfying $\{s = \epsilon\}S_1\{s = \langle c!!5, d!!3\rangle\}$, so initially s is empty and upon termination s contains the communication records $c!!5$ and $d!!3$, in that order. Clearly, $S = c!!5; d!!3$ is a correct implementation of the specification. However it can be shown that $S' = d!!3; c!!5$ is semantically indistinguishable from S, in the sense that there exists no *context* which, when applied to S, gives rise to a different state-transformation then when applied to S'. But S' does *not* satisfy the above (interface) specification. Thus we conclude that the specification includes irrelevant information with respect to the observable behavioural properties of programs. This would prohibit an efficient implementation in the case of two environmental processes S_2 and S_3 which are given by $S_2 = d??x; e!!(x + 1)$ and $S_3 = e??y; c??z$. Note that S_3 needs input from S_2 before it can read channel c; therefore there is no point for S_1 in sending over channel c first.

To obtain a more appropriate level of abstraction one could simply introduce in the assertion language a binary predicate on histories $R(s_1, s_2)$ which expresses that s_2 is a permutation (allowed by the fully abstract semantics) of s_1. Thus we would have, for example, the following axiom for calculating the weakest precondition of an output $c!!e$:

$$\{\exists s'[p[s' \cdot c!!e/s] \wedge R(s', s)]\}c!!e\{p\}$$

where s' is a new history variable, and $s' \cdot c!!e$ denotes the result of appending the communication event $c!!v$, with v the value of e, to the sequence denoted by s'; substitution of a term t for a variable x in an assertion p is denoted by $p[t/x]$. However the obvious disadvantage of this approach is that to express the predicate $R(s_1, s_2)$ one needs either quantification over (finite) sequences of histories or the introduction of recursively defined predicates, since it involves the transitive closure of a relation $s_1 \rightarrow s_2$, which expresses that s_2 can be obtained from s_1 by swapping two elements (as allowed by the fully abstract semantics). As such it highly complicates the reasoning process.

A more manageable and direct description of the interface of a local process can be based on the following observation. Let s be a sequence of communication records, and $[s]$ denote the set of permutations of s resulting from input and output swaps (on different channels). In the following, let I, O denote functions (also called streams) from C to $\mathbb{N}^*$. Let, for arbitrary s, IO_s be a function which transforms input streams into output streams, such that $IO_s(\mathrm{I}) = \mathrm{O}$ iff there exists a prefix s' of s ending in an output which is not immediately followed in s by another output, such that I records for each (input) channel the sequence of values read in s' and O records for each (output) channel the sequence of values sent in s'. (In case s does not contain outputs we define $IO_s(\mathrm{I}) = \mathrm{O}$ iff I records for each input channel of s the sequence of values read and O assigns to each output channel the empty sequence.) We then have that $s' \in [s]$ iff $IO_{s'} = IO_s$ and the projection of s and s' onto any input channel gives the same result (this last condition takes care of trailing inputs, namely those inputs which are not followed by any output). Thus the function IO_s (with the additional information about trailing inputs) is a canonical representative of the equivalence class $[s]$.

Example 2. Consider the history $s = \langle c??0, c??1, d!!0, e!!0, f??0, e!!1 \rangle$. Then with the output $e!!0$ of s there corresponds a pair $\langle I, O \rangle$ such that $I(c) = \langle 0, 1 \rangle$, $I(f) = \epsilon$, and $O(d) = \langle 0 \rangle$, $O(e) = \langle 0 \rangle$ (here ϵ denotes the empty sequence). With the last output $e!!1$ there corresponds a pair $\langle I, O \rangle$ such that $I(c) = \langle 0, 1 \rangle$, $I(f) = \langle 0 \rangle$, and $O(d) = \langle 0 \rangle$, $O(e) = \langle 1 \rangle$.

Our proof theory is based on the following representation of the above defined canonical representative of the equivalence class $[s]$ of a sequence of communication records s. We introduce input/output variables $c??$ and $c!!$ which record the values read from the input channel c and the values sent to the output channel c, respectively. Note that these input/output variables abstract from the order of the communications on different channels. We denote the set of variables $c??$ and $c!!$ by $\mathcal{I}$ resp. $\mathcal{O}$; their union is denoted $\mathcal{IO}$. Moreover, the set of variables $c??$ where c is an input channel of process i, and the set of variables $c!!$ where c is an output channel of process i, will be denoted by $\mathcal{I}_i$ and $\mathcal{O}_i$, respectively. The union of $\mathcal{I}_i$ and $\mathcal{O}_i$ we denote by $\mathcal{IO}_i$. The additional information about the relevant ordering between communications on different channels can be described as a function h which transforms *multisets* of channel names, i.e. $h \in \mathcal{P}_m(C) \to \mathcal{P}_m(C)$, where $\mathcal{P}_m(C)$ denotes the set of all finite multisets of elements of C. Typical multisets will be represented by I, O. The idea is that the argument I in $h(I) = O$ contains the number of inputs which are necessary for the outputs of O to take place. For example, $h(\{c, c\}) = \{d, d\}$ indicates that the process needs at least two inputs on c two produce two outputs on d. Thus the number of occurrences of a channel c in I (O) corresponds to the number of input (output) actions on c. It is not difficult to see that indeed we can thus represent IO_s as a function $h \in \mathcal{P}_m(C) \to \mathcal{P}_m(C)$ and a function which assigns to each input/output variable a sequence of values. An element of $\mathcal{P}_m(C) \to \mathcal{P}_m(C)$ we call an *abstract history*.

Example 3. Consider the process $c??x; d!!0; c??y; e!!1$. Its abstract history consists of the pairs $\langle \emptyset, \emptyset \rangle$, $\langle \{c\}, \{d\} \rangle$, $\langle \{c, c\}, \{d, e\} \rangle$. Thus the pair $\langle \{c, c\}, \{d, e\} \rangle$ for example indicates that the process needs two inputs on c to output once on d and e. The pair $\langle \emptyset, \emptyset \rangle$ indicates that the process is not able to output when no inputs are given. Assuming that first 0 and then 1 has been read from c we have that the input variable $c??$ denotes the sequence $\langle 0, 1 \rangle$, and the output variables $d!!$ and $e!!$ denote the sequences $\langle 0 \rangle$, $\langle 1 \rangle$, respectively.

Together with the information of its input/output variables the abstract history determines the communication interface of a local process. Note that the input/output variables thus can be considered as the data component of the communication interface, whereas the control component, which specifies the relevant order between the communication events, is described by the abstract history.

The local proof system formalizes reasoning about the correctness of a process in terms of its communication interface as specified by its abstract history and its input/output variables as defined above. Therefore we assume given a many-sorted assertion language (defined formally in the full paper) which, besides the usual vocabulary for describing properties of integers, includes a variable h which denotes an abstract history; input/output variables $c??$, $c!!$, along with sequence operations like append, prefixing etc; the set C of channel names as constants, and variables which range over multisets of channel names. We include the relation $\subseteq$ of multiset-inclusion, the operation $\cap$ of multiset-intersection, and for each channel name c the unary multiset operation S_c, which consists of adding a copy of c. In order to reason about the abstract history h we introduce terms of the form h_i, where i denotes the index of a local process. A term h_i denotes the *projection* of the (global) history h onto the input/output variables of the process i. Formally, the meaning of a term h_i is given by the following formula

$$\forall I \forall O [h_i(I) = O \leftrightarrow \exists I' \exists O' [h(I') = O' \land I = I' \cap \mathcal{I}_i \land O = O' \cap \mathcal{O}_i]]$$

where I, I', O, O' are multiset variables. Note that for this notion of projection to be well-defined we have to require that

$$\forall I \forall I' [I \cap \mathcal{I}_i = I' \cap \mathcal{I}_i \rightarrow h(I) \cap \mathcal{O}_i = h(I') \cap \mathcal{O}_i]$$

Finally, we also include expressions of the form $h(e_1) := e_2$, where e_1 and e_2 are multiset expressions, the meaning of which is given by the formula

$$\forall I [I \neq e_i \rightarrow (h(e_1) := e_2)(I) = h(I) \land I = e_1 \rightarrow (h(e_1) := e_2)(I) = e_2]$$

This notation for describing an update to the abstract history is derived from the axiomatization of assignments to arrays (see [Gri87]).

In the assertion language quantification is only allowed over integer variables and variables ranging over multisets of channel names. Assertions will be denoted by $p, q, \ldots$.

Definition 3. Local correctness formulas are of the form

$$\{p\} S \{q\},$$

where it is implicitly assumed that the free integer variables of p and q are included in the program variables of S, and p and q only refer to the input/output variables of S. These syntactical conditions ensure that local specifications are free from *interference* (occurrences of the abstract history variable h will be interpreted at this level as the local history of S, only when combining the local specifications we substitute h by h_i, see rule 5).

Global correctness formulas are of the form

$$\{p\}P\{q\}.$$

Both type of correctness formulas are provided with a partial correctness interpretation: for example, $\{p\}S\{q\}$ is valid if every terminating computation of S starting in a state satisfying precondition p results in a state satisfying postcondition q.

3.2 Axioms and Rules

Next we discuss the axioms and rules of the proof system. We have the following well-known axiom for the assignment:

Axiom 1 *(assignment)* $\{p[e/x]\}x := e\{p\}$

Here $p[e/x]$ denotes the result of substituting occurrences of x in p by e. Simultaneous substitution of $e_1, \ldots e_n$ for the variables $x_1, \ldots, x_n$ in p will be denoted by $p[e_1/x_1, \ldots, e_n/x_n]$.

An input statement $c??x$ is axiomatized by a multiple assignment to the input variable $c??$, the variable x, and a distinguished multiset variable I. The variable I indicates the number of inputs which have been executed so far. So if, for example, $I = \{c, c, d\}$ holds in the current state, this means that until now, the process has read twice from channel c and once from d. The assignment to the input variable $c??$ models the operation of appending the value read to $c??$ and the assignment to the variable x models the storage of the value read in the local memory. The value read is represented by a new integer variable v. Since the value of v is not known locally, the variable v is universally quantified.

Axiom 2 *(input)* $\{\forall v[p[v/x, c?? \cdot v/c??, S_c(I)/I]]\}c??x\{p\}$

Here the operation of appending an element to a sequence is denoted by '$\cdot$'. Note that $S_c(I)$ denotes the result of adding a copy of c to I. Observe that an input statement does not affect the abstract history.

An output statement $c!!e$ is axiomatized by a multiple assignment to the output variable $c!!$, the abstract history variable h, and a distinguished multiset variable O, which indicates the number of outputs which have been executed so far. The assignment to the output variable $c!!$ models the operation of appending the value sent to $c!!$ and the assignment to the abstract history records the causal dependencies between the outputs executed so far and the inputs that have been executed until now, and which are represented by the multiset variables I and O, respectively.

Axiom 3 *(output)*

$$\{\forall I'[I \subseteq I' \to p[c!! \cdot e/c!!, (h(I') := S_c(O))/h, S_c(O)/O]]\}c!!e\{p\}$$

Here I' denotes a new multiset variable. Note that we update the abstract history for an arbitrary I' which contains I, where I records the number of inputs which have been executed so far. This corresponds with the monotonicity property that if a multiset I of inputs enables a multiset O of outputs then any $I' \supseteq I$ enables O. The monotonicity property allows abstraction from the order between an output and a subsequent input as illustrated in example 4.

The following rules for sequential composition, the guarded statement and the guarded iteration are the usual ones.

Rule 1 *(sequential composition)*

$$\frac{\{p\}S_1\{r\}, \ \{r\}S_2\{q\}}{\{p\}S_1;S_2\{q\}}$$

Rule 2 *(guarded statement)*

$$\frac{\{p \wedge b_i\}c_i??x_i; S_i\{q\}}{\{p\}\|_i[b_i; c_i??x_i \to S_i]\{q\}}$$

Rule 3 *(guarded iteration)*

$$\frac{\{p\}\|_i b_i; c_i??x_i \to S_i\{p\}}{\{p\} \star \|_i[b_i; c_i??x_i \to S_i]\{p \wedge \bigwedge_i \neg b_i\}}$$

Moreover we have the following consequence rule.

Rule 4 *(Local consequence rule)*

$$\frac{\models p \to p', \ \{p'\}S\{q'\}, \ \models q' \to q}{\{p\}S\{q\}}$$

We have the following rule for parallel composition.

Rule 5 *(parallel composition)*

$$\frac{\{p_i \wedge Init_i\}S_i\{q_i'\}, \ (q_i' \wedge \forall I'[h(I') \neq \emptyset \to I' \subseteq I]) \to q_i}{\{\bigwedge_i p_i[h_i/h]\}[S_1 \| ... \| S_n]\{\bigwedge_i q_i[h_i/h]\}}$$

Here $Init_i$ denotes the assertion $h = \emptyset \wedge I = \emptyset \wedge O = \emptyset \wedge \bigwedge_{c?? \in \mathcal{I}_i}(c?? = \epsilon) \wedge \bigwedge_{c!! \in \mathcal{O}_i}(c!! = \epsilon)$. (In $h = \emptyset$ the function which assigns to each multiset the empty multiset is denoted by $\emptyset$, whereas in $I = \emptyset$ $(O = \emptyset)$, $\emptyset$ denotes the empty multiset. The empty sequence is denoted by ϵ.) The additional information expressed by $\forall I'[h(I') \neq \emptyset \rightarrow I' \subseteq I]$ ensures that the choices for the input set in the output axiom are consistent with the final set of inputs. It is implicitly assumed that p_i and q_i do not contain the logical variables I and O (these variables are only used locally to generate the abstract history, globally they are irrelevant). When combining the local specifications in the conclusion of the rule we substitute the abstract history variable h by its corresponding projection.

We now arrive at a suitable point to illustrate the use of the output axiom.

Example 4. Let $S_1 = c!!0; d??x$ and $S_2 = [true \rightarrow c!!0; d??x | d??x \rightarrow c!!0]$. It is not difficult to see that S_1 and S_2 are observationally equivalent, that is in every context they give rise to the same state-transformation. Using the above calculus we can derive the postcondition $\exists I'[\emptyset \subseteq I' \wedge h = \{\langle I', \{c\}\rangle\}] \wedge I = \{d\}$ for S_1. Thus using the additional information $\forall I'[h(I') \neq \emptyset \rightarrow I' \subseteq I]$ we derive the postcondition $h = \{\langle \emptyset, \{c\}\rangle\} \vee h = \{\langle \{d\}, \{c\}\rangle\}$, which is also satisfied by S_2. In other words, S_1 and S_2 are provably equivalent.

The following rule allows to strengthen the postcondition of a program with the information that the sequence of values read from a channel is a prefix of the sequence of values sent.

Rule 6 *(FIFO rule)*

$$\frac{\{p\}P\{q\}}{\{p\}P\{q \wedge c?? \preceq c!!\}}$$

Here $\preceq$ denotes the prefix relation on sequences.

Next we introduce a rule which allows to strengthen the postcondition of a program with additional information about the global history.

Rule 7 *(Compatibility predicate)*

$$\frac{\{p\}P\{q\}}{\{p\}P\{q \wedge compat(h)\}}$$

Here the compatibility predicate $compat(h)$ is defined as follows:

$$\forall I(I \neq \emptyset \wedge h(I) \neq \emptyset \rightarrow \exists I' \subset I(I \subseteq h(I')))$$

It roughly expresses that each input of h must be generated by a proper subset. In the full paper we show on the basis of a formally defined semantics that this requirement ensures that there exists an execution of P which complies with the condition that on each channel, each value should be written before it is read. This is best explained by a simple example.

Example 5. Consider again the sequential processes

$$S_1 = [c??x \rightarrow c??y \| true \rightarrow c??y]; d!!0$$

and

$$S_2 = c!!0; [d??z \rightarrow c!!1]$$

After termination of $[S_1 \| S_2]$ we have that $y = 0$. This can be proved by deriving locally the postcondition

$$p_1 = (h = \{\langle\{c, c\}, \{d\}\rangle\} \wedge \forall u, v[c?? = \langle u, v \rangle \rightarrow y = v]) \vee$$
$$(h = \{\langle\{c\}, \{d\}\rangle\} \wedge \forall u[c?? = \langle u \rangle \rightarrow y = u])$$

for S_1 and the postcondition

$$p_2 = (h = \{\langle\emptyset, \{c\}\rangle, \langle\{d\}, \{c, c\}\rangle\} \wedge c!! = \langle 0, 1 \rangle)$$

for S_2. Then we have that $(p_1 \wedge p_2 \wedge compat(h) \wedge c?? \preceq c!!) \rightarrow y = 0$. This can be seen as follows: we consider the following two cases. Let h_1 denote the local history of S_1 and h_2 the local history of S_2:

1. $h_1 = \{\langle\{c, c\}, \{d\}\rangle\}$: there are a number of possible global histories that obey the projection restriction, i.e. are such that their respective projections yield h_1 and h_2. We only list a few below:

   - $h = \{\langle\emptyset, \{c\}\rangle, \langle\{d\}, \{c, c\}\rangle, \langle\{c, c\}, \{d\}\rangle\}$
   - $h = \{\langle\{c, c\}, \{c, d\}\rangle, \langle\{d\}, \{c, c\}\rangle\}$
   - $h = \{\langle\{c, c\}, \{c, d\}\rangle, \langle\{d\}, \{c, c\}\rangle, \langle\emptyset, \{c\}\rangle\}$
   - $h = \{\langle\emptyset, \{c\}\rangle, \langle\{c, c, d\}, \{c, c, d\}\rangle\}$
   - $h = \{\langle\{c, c\}, \{c, d\}\rangle, \langle\{c, c, d\}, \{c, c, d\}\rangle, \langle\emptyset, \{c\}\rangle, \langle\{d\}, \{c, c\}\rangle, \langle\{c, c\}, \{d\}\rangle\}$

   None of these possible global histories is compatible. For instance, in the first case the pair $\langle\{c, c\}, \{d\}\rangle$ has no predecessor as described in the definition of *compat* because the multiset $\{c, c\}$ cannot be generated. Note that $\{d\}$ generates $\{c, c\}$, but $\{d\} \not\subseteq \{c, c\}$. Without this requirement that $\{c, c\}$ should be generated by a proper subset we thus would allow circularities: $\{d\}$ generates $\{c, c\}$ and $\{c, c\}$ in its turn generates $\{d\}$.

2. $h_1 = \{\langle\{c\}, \{d\}\rangle\}$: again we list some representative possible global histories:

- $h = \{\langle \emptyset, \{c\}\rangle, \langle \{d\}, \{c,c\}\rangle, \langle \{c\}, \{d\}\rangle\}$
- $h = \{\langle \{c\}, \{c,d\}\rangle, \langle \{d\}, \{c,c\}\rangle\}$
- $h = \{\langle \emptyset, \{c\}\rangle, \langle \{c,d\}, \{c,c,d\}\rangle\}$
- $h = \{\langle \{c\}, \{c,d\}\rangle, \langle \{c,d\}, \{c,c,d\}\rangle, \langle \emptyset, \{c\}\rangle\}$

Out of these possible h's, for instance the last one listed here fulfils the *compat*-demands.

Therefore we conclude that $compat(h)$ implies that the first disjunct of p_1 should be discarded of, and hence from $\forall u[c?? = \langle u\rangle \to y = u]$, $c!! = \langle 0,1\rangle$ and $c?? \preceq c!!$ we conclude $y = 0$.

We conclude the exposition of the proof system with the global consequence rule and the substitution rule.

Rule 8 *(global consequence rule)*

$$\frac{\models p \to p', \ \{p'\}P\{q'\}, \ \models q' \to q}{\{p\}P\{q\}}$$

Rule 9 *(Substitution rule)*

$$\frac{\{p\}P\{q\}}{\{p[z/x]\}P\{q\}}$$

where x is a variable not occurring in P or q, and z is a variable of the same sort as x.

4 Multiset Logic

In this section, we look a bit closer at the subset of the logic that is needed in order to formalize reasoning about multisets. Formally, we introduce the following logic of multisets: Consider a structure $\langle \mathcal{P}_m(C), S_{c_1}, ..., S_{c_n}, \leq, \cup, \cap, \emptyset\rangle$, where $\mathcal{P}_m(C)$ denotes the set of multisets of elements of the finite set $C = \{c_1, ..., c_n\}$; S_{c_i}, for $c_i \in C$, denotes the —unary— c_i-successor function; $\leq$ is the subset-relation between multisets and $\emptyset$ denotes the empty multiset. Furthermore, we add two binary operators on multisets: the least upperbound (lub, denoted by $\cup$) and the greatest lowerbound (glb, denoted by $\cap$). Note that the glb of two elements of $\mathcal{P}_m(C)$ corresponds with the usual multiset intersection, whereas the least upperbound of two multisets x and y of $\mathcal{P}_m(C)$ corresponds to the multiset which contains for each element the maximal number of occurrences in x and

y. Hence the least upperbound operation differs from the operation of multiset addition, which *adds* the number of occurrences: consider for instance the multisets $\{c, d\}$ and $\{c, c, d\}$. Their least upperbound is $\{c, c, d\}$ whereas their multiset addition is $\{c, c, c, d\}$.

Given multiset variables $x, y, \ldots$ ranging over $\mathcal{P}_m(C)$, terms and formulas in this logic are given by

$$t ::= \emptyset \mid x \mid S_{c_i}(t) \mid t_1 \cup t_2 \mid t_1 \cap t_2$$

$$\varphi ::= t_1 = t_2 \mid t_1 \leq t_2 \mid \neg\varphi \mid \varphi_1 \wedge \varphi_2 \mid \exists x[\varphi].$$

The logic of multisets includes for each successor function its logic of discrete time, and consists of the following set T of axioms.

Firstly, we have the axioms concerning the ordering relation:

MS-REFL	$\forall x[x \leq x]$
MS-ANTISYM	$\forall x \forall y[x \leq y \wedge y \leq x \to x = y]$
MS-TRANS	$\forall x \forall y \forall z[x \leq y \wedge y \leq z \to x \leq z]$
MS-LEASTEL	$\forall x[\emptyset \leq x]$
MS-LUB	$\forall x \forall y[\ x \leq (x \cup y) \wedge y \leq (x \cup y)$
	$\qquad\qquad \wedge \forall z[x \leq z \wedge y \leq z \to (x \cup y) \leq z]]$
MS-GLB	$\forall x \forall y[x \geq (x \cap y) \wedge y \geq (x \cap y)$
	$\qquad\qquad \wedge \forall z[x \geq z \wedge y \geq z \to (x \cap y) \geq z]]$

Then, we have axioms concerning the successor functions:

MS-INJ	$\forall x \forall y[S_{c_i}(x) = S_{c_i}(y) \to x = y]$
MS-IMMSUC	$\forall x[\ x \leq S_{c_i}(x) \wedge x \neq S_{c_i}(x)$
	$\qquad \wedge \neg \exists y[x \leq y \wedge y \leq S_{c_i}(x) \wedge x \neq y \wedge y \neq S_{c_i}(x)]]$
MS-PRED	$\forall x[S_{c_i}(\emptyset) \leq x \to \exists y[S_{c_i}(y) = x]]$
MS-SUCDIFF	$\forall x[S_{c_i}(x) \neq S_{c_j}(x)]$ (for $i \neq j$)
MS-COMM	$\forall x[S_{c_i}(S_{c_j}(x)) = S_{c_j}(S_{c_i}(x))]$ (successors commute)

The following axiom allows to factorize a term t without occurrences of the $\cup$ and $\cap$ operations into a union of terms t_i, where t_i only contains the S_{c_i} successor function (from here on, $S_{c_i}^{k_i}(x)$ denotes the term resulting from applying S_{c_i} k_i times to x):

MS-SPLIT	$\forall x[S_{c_1}^{k_1} \cdots S_{c_n}^{k_n}(x) = \bigcup_i S_{c_i}^{k_i}(x)]$

Next we have an axiom (actually a family of axioms for $n, m \geq 0$ and each successor function S_{c_i}) which states in a sense that terms which only contain the successor operation S_{c_i} are totally ordered:

MS-TOT $\qquad \forall x \forall y [S_{c_i}^n(x) \leq x \cup S_{c_i}^m(y) \vee S_{c_i}^m(y) \leq y \cup S_{c_i}^n(x)]$

Note that the occurrence of x in the right hand side of $S_{c_i}^n(x) \leq x \cup S_{c_i}^m(y)$ causes the inequality to be valid automatically for the non-c_i elements of x. In this way, x serves as a 'mask' which filters out the irrelevant ordering information.

The following axiom allows to reduce basic formulas of the form $S_{c_j}^n(x) \leq \bigcup_i S_{c_i}^{k_i}(y)$ to a conjunction of formulas $t_1^i \leq t_2^i$, where t_1^i and t_2^i contain only the S_{c_i} successor function:

MS-COMP $\qquad \forall x \forall y [\ S_{c_j}^n(x) \leq \bigcup_i S_{c_i}^{k_i}(y) \longleftrightarrow \bigwedge_{i \neq j}(S_{c_i}(x) \leq x \cup S_{c_i}^{k_i+1}(y))$
$\qquad\qquad\qquad \wedge (S_{c_j}^{n+1}(x) \leq x \cup S_{c_j}^{k_j+1}(y))]$

Finally we have an axiom which allows to distribute existential quantification over a conjunction of formulas which do not share occurrences of the same successor function: let $Succ(\phi)$ denote the set of successor functions occurring in ϕ.

MS-CONSPLIT $\qquad \exists x[\phi_1 \wedge \phi_2] \longleftrightarrow (\exists x[\phi_1] \wedge \exists x[\phi_2])$
$\qquad\qquad\qquad$ (provided $Succ(\phi_1) \cap Succ(\phi_2) = \emptyset$)

We have the following theorem:

Theorem 4. *The theory T admits elimination of quantifiers, i.e. for any formula ϕ there exists a quantifier free formula ψ such that $T \vdash \phi \leftrightarrow \psi$; hence T is complete, and thus the theory of the structure $(\mathcal{P}_m(C), S_{c_1}, ..., S_{c_n}, \leq, \cup, \cap, \emptyset)$ is decidable.*

The proof is given in the full paper. Globally, we proceed as follows: it suffices to show that for any quantifier free formula ϕ the formula $\exists x \phi$ is equivalent (with respect to the above axioms) to a quantifier free formula. So let ϕ be a quantifier free formula. It is not difficult to transform, using the axioms, ϕ into a equivalent formula ψ which is constructed from basic formulas of the form $S_{c_i}^n(t) \leq t \cup S_{c_i}^m(t')$, where t and t' are either a variable or the constant $\emptyset$. Transform the resulting formula ψ into disjunctive normal form, and distribute the $\exists x$ over the disjunction. Now each disjunct is of the form $\exists x \bigwedge_i \phi_i$, where each ϕ_i is a conjunction of basic formulas which only contain the successor function S_{c_i}. Using the last axiom we can distribute the $\exists x$ over the conjuncts ϕ_i. Thus we obtain formulas $\exists x \phi_i$, where ϕ_i only contains the successor function S_{c_i}. But to these formulas we can apply the well-known theorem which states that the theory of one successor function admits elimination of quantifiers. Note that indeed our axioms contain for each successor function S_{c_i} the standard theory of one successor function, consisting of the axioms MS-REFL, MS-ANTISYM, MS-TRANS, MS-LEASTEL, MS-IMMSUC, MS-PRED and MS-TOT.

5 Conclusion and Future Work

The present paper presents a proof methodology which supports reasoning about the correctness of asynchronously communicating processes at an abstraction level at least as high as that of the programming language.

In the full paper we have proved that the proof system is *sound*, i.e. every derivable correctness formula is valid, and *(relative) complete*, i.e. every valid correctness formula is derivable. The formal justification is given with respect to a formally defined fully abstract semantics. Due to a close correspondence of the proof rules and the semantics, the proofs of soundness and completeness are fairly straightforward.

Because of its high level of abstraction the proof system provides a suitable basis for top-down program development along the lines of a refinement calculus as defined in [Bac80]. Such a refinement calculus for asynchronously communicating processes we are currently investigating.

Additionally, to study the practical usage of the presented proof methodology we plan to investigate some case studies.

Exploiting the fact that our multiset logic is decidable, we can transform our rules in a format amenable for use by verification tools; in particular, we use PVS (Prototype Verification System, see [SOS92]) to study the impact of automated theorem proving techniques in our setting. PVS allows for interactive generation of proofs, defining of strategies and decision procedures for arithmetic, thus alleviating the user from trivial but tedious tasks.

In this way, using the proof system from [dBvH94], we already verified the problem of determining a network topology by means of a so-called heartbeat algorithm (see also [And91]). The algorithm entails for each participating process to repeatedly send and receive information about network links to its direct neighbours, which finally leads to a complete picture of the networks topology. (The topology information can be used by the processes for instance to route their messages efficiently along the links of the network.)

Finally, we are currently investigating the decidability of the extension of our multiset logic with the operation of multiset addition, denoted by $\oplus$ and defined by:

$$x \oplus \emptyset = x$$
$$x \oplus S_{c_i}(y) = S_{c_i}(x \oplus y)$$

References

[AdB94] P.H.M. America and F.S. de Boer. Reasoning about dynamically evolving process structures. *Formal Aspects of Computing*, 6:269–316, 1994.

[AFdR80] K.R. Apt, N. Francez, and W.-P. de Roever. A proof system for communicating sequential processes. *ACM-TOPLAS*, 2(3):359–385, 1980.

[And91] Gregory R. Andrews. *Concurrent Programming, Principles and Practice*. The Benjamin/Cummings Publishing Company, Inc., 1991.

[Bac80] R.J.R. Back. *Correctness Preserving Program Refinements: Proof Theory and Applications*. Number 131 in Mathematical Centre Tracts. Mathematical Centre, Amsterdam, 1980.

[dBvH94] F.S. de Boer and M. van Hulst. A proof system for asynchronously communicating deterministic processes. In B. Rovan I. Prívara and P. Ružička, editors, *Proc. MFCS '94*, volume 841 of *Lecture Notes in Computer Science*, pages 256–265. Springer-Verlag, 1994.

[Fra92] N. Francez. *Program Verification*. Addison Wesley, 1992.

[Gri87] David Gries. *The Science of Programming*. Texts and Monographs in Computer Science. Springer, 4th print edition, 1987.

[HdR86] J. Hooman and W.-P. de Roever. The quest goes on: a survey of proof systems for partial correctness of CSP. In *Current trends in concurrency*, volume 24 of *Lecture Notes in Computer Science*, pages 343–395. Springer-Verlag, 1986.

[Jon89] B. Jonsson. A fully abstract trace model for dataflow networks. In *Proc. POPL '89*, 1989.

[Jos92] M.B. Josephs. Receptive process theory. *Acta Informatica*, 29, 1992.

[OG76] S. Owicki and D. Gries. An axiomatic proof technique for parallel programs I. *Acta Informatica*, 6:319–340, 1976.

[Pan88] P.K. Pandya. *Compositional Verification of Distributed Programs*. PhD thesis, Tata Institute of Fundamental Research, Homi Bhabha Road, Bombay 400 005, INDIA, 1988.

[SOS92] J. Rushby S. Owre and N. Shankar. PVS: A prototype verification system. In *11th Conference on Automated Deduction*, volume 607 of *Lecture Notes in Artificial Intelligence*, pages 748–752. Springer-Verlag, 1992.

[Zwi88] J. Zwiers. *Compositionality, Concurrency and Partial Correctness*. PhD thesis, Technical University Eindhoven, 1988.

A Graphical Calculus

Sharon Curtis and Gavin Lowe

Oxford University Computing Laboratory, Parks Road, Oxford, OX1 3QD, UK.

Abstract. We present a graphical calculus, which allows mathematical formulae to be represented and reasoned about using a visual representation. We define how a formula may be represented by a graph, and present a number of laws for transforming graphs, and describe the effects these transformations have on the corresponding formulae. We then use these transformation laws to perform proofs. We illustrate the graphical calculus by applying it to the relational and sequential calculi. The graphical calculus makes formulae easier to understand, and so often makes the next step in a proof more obvious. Furthermore, it is more expressive, and so allows a number of proofs that cannot otherwise be undertaken in a point-free way.

1 Introduction

Traditionally, mathematical formulae are written down on a single line. For example, in the relational calculus [9], given four relations P, Q, R and S, we can write $P;Q \cap R;S$ to represent the relation that relates two elements x and y iff there exist u and v such that P relates x to u, Q relates u to y, R relates x to v, and S relates v to y:

$$x(P;Q \cap R;S)y \;\Leftrightarrow\; \exists u,v \bullet x\,P\,u \wedge u\,Q\,y \wedge x\,R\,v \wedge v\,S\,y.$$

But suppose that we also want to specify that u and v are related by T. Traditional mathematics has no way of writing down such a relation in a point-free style using only the composition and intersection operators. In other words, the language of intersection and composition is expressively incomplete.

In this paper we develop a calculus of graphs for defining and reasoning about relations. For example, we represent the relation $P;Q \cap R;S$ by the graph in figure 1. Each edge represents the relation with which it is labelled; two consecutive

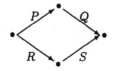

Fig. 1. A graph representing $P;Q \cap R;S$.

edges represent the composition of the corresponding relations; two paths with the same start and end points represent the intersection of the corresponding relations.

If we want to add the above condition that the intermediate points are related by T then we simply add a corresponding edge labelled T:

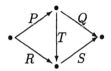

We will develop a number of *graph transformation rules*. Transforming a graph according to these rules alters the corresponding relation: for example, we will show that removing an edge from a graph makes the corresponding relation larger.

The graphical calculus provides a useful tool for doing proofs about relations: sometimes the proof without graphs is very unobvious and complicated, whereas the graphical proof is much more straightforward; and in some cases, we have proved results using the graphical calculus that we have been unable to do otherwise. The calculus gives us a way of getting at the internal structure of a relation; and because the representation is very visual, it is normally easy to see what is the correct next step in a proof.

In fact, the graphical calculus applies to more calculi than just the relational calculus. It provides a general way of representing many mathematical formulae that cannot be written down on one line in the normal way. It then provides rules for transforming these representations. We give examples of other calculi that can be represented in the graphical calculus.

In the next section we apply the graphical calculus to the relational calculus: we give a brief overview of the relational calculus, formally define how a relation can be represented by a graph, present eleven graph transformation rules, and illustrate the calculus with two examples. In section 3, we consider the sequential calculus of [10]: we describe the calculus, define how elements of the calculus can be represented by graphs, present nine graph transformation rules (eight of which are the same as in the relational calculus), and use the graph calculus to prove a result which has not otherwise been proved in the sequential calculus. In section 4 we discuss various other points of interest.

2 The relational calculus

We define a *relation* of type $A \leftrightarrow B$ to be a subset R of $A \times B$, and write xRy when $(x, y) \in R$. Composition and converse are defined in the normal way:

$$P;Q \mathrel{\widehat{=}} \{(x, z) \mid \exists y \bullet xPy \wedge yQz\}$$
$$P^{\circ} \mathrel{\widehat{=}} \{(y, x) \mid xPy\}.$$

Union and intersection of relations are simply the corresponding set relations. We use the convention that composition binds more tightly than union and intersection. The identity relation on A is denoted by Id_A, and the universal relation on $A \times B$ by $\Pi_{A \times B}$:

$$Id_A \cong \{(x,x) \mid x \in A\}$$
$$\Pi_{A \times B} \cong \{(x,y) \mid x \in A \wedge y \in B\};$$

the subscripts are usually omitted, and inferred from context.

We will use two operators which return the domain and range of a relation. It is convenient to define these such that they return a relation, i.e. a set of pairs. They can be defined in a point-wise manner by:

$$dom\ R \cong \{(x,x) \mid \exists y \cdot xRy\}$$
$$ran\ R \cong \{(y,y) \mid \exists x \cdot xRy\}.$$

However, for calculations it is more convenient to have a point-free definition:

$$dom\ R \cong Id \cap R;R^\circ$$
$$ran\ R \cong Id \cap R^\circ;R.$$

We will also use the quotient operator, defined as follows:

$$R \backslash S \cong \{(x,y) \mid \forall z \cdot zRx \Rightarrow zSy\}.$$

The operator may also be defined by a Galois connection:

$$R;T \subseteq S \Leftrightarrow T \subseteq R \backslash S.$$

For example, $\in \backslash \in$ represents the subset relation (where $\in$ is the set membership relation).

2.1 Representing relations by graphs

As described in the introduction, we will represent relations by graphs: each edge represents the relation with which it is labelled; composition is represented by arrows in sequence; and intersection is represented by arrows in parallel. For example, the relation $(P;Q^\circ \cap (R \cup S));T$ can be represented by:

As we will see later, arrows can be reversed to give the converse of a relation, and union can be represented by splitting the graph; so the above relation may also be represented by:

Formally, we consider graphs of the form (V, s, t, A) where V is a finite set of vertices, $s \in V$ is the source, $t \in V$ is the target, and $A \in \mathbf{P}(V \times S \times V)$ is a finite set of edges labelled with elements of S representing relations: the edge (v, R, v') represents an edge from v to v' labelled R. When we draw a graph, the source and target will not be explicitly labelled: they will be the left-most and right-most vertices, respectively.

Note that we have no conditions concerning the connectivity of graphs. Note also that we use *sets* of edges, rather than multisets (bags); this means that a graph with two edges from v to v' labelled R is the same as the corresponding graph with only one such edge.

We can now formally define the way in which a graph represents a relation.

Definition 1. The graph $G = (\{v_0, \ldots, v_n\}, v_0, v_n, A)$ represents the relation R where

$$x \mathrel{R} y \ \textit{iff}\ \exists x_0, \ldots, x_n \bullet x = x_0 \wedge y = x_n \wedge \forall (v_i, S, v_j) \in A \bullet x_i \mathrel{S} x_j.$$

We call R the *interpretation* of G.

The graph represents the relation that relates x and y iff there is some way of labelling the vertices with elements such that x labels the source, y labels the target, and if there is an edge labelled S between two vertices then the corresponding elements are related by S.

For example, the graph in figure 1 relates x and y iff

$$\exists x_0, x_1, x_2, x_3 \bullet x = x_0 \wedge y = x_3 \wedge x_0 \mathrel{P} x_1 \wedge x_1 \mathrel{Q} x_3 \wedge x_0 \mathrel{R} x_2 \wedge x_2 \mathrel{S} x_3,$$

that is, the graph indeed represents the relation $P;Q \cap R;S$.

In the following we will use graphs when formally we mean the relations represented by those graphs. So, for example, we write $G_1 \subseteq G_2$ when the relation corresponding to G_1 is a subset of the relation corresponding to G_2; we write $G_1 \cong G_2$ when the relations are equal.

We define a number of graph transformation laws: some of these transformations leave the corresponding relation unchanged; others produce a superset of the original relation. Each of the laws may easily be proved sound with respect to the above definition.

We may enlarge the relation labelling any edge; this enlarges the relation represented by the whole graph:

Law 1 (Monotonicity) *If $R \subseteq S$ then*

$$(V, s, t, A \cup \{(v, R, v')\}) \subseteq (V, s, t, A \cup \{(v, S, v')\}).$$

This law allows us to incorporate techniques from the relational calculus into the graph calculus: we may use the relational calculus to prove $R \subseteq S$, and then use law 1 to replace an edge labelled R by one labelled S.

The next law uses the concept of a graph homomorphism:

Definition 2 (Homomorphism). Given graphs $G = (V, s, t, A)$ and $G' = (V', s', t', A')$, a *homomorphism* from G to G' is a function $\phi : V \to V'$ such that: (1) $\phi(s) = s'$; (2) $\phi(t) = t'$; and (3) for each edge $(v, P, v') \in A$, there is a corresponding edge $(\phi(v), P, \phi(v')) \in A'$.

For example, there is a homomorphism from the left hand graph to the right hand graph below, mapping u_0 to v_0, u_1 and u_2 to v_1, and u_3 to v_3.

Law 2 (Homomorphism) *If there is a homomorphism from G to G' then $G \supseteq G'$.*

Note that if there is a homomorphism ϕ from G to G', and another homomorphism ψ from G' to G, then $G \cong G'$. This allows us to identify the following two graphs, for example:

and

The following law states that we may always remove edges to make the corresponding relation larger. It can be proved as a corollary of the previous law, but it is sufficiently useful to be worth stating explicitly.

Law 3 (Remove edges) $(V, s, t, A \cup \{(v, R, v')\}) \subseteq (V, s, t, A)$.

An edge labelled with R may be replaced by a graph representing R:

Law 4 (Replace edge by graph) *If the relation R is represented by the graph (V', s', t', A'), and $V \cap V' = \{s', t'\}$, then*

$$(V, s, t, A \cup \{(s', R, t')\}) \cong (V \cup V', s, t, A \cup A').$$

The next four laws show how the operations of composition, intersection and union are represented in the graph calculus. If an edge is labelled by a relational composition then we may split it into two:

Law 5 (Split composition) *If v'' is a vertex not in V, then*

$$(V, s, t, A \cup \{(v, R;S, v')\}) \cong (V \cup \{v''\}, s, t, A \cup \{(v, R, v''), (v'', S, v')\}).$$

If we have two successive edges labelled with relations R and S, we may add another edge labelled with $R;S$ (this may be proved as a corollary of the previous law and the homomorphism law):

Law 6 (Composition) *If* $(v, R, v'), (v', S, v'') \in A$ *then*

$$(V, s, t, A) \cong (V, s, t, A \cup \{(v, R;S, v'')\}).$$

An edge labelled with an intersection $R \cap S$ may be replaced by two edges with the same start and end points, labelled with R and S, and vice versa:

Law 7 (Intersection)

$$(V, s, t, A \cup \{(v, R \cap S, v')\}) \cong (V, s, t, A \cup \{(v, R, v'), (v, S, v')\}).$$

If an edge of a graph is labelled with the union of two relations, R and S, then the graph may be replaced by the union of two graphs with corresponding edges labelled by R and by S:

Law 8 (Union)

$$(V, s, t, A \cup \{(v, R \cup S, v')\}) \cong (V, s, t, A \cup \{(v, R, v')\})$$
$$\cup (V, s, t, A \cup \{(v, S, v')\}).$$

The above laws allow a graph to be reduced to a normal form: laws 5, 7 and 8 allow compound labels to be broken down into simple labels (i.e. labels without compositions, intersections or unions); law 2 then allows redundant edges to be removed. Further, the laws—along with the observation that a graph with a single edge labelled R represents the relation R—justify our informal description of how to represent a relation by a graph.

In the above we have used graphs to represent *relations*. However, we can also use graphs to represent other sorts of mathematical formulae. Given any space S with operators $\cap$, $\cup$ and ; and a preorder $\subseteq$, we define a *graphical calculus* over S to be a calculus of graphs labelled with members of S, such that we have some way of interpreting a graph as a member of S, such that the above eight transformation rules are satisfied. For example, in the above we took S to be a space of relations, and $\cap$, $\cup$, ; and $\subseteq$ had the normal interpretations of intersection, union, relational composition and subset. In later sections we will look at other instances of graphical calculi.

Particular instances of the graphical calculus may satisfy additional laws. For example, in the relational calculus three additional laws concern the converse operator, the universal relation and the identity relation.

An edge labelled R may be reversed in direction and relabelled with the converse of R:

Law 9 (Converse)

$$(V, s, t, A \cup \{(v, R, v')\}) \cong (V, s, t, A \cup \{(v', R^\circ, v)\}).$$

Any two vertices are connected via the universal relation:

Law 10 (Universal relation) *If v,v' are two vertices in V, then*

$$(V, s, t, A) \cong (V, s, t, A \cup \{(v, \Pi, v')\}).$$

If two vertices are related by the identity, then they may be fused together:

Law 11 (Fusion)

$$(V, s, t, A \cup \{(v, Id, v')\}) \cong$$
$$(\{ren\, u \mid u \in V\}, ren\, s, ren\, t, \{(ren\, u, R, ren\, u') \mid (u, R, u') \in A\}),$$
$$where\ ren\, u = \begin{cases} v, & if\ u = v' \\ u, & otherwise. \end{cases}$$

The function *ren* renames the node v' to v.

2.2   Example: the modular law

One law commonly used in the relational calculus is the modular law, also known as the Dedekind law:

$$A \cap B;C \subseteq (A;C^\circ \cap B);C.$$

This law cannot be proved by calculation using only the properties of intersection, converse and composition in a point-free manner (there exist frameworks that satisfy these properties but not the modular law). The proof may either be executed in a point-wise fashion, or by using tabulation of relations (expressing a relation as the converse of a function followed by a function). Either method is more complicated than the proof using the graph calculus:

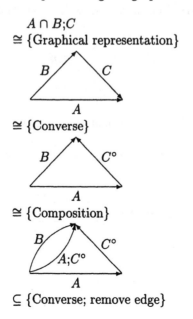

$$A \cap B;C$$
$$\cong \{\text{Graphical representation}\}$$

$$\cong \{\text{Converse}\}$$

$$\cong \{\text{Composition}\}$$

$$\subseteq \{\text{Converse; remove edge}\}$$

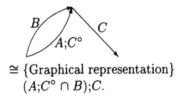

$\cong$ {Graphical representation}
$(A;C° \cap B);C.$

2.3 Example: an arithmetical lemma

Another example concerns a lemma pertaining to sets of natural numbers. Writing $\ni$ for $\in°$, we define the minimum with respect to a relation by:

$$min\, R = \ni \cap \in \backslash R°.$$

(The pair (X, x) is in this relation if $X \ni x$ and for all y, $y \in X \Rightarrow x\, R\, y$.) Our lemma states:

$$dom \ni \; ; \in\backslash\in \; ; min \leq \; \subseteq \; min \leq \; ; \geq,$$

If a pair (X, y) is in the left hand side then X is non-empty, and there is some superset Y of X such that y is the minimum element of Y. The lemma states that X has a minimum x which is at least as large as y. That is, the minimum of a non-empty set of numbers is at least as large as the minimum of any superset.

Before embarking on the graphical proof, we note how the law $S; S\backslash R \subseteq R$ of the relational calculus may be translated into the graph calculus. If we have in our graph a subgraph

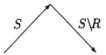

then the following arrow may be added without altering the interpretation of the graph:

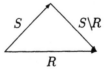

We will refer to this law as the quotient law. It may be proved using laws 1, 3 and 6.

Note also that the domains and ranges of relations may be simply represented within graphs. For example:

(Recall that the sources and targets of the graphs are the left-most and right-most nodes.)

The proof of the above lemma goes as follows:

$$dom \ni ; \in \setminus \in ; min \leq$$
$$= \{\text{Well-foundedness of } \geq\}$$
$$dom(min \leq); \in \setminus \in ; min \leq$$
$$\cong \{\text{Graphical representation}\}$$

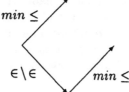

$$\cong \{\text{Definition of } min; \text{ intersection}\}$$

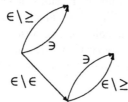

$$\cong \{\text{Converse; quotient; converse}\}$$

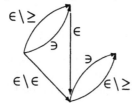

$$\cong \{\text{Quotient}\}$$

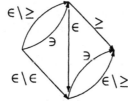

$$\subseteq \{\text{Remove edges; definition of } min\}$$

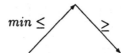

$$\cong \{\text{Graphical representation}\}$$
$$min \leq ; \geq .$$

This proof illustrates a common technique in the graph calculus, namely adding all the arrows we need, and removing superfluous ones at the end.

3 Sequential calculus

The sequential calculus [10] aims to provide a common framework of algebraic laws applicable to many models of reactive systems. In this section, we examine how the sequential calculus can be modelled in the graphical calculus.

Central to the sequential calculus is the notion of an *observation*. In the calculus of intervals [1], an observation is a pair (s, t) of times—the start and termination times—with $s \leq t$. In regular expressions [8], an observation is a finite sequence of letters drawn from some alphabet A. In the regularity calculus [4], the sequences are given the structure of a group. In interval temporal logic [11], observations are functions from time intervals to states. In the traces model of CSP [6], observations are traces of visible actions. The relational calculus is also a sequential calculus, where an observation is a pair (x, y) such that x is related to y.

In each of these calculi, two observations can be composed via an associative composition operator, ";". For regular expressions, the composition operator is simply concatenation of strings. For the other calculi, composition is a partial operator; for example, in the relational calculus two observations may be composed iff the second element of the first observation is the same as the first element of the second observation; in this case the intermediate point is omitted:

$$(r, s);(s, t) = (r, t).$$

We say that observation x is a prefix of y, written $x \leq y$, if x can be extended to y:

$$x \leq y \Leftrightarrow \exists z \bullet x;z = y.$$

In each calculus, a system may be represented by a *set* of observations, termed a *sequential relation*. These form a Boolean algebra under the union and intersection operators. The composition operator may be lifted point-wise to sets:

$$P;Q \;\hat{=}\; \{p;q \mid p \in P \wedge q \in Q\}.$$

We denote the universal set of observations by Π. The main difference between the relational and sequential calculi is the lack of a converse operator in the sequential calculus.

An important concept is that of units. Each observation x has a left unit $\overleftarrow{x}$ and a right unit $\overrightarrow{x}$ such that

$$\overleftarrow{x};x \;=\; x \;=\; x;\overrightarrow{x}.$$

For example, in the relational and interval calculi, $\overleftarrow{(x, y)} = (x, x)$ and $\overrightarrow{(x, y)} = (y, y)$. We denote the set of all units by Id:

$$Id \;\hat{=}\; \{x \mid \overleftarrow{x} = x = \overrightarrow{x}\}.$$

In [10], a number of algebraic laws are developed for reasoning about sequential relations, rather than reasoning about individual observations; for example:

$$R;Id = R = Id;R, \qquad P;(Q \cup R) = P;Q \cup P;R, \qquad P;(Q \cap R) \subseteq P;Q \cap P;R.$$

3.1   Representing sequential relations by graphs

We may use the graph calculus to represent sequential relations in the obvious way. For example, if in figure 1 the labels are interpreted as sequential relations then the graph represents the sequential relation $P;Q \cap R;S$. Each edge represents the sequential relation with which it is labelled; a path through the graph represents the composition of the corresponding relations; two paths with common source and target represent the intersection of the corresponding relations.

We formalize our representation as follows:

Definition 3. The graph $G \cong (\{v_0, \ldots, v_n\}, v_0, v_n, A)$ represents the sequential relation

$$\{x \mid \exists x_0, \ldots, x_n \bullet x_0 = \overleftarrow{x} \wedge x_n = x \wedge \forall i \in 0 \ldots n \bullet x_i \leq x$$
$$\wedge \forall (v_i, S, v_j) \in A \bullet \exists y \in S \bullet x_i;y = x_j\}.$$

We call this sequential relation the *interpretation* of G.

An observation x is in the interpretation of G if for each vertex v_i there is a corresponding observation x_i, such that:

- the observation corresponding to the source is the left unit of x;
- the observation corresponding to the target is x;
- each observation is a prefix of x;
- and for each edge (v_i, S, v_j) there is an observation y of S which when composed with x_i gives x_j.

The idea is that we start off at the source with a unit observation, and traverse the graph; on each edge we extend the observation with an observation from the edge's label, until we get to the target. Each intermediate observation is compatible with (i.e. is a prefix of) the final observation.

It is easy to prove the following theorem from the above definition:

Theorem 4 (Laws of the sequential calculus). *Each of the graph transformation laws 1–8 hold for the sequential calculus.*

The relational calculus is a particular example of a sequential calculus, so we would hope that the two ways of interpreting a graph—as a relation or as a sequential relation—are compatible; the following lemma shows that this is indeed the case.

Lemma 5. *Given a graph G labelled with relations, let R be the corresponding relation (as in definition 1) and let S be the corresponding sequential relation (as in definition 3); then:*

$$x \, R \, y \Leftrightarrow (x, y) \in S.$$

Proof. Let $G = (\{v_0, \ldots, v_n\}, v_0, v_n, A)$, and let R and S be as above. Suppose $x\,R\,y$. Then, from definition 1, there exist $y_0, \ldots, y_n$ (labelling the vertices) such that

$$x = y_0 \land y = y_n \land \forall(v_i, P, v_j) \in A \cdot y_i \, P \, y_j.$$

Then to show $(x, y) \in S$, we label the vertices with $(x, y_0), \ldots, (x, y_n)$; to meet the requirements of definition 3 we need to check:

$$(x, y_0) = \overleftarrow{(x, y)} \land (x, y_n) = (x, y) \land \forall i \in 0 \ldots n \cdot (x, y_i) \leq (x, y)$$
$$\land \forall(v_i, P, v_j) \in A \cdot \exists(x', y') \in P \cdot (x, y_i); (x', y') = (x, y_j),$$

which is trivial.

Conversely, suppose $(x, y) \in S$. Then, from definition 3, there exist $(x_0, y_0), \ldots, (x_n, y_n)$ such that

$$(x_0, y_0) = \overleftarrow{(x, y)} \land (x_n, y_n) = (x, y) \land \forall i \in 0 \ldots n \cdot (x_i, y_i) \leq (x, y)$$
$$\land \forall(v_i, P, v_j) \in A \cdot \exists(x', y') \in P \cdot (x_i, y_i); (x', y') = (x_j, y_j),$$

from which it follows that $\forall i \in 0 \ldots n \cdot x_i = x$. To show $x\,R\,y$, we label the vertices with $y_0, \ldots, y_n$; to meet the requirements of definition 1 we need to check:

$$x = y_0 \land y = y_n \land \forall(v_i, P, v_j) \in A \cdot y_i \, P \, y_j,$$

which is again trivial.

3.2 Local linearity

Many sequential calculi satisfy an additional axiom, that of *local linearity*. This is expressed at the level of observations as follows:

Definition 6 (Local linearity).

$$x;y = x';y' \Rightarrow \exists w \cdot x;w = x' \land w;y' = y$$
$$\lor \exists w \cdot x';w = x \land w;y = y'.$$

This may be expressed as a pair of commuting diagrams:

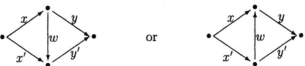

Lifting the axiom of local linearity to the level of sets of observations has proved difficult. One formulation is

$$P;Q \cap R;S = (P \cap R;\Pi);Q \cap R;(\Pi;Q \cap S)$$
$$\cup (P;\Pi \cap R);S \cap P;(Q \cap \Pi;S).$$

However, this formulation does not seem to be strong enough for all our requirements.

In the graph calculus, the axiom of local linearity can be expressed as follows: if we have a graph G containing two edges with start points v_i and v_j, and common end point v_k, then we can add an edge labelled with the universal relation Π either from v_i to v_j or from v_j to v_i:

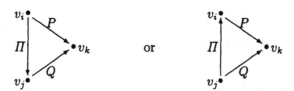

(Note that the above pictures may be subgraphs of the complete graph.) This is formalized as follows:

Law 12 (Local linearity) *If* $(v_i, P, v_k), (v_j, Q, v_k) \in A$ *then*

$$(V, s, t, A) \cong (V, s, t, A \cup \{(v_i, \Pi, v_j)\}) \cup (V, s, t, A \cup \{(v_j, \Pi, v_i)\}).$$

Proof. Obviously, from the law for removing edges (law 3), the right hand side is a subset of the left hand side.

Let $G = (V, s, t, A)$ be such that $(v_i, P, v_k), (v_j, Q, v_k) \in A$. Let R be the sequential relation represented by G, and let $x \in R$. Then there exist $x_0, \ldots, x_n$ such that

$$x_0 = \overleftarrow{x} \wedge x_n = x \wedge \forall i \in 0 \ldots n \cdot x_i \leq x$$
$$\wedge \forall (v_i, S, v_j) \in A \cdot \exists y \in S \cdot x_i; y = x_j.$$

In particular, there exist $p \in P$ and $q \in Q$ such that $x_i; p = x_j; q = x_k$. Then by the axiom of local linearity,

$$\exists w \cdot x_i; w = x_j \wedge w; q = p \quad \text{or} \quad \exists w \cdot x_j; w = x_i \wedge w; p = q.$$

In the first case, consider the graph $G' = (V, s, t, A \cup \{(v_i, \Pi, v_j)\})$. Then x is a member of the sequential relation represented by G': to show this we simply label G' with the same observations $x_0, \ldots, x_n$ as above, and note that $\exists w \in \Pi \cdot x_i; w = x_j$.

Similarly, in the second case x is a member of the sequential relation represented by $(V, s, t, A \cup \{(v_j, \Pi, v_i)\})$.

3.3 Example: the 3-◇ law

We will now use the above graph transformation rule to prove a law known as the 3-◇ law. Define

$$\diamond X \cong \Pi; X; \Pi.$$

Note that $\diamond X$ corresponds to the "somewhere X" of interval temporal logic: it contains all observations that include an element of X as a subobservation.

The 3-$\diamond$ law states:

$$P;Q;R \cap \diamond X \subseteq P;(Q;R \cap \diamond X) \cup (P;Q \cap \diamond X);R \cup \diamond(X \cap \diamond Q).$$

That is, if an observation of X occurs sometime during an observation of $P;Q;R$, then either it occurs during $Q;R$, or it occurs during $P;Q$, or Q occurs during X. Much effort has gone into proving this law using the standard axioms of the sequential calculus, but without success.

Using the graph calculus version of the axiom of local linearity, the proof is extremely straightforward:

$P;Q;R \cap \diamond X$
$\cong \{$Graph representation$\}$

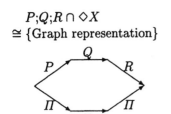

$\cong \{$Local linearity$\}$

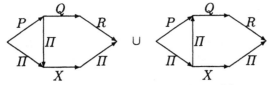

$\subseteq \{$Local linearity applied to second graph$\}$

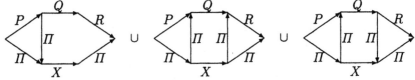

$\subseteq \{$Removing edges$\}$

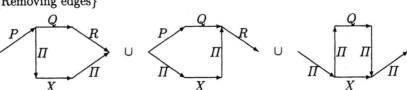

$\cong \{$Relations corresponding to graphs$\}$
$\quad P;(Q;R \cap \diamond X) \cup (P;Q \cap \diamond X);R \cup \diamond(X \cap \diamond Q).$

4 Discussion

In this paper we have presented a graphical calculus. We have described how to represent mathematical formulae—for example relations or sequential relations—by graphs. We have presented rules for transforming graphs and explained how these rules affect the corresponding formulae. In this final section we discuss a few other points of interest.

4.1 Related work

Brown and Hutton [2] have developed a calculus of pictures, oriented towards circuit design. Their pictures are built up from basic cells and wires using sequential composition, intersection and reciprocation. They give a semantics to pictures in terms of relations, in a manner very similar to our approach. In [2, 3] it is shown that their calculus is complete in that two pictures are equivalent with respect to their transformation rules if and only if they represent the same relation for all interpretations of the basic cells; this proof proceeds by viewing pictures as arrows in a unitary pretabular allegory [5].

Our approach is more general: their approach is restricted to calculi with intersection, composition and converse, whereas ours includes the union operator, or can exclude the converse operator. Furthermore, their approach is more oriented towards treating basic cells as simply symbols, and proving circuits equivalent in an automated manner [7]; whereas our calculi—particularly the relational calculus—are more oriented towards using the properties of the basic relations themselves in order to manually prove results concerning those relations. The Brown–Hutton pictures seem to be the easier to use for circuit design, whereas our graphs are suitable for more abstract calculi.

4.2 Other graphical calculi

We believe that many other calculi can also be fitted into the framework of the graphical calculus. For example, consider graphs labelled with positive numbers—to represent lengths—and where the interpretation of a graph is the length of the shortest path from source to target. This is a graphical calculus when one interprets the operations $\cup, \cap,$; and $\subseteq$ as maximum ($\sqcup$), minimum ($\sqcap$), addition ($+$) and less-than ($\leq$), respectively. We leave it to the reader to check that the graph transformation laws 1–8 are satisfied.

While this calculus is not very interesting in its own right, it does provide some evidence that the graph calculus may be of more general applicability.

We have tried to provide a general framework for others to produce their own graphical calculus: they have only to formally define the way in which a graph represents a formula in their setting, check that the eight graph transformation laws 1–8 hold, and derive other laws particular to their calculus. Any law in the underlying calculus will have a counterpart in the graphical calculus (because of the monotonicity law), but in some cases the graphical law will be stronger (for example, the local linearity law of the sequential calculus).

4.3 Advantages of the graph calculus

One major advantage of the graph calculus is that expressive power is increased, allowing us to define and reason about more formulae. For example, Tarski [9] gives an example of a predicate not expressible as a sentence of the relational calculus:

$$\exists w, x, y, z \bullet x\,R\,y \wedge x\,R\,z \wedge x\,R\,w \wedge y\,R\,z \wedge y\,R\,w \wedge w\,R\,z.$$

We may express this predicate in the graphical calculus as follows:

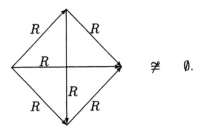

$$\neq \quad \emptyset.$$

If the relation represented by the above graph is non-empty then the vertices in the graph can be labelled by w, x, y and z (clockwise from the bottom) such that $x\,R\,y \wedge x\,R\,z \wedge x\,R\,w \wedge y\,R\,z \wedge y\,R\,w \wedge w\,R\,z$, and conversely. We are grateful to C. A. R. Hoare for referring us to this example.

The extra expressive power of the graphical calculus makes some proofs possible that cannot be done otherwise, for example the proofs of the modular law and the 3-$\diamond$ law above. Even in short proofs, the steps taken often result in intermediate graphs that are not directly translatable back to the underlying calculus. Even when the extra expressive power of the graphical calculus is not used, graphical proofs can be easier because they give a very visual representation of formulae, and this can make the next step more obvious.

Some formulae themselves may be simpler as graphs. For example, in the relational calculus, formulae involving dom, ran, Id or Π are often greatly simplified in the graphical representation.

Products of relations are also easily represented, by graphically interpreting their definition in terms of projections:

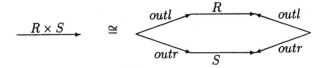

where $outl$ and $outr$ are the normal projection relations. This yields the pictorially intuitive idea of products being represented as parallel arrows; the graphical representation makes it easier to reason about each element of the pair separately.

4.4 Generalizing the graph calculus

In this paper we defined a graphical calculus to be defined over any structure S with operators $\cap$, $\cup$ and ; and a preorder $\subseteq$ such that the laws 1–8 hold. The question then arises as to whether we need all these laws, or even whether we need more. It may be that we can find calculi that we would like to consider as graphical calculi, but which satisfy only some of these laws; for example, if the underlying structure includes only composition and intersection operators, then we would not have the union law. Further investigations will be needed to find the laws common to all graphical calculi.

So far we have been considering graphs with two special vertices, the source and the target. We can easily generalise this to allow graphs with k special nodes, representing a k-ary relation. Tarski [9] gave another example of a predicate not expressible in the relational calculus:

$$\forall x, y, z \bullet \exists u \bullet x\,R\,u \wedge y\,R\,u \wedge z\,R\,u.$$

This can be represented using a graph representing a ternary relation, with the three outermost nodes representing the three components of the relation:

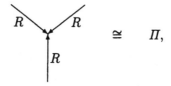 $\cong \quad \Pi,$

The graph represents the ternary relation that relates x, y and z if there is some way of labelling the central node with u such that $x\,R\,u \wedge y\,R\,u \wedge z\,R\,u$; if this is the universal relation then R satisfies the above predicate.

The graph calculus can be extended to use *hyperedges* within graphs (i.e. edges with more than two ends) to represent k-ary relations; then composition of relations would be simply represented by hyperedges sharing nodes. We hope that a suitable pictorial representation could be found that would make reasoning about such relations easier.

Acknowledgements

We are grateful to Tony Hoare, He Jifeng, Oege de Moor, Graham Hutton, and the anonymous referees for useful comments, suggestions and encouragement.

References

1. Stephen Brien. A time-interval calculus. In R. Bird, C. Morgan, and J. Woodcock, editors, *Mathematics of Program Construction*, volume 669 of *LNCS*. Springer Verlag, 1992.
2. Carolyn Brown and Graham Hutton. Categories, allegories and circuit design. In *Ninth Annual IEEE Symposium on Logic in Computer Science*, pages 372–381, 1994.
3. Carolyn Brown and Alan Jeffrey. Allegories of circuits. In *Third International Symposium, Logical Foundations of Computer Science*, volume 813 of *Lecture Notes in Computer Science*, pages 56–68. Springer-Verlag, 1994.

4. E. W. Dijkstra. The unification of three calculi. In M. Broy, editor, *Program Design Calculi*, pages 197–231. Springer Verlag, 1993.

5. Peter Freyd and Andre Scedrov. *Categories, Allegories*. North-Holland, 1990.

6. C. A. R. Hoare. *Communicating Sequential Processes*. Prentice Hall, 1985.

7. Graham Hutton, Erik Meijer, and Ed Voermans. A tool for relational programmers. Available on WWW from `http://www.cs.ruu.nl/people/graham/allegories.txt`, 1994.

8. S. Kleene. Representation of events in nerve nets and finite automata. In Shannon and McCarthy, editors, *Automata Studies*, pages 3–42. Princeton University Press, 1956.

9. A. Tarski. On the calculus of relations. *Journal of Symbolic Logic*, 6:73–89, 1941.

10. Burghard v. Karger and C. A. R. Hoare. Sequential calculus. *Information Processing Letters*, 53:123–130, 1995.

11. Chaochen Zhou, C. A. R. Hoare, and Anders P. Ravn. A calculus of durations. *Information Processing Letters*, 40:269–276, 1992.

A simple, efficient, and flexible implementation of flexible arrays

Victor J. Dielissen[1] and Anne Kaldewaij[2]

[1] Department of Mathematics and Computing Science,
Eindhoven University of Technology,
P.O. Box 513, 5600 MB Eindhoven, The Netherlands
[2] Department of Mathematics and Computer Science,
University of Amsterdam,
Plantage Muidergracht 24, 1018 TV Amsterdam, The Netherlands

Abstract. Flexible arrays can grow and shrink at both sides. Operations on flexible arrays are the usual ones: element inspection and assignment of a value to an array element. Additional operations are *hiext*, extending the array at its high end with an entry; *loext*, extension at the low end; *hirem*, removing the last element of the array; and *lorem*, removing the first element of the array.

It is shown how so-called leaf trees can be used to implement flexible arrays efficiently. The implementation is simple (no rotations are involved) and yields nicely shaped trees. The implementation is flexible, in the sense that a large class of additional operations, such as computation of the minimum and maximum of the array, can be easily added to the repertoire of operations without affecting time complexities. The standard flexible array operations take $\mathcal{O}(\log n)$ time, where n is the size of the flexible array. Additional operations, such as minimum and maximum take $\mathcal{O}(1)$ time.

1 Introduction

Flexible arrays, as described in [3], are an extension of static arrays. In addition to inspection and array element assignment, the size of the array can be changed. A flexible array can grow and shrink at both ends. Flexible array x with elements of type T is characterized by three components: the low bound $x.lb$, the high bound $x.hb$, and $x.v$ ("the array"), which is a function defined on the interval $[x.lb .. x.hb)$ of the integers. Hence,

$$x.v \colon [x.lb .. x.hb) \to T$$

Operations on x are inspections and updates. The value of $x.v$ in i, for $x.lb \le i < x.hb$, is, as usual, denoted as $x[i]$, and an assignment to this entry is denoted as $x[i] := E$, where E is an expression of type T.

More interesting are the operations hiext.$w.x$ and loext.$w.x$ (high extend and low extend), defined by

$$
\begin{aligned}
&\text{hiext.}w.x: \quad x.hb := x.hb + 1 \,;\; x[x.hb - 1] := w\\
&\text{loext.}w.x: \quad x.lb := x.lb - 1 \,;\; x[x.lb] := w
\end{aligned}
$$

Shrinking is possible by operations hirem and lorem (high remove and low remove), given by

| hirem.x: | $x.hb := x.hb - 1$ |
| lorem.x: | $x.lb := x.lb + 1$ |

Flexible arrays are especially useful for representations of strings to which various operations like substring selection and substring replacement can be applied. The usefulness of being able to extend array bounds by small amounts had been emphasized by Lindsey in [9], who used the simple example of reading in an array of an unknown number of items.

Implementations of flexible arrays can, for instance, be found in [1] and [2]. The implementation described in [1], which appears in a derivational style in [4], uses binary trees. The idea proposed in [1] is to store the array values in the internal nodes of a tree in such a way that sizes of left and right subtrees differ by at most one. This implementation, however, cannot be easily extended to accommodate additional operations defined on *segments* of the array.

In [2], (2,3)-trees are used (only hiext and hirem are implemented: the arrays are extendable at one end only). The values are stored in the leaves and the standard node splitting and node fusion algorithms for (a,b)-trees are used (cf. [7]). Although conceptually simple, implementations of these algorithms are rather complicated.

In this paper we use the binary leaf tree (as we call it): the elements of the array represented by the tree are stored in the leaves. It turns out that reasoning about binary leaf trees, and extending leaf trees in such a way that efficient implementations of required operations are obtained is much easier than in the case of node-oriented trees (cf. [8]) . The resulting programs are simple and the resulting trees turn out to have nice properties.

An important aspect in the derivation of leaf tree structures and accompanying programs is the decomposability of functions. In [10], decomposability is described in terms of sets in a more theoretical setting, which is not easily transformed into a program. In our approach, a function on trees is called decomposable if the function value of a tree can be easily expressed in terms of the function values of its subtrees. A systematic use of decomposability can be found in [6].

The implementation presented in this paper yields $\mathcal{O}(\log n)$ time complexity for the flexible array operations, where n is the size of the array. Additional decomposable operations (e.g., computing the maximum and the minimum of the array, or computing the maximal sum of elements of consecutive array segments of the array, cf. [5]) can be implemented such that their execution takes $\mathcal{O}(1)$ time.

Overview

Definitions, notations and the idea of decomposability are presented in Section 2.

Section 3 discusses the derivation of an implementation of restricted flexible arrays: growing and shrinking is only at one end of the array.

In Section 4 we show how an implementation of a complete flexible array can be constructed from the restricted flexible array.

2 Leaf trees

Leaf trees are defined as follows. Let T be a set. The set $\mathcal{L}$ of *leaf trees* over T is the smallest set for which

(i) $\langle\rangle \in \mathcal{L}$ (the *empty* tree)
(ii) $a \in T \Rightarrow \langle a \rangle \in \mathcal{L}$ (a *leaf*)
(iii) $l, r \in \mathcal{L} \backslash \{\langle\rangle\} \Rightarrow \langle l, r \rangle \in \mathcal{L}$ (a *node*)

Note that the empty tree does not occur as subtree of a non-empty tree. Leaf trees are full binary trees: nodes have two successors and leaves have zero successors.

Function application is denoted by an infix dot, i.e., we write $f.x$ instead of $f(x)$. A function $f: \mathcal{L} \rightarrow V$ for some set V, is called *decomposable* if

$$f.\langle l, r \rangle = f.l \oplus f.r \text{ for some } \mathcal{O}(1) \text{ operator } \oplus \text{ on } V.$$

Examples of decomposable functions are the height and the size of a tree. The height of a tree is defined as follows:

$$
\begin{aligned}
\text{h.}\langle\rangle &= 0 \\
\text{h.}\langle a \rangle &= 0 \\
\text{h.}\langle l, r \rangle &= 1 + (\text{h.}l \uparrow \text{h.}r)
\end{aligned}
$$

where $a \uparrow b$ denotes the maximum of a and b.
The size of a tree is defined by

$$
\begin{aligned}
\text{size.}\langle\rangle &= 0 \\
\text{size.}\langle a \rangle &= 1 \\
\text{size.}\langle l, r \rangle &= \text{size.}l + \text{size.}r
\end{aligned}
$$

Another (boolean) function that plays a role in the sections that follow is the property of being *perfect* (cf. [12]). In a perfect tree all leaves are at the same level. It is formally defined by

$$
\begin{aligned}
\text{perfect.}\langle\rangle &= \text{true} \\
\text{perfect.}\langle a \rangle &= \text{true} \\
\text{perfect.}\langle l, r \rangle &= \text{perfect.}l \wedge \text{perfect.}r \wedge h.l = h.r
\end{aligned}
$$

Function perfect is not (strictly) decomposable, however, the pair $(\text{perfect}, h)$ is a decomposable function.
Note that the height of a non-empty perfect leaf tree with n elements is $\log_2 n$.

As a final example of a decomposable function, we consider the maximum of a non-empty tree over a totally ordered set, which can be defined by

$$
\begin{aligned}
\text{max.}\langle a \rangle &= a \\
\text{max.}\langle l, r \rangle &= \text{max.}l \uparrow \text{max.}r
\end{aligned}
$$

For leaf tree t, we define the list of t by the so-called *abstraction function* list, given by

$$\begin{aligned} \text{list.}\langle\rangle &= [\,] && \text{(the empty list)} \\ \text{list.}\langle a\rangle &= [a] && \text{(a singleton list)} \\ \text{list.}\langle l, r\rangle &= \text{list.}l \mathbin{+\!\!+} \text{list.}r && \text{(concatenation of lists)} \end{aligned}$$

The implementation of leaf trees at a pointer level is straightforward. The empty tree is represented by the constant nil; a leaf by its value, and a node by two pointers to its constituting subtrees.

Let T be a leaf tree with n leaves and let f be a decomposable function. To obtain an efficient implementation for the computation of $f.T$, the f-values of each subtree are stored at the root of that subtree. When a local change is made to the tree, the values of f for the unchanged subtrees can be used to recompute f for the changed subtrees, including T.

Hence, to each subtree (each node and each leaf) an attribute is added that has as value the function value of that subtree. Since f is decomposable, recomputing $f.\langle l, r\rangle$ from $f.l$ and $f.r$ takes $\mathcal{O}(1)$ time. Computation of the function value of the tree takes $\mathcal{O}(1)$ as well, since it is recorded in the root. A change of the value of a leaf, or the addition of a leaf, leads to updates of all f-values at the nodes on the path from that leaf to the root of the tree.

We use a functional notation for our programs. Since these program definitions follow a regular recursive pattern, they can be easily transformed into imperative constructs (functions, procedures or repetitions). In such implementations, trees that occur as argument of a function are not copied, but their representations are used to obtain a representation of the resulting value, as described in [11]. For instance, function "pair", which combines two leaf trees into one, defined by

$$\begin{aligned} \text{pair.}\langle\rangle.t &= t \\ \text{pair.}s.\langle\rangle &= s \\ \text{pair.}s.t &= \langle s, t\rangle, \; s \neq \langle\rangle \wedge t \neq \langle\rangle \end{aligned}$$

is considered as an $\mathcal{O}(1)$ program: for the last case a new node is created that has s and t as subtrees.

3 One-sided flexible arrays

In this section, we consider inspection, update, hiext and hirem only. In the next section it is shown how loext and lorem can be added to the repertoire of operations. As lower bound of the arrays, we choose 0, hence, array x is defined on $[0 .. x.hb)$. As representation of x, we use $x.hb$ and a leaf tree t, such that

$$\text{list.}t = x.v[0 .. x.hb)$$

Programs for the computation of the i-th element of list.t and for an update thereof are easily derived. Since these are the easy parts, we present the solutions without derivation or proof.

A program for the computation of the i-th element of x is given by

$$\text{elt}.i.\langle a \rangle \quad = a$$
$$\text{elt}.i.\langle l, r \rangle = \text{elt}.i.l, \qquad\qquad 0 \leq i < \text{size}.l$$
$$\text{elt}.(i - \text{size}.l).r, \text{size}.l \leq i < x.hb$$

Similarly, a program corresponding to the assignment of w to the i-th element is given by

$$\text{upd}.i.w.\langle a \rangle \quad = \langle w \rangle$$
$$\text{upd}.i.w.\langle l, r \rangle = \langle \text{upd}.i.w.l, r \rangle, \qquad\qquad 0 \leq i < \text{size}.l$$
$$\langle l, \text{upd}.(i - \text{size}.l).w.r \rangle, \text{size}.l \leq i < x.hb$$

The number of unfoldings that result when these functions are evaluated is bounded by the height of t, hence, their time complexity is $\mathcal{O}(h.t)$.
Function size is decomposable and can thus be stored in each node of the tree (its value is not affected by inspections or updates). As will be explained later, functions elt and upd can also be defined without the use of function size.

The more interesting operations are hiext and hirem, since these operations will affect the structure of the tree involved. We consider high extension first, and we denote the extension of tree t with a value w as $\text{hiext}.w.t$. Its specification is

$$\text{list}.(\text{hiext}.w.t) = \text{list}.t + [w]$$

Substitution of $\langle \rangle$ for t yields for the right-hand side

$$\text{list}.\langle \rangle + [w]$$
$$= \qquad \{ \text{definition of list} \}$$
$$[] + [w]$$
$$= \qquad \{ \text{definition of concatenation} \}$$
$$[w]$$
$$= \qquad \{ \text{definition of list} \}$$
$$\text{list}.\langle w \rangle$$

Hence, $\text{hiext}.w.\langle \rangle = \langle w \rangle$ is appropriate. A similar derivation for $\text{hiext}.w.\langle a \rangle$ yields as result

$$\text{hiext}.w.\langle a \rangle = \langle \langle a \rangle, \langle w \rangle \rangle$$

For $t = \langle l, r \rangle$, we have

$$\text{list}.(\text{hiext}.w.\langle l, r \rangle)$$
$$= \qquad \{ \text{specification of hiext} \}$$
$$\text{list}.\langle l, r \rangle + [w]$$
$$= \qquad \{ \text{definition of list} \}$$
$$\text{list}.l + \text{list}.r + [w]$$

This concatenation can be parenthesized in two ways:

$(\text{list}.l + \text{list}.r) + [w]$, which equals $\text{list}.\langle \langle l, r \rangle, \langle w \rangle \rangle$, and
$\text{list}.l + (\text{list}.r + [w])$, which equals (by induction) $\text{list}.\langle l, \text{hiext}.w.r \rangle$

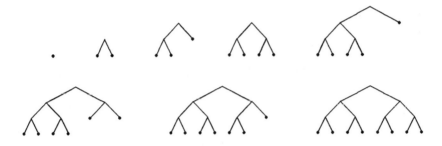

Figure 1: trees corresponding to arrays of sizes 1 through 8

Hence, two solutions are at hand, viz

$$\text{hiext}.w.\langle l, r \rangle = \langle \langle l, r \rangle, \langle w \rangle \rangle \quad \text{and}$$
$$\text{hiext}.w.\langle l, r \rangle = \langle l, \text{hiext}.w.r \rangle$$

The first one is attractive, since it is an $\mathcal{O}(1)$ operation. It yields, however, an increase of the height of the tree to which it is applied. Since the time complexities of inspection and update are related to this height, we wish to keep heights as small as possible. The idea is to apply the first alternative only when adding an element to the tree will *inevitably* increase its height, whatever algorithm is used.

This is precisely the case when the tree is *perfect*, i.e., when all leaves are at the same depth. Hence, as a complete solution, we propose

$$\text{hiext}.w.\langle \rangle \quad = \langle w \rangle$$
$$\text{hiext}.w.\langle a \rangle \quad = \langle \langle a \rangle, \langle w \rangle \rangle$$
$$\text{hiext}.w.\langle l, r \rangle = \langle \langle l, r \rangle, \langle w \rangle \rangle, \quad \text{perfect}.\langle l, r \rangle$$
$$\langle l, \text{hiext}.w.r \rangle, \neg \text{perfect}.\langle l, r \rangle$$

For hirem (being the left inverse of hiext) there is hardly a choice: the right-most element has to be removed. This yields

$$\text{hirem}.\langle a \rangle \quad = \langle \rangle$$
$$\text{hirem}.\langle l, r \rangle = \langle l, \text{hirem}.r \rangle$$

where $\langle t, \langle \rangle \rangle$ should be read as t, i.e., function "pair" introduced in the previous section is tacitly applied to the resulting trees. (Recall that a non-empty leaf tree does not have empty subtrees.)

These programs yield as result leaf trees whose shapes are completely determined by their sizes. Figure 1 shows the shapes of the trees corresponding to flexible arrays of sizes one through eight. The dots indicate the leaves. The class of trees obtained by successive applications of hiext has a number of nice properties that are easily proved by induction. One important property is being *left-perfect*: all left subtrees are perfect. Formally this predicate is defined by

$$\text{left-perfect.}\langle\,\rangle \quad = \text{true}$$
$$\text{left-perfect.}\langle a\rangle \quad = \text{true}$$
$$\text{left-perfect.}\langle l,r\rangle = \text{perfect.}l \wedge \text{left-perfect.}r$$

Note that a perfect tree is left-perfect as well. Trees obtained by these operations are also what we call *leftist* trees, i.e., for all subtrees the height of the left subtree is at least the height of the right subtree. Formally this predicate is defined by

$$\text{leftist.}\langle\,\rangle \quad = \text{true}$$
$$\text{leftist.}\langle a\rangle \quad = \text{true}$$
$$\text{leftist.}\langle l,r\rangle = h.l \geq h.r \wedge \text{leftist.}l \wedge \text{leftist.}r$$

Since the shape of a leftist left-perfect tree is determined by its size, the class of trees generated by hiext and hirem operations, starting with the empty tree, is precisely the class of leftist left-perfect trees.

For a leftist tree $\langle l,r\rangle$, we have $h.\langle l,r\rangle = 1 + h.l$. Since the trees of this class are left-perfect as well, we have $h.l = \log_2(\text{size.}l)$, and, hence

$$h.\langle l,r\rangle = 1 + \log_2(\text{size.}l)$$

We conclude that this implementation of (one-sided) flexible arrays yields logarithmic time complexities for the operations required. As additional information in the nodes of the tree, perfect (a boolean) and height (logarithmic in the size) are needed for hiext. For inspection and assigment the size of each subtree should be recorded as well. Since the trees are left-perfect and leftist, the leaf containing the i-th element can also be computed from $x.hb$ (the size of the tree) and the binary representation of i.

4   Fully flexible arrays

In the previous section, we showed how one-sided flexible arrays can be implemented. If only operations hiext and hirem are used, this gives rise to the class of leftist left-perfect leaf trees, which we will call ll-trees for short. Of course, its symmetric counterpart, in which only operations loext and lorem are used, yields the class of rightist right-perfect leaf trees, called rr-trees for short. The problem is how to combine these into a structure that allows all operations.

One idea is to represent flexible array x by a pair (s,t), such that s is an rr-tree, t is an ll-tree and

$$x[x.lb\,..\,x.hb) = \text{list.}s \,+\!\!+\, \text{list.}t$$

This works well, but leads to case-analysis for hirem and lorem that complicates the resulting programs. Instead, we use the programs as obtained for the one-sided versions by again considering the cases "perfect" and "not perfect". This results in the following simple and elegant programs:

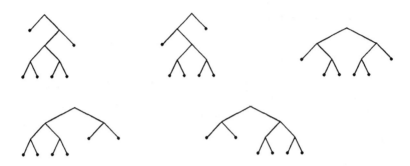

Figure 2: the trees corresponding to arrays of size 6

$$\text{hiext}.w.\langle\,\rangle \quad = \langle w\rangle$$
$$\text{hiext}.w.\langle a\rangle \quad = \langle\langle a\rangle, \langle w\rangle\rangle$$
$$\text{hiext}.w.\langle l, r\rangle = \langle\langle l, r\rangle, \langle w\rangle\rangle, \qquad \text{perfect}.\langle l, r\rangle$$
$$\langle l, \text{hiext}.w.r\rangle, \neg\text{perfect}.\langle l, r\rangle$$

$$\text{loext}.w.\langle\,\rangle \quad = \langle w\rangle$$
$$\text{loext}.w.\langle a\rangle \quad = \langle\langle w\rangle, \langle a\rangle\rangle$$
$$\text{loext}.w.\langle l, r\rangle = \langle\langle w\rangle, \langle l, r\rangle\rangle, \qquad \text{perfect}.\langle l, r\rangle$$
$$\langle \text{loext}.w.l, r\rangle, \neg\text{perfect}.\langle l, r\rangle$$

$$\text{hirem}.\langle a\rangle \quad = \langle\,\rangle$$
$$\text{hirem}.\langle l, r\rangle = \langle l, \text{hirem}.r\rangle$$

$$\text{lorem}.\langle a\rangle \quad = \langle\,\rangle$$
$$\text{lorem}.\langle l, r\rangle = \langle \text{lorem}.l, r\rangle$$

It is easily shown (using induction) that for a tree $\langle l, r\rangle$ corresponding to a flexible array, its left subtree l is an rr-tree and its right subtree r is an ll-tree. As shown in the previous section the heights of these subtrees are logarithmic in their sizes. Hence, the height of tree $\langle l, r\rangle$ is logarithmic in its size. Figure 2 shows the possible trees corresponding to an array of size 6.

Programs for inspection and assignment are similar to those in the previous section. In this general case, the index of an element is related to the bounds of the array and an element with index i in the array corresponds to the element with index $i - x.lb$ in the list of the tree representing the array.

5   Concluding Remarks

We showed how flexible arrays can be implemented by leaf trees, in such a way that the height of trees are logarithmic in their sizes. The programs for the operations are simple and no rotations for balancing are needed. The translation of the abstract leaf tree structure into pointer level structures is straightforward. Additional operations such as the priority queue operations minimum and maximum, can also be added easily, since these functions are decomposable. The resulting trees have a number of nice properties. Left subtrees are rightist and right-perfect; right subtrees are leftist and left-perfect. The sizes of left and right subtree completely determine the shape of the tree. This property can be used to obtain low-level implementations that require a minimum amount of information stored at the nodes of the trees.

Other applications are abstract data types in which lists play a rôle and where apart from the usual "head" and "tail" also additional operations (e.g., the minimum of the list) are required. The algebra of double-ended lists (also known as "cons-snoc lists") is another example for which the programs of this paper can be used.

It is our experience that leaf trees lead to much simpler programs than node oriented trees. During the derivation of a function or program, additional functions (such as the height or the size of a tree) may be needed. For these functions a decomposition is derived (if possible) which leads to new attributes for the nodes of the trees. In this way, programs are systematically derived from their specifications. They are easily transformed into their imperative counterparts.

6 Acknowledgements

We thank the members of the Eindhoven Algorithm Club and their guest Dieter Kratsch for stimulating criticisms on earlier parts of this paper.

References

1. Braun W. and Rem M.,
   A logarithmic implementation of flexible arrays,
   Memorandum MR83/4, University of Technology Eindhoven, 1983.
2. Challab D.J.,
   Implementation of flexible arrays using balanced trees,
   The Computer Journal, vol. 34, no. 5. 1991, pp 386-396.
3. Dijkstra, E. W., A discipline of programming,
   Prentice Hall, Englewood Cliffs, 1976.
4. Hoogerwoord, R.R.,
   A logarithmic implementation of flexible arrays
   in Mathematics of Program Construction: second international conference, Oxford U.K., June 29-July 3, 1992: proceedings/R.S. Bird, C.C. Morgan, J.C.P. Woodcock, eds,
   LCNS 669, Springer-Verlag, Berlin Heidelberg 1993, pp 191-207.
5. Kaldewaij A.,
   Programming, The derivation of algorithms,
   Prentice Hall International Series in Computer Science, 1990, pp 67-69
6. Kaldewaij A. and Dielissen V.J.,
   Decomposable functions and leaf trees: a systematic approach,

in Programming, concepts, methods and calculi: proceedings of the IFIP TC2/WG2.1/WG2.2/WG2.3 Working Conference on Programming Concepts, Methods and calculi (PROCOMET'94), San Miniato, Italy, 6-10 June 1994 / edited by Ernst-Rüdiger Olderog, Elsevier, Amsterdam, 1994, pp 3-17.

7. Knuth, D.E.,
   The art of computer programming 3: Sorting and searching,
   Addison-Wesley, Reading, Mass. (1973).

8. Lewis H.R. and Denenberg L.,
   Data structures and their algorithms,
   Harper Collins Publishers, 1991.

9. Lindsey, C.H.,
   ALGOL-68 with fewer tears,
   Algol Bulletin 28 (1968), Science Reference Library, London UK.

10. Overmars M.H.,
    Dynamization of order decomposable set problems,
    J. Algorithms 2 (1981), pp 245-260.

11. Wadler P.,
    Linear types can change the world!
    in M. Broy, C.B. Jones (eds.), Programming concepts and methods,
    North-Holland, Amsterdam (1990), pp 561-581.

12. Wood D.,
    Data structures, algorithms, and performance,
    Addison-Wesley (1993).

Induction and Recursion on Datatypes

Henk Doornbos and Roland Backhouse

Department of Mathematics and Computing Science, Eindhoven University of
Technology, P.O. Box 513, 5600 MB Eindhoven, The Netherlands

Abstract. A new induction principle is introduced. The principle is
based on a property of relations, called reductivity, that generalises the
property of admitting induction to one relative to a given datatype. The
principle is used to characterise a broad class of recursive equations that
have a unique solution and is also related to standard techniques for
proving termination of programs. Methods based on the structure of the
given datatype for constructing reductive relations are discussed.
The principle is formulated in the point-free calculus of relations guaran-
teeing concision without loss of precision and thus ensuring its amenabil-
ity to calculation.

1 Introduction

A central element in any programming algebra is the definition of programs as
solutions of (recursive) equations. A central element in any programming algebra's metatheory is the characterisation of classes of equations that have unique
solutions; first, because uniqueness guarantees well-definedness, second, because
it affords much stronger calculational properties than does mere existence of solutions and, third, because there is a close connection between proofs of unicity
and proofs of termination.

Unicity is typically established by an inductive argument —more often than
not by induction over the datatype of natural numbers. In this paper we introduce a notion of induction over an arbitrary datatype and go on to show how
the notion is used to establish unicity of a certain (broad) class of equations.
Our overall goal is to develop a *calculational* theory of mathematical induction.
That is, we want to be able to *calculate* relations on which inductive arguments
may be based, using laws that relate "admitting induction" to the mechanisms
for constructing datatypes. We also want to incorporate such calculations into
a methodology for *calculating* inductive hypotheses rather than leaving their
creation to inspired guesswork. This is a bold aim, in view of the vast body of
knowledge and experience that already exists on proof by induction, but recent
advances in understanding the rôle played by Galois connections in the calculus
of relations have led us to speculate that some progress can be made in the short
term.

The theory developed in this paper is general and not specific to any particular datatype. We define a notion of F-reductivity (so called in order to avoid
confusion with existing notions of inductivity), where F stands for a "relator",
and show that F-reductive relations always exist, whatever the value of F. We

also give laws for constructing reductive relations from existing reductive relations. Finally, we show a connection between proofs of unicity using reductivity arguments and termination proofs.

The general context of this work is a relational algebra of datatypes developed in close cooperation with our own group at Eindhoven University [2], Lambert Meertens at Utrecht University, and Richard Bird and Oege de Moor at Oxford University [5].

2 Preliminaries

Nondeterministic programs can be viewed as (input-output) relations. So a calculus of programs is a calculus of relations. In this section we give a brief introduction to the relational calculus. We use the notation and calculational style as introduced in [2]. In addition we mention some results from the theory of Galois connections, because they are useful for the introduction of some of the operators.

2.1 Galois connections

The concept of Galois connection is well-known, see e.g. [6, 7], but perhaps not as well known as it deserves to be. Given two preorders $\leq$ and $\sqsubseteq$, two functions f and g form a *Galois connection* if the following formula holds for all x and y:

$$f.x \leq y \;\equiv\; x \sqsubseteq g.y \;. \tag{1}$$

Function f will be called the *lower adjoint* and function g the *upper adjoint*. (These names are chosen because (1) is a special case of the categorical notion of adjoint situation.) Galois connections are interesting because as soon as we recognise one we get a large number of properties of the adjoints for "free", in a manner of speaking. First of all, we have the two *cancellation properties* $x \sqsubseteq g.(f.x)$ and $f.(g.y) \leq y$. These are obtained by instantiating (1) in such a way that either the lefthand or the righthand side becomes true. Furthermore, if the two orders are complete lattices (which is the case for the inclusion order on relations), then it can be shown that the lower adjoint distributes over arbitrary joins and the upper adjoint distributes over arbitrary meets.

Another important fact is that if a function on a complete lattice distributes over arbitrary joins, then it has an upper adjoint; dually, if it distributes over arbitrary meets, then it has a lower adjoint. This fact allows us to define new operators: e.g. if f is a function that distributes over arbitrary joins then there is a function $f^\sharp$ with properties

$$f.A \leq B \equiv A \sqsubseteq f^\sharp.B \quad \text{and} \quad f.(f^\sharp.A) \leq A \;. \tag{2}$$

Finally, the recognition of Galois connections is often vital to effective calculation with fixed points. In particular we have the following μ-*fusion* lemma (where μg denotes the least fixed point of g).

Lemma 1 (μ-fusion). *If g and h are monotone functions on a complete lattice (with order $\preceq$) and if, furthermore, f is a function that has an upper adjoint, then:*

$$f \cdot \mu g \preceq \mu h \;\; \Leftarrow \;\; \forall(x :: f.(g.x) \preceq h.(f.x)) \;.$$

For a discussion of μ-fusion and a proof of Lemma 1, see [12]. For a complete account of the theory of Galois connections, including proofs of the other properties mentioned here, see [1].

2.2 Basic Operators

A binary relation on a set $\mathcal{A}$ is a subset of the cartesian product $\mathcal{A} \times \mathcal{A}$. In other words a relation is an element of the powerset $\mathcal{P}(\mathcal{A} \times \mathcal{A})$. Therefore, the first axiom of the relational calculus is that the relations form a complete lattice. The top of this lattice is denoted by $\top\!\top$, its interpretation being the total relation $\mathcal{A} \times \mathcal{A}$. The bottom, denoted by $\bot\!\bot$, has as its interpretation the empty relation. We write $\subseteq$ for the order on the lattice and $\cup$ and $\cap$ for the join and the meet, respectively.

Relations can be composed in the usual way:

$$x(R \cdot S)y \;\; \equiv \;\; \exists(z : x(R)z : z(S)y) \;.$$

Composition is associative and has the identity relation as unit, so we have as an axiom that $(I, \cdot)$ is a monoid. The interpretation of I is the identity relation: $x(I)y \equiv x = y$. An additional axiom is that the sections $(R \cdot)$ and $(\cdot R)$ distribute over arbitrary joins. As a consequence of this axiom, operator $\cdot$ is monotone in both its arguments with respect to $\subseteq$. From now on if we say that an operator is monotone it is to be understood that this is with respect to $\subseteq$.

2.3 Monotypes and the Domain Operators

Following [2], relations R that satisfy $R \subseteq I$ are called *monotypes*. (Elsewhere [10] they are called *coreflexives*.) Monotypes will be denoted by upper case identifiers A, B, C. In the relational model of the calculus, monotypes are partial identity relations and can be identified with subsets of the universe $\mathcal{A}$. Therefore we write $x \in A$ as a shorthand for $x(A)x$. An important fact is that meet and composition coincide on monotypes: $A \cap B = A \cdot B$.

A relation R induces two monotypes: the right domain, denoted by $R\!\!>$, and the left domain, denoted by $R\!\!<$. These are to be interpreted as follows:

$$x \in R\!\!< \equiv \exists(y :: x(R)y) \quad \text{and} \quad x \in R\!\!> \equiv \exists(y :: y(R)x) \;,$$

so they can indeed be interpreted as domain operators on relations. The domain operators are defined by the Galois connections

$$R\!\!> \subseteq A \equiv R \subseteq \top\!\top \cdot A \quad \text{and} \quad R\!\!< \subseteq A \equiv R \subseteq A \cdot \top\!\top \;.$$

That these are indeed Galois connections, and thus proper definitions, follows from the fact that $(\pi \cdot)$ and $(\cdot \pi)$ both distribute over arbitrary meets of monotypes. An immediate consequence is that the domain operators, being lower adjoints, distribute over arbitrary joins and therefore are monotone. Another property is:

$$R{<} \cdot R = R = R \cdot R{>} \ . \tag{3}$$

From equation (3) it can be seen that the domain operator indeed yields a domain as result. Composition with a monotype can be seen as a (domain) restriction of the relation: $x(R{\cdot}A)y$ holds iff $x(R)y$ and $y{\in}A$. So $R{\cdot}A$ is the relation R restricted on the right to elements of A. Equation (3) therefore expresses the fact that restricting a relation to its domain has no effect.

2.4 The Monotype Factor

The *monotype factor* is defined by the Galois connection

$$A \subseteq R{\backslash}B \ \equiv \ (R \cdot A){<} \subseteq B \ . \tag{4}$$

That this is a proper definition follows again from the theory of Galois connections and the join-distributivity properties of composition and the domain operators. It should be noted that $R{\backslash}B$ is by definition a monotype.

The interpretation of $R{\backslash}B$ is the following:

$$x \in R{\backslash}B \ \equiv \ \forall(y : y(R)x : y{\in}B) \ . \tag{5}$$

Viewing relation R as a program that takes its input on the right (like functions, which have their arguments on the right but unlike imperative programs, which are usually thought to have their input on the left) we see that $R{\backslash}B$ is the greatest set such that if program R is started with a value from that set, the result will be in the set B. In other words it is a weakest (liberal) precondition. Note that $x \in R{\backslash}B$ also holds when $x \notin R{>}$.

Because the monotype factor plays an important role in the remainder of this paper we now give a rather long list of properties. All are rather easy to prove using the defining Galois connection and the properties of the domain operator documented in [2]. Also, we give some connection with the properties of the weakest precondition function to support the interpretation.

First note that the function $(R{\backslash})$, being an upper adjoint, distributes over arbitrary meets of monotypes. Because meet on monotypes coincides with composition it follows that $R{\backslash}$ distributes over composition: $R{\backslash}(A{\cdot}B) = (R{\backslash}A) \cdot (R{\backslash}B)$. This corresponds to the fact that the function wlp.r is universally conjunctive.

From (4) we obtain the cancellation property:

$$(R \cdot R{\backslash}B){<} \subseteq B \ . \tag{6}$$

Often this property is used in a slightly different form:

$$R \cdot R{\backslash}B \subseteq B \cdot R \ . \tag{7}$$

Both (6) and (7) express that program R produces a result from set B when started in a state satisfying $R \backslash B$. It can be shown that, if R is a monotype, (6) can be strengthened to an equality. Next:

$$A \cdot A \backslash B = A \cdot B . \tag{8}$$

We call (8) the rule of modus ponens. The reason is that if monotypes are interpreted as predicates then, when restricted to monotypes only, the operator $\cdot$ and the operator $\backslash$ are interpreted as conjunction and implication, respectively. Thus (8) is the statement $A \wedge A \Rightarrow B \equiv A \wedge B$.

A consequence of the cancellation property that is sometimes useful is:

$$R> \cdot R \backslash A \subseteq (A \cdot R)> . \tag{9}$$

The righthand side of (9) is the set of states $x \in R>$ such that when R is started in x the result *may* satisfy A. The lefthand side is the set of states x such that $x \in R>$ and that when R is started in x the result is *guaranteed* to satisfy A.

If R is a functional relation, then this inclusion can be strengthened to an equality:

$$R \text{ is a function} \quad \Rightarrow \quad R> \cdot R \backslash A = (A \cdot R)> . \tag{10}$$

This expresses that for functions (or deterministic programs), what *may* happen is the same as what is *guaranteed* to happen.

From associativity of composition we obtain:

$$R \backslash (S \backslash A) = (S \cdot R) \backslash A . \tag{11}$$

This corresponds to the rule wlp.$(r;s).p = $ wlp.$r.($wlp.$s.p)$.

Combining (8) and (11) we get the following:

$$A \cdot R \backslash B = A \cdot (R \cdot A) \backslash B . \tag{12}$$

Finally we mention the monotonicity properties of the monotype factor: $(R \backslash)$ is monotone and $(\backslash A)$ is antimonotone. This concludes our short introduction to the monotype factor. For a more extensive treatment see [4].

2.5 The Induction Principle

Now we have all the machinery to define the induction principle in the relation calculus. A more or less standard definition is: relation R admits induction if and only if:

$$\forall(y : \forall(x : x(R)y : x \in A) : y \in A) \quad \Rightarrow \quad \forall(y :: y \in A) \quad \text{for all sets } A . \tag{13}$$

To arrive at a definition without dummies first notice that $\forall(y :: y \in A)$, the (understood) domain of y being I, can be rewritten as $I \subseteq A$. Furthermore, the expression in the domain of the antecedent, $\forall(x : x(R)y : x \in A)$, is just $y \in R \backslash A$, see (5). So the notion of admitting induction can be drastically simplified to: relation R admits induction if and only if

$$R \backslash A \subseteq A \quad \Rightarrow \quad I \subseteq A \quad , \quad \text{for all monotypes } A . \tag{14}$$

Property (14) is, in our view, a very attractive calculational formulation of the notion of admitting induction. Note first its compactness. Now note its form: it is a rule for establishing that a property (A) is universal $(I \subseteq A)$. The mechanism to do so is to establish a property that is formally much weaker, namely $R \backslash A \subseteq A$. The proof of $R \backslash A \subseteq A$ is what is usually called the induction step, and $R \backslash A$ is the induction hypothesis.

In Sect. 4 this definition will be generalised.

3 Relators and Datatypes

In category theory, datatypes are modelled using functors. A functor is a pair of mappings, one from objects to objects and one from arrows to arrows. For instance, in the category of sets the object map of a functor is a mapping of sets to sets: this can be viewed as a *type* constructor. The other part, the arrow map, is a mapping of functions to functions: this is a way to construct functions on the datatype constructed by the object map.

As a typical example consider lists; this datatype can be seen as constructed by a functor F. The object map of F transforms a set A into the set of lists over A, the arrow map is the well-known function map: $(F.f).[x,y,z] = [f.x, f.y, f.z]$.

In general, the object map of functor F maps a set A to the set of F-structures over A and the arrow map of F maps a function f on a set A to a function on F-structures over A, which may be thought of as "f applied element-wise".

If we want to introduce a functor-like notion in the relation calculus –call it a relator– we need a function that consists of two mappings: a function from sets to sets –the proper type constructor– and a function from relations to relations. In the relation calculus we choose not to make a distinction between sets and relations. Both are modelled as relations, so we don't need two functions: a relator is a function from relations to relations. It turns out that all relators we want to consider have the property that they are monotone. Of course we still want a relator to map sets to sets; this is the case if we require that $F.I \subseteq I$. Together with monotonicity of F this implies that F maps monotypes to monotypes. Inspired by category theory, we furthermore require that relators distribute over composition.

Definition 2 (Relators). A function F from relations to relations is a *relator* if it enjoys the following properties:

1. F is monotone,
2. F distributes over composition,
3. $F.I \subseteq I$.

Examples of relators are the identity relator Id (Id.$R = R$) and the constant relators, i.e. relators F such that $F.R = A$ for a fixed monotype A.

A more substantial example is the product relator, denoted by $\times$. It is introduced by assuming that the universe $\mathcal{A}$ is closed under pair forming. The interpretation of $x(R \times S)y$ is that x is a pair (a,b), y is a pair (c,d), and furthermore that $a(R)c$ and $b(S)d$. Closely connected with the product relator is the function "split" (denoted by ⌃). It has as interpretation that $(x,y)(R{\scriptstyle\vartriangle} S)z$ holds exactly when $x(R)z$ and $y(S)z$ hold. From a computational point of view, the function split corresponds, therefore, to a kind of fork operation.

Another example of a relator, a kind of dual to the product, is the disjoint sum. It is introduced by assuming that we have two total injections, *inl* and *inr* with disjoint ranges. These two functions can then be seen as tagging operations. The interpretation of $x(R+S)y$ is that either $x = inl.a$ and $y = inl.b$, for some a and b (this can also be expressed as x and y are tagged by *inl*) and that $a(R)b$ holds, or that $x = inr.a$ and $y = inr.b$, for some a and b, and $a(S)b$ holds. Operationally this is: test whether the input is tagged by *inl* or *inr*; in the first case apply R and tag the result with *inl*; in the second case apply S and tag the result with *inr*.

As a "dual" of split we have the function *cojunc*, denoted by ▼ . The interpretation of $x(R{\blacktriangledown}S)y$ is: there exists a z such that either $x = inl.z$ and $z(R)y$ or $x = inr.z$ and $z(S)y$. Operationally: make a nondeterministic choice between applying R and tagging the result with *inl* and applying S and tagging the result with *inr*.

From the operational interpretation it is clear that disjoint sum can be used to model non-deterministic choice and if-statements. If we write $\sim\!A$ for the complement of monotype A and strip for the function that strips the tag from its argument, the relation

$$\text{strip} \cdot (R+S) \cdot (A \blacktriangledown \sim\!A)$$

corresponds to the program

$$\text{if } a \to R \ [\!] \ \neg a \to S \text{ fi },$$

where a denotes the predicate corresponding to A.

The correspondence between disjoint sum and nondeterministic choice can also be seen in the following identity:

$$(R{\blacktriangledown}S){\scriptstyle\backslash}(A+B) \ = \ R{\scriptstyle\backslash}A \cap S{\scriptstyle\backslash}B . \tag{15}$$

The relators built from the identity, constant, product and disjoint sum relators are called polynomial relators. In fact there is a fifth kind of polynomial relator. With $\otimes$ denoting a binary polynomial relator, it can be shown that the function that maps R to $\mu(R\otimes)$ is a relator too. This is how relators like the list or tree formers can be constructed. See [3] for more details.

Finally we mention a property connecting relators and the monotype factor. Relators distribute over the monotype factor in the sense that

$$F.(R{\scriptstyle\backslash}A) \subseteq (F.R){\scriptstyle\backslash}(F.A) . \tag{16}$$

This property follows because relators distribute over composition and commute with the domain operators.

3.1 Natural Transformations for Monotypes

The concept "natural transformation" is well known in category theory. In this paper we need the following variant.

Definition 3. Let R be a relation and let F and G be relators. We say that $R \in G \leadsto F$ ("R is from G to F") if and only if for all monotypes A:

$$R \cdot G.A \subseteq F.A \cdot R .$$

In words, this means that R preserves properties of the elements of the data structure it acts on. As an example, let F be the tree relator and G be the list relator. The fact that $x \in G.A$ is then interpreted as: all elements of list x are elements of A (or satisfy property A). If furthermore $y(R)x$, we may conclude from $R \in G \leadsto F$ that y is a tree and all elements of this tree also satisfy property A.

A (not very surprising) observation is that $R \in G \leadsto F$ can also be expressed using the monotype factor.

Lemma 4. $R \in G \leadsto F \;\equiv\; \forall(A : A \subseteq I : G.A \subseteq R \backslash F.A)$.

Proof.
$$G.A \subseteq R \backslash F.A$$
$$\equiv \qquad \{ \quad \text{factors: (4)} \quad \}$$
$$(R \cdot G.A){<} \subseteq F.A$$
$$\equiv \qquad \{ \quad \text{domains: } X{<} \subseteq A \;\equiv\; X \subseteq A \cdot X \quad \}$$
$$R \cdot G.A \subseteq F.A \cdot R \cdot G.A$$
$$\equiv \qquad \{ \quad (\Rightarrow): G.A \subseteq I; (\Leftarrow): G.A \cdot G.A = G.A \quad \}$$
$$R \cdot G.A \subseteq F.A \cdot R$$

$\square$

4 *F*-reductivity

This section is begun by giving a compact point-free definition of the notion of *F-reductive* relation (where F is a relator). This definition generalises the notion of a well-founded relation. Following its definition, we present a theorem giving alternative characterisations of the notion. These alternative characterisations help to justify its relevance and usefulness. In later sections we amplify on this aspect by considering several (abstract and concrete) applications. (From here on we use the operator $\circ$ to denote composition of functions on relations.)

Definition 5 (*F*-reductivity). Relation R is said to be *F-reductive* if and only if it enjoys the property:

$$\mu((R \backslash) \circ F) = I . \tag{17}$$

Note that R is Id-reductive if and only if R admits induction.

Theorem 6 (Characterisations of *F*-reductivity). *The following three formulations are equivalent:*

1. R is F-reductive ,
2. $\forall(A : A \subseteq I : R \backslash\!\!\backslash F.A \subseteq A \Rightarrow I \subseteq A)$,
3. $\forall(A : A \subseteq I : R \backslash\!\!\backslash F.A = A \Rightarrow R\!\!> \subseteq A)$.

Proof. The proof is by cyclic implication. That (1.) implies (2.) is an immediate consequence of the Knaster-Tarski fixpoint theorem. The implication (2.)$\Rightarrow$(3.) is also easy: by reflexivity of $\subseteq$ and the fact that $R\!\!> \subseteq I$. The more difficult step is that from (3.) to (1.); we show the (formally) stronger: clause (3.) implies that *every* fixpoint of the function $(R\backslash\!\!\backslash) \circ F$ is I. Assume :

$$R \backslash\!\!\backslash F.A = A ,$$

i.e. A is a fixpoint of $(R\backslash\!\!\backslash) \circ F$, and (c). Then

$$
\begin{aligned}
& I = A \\
\equiv \quad & \{ \quad A \subseteq I, \text{ assumption } \} \\
& I \subseteq R \backslash\!\!\backslash F.A \\
\equiv \quad & \{ \quad \text{factors: (4) } \} \\
& R\!\!< \subseteq F.A \\
\equiv \quad & \{ \quad \text{domains: (3) } \} \\
& (R \cdot R\!\!>)\!\!< \subseteq F.A \\
\equiv \quad & \{ \quad \text{factors: (4) } \} \\
& R\!\!> \subseteq R \backslash\!\!\backslash F.A \\
\equiv \quad & \{ \quad \text{assumption } \} \\
& R\!\!> \subseteq A \\
\Leftarrow \quad & \{ \quad 6(3.) \} \\
& R \backslash\!\!\backslash F.A = A \\
\equiv \quad & \{ \quad \text{assumption } \} \\
& true
\end{aligned}
$$

$\square$

Of the three different forms of the definition of F-reductivity the first (i.e. (17)) is clearly the most compact, and hence the most suited to abstract reasoning about the notion. The second form 6(2.) is closest to the way proof by induction is normally presented. The third alternative, because it is formally weaker than the other two, is often useful to *prove* that a given relation is F-reductive.

Comparing 6(2.) with (14) one sees that F-reductivity is a generalisation of inductivity (or well-foundedness): Id-reductivity is the same as admitting induction. Indeed 6(2.) is a kind of induction principle with respect to a datatype represented by the relator F. In a formulation using points, it reads:

$$\forall(y : \forall(x : x(R)y : x \in F.A) : y \in A) \quad \Rightarrow \quad \forall(y :: y \in A) . \tag{18}$$

In words: we may conclude that all elements satisfy property A if we can show that any element y such that any R predecessor x of y is an F-structure containing only elements satisfying A (i.e. $x \in F.A$) satisfies A. One may wonder why we use the term reductivity instead of inductivity. The reason is that the term

F-inductivity seems to be reserved traditionally for the notion that is expressed by the following formula:

$$\forall(y : \exists(x : y(R)x : x \in F.A) : y \in A) \quad \Rightarrow \quad \forall(y : y \in R< : y \in A) .$$

5 Hylomorphisms

A relation is said to be a *hylomorphism* if it is the least solution of the equation

$$X :: X = S \cdot F.X \cdot R , \tag{19}$$

for some relations R and S. Such an equation is called a *hylo equation*. (In fact, the name hylomorphisms for the least solution of a hylo equation appeared in [8].)

These equations are interesting because they represent a recursion pattern that occurs frequently in practice. Operationally it is as follows: program R constructs from the input an F-structure (think of a list); then program X is applied to every element of the F-structure by $F.X$; finally, the results of the recursive calls are combined by program S. Consider, for instance, the program known as "merge sort": R represents the "splitting" step, $F.X$ the recursive call, and S the "merge" step.

The hylo equation generalises many of the defining equations of the "morphisms" from the "squiggol" literature. Examples are catamorphisms (see e.g. [11] and [14]), which are defined as the unique solution of

$$X :: X = f \cdot F.X \cdot out , \tag{20}$$

and paramorphisms (see [13]), which have as defining equation:

$$X :: X = f \cdot (I \triangle F.X) \cdot out . \tag{21}$$

Here *out* is the inverse of the so-called initial F-algebra. The relation *out* is a kind of pattern matching function that makes case distinctions according to the structure of its input. For instance, for lists it captures the case distinction between the empty list and non-empty lists; for the natural numbers it captures the case distinction between zero and non-zero (see e.g. [8] for more details). So, catamorphisms capture structural recursion whereas paramorphisms capture primitive recursion: for paramorphisms the output is constructed from the result of the recursive call and the original input.

Another, perhaps more familiar example, is the do-statement. This statement is a solution of the recursive equation:

$$x = \text{if } \neg b \rightarrow \text{skip } [] \ b \rightarrow s;x \text{ fi} . \tag{22}$$

Using the fact that skip (do nothing) corresponds to the relation I and writing B for the monotype corresponding to predicate b, we may express (22) using the disjoint sum as:

$$X = \text{strip} \cdot (I+X) \cdot (\sim B \blacktriangledown (S \cdot B)) , \tag{23}$$

(recall that input is from the right). So, the do-statement is a solution of a hylo equation.

Typically, equation (19) will not have a unique solution. The purpose of this section is to show, however, that it does have a unique solution, whatever the value of S, when R is an F-reductive relation.

Theorem 7 (Hylomorphism UEP). *Let S be an arbitrary relation and R be an F-reductive relation. Then the equation*

$$X \quad :: \quad X = S \cdot F.X \cdot R \tag{24}$$

has a unique solution.

Proof. That (24) has a least solution follows by the Knaster-Tarski theorem from the fact that the function g defined by $g.X = S \cdot F.X \cdot R$ is a monotonic function of X. To prove that there is a unique solution, we now show that any solution is equal to the least solution μg .

Assume that $X = g.X$ and R is F-reductive.

$$
\begin{aligned}
&X = \mu g \\
\equiv \quad &\{ \quad \mu g \text{ is least solution; } X \text{ is a solution;} \\
&\qquad R \text{ is } F\text{-reductive } \} \\
&X \cdot \mu(R \backslash \circ F) \subseteq \mu g \\
\Leftarrow \quad &\{ \quad \mu\text{-fusion; for any } A \quad \} \\
&X \cdot R \backslash F.A \subseteq g.(X \cdot A) \\
\equiv \quad &\{ \quad \text{Definition of } g \text{ and assumption } X = g.X \quad \} \\
&S \cdot F.X \cdot R \cdot R \backslash F.A \subseteq S \cdot F.(X \cdot A) \cdot R \\
\Leftarrow \quad &\{ \quad \text{monotype factors (7) and monotonicity } \} \\
&S \cdot F.X \cdot F.A \cdot R \subseteq S \cdot F.(X \cdot A) \cdot R \\
\equiv \quad &\{ \quad \text{relators distribute over composition } \} \\
&\text{true}
\end{aligned}
$$

□

In the case of the do-statement, the equation (23) in X has a unique solution if the relation $\sim B \blacktriangledown (S \cdot B)$ is $(I+)$-reductive or $\mu((\sim B \blacktriangledown (S \cdot B)) \backslash \circ (I+)) = I$. It is not difficult to show that this is the same as $\mu((S \cdot B) \backslash) = I$, or $S \cdot B$ admits induction which, in turn, is equivalent to $S \cdot B$ is well-founded. This is exactly what we have to show in a proof of termination of a do-loop. This gives some evidence that a proof of unicity using F-reductivity can also be viewed as a proof of termination. In Sect. 7 we will give more evidence why this is so.

6   Basic F-reductive Relations

We have seen that the notion of F-reductivity is an important one. It is therefore desirable to be able to *construct* relations enjoying this property. Remarkably, it is always possible to turn a given relation into an F-reductive relation by restricting it by a certain monotype.

Theorem 8. *For any relation R the relation $R \cdot \mu((R\backslash) \circ F)$ is F-reductive.*

Proof. Let E be $\mu((R\backslash) \circ F)$. By Theorem 6 we have to show for any monotype A:
$$(R \cdot E)\backslash F.A = A \Rightarrow (R \cdot E)^> \subseteq A .$$
This is done in the following calculation.

$$
\begin{aligned}
&(R \cdot E)^> \subseteq A \\
\Leftarrow \quad &\{ \quad \text{domains: } (R \cdot A)^> \subseteq A \quad \} \\
&E \subseteq A \\
\Leftarrow \quad &\{ \quad \text{Knaster-Tarski, definition of } E \quad \} \\
&R\backslash F.A \subseteq A \\
\equiv \quad &\{ \quad \text{assume: } (R \cdot E)\backslash F.A = A \quad \} \\
&R\backslash F.A \subseteq (R \cdot E)\backslash F.A \\
\equiv \quad &\{ \quad \text{antimonotonicity of } \backslash B \quad \} \\
&R \cdot E \subseteq R \\
\equiv \quad &\{ \quad \text{domain restriction} \quad \} \\
&true
\end{aligned}
$$

□

Another easy consequence is that for any relator F there is an F-reductive relation:

Corollary 9. *μF is F-reductive.*

Proof. Instantiate R in Theorem 8 to I and observe that $(I\backslash)$ is the identity function. □

This is a nice result because μF is the "pattern matching" function *out*. So this proves that catamorphisms are the unique solution of their defining equation (20).

7 New F-reductive Relations from Old

This section is intended to show how, given an F-reductive relation, other reductive relations can be constructed. The first construction is simple enough:

Theorem 10. *If R is F-reductive and $S \subseteq R$ then S is F-reductive.*

Proof. Immediate from Theorem 6(2.) and the monotonicity properties of the monotype factor. □

The next two theorems can be used to change the "kind of reductivity", i.e. to construct F-reductive relations from G-reductive relations.

Theorem 11. *Let Q be G-reductive and $S \in \mathsf{Id} \rightsquigarrow F$. Then relation $F.Q \cdot S$ is $F \circ G$-reductive.*

254

Proof. $I \subseteq A$

$\Leftarrow$ $\{$ Q is G-reductive $\}$

          $Q \backslash G.A \subseteq A$

$\Leftarrow$ $\{$ $S \in \text{Id} \leadsto F$ Lemma 4 $\}$

          $S \backslash F.(Q \backslash G.A) \subseteq A$

$\Leftarrow$ $\{$ factors and relators: (16) $\}$

          $S \backslash (F.Q \backslash F.(G.A)) \subseteq A$

$\equiv$ $\{$ factors: (11) $\}$

          $(F.Q \cdot S) \backslash F.(G.A) \subseteq A$

$\square$

A typical use of Theorems 10 and 11 is: R is F-reductive follows from the fact that there is a well-founded relation Q and a relation $S \in \text{Id} \leadsto F$ such that $R \subseteq F.Q \cdot S$.

A particularly important F-reductivity theorem is:

Theorem 12. *Let R be F-reductive, $S \in G \circ F \leadsto H \circ G$, and G be a relator that distributes over all joins of monotypes. Then $S \cdot G.R$ is H-reductive.*

Proof. We aim to prove (3.) in Theorem 6 with the instantiations $R := S \cdot G.R$ and $F := H$.

          $(S \cdot G.R){>} \subseteq A$

$\Leftarrow$ $\{$ domains $\}$

          $G.I \subseteq A$

$\equiv$ $\{$ G distributes over all joins $\}$

          $I \subseteq G^{\text{I}}.A$

$\Leftarrow$ $\{$ R is F-reductive $\}$

          $R \backslash F.(G^{\text{I}}.A) \subseteq G^{\text{I}}.A$

$\equiv$ $\{$ G distributes over all joins $\}$

          $G.(R \backslash F.(G^{\text{I}}.A)) \subseteq A$

$\Leftarrow$ $\{$ relators and factors: (16) $\}$

          $G.R \backslash G.(F.(G^{\text{I}}.A)) \subseteq A$

$\Leftarrow$ $\{$ $S \in G \circ F \leadsto H \circ G$; Lemma 4 $\}$

          $G.R \backslash (S \backslash H.(G.(G^{\text{I}}.A))) \subseteq A$

$\Leftarrow$ $\{$ factors: (11); cancellation (2) $\}$

          $(S \cdot G.R) \backslash H.A \subseteq A$

$\square$

The restriction imposed on relator G in this theorem is rather severe. However, one important class of relators satisfy it: the sections of the product relator. This enables us to define functions that are defined on the product of an "inductive" domain and another domain (such as the summation function on pairs of natural numbers or the concatenation function on pairs of lists) as the unique solution of a hylo equation. In other words, it enables us to define recursive programs having additional parameters.

Another example of a relator that distributes over any join is of course the identity relator, so we have the following corollary of Theorem 12.

Corollary 13. *If R is F-reductive and $S \in F \rightsquigarrow H$ then $S \cdot R$ is H-reductive.*

Proof. Instantiate Theorem 12 with the (join-distributive) identity relator. □

Using this corollary (together with Corollary 9) it is straightforward to prove that equations such as the "paramorphism" equation

$$X :: X = R \cdot (I \vartriangle F.X) \cdot out$$

have unique solutions.

Also, Corollary 13 gives some more insight into the connection between termination proofs and unicity proofs. Freyd, Hoogendijk and De Moor [9] have shown that it is possible to define a membership relation for any polynomial relator, say *mem*. For example, for datatype list this relation holds between an element and a list if the element is in the list. For product, the relation holds between x and (x,y) and also between y and (x,y). This membership relation is of type $F \rightsquigarrow \mathsf{Id}$; combining this with Corollary 13, we deduce that the composition of the membership relation and an F-reductive relation admits induction, or is well-founded. Now consider the hylo equation. When interpreted operationally we see that each recursive call has as argument an element that is related to the original input by the relation $mem \cdot R$. If R is F-reductive this gives us the traditional termination argument using a well-founded relation.

8 Conclusion

We have given an induction principle over arbitrary datatypes and a class of equations that can be proved to have unique solutions using this induction principle. A topic for future research is: are there other classes of equations such that one of the induction principles can be used to give uniqueness proofs? In this respect, an interesting class is the class of equations of the form:

$$X :: X = R \cdot F.X \cdot G.X \cdot S . \tag{25}$$

(For instance, the Ackermann function satisfies an equation of this form.)

Another question is how we can weaken the restriction on S in Corollary 13. This is important because it turns out that for some applications the requirement $S \in F \rightsquigarrow H$ is simply too strong.

Also it has to be investigated what other rules there are to construct new F-reductive relations. For instance, how can two reductive relations be combined into one, thereby generalising the result that, under certain conditions, the join of two well-founded relations is well-founded again? In connection with this question, we would like to remark that there seems to be a strong connection between the laws from the μ-calculus from [12] and rules to construct reductive relations. This means that it should be possible to use the μ-calculus as a source of inspiration to predict reductivity lemmas.

Acknowledgements

We owe a great debt to the team spirit in the Eindhoven Mathematics of Program Construction group, in particular we thank Netty van Gasteren, Paul Hoogendijk and Jaap van der Woude for commenting on an earlier version of this paper. The inspiration for the notion of F-reductivity came from Oege de Moor during an extended visit he made to Eindhoven in October 1992.

References

1. C.J. Aarts. Galois connections presented calculationally. Afstudeer verslag (Graduating Dissertation), Department of Computing Science, Eindhoven University of Technology, 1992.
2. C.J. Aarts, R.C. Backhouse, P. Hoogendijk, T.S. Voermans, and J. van der Woude. A relational theory of datatypes. Available via anonymous ftp from ftp.win.tue.nl in directory pub/math.prog.construction, September 1992.
3. R.C. Backhouse, P. de Bruin, P. Hoogendijk, G. Malcolm, T.S. Voermans, and J. van der Woude. Polynomial relators. In M. Nivat, C.S. Rattray, T. Rus, and G. Scollo, editors, *Proceedings of the 2nd Conference on Algebraic Methodology and Software Technology, AMAST'91*, pages 303–326. Springer-Verlag, Workshops in Computing, 1992.
4. R.C. Backhouse and J. van der Woude. Demonic operators and monotype factors. *Mathematical Structures in Computer Science*, 3(4):417–433, December 1993.
5. Richard S. Bird and Oege de Moor. The algebra of programming. Programming Research Group, Oxford University. Textbook in preparation.
6. Garrett Birkhoff. *Lattice Theory*, volume 25 of *American Mathematical Society Colloquium Publications*. American Mathematical Society, Providence, Rhode Island, 3rd edition, 1967.
7. B. A. Davey and H. A. Priestly. *Introduction to Lattices and Order*. Cambridge Mathematical Textbooks. Cambridge University Press, first edition, 1990.
8. Maarten M. Fokkinga. *Law and Order in Algorithmics*. PhD thesis, Universiteit Twente, The Netherlands, 1992.
9. Peter Freyd, Paul Hoogendijk, and Oege de Moor. Membership of datatypes. Unpublished draft.
10. P.J. Freyd and A. Scedrov. *Categories, Allegories*. North-Holland, 1990.
11. G. Malcolm. Homomorphisms and promotability. In J.L.A. van de Snepscheut, editor, *Conference on the Mathematics of Program Construction*, pages 335–347. Springer-Verlag LNCS 375, 1989.
12. Eindhoven University of Technology Mathematics of Program Construction Group. Fixed point calculus. *Information Processing Letters*, 53(3):131–136, February 1995.
13. L. Meertens. Paramorphisms. *Formal Aspects of Computing*, 4(5):413–424, 1992.
14. E. Meijer, M.M. Fokkinga, and R. Paterson. Functional programming with bananas, lenses, envelopes and barbed wire. In *FPCA91: Functional Programming Languages and Computer Architecture*, volume 523 of *LNCS*, pages 124–144. Springer-Verlag, 1991.

Program Construction by Parts*

M. Frappier[1], A. Mili[1] and J. Desharnais[2]

[1] Department of Computer Science, University of Ottawa, Ottawa, Ont. K1N 6N5
fax: (613) 564 5045, email: {mfrappie,amili}@csi.uottawa.ca
[2] Département d'Informatique, Université Laval, Québec, Qué. G1K 7P4
fax: (418) 656 2324, email: desharn@ift.ulaval.ca

Abstract. Given a specification that includes a number of user requirements, we wish to focus on the requirements in turn, and derive a partly defined program for each; then combine all the partly defined programs into a single program that satisfies all the requirements simultaneously. In this paper we introduces a mathematical basis for solving this problem; and we illustrate it by means of a simple example.

1 Introduction and Motivation

We propose a program construction method whereby, given a specification that includes a number of user requirements, we focus on the requirements in turn, and derive a partly defined program for each; then combine all the partly defined programs into a single program that satisfies all the requirements simultaneously. In this paper we discuss this programming paradigm, which we call *program construction by parts*, and introduce a mathematical foundation for this paradigm.

Our paradigm is based on the premise that program specifications are represented by homogeneous binary relations, and that program construction proceeds by correctness-preserving stepwise transformations of relations; in Sect. 2, we introduce the mathematical background that is needed for our discussions, in terms of relation algebras. In Sect. 3, we introduce a number of relational operators that are useful for structuring specifications; some of these operators are original, others have been introduced by other researchers. In Sect. 4, we introduce our programming paradigm, which is based on the following premise: in previous work [7], we have found that complex program specifications are naturally structured as aggregates of simpler specifications by means of lattice-like relational operators; the crux of our proposed paradigm is to solve the subspecifications one at a time by means of partially defined programs, then to combine these partially defined programs into a fully defined program that solves the overall specification. The paradigm is presented by discussing in turn how to solve subspecifications then how to combine the partially defined programs that

---

* This research is supported by NSERC (Natural Sciences and Engineering Research Council) of Canada and by FCAR (Fonds pour la Formation de Chercheurs et l'Aide à la Recherche) of Québec

are so obtained. Section 5 illustrates our discussions by means of a simple example, and Sect. 6 summarizes our findings and sketches our prospects for future work.

2 Mathematical Background

Our work is based on the premise that specifications are binary homogeneous relations and that program construction proceeds by stepwise transformation of relations. In this section we introduce some mathematical background on binary relations.

2.1 Abstract Relation Algebra

Our definition of abstract relation algebra comes from [22], as do most of the other relational notions presented in this section. An interesting presentation of relation algebras can also be found in [2]. Relations have been used for specification and design in various domains (e.g. [6, 14, 17]).

Definition 1. A *homogeneous relation algebra* is a structure $(\mathcal{R}, \cup, \cap, ^-, \hat{}, \circ)$ over a non-empty set $\mathcal{R}$ of elements, called *relations*. The following conditions are satisfied.

1. $(\mathcal{R}, \cup, \cap, ^-)$ is a complete atomic Boolean algebra, with *zero* element $\emptyset$ and *universal* element L. The elements of $\mathcal{R}$ are ordered by *inclusion*, denoted by $\subseteq$.
2. For every relation R there exists a *converse* relation $\hat{R}$ (we will write $(R)^{\hat{}}$ rather than $\widehat{(R)}$ for parenthesized expressions).
3. *Composition*, denoted by $\circ$, is an associative operation with an identity element, which is denoted by I.
4. The Schröder rule is satisfied: $P \circ Q \subseteq R \Leftrightarrow \hat{P} \circ \overline{R} \subseteq \overline{Q} \Leftrightarrow \overline{R} \circ \hat{Q} \subseteq \overline{P}$.
5. $L \circ R \circ L = L$ holds for every $R \neq \emptyset$ (Tarski rule).   □

The precedence of the relational operators, from highest to lowest, is the following: $^-$ and $\hat{}$ bind equally, followed by $\circ$, followed by $\cap$ and finally by $\cup$. The scope of $\bigcup_i$ and $\bigcap_i$ goes to the right as far as possible. From now on, the composition operator symbol $\circ$ will be omitted (that is, we write QR for $Q \circ R$). The precedence of logical operators, from highest to lowest, is: $\neg$, $\wedge$, $\vee$, $(\Leftarrow, \Rightarrow)$, $\Leftrightarrow$, $(\forall, \exists)$, $\triangleq$. Relational operators and "=" bind stronger than logical operators.

A *concrete* (homogeneous) relation R on a set S (state space) is a subset of the Cartesian product $S \times S$. We denote the *universal relation* ($S \times S$) by L, the *empty relation* by $\emptyset$ and the *identity relation* ($\{(s, s')|s' = s\}$) by I. Also, the complement $\overline{R}$ is the set difference $L - R$; the relational product $R \circ R'$ is defined by $\{(s, s')|\exists t : (s, t) \in R \wedge (t, s') \in R'\}$; the ith relative power of relation R is denoted by R^i and represents the product of R by itself i times (with $R^0 = I$); finally, the converse $\hat{R}$ is $\{(s, s')|(s', s) \in R\}$. We admit without proof that the algebra of concrete relations, provided with the set theoretic operations of union, intersection and complement, and the relational operations of product and converse defines a *relation algebra* in the sense of definition 1 above [22]. We use abstract relation algebra for studying the properties of refinement, and we use the algebra of concrete relations for writing specifications.

Our sets are typically structured as Cartesian products of elementary sets, and are declared in a Pascal-like fashion. Hence, e.g. the declaration

var a : **Natural**, b : **Integer**

defines a set S as: $S =$ **Natural** $\times$ **Integer**. Given that s is an element of S, we let $a(s)$ and $b(s)$ denote its $a-$ and $b-$ components.

2.2 Properties of Relations

We present in turn some relational operators then some relational properties; these definitions are taken from [22] and [8].

The *transitive closure* of relation R is denoted by R^+ and defined by $\bigcup_{i>0} R^i$; the *reflexive transitive closure* of relation R is denoted by R^* and is given by $R^+ \cup I$ or, equivalently, $\bigcup_{i\geq 0} R^i$; the *conjugate kernel* of relation R and Q is denoted by $\kappa(R,Q)$ and is given by $\overline{\overline{R}\widehat{Q}} \cap L\widehat{Q}$; the *left residue* of relation R by relation Q is denoted by R/Q and is given by $\overline{\overline{R}\widehat{Q}}$; the *right residue* of relation R by relation Q is denoted by $Q\backslash R$ and is given by $\overline{\widehat{Q}\overline{R}}$.

We say that a relation t is a *left vector* if and only if $t = tL$; the converse $\widehat{t}$ of a left vector t is called a *right vector*. A relation R is said to be *progressively finite* if and only if for any left vector t, $t \subseteq Rt \Rightarrow t = \emptyset$ (equivalently, we also say that $\widehat{R}$ is well-founded).

As a convention, we use symbols P, Q, R (possibly subscripted) for relations, we use t, u, v for left vectors, and we use $\mathcal{A}$ for an arbitrary non-empty set of relations. The *domain* and *range* of a relation R can be characterized by left vectors RL and $\widehat{R}L$ respectively.

2.3 Refinement Ordering

We let a *specification* be defined by a set S, called the *space*, and a binary homogeneous relation R on S, called the *relation* of the specification. When the space is implicit from the context, we equate the specification with the relation R. A relation R has the following informal meaning: if a computation starts on a state s in the domain of relation R, then it must terminate on a state s' such that $(s, s') \in R$. If a computation starts on a state not in the domain of R, then any outcome is acceptable, including nontermination.

We wish to define an ordering on specifications whose interpretation is that a specification P is *weaker* than a specification Q, in the sense that any program totally correct with respect to Q is totally correct with respect to P.

Definition 2. Relation P is said to be *refined* by relation Q, denoted by $P \sqsubseteq Q$, if and only if

$$PL \subseteq QL \wedge Q \cap PL \subseteq P \ . \qquad \square$$

We leave it to the reader to check that this defines a partial ordering (reflexive, antisymmetric and transitive); we refer to this as the *refinement ordering*. To illustrate this definition, we consider space $S=$**real** and we let P and Q be defined as follows:

$$P = \{(s, s') | s - 3 \le s' \le s + 3\},$$
$$Q = \{(s, s') | s - 1 \le s' \le s + 1\}.$$

Then P is refined by Q because they have the same domain and Q is a subset of P. If we now consider the following definitions of P and Q:

$$P = \{(s, s') | 0 \le s \le 100 \wedge s - 3 \le s' \le s + 3\},$$
$$Q = \{(s, s') | s - 3 \le s' \le s + 3\},$$

then we find again that P is refined by Q because P has a smaller domain, and they both have the same image sets.

3 Structuring Relational Specifications

With the introduction of the refinement ordering, we can now be more explicit as to what represents a *correctness-preserving* transformation. In the process of transforming a specification into a program, we must ensure that each step maps a relation R into a relation R' such that $R \sqsubseteq R'$. Also, as a measure of separation of concerns, we wish to ensure that whenever a component of a specification is refined, the whole specification is refined; to do so, we take the position that all the operators that we use to structure our specifications must be monotonic with respect to the refinement ordering. In this section, we introduce a number of relational operators that we use to structure our specifications; for each such operator, we give a simple illustration, a formal semantic definition, and a brief argument to the effect that the operator is indeed monotonic with respect to the refinement ordering.

3.1 Demonic Join

In [7], we had found that the refinement ordering confers the set of relations (interpreted as specifications) a lattice-like structure, where the join (least upper bound) exists conditionally. The demonic join operator is defined if and only if the following condition is satisfied:

$$cs(P, Q) \triangleq PL \cap QL = (P \cap Q)L \ . \tag{1}$$

Whenever the condition is satisfied, the join is defined by

$$P \sqcup Q \triangleq (P \cap \overline{QL}) \cup (P \cap Q) \cup (\overline{PL} \cap Q) \ . \tag{2}$$

In [7], we had found that condition 1 can be interpreted as: P and Q are mutually consistent, i.e. they do not contradict each other; we call this the *consistency condition*. Two relations contradict each other when they provide disjoint sets of outputs for some input where they are both defined. Also, we have found that the join can be interpreted as: the specification that carries all the requirements of P and all the requirements of Q and nothing more; hence the join is in effect adding up the specifications.

By its very definition, a join (in any lattice) is monotonic with respect to the ordering that defines it. However, consistency may be lost while refining the components of our join, thereby obtaining an undefined join. We will discuss this issue in Sect. 4.

To illustrate this operator, we consider the case where we want a program that merges two sorted lists l_1 and l_2 into a list l_3. The following is a possible specification:

$$\{(s, s')|perm(l_1(s) \bullet l_2(s), l_3(s'))\} \sqcup$$
$$\{(s, s')|sorted(l_1(s)) \wedge sorted(l_2(s)) \wedge sorted(l_3(s'))\} \ .$$

This specifications requires a program to produce a list l_3 which is a permutation of the concatenation of the input lists l_1 and l_2. Moreover, when the input lists are sorted, the final list l_3 is also sorted.

3.2 Demonic Meet

In [7], we had found that any pair of relations has a meet (greatest lower bound) in the refinement ordering. It is defined as follows:

$$P \sqcap Q \triangleq (PL \cap Q) \cup (P \cap QL) \ . \tag{3}$$

Demonic meet offers a choice between two specifications. As an illustration of this operator, consider the following equalities:

$$\{(s, s')|s'^2 = s \wedge s' \geq 0\} \sqcap \{(s, s')|s'^2 = s \wedge s' \leq 0\} = \{(s, s')|s'^2 = s\} \ ,$$
$$\{(s, s')|s'^2 = s\} \sqcap \{(s, s')|-(s'^2) = s\} = \{(s, s')|s' = s = 0\} \ .$$

A demonic join is defined only on the intersection of the domains of the components; its outputs are the union of the outputs of the components. We assign to $\sqcup, \sqcap$ the same precedence as $\cup, \cap$. Demonic join and demonic meet take simple forms when some conditions are met.

(a) $P \cap QL = PL \cap Q \Rightarrow P \sqcap Q = P \cap Q$ and $P \sqcup Q = P \cup Q$
(b) $t \sqcap u = t \cap u$
(c) $t \sqcup u = t \cup u$
(d) $PL = QL = (P \cap Q)L \Rightarrow P \sqcap Q = P \cup Q$ and $P \sqcup Q = P \cap Q$
(e) $\hat{t} \sqcap \hat{u} = \hat{t} \cup \hat{u}$
(f) $t \cap u \neq \emptyset \Rightarrow \hat{t} \sqcup \hat{u} = \hat{t} \cap \hat{u}$

$$(4)$$

The definitions of join and meet can be generalized for the infinitary case. To this effect, we cite one last result which was proved in [4].

Proposition 3. *Let $\mathcal{R}$ be a relation algebra. The structure $(\mathcal{R}, \sqsubseteq)$ is a complete $\sqcap$-semilattice.* $\square$

When the necessary joins are defined, the following identities hold ([4]).

(a) $P \sqcup \bigsqcap_{Q \in \mathcal{A}} Q = \bigsqcap_{Q \in \mathcal{A}} P \sqcup Q$

(b) $P \sqcap \bigsqcup_{Q \in \mathcal{A}} Q = \bigsqcup_{Q \in \mathcal{A}} P \sqcap Q$

(c) $(P \sqcup Q)L = PL \cup QL$

(d) $(P \sqcap Q)L = PL \cap QL$

(e) $t \cap (Q \sqcap R) = (t \cap Q) \sqcap (t \cap R)$

(f) $t \cap (Q \sqcup R) = (t \cap Q) \sqcup (t \cap R)$ (5)

(g) $(t \sqcap u)\widehat{\ } = \widehat{t} \sqcup \widehat{u}$

(h) $(t \sqcup u)\widehat{\ } = \widehat{t} \sqcap \widehat{u}$

(i) $R = t \cap R \sqcup \overline{t} \cap R$

(j) $P \sqcap Q \sqsubseteq P \sqcup Q$

3.3 Demonic Composition

Given a specification R that we wish to decompose as the sequential composition of two subspecifications R_0 and R_1; it seems natural to rewrite R as $R = R_0 \circ R_1$. Unfortunately, this is not acceptable, because the traditional relational product (represented by $\circ$) is not monotonic with respect to the refinement ordering; so that if we now refine R_0 by R_0', we have no assurance that $R_0' \circ R_1$ refines $R_0 \circ R_1$. Hence we introduce the *demonic composition* operator [3, 5], which captures the idea of sequential composition and is monotonic with respect to the refinement ordering:

$$P \,\square\, Q \stackrel{\triangle}{=} PQ \cap \overline{P\overline{QL}} \ . \tag{6}$$

In [9], it is shown how the definition of demonic composition can be obtained from *flow diagrams* [22], which are used to provide a general definition of programming constructs.

The equivalent set-theoretic definition of demonic composition is more intuitive:

$$(s, s') \in P \,\square\, Q \Leftrightarrow (s, s') \in PQ \wedge s.R \subseteq dom(Q) \ ,$$

where $s.P$ stands for the set of images of s by relation P, and $dom(Q)$ stands for the domain of relation Q. It is noteworthy that when P is deterministic, the demonic product of P by Q is the same as the traditional relational product.

As an example of demonic composition, we have the following equalities:

$$\{(s, s') | s'^2 = s\} \,\square\, \{(s, s') | s'^2 = s\} = \{(s, s') | s = s' = 0\} \ ,$$
$$\{(s, s') | s'^2 = s \wedge s' \geq 0\} \,\square\, \{(s, s') | s'^2 = s\} = \{(s, s') | s'^4 = s\} \ .$$

We assign to $\square$ the same precedence as $\circ$. The following laws hold when the necessary joins exist.

(a) $P \,\square\, (Q \,\square\, R) = (P \,\square\, Q) \,\square\, R$

(b) $P \,\square\, I = I \,\square\, P = P$

(c) $Q \sqsubseteq R \Rightarrow P \,\square\, Q \sqsubseteq P \,\square\, R$

(d) $P \sqsubseteq Q \Rightarrow P \,\square\, R \sqsubseteq Q \,\square\, R$

(e) $P \,\square\, \bigsqcap_{Q \in \mathcal{A}} Q = \bigsqcap_{Q \in \mathcal{A}} P \,\square\, Q$

(f) $(\bigsqcap_{P \in \mathcal{A}} P) \,\square\, Q = \bigsqcap_{P \in \mathcal{A}} P \,\square\, Q$

(g) $P \,\square\, \bigsqcup_{Q \in \mathcal{A}} Q \sqsupseteq \bigsqcup_{Q \in \mathcal{A}} P \,\square\, Q$

(h) $(\bigsqcup_{P \in \mathcal{A}} P) \,\square\, Q \sqsupseteq \bigsqcup_{P \in \mathcal{A}} P \,\square\, Q$ (7)

(i) $\widehat{P}P \subseteq I \Rightarrow P \,\square\, Q = PQ$

(j) $\widehat{P}L \subseteq QL \Rightarrow P \,\square\, Q = PQ$

(k) $Q \subseteq R \Rightarrow P \,\square\, Q \subseteq P \,\square\, R$

(l) $t \cap (P \,\square\, Q) = (t \cap P) \,\square\, Q$

(m) $P \,\square\, (t \cap Q) = P \,\square\, t \cap P \,\square\, Q$

(n) $\widehat{t} = L \,\square\, \widehat{t}$

3.4 Demonic Closure

If we consider that specification R can be satisfied by a sequential combination of specification Q an arbitrary number of times, we use the *demonic closure* operator, which is defined as follows.

Definition 4. The *demonic reflexive transitive closure* (or simply *demonic closure* for short) of a relation R is defined as

$$R^{\boxplus} \triangleq \bigsqcap_{i \geq 0} R^{\boxed{i}}$$

where $R^{\boxed{0}} \triangleq I$ and $R^{\boxed{i+1}} \triangleq R \circ R^{\boxed{i}}$. □

As an illustration of demonic closure, we consider the specification of a permutation. If we observe that a natural way to define a permutation of an array is by an arbitrary number of swaps of pairs of cells, then we can write a permutation Prm as:

$$Prm = Swap^{\boxplus} \ .$$

Because it is based on demonic product, demonic closure may differ significantly from the angelic closure (*), as the following example illustrates it:

$$\{(s, s') | s'^2 = s\}^* = \{(s, s') | \exists n \geq 0 : sq^n.s' = s\} \ ,$$
$$\{(s, s') | s'^2 = s\}^{\boxplus} = \{(s, s') | s = s' = 0\} \ ,$$

where $sq.x \triangleq x^2$ and sq^n is the usual exponential of a function. Our demonic closure can be understood as an iteration without an exit condition. This is not an acceptable construct in programming languages, but is quite acceptable in our specification language: the demonic closure knows what to do at each iteration but does not know when to stop doing it; typically, this will be combined (by the demonic join) with another specification which will provide the exit condition. An illustrative example of this pattern is the specification of the sort program, which can be written as:

$$Sort = Swap^{\boxplus} \sqcup Sorted \ ,$$

where $Sorted$ indicates that the output array is sorted. In practice, it is quite typical that specifications be structured as the join of two specifications: a binary specification, which defines a link between inputs and outputs, and can be formulated as the demonic closure of a simpler specification; a unary specification, which defines desirable properties of the output, and can be represented by a right vector.

We assign to $\boxplus$ the same precedence as $\widehat{}$ and $\overline{}$. The next proposition provides an alternative definition of the *demonic closure*, based on the notion of greatest fixpoint.

Proposition 5. *Let R be a relation; let f be the function given by $f.X \triangleq I \sqcap R \sqcap X \circ X$. The greatest fixpoint of f wrt $\sqsubseteq$ exists, and it is given by $R^{\boxplus}$.*

PROOF. Let $f^0.X \triangleq X$, and $f^{n+1}.X \triangleq f.f^n.X$. By induction, we can show that $f^n.I \sqsubseteq I$ for all n. It is easy to show that f is $\sqcap$-continuous, using law 7(e). Therefore, we have

$$f. \bigsqcap_{n \geq 0} f^n.I$$
$$= \qquad \{ f \text{ is } \sqcap\text{-continuous} \}$$
$$\bigsqcap_{n \geq 1} f^n.I$$
$$= \qquad \{ f^n.I \sqsubseteq I \text{ for all } n \}$$
$$\bigsqcap_{n \geq 0} f^n.I .$$

Hence, $\bigsqcap_{n \geq 0} f^n.I$ is a fixpoint of f. Let Z be a fixpoint of f. We have $Z = I \sqcap R \sqcap Z \circ Z \sqsubseteq I$. Since f is monotonic, it is easy to show by induction that $Z \sqsubseteq f^n.I$ for all n. Hence, $Z \sqsubseteq \bigsqcap_{n \geq 0} f^n.I$, and $\bigsqcap_{n \geq 0} f^n.I$ is the greatest fixpoint of f. Now, a simple induction shows that $\bigsqcap_{n \geq 0} f^n.I = R^{\boxdot}$. $\qquad \square$

The demonic closure satisfies properties similar to its angelic counterpart (R^*). We only mention four of them.

$$
\begin{array}{ll}
\text{(a) } P \sqsubseteq Q \Rightarrow P^{\boxdot} \sqsubseteq Q^{\boxdot} & \text{(b) } P \sqsubseteq I \wedge P \sqsubseteq P \circ P \Leftrightarrow P = P^{\boxdot} \\
\text{(c) } P^{\boxdot} = P^{\boxdot} \circ P^{\boxdot} & \text{(d) } P^{\boxdot} \sqsubseteq (t \cap P \sqcup \bar{t} \cap I)^{\boxdot}
\end{array}
\qquad (8)
$$

PROOF. Identity (a) follows easily from the definition of $^{\boxdot}$, since meet and demonic composition are monotonic. For (b), we have

$$P \sqsubseteq I \wedge P \sqsubseteq P \circ P$$
$$\Leftrightarrow \qquad \{ \text{reflexivity of } \sqsubseteq \}$$
$$P \sqsubseteq I \wedge P \sqsubseteq P \circ P \wedge P \sqsubseteq P$$
$$\Leftrightarrow \qquad \{ \text{property of meet} \}$$
$$P \sqsubseteq I \sqcap P \sqcap P \circ P$$
$$\Leftrightarrow \qquad \{ I \sqcap P \sqcap P \circ P \sqsubseteq P, \text{ by def. of meet} \}$$
$$P = I \sqcap P \sqcap P \circ P$$

Therefore, P is a fixpoint of $f.X = I \sqcap P \sqcap X \circ X$. It is also the greatest fixpoint: let Y be a fixpoint of f; then $Y = I \sqcap P \sqcap Y \circ Y \sqsubseteq P$. By Proposition 5, we have $P = P^{\boxdot}$. For the reverse implication, we have:

$$P = P^{\boxdot}$$
$$\Rightarrow \qquad \{ \text{Proposition 5} \}$$
$$P = I \sqcap P \sqcap P \circ P$$
$$\Leftrightarrow \qquad \{ \text{property of meet} \}$$
$$P \sqsubseteq I \wedge P \sqsubseteq P \wedge P \sqsubseteq P \circ P$$
$$\Rightarrow \qquad \{ \text{property of } \wedge \}$$
$$P \sqsubseteq I \wedge P \sqsubseteq P \circ P .$$

For (c), we have

$$P^{\boxdot}$$
$$= \qquad \{ \text{Proposition 5} \}$$
$$I \sqcap P \sqcap P^{\boxdot} \circ P^{\boxdot}$$
$$\sqsubseteq \qquad \{ \text{property of meet} \}$$
$$P^{\boxdot} \circ P^{\boxdot}$$
$$\sqsubseteq \qquad \{ P^{\boxdot} \sqsubseteq I, \text{ monotonicity of } \circ \}$$

$$P^{\boxplus} \circ I$$
$$= \qquad \{\ 7(b)\ \}$$
$$P^{\boxplus}\ .$$

For (d), we have

$$P^{\boxplus}$$
$$= \qquad \{\ \text{Proposition 5}\ \}$$
$$I \sqcap P \sqcap P^{\boxplus} \circ P^{\boxplus}$$
$$\sqsubseteq \qquad \{\ \text{property of meet}\ \}$$
$$I \sqcap P$$
$$= \qquad \{\ \text{law 5(i)}\ \}$$
$$t \cap (I \sqcap P) \sqcup \bar{t} \cap (I \sqcap P)$$
$$\sqsubseteq \qquad \{\ \text{property of meet, monotonicity}\ \}$$
$$t \cap P \sqcup \bar{t} \cap I$$

In addition, since $P^{\boxplus} = I \sqcap P \sqcap P^{\boxplus} \circ P^{\boxplus}$, we also have $P^{\boxplus} \sqsubseteq I$ and $P^{\boxplus} \sqsubseteq P^{\boxplus} \circ P^{\boxplus}$. From 8(b), it follows that $P^{\boxplus} = P^{\boxplus\,\boxplus}$. Hence,

$$P^{\boxplus} = P^{\boxplus\,\boxplus} \sqsubseteq (t \cap P \sqcup \bar{t} \cap I)^{\boxplus}\ . \qquad \square$$

3.5 Prerestriction

Whenever we want to limit the domain of a specification (relation) P to a particular subset defined by the left vector t, we use the *prerestriction* operator, which we write as follows:

$$t \to P \triangleq t \cap P\ . \tag{9}$$

While intersection is not monotonic with respect to the refinement ordering, this particular form of intersection (by a left vector) is:

$$t \sqsubseteq u \wedge P \sqsubseteq Q \Rightarrow t \to P \sqsubseteq u \to Q\ . \tag{10}$$

We refer the reader to the left vector laws of (5) and (7), which can be interpreted as properties of $\to$. We assign to $\to$ the same precedence as $\cap$ and $\sqcap$. Given a relation P and a set defined by V, we can define the restriction of P to V in one of two ways: either by means of left vectors, as we just did; or by means of monotypes, as $I(V) \circ P$, where $I(V) = \{(s, s') | s' = s \wedge s \in V\}$. The latter form is strongly advocated in [2], with ample justifications. In the context of this work, we have chosen to use left vectors, because vectors arise naturally in join-based specifications.

3.6 Preserve

In program construction by parts, we may sometimes want to keep the program state within some set in order to satisfy a particular requirement. This occurs quite typically in loops: in order to satisfy the loop invariant, we must keep the program state within a particular set from one iteration to the next. The specification that provides that states originating in set V (defined by left vector t) remain in V is defined by:

$$t^\circ \triangleq t \to \hat{t} \ . \tag{11}$$

The following identities follow readily from the definition of the preserve construct, and hold whenever the joins are defined.

$$
\begin{array}{ll}
\text{(a) } (t \sqcap u)^\circ = (t \sqcap u) \to (\hat{t} \sqcup \hat{u}) & \\
\text{(c) } (t \sqcup u)^\circ = (t \sqcup u) \to (\hat{t} \sqcap \hat{u}) & \text{(b) } (t \sqcap u)^\circ \sqsubseteq t^\circ \sqcup u^\circ \\
\text{(e) } t^\circ = t^\circ \circ t^\circ & \text{(d) } t^\circ \sqsubseteq I \\
\text{(g) } \hat{t} = \hat{t} \circ t^\circ & \text{(f) } t^\circ = t^{\circ \boxplus}
\end{array} \tag{12}
$$

We assign to $^\circ$ the same precedence as $\hat{\ }$, $^-$ and $\boxplus$. For simplicity, if a is a right vector, we write a° instead of $\hat{a}^\circ$ (in fact, both forms are equivalent if we extend the definition of $^\circ$ to take right vectors as operands).

As an illustration of the *preserve* construct, we consider the preservation of the condition "the array is partially sorted" (an invariant), as it would occur in a typical sorting problem:

$$inv = PartlySorted^\circ \ .$$

3.7 Local Variables

In the process of refining a specification, it is sometimes necessary to introduce a new variable in order to find suitable refinements. The expression

var $x : T \ P$

introduces a local variable x of type T. The initial value of x is arbitrary in type T; its final value is lost when the execution of P is completed. The *scope* of a declaration **var** $x : T$ extends as far as possible on the right, and is limited by parentheses if necessary. The *context* of a relation R is the set of declarations whose scope contains R.

Let w be the context of statement **var** $x : T \ P$. The space of P is the context w extended by variable x. We denote it by S_{w+x}. The space of **var** $x : T \ P$ is denoted by S_w. Variable x must not already be declared in w. The semantics of **var** $x : T \ P$ is the projection of the semantics of P on space S_w. We express this formally as

var $x : T \ P \triangleq \hat{\Pi} \circ P \circ \Pi$

where Π is a *projection relation* defined as

$$\Pi = \{(s, s') \in S_{w+x} \times S_w \,|\, \exists t : s = \langle s', t \rangle\} \ .$$

The following laws hold.

$$\text{(a) } P \sqsubseteq Q \Rightarrow \textbf{var } x : T \ P \sqsubseteq \textbf{var } x : T \ Q \qquad \text{(b) } P \sqsubseteq \textbf{var } x : T \ P \tag{13}$$

4 Program Construction by Parts

4.1 A Programming Paradigm

We consider a specification R that is structured as a join of simpler specifications, say R' and R'': $R = R' \sqcup R''$. Specifications R' and R'' are typically simpler than R, because they capture partial requirements. As a matter of separation of concerns, we propose to solve R' and R'' in turn, then combine their solutions to find a solution for R. This is the paradigm of *program construction by parts*. In the sequel we discuss in turn: how to refine subspecifications; then how to combine partial solutions to form a solution for the whole specification.

4.2 Refining Subspecifications

Given a specification R structured as the join of two subspecifications R' and R'', we consider the question of how to refine R' and R'' in turn. The refinement of a subspecification (say, R') involves a tradeoff between two requirements: refine R' sufficiently to register some progress in the refinement process; do not refine R' too much, for fear that it becomes irreconcilable with R'' (i.e. R' and R'' no longer satisfy the consistency condition).

To illustrate this tradeoff, we consider again the specification of a sort program:
$$Sort = Prm \sqcup Sorted \ .$$

Relation Prm is refined by the identity relation, I. Yet, $Sort$ is not refined by $I \sqcup Sorted$ because I and $Sorted$ do not satisfy the consistency condition. This is a case where excessive refinement leads to a dead end in the refinement process. A more reasonable refinement of Prm would be to rewrite Prm as the demonic closure of specification $Swap$, which we presented in Sect. 3.4. Then $Sort$ can be refined as follows:
$$Sort \sqsubseteq Swap^{\boxdot} \sqcup Sorted \ .$$

We leave it to the reader to check that the components of the join do satisfy the consistency condition.

This example raises the issue of whether we must check the consistency of two subspecifications whenever we perform a refinement. The proposition below provides that the programmer may check consistency arbitrarily seldom in the refinement process.

Proposition 6. *Let P, P', Q, Q' be relations such that $P \sqsubseteq P'$ and $Q \sqsubseteq Q'$. If specifications P' and Q' satisfy the consistency condition, then so do specifications P and Q.*

PROOF. We prove $cs(P',Q') \Rightarrow cs(P,Q)$. Assume $cs(P',Q')$.

$PL \cap QL$
$=$ { $PL \subseteq P'L$ and $QL \subseteq Q'L$ from $P \sqsubseteq P'$ and $Q \sqsubseteq Q'$ }
$PL \cap QL \cap P'L \cap Q'L$

$$= \qquad \{ P'L \cap Q'L = (P' \cap Q')L \text{ from } cs(P', Q') \}$$
$$PL \cap QL \cap (P' \cap Q')L$$
$$= \qquad \{ \text{ relational law } t \cap RR' = (t \cap R)R' \}$$
$$(PL \cap QL \cap P' \cap Q')L$$
$$\subseteq \qquad \{ P' \cap PL \subseteq P \text{ and } Q' \cap QL \subseteq Q \text{ from } P \sqsubseteq P' \text{ and } Q \sqsubseteq Q' \}$$
$$(P \cap Q)L \qquad \square$$

4.3 Combining Subspecifications

The problem that we address in this section is the following: given that we have refined the arguments of our join, we must now combine them into a single program. In this section we give the rewriting rules that allow us to carry out this transformation. One of the objectives of the rules is to eliminate join operators from specifications, because the join is not executable.

Eliminating Joins. A trivial way to get rid of a join is when the arguments of the join are identical.

Proposition 7. *A specification of the form $P \sqcup P$ is refined by P.*

This proposition stems readily from the idempotence of lattice operators. It represents the *bottom of recursion* of a recursive process which consists in pushing joins deeper and deeper into the nesting structure of the specification. The inductive step of this recursive process is discussed in Sect. 4.3.

Another way to eliminate joins is to substitute a specification pattern by a Pascal-like statement. The following propositions identify several patterns, as well as their associated Pascal-like statement. These propositions are given without proof; their proofs can be found in [11].

Proposition 8. *Let $x_1, \ldots, x_n$ be the variables of a specification, and let $e(s)$ be an expression on space S. A specification of the form*

$$\{(s, s') | x_i(s') = e(s) \land \forall j \in 1..n : i \neq j \Rightarrow x_j(s') = x_j(s)\}$$

is equivalent to

$$x_i(s) := e(s) \qquad \square$$

Proposition 9. *If specifications P and Q satisfy the following condition $P \cap QL \subseteq Q$ then they are mutually consistent, and their join $(P \sqcup Q)$ is equivalent to*

$$\textbf{if } t \textbf{ then } P \textbf{ else } Q \textbf{ end },$$

where t is defined by $t = PL$.

Proposition 10. *A specification of the form*

$$t \to P \sqcup \bar{t} \to Q$$

is equivalent to

if t **then** P **else** Q **end,**

according to the traditional semantics associated with the **if-then-else** *statement [1, 15, 18].* □

As usual, we define the conditional as:

if t **then** P **end** $\stackrel{\wedge}{=}$ **if** t **then** P **else** I **end.**

Proposition 11. *When a specification of the form*

if t **then** P **end**$^{\boxminus}$ $\sqcup$ $\widehat{t}$

satisfies the conditions

1. $t \to P$ is progressively finite,
2. $t \subseteq PL$;

then it is defined (join exists), and it is equivalent to

while t **do** P **end,**

according to the traditional least fixpoint semantics (wrt $\sqsubseteq$) associated with the **while-do** *statement [1, 15, 18].* □

Propagating Joins. If two relational expressions combined with a join share the same structure, then the join can be pushed inside the structure. The resulting joins are made of smaller expressions, and hopefully they become easier to eliminate. We express this law for generic monotonic operators in the following proposition.

Proposition 12. *Let $\Phi(P_1, \ldots, P_n)$ be a monotonic operator with respect to $\sqsubseteq$. Then the following holds if the joins are defined:*

$$\Phi(P_1, \ldots, P_n) \sqcup \Phi(Q_1, \ldots, Q_n) \sqsubseteq \Phi(P_1 \sqcup Q_1, \ldots, P_n \sqcup Q_n) \ .$$

PROOF.

$\qquad \Phi(P_1, \ldots, P_n) \sqcup \Phi(Q_1, \ldots, Q_n)$
$\sqsubseteq \qquad \{\ P_i \sqsubseteq P_i \sqcup Q_i, \text{ monotonicity of } \Phi \text{ and } \sqcup\ \}$
$\qquad \Phi(P_1 \sqcup Q_1, \ldots, P_n \sqcup Q_n) \sqcup \Phi(Q_1, \ldots, Q_n)$
$\sqsubseteq \qquad \{\ Q_i \sqsubseteq P_i \sqcup Q_i, \text{ monotonicity of } \Phi \text{ and } \sqcup\ \}$
$\qquad \Phi(P_1 \sqcup Q_1, \ldots, P_n \sqcup Q_n) \sqcup \Phi(P_1 \sqcup Q_1, \ldots, P_n \sqcup Q_n)$
$= \qquad \{\ \text{idempotence of } \sqcup\ \}$
$\qquad \Phi(P_1 \sqcup Q_1, \ldots, P_n \sqcup Q_n) \qquad$ □

Using this proposition, we derive one law for each monotonic operator used in the construction of programs. Of course, these laws hold if the joins are defined.

$$P_1 \mathbin{\square} P_2 \;\sqcup\; Q_1 \mathbin{\square} Q_2 \;\sqsubseteq\; (P_1 \sqcup Q_1) \mathbin{\square} (P_2 \sqcup Q_2) \tag{14}$$

$$P^{\boxplus} \;\sqcup\; Q^{\boxplus} \;\sqsubseteq\; (P \sqcup Q)^{\boxplus} \tag{15}$$

$$t \to P \;\sqcup\; u \to Q \;\sqsubseteq\; (t \sqcup u) \to (P \sqcup Q) \tag{16}$$

$$\textbf{var } x : T \; P \;\sqcup\; \textbf{var } x : T \; Q \;\sqsubseteq\; \textbf{var } x : T \; P \sqcup Q \tag{17}$$

$$\textbf{if } t \textbf{ then } P_1 \textbf{ else } Q_1 \textbf{ end } \;\sqcup\; \textbf{if } t \textbf{ then } P_2 \textbf{ else } Q_2 \textbf{ end } \sqsubseteq \atop \textbf{if } t \textbf{ then } P_1 \sqcup P_2 \textbf{ else } Q_1 \sqcup Q_2 \textbf{ end} \tag{18}$$

$$\textbf{while } t \textbf{ do } P \textbf{ end } \;\sqcup\; \textbf{while } t \textbf{ do } Q \textbf{ end } \;\sqsubseteq\; \textbf{while } t \textbf{ do } P \sqcup Q \textbf{ end} \tag{19}$$

A typical use of the refinement rule 14 arises in cases where the specification at hand has the form $(P_1 \mathbin{\square} P_2) \sqcup Q$. In order to apply the refinement, we may decompose Q as $Q \mathbin{\square} X$, if we wish to match Q with P_1, or as $X \mathbin{\square} Q$, if we wish to match Q with P_2. In both cases, X must be chosen in such a way as to be minimal in the refinement ordering. We briefly review some results we had found in [4] regarding these problems.

The least solution in X, wrt $\sqsubseteq$, of the equation $R \sqsubseteq X \mathbin{\square} Q$ exists if $RL \sqsubseteq \kappa(R,Q)L$ [4]. In this case, the solution is denoted by $R /\!\!/ Q$ (*demonic left residue*), and is given by $\kappa(R,Q)$. Similarly, the least solution in X, wrt $\sqsubseteq$, of the equation $R \sqsubseteq Q \mathbin{\square} X$ exists if $RL \subseteq QL$ and $L \subseteq ((RL \cap Q)\backslash R)L$ [4]. In that case, the solution is denoted by $Q \backslash\!\backslash R$ (*demonic right residue*), and is given by $\kappa(\widehat{R}, (RL \cap Q)\widehat{})\widehat{}$. The computation of the kernels is, in general, rather unwieldy. However, when $R = R\widehat{Q}Q$ (i.e. Q is *regular relatively to* R [8]), then $\kappa(R,Q)$ is given by $R\widehat{Q}$. Among the properties of $/\!\!/$ and $\backslash\!\backslash$, we mention the following, because they proved useful in the construction of loops.

$$\text{(a) } P /\!\!/ P = (P /\!\!/ P)^{\boxplus} \qquad \text{(b) } P \backslash\!\backslash P = (P \backslash\!\backslash P)^{\boxplus} \tag{20}$$

PROOF. For (a): we have $P \sqsubseteq I \mathbin{\square} P$; therefore, I is a solution of $P \sqsubseteq X \mathbin{\square} P$; from the definition of $/\!\!/$, it follows that $P /\!\!/ P \sqsubseteq I$. Also,

$$
\begin{array}{ll}
P & \\
\sqsubseteq & \{ \text{ definition of } /\!\!/ \} \\
(P /\!\!/ P) \mathbin{\square} P & \\
\sqsubseteq & \{ \text{ definition of } /\!\!/, \text{ monotonicity of } \mathbin{\square} \} \\
(P /\!\!/ P) \mathbin{\square} (P /\!\!/ P) \mathbin{\square} P &
\end{array}
$$

Hence, $(P/\!\!/P) \circ (P/\!\!/P)$ is a solution of $P \sqsubseteq X \circ P$; from the definition of $/\!\!/$, it follows that $P/\!\!/P \sqsubseteq (P/\!\!/P) \circ (P/\!\!/P)$. From $P/\!\!/P \sqsubseteq I$ and $P/\!\!/P \sqsubseteq (P/\!\!/P) \circ (P/\!\!/P)$, we conclude $P/\!\!/P = (P/\!\!/P)^{\boxplus}$ by virtue of law 8(b). The proof of (b) is similar.
□

The following proposition provides that it is not possible to propagate an undefined join and obtain defined joins.

Proposition 13. *Let P_1, P_2, Q_1, Q_2 be relations; let Φ be a monotonic operator wrt $\sqsubseteq$ on relations. Then, we have:*

$$cs(P_1, Q_1) \land cs(P_2, Q_2) \Rightarrow cs(P_1 \Phi P_2, Q_1 \Phi Q_2) \ .$$

PROOF.

$\quad cs(P_1, Q_1) \land cs(P_2, Q_2)$
$\Rightarrow \quad \{ \ cs(P_i, Q_i) \text{ implies } P_i \sqcup Q_i \text{ exists } \}$
$\quad cs((P_1 \sqcup Q_1)\Phi(P_2 \sqcup Q_2), (P_1 \sqcup Q_1)\Phi(P_2 \sqcup Q_2))$
$\Rightarrow \quad \{ \ P_1 \sqsubseteq P_1 \sqcup Q_1, \text{ monotonicity of } \Phi, \text{ Proposition 6 } \}$
$\quad cs(P_1\Phi(P_2 \sqcup Q_2), (P_1 \sqcup Q_1)\Phi(P_2 \sqcup Q_2))$
$\Rightarrow \quad \{ \ P_2 \sqsubseteq P_2 \sqcup Q_2, \text{ monotonicity of } \Phi, \text{ Proposition 6 } \}$
$\quad cs(P_1\Phi P_2, (P_1 \sqcup Q_1)\Phi(P_2 \sqcup Q_2))$
$\Rightarrow \quad \{ \ Q_1 \sqsubseteq P_1 \sqcup Q_1, \text{ monotonicity of } \Phi, \text{ Proposition 6 } \}$
$\quad cs(P_1\Phi P_2, Q_1\Phi(P_2 \sqcup Q_2))$
$\Rightarrow \quad \{ \ Q_2 \sqsubseteq P_2 \sqcup Q_2, \text{ monotonicity of } \Phi, \text{ Proposition 6 } \}$
$\quad cs(P_1\Phi P_2, Q_1\Phi Q_2)$ □

A consequence of this proposition is that the programmer may delay the verification of the consistency condition, even if joins are propagated. In fact, it is seldom required to prove consistency using definition 1: if one is successful in removing a join using laws 7, 9, 10 or 11, then consistency is proved as a byproduct. One would need to prove consistency using the definition only if it seems impossible to eliminate the join, as a mean of determining if components were refined up to a point where they can no longer agree.

5 The Naur Problem

In this section, we apply our program construction paradigm to the Naur problem. Note that the purpose of this section is not to solve the Naur problem as much as it is to illustrate our method. In order to illustrate the versality of our notation and method, we will leisurely contemplate alternative design choices and discuss their merits. If our purpose were to find a solution to the problem, as opposed to illustrate our method, then our discussion would have been a great deal shorter.

5.1 The User Requirements

First, we present the English version of this problem, as given by [16].

"Given are a non-negative integer M and a character set which includes two *break* characters, viz. $\flat$ (*blank*) and $\sharp$ (*newline*). For a sequence s of characters, we define a *word* as a non-empty sequence of consecutive non-break characters embedded between break characters or the endpoints of s (i.e. the beginning and end of sequence s). The program shall accept as input a finite sequence of characters and produce as output a sequence of characters satisfying the following conditions.

1. If the input includes at least one break character for any consecutive $M + 1$ characters, then all the words of the input appear in the output, in the same order; all the words of the output appear in the input.

2. Furthermore, the output must meet the following conditions:
   (a) It contains no leading or trailing breaks, nor does it have two consecutive breaks.
   (b) Any sequence of $M + 1$ consecutive characters includes a newline.
   (c) Any sequence made up of no more than M consecutive characters and embedded between (the head of the output or a newline on the left) and (the tail of the output or a break on the right) does not contain a newline character".

5.2 The Relational Specification

Before we proceed with writing a formal specification for this problem, we introduce the following notations: we denote by chr the set of characters under consideration, including the *newline* symbol; also, we let this set be partitioned into the set of *text* characters, which we denote by txt and the set of *breaks*, which we denote by brk; we let $x \bullet y$ stand for the concatenation of sequences x and y; we let ϵ denote the empty sequence; we let X^+ denote the closure under "$\bullet$" of the set of sequences X; we let X^* denote $X^+ \cup \{\epsilon\}$; we let $\#.x$ denote the length of sequence x; we let $x \preceq y$ be the predicate "x is a subsequence of consecutive characters of y"; we let $fw.x$ denote the first word of sequence x, provided that x contains a word; we let $rw.x$ denote the sequence beginning after the first word of x and terminating at the end of x, provided that x contains a word; we let $lw.x$ be the Boolean value "sequence x contains a word of length $> M$"; we let $lfw.x$ be the Boolean value "the length of the first word of sequence x is $> M$"; we let sw be a function that maps a sequence of characters x to the sequence of words of x (e.g. $sw.\langle ab\flat cd\rangle = \langle\langle ab\rangle\langle cd\rangle\rangle$). Function sw satisfies the following condition:

$$sw.x = sw.y \bullet sw.z \Rightarrow (lw.x \Leftrightarrow lw.y \vee lw.z) \ . \tag{21}$$

Given that x is a program variable, we write logical expressions using x and x' instead of $x(s)$ and $x(s')$ respectively, for the sake of brevity. Also, instead of writing our relations in the form $\{(s, s')|p(s, s')\}$, we simply write $\{p(s, s')\}$.

The space of our specification is given by the following declaration:

var in, out : **seq** chr .

We let relation $binary$ represent clause 1 of the user requirements. It can be written as

$$binary \triangleq \{\neg lw.in \wedge sw.in = sw.out'\} \quad .$$

Clauses 2a, 2b and 2c are conditions on the output only. They are represented, respectively, by the following right vectors:

$$exb \triangleq \{out' \in txt^+ \bullet (brk \bullet txt^+)^* \cup \{\epsilon\}\}$$

$$sht \triangleq \{\forall x : x \preceq out' \wedge \#.x = M+1 \Rightarrow \not| \preceq x\}$$

$$lng \triangleq \{\forall x, y, z : out' = x \bullet y \bullet z \wedge x \in chr^* \bullet \not| \cup \{\epsilon\} \wedge \#.y \leq M \wedge$$
$$z \in brk \bullet chr^* \cup \{\epsilon\} \Rightarrow \not| \not\preceq y\}.$$

Given exb, sht and lng, we let $unary$ be defined as:

$$unary \triangleq exb \sqcup sht \sqcup lng.$$

The complete specification of the Naur problem is given by the following:

$$binary \sqcup unary \quad .$$

We leave it to the reader to check that the components are consistent, hence the join is defined. The structure of the Naur specification is typical of join-structured specifications: some components represent the relationship between initial states and final states (i.e. $binary$), whereas others, defined by right vectors, represent a condition on the output (i.e. $unary$).

5.3   The Solution

Our strategy is to solve $binary$ and $unary$ independently, and then to progressively combine their solutions to come up with a program satisfying the complete specification.

Solving Unary. Each component in $unary$ has a simple solution. For instance,

$$
\begin{aligned}
&\quad unary \\
&= \qquad \{ \text{ definition of } unary \} \\
&\quad exb \sqcup sht \sqcup lng \\
&\sqsubseteq \qquad \{ \text{ refine each component by } out := \epsilon \} \\
&\quad out := \epsilon \sqcup out := \epsilon \sqcup out := \epsilon \\
&= \qquad \{ \text{ idempotence of } \sqcup \} \\
&\quad out := \epsilon
\end{aligned}
$$

is a valid refinement of *unary*. However, it is not consistent with *binary*, so that the join

$$out := \epsilon \sqcup binary$$

is not defined. By applying precipitous refinements, we have come to a dead end in the design process. It is crucial to leave our design options open, and not to fall into abrupt refinements. We propose an iterative solution for *unary*, which is general enough to preserve consistency with *binary*, but highlights the structure of a solution to *unary*.

$$
\begin{aligned}
&unary \\
= \quad &\{ \text{law 12(g)} \} \\
&unary \sqcap unary^\circ \\
= \quad &\{ \text{law 12(f)} \} \\
&unary \sqcap unary^{\circ \boxdot}
\end{aligned}
$$

We stop the refinement process at this point in order not to overcommit ourselves. However, it is interesting to see that this solution can be developed further to derive a real solution to *unary*, that is, a solution that would generate all possible final values of *out* satisfying the specification, assuming that a nondeterministic implementation of the language is available. The term *unary* may be refined by $out := \epsilon$, as we saw earlier. The refinement of $unary^\circ$ is more complex. One possible solution is to nondeterministically generate a word of length $\leq M$, and to append it to *out*. In doing so, we must make sure that lines are not too short and not too long, and that only one break separates each word. That requires "scanning" variable *out* to determine if a $\flat$ or a $\natural$ must be inserted before the word to append. Adding a variable which keeps track of the length of the last line of *out* removes this obligation of scanning *out*. We introduce a new variable k, by virtue of rule 13(b), and we define the following right vector:

var k : **Integer**
$$count \triangleq \{\exists x : \natural \not\preceq x \wedge out' \in (chr^* \bullet \natural)^* \bullet x \wedge k = \#.x\}$$

We modify the specification of *unary* to include *count*:

$$unary \triangleq exb \sqcup sht \sqcup lng \sqcup count \ .$$

An adequate solution for *unary* must now take into account *count*. We propose the following right vector: $\{out' = \epsilon \wedge k' = 0\}$. Before proceeding with the refinement of $unary^\circ$, let us introduce the following notation:

$$words \triangleq \bigcup_{i=1}^{M} txt^i \ ,$$
$$aw(x,y) \triangleq out' = out \bullet x \bullet y \wedge (x = \natural \Rightarrow k' = \#.y) \wedge$$
$$(x \neq \natural \Rightarrow k' = k + \#.x + \#.y) \ ,$$
$$filled(x) \triangleq k + \#.x \geq M \ .$$

The refinement of $unary^\circ$ consists of the following steps:

$$
\begin{aligned}
&unary^\circ \\
= \quad &\{ \text{case analysis: law 5(i)} \}
\end{aligned}
$$

$$out = \epsilon \rightarrow unary^\diamond \ \sqcup \ out \neq \epsilon \rightarrow unary^\diamond$$
$$\sqsubseteq \quad \{ \text{ refining first case } \}$$
$$out = \epsilon \rightarrow \{\exists w \in words : aw(\epsilon, w)\} \ \sqcup \ out \neq \epsilon \rightarrow unary^\diamond$$
$$\sqsubseteq \quad \{ \text{ refining second case } \}$$
$$out = \epsilon \rightarrow \{\exists w \in words : aw(\epsilon, w)\} \ \sqcup$$
$$out \neq \epsilon \rightarrow \{\exists w \in words : filled(w) \wedge aw(\natural, w) \vee \neg filled(w) \wedge aw(\flat, w)\}$$

Further refinements to a complete solution in terms of programming constructs are simple. Assuming that we have available a nondeterministic assignment statement " $:\in$ " defined as

$$x_i :\in E \triangleq \{(s, s')|x_i(s') \in E(s) \wedge \forall j \in 1..n : i \neq j \Rightarrow x_j(s') = x_j(s)\} \quad,$$

a complete solution to *unary* is:

```
out := ε □ k := 0 □
(var w: seq chr
w :∈ ⋃ᵢ₌₁ᴹ txtⁱ □
if out = ε then {aw(ε, w)}
else if filled(w) then {aw(♮, w)}
    else {aw(♭, w)} end
end)▣
```

Solving Binary. We are targetting an iterative solution for *binary*. Our strategy consists in decomposing *binary* into a format such that one component allows the introduction of a demonic closure. Considering the rules provided in this paper, it means that this component satisfies law 8(b)); in particular this component can be a preserve (law 12(f)) or a demonic residue (laws 20). The latter form is more appropriate for the solution of *binary*, as we shall see in the sequel.

$$binary$$
$$= \quad \{ \text{ def. of } binary \}$$
$$\{\neg lw.in \wedge sw.in = sw.out'\}$$
$$\sqsubseteq \quad \{ \epsilon \text{ is the identity of } \bullet \}$$
$$\{\neg lw.in \wedge sw.in = sw.out' \bullet sw.in' \wedge sw.in' = \epsilon\}$$

Let us introduce the following abbreviations which will be used in the sequel:

$$init \triangleq \{\neg lw.in \wedge sw.in = sw.out' \bullet sw.in'\} \quad,$$
$$mw \triangleq \overline{\{sw.in = \epsilon\}} \quad.$$

Abbreviation *init* corresponds to the first and second terms of the conjunction in the previous refinement. Abbreviation *mw* is the unprimed negation of the third term of the conjunction; it stands for "more words", i.e. *in* contains at least one word. We pursue the refinement of *binary*.

$$= \qquad \{ \text{ abbreviations above, set theoretic definition of } \cap \}$$
$$init \cap \widehat{\overline{mw}}$$
$$\sqsubseteq \qquad \{ \text{ law 5(j) } \}$$
$$init \sqcup \widehat{\overline{mw}}$$
$$\sqsubseteq \qquad \{ \text{ definition of } \backslash\!\backslash \text{ (Sect. 4.3) } \}$$
$$init \circ (init \backslash\!\backslash init) \sqcup \widehat{\overline{mw}}$$

Let us introduce another abbreviation: *init* is regular relatively to itself (Sect. 4.3), therefore $init \backslash\!\backslash init = \widehat{init} \, init$.

$$pw \triangleq init \backslash\!\backslash init = \{ \neg lw.in \wedge \neg lw.out \wedge sw.out \bullet sw.in = sw.out' \bullet sw.in' \}$$

Abbreviation *pw* stands for "preserve word sequence". We pursue the refinement of *binary*.

$$= \qquad \{ \text{ abbreviation } pw \}$$
$$init \circ pw \sqcup \widehat{\overline{mw}}$$
$$= \qquad \{ \text{ law 20(b) } \}$$
$$init \circ pw^{\boxplus} \sqcup \widehat{\overline{mw}}$$

We are close to a relational expression equivalent to a **while** loop (Proposition 11). The next steps will bring us up to that point.

$$= \qquad \{ \text{ law 7(n) } \}$$
$$init \circ pw^{\boxplus} \sqcup L \circ \widehat{\overline{mw}}$$
$$\sqsubseteq \qquad \{ \text{ law 14 } \}$$
$$(init \sqcup L) \circ (pw^{\boxplus} \sqcup \widehat{\overline{mw}})$$

The second join clearly has a structure appropriate for a conversion into a **while**, given some additional refinements. We postpone these refinements to the next paragraph.

Merging Binary with Unary. We now merge the solutions of *binary* and *unary*. The process is almost a mechanical application of laws, except for the selection of a progressively finite relation in the second-to-last step.

$$binary \sqcup unary$$
$$\sqsubseteq \qquad \{ \text{ refinement of } unary \text{ and } binary \text{ above } \}$$
$$unary \circ unary^{\diamond \boxplus} \sqcup$$
$$(init \sqcup L) \circ (pw^{\boxplus} \sqcup \widehat{\overline{mw}})$$
$$\sqsubseteq \qquad \{ \text{ law 14 } \}$$
$$(unary \sqcup init \sqcup L) \circ$$
$$(unary^{\diamond \boxplus} \sqcup pw^{\boxplus} \sqcup \widehat{\overline{mw}})$$

The first component of the sequence in the last step has a simple refinement: $\{ out' = \epsilon \wedge in' = in \}$. We pursue the refinement for the second component of the sequence.

$$(unary^{\diamond\boxplus} \sqcup pw^{\boxplus} \sqcup \overline{mw}^{\frown})$$
$\sqsubseteq$ { law 15 }
$$(unary^{\diamond} \sqcup pw)^{\boxplus} \sqcup \overline{mw}^{\frown}$$
$\sqsubseteq$ { law 8(d), Proposition 10 }
if mw **then** $unary^{\diamond} \sqcup pw$ **end**$^{\boxplus} \sqcup \overline{mw}^{\frown}$
$\sqsubseteq$ { $pf \triangleq \{in' = rw.in\}$ }
if mw **then** $unary^{\diamond} \sqcup pw \sqcup pf$ **end**$^{\boxplus} \sqcup \overline{mw}^{\frown}$
$=$ { Proposition 11 }
while mw **do** $unary^{\diamond} \sqcup pw \sqcup pf$ **end**

Let us now pause for a moment and see how the merge was done. The solutions of *unary* and *binary* share the same structure, therefore it is possible to push the join inside the structure. The result is a sequence of two joins. The first one being quite easy to refine, we focus our attention on the second component. Its structure is close to a pattern transformable into a **while** loop. We apply two rules to refine it into a pattern equivalent to a **while-do**.

Solving the Loop Body. We now solve the body of the loop resulting from the merge of the solutions of *unary* and *binary*.

$unary^{\diamond} \sqcup pw \sqcup pf$
$=$ { case analysis: law 5(i) }
$lfw.in \rightarrow (unary^{\diamond} \sqcup pw \sqcup pf) \sqcup \neg lfw.in \rightarrow (unary^{\diamond} \sqcup pw \sqcup pf)$
$\sqsubseteq$ { refining first case, relational calculus }
$lfw.in \rightarrow in := rw.in \sqcup \neg lfw.in \rightarrow (unary^{\diamond} \sqcup pw \sqcup pf)$

In the refinement of the second case, we are facing a problem similar to the one we encountered when proposing a complete solution for *unary* (Sect. 5.3). The term $pw \sqcup pf$ appends the first word from *in* to *out*. To determine if a $\flat$ or a $\sharp$ is to be inserted, we use the same strategy as we did for *unary*: we add a new variable k; we modify the definition of *unary* to include right vector *count* which requires k to be equal to the length of the last line of *out'*.

var k : **Integer**
$count \triangleq \{\exists x : \sharp \not\preceq x \land out' \in (chr^{*} \bullet \sharp)^{*} \bullet x \land k = \#.x\}$,
$unary \triangleq exb \sqcup sht \sqcup lng \sqcup count$.

We may now pursue the refinement of the second case, using the solution we derived for *unary* in Sect. 5.3.

$\neg lfw.in \rightarrow (unary^{\diamond} \sqcup pw \sqcup pf)$
$=$ { law 5(f) }
$\neg lfw.in \rightarrow unary^{\diamond} \sqcup \neg lfw.in \rightarrow (pw \sqcup pf)$
$\sqsubseteq$ { refine first $\sqcup$ component, see Sect. 5.3 }
$\neg lfw.in \rightarrow$
     $(out = \epsilon \rightarrow \{\exists w \in words : aw(\epsilon, w)\} \sqcup$
     $out \neq \epsilon \rightarrow \{\exists w \in words : filled(x) \land aw(\sharp, w) \lor \neg filled(x) \land aw(\flat, w)\})$
     $\sqcup$
$\neg lfw.in \rightarrow (pw \sqcup pf)$

It is possible to refine the first component of the join above sufficiently high in the semilattice so that it also refines the second component. All we need to do is append the first word of *in* instead of an arbitrary word. We use the predicate *cw* (*copy word*) defined below instead of *aw*.

$$cw(x) \stackrel{\triangle}{=} aw(x, fw.in) \wedge in' = rw.in$$

We obtain the following refinement:

$$
\neg lfw.in \rightarrow \\
\quad (out = \epsilon \rightarrow \{cw(\epsilon)\} \sqcup \\
\quad out \neq \epsilon \rightarrow \{filled(fw.in) \wedge cw(\sharp) \vee \neg filled(fw.in) \wedge cw(\flat)\}).
$$

The refinement of *cw* is simple, and it is not presented here. If we piece all the parts together, and if we replace relational patterns by their equivalent programming constructs, we obtain the final program shown below.

```
out := ε □ k := 0 □
while mw do
  if lfw.in then in := rw.in
  else if out = ε then {cw(ε)}
    else if filled(fw.in) then {cw(♯)}
      else {cw(♭)} end
    end
  end
end
```

If we provide an appropriate implementation of the type sequence using external files in Pascal, our solution is comparable to the solution of Myers in [20], both in terms of length and algorithmic complexity. Myers' solution is 63 lines long (in PL/I), and $O(\#.in)$ in complexity, versus 100 lines and $O(\#.in)$ for ours. The difference in length is explained by the fact that we have an additional layer of abstraction by implementing a sequence data type, whereas Myers is directly using files and global variables for composing his solution.

6 Conclusion

In earlier work we had shown that specifications are naturally structured as aggregates of component specifications, using the lattice based join operator. In this paper we discuss how this structure can be used as a basis for separation of concerns in program construction: we can refine each argument of the join separately then combine the refinements to get a solution to the overall specification. To be sure, the refinements of the individual components are not totally independent: while refining a component, we must keep an eye on the neighboring components, with a view to remaining consistent with them. This could be viewed as a constraint; we prefer to view it as a means to guide the programmer, in the sense that the structure of one component is hinted by the structure of its neighboring component(s). The mathematics we have developed for our programming paradigm appear to be satisfactory: first, they enable us to produce arbitrarily nondeterministic solutions to the component specifications; second, they faithfully reflect the stepwise negotiation process whereby two component specifications negotiate a common refinement; third, they do show how the refinement of individual components may lead to failure if it is carried out too independently. We have illustrated our method on a simple example, where our emphasis is more on illustrating the method than on solving the example.

Among the features highlighted by the example, we mention an interesting aspect of separation of concerns. In most refinement calculi, program refinement steps can be divided into two categories: viz. creative steps, where the programmer must derive an original solution to a problem; and bookkeeping steps, where the programmer must refine his or her solution within the confines of correctness preservation. We have found that our pattern separates these two steps chronologically and by difficulty: the creative steps are all concentrated at the beginning of the refinement process and are applied to subspecifications, rather than to the overall specification (hence are arbitrarily easy); by contrast, the bookkeeping steps, which consist in negotiating common refinements for various components, are done in later stages and are driven by clerical formal manipulations (requiring less creativity). Hence at no time does the programmer have to grasp the whole specification in all its complexity.

Program construction by parts is not new: Hehner discusses it in [12], in the case where specifications are represented by predicates. Taking the least upper bound of programs is not new: Hoare *et al* talk about it in [13], in the case where the programs at hand are simple assignments. Our work differs from Hehner's work by the representation of specifications (predicates vs. relations) and by their interpretations: termination is implicit in our specifications whereas it is expressed as timing constraints in Hehner's. Our work generalizes the idea of Hoare *et al* by taking the least upper bound of arbitrary programs (i.e. arbitrarily partial and arbitrarily nondeterministic). It differs from Morgan's work [19] by designing an integrated specification and design language, rather than by adding a *specification* statement to an existing design language (viz. Dijkstra's guarded command language). We share with the work of Sekerinski [23] (and Z) the same specification model where the focus is on input-output pairs for which a program must terminate. Like Sekerinski, our specifications are simpler than Hehner's and Morgan's. Any relation is a specification. In Hehner's calculus, specifications must be *implementable* (total). The domain of a specification does not need to be explicitly stated with a precondition, as in Morgan's calculus. For instance, a relation $\{s'^2 = s\}$ is written as $[s \geq 0, s^2 = s_0]$ in Morgan's calculus. On the other hand, our definitions of refinement and language constructs are more complex than Hehner's, because we must cater for nontermination.

Our plan for future research includes two directions. On the practical side, we wish to experiment further with the proposed method, by attempting increasingly complex and increasingly large examples. On the other hand, we have found that a number of problems pertaining to large-scale software development can be formulated as the refinement of join-structured specifications, hence they can be solved using the same discipline that we have presented for program construction by parts. These problems include: software reuse, software merging and software maintenance.

Acknowledgements. The authors are grateful to the anonymous reviewers for their patience and attention in reviewing previous versions of this paper and improving it.

References

1. Alikacem, A., S.B.M. Sghaier, J. Desharnais, M. El Ouali, and F. Tchier. From Demonic Semantics to Loop Construction: A Relation Algebraic Approach. *3rd Maghrebian Conf. on Software Engineering and Artificial Intelligence*, April 11–14, Rabat, Morocco (1994) 239–248.
2. Backhouse, R.C. *et al.* A Relational Theory of Data Types. Dept. of Math. and Comp. Sc., Eindhoven University of Technology, Netherlands, 1992.
3. Backhouse, R. C. and J. van der Woude. Demonic Operators and Monotype Factors. Dept. of Math. and Comp. Sc., Eindhoven University of Technology, Netherlands, 1993.
4. Belkhiter, N., S.B.M. Sghaier, J. Desharnais, F. Tchier, A. Jaoua, A. Mili, and N. Zaguia. Embedding a Demonic Semi-Lattice in a Relation Algebra. Rapport de recherche DIUL-RR-9302, Département d'Informatique, Université Laval, Québec, Canada, 1993.
5. Berghammer, R. and H. Zierer. Relational Algebraic Semantics of Deterministic and Nondeterministic Programs. *Theoretical Computer Science* **43** (1986) 123–147.
6. Berghammer, R. *Relational Specifications.* In: C. Rauszer (editor), XXXVIII Banach Center Semesters on Algebraic mathods in Logic and their Computer Science Applications, 1991.
7. Boudriga, N., F. Elloumi, and A. Mili. On The Lattice of Specifications: Applications to a Specification Methodology. *Formal Aspects of Computing* **4** (1992) 544–571.
8. J. Desharnais, A. Jaoua, F. Mili, N. Boudriga and A. Mili. A Relational Division Operator: The Conjugate Kernel. *Theoretical Computer Science* **114** (1993) 247–272.
9. J. Desharnais, F. Tchier and Ridha Khédri. Demonic Relational Semantics of Sequential Programs. Research Report DIUL-RR-9406, Département d'informatique, Université Laval, Québec City, Canada, 1994.
10. Dijkstra, E.W. *A Discipline of Programming.* Prentice Hall, 1976.
11. M. Frappier. *A Relational Basis for Program Construction by Parts.* Dept. of Computer Science, University of Ottawa, 1994.
12. Hehner, E.C.R. *A Practical Theory of Programming.* Springer Verlag, 1993.
13. Hoare, C.A.R., I.J. Hayes, H. Jifeng, C.C. Morgan, A.W. Roscoe, J.W. Sanders, I.H. Sorenson, J.M. Spivey, and B.A. Sufrin. Laws of Programming. *Communications of the ACM* **30**(8) (1987) 672–686.
14. Jones, G. and M. Sheeran. Designing Arithmetic Circuits by Refinement in Ruby. in *Mathematics of program construction : second international conference.* R.S. Bird, C.C. Morgan and J.C.P. Woodcock, eds, Oxford, 1992, LNCS 669, Springer-Verlag, 1993.

15. Mili, A. A Relational Approach to the Design of Deterministic Programs. *Acta Informatica* **20** (1983) 315–328.
16. Mili, A., Y. Qing, and W.X. Yang. A Relational Specification Methodology. *Software- Practice and Experience*, **16**(11) (1986) 1003–1030.
17. Möller, B. Relations as a Program Development Language, In: Möller, B, ed. *Constructing Programs from Specifications*. Proc. IFIP TC 2/WG 2.1 Pacific Grove, CA, USA, May 13-16, North-Holland (1991) 373–397.
18. Mills, H.D., V.R. Basili, J.D. Gannon and R.G. Hamlet. *Principles of Computer Programming: A Mathematical Approach.* Allyn and Bacon, 1987.
19. Morgan, C. *Programming from Specifications.* Prentice Hall, 1990.
20. Myers, G.J. A Controlled Experiment in Program Testing and Code Walkthroughs / Inspections. *CACM* **21**(9) (1978) 760–768.
21. Naur, P. Programming by Action Clusters. *BIT* **9**(3) (1969) 250–258.
22. Schmidt, G. and T. Ströhlein. *Relations and Graphs.* Springer Verlag, 1993.
23. Sekerinski, E. A Calculus for Predicative Programming. in *Mathematics of program construction : second international conference.* R.S. Bird, C.C. Morgan and J.C.P. Woodcock, eds, Oxford, 1992, LNCS 669, Springer-Verlag, 1993.

An initial-algebra approach to directed acyclic graphs

Jeremy Gibbons*

Department of Computer Science, University of Auckland, Private Bag 92019, Auckland, New Zealand. Email: jeremy@cs.auckland.ac.nz

Abstract. The initial-algebra approach to modelling datatypes consists of giving *constructors* for building larger objects of that type from smaller ones, and *laws* identifying different ways of constructing the same object. The recursive decomposition of objects of the datatype leads directly to a recursive pattern of computation on those objects, which is very helpful for both functional and parallel programming.

We show how to model a particular kind of directed acyclic graph using this initial-algebra approach.

Keywords. Graphs, data types, catamorphisms, initial algebras, Bird-Meertens Formalism, program derivation.

1 Introduction

It is now widely recognized that the traditional ad-hoc approaches to program construction do not yield reliable software; a more systematic and formal approach is required. One such approach consists of *program verification*—proving after the fact that a given program satisfies its formal specification. This approach turns out to be difficult to implement, not least because the vast majority of programs would *not* satisfy their specification, even if they had one, but more importantly, because program verification gives no direct help in actually constructing the program in the first place.

An alternative approach is provided by *program derivation*, whereby a program is *calculated* from its formal specification by the application of a series of correctness-preserving transformations. The resulting program is guaranteed to satisfy its specification (assuming that the calculation is carried out correctly), but now its construction and verification are performed together, allowing insights from each to help with the other.

---

* Copyright ©1994 Jeremy Gibbons. This work was partially supported by University of Auckland Research Committee grant numbers A18/XXXXX/62090/3414013, /3414019 and /3414024.

Such a calculational approach necessitates having a body of *notations* for writing programs and *theorems* for proving equalities between them—that is, a *calculus* of programs. The Bird-Meertens Formalism [20, 5, 1] is one such calculus; it relies on tightly-coupled notions of *data* and *program* structure to yield its notations and theorems. In particular, datatypes are defined as extreme (initial or terminal) objects in categories of algebras—equivalently, extreme solutions of recursive systems of equations—and various morphisms representing common patterns of computation on those datatypes defined as the corresponding unique arrows from or to those objects. In this paper, we consider only initial algebras and *catamorphisms*, the corresponding morphisms; how well the ideas translate to final algebras and other morphisms remains to be seen.

Defining a datatype as an initial algebra essentially consists of giving two kinds of object:

- *constructors* for building larger elements of that type from smaller elements, and
- *laws* identifying syntactically different but semantically equivalent ways of constructing an element of that type.

Studying the initial algebra corresponding to a datatype gives new ways of implementing that datatype, and new insight into old algorithms—and sometimes even new algorithms—on that datatype. Moreover, the initial-algebra approach to datatypes appears to be particularly suitable for implementation in functional languages and in languages for parallel execution [29].

We have a good understanding of initial algebras corresponding to many common datatypes, such as lists [5], sets and bags [1, 14, 7], trees [21, 15, 12], and arrays [30, 6, 16]. One datatype ubiquitous in computing but conspicuous by its absence from this collection is that of *graphs*. The reason for this absence is that in order to model graphs, it appears that some means of 'naming' subcomponents is required. In contrast, the initial-algebra approach permits only 'structural' references to subcomponents.

In this paper we take steps towards remedying this absence, by defining and exploring an initial algebra corresponding to directed acyclic graphs. We show that naming is not necessary for modelling directed acyclic graphs. However, these are only the first steps; for one thing, the algebra does not correspond exactly to directed acyclic graphs, and for another, there are other kinds of graphs (for example, undirected graphs and directed cyclic graphs) to consider. These are topics for further study.

The rest of this paper is organized as follows. In Section 2, we review the initial-algebra approach to modelling datatypes. In Section 3, we present an initial-algebra definition of unlabelled directed acyclic graphs. In Section 4, we discuss catamorphisms on graphs. In Section 5, we generalize the construction of Section 3 to labelled directed acyclic graphs. In Section 6, we discuss other approaches to representing graphs in a style suitable for functional programming. Finally, Section 7 summarizes and presents directions for further work.

Throughout this paper, we write '.' for function application, which associates to the right, and '∘' for function composition, which is associative:

$$(g \circ f).a = g.(f.a) = g.f.a$$

We write '$a : A$' for 'a has type A', and 'IN' for the type of natural numbers including zero. For associative operator $\oplus$, we write $copy(n, \oplus, x)$ as an abbreviation for $x \oplus x \oplus \cdots \oplus x$ with n occurrences of x. For any x, $copy(0, \oplus, x)$ is the unit of $\oplus$ if it exists.

2 Initial Algebras and Catamorphisms

We introduce the initial-algebra approach to datatypes by way of a simple familiar example, the algebra of *join lists*. We use what may seem like unnecessarily heavy machinery for this simple example; the reason is that the machinery is necessary for the more complex algebra of directed acyclic graphs that is the subject of this paper.

2.1 Unlabelled Join Lists

We start by considering 'unlabelled join lists' (UJLs), which are finite possibly-empty chains of unlabelled nodes. For example, the UJL with three nodes might be drawn as in Figure 1. UJLs are built using three constructors: the constants *null* and *node*, respectively representing the empty list and the list with one node, and the binary operator ++ (pronounced 'join') which joins two lists to make a (usually) longer list.

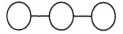

Fig. 1. An unlabelled join list

These constructors obey some laws, identifying different ways of building the same list. These laws are that ++ is associative and has unit *null*. (In other words, the constructors form a monoid.) For example, the list in Figure 1 is represented by (among others) the expression

$$node \mathbin{+\!\!+} node \mathbin{+\!\!+} node$$

Because of associativity, no parentheses are needed.

UJLs can be modelled as a category. Recall that a *category* consists of a collection of objects and a collection of arrows between objects. We write '$x : m \to n$' to indicate that arrow x goes from object m to object n. Compatible arrows can be composed; if $x : m \to n$ and $y : n \to p$ then $x; y : m \to p$.

Composition is associative, and for every object m there is an *identity arrow* $id_m : m \to m$ which is the unit of composition to or from that object.

In the case of UJLs, the category has a single object, corresponding to the type of all UJLs, and arrows corresponding to the lists themselves. Composition of arrows corresponds to joining lists; since there is but a single object, all pairs of arrows are composable. The identity arrow corresponds to the empty list. We require an arrow corresponding to the list *node* with a single element; since the collection of arrows is closed under composition, there is then necessarily an arrow corresponding to every UJL.

If we now consider those categories with a single object, they in turn form a category $\mathcal{L}$, with objects the categories in question and arrows the functors between these categories. (A *functor* F from category B to category C is a morphism on categories taking objects of B to objects of C and arrows of B to arrows of C such that, if $x : m \to n$ in B then $F.x : F.m \to F.n$ in C, and moreover $F.id_m = id_{F.m}$ and $F.(x;y) = F.x;F.y$.) We define the algebra of UJLs to be the *initial* object in $\mathcal{L}$, that is, the object in $\mathcal{L}$ from which there is a unique arrow to any other object in $\mathcal{L}$. (The initial object is unique up to isomorphism, and can be shown to exist.) Informally, this states that UJLs form the *smallest* algebra closed under the constructors in which the given laws hold, and no other laws do.

2.2 Labelled Join Lists

Of course, the type of UJLs is not very interesting; it is isomorphic to the natural numbers. We presented it simply because it happens to be the list-like algebra closest to the unlabelled directed acyclic graphs that we introduce later.

We can generalize UJLs to *labelled join lists* (LJLs) with nodes labelled by elements of some type A. The node constructor changes, so that now *node.a* is a LJL for every $a : A$, but the two constructors *null* and ⧺ and the laws do not change. For example, the LJL in Figure 2 is represented by the expression

$$node.3 ⧺ node.1 ⧺ node.6$$

where the label type is $\mathbb{N}$.

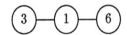

Fig. 2. A labelled join list

LJLs with labels of type A are by definition the initial object in the category consisting of categories with just one object and an arrow corresponding to every element of type A.

UJLs are isomorphic to LJLs with labels drawn from the unit type (the type with exactly one element), so from now on we will use the term 'join lists' to refer to LJLs.

2.3 Catamorphisms on Join Lists

Since the algebra of join lists was defined to be the initial object in the appropriate category, there is by definition a unique morphism from that algebra to any target algebra in the category. Such a morphism is called a *join list catamorphism*, and is uniquely determined by that target algebra.

Put another way, a function h from join lists with labels of type A to another type B is a join list catamorphism iff there exist a constant $b : B$, a function $f : A \rightarrow B$ and a binary operator $\oplus : B \times B \rightarrow B$ such that

$$h.null = b$$
$$h.node.a = f.a$$
$$h.(x \mathbin{+\!\!+} y) = h.x \oplus h.y$$

and such that $\oplus$ is associative and has unit b. (The target category in this case has a single object B and arrows corresponding to elements of B; composition of arrows corresponds to $\oplus$, and the identity arrow is b.) We write '$([b, f, \oplus])$' for such an h.

There are many examples of interesting join list catamorphisms. A few simple ones are as follows. The identity function on join lists is $([null, node, +\!\!+])$. The function *length*, returning the number of nodes in a list, is $([0, f, +])$ where $f.a = 1$ for each a. The function *reversel*, which reverses a join list, is $([null, node, \oplus])$ where $t \oplus u = u \mathbin{+\!\!+} t$.

3 Unlabelled Directed Acyclic Graphs

In this section, the main part of the paper, we present an initial-algebra definition of a particular kind of directed acyclic graph.

3.1 Directed Acyclic Multigraphs

The particular kind of graph we will model is that of directed acyclic graphs, but with a few unconventional aspects:

- there may be more than one edge between a given pair of vertices (thus, these are *multigraphs* rather than simply graphs)
- the incoming and outgoing edges of a vertex are ordered (that is, they form a sequence, rather than a bag or set)

- the graph as a whole has a sequence of incoming edges ('entries') with targets but no sources, and a sequence of outgoing edges ('exits') with sources but no targets; entries and exits are collectively called 'connections'

We call such a graph a *directed acyclic multigraph*, or DAMG (pronounced 'damage') for short.

For $m, n : \mathbb{N}$, the type $G_{m,n}$ consists of DAMGs with m entries and n exits. Thus, a graph of type $G_{3,4}$ has the form pictured in Figure 3. We write G for the type of all DAMGs.

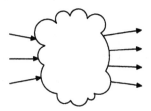

Fig. 3. The form of a graph of type $G_{3,4}$

3.2 Constructors

DAMGs are built from six constructors, as explained below.

Vertices. Vertices are represented by a set *vert* indexed by pairs of natural numbers, such that $vert_{m,n} : G_{m,n}$ for $m, n : \mathbb{N}$. The intention is that $vert_{m,n}$ represents a single vertex with m entries and n exits. For example, $vert_{3,2}$ might be drawn as in Figure 4.

Fig. 4. The vertex $vert_{3,2}$

Edges. The constant *edge* : $G_{1,1}$ is simply an edge, with a single entry and a single exit. It would be drawn as in Figure 5.

Fig. 5. An edge

Beside. If $x : G_{m,n}$ and $y : G_{p,q}$ then $x \parallel y$ (pronounced 'x beside y') is of type $G_{m+p,n+q}$. Informally, $x \parallel y$ consists of x 'in parallel with' y; for example, $vert_{1,2} \parallel vert_{2,1}$ (of type $G_{3,3}$) might be drawn as in Figure 6. (In drawings of graphs, we order connections from top to bottom, and direct them from left to right.)

Fig. 6. $vert_{1,2} \parallel vert_{2,1}$

The constructor $\parallel$ is associative, so $x \parallel (y \parallel z) = (x \parallel y) \parallel z$. We write '$m \times x$' as an abbreviation for $copy(m, \parallel, x)$; we see later that $\parallel$ has a unit, so $0 \times x$ is defined.

Before. If $x : G_{m,n}$ and $y : G_{n,p}$, then $x \, \mathbin{\S} \, y$ (pronounced 'x before y') has type $G_{m,p}$, and is formed by connecting the exits of x to the entries of y. For example, $vert_{0,1} \, \mathbin{\S} \, vert_{1,0}$ might be drawn as in Figure 7.

Fig. 7. $vert_{0,1} \, \mathbin{\S} \, vert_{1,0}$

The constructor $\mathbin{\S}$ is associative; that is, $x\mathbin{\S}(y\mathbin{\S}z) = (x\mathbin{\S}y)\mathbin{\S}z$ if both expressions are correctly typed. (Note that if either expression is incorrectly typed, then both are.)

We write '$\mathbin{\S}_m$' for the restriction of $\mathbin{\S}$ to pairs of DAMGs with exactly m intermediate connections. Note that $\mathbin{\S}_m$ has unit $m \times edge$.

A further property enjoyed by $\parallel$ and $\mathbin{\S}$ is the so-called *abiding law*. If $w : G_{m,n}$, $x : G_{n,p}$, $y : G_{q,r}$ and $z : G_{r,s}$, then

$$(w \mathbin{\S}_n x) \parallel (y \mathbin{\S}_r z) = (w \parallel y) \mathbin{\S}_{n+r} (x \parallel z)$$

For example,

$$(vert_{2,1} \mathbin{\S} vert_{1,1}) \parallel (vert_{1,1} \mathbin{\S} vert_{1,2}) = (vert_{2,1} \parallel vert_{1,1}) \mathbin{\S} (vert_{1,1} \parallel vert_{1,2})$$

—in pictures, both sides might be drawn as in Figure 8. Notice that the type information is important here; without it, $(w \parallel y) \, _9^\circ \, (x \parallel z)$ may be well-typed when $(w \, _9^\circ \, x) \parallel (y \, _9^\circ \, z)$ is not.

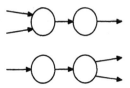

Fig. 8. An instance of the abiding law

The name 'abiding' is due to Bird [6]. He coined it as a contraction of 'above' and 'beside', operators which he used for building a larger array by putting one smaller array above or beside another.

Empty. We introduce a constructor *empty* for the empty graph, largely because of the elegant properties that it enjoys. It would be drawn as a blank picture. The empty graph satisfies the following two laws.

- *empty* is the unit of $\parallel$ (and so, for any x, $0 \times x = empty$)
- *empty* (being $0 \times edge$) is also the unit of $_9^\circ_0$

From these we can conclude that, if $x : G_{m,0}$ and $y : G_{0,n}$, then $x \, _9^\circ_0 \, y = x \parallel y$, since

$$
\begin{aligned}
& x \, _9^\circ_0 \, y \\
=\ & \quad \{empty \text{ is the unit of } \parallel\} \\
& (x \parallel empty) \, _9^\circ_0 \, (empty \parallel y) \\
=\ & \quad \{abiding\} \\
& (x \, _9^\circ_0 \, empty) \parallel (empty \, _9^\circ_0 \, y) \\
=\ & \quad \{empty \text{ is the unit of } _9^\circ_0\} \\
& x \parallel y
\end{aligned}
$$

For example, both $vert_{2,0} \, _9^\circ_0 \, vert_{0,1}$ and $vert_{2,0} \parallel vert_{0,1}$ could be drawn as in Figure 9. We call this the *dislocation law*. Symmetrically, $x \, _9^\circ_0 \, y = y \parallel x$.

Swap. The five constructors we have seen so far can construct only planar graphs. The constructor *swap* escapes from planarity. For $m, n \in \mathbb{N}$, $swap_{m,n}$ has type $G_{m+n,n+m}$, and consists of m edges connecting the first m entries to the last m exits, and n edges connecting the last n entries to the first n exits. For example, $swap_{3,2}$ has type $G_{5,5}$, and might be drawn as in Figure 10.

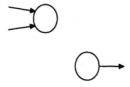

Fig. 9. An instance of the dislocation law

Fig. 10. $swap_{3,2}$

Swaps satisfy a number of laws. The first of these laws states that swapping zero connections makes no difference:

$$swap_{m,0} = m \times edge$$

The second law shows that swapping $n+p$ connections can be done by swapping n connections and then swapping p connections:

$$swap_{m,n+p} = (swap_{m,n} \, [\![\, (p \times edge)) \, \S \, ((n \times edge) \, [\![\, swap_{m,p})$$

The right-hand side of this equation is illustrated in Figure 11, in the case when $m = 1$, $n = 2$ and $p = 3$. We call these last two laws the *swap simplification laws*.

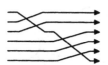

Fig. 11. Breaking down a larger *swap*

The third law relates swaps to other constructs. If $x : G_{n,p}$ and $y : G_{m,q}$ then

$$swap_{m,n} \, \S \, (x \, [\![\, y) \, \S \, swap_{p,q} = y \, [\![\, x$$

We call this the *swap law*. The left-hand side of this equation is illustrated in Figure 12, in the case when $x = vert_{2,1}$ and $y = vert_{1,2}$; then the right-hand side is as in Figure 6.

In the special case when $n = p$, $x = n \times edge$, $m = q$ and $y = m \times edge$, the swap law simplifies to

$$swap_{m,n} \, \S \, swap_{n,m} = (m+n) \times edge$$

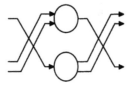

Fig. 12. An instance of the swap law

From this law and the earlier simplification laws we can deduce simplification laws for the first index too:

$$swap_{0,n} = n \times edge$$

and

$$swap_{m+n,p} = ((m \times edge) \parallel swap_{n,p}) \, \S \, (swap_{m,p} \parallel (n \times edge))$$

Note that, in view of the swap simplification laws, any swap can be built from $swap_{1,1}$ and edges using $\parallel$ and $\S$, so in that sense we could replace the family of swap constructors with just $swap_{1,1}$. However, it appears that the general form of the swap law is then difficult to express.

3.3 An Example Graph

As an example, we show how to construct the graph in Figure 13.

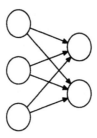

Fig. 13. An example graph

'Teasing' apart the edges, we see that this graph is equivalent to the exploded graph in Figure 14. Hence the graph is represented by the expression

$$(3 \times vert_{0,2}) \, \S \, (edge \parallel ((2 \times swap_{1,1}) \, \S \, (edge \parallel swap_{1,1} \parallel edge)) \parallel edge) \, \S \, (2 \times vert_{3,0})$$

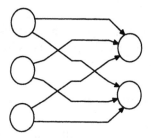

Fig. 14. An 'exploded view' of the graph in Figure 13

3.4 DAMGs As Symmetric Strict Monoidal Categories

It turns out that the algebra of DAMGs is essentially a *symmetric strict monoidal category* [19] enriched with objects representing vertices. We expand here on this observation.

A *strict monoidal category* (SMC) $(B, +, e)$ is a category B in which:

- the objects of B form a monoid with respect to $+$ (as a binary operation on objects of B) and e (as an object of B)
- the operator $+$ also acts on arrows of B; if $x : m \to n$ and $y : p \to q$ then $x + y : m + p \to n + q$; moreover, $+$ satisfies the laws

$$(x + y) + z = x + (y + z)$$
$$id_e + x = x$$
$$x + id_e = x$$
$$id_m + id_n = id_{m+n}$$
$$(w + x); (y + z) = (w; y) + (x; z)$$

provided in the last case that all the compositions are defined.

A *symmetric strict monoidal category* (SSMC) $(B, +, e, \gamma)$ is a SMC $(B, +, e)$ with a family of arrows $\gamma_{m,n} : m + n \to n + m$ for all objects m and n of B, for which the following laws hold:

$$\gamma_{m,0} = id_m$$
$$\gamma_{m,n+p} = (\gamma_{m,n} + id_p); (id_n + \gamma_{m,p})$$
$$\gamma_{m,n}; (x + y); \gamma_{p,q} = y + x$$

provided in the last case that $x : n \to p$ and $y : m \to q$.

Clearly, the algebra of DAMGs forms a SSMC $(B, \mathbb{I}, empty, swap)$ in which the category B has as objects the natural numbers, and arrows $x : m \to n$ corresponding to DAMGs x in $G_{m,n}$. Composition of arrows is $\mathring{,}$, and the identity object on m is $m \times edge$.

Now consider SSMCs in which the objects of the base category B are the natural numbers, and the collection of arrows of B also contains arrows $v_{m,n} : m \to n$ for each pair of naturals m, n. We call such a SSMC an *enriched* SSMC, and write $\mathcal{G}$ for the category of all enriched SSMCs (with functors between SSMCs as arrows). We define the algebra of DAMGs to be the *initial* SSMC in the category $\mathcal{G}$. Informally, this says that DAMGs form the smallest algebra closed under the constructors in which all and only the DAMG laws hold.

3.5 Soundness and Completeness of the Laws

When axiomatizing a datatype, it is usually obvious whether sufficient constructors have been chosen to represent all elements of the intended model. If there are not enough constructors, extra ones can be added as necessary, and the worst that can happen is some redundancy in the resulting datatype.

It is more difficult to tell whether the right collection of laws has been chosen, since this collection must be neither too strong nor too weak. The collection must satisfy the following two properties.

Soundness: The given collection of laws must certainly be true of the intended model. That is, the laws must not be too strong, identifying distinct elements of the intended model.

Completeness: Soundness can be attained simply by having no laws at all. The competing requirement is that the collection of laws must be complete. That is, the laws must be sufficient to identify any two representations of the same element in the intended model. In other words, the collection of laws must also not be too weak.

We have just seen that the five constructors *edge*, $\S$, $\|$, *empty* and *swap*, together with all the laws (that is, the whole algebra except the vertices), form exactly a SSMC in which the objects are the natural numbers. Căzănescu and Ştefănescu [10] show that such a category axiomatizes bijective relations; bijective relations are the initial algebra with those five constructors and those laws.

Since none of the laws involve the vertices, the whole algebra (all six constructors together with the laws) axiomatizes vertices with bijections for 'plumbing' between them. This is clearly exactly the datatype of directed acyclic multigraphs; the laws we have defined are indeed sound and complete.

4 DAMG Catamorphisms

We defined the algebra of DAMGs to be the initial object in the category $\mathcal{G}$ of enriched SSMCs. By definition, therefore, there is a unique morphism from the algebra of DAMGs to any other enriched SSMC. Such a morphism is called a DAMG *catamorphism*, and is uniquely determined by that other enriched SSMC.

Put another way, a function $h : G \to B$ is a DAMG catamorphism iff there exist constants $a, b : B$, families of constants $v_{m,n} : B$ and $s_{m,n} : B$ indexed by pairs of naturals m, n, and binary operators $\oplus : B \times B \to B$ and $\otimes : B \times B \to B$

such that

$$h.empty = a$$
$$h.edge = b$$
$$h.vert_{m,n} = v_{m,n}$$
$$h.swap_{m,n} = s_{m,n}$$
$$h.(x \parallel y) = h.x \oplus h.y$$
$$h.(x \, \S \, y) = h.x \otimes h.y$$

(in fact, $h.x \otimes h.y$ need only be defined when x and y are compatible) and such that these constants and functions form an enriched SSMC in the obvious way. We write '$(\!| a, b, v, s, \oplus, \otimes |\!)$' for such an h; these six items uniquely determine h.

4.1 Examples of DAMG Catamorphisms

Some simple examples of DAMG catamorphisms are as follows. The identity function on G is $(\!| empty, edge, vert, swap, \parallel, \S |\!)$. The function *nvertices*, which returns the number of vertices, is $(\!| 0, 0, 1, 0, +, + |\!)$. (We write simply '1' for the family of constants indexed by pairs of naturals, each member of which is 1.) The function *reverseg*, which reverses a DAMG, is $(\!| empty, edge, vert, s, \parallel, \otimes |\!)$ where $s_{m,n} = swap_{n,m}$ and $t \otimes u = u \, \S \, t$.

A more interesting example is the function *sp*, which returns the length of the shortest path from each entry to each exit; *sp* takes a DAMG of type $G_{m,n}$ and returns an $m \times n$ matrix of values in $\mathbb{N} \cup \{\infty\}$. We have

$$sp = (\!| a, b, v, s, \oplus, \otimes |\!)$$

where

- a is the 0×0 matrix
- b is the 1×1 matrix containing a 0
- $v_{m,n}$ is the $m \times n$ matrix consisting entirely of 1s
- $s_{m,n}$ is the $(m + n) \times (n + m)$ matrix of the form $\begin{pmatrix} A & B \\ C & D \end{pmatrix}$ in which A and D are $m \times n$ and $n \times m$ submatrices consisting entirely of ∞s, and B and C are $m \times m$ and $n \times n$ submatrices with zeroes on the leading diagonals and ∞s elsewhere
- if t and u are $m \times n$ and $p \times q$ matrices, respectively, then $t \oplus u$ is the $(m + p) \times (n + q)$ matrix $\begin{pmatrix} t & \infty \\ \infty & u \end{pmatrix}$—that is, with elements from t and u in the top left and bottom right quadrants, and ∞ filling the other two quadrants
- if t and u are $m \times n$ and $n \times p$ matrices, respectively, then $t \otimes u$ is the matrix product of t and u in the closed semiring $(min, +)$—that is,

$$(t \otimes u)_{i,j} = \min_{1 \le k \le n} (t_{i,k} + u_{k,j}) \qquad \text{for } 1 \le i \le m, \, 1 \le j \le p$$

where ∞ is the zero of addition and the unit of *min*.

For example, the DAMG in Figure 15 is represented by the expression:

$$vert_{1,2} \, \S \, ((vert_{1,1} \, \S \, vert_{1,1}) \, \| \, vert_{1,1}) \, \S \, vert_{2,1}$$

and one way of computing its single shortest path could be as illustrated in Figure 16. Thus, the shortest path between the connections of $vert_{1,1}$ has just one vertex, and that between the connections of $vert_{1,1} \, \S \, vert_{1,1}$ has two; the shortest paths between the four possible pairs of connections of $(vert_{1,1} \, \S \, vert_{1,1}) \, \| \, vert_{1,1}$ have lengths $2, \infty, \infty$ and 1. The shortest path from the only entry to the only exit of the whole graph has three vertices.

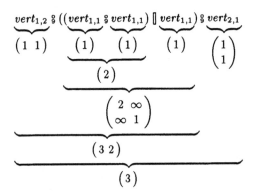

Fig. 15. Another example graph

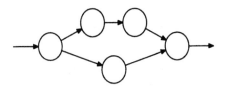

Fig. 16. The shortest path between connections of the graph in Figure 15

We should check that sp really is a DAMG catamorphism, that is, that the six components really do form an enriched SSMC. We leave it to the reader to verify (writing i_m for $copy(m, \oplus, b)$, the $m \times m$ matrix with 0s on the leading diagonal and ∞s elsewhere) that:

- $\oplus$ is associative, and has unit a
- $\otimes$ is associative, and has unit i_m (for suitable value of m)
- $(w \otimes x) \oplus (y \otimes z) = (w \oplus y) \otimes (x \oplus z)$ for compatible matrices w, x and y, z
- $s_{m,0} = i_m$
- $s_{m,n+p} = (s_{m,n} \oplus i_p) \otimes (i_n \oplus s_{m,p})$

$-\ s_{m,n} \otimes (x \oplus y) \otimes s_{p,q} = y \oplus x$ for $n \times p$ matrix x and $m \times q$ matrix y

If still keen after doing so, the reader may also wish to verify that the function that computes the *longest* path between any pair of connections is also a catamorphism.

5 Labelled DAMGs

In this section we discuss labelling the vertices and edges of a DAMG.

5.1 Vertex-Labelled DAMGs

We can generalize to vertex-labelled DAMGs easily. We write $G_{m,n}.A$ for the type of DAMGs with m entries and n exits and vertices labelled with elements of A, and $G.A$ for the type of vertex-labelled DAMGs with any number of connections. Then, for a of type A, $vert_{m,n}.a$ is of type $G_{m,n}.A$, and consists of a single vertex with m entries and n exits and label a. The other five constructors and all the laws remain unchanged.

Thus, the expression

$$vert_{1,2}.3 \, \text{\textsection} \, ((vert_{1,1}.2 \, \text{\textsection} \, vert_{1,1}.5) \, [\!] \, vert_{1,1}.9) \, \text{\textsection} \, vert_{2,1}.7$$

represents the vertex-labelled DAMG of type $G_{1,1}.\mathbb{N}$ in Figure 17.

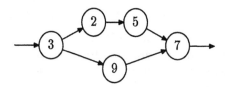

Fig. 17. A vertex-labelled DAMG

5.2 Edge-Labelled DAMGs

It is more difficult to model edge-labelled DAMGs satisfactorily. For example, should we label all connections? If so, what happens when connections matched by ⵗ do not have the same label? Should ⵗ be a partial operator, undefined in such cases? Or should it be asymmetric, taking (say) the labels from its first argument? Alternatively, we could label only 'complete edges'—edges with a vertex at each end—and leave 'dangling' connections unlabelled; then ⵗ could take also a list of of the appropriate number of labels with which to label connections. Another alternative would be to label the connections with elements of a monoid (for example, lists), and combine the labels on matched connections using the binary operation of the monoid.

It is not at all clear which is the best approach to take.

5.3   Topological Sort

One operation suitable for vertex-labelled DAMGs is topological sort; given a
DAMG, return the vertex labels as a list whose ordering respects the edge ordering
of the graph. Is topological sort a catamorphism?

It would appear so. Topological sort ts satisfies the following properties.

- $ts.empty$, $ts.edge$ and $ts.swap_{m,n}$ are all just $null$, since these graphs have
  no vertices
- $ts.vert_{m,n}.a$ is $node.a$
- $ts.(x \mathbin{\S} y)$ is $ts.x \mathbin{+\!\!+} ts.y$
- $ts.(x \mathbin{\|} y)$ is any interleaving of $ts.x$ and $ts.y$—for example, $ts.x \mathbin{+\!\!+} ts.y$

In other words, we can topologically sort a DAMG by deleting from the expression
by which it was constructed everything except the labels; this necessarily gives
the correct labels in a correct order.

Unfortunately, things are not so straightforward. In general, a DAMG has
many topological sorts, but the function ts can return only one of them. Moreover, with the way we have defined ts above, the particular topological sort
returned will depend on the way that the graph was constructed. For example,
suppose that we take $ts.(x \mathbin{\|} y) = ts.x \mathbin{+\!\!+} ts.y$, as suggested above. Then the two
graphs

$$(vert_{1,1}.1 \mathbin{\S} vert_{1,1}.2) \mathbin{\|} (vert_{1,1}.3 \mathbin{\S} vert_{1,1}.4)$$

and

$$(vert_{1,1}.1 \mathbin{\|} vert_{1,1}.3) \mathbin{\S} (vert_{1,1}.2 \mathbin{\|} vert_{1,1}.4)$$

(which by the abiding law are equal) will have different images, $[1, 2, 3, 4]$ and
$[1, 3, 2, 4]$, under ts. Both images are valid topological sorts of the graph, but if
ts is to be well-defined it must return exactly the same topological sort as result
given the same graph as argument.

Put another way, the sextuple of components $(null, null, node, null, +\!\!+, +\!\!+)$
does not form an enriched SSMC, since it does not satisfy all the DAMG laws.
Neither does $(null, null, node, null, \oplus, +\!\!+)$ for any $\oplus$ such that $x \oplus y$ is an interleaving of x and y; in particular, $+\!\!+$ does not abide with any deterministic
interleave operator. The problem is that a single topological sort of each of x
and y is sufficient information to compute one topological sort of $x \mathbin{\S} y$, but
not in general to compute all topological sorts. Topological sort is not a DAMG
catamorphism.

(The problem appears to do with the deterministic interleaving for $ts.(x \mathbin{\|} y)$,
which suggests that although topological sort is not a $functional$ catamorphism,
it might be a $relational$ catamorphism [2]. The topological sorts of $x \mathbin{\|} y$ would
be any interleaving of the topological sorts of x and of y. Unfortunately, given
topological sorts s and t of x and y, still the only list guaranteed to be a topological sort of $x \mathbin{\S} y$ is $s \mathbin{+\!\!+} t$—although other interleavings of s and t may also be.
The two different representations of the same graph above will still have different
topological sort relations—the first representation allows $[1, 2, 3, 4]$ whereas the
second does not. Intuitively, the non-determinism is 'too local'; it turns out that

'more global' non-determinism is needed. In fact, the function that returns the set of *all* topological sorts of a DAMG *is* a functional catamorphism [27].)

6 Other Approaches to Modelling Graphs

In this section we discuss a number of other approaches to modelling graphs, and compare them to the initial-algebra approach presented here.

6.1 Traditional Representations

Graphs are traditionally represented in one of three ways:

- a set of vertices and a set of edges
- a collection of adjacency lists
- an adjacency matrix

None of these representations are particularly suitable for implementing graph algorithms in a functional language. More to the point, however, none of these representations recursively composes larger graphs out of smaller ones, and so none of them provides for free a pattern of computation on graphs that recursively decomposes its argument into smaller graphs. Such patterns of computation—catamorphisms—seem very useful for functional and parallel programming.

6.2 Graphs in Functional Languages

Directed graphs can be represented in a lazy functional language using cyclic data structures [4]. For example, the Gofer definition

```
[node1,node2,node3] where node1 = (1, [node2,node3])
                          node2 = (2, [node1])
                          node3 = (3, [])
```

represents the cyclic graph in Figure 18 as a list of vertices where each vertex is a pair consisting of a label and an adjacency list. The disadvantage of this approach is that a cyclic graph is operationally indistinguishable from an infinite tree. Kashiwagi and Wise [17] use this approach to implement some graph algorithms (strong components, connected components, acyclicity) by having a stream of 'updateable' values at each node and a problem-specific method of finding fixed points on those streams. This produces a graph labelled with results, which, if cyclic, is again indistinguishable from an infinite tree.

A related approach [28] is to represent the graph as a function of type $N \rightarrow F.N$, where N is the type of node identifiers and F is some functor.

King and Launchbury [18] implement some graph algorithms (topological sort, connected components, strong components, reachability) by imperatively performing a depth-first search on the graph, and declaratively manipulating the resulting depth-first-search forest.

Burton and Yang [8] implement graphs in a pure functional language effectively by implementing an imperative store and threading this through the program.

Fig. 18. A cyclic graph

6.3 Formal Languages and Relations

Möller [24, 25, 26] uses formal languages, and in particular multiary relations, to model graphs. He derives a number of graph algorithms, such as reachability, topological sort and cycle detection.

This approach gives concise specifications and calculations. However, graphs are still modelled monolithically—there is no recursive decomposition, and so no direct help in that way in constructing programs. (Help does come from another direction, though: from familiar properties of relations and formal languages.)

6.4 Graph Grammars

There is a large body of work in the field of *graph grammars*. Courcelle [11] gives definitions in terms of directed *hypergraphs*, in which edges may have arbitrarily many endpoints; to avoid too much extra notation, we discuss here just the specialization to edges with exactly two endpoints.

A graph has a *source*, a sequence consisting of some of the vertices of the graph (perhaps with omissions and duplication). Vertices in the source are 'external' and are available for connection to other graphs; other vertices are 'internal' and are hidden.

There are five constructors:

vertex: a single vertex, which is the sole element of the source
edge: a single edge, with two vertices that form the source
disjoint union: combines two graphs into a larger graph, concatenating the sources
source fusion: takes a graph and an equivalence relation δ on its sources, and identifies the vertices equivalent under δ
source redefinition: rearranges the source of a graph (perhaps omitting some vertices and duplicating others) according to a given mapping

There are eleven laws; these are sufficient to transform any term built from the above constructors into a (non-unique) normal form consisting of the disjoint union of some vertices and edges, submitted to a single source fusion and then a single source redefinition.

Graph grammars are appropriate as a basis for describing graph rewriting systems, but they seem less so for more general graph algorithms.

6.5 Skillicorn's Definition

Skillicorn [29] defines an algebra of connected undirected vertex-labelled graphs, using three constructors:

- an injection, mapping labels to vertices,
- a binary operator 'connect', connecting two disjoint graphs with a single edge, and
- a unary operator 'close', adding an edge to a graph, thereby creating a cycle.

In order to indicate which two vertices are connected by the 'connect' or 'close' operators, Skillicorn says that the two constructors 'are drawn as simple straight lines connecting the two vertices', which seems to imply that his graphs can be represented faithfully only by two-dimensional pictures, and not by one-dimensional terms in an algebra.

Moreover, Skillicorn does not state the laws needed to distinguish this algebra from an algebra of trees in which each node can have zero, one or two children. He is therefore forced to decompose a graph in exactly the same way as it was built, precluding any attempt at load-balancing for parallel execution.

6.6 Free Net Algebras

Molitor [22] defines an algebra of 'nets', modelling VLSI circuits. The constructors of this algebra are:

- a collection of basic 'cells',
- some wiring components (straight wires, corners, T-junctions and a 'crossover'), and
- two partial binary operators 'above' and 'beside' which compose circuit diagrams vertically and horizontally, provided that the edges to be matched have the same number of connections.

He gives a collection of fourteen rather complex laws, and claims that they are sound and complete. (The proof is omitted from Molitor's paper, and the reader referred to his thesis.)

This work may lead to an algebra of undirected hypergraphs, in which an 'edge' connects arbitrarily many vertices.

7 Conclusions

7.1 Summary

We have presented an initial algebra modelling a particular (and rather unconventional) kind of directed acyclic graph. We have shown that quite a few natural functions on these graphs are catamorphisms on the algebra we have defined; we have also seen one natural function (topological sort) that appears not to be a catamorphism. (We believe that this is no fault of the particular algebra presented here, but is inherent in any initial-algebra model of directed acyclic graphs.) We have also discussed a number of other approaches to representing graphs.

7.2 Further Work

There are several directions for further work that appear quite promising. A few of these are outlined below.

- One question that remains to be answered is whether the algebra presented here is practically useful. Many natural simple problems on DAMGs turn out to be DAMG catamorphisms, but we have not yet seen any more complicated problems whose solution was simplified by this algebra of DAMGs.

- A problem with the algebra we have defined here is that it does not model directed acyclic graphs particularly closely. We have had to introduce 'connections' (incoming edges with targets but no sources, and outgoing edges with sources but no targets) for the whole graph, allow multiple edges between a pair of vertices, and consider the ordering of the incoming and outgoing edges of a vertex to be significant, all in order to come up with an algebra at all. Is it possible to adapt this approach to yield an algebra that more closely models directed acyclic graphs?

- The 'symmetric strict monoidal category' approach we have used here is based heavily on the work of Căzănescu and Ştefănescu. They use it to obtain initial-algebra models of sixteen classes of finite relations, corresponding to all sixteen combinations of totality, surjectivity, univocality (that is, being single-valued or functional) and injectivity [10]. They go on [9] to present an algebraic theory of 'flownomials'—flowcharts abstracted on both the individual statements and the interconnection pattern; the algebra of cyclic flownomials consists of the algebra of acyclic flownomials (similar to our DAMGs) endowed with 'feedback' operator that cyclically connects the first few exits to the corresponding number of entries. This may present a way to adapt our approach to model also possibly cyclic graphs.

- Modelling undirected graphs appears to be more difficult, because vertex connections are not partitioned into two groups according to direction, and it is therefore less obvious how to connect subgraphs together.

- With all the other initial-algebra definitions of datatypes that have been explored to date, the concept of an *accumulation* has proved to be very powerful [13]. Essentially, an accumulation records all the partial results from the computation of a catamorphism. One application of 'forwards and backwards accumulations' on directed acyclic graphs might be to compute 'earliest and latest possible finishing times' for tasks in a project, in which the tasks are represented by the vertices of a graph (labelled with task duration) and their dependencies by the edges. However, all these other initial algebras have been 'free', that is, with no laws. It is not immediately obvious how to define accumulations on types with laws, since for these there may be different ways of representing the same object, and hence different ways of computing the same catamorphism on that object. These different computations necessarily return the same results, but may well do so with different collections of partial results; which computation should the accumulation record?

7.3 Acknowledgements

The author wishes to thank Bob Paige for pointing out the dislocation law, and other members of IFIP WG2.1 and the anonymous referees for many helpful comments. Also, this presentation would have been a lot less elegant without the help of Virgil Căzănescu and Gheorghe Ştefănescu's work on SSMCs.

References

1. Roland Backhouse. An exploration of the Bird-Meertens formalism. In *International Summer School on Constructive Algorithmics, Hollum, Ameland.* STOP project, 1989. Also available as Technical Report CS 8810, Department of Computer Science, Groningen University, 1988.
2. Roland Backhouse, Peter de Bruin, Grant Malcolm, Ed Voermans, and Jaap van der Woude. Relational catamorphisms. In Möller [23], pages 287–318.
3. R. S. Bird, C. C. Morgan, and J. C. P. Woodcock, editors. *LNCS 669: Mathematics of Program Construction.* Springer-Verlag, 1993.
4. Richard S. Bird. Using circular programs to eliminate multiple traversals of data. *Acta Informatica*, 21:239–250, 1984.
5. Richard S. Bird. An introduction to the theory of lists. In M. Broy, editor, *Logic of Programming and Calculi of Discrete Design*, pages 3–42. Springer-Verlag, 1987. Also available as Technical Monograph PRG-56, from the Programming Research Group, Oxford University.
6. Richard S. Bird. Lectures on constructive functional programming. In Manfred Broy, editor, *Constructive Methods in Computer Science.* Springer-Verlag, 1988. Also available as Technical Monograph PRG-69, from the Programming Research Group, Oxford University.
7. Alex Bunkenburg. The Boom hierarchy. In Kevin Hammond and John T. O'Donnell, editors, *1993 Glasgow Workshop on Functional Programming.* Springer, 1993.
8. F. Warren Burton and Hsi-Kai Yang. Manipulating multilinked data structures in a pure functional language. *Software—Practice and Experience*, 20(11):1167–1185, November 1990.
9. Virgil Emil Căzănescu and Gheorghe Ştefănescu. Towards a new algebraic foundation of flowchart scheme theory. *Fundamenta Informaticae*, XIII:171–210, 1990.
10. Virgil-Emil Căzănescu and Gheorghe Ştefănescu. Classes of finite relations as initial abstract data types I. *Discrete Mathematics*, 90:233–265, 1991.
11. Bruno Courcelle. Graph rewriting: An algebraic and logic approach. In Jan van Leeuwen, editor, *Handbook of Theoretical Computer Science*, volume B, chapter 5. Elsevier, 1990.
12. Jeremy Gibbons. *Algebras for Tree Algorithms.* D. Phil. thesis, Programming Research Group, Oxford University, 1991. Available as Technical Monograph PRG-94.
13. Jeremy Gibbons. Upwards and downwards accumulations on trees. In Bird et al. [3], pages 122–138. A revised version appears in the Proceedings of the Massey Functional Programming Workshop, 1992.
14. Paul Hoogendijk. Relational programming laws in the Boom hierarchy of types. In Bird et al. [3], pages 163–190.

15. Johan Jeuring. Deriving algorithms on binary labelled trees. CWI, Amsterdam, July 1989.
16. Johan Jeuring. The derivation of hierarchies of algorithms on matrices. In Möller [23], pages 9–32.
17. Yugo Kashiwagi and David S. Wise. Graph algorithms in a lazy functional programming language. Technical Report 330, Department of Computer Science, Indiana University, April 1991.
18. David J. King and John Launchbury. Lazy depth-first search and linear graph algorithms in Haskell. Department of Computer Science, University of Glasgow, 1993.
19. Saunders Mac Lane. *Categories for the Working Mathematician.* Springer-Verlag, 1971.
20. Lambert Meertens. Algorithmics: Towards programming as a mathematical activity. In J. W. de Bakker, M. Hazewinkel, and J. K. Lenstra, editors, *Proc. CWI Symposium on Mathematics and Computer Science,* pages 289–334. North-Holland, 1986.
21. Lambert Meertens. First steps towards the theory of rose trees. CWI, Amsterdam; IFIP Working Group 2.1 working paper 592 ROM-25, 1988.
22. Paul Molitor. Free net algebras in VLSI-theory. *Fundamenta Informaticae,* XI:117–142, 1988.
23. B. Möller, editor. *IFIP TC2/WG2.1 Working Conference on Constructing Programs from Specifications.* North-Holland, 1991.
24. Bernard Möller. Derivation of graph and pointer algorithms. In Bernhard Möller, Helmut Partsch, and Steve Schumann, editors, *LNCS 755: IFIP TC2/WG2.1 State-of-the-Art Report on Formal Program Development,* pages 123–160. Springer-Verlag, 1993.
25. Bernhard Möller. Algebraic calculation of graph and sorting algorithms. In Dines Bjørner, Manfred Broy, and Igor V. Pottosin, editors, *LNCS 735: Formal Methods in Programming and Their Applications,* pages 394–413. Springer-Verlag, 1993.
26. Bernhard Möller and Martin Russling. Shorter paths to graph algorithms. In Bird et al. [3], pages 250–268.
27. Bob Paige. Comment at IFIP Working Group 2.1 meeting, Renkum, January 1994.
28. Ross Paterson. Interpretations of term graphs. Draft. Department of Computing, Imperial College, 1994.
29. David B. Skillicorn. *Foundations of Parallel Programming.* Cambridge University Press, 1994.
30. Chris J. Wright. A theory of arrays for program derivation. Transferral dissertation, Programming Research Group, Oxford University, 1988.

Algebraic Proof Assistants in HOL

Rix Groenboom, Chris Hendriks, Indra Polak,
Jan Terlouw, Jan Tijmen Udding

Department of Computing Science
Groningen University, P.O. Box 800
9700 AV Groningen
The Netherlands
Phone +31 50 63 39 39, Fax +31 50 63 38 00.
Internet: {rix,chris,indra,terlouw,jtu}@cs.rug.nl

Abstract. We explore several ways to formalize the algebraic laws of
CSP-like languages in HOL. The intent of the paper is to show how
HOL can be tailored to acting as a proof assistant. The emphasis is
therefore on the consequences of various choices to be made during the
formalization for writing tactics. We end up with a proof assistant that
allows a user to make steps of the granularity of an algebraic law. It is
not the purpose of this paper to show in HOL that the algebraic laws of
some CSP-like language are sound; the purpose is to show how HOL can
be used to apply the algebraic laws and act as a rewrite system.

1 Introduction

We report on our attempts to tailor the automated proof checker HOL [GM93]
to the verification of proofs in CSP-like process algebras. Although it is technically feasible to prove the correctness of processes operating in parallel, this is
often a long and tedious, and therefore extremely error-prone task. Reliable tools
that can assist in proving concurrent programs correct are indispensable, if we
ever want the programming practitioners to prove their programs correct. The
goal of making program correctness proofs common practice in industry will fail
miserably, if we cannot supply adequate tool support. Toy problems and their
solutions simply do not scale to problems of industrial size.

For these reasons, we aim at the mechanization of reasoning about concurrent
programs, CSP-like programs in particular. One can think of two approaches to
achieve this goal: build something from scratch, or tailor some existing proof
checker/formula manipulator to one's needs. Since the feasibility of the latter
can be checked in a relatively short amount of time, we decided to pursue this
option first. We chose HOL for a number of reasons. After looking briefly at
the Boyer-Moore theorem prover [BM88], we decided, in view of the type of
verification we wanted to do, that a formalism that could support higher order
functions would be very beneficial. We then chose for HOL for the fact that it
has been around for a long time, is well supported, and well known.

The particular algebra that we formalize in HOL is DI-algebra [JU93]. This
is a CSP-like formalism to reason about asynchronous circuits. At this point, it

is good to make clear what this paper is *not* about. It is not about proving this algebra sound, by providing a semantics, and showing that the algebraic laws hold with respect to that semantics. This is a well-trodden path, and has for example been done for CSP by Camilleri [C91] and CCS by Nesi [N92]. Moreover, it is not about a proof for a particular (hardware) design, like a correctness proof for a microprocessor [H89] or an SECD-machine [BG90].

This paper, and the entire project for that matter, aims at providing an environment in which a user can prove *any* design at hand, with the same granularity of proof steps as in a manual proof. Such a proof assistant increases the proof reliability, and also alleviates the burden of spelling out each of the intermediate terms, for human beings a tedious and extremely error-prone task. In this respect, it is much more like the formalization of ACP in Coq by Sellink [S94], which has been applied to various correctness proofs for communication protocols like the Alternating Bit Protocol [BG93]. An intermediate layer is built upon an existing proof checker, which has already been shown useful in the proofs of individual instances, so as to facilitate program correctness proofs. The tool KIV (Karlsruhe Interactive Verifier [HRS90]) is similar in approach, although the aim is to verify sequential programs and it has been built from scratch.

Although the results are only preliminary, we can draw a few conclusions. Formalizing a process algebra in HOL requires some effort in order not to introduce any inconsistencies, but is rather straightforward. Much effort has to go into hiding all internal steps that HOL has to take when applying just one algebraic law. However, the approach is feasible, and requires a relatively small amount of work, compared to building a similar environment from scratch.

In the rest of this paper, we first give an outline of DI-algebra. It is only used to show the points that we want to make about this approach. Next is the formalization of the algebra in HOL. We discuss two possible approaches to such a formalization: a syntactic approach and an algebraic approach. They are similar as far as the formalization itself is concerned. For the actual tailoring of HOL to the algebra it turns out to have major consequences, both for the tactics to be written and for the speed with which HOL can eventually apply those tactics. The design of the tactics and their applications to some small examples is discussed in the subsequent sections. We conclude with a number of remarks, gained insights, and ideas for future research.

2 DI-Algebra

We briefly explain the syntax of DI-Algebra and some of its laws. For the purposes of this paper, the exact syntax and semantics are not essential. The development of a proof assistant in HOL for any CSP-like language could be carried out along the same lines. Yet, in order to get some points across, we stick to one concrete syntax and semantics, viz. that of DI-algebra.

In DI-Algebra, a process is a mathematical model at a certain level of abstraction of the way in which a circuit interacts with its environment. A circuit receives signals from its environment on certain wires and sends signals to its environment on certain other wires. Thus with each process is associated an alphabet of input wires and an alphabet of output wires. These alphabets are finite and disjoint. Their union is referred to as the alphabet of a process.

The algebra is intended for the design of asynchronous processes. A process does not model the time it takes for a signal to traverse a wire, which may vary from wire to wire or from signal to signal. A circuit can never block a signal, even one which would cause it to enter an undesirable state, e.g., a state in which a glitch or non-digital signal may result. Thus the environment must not send a signal along a wire when the circuit is not ready for it and this situation will persist until the circuit indicates otherwise by outputting on another wire. This is because, without assuming anything about timing, it is not possible to know whether a circuit has changed state simply by waiting, or by providing an input on another wire.

Typical names for processes are P and Q. Typical names for input wires are a and b; typical names for output wires are c and d. There is a refinement ordering on processes in which $\perp$, Chaos, is the least element. The ordering is intimately connected with nondeterministic choice. Process $P \sqcap Q$ is allowed to behave either as P or as Q. It reflects the designer's freedom to implement such a process by either P or Q. (Thus $\sqcap$ is obviously commutative, associative and idempotent.)

Defining a process by recursion is useful in specifying cyclic behavior. Formally, the meaning of $\mu X.F(X)$ is the least fixed point of F. Its successive approximations are $\perp$, $F(\perp)$, $F(F(\perp))$, etc., and fortunately all operators that we use to define processes are continuous [L94]. Note that continuity implies monotonicity, but all the operators except for recursion enjoy the stronger property of being distributive (with respect to nondeterministic choice).

We write $a?; P$ to denote a process that must wait for a signal to arrive on a before it can behave like P. It is quite permissible for the environment to send a signal along any other input wire b. Such a signal is ignored at least until a signal is sent along a (or a second signal is sent along b causing interference).

Complementary to input-prefixing $a?; P$ is output-prefixing $c!; P$. This is a process that outputs on c and then behaves like P. The environment may send a signal on any input wire even before it receives the signal on c; whether or not it can do so safely depends on P.

A more general form of input-prefixing is guarded choice. Such a choice allows a process to take different actions depending upon the input received. The choice is made between a number of alternatives of the form $a? \rightarrow P$, $skip \rightarrow P$, and $c! \rightarrow P$. For S a finite set of alternatives, the guarded choice $[S]$ selects one of them. An input alternative, $a? \rightarrow P$, can be selected only if a signal has been received on a. An output or $skip$ alternative can always be selected. The choice cannot be postponed indefinitely once one or more alternatives become selectable.

The process $P/a?$ behaves like P after its environment has sent it a signal on a. Notice that this does not mean that P has received this input yet; the signal may still be on its way. Indeed it is impossible to tell whether P has received the signal until some acknowledging signal has been received from P.

With parallel composition we can determine the overall behavior of a circuit from the individual behavior of its components. It is understood that if the output wire of one component has the same name as the input wire of another, then these wires are supposed to be joined together; any signals transmitted along such a connection are hidden from the environment.

Parallel composition is denoted by the infix binary operator $\|$. All the operators we have met so far do not affect the input and output alphabets of their operands; so, for example, in the nondeterministic choice $P \sqcap Q$, we insist that the input alphabet of P is the same as that of Q, and declare that it is the same as that of $P \sqcap Q$. In the parallel composition $P \| Q$, however, the input alphabet of P should be disjoint from that of Q; likewise, the output alphabet of P should be disjoint from that of Q. (These rules prohibit fan-in and fan-out of wires; the explicit use of Merges and Forks is required.) The input alphabet of $P \| Q$ then consists of those input wires of each process P and Q which are not output wires of the other. Similarly, the output alphabet of $P \| Q$ consists of those output wires of each process which are not input wires of the other.

3 Implementation in HOL

We have formalized the algebra described in the previous section in HOL. That is, we have defined a process syntax in HOL, and we have also formalized the algebraic laws that govern the algebra. It should be clear that there are many ways to do this. We have chosen two quite different approaches. The first approach, which we call the syntactic approach, defines a constructor for each operator in the algebra. The second approach, called the algebraic approach, stipulates a space of abstract processes, on which the algebraic operators are defined as functions. This choice has far reaching consequences for the formalization of the laws and for substitution, as we demonstrate in the next sections.

First, however, we describe the environment that we would like to create with HOL, using either approach. Proving processes correct in an algebra basically amounts to proving $P = Q$, for some processes P and Q, using only the algebraic laws[1]. We want HOL to apply the algebraic laws. It should act as a proof assistant, a proof checker, and be able to make steps of the same size as those of a human being.

We conform to HOL's ability to set a goal, and to subsequently, using tactics, reduce a goal to (smaller) subgoals. We assume that a theorem to be proved has the form $P = Q$, and that it will be proved by repeated algebraic rewrites of P until it has been rewritten to Q. Our aim is to formalize the laws in HOL, and then to write two tactics for each law. One that will transform the left hand side of *any* goal using the law from left to right (on some subexpression). The other one will apply the law from right to left. Each tactic should be such that it will,

---

[1] Actually, there is a refinement relation $\sqsubseteq$ between processes, and one usually proves that an implementation Q is at least as good as its specification P. For the points we want to make in this paper, however, it suffices to consider only equality.

in one step, apply the corresponding law as a human being would. That is, it should find the subexpressions that match (by substitution) one side of the law, calculate the corresponding other side of the law, and calculate the resulting expression. Depending upon the law, the latter may involve the calculation of the cartesian product of alternatives in two guarded choices, or the calculation of the difference and intersection of arbitrary (finite) sets. HOL should do all of this in one step.

In the next sections we show how we have used HOL for the formalization of the algebra and its laws. The frame boxed expressions are HOL code. A reader with some knowledge of functional programming languages should be able to grasp the intended meaning.

3.1 The syntactic approach

In the syntactic approach, there is a constructor for each operator in the algebra. First we define a few abbreviations. A channel is just a string, and an alphabet is a set of channels. Furthermore, in order to express recursion, we need variables of type ProcVar, variables over processes, which are simply strings.

```
new-type-abbrev('ProcVar', ":string");;
new-type-abbrev('Channel', ":string");;
new-type-abbrev('Alphabet', ":(Channel)set");;
```

Then, in order to express prefixing and guarded choice we must be able to make a channel an input or output channel.

```
let CommExpr = define-type
                'CommExpr'
                'CommExpr = INPUT Channel
                          | OUTPUT Channel';;
```

Finally, in addition to input and output guards, a guarded choice may contain skip guards, for which we introduce a guard expression.

```
let GuardExpr =define-type
                'GuardExpr'
                'GuardExpr = SKIP
                           | COMM CommExpr';;
```

Now we are able to define how a process expression is to be constructed.

```
let ProcExpr =
 define-type
 'ProcExpr'
 'ProcExpr = CHAOS Alphabet Alphabet
            | STOP Alphabet Alphabet
            | PROCVAR ProcVar Alphabet Alphabet
            | ND ProcExpr ProcExpr
            | PREFIX CommExpr ProcExpr
            | AFTER ProcExpr CommExpr
            | GC GuardExpr ProcExpr ProcExpr
            | PC ProcExpr ProcExpr
            | MU ProcVar ProcExpr';;
```

A few things are worth noticing. First of all, care has to be taken with the alphabets of a process. In a formal description we have to explicitly state the input and the output alphabet of a process. In order to calculate the parallel composition of two processes, and, indeed, formally check whether two processes can be composed, HOL needs to be able to compute the alphabet of a process. In a constructor that takes two alphabets as its arguments, the first argument is to be interpreted as the input alphabet, the second as the output alphabet. A second thing worth noticing is that HOL does not allow a recursive type definition involving lists. That is, we were not able to define a guarded choice as a list of alternatives of the form (GuardExpr, ProcExpr). Also, HOL does not allow mutual recursion, so we could not define ProcExpr and GC in terms of one another. Therefore, GC is a ternary operator, the first two arguments forming an alternative, the last argument being another process expression, representing the rest of the guarded choice. This also meant that we had to explicitly introduce a representation of the guarded choice without alternatives: STOP with an input and an output alphabet.

Clearly, it is not the case that anything that satisfies the syntax of ProcExpr represents a process. There are conditions to be imposed on the alphabets of a process, or of processes that are composed in parallel. Also, the third argument of a GC should be a GC itself or STOP. A function IsProcess has been defined that determines whether a process expression represents a process. Of course, the property of an expression to represent a process is invariant under the application of a law.

Next we demonstrate how we have introduced the algebraic laws in HOL. Taking a simple example first, we discuss the law that expresses that the order in which inputs arrive is immaterial: $a?; b?; P = b?; a?; P$ for any process P and channels a and b.

Our first concern is the equality in this law. As syntactic expressions, $a?; b?; P$ is not equal to $b?; a?; P$, unless $a = b$. Hence, an axiom that would force this equality to hold, using HOL's built-in $=$, would introduce an inconsistency. Therefore, we are forced to define a semantic process equivalence, called eq, that will serve as the equality for processes. For eq we introduce the obvious axioms of reflexivity, symmetry, and transitivity. The most important axiom, however, is the one that expresses that replacement of P by Q in any process expression R does not change the meaning of R, provided that P and Q are (semantically) equal. A first attempt at this was to define a function SubstProc p q r over the syntax of r, that would replace every occurrence of p by q in r, and to introduce as axiom that the meaning of r would not change:

```
let eqSubst = new-axiom(
          'eqSubst',
          "(p eq q) ==> (r eq SubstProc p q r)"
          );;
```

At least two objections can be made to this axiom. First of all, it replaces *every* occurrence of p by q. It is hard, although not impossible, to replace only *some* occurrences of p by q in r. A much bigger problem becomes apparent when we try to prove algebraic theorems containing process variables. Remember that the purpose is to rewrite the left hand side of an arbitrary goal of the form r eq s. The idea is to transform this goal to the new goal (SubstProc p q r) eq s, for some p equivalent to q, and then to remove the function SubstProc by applying it to its arguments (all to be done by HOL). The problem is, if r contains variables then HOL cannot by itself eliminate SubstProc, since the result of SubstProc depends on what will be substituted for these variables! Recognizing those places where SubstProc has not disappeared, and then resorting to different means to prove equality, is possible in each individual case, of course. However, we were unable to write a tactic that would silently do this in any arbitrary case.

Both problems are solved if we use a boolean function that will check the correctness of a substitution, rather than a function that will perform the substitution, like SubstProc. Hence, we use the function Subst p q r s that checks whether s can be conceived of as being the result of replacing some expressions p in r by q. The substitution law then becomes:

```
let eqSubst = new-axiom(
          'eqSubst',
          "((p eq q) ∧ (Subst p q r s)) ==> (r eq s)"
          );;
```

The previous axiom can now be proved to be a theorem. Finally, we can state the law that the order of two inputs is immaterial.

```
let INCOMMLaw = new-axiom (
             'INCOMMLaw',
             "(PREFIX (INPUT a) (PREFIX (INPUT b) p)) eq
             (PREFIX (INPUT b) (PREFIX (INPUT a) p))"
             );;
```

A second, and much more involved, law is that of parallel composition through guarded choice. In the algebra it is stated as follows. For any two sets of alternatives S_0 and S_1

$[S_0] \parallel [S_1] = [S]$,

where S is formed from the alternatives in S_0 and S_1 in the following way. For each alternative in S_0 of the form $skip \to P$, we have $skip \to (P \parallel [S_1])$ in S. For each alternative in S_0 of the form $a? \to P$ with a not in the output alphabet of $[S_1]$, we have $a? \to (P \parallel [S_1])$ in S. For each alternative in S_0 of the form $c! \to P$ with c not in the input alphabet of $[S_1]$, we have $c! \to (P \parallel [S_1])$ in S. Finally, for each alternative in S_0 of the form $c! \to P$ with c in the input alphabet of $[S_1]$, we have $skip \to (P \parallel ([S_1]/c?))$ in S. The alternatives in S_1 contribute to the alternatives in S in a similar way.

Apparently, we need functions InProc and OutProc that determine the input alphabet and the output alphabet of a process. These can be easily defined, although care has to be taken to avoid mutual recursion, since the input alphabet of $P \parallel Q$ is expressed using both input and output alphabets of P and Q. Next we define a function PCThruGCL, which calculates the contribution of the left operand $[S_0]$ of the parallel composition to the result $[S]$. It need only be defined for a guarded choice, hence for the constructs GC and STOP. In order to determine whether a channel belongs to the alphabet of the other process, we need to unwrap a guard. The function CommChan strips away the COMM constructor, if the guard is not a skip-guard. The function GuardComm strips away the INPUT or OUTPUT constructor. What remains in this way is a channel. The definition of PCThruGCL then becomes:

```
let PCThruGCL =
new-recursive-definition
false
ProcExpr
'PCThruGCL'
"(PCThruGCL (STOP InP OutP) e =
(STOP (UNION (DIFF InP (OutProc e))
             (DIFF (InProc e) OutP))
      (UNION (DIFF OutP (InProc e))
             (DIFF (OutProc e) InP)))) /\
(PCThruGCL (GC g p0 p1) e =
(IsSKIP g) => GC g (PC p0 e) (PCThruGCL p1 e)
| (IsInput (GuardComm g)) =>
  (CommChan (GuardComm g) IN (OutProc e)) =>
  PCThruGCL p1 e | GC g (PC p0 e) (PCThruGCL p1 e)
| (CommChan (GuardComm g) IN (InProc e)) =>
  GC SKIP
    (PC p0 (AFTER e (INPUT (CommChan (GuardComm g)))))
    (PCThruGCL p1 e)
  | GC g (PC p0 e) (PCThruGCL p1 e))";;
```

In order to define PCThruGC we apply PCThruGCL twice, once for the first guarded choice and once for the second. However, then we are left with two guarded choices, which should be combined into one. This basically means that the last STOP construct in the first guarded choice, be replaced by the second guarded choice.

```
let CombGC =
  new-recursive-definition
  false
  ProcExpr
  'CombGC' "(CombGC (STOP InP OutP) e = e) /\
  (CombGC (GC g p0 p1) e = GC g p0 (CombGC p1 e))";;
```

The definition of the function that computes a parallel composition through guarded choice is now trivial

```
let PCThruGC =
  new-definition(
  'PCThruGC',
  "PCThruGC p0 p1 =
  CombGC (PCThruGCL p0 p1) (PCThruGCL p1 p0)"
  );;
```

All of the above are only definitions, so as to be able to express the law for parallel composition. The law itself, however, is now easy to define and understand.

```
let PCThruGCLaw = new-axiom(
                  'PCThruGCLaw'
                  "(PC p0 p1) eq (PCThruGC p0 p1)"
                  );;
```

The law for parallel composition through guarded choice is by far the most complicated. All of the other laws in the algebra can be axiomatized in HOL in a similar but simpler way. We refrain from doing so in this paper.

3.2 The Algebraic Approach

In the algebraic approach, we stipulate an abstract space of processes. The operators of the algebra are not inductively defined, but they are introduced as functions on this space by giving only their types. In order to do this we first introduce a new type that corresponds with the notion of 'process'. Then functions are introduced for each operator on processes. Consequently, axioms have to be used to state properties of these functions. The definitions for ProcVar, Alphabet, CommExpr, and GuardExpr remain unchanged.

We define the new process type P for Process as follows:

```
new-type 0 'P';;
```

The zero means that the type P has arity 0. The algebraic operators are now introduced as functions:

```
new-constant('CHAOS', ":Alphabet -> Alphabet -> P");;
new-constant('STOP', ":Alphabet -> Alphabet -> P");;
new-constant('PROC-VAR', ":ProcVar -> Alphabet -> Alphabet -> P");;
new-constant('ND', ": P -> P -> P");;
new-constant('PREFIX', ": CommExpr -> P -> P");;
new-constant('AFTER', ": P -> CommExpr -> P");;
new-constant('GC', ": GuardExpr -> P -> P -> P");;
new-constant('PC', ": P -> P -> P");;
new-constant('MU', ": ProcVar -> P -> P");;
```

In this way we have represented the signature of the algebra. It remains to represent the laws of the algebra. We do this by introducing exactly the same axioms, now expressed in terms of the newly introduced functions and the syntactic equality '=' of HOL, rather than eq as in the syntactic approach. For example, the axiom that implements the law $a?; b?; P = b?; a?; P$ is:

```
let INCOMMLaw = new-axiom(
                'INCOMMLaw',
                "(PREFIX (INPUT a) (PREFIX (INPUT b) p)) =
                (PREFIX (INPUT b) (PREFIX (INPUT a) p))"
                );;
```

Such axioms change the original meaning of the =-relation. More terms can be proved equal in HOL than before. In general this is a very dangerous approach, since equality plays a crucial role within HOL. Care has been taken to ensure that the axioms only express equalities of terms of type ":P". Now there can only be an inconsistency if the algebraic axioms are unsound or HOL itself. We have sufficient reason to assume that this is not the case.

In the syntactic approach we can prove

```
(PREFIX (INPUT a) (PREFIX (INPUT b) p)) ≠
(PREFIX (INPUT b) (PREFIX (INPUT a) p))
```

as a consequence of the induction theorem that is returned when defining an inductive type. All constructors are distinct by definition. In the algebraic approach, however, a property of a function will only hold if we explicitly state it . In some settings the syntactic approach is to be preferred to the algebraic approach. For instance, when proving the algebra sound with respect to a given semantics, introducing the operators through an inductive definition is the obvious way to go. Also, one can make a mistake when formalizing a law in HOL. This is a valid argument for not using axioms at all. We agree that to be absolutely sure one should not use an axiom. Presently, however, we mainly want to investigate whether it is at all feasible to use HOL as an algebraic term rewriter. In a later stage one can then make use of the full power of HOL and formalize the semantics of the algebra and replace all axioms by theorems.

The way in which we have formalized the algebra in HOL is completely general in the sense that we can do this for *any* algebra in the same way. In a similar way, also the tactics, which we discuss in the next section, are completely general. This leads to the conjecture that it is possible to automatically generate a proof-assistant in HOL from any given algebra.

3.3 Tactics

As stated earlier, the purpose of formalizing DI-algebra in HOL is not to prove the soundness of the laws, but to develop a proof assistant that can apply the algebraic laws, and in that way assist a user in checking his proofs. This is only feasible, if HOL can apply steps of the same granularity as a human being. From the previous sections, it should have become clear, that applying a law may involve quite a number of additional functions (like PCThruGC, InProc, etc.). Also in the case of the syntactic approach, it requires HOL to apply the usually tacitly understood laws for substitution, and transitivity, symmetry, and reflexivity of equality. For the algebraic approach the latter transformations come for free. Our aim is that none of those auxiliary functions will ever appear in an expression. HOL should see to it that they disappear, when a law is to be applied, before the next goal becomes visible on the screen.

For that purpose, HOL allows one to write tactics. As explained in Section 3, we assume that a goal will always have the form p eq q, and that p is to be rewritten until it has become q. Then it is our task to write two tactics for every law that a user wishes to be applied to p, one for each direction in which the law is to be applied. We give one example of such a tactic. Typically, each tactic is about one page long. We take the example of the law that we have seen earlier: $a?; b?; P = b?; a?; P$. In this particular case, there will of course be only one tactic.

Each tactic for a law has one argument, **arg**, being the (sub)expression to which the law should be applied. Informally, what a tactic should do with this argument and goal p eq q is:

1. Bring **arg** in such a form that it matches one side of the law to be applied.

2. Prove a theorem, stating that **arg** equals some u, using the law.

3. Reduce the goal by substituting u for **arg** in p.

4. Remove all internal functions.

A more sophisticated tactic would allow the substitution of **arg** at only some places. The basic algorithm, however, remains the same. The implementation of the algorithm in the syntactic approach differs considerably from the algorithm in the algebraic approach.

Tactics for the Syntactic Approach Typically, each tactic begins with a number of abbreviations, giving names to subterms in the goal to be rewritten, and to the individual components of the argument **arg**. Moreover, the tactic has to construct the other side of the law somehow, and some new term, whose purpose will become clear momentarily. As we shall see, these constructions are not necessary in the algebraic approach, which makes those tactics considerably faster.

```
let s t = snd (dest-comb (t)) and
    f t = fst (dest-comb (t)) in
  let p = s (f (s (top-goal ())))) and
      a = s (s (f (arg))) and
      b = s (s (f (s (arg)))) and
     p0 = s (s (arg)) in
         let rhs = mk-comb
                     ( mk-comb ("COMM", b)
                     , mk-comb
                         ( mk-comb ("COMM", a)
                         , p0)) in
         let nt  = mk-comb
                     ( mk-comb
                         ( mk-comb ("SubstProc", p0)
                         , rhs)
                     , p)
```

The functions dest-comb en mk-comb are predefined functions. The function dest-comb takes a function application of the form f g, and yields the pair (f,g), that can then be picked apart with fst and snd. The function mk-comb does the inverse. Finally, top-goal() yields the pair of current assumptions and the current goal, which is assumed to be of the form p eq q. By these definitions, the concrete a, b, and p0, are going to correspond to the parameters a, b, and P, in the law $a?; b?; P = b?; a?; P$. The term p is the term that is going to be rewritten, the left hand side of the equality in the goal. Notice that two new terms are constructed, rhs, which is the right hand side of the law, and nt, the new left hand side of the equation of the goal.

Now each tactic typically proceeds as follows. First, the argument needs to be proved equal to some instantiation of one of the sides of the law. In this case, this is a trivial step, since the law is so simple, i.e. a matches a, b matches b, and p0 matches P. In a more general case, the law may contain functions like InProc and OutProc, and then instantiating the law and proving equality is not so trivial.

When that has been done, the idea is to transform the goal p eq q to

```
p eq (SubstProc arg rhs p) ∧ (SubstProc arg rhs p) eq q
```

by explicitly using the transitivity of eq. Then the first conjunct is removed by the proper instantiation of the corresponding law and the substitution theorem. What remains is a goal that has the right form, but in which the function SubstProc occurs still. (When writing more complicated tactics, other "internal" functions will turn out to appear.) By letting HOL rewrite this function and all new functions that appear as a result of those rewrites, we eventually arrive at a form in which none of these internal functions appear still. This requires the use of many conversion theorems for sets and strings. Especially, the calculation of set operations like intersection and union is very involved. For example, in order to calculate $\{a\} \cap \{b\}$ autonomously, HOL needs to know whether $a = b$, which it should somehow deduce from the assumptions. The tactics INT-FUNC-TAC, SET-REWRITE-TAC, and SYM-TAC perform together all the necessary work to remove the internal functions from arbitrary terms. The tactic INT-FUNC-TAC removes all internal functions that are specifically defined for the formalization of the algebra. The tactic SET-REWRITE-TAC removes all set operations and SYM-TAC is a tactic that changes all equalities $x = y$ in all subterms of a goal to $y = x$. This proved to be necessary to account for all possible inequalities of channel names without having to state them all in the goal.

Tactics for the algebraic approach The tactics for the algebraic approach proved to be much easier to write, and also, faster to execute. All problems concerning substitution and equality are absent. HOL's efficient and built-in rewrite and substitution tactics could directly be used. However, only some gain is made with respect to the last step in the tactic algorithm: the removal of internal functions. The function SubstProc is unnecessary, but the removal of set functions like UNION and DIFF, or InProc and OutProc is still a substantial task, not only when writing a tactic, but also with respect to run-time.

Looking at the same example as with the syntactic approach, also in this case we define abbreviations, but only the ones necessary to pick the argument **arg** apart. The terms dealing with the transitivity of **eq** and the new goal are no longer necessary. As a matter of fact, the rest of this tactic is a one-liner that instantiates the axiom, and does the proper substitutions in the goal.

```
SUBST-TAC [(SPECL [a;b;p] (axiom '-' 'INCOMMLaw))];;
```

For more complicated laws we need to rewrite **arg** in the beginning and remove internal functions at the end, similar to the syntactic approach.

4 Proving Compositions Correct

Using the formalization and the tactics discussed above, we have proved several compositions correct. The first thing we tried was the composition of two wires, where a wire is defined as $W(a, b) = a?; b!; W(a, b)$. Here, the wire is implicitly given as the unique solution of a fixed point equation. With the formalization above, the definition of a wire is:

```
let Wire = new-definition
          ('Wire',
          "Wire a b = (MU 'W' (PREFIX (INPUT a)
                              (PREFIX (OUTPUT b)
                              (PROCVAR 'W' a b)))))");;
```

The theorem to be proved is $W(a, b) \parallel W(b, c) = a?; c!; (W(a, b) \parallel W(b, c))$, given of course that all of the channel names are different. In HOL this is expressed by the goal

```
¬(a=b) ∧ ¬(a=c) ∧ ¬(b=c) ==>
(PC (Wire a b) (Wire b c)) eq
(PREFIX (INPUT a)
(PREFIX (OUTPUT c)
(PC (Wire a b) (Wire b c))))
```

The manual proof consists of 19 steps, each one applying one law or pre-proven theorem. The proof in HOL consists of exactly the same 19 steps in addition to which one or two steps are needed. The first one serves to set things up properly. The left hand side of the implication, expressing that all channels are different, is to become an assumption, and the definition of the Wire above has to be retrieved.

```
e(DISCH-TAC THEN
      REWRITE-TAC [definition '-' 'Wire']);;
```

Moreover, but only in case of the syntactic approach, we need an explicit reference to the reflexivity of eq, to prove that q eq q at the end.

```
e(REWRITE-TAC[axiom '-' 'eqRef']);;
```

The main difference between the two approaches is the time that it takes HOL to prove this theorem. The tactics in the algebraic approach turn out to be about two to three times as fast. All times in the next table are in seconds.

Table 1. Timings of a small proof.

Approach	CPU time	Garbage Collection	Intermediate Theorems
Syntactic	76.3	152.8	24,441
Algebraic	27.2	38.3	9,422

We have also proved a somewhat more elaborate theorem, viz. that the composition of a Fork, an element that duplicates its inputs, and a Join, an element that waits for two inputs and then produces an output, behaves as a Wire. The formal specification of a Join is

```
let Join = new-definition
          ('Join',
          "Join a b c = (MU 'C' (PREFIX (INPUT a)
                              (PREFIX (INPUT b)
                              (PREFIX (OUTPUT c)
                              (PROCVAR 'C' a,b c)))))");;
```

and of a Fork is

```
let Fork = new-definition
           ('Fork',
            "Fork a b c = (MU 'F' (PREFIX (INPUT a)
                                  (PREFIX (OUTPUT b)
                                  (PREFIX (OUTPUT c)
                                  (PROCVAR 'F' a b,c)))))");;
```

The goal is to prove that $Fork(a, b, c) \parallel Join(b, c, d) = a?; d!; (Fork(a, b, c) \parallel Join(b, c, d)$, which is expressed in HOL as the goal

```
(¬(a=b) ∧ ¬(a=c) ∧ ¬(a=d) ∧ ¬(b=c) ∧ ¬(b=d) ∧ ¬(c=d)) ==>
(PC (Fork a b c) (Join c b d)) eq
(PREFIX (INPUT a)
    (PREFIX (OUTPUT d)
    (PC (Fork a b c) (Join c b d)))))";;
```

Also this time, we need an additional step for setting things up properly. And in case of the syntactic approach we also need to appeal to the reflexivity of eq. Other then that, the proof requires exactly the same steps as a manual proof, being 28. Again the algebraic tactics were faster by a factor of about two to three.

Table 2. Timings of a longer proof.

Approach	CPU Time	Garbage Collection	Intermediate Theorems
Syntactic	316.7	608.1	74,322
Algebraic	147.6	292.4	47,224

5 Future Work

Eventually we want to create an environment in which a user can apply laws and theorems to a term, assisted by the system that will quickly and correctly perform the operations involved. At this moment, we have only shown the feasibility of such an approach. In a practical tool, a user should be able to enter algebraic expressions graphically, rather than by using HOL's internal representation. Also, output from HOL should be translated back into this format. A system like this should also be able to give hints as to what law or theorem to apply next.

Currently, we are working on incorporating communication with data. For example, $a?x$, means that on channel a a value arrives that is assigned to a (local) variable x. The subsequent behavior may depend on the value received.

In order to be able to specify interesting processes in the presence of data, we have to allow mutual recursion between processes in a more elegant way than using only the MU operator. We are still investigating how this can be done best. Also, we are looking at the formalization of different proof techniques, like recursion induction, again keeping the proof in HOL as close as possible to the manually written one.

Now we have shown the feasibility of this approach, we may decide to set things up properly, and actually *prove* the axioms that we have now assumed. However, that is not the major concern at the moment.

Another point is the automatic generation of tactics as mentioned earlier. We believe this should be possible for reasonably arbitrary algebras.

6   Conclusions

We have demonstrated how HOL can be used as a term rewriting facility, that allows proof steps of the size of proof steps in a manual proof. The gained advantage is of course the fact that HOL takes care of the proof administration and will flawlessly perform the rewritings. We have used DI-Algebra as vehicle for the experiment and formalized its syntax and its algebraic laws in HOL. It turned out that there are at least two viable approaches to the formalization, a syntactic and an algebraic one. But either way, the proofs of a few simple cases turned out to have the same granularity as the manual proofs.

The more conservative syntactic approach required an elaborate set of functions and axioms in order to introduce substitution and semantic equality of processes. The algebraic approach could easily use the built-in functions and tactics for equality, and as a result proof checking turned out to be faster by a factor of three in the latter case. In either case, we did not reach our original goal to build an interactive proof checker, with which a user could in a matter of seconds see the result of applying a particular law or theorem. It may be that we can still optimize the tactics that we have written, but it seems that some laws, especially parallel composition through guarded choice, take too much time, even in very simple cases. However, for proof checking afterwards, a manual proof can be directly translated into a proof that HOL can verify.

We have also noticed that the tactics that we have written all share the same pattern. Thus, in principle the tactics could be generated automatically given a specific algebra. This makes our approach generally applicable to any algebra. Even from scratch and without any knowledge of HOL, it turned out to be only a matter of a few months to write a reliable algebraic proof checker.

References

[BG93] M.A. Bezem and J.F. Groote. *A formal verification of the alternating bit protocol in the calculus of constructions.* Technical Report 88, Logic Group Preprint Series, Utrecht University, March 1993.

[BG90] G. Birtwistle and B. Graham. Verifying SECD in HOL. In Proceedings of the *IFIP TC10/WG10.5 Summer School on Formal Methods for VLSI Design*, North Holland, 1990.

[BM88] Robert S. Boyer and J Strother Moore. *A Computational Logic Handbook.* Academic Press, 1988.

[C91] A.J. Camilleri. A Higher Order Logic Mechanization of the CSP Failure-Divergence Semantics. In Proceedings of the *4th Banff Higher Order Workshop*, G. Birtwistle (ed.), Workshops in Computing Series, Springer Verlag, 1991, pp. 123 – 150.

[GM93] M.J.C. Gordon en T.F. Melham. *Introduction to HOL.* Cambridge University Press, 1993.

[HRS90] M. Heisel, W. Reif and W. Stephan, Tactical Theorem Proving in Program Verification, In: *Conference on Automated Deduction*, Siekmann (ed), LNCS 449, Spinger Verlag, 1990, pp. 117-131.

[H89] Warren A. Hunt, Jr, Microprocessor Design Verification. *Journal of Automated Reasoning*, Vol 5, Nr 4, December 1989, pp. 429–460.

[JU93] M.B. Josephs and J.T. Udding, An Overview of DI Algebra. In: *Proc. Hawaii International Conf. System Sciences*, T.N. Mudge and V. Milutinovic and L. Hunter (eds), Vol. I, IEEE Computer Society Press, 1993, pp. 329-338.

[L94] P. G. Lucassen. *A Denotational Model and Composition Theorems for a Calculus of Delay-Insensitive Specifications.* PhD thesis, Dept. of C.S., Univ. of Groningen, The Netherlands, May 1994.

[N92] M. Nesi. *A Formalization of the Process Algebra CCS in Higher Order Logic.* Technical Report 278, University of Cambrigde Computer Laboratory, December 1992.

[S94] M.P.A. Sellink. Verifying Process Algebra Proofs in Type Theory, In: *Proceedings of Workshop in Semantics of Specification Languages*, D.J. Andrews, J.F. Groote and C.A. Middelburg (eds), October 1993, Utrecht, Springer Verlag, 1994, pp. 315–339.

Angelic termination in Dijkstra's calculus

Wim H. Hesselink[1]

Dept. of Mathematics and Computing Science
Rijksuniversiteit Groningen
Postbox 800, 9700 AV Groningen
The Netherlands

Abstract. As a variation of a recent proposal of Broy and Nelson's, a construct for nondeterministic choice is proposed that terminates if at least one of the branches terminates and that for all other aspects serves as a demonic choice. Two versions of the operator are discussed. In contrast to the Broy–Nelson proposal, the semantics are given by monotonic predicate transformers and monotonic operations on them. In this way the semantics of recursion is completely standard. The paper concludes with proof rules for recursive procedures and a small example of their applications.

Key words: predicate transformer, nontotal command, nondeterminism (demonic, angelic), termination, proof rule.

1 Introduction

In [2], Broy and Nelson propose a choice operator dovetail ∇ for imperative languages. This operator is described operationally as follows: "$A \nabla B$ is the command to execute A and B fairly in parallel, on separate copies of the state, accepting as outcome any proper (i.e. nonlooping) outcome of either A or B." In our view, the intention of [2] is captured somewhat better by: "$A \nabla B$ is executed by letting A and B be executed in parallel by separate processors on separate copies of the state, accepting as an outcome any proper (i.e. nonlooping) outcome of either processor." So, $A \nabla B$ terminates if and only if A or B terminates.

As shown in [2], the dovetail can be combined with recursive procedures to yield unbounded nondeterminacy. For example, procedure $h0$ declared by

$$\textbf{body}.h0 \;\; = \;\; (n := 0) \; \nabla \; (h0 \; ; \; n := n + 1)$$

necessarily terminates and has the effect to give n an arbitrary value in the natural numbers. If procedure $h0$ is modified by replacing the dovetail by a demonic choice $[\!]$, however, it clearly need not terminate since the second branch can always be chosen.

In [2], the dovetail is described as a fair choice operator. The following example shows that it is more than fair. Let procedure $h1$ be declared by

[1] email: wim@cs.rug.nl

body.$h1$ =
    if $n = 0$ **then** *skip*
    else $(n := n + 1 ;$ $h1)$
          $\nabla \, (n := n - 1 ;$ $h1)$
  fi .

Procedure $h1$ necessarily terminates, since it terminates for $n = 0$ and otherwise the dovetail can choose a terminating branch. If procedure $h1$ is modified by replacing the dovetail by a demonic choice ⫿, however, it need not terminate even for many fair execution sequences. We therefore prefer to speak of "angelic termination" instead of "fair choice".

It should be mentioned that procedure $h2$ declared by

body.$h2$ =
    if $n = 0$ **then** *skip*
    else $(n := n + 1 \, \nabla \, n := n - 1) ; h2$
  fi

need not terminate, since the dovetail of two terminating commands is just demonic choice. This shows that postcomposition does not distribute over dovetail.

In the conclusion of [2], it is admitted that "the formal treatment of dovetail is somewhat curious: a function f is proved to have a least fixed point with respect to an order $\leq$, although f is not monotonic with respect to $\leq$ ..." Investigation of the results of [2] shows, however, that the formal treatment of dovetail has been complicated by two design choices inherited from [14], viz. the combination of *wp* and *wlp* into one function and the incorporation of Nelson's else operator ⧖.

It is the purpose of this paper to show that the formal treatment of dovetail by means of monotonic predicate transformers is completely standard. It can even be combined easily with angelic nondeterminacy as proposed in [1, 8, 11, 12, 13].

The informal description of the dovetail that we gave above easily leads to a formal definition that differs from the formal definition given in [2]. We therefore consider two versions of the dovetail. We shall distinguish them as the simple dovetail ∇ and the dotted dovetail $\dot{\nabla}$. Indeed, ∇ is the simpler operator, but $\dot{\nabla}$ is the dovetail introduced in [2]. The two versions only differ when applied to nontotal commands. The differences between ∇ and $\dot{\nabla}$ will be discussed in Section 4.

One of the referees pointed out to us that, in [5], Doornbos proposes a fair choice operator $\Diamond$ which is the same as our simple dovetail ∇. We prefer to use the symbol ∇ instead of $\Diamond$ because of the similarity of $\Diamond$ to the symbol $\diamondsuit$ for the angelic choice, cf. [8]. The arguments of Doornbos show that ∇ is easily compatible with the relational semantics of programs.

We introduce the weakest precondition functions and the operator ∇ in Section 2. In Section 3, we discuss the termination rule and the refinement relation of commands. The dotted dovetail $\dot{\nabla}$ is introduced and discussed in Section 4. We define the semantics of recursive procedures (possibly with ∇ and $\dot{\nabla}$) in Section 5. In Section 6, we show that the proof rules for *wp* and *wlp* of [7] can be used in a formal correctness proof for procedure $h1$ above. Conclusions are drawn in Section 7.

2 Weakest preconditions

We write $\mathbb{P}$ to denote the set of the predicates on the state space. For $P \in \mathbb{P}$, the assertion $[P]$ means that P holds everywhere on the state space, cf. [4]. Predicate P is said to be *stronger* than Q if and only if $[P \Rightarrow Q]$. We write PT for the set of functions $\mathbb{P} \to \mathbb{P}$. The elements of PT are called *predicate transformers*. A predicate transformer $f \in PT$ is called *monotonic* if and only if

$$(\forall\, P, Q \in \mathbb{P} : [P \Rightarrow Q] : [f.P \Rightarrow f.Q])\ .$$

We write MT to denote the set of the monotonic predicate transformers.

Following [3, 4] (and also [2, 14]), the semantics of a command S is expressed by two monotonic predicate transformers $wp.S$ and $wlp.S$. For a predicate P, the predicate $wp.S.P$ is regarded as the weakest precondition such that execution of S terminates in a state where P holds. Similarly, $wlp.S.P$ is regarded as the weakest precondition such that, if execution of S terminates, the final state satisfies P.

Given commands S and T, the sequential composition $S;T$ and the demonic choice $S[\!]T$ are given by

$$
\begin{aligned}
w.(S;T).P &= w.S.(w.T.P)\ , \\
w.(S[\!]T).P &= w.S.P \wedge w.T.P\ ,
\end{aligned}
$$

where w ranges over $\{wp, wlp\}$.

Following [10, 13, 14], we allow nontotal commands (commands S such that $wp.S.false \neq false$). If $wp.S.false$ holds in some state, command S is said to perform a miracle in that state. The most important examples are guards. If B is a predicate, the guard $?B$ is the simple command with

$$w.(?B).P = (\neg B \vee P)$$

where w ranges over $\{wp, wlp\}$. As is well known, cf. [6] Section 1.5, it follows that the conditional choice can be expressed by

$$\textbf{if } B \textbf{ then } S \textbf{ else } T \textbf{ fi} = (?B\ ;\ S\ [\!]\ ?\neg B\ ;\ T)\ .$$

We now come to the dovetail operator. According to the informal description, command $S\nabla T$ can yield all proper results delivered by both S and T, but $S\nabla T$ terminates if and only if at least one of the two terminates. This suggests the rules

$$
\begin{aligned}
(0) &\quad wlp.(S\nabla T) = wlp.(S[\!]T)\ , \\
(1) &\quad wp.(S\nabla T).P = (wp.S.P \wedge wlp.T.P)\ \vee\ (wp.T.P \wedge wlp.S.P)\ .
\end{aligned}
$$

Formula (1) differs from the choice of [2], which will be discussed in Section 4. The semantics of recursive procedures with ∇ and ∇ will be defined in Section 5.

3   The termination rule and refinement

A command S is said to satisfy the *termination rule* if

(2) $wp.S.P = wp.S.true \land wlp.S.P$ for every predicate P.

Traditionally, this rule is postulated for all commands, cf. [2, 4, 5, 6]. Under assumption of (2), formula (1) can be rewritten to

$$wp.(S\nabla T).P = (wp.S.true \lor wp.T.true) \land wlp.S.P \land wlp.T.P .$$

This is the same rule as given in (31) of [5]. So, under assumption of (2), the operators ∇ and $\diamond$ are identical.

(3) **Theorem.** If both S and T satisfy the termination rule then $S\nabla T$ does so as well.

Proof. It suffices to observe that, for every predicate P,

$$
\begin{aligned}
&wp.(S\nabla T).true \land wlp.(S\nabla T).P \\
=\quad & \{(0), (1)\} \\
&((wp.S.true \land wlp.T.true) \lor (wp.T.true \land wlp.S.true)) \\
&\land\ wlp.S.P \land wlp.T.P \\
=\quad & \{\text{distribution}\} \\
&(wp.S.true \land wlp.T.true \land wlp.S.P \land wlp.T.P) \\
&\lor (wp.T.true \land wlp.S.true \land wlp.S.P \land wlp.T.P) \\
=\quad & \{wlp.S \text{ and } wlp.T \text{ are monotonic}\} \\
&(wp.S.true \land wlp.S.P \land wlp.T.P) \\
&\lor (wp.T.true \land wlp.S.P \land wlp.T.P) \\
=\quad & \{S \text{ and } T \text{ satisfy } (2)\} \\
&(wp.S.P \land wlp.T.P) \lor (wp.T.P \land wlp.S.P) \\
=\quad & \{(1)\} \\
&wp.(S\nabla T).P .
\end{aligned}
$$

(End of proof)

We now briefly discuss the monotonicity of the programming operators with respect to the relation of refinement. Since both *wp* and *wlp* are concerned, we define the refinement relation $\sqsubseteq$ between commands by

(4) $S \sqsubseteq T \equiv (\forall P :: [wp.S.P \Rightarrow wp.T.P] \land [wlp.S.P \Rightarrow wlp.T.P])$.

It is easy to verify that the operators ";", "⫿", and "∇" are monotonic with respect to refinement:

(5) $S \sqsubseteq S' \land T \sqsubseteq T'$
$\Rightarrow S;T \sqsubseteq S';T' \land S⫿T \sqsubseteq S'⫿T' \land S\nabla T \sqsubseteq S'\nabla T'$.

This monotonicity is important since it allows compositional refinement of commands.

Remark. The dovetail operator ∇ is not monotonic with respect to Nelson's approximation order $\sqsubseteq_N$ (cf. [14, 2]), which is given by

$$S \sqsubseteq_N T \equiv (\forall P :: [wp.S.P \Rightarrow wp.T.P] \land [wlp.S.P \Leftarrow wlp.T.P]) .$$

This nonmonotonicity only presents a difficulty if one wants to use the method of [14] for the definition of recursive procedures. (End of remark)

4 The dotted dovetail

As announced above, we write ∇ for the dovetail operator of [2]. In order to define and discuss this operator, we define, for a command S, predicates $hlt.S$, $grd.S$, and $sg.S$ by

$$
\begin{aligned}
(6) \qquad hlt.S &= wp.S.true , \\
grd.S &= \neg wp.S.false , \\
sg.S &= \neg wlp.S.false .
\end{aligned}
$$

Predicate $hlt.S$ (halt) holds in the states where S necessarily terminates. Predicate $grd.S$ (guard) holds where S need not perform a miracle. Predicate $sg.S$ (strong guard) holds in the states where S has a (nonmiraculous) terminating computation.

In the remainder of this section, we assume that all commands satisfy termination rule (2). It follows from (2) and (6) that

$$(7) \qquad grd.S = \neg hlt.S \lor sg.S .$$

This implies

$$(8) \qquad grd.S \land hlt.S = sg.S \land hlt.S .$$

The dovetail operator of [2] (see p. 929) is characterized by

$$
\begin{aligned}
(9) \qquad wlp.(S\nabla T) &= wlp.(S[\!]T) , \\
(10) \qquad hlt.(S\nabla T) &= (hlt.S \land hlt.T) \lor (grd.S \land hlt.S) \lor (grd.T \land hlt.T) .
\end{aligned}
$$

We claim that this implies

$$
\begin{aligned}
(11) \qquad wp.(S\nabla T).P = \ &(wp.S.P \land wp.T.P) \\
\lor \ &(wp.S.P \land sg.S \land wlp.T.P) \\
\lor \ &(wp.T.P \land sg.T \land wlp.S.P) .
\end{aligned}
$$

This is proved in

$$
\begin{aligned}
&wp.(S\nabla T).P \\
= \ &\{\text{termination rule (2) for } S\nabla T\} \\
&wp.(S\nabla T).true \ \land \ wlp.(S\nabla T).P \\
= \ &\{(6), (10), (8), (9)\} \\
&((hlt.S \land hlt.T) \ \lor \ (sg.S \land hlt.S) \ \lor \ (sg.T \land hlt.T)) \\
&\land \ wlp.S.P \ \land \ wlp.T.P
\end{aligned}
$$

$=$ {distribution}
$$(hlt.S \land hlt.T \land wlp.S.P \land wlp.T.P)$$
$$\lor \quad (sg.S \land hlt.S \land wlp.S.P \land wlp.T.P)$$
$$\lor \quad (sg.T \land hlt.T \land wlp.S.P \land wlp.T.P)$$
$=$ {(6) and termination rule (2) for S and T}
$$(wp.S.P \land wp.T.P)$$
$$\lor \quad (wp.S.P \land sg.S \land wlp.T.P)$$
$$\lor \quad (wp.T.P \land sg.T \land wlp.S.P) \ .$$

So the only difference between ∇ and $\triangledown$ is the difference between (1) and (11). Since (1) is simpler than (11), ∇ is simpler than $\triangledown$. We leave it to the reader to prove

$$S \| T \quad \sqsubseteq \quad S \nabla T \quad \sqsubseteq \quad S \triangledown T \ .$$

One can also prove that

$$[\, grd.S \land grd.T \land wp.(S \triangledown T).P \quad \Rightarrow \quad wp.(S \nabla T).P \,] \ .$$

In particular, if S and T are total, then $S \nabla T = S \triangledown T$. This shows that ∇ and $\triangledown$ are equal for total commands. Since formula (1) is simpler than (11), it follows that ∇ is preferable when only total commands are concerned.

Since function sg involves a negation, the operator $\triangledown$ is not monotonic with respect to refinement, i.e. in formula (5) the operator ∇ cannot be replaced by $\triangledown$. In fact, we have $?true \sqsubseteq \, ?false$, but if $abort$ is defined by

$$wp.abort.P = false \quad , \quad wlp.abort.P = true \quad \text{for all } P,$$

then one can easily verify

$$\neg \, (?true \triangledown abort \sqsubseteq \, ?false \triangledown abort) \ .$$

For us this indicates that ∇ is not only simpler than $\triangledown$ but also more useful. In the remainder of this paper, we treat both ∇ and $\triangledown$, but the only reason for including $\triangledown$ is that it does not require much additional work. We do not treat $\triangledown$ in the example, since the additional work would be substantial.

In [2], no motivation is given for the choice of $\triangledown$ instead of ∇. We have the impression that $\triangledown$ is chosen there to save implementability of Nelson's else operator $⋈$. The underlying issue is the role of the nontotal commands. Nelson's operator $⋈$ uses the nontotality of commands to determine the flow of control. We regard nontotal commands as useful in a (refinement) calculus of commands, but we would not allow them in implementable programs. We have therefore no need for the operators $⋈$ and $\triangledown$.

Remark. One of the referees considered our operator ∇ misconceived because it is hard to implement and unintuitive to reason with. Since ∇ and $\triangledown$ are equal for total commands, the difference lies in the treatment of nontotal commands. In our view, nontotal commands are hard to implement and unintuitive to reason with, and yet very useful for calculational purposes. As an example of the difference, consider the choice between $?false$ and $abort$. It is easy to verify that

$$?false \; \nabla \; abort \quad \cong \quad ?false \; ,$$
$$?false \; \nabla \; abort \quad \cong \quad abort \; ,$$

where $S \cong T$ means that S and T have the same wp and wlp. Indeed, command $?false$ "establishes" every postcondition in the sense that $wp.(?false).P = true$, but this miracle is due to $?false$, not to ∇. The simple dovetail ∇ cannot be blamed for not resolving the miracles of nontotal commands like $?false$. (End of remark)

5 The semantics of recursion

In this section we define the semantics of recursive procedures, possibly mutual, in such a way that both operators ∇ and ∇ are allowed. Note that recursive procedures with parameters can be regarded as a special case of mutual recursion.

For our present proposal there is no need to consider mutual recursion. Yet we have chosen to treat mutual recursion, since its treatment is completely standard and we have fruitfully used the same machinery in a number of other situations, cf. [6, 8, 9].

The programming language consists of commands. These are built from elementary commands by means of the operators ";" for sequential composition, "⫴" for demonic nondeterminate choice, and the new operators ∇ and ∇ (later we shall show that angelic choice can also be included). We use the following syntax for commands. Let A be a set of symbols. The elements of A are called *elementary commands*. Starting from A, we define the class Cmd of command expressions inductively by the clauses

- $A \subseteq Cmd$,
- if $S, T \in Cmd$ then $(S;T)$, $(S\|T)$, $(S\nabla T)$, and $(S\nabla T) \in Cmd$.

We give the operators "⫴", "∇", and "∇" an equal priority that is lower than ";".

The semantics of the commands will be determined by the semantic functions wlp and $wp \in Cmd \rightarrow MT$. We assume that the set of commands A is the disjoint union of two sets Smp and H, which may be infinite. The elements of Smp are called *simple commands*. We assume that functions ws and $wls \in Smp \rightarrow MT$ are given, which will serve as restrictions of wp and wlp to Smp. For definiteness, we provide at least the following simple commands: assignments $x := E$ for program variable x and expression E and guards $?B$ for predicate B.

The elements of the set H are called *procedures* or *procedure names*. Every procedure $h \in H$ is supposed to be equipped with a body **body**.$h \in Cmd$. In this way recursion is possible. For example, a repetition

$$L \;\; = \;\; \textbf{while } B \textbf{ do } S \textbf{ od}$$

is an abbreviation of a recursive procedure $L \in H$ with

$$\textbf{body}.L \;\; = \;\; (?B; S; L \,\|\, ?\neg B) \; .$$

We shall construct wp and wlp in such a way that they are functions $w \in Cmd \to MT$ that satisfy $w.h = w.(\textbf{body}.h)$ for all $h \in H$. This will be expressed by saying that w respects the declaration.

It is well known that the sets $\mathbb{P}$ of the predicates, PT of the predicate transformers, and MT of the monotonic predicate transformers, all three with the implication orders, are complete lattices. Occasionally, we use $\leq$ to denote this implication order. Recall that the well known theorem of Knaster–Tarski asserts that, for any complete lattice W, a monotonic function $D \in W \to W$ has a least fixpoint and a greatest fixpoint.

We begin with the construction of wlp, which is completely standard. Let a function $w \in Cmd \to MT$ be called a homomorphism if it satisfies, for all S, $T \in Cmd$ and all $P \in \mathbb{P}$,

(12) $\begin{aligned} w.(S;T).P &= w.S.(w.T.P)\,, \\ w.(S\|T).P &= w.S.P \wedge w.T.P\,, \\ w.(S\nabla T) &= w.(S\nabla T) = w.(S\|T)\,. \end{aligned}$

In view of (0) and (9), we want function wlp to be a homomorphism. By induction over the structure of Cmd, one can easily prove that, for every function $v \in A \to MT$, there is precisely one homomorphism $w \in Cmd \to MT$ with restriction $(w|A) = v$. This function w is called the homomorphic extension $hom.v$ of v. Moreover, the function hom is monotonic: if $u \leq v$ then $hom.u \leq hom.v$. One can prove this using induction over the structure of Cmd and monotonicity of the functions $hom.u.c \in MT$. Notice that hom is a function $(A \to MT) \to (Cmd \to MT)$.

In order to define wlp, we have to extend the given function wls to the set Cmd in such a way that it is a homomorphism that respects the declaration. For any function $x \in H \to MT$ (which gives meaning to the procedure names), we write $wls + x$ to denote the function $A \to MT$ with the restrictions wls to Smp and x to H. Now one can verify that a function $w \in Cmd \to MT$ is a homomorphism that extends wls and respects the declaration if and only if $w = hom.(wls + (w \circ \textbf{body}))$. The latter condition is equivalent to $w = D.w$ where function D is given by

$$D.w = hom.(wls + (w \circ \textbf{body}))\,.$$

Function $D \in (Cmd \to MT) \to (Cmd \to MT)$ is easily seen to be monotonic. By the theorem of Knaster–Tarski, the function D has a least fixpoint and a greatest fixpoint. Following [4, 6], we define wlp to be the greatest fixpoint of D. It follows that, indeed, wlp is a homomorphism that extends wls and respects the declaration.

Now that wlp has been constructed, we use (6) to define function sg. In view of (1) and (11), we want wp to be a "dovetail morphism", where a function $w \in Cmd \to MT$ is called a dovetail morphism if it satisfies, for all $S, T \in Cmd$ and all $P \in \mathbb{P}$,

(13) $\begin{aligned} w.(S;T).P &= w.S.(w.T.P)\,, \\ w.(S\|T).P &= w.S.P \wedge w.T.P\,, \end{aligned}$

$$w.(S \triangledown T).P = (w.S.P \wedge wlp.T.P) \quad \vee \quad (w.T.P \wedge wlp.S.P) \,,$$
$$w.(S \triangledown T).P = (w.S.P \wedge w.T.P)$$
$$\vee \quad (w.S.P \wedge sg.S \wedge wlp.T.P)$$
$$\vee \quad (w.T.P \wedge sg.T \wedge wlp.S.P) \,.$$

Again, by induction over the structure of Cmd, one can prove that, for every function $v \in A \to MT$, there is precisely one dovetail morphism $w \in Cmd \to MT$ with restriction $(w|A) = v$. This function w is called the dovetail extension $dov.v$ of v. Again, the function dov is monotonic.

In order to define wp, we have to extend the given function ws to the set Cmd in such a way that it is a dovetail morphism that respects the declaration. As before, we write $ws + x$ to denote the function $A \to MT$ with the restrictions ws to Smp and x to H. Just as before, we have that a function $w \in Cmd \to MT$ is a dovetail morphism that extends ws and respects the declaration if and only if $w = dov.(ws + (w \circ \mathbf{body}))$. The latter condition is equivalent to $w = E.w$ where function E is given by

$$E.w = dov.(ws + (w \circ \mathbf{body})) \,.$$

Again, function $E \in (Cmd \to MT) \to (Cmd \to MT)$ is easily seen to be monotonic. By the theorem of Knaster–Tarski, function E has a least fixpoint and a greatest fixpoint. Following [4, 6], we define wp to be the least fixpoint of D. Again, it follows that wp is a dovetail morphism that extends ws and respects the declaration.

Remarks. (a) In Theorem 1 of [2], the pair of wlp and wp is constructed as a least fixpoint of a certain lexicographic ordering. This corresponds to the fact that we first constructed wlp and then wp in a second step. The separation of wlp and wp makes the construction much easier.

(b) The dovetail operators respect the two fundamental healthiness laws, the universal conjunctivity of wlp and the termination rule. In fact, if we assume that $wlp.S$ is universally conjunctive for every simple command S then $wlp.S$ is universally conjunctive for every command $S \in Cmd$. If, moreover, every simple command satisfies the termination rule, then every command satisfies the termination rule. These facts can be proved easily with the methods of [6], Chapter 4.

(c) Above we treated the simple case with only binary demonic choice. It is a completely standard exercise to extend the language with both unbounded demonic choices ($\|\, i \in I :: S.i$) and unbounded angelic choices ($\Diamond\, i \in I :: S.i$), as considered in [8]. As is well known, however, the angelic choice operator leads to violation of the two healthiness laws mentioned in (b). (End of remarks)

6 Proof rules for recursive procedures

Consider a family of procedures $h.i$ with preconditions $P.i$ and postconditions $Q.i$, where i ranges over some set I. In this section, we give a rule to prove

$$[P.i \;\;\Rightarrow\;\; wp.(h.i).(Q.i)] \quad \text{for all } i.$$

Since formulae (1) and (11) also need *wlp*, we also give a similar rule for *wlp*. Both rules are minor variations of rules given in [6, 7]. They are given here to show that there is no reason for new rules and to give a formal proof of the second example in the introduction.

The rule for *wp* is as follows, cf. [7], theorem (19):

(14) **Theorem.** For every $i \in I$, let $vf.i$ be an integer valued state function. Assume that, for every integer m,

$$(\forall\, i \in I :: [\, P.i \;\wedge\; vf.i < m \;\wedge\; m \geq 0 \;\Rightarrow\; wp.(h.i).(Q.i)\,])$$
$$\Rightarrow\;\; (\forall\, i \in I :: [\, P.i \;\wedge\; vf.i = m \;\Rightarrow\; wp.(\mathbf{body}.(h.i)).(Q.i)\,])\,.$$

Then $[\, P.i \;\Rightarrow\; wp.(h.i).(Q.i)\,]$ for all i.

The proof of this theorem is based on induction over the state space by means of the variant functions $vf.i$. In [7], we gave a version where the variant function can have values in an arbitrary well-founded set.

The rule for *wlp* is called Hoare's induction rule. Instead of induction over the state space it is based on an induction over the generalizations of the semantic function *wlp*.

(15) **Theorem.** Assume that, for every homomorphism $w \in Cmd \to MT$ with $w|Smp = wls$, we have

$$(\forall\, i \in I :: [\, P.i \;\Rightarrow\; w.(h.i).(Q.i)\,])$$
$$\Rightarrow\;\; (\forall\, i \in I :: [\, P.i \;\Rightarrow\; w.(\mathbf{body}.(h.i)).(Q.i)\,])\,.$$

Then $[\, P.i \;\Rightarrow\; wlp.(h.i).(Q.i)\,]$ for all i.

The proof is analogous to the proofs given in [6], Section 4.9.

Example. We use the proof rules to analyse procedure $h1$ of the introduction. In the formal syntax, the declaration becomes

$$\mathbf{body}.h1 \;=$$
$$(?n = 0 \;[\!]\; ?n \neq 0 \,;\, (n := n + 1 \,;\, h1 \,\nabla\, n := n - 1 \,;\, h1))\,.$$

The goal is to prove $[\, wp.h1.(n = 0)\,]$: procedure $h1$ terminates in a state with $n = 0$.

We need both rules (14) and (15). In both cases, the set I is a singleton set. Therefore, the indices i can (and will) be omitted. In both cases, we use $P = true$ and $Q = (n = 0)$. Since $[\, true \Rightarrow R\,]$ is equivalent to $[R]$, the fragment "$true \Rightarrow$" will be omitted.

We begin with partial correctness. So we use theorem (15) to prove that $[\, wlp.h1.(n = 0)\,]$. For this purpose, it suffices to prove that every homomorphism w with $w|Smp = wls$ satisfies

$$(16) \qquad [\, w.h1.(n = 0)\,] \;\;\Rightarrow\;\; [\, w.(\mathbf{body}.h1).(n = 0)\,]\,.$$

Proof obligation (16) is proved by proving the consequent under assumption of the antecedent.

$$w.(\textbf{body}.h1).(n = 0)$$
$$= \quad \{\text{declaration, } w \text{ homomorphism}\}$$
$$w.(?n = 0).(n = 0)$$
$$\wedge \quad w.(?n \neq 0) . (\, w.(n := n + 1).(w.h1.(n = 0))$$
$$\wedge \, w.(n := n - 1).(w.h1.(n = 0)) \,)$$
$$= \quad \{\text{assumption: antecedent of (16)}\}$$
$$w.(?n = 0).(n = 0)$$
$$\wedge \quad w.(?n \neq 0).(w.(n := n + 1).true \, \wedge \, w.(n := n - 1).true)$$
$$= \quad \{w|Smp = wls, \text{ definitions of guards and assignments}\}$$
$$(n \neq 0 \vee n = 0) \quad \wedge \quad (n = 0 \vee (true \wedge true))$$
$$= \quad \{\text{calculus}\}$$
$$true .$$

This proves $[\, wlp.h1.(n = 0)\,]$.

We now prove $[\, wp.h1.(n = 0)\,]$. Because of termination rule (2), it suffices to prove $[\, wp.h1.true\,]$. This is done by means of theorem (14). In the course of this proof we shall use the universal conjunctivity of wlp, i.e., we shall use that $[\, wlp.S.true\,]$ holds for every command S.

In order to apply theorem (14), it suffices to provide a state function vf and to prove that, for every integer m:

(17) $\qquad [\, vf < m \ \wedge \ m \geq 0 \ \Rightarrow \ wp.h1.true\,]$
$$\Rightarrow \ [\, vf = m \ \Rightarrow \ wp.(\textbf{body}.h1).true\,] .$$

Again, we are going to prove the consequent of this proof obligation under assumption of the antecedent.

$$wp.(\textbf{body}.h1).true$$
$$= \quad \{\text{declaration, } wp \text{ dovetail morphism}\}$$
$$wp.(?n = 0).true$$
$$\wedge \quad wp.(?n \neq 0) . (wp.(n := n + 1 \, ; \, h1 \, \nabla \, n := n - 1 \, ; \, h1).true)$$
$$\Leftarrow \quad \{wp \text{ of guards}\}$$
$$n = 0 \ \vee \ wp.(n := n + 1 \, ; \, h1 \, \nabla \, n := n - 1 \, ; \, h1).true$$
$$= \quad \{wp \text{ dovetail morphism and } [\, wlp.S.true\,] \text{ for every } S\}$$
$$n = 0 \ \vee \ wp.(n := n + 1).(wp.h1.true)$$
$$\vee \ wp.(n := n - 1).(wp.h1.true)$$
$$\Leftarrow \quad \{\text{assumption: antecedent of (17)}\}$$
$$n = 0 \ \vee \ wp.(n := n + 1).(vf < m \wedge m \geq 0)$$
$$\vee \ wp.(n := n - 1).(vf < m \wedge m \geq 0) .$$

At this point we choose the variant function $vf = abs.n$. Then the latest expression becomes:

$$n = 0 \ \vee \ wp.(n := n + 1).(abs.n < m \wedge m \geq 0)$$
$$\vee \ wp.(n := n - 1).(abs.n < m \wedge m \geq 0)$$

$$= \quad \{wp \text{ of assignment}\}$$
$$n = 0 \quad \lor \quad (abs.(n+1) < m \land m \geq 0)$$
$$\lor \quad (abs.(n-1) < m \land m \geq 0)$$
$$\Leftarrow \quad \{\text{arithmetic}\}$$
$$abs.n = m \ .$$

This concludes the proof of (17), and thus of $[\,wp.h1.true\,]$. (End of example)

Remark. If we would use ∇ instead of ∇ in this example, we would have to prove $[\,sg.h1\,]$. This fact is operationally obvious, since, for every initial state, $h1$ clearly has a (nonmiraculous) terminating computation. Since $sg.h1 = \neg wlp.h1.false$, a formal proof of $[\,sg.h1\,]$ cannot be based on rule (15), but needs the necessity rule for wlp, cf. [7] theorem (31), which uses a variant function. Indeed, the complexity of ∇ (in comparison with ∇) is a handicap in every application. (End of remark)

7 Conclusions

The dovetail operator proposed by Broy and Nelson is an interesting operator that expresses demonic choice with angelic termination. The version ∇ is simpler and more useful than the version ∇ proposed originally. In particular, ∇ is monotonic with respect to refinement while ∇ is not. If wp and wlp are handled separately, the semantics of recursive procedures can be treated in a completely standard way. The proof rules for recursive procedures can easily be applied to procedures with ∇. Procedures with ∇ can also be treated but require more work.

Acknowledgements. We are indebted to one referee for the reference to [5] and for two improvements in the treatment of our final example.

References

1. R.J.R. Back, J. von Wright: Refinement calculus, Part I: Sequential Nondeterministic Programs. In: J.W. de Bakker, W.-P. de Roever, G. Rozenberg (eds.) Stepwise Refinement of Distributed Systems. Lecture Notes in Computer Science 430 (Springer, Berlin, 1990) pp. 42–66.
2. M. Broy, G. Nelson: Adding fair choice to Dijkstra's calculus. ACM Transactions on Programming Languages and Systems, **16** (1994) 924–938.
3. E.W. Dijkstra: A discipline of programming. Prentice–Hall 1976.
4. E.W. Dijkstra, C.S. Scholten: Predicate calculus and program semantics. Springer V. 1990.
5. H. Doornbos: A relational model of programs without the restriction to Egli–Milner–monotone constructs. In: E.-R. Olderog: Programming Concepts, Methods and Calculi. North-Holland, 1994, pp. 363–382.
6. W.H. Hesselink: Programs, Recursion and Unbounded Choice. Cambridge Tracts in Theoretical Computer Science 27. Cambridge University Press 1992. ISBN 0521 404363.

7. W.H. Hesselink: Proof rules for recursive procedures. Formal Aspects of Computing **5** (1993) 554–570.

8. W.H. Hesselink: Nondeterminacy and recursion via stacks and games. Theoretical Computer Science **124** (1994) 273–295.

9. W.H. Hesselink: Safety and progress of recursive procedures. Formal Aspects of Computing (to appear).

10. C.C. Morgan: Data refinement by miracles. Information Processing Letters 26 (1987/88) 243–246.

11. C. Morgan: Programming from Specifications. Prentice Hall, Englewood Cliffs, NJ, 1990.

12. C. Morgan, P.H.B. Gardiner: Data refinement by calculation. Acta Informatica **27** (1990) 481–503.

13. J.M. Morris: A theoretical basis for stepwise refinement and the programming calculus. Science of Comp. Programming **9** (1987) 287–306.

14. G. Nelson: A generalization of Dijkstra's calculus. ACM Transactions on Programming Languages and Systems, **11** (1989) 517–561.

Extracting Programs with Exceptions in an Impredicative Type System

Jean-François Monin

France Télécom CNET, LAA/EIA/EVP
Technopôle Anticipa, 2 avenue Pierre Marzin
F-22307 Lannion Cedex, France
monin@lannion.cnet.fr

Abstract. This paper is about exceptions handling using classical techniques of program extraction. We propose an impredicative formalization in the calculus of constructions and we illustrate the technique on two examples. The first one, though simple, allows us to experiment various techniques. The second one is an adaptation of a bigger algorithm previously developed in Coq by J. Rouyer, namely first order unification. Only small changes were needed in order to get a more efficient program from the original one.

1 Introduction

Several paradigms have been proposed for constructing correct programs from a formal specification. Let us sketch some among the most significant ones:

- Program calculation [6]: a program is obtained in a calculational manner as the solution of a logical assertion of the form $P \Rightarrow \text{wp}.S.Q$ where P is the precondition, Q the postcondition and S the unknown (a command).
- Specification refinement [1, 13]: for instance an abstract command involving a quantifier can sometimes be refined using a loop; another kind of refinement, *data refinement*, consists roughly of replacing abstract data structures by concrete ones[1].
- Program extraction [11, 15]: one tries to build a constructive proof of a specification $\forall x\ P(x) \rightarrow \exists y\ Q(x, y)$. Such a proof can be considered a functional program through "Curry-Howard isomorphism":

$$formula = type,$$
$$proof = program.$$

Using a suitable realizability interpretation, it is also possible to remove irrelevant (from an algorithmic point of view) parts of the proof. A general result of the related meta-theory ensures that the extracted program f satisfies its specification, i.e. $\forall x\ P(x) \rightarrow Q(x, f(x))$. Such a mechanism is implemented in Coq, a general proof assistant devoted to the *Calculus of Inductive Constructions* [7].

---

[1] Refinement has also been extensively studied in the framework of algebraic specifications.

Each approach has its strong and weak points. For instance the two first are better appropriate to imperative programming (we mean "based on state transformation"); but constructing algorithms on recursive data structures is not always easy. Conversely the third approach is well suited to functional programming and can already deal with reasonably complex programs such as a mini-ML compiler.

In both the imperative and the functional world escapements – typically goto statements and exceptions – are generally considered as difficult to handle. The problem is perhaps more important in functional programming: during the design of ML, which was originally the tactics language of LCF, exceptions were considered as an essential feature. Nowadays ML is used as a general purpose language, and it is a current practice to use exceptions: not only in exceptional situations, and not only for efficiency reasons.

Therefore we consider that dealing with exceptions in recursive programs is an important step if we want to tackle real problems. The first work in this direction to our knowledge, at least in the context of Coq, is due to Pierre Castéran [3]. Recall the main steps for developing an algorithm by program extraction in Coq:

1. State the specification, a logical formula, as a goal to be proved.
2. Prove it, typically by induction on one or several variables.
3. Ask the system to extract the algorithmic content of the proof.

Castéran showed on a simple example – multiplying the leaves of a binary tree – that stating a goal of the right form very naturally leads the user to an algorithm in continuation passing style (CPS). More specifically, instead of proving the goal $\forall t$:tree RESU(t) by induction on t, where RESU$(t) = \{n$:nat $\mid n = $ leavemult$(t)\}$ and where leavemult is the obvious function – this would be *direct style* – he considered $\forall t, t'$:tree $(\forall n'$:nat $n' = $ leavemult$(t')\rightarrow$RESU$(t))\rightarrow$RESU(t) and proved it by induction on t'; the desired RESU(t) was obtained by application of this function to t, t and $\lambda n. \lambda h. \langle n, h \rangle$ whose algorithmic content is the identity function. Moreover this proof/function was optimized in an elegant way by raising an exception as soon as a zero was detected on a leaf.

In other respects *control operators* such as Abort and Callcc have been studied in the formulae-as-type framework in the early 90's [10, 14]. It camed out that CPS transformation, which makes the interpretation of control operators possible in a purely functional setting, corresponds on the logical side to a Gödel translation. In other words, control operators are typed using *classical* theorems, hence in order to get a constructive interpretation of them we first translate them in intuitionistic logic by means of double negations[2]. As a simple example, if a has atomic type A, its translation is $\lambda k. ka$ whose type is $(A\rightarrow\perp)\rightarrow\perp$. In fact one often consider a variant where the empty type $\perp$ is replaced by the type of

---

[2] It is well known that classical logic is not constructive: the structure of the set of proofs of any theorem is made trivial by the behaviour of cut-elimination. This is discussed in depth in [9, 8].

the result of the main program, say R. The function k of type $A{\rightarrow}R$ is called a *continuation*, i.e. a function to be applied on a in order to get the final result. On the above example we could take $\text{RESU}(t)$ for R, $\text{RESU}(t')$ for A, and get an equivalent formulation.

The work of Castéran is extended in several directions in this paper. First the type of the final result is universally quantified. We need a further assumption on this type: in the simplest case it must have at least one value. We show that the gain in abstraction obtained in this way helps to nicely handle situations arising in practice, for instance when an auxilliary function is locally defined, or when an "accumulator" is used. Furthermore we gain in modularity: a function f possibly raising an exception $e{:}E$ can then be used in several contexts.

The type of the result of such a f is similar to $E \vee A$ as (impredicatively) defined in system F, i.e. $\forall X\ (E{\rightarrow}X){\rightarrow}(A{\rightarrow}X){\rightarrow}X$. This means that even if we develop a program using only propositional types, this typing is already more informative than the conventional one of, say, ML^3.

We introduce a general datatype called Nx for this kind of disjunction. Nx is equiped with a few constructors and destructors, namely Nx_unit, Nx_raise, Nx_handle and Nx_elim_Nx. Thanks to these abstract definitions it is possible to hide the CPS translation and to develop a program as in a functional language extended with exceptions. As a non trivial example it becomes possible to adapt the development of a first order unification algorithm [18] almost without modification.

Finally we consider handling several exceptions and a different Catch/Throw mechanism. An interesting remark is that the impredicativity of our typing can be very useful. Using impredicativity seems to be new in this context.

The rest if this paper is organized as follows. Section 2 is a very quick and informal introduction to the calculus of constructions with inductive definitions, as used in the Coq system. Section 3 introduces general definitions enabling the development of programs with exceptions. Section 4 illustrates their use on two examples. The first one is about computing the weight of a binary tree unless a threshold is reached. The second example is an adaptation of a bigger algorithm previously developed by other people, namely first order unification. Only small changes were needed in order to get a more efficient program from the original one. In the last section we discuss how far the Coq system suits our needs.

2 General Framework and Notations

2.1 The Calculus of Constructions

The Calculus of Constructions is a typed λ-calculus. Objects of the first level are constants like 0 or the successor function. They inhabit objects of the second

---

[3] The type of the result of f would be A, and the type of any subexpression raise e would be an undeterminate α. Here we loose the fact that in the body of f an exception carrying a value of type E can be raised.

level, which are propositions seen as set of proofs, themselves of type Prop. Typed abstraction is denoted by $\lambda x^A B$ or [x:A]B. Application is denoted $(A\ B)$. Products are denoted by $\forall x{:}A\ B$ or (x:A)B; when B does not depend on A, the simpler notation $A{\to}B$ is generally used. Application associates to the left and arrow to the right. The reader is refered to [4, 2] for a detailed presentation.

Examples. The type of natural numbers can be represented in system F style by nat $= \forall X{:}\text{Prop}\ X{\to}(X{\to}X){\to}X$. The constant 0 of type nat is $0 = \lambda X^{\text{Prop}} \lambda x^X \lambda f^{X\to X}\ x$; nat is itself of type Prop. Predicates on natural numbers, are objects of type nat$\to$Prop. Logical operations such as $\vee$ are of type Prop$\to$Prop$\to$Prop.

For program extraction purposes Coq distinguishes in fact two sorts of props: Prop and Set. Only data and functions of sort Set are kept by program extraction. Objects of sort Prop are used to handle logical information on data and functions during program construction. For example, in the definition of nat above we would use Set instead of Prop.

Finally, for theoretical and practical reasons, the system allows the user to define *inductive definitions* in a secure way. The simpler ones correspond to concrete data types of ML. For example the definition of nat actually used is

```
Inductive nat : Set :=
   0 : nat  |  S : nat→nat.
```

Predicates and n-ary relations can also be inductively defined à la Prolog, for instance :

```
Inductive even : nat→Prop :=
   ev0 : (even 0)  |  evSS : (n:nat)(even n)→(even (S (S n))).
```

It is then possible to define the type of even numbers as

```
Inductive even_nat : Set :=
   en_intro : (n:nat)(even n)→even_nat.
```

Such a type can also be defined using $\{x{:}A \mid (P\ x)\}$ which is a general purpose inductive type for the set of ordered pairs $\langle x,p \rangle$ where p is a proof of $(P\ x)$. During program extraction p is removed and this type becomes just A.

Each inductively defined type is automatically equiped with a general elimination principle enabling inductive reasoning and the definition of primitive recursive functions. Further information on inductive definitions and their use in Coq can be found in [5, 16, 17].

2.2 Impredicativity

A definition of some object p is said to be *impredicative* when it involves a quantification over objects including p. A type system is impredicative when impredicative definition of types are allowed.

For instance the first definition of nat given above is impredicative because it is of the form nat $= \forall X{:}\text{Prop} \cdots$ and nat is of type Prop.

Impredicative type systems are very powerful. It is possible in system F to define many data structures like polymorphic lists, binary trees, and other mathematical objects like infinitely branching trees, streams and ordinal numbers. It is also possible, using only (higher order) primitive recursion, to define much more functions than in simple type systems.

Impredicative definitions are potentially dangerous, because they involve a kind of circularity. It is then an important and non trivial matter to ensure that an impredicative type system remains consistent, i.e. that it does not leave room for a logical paradox such as Russel's paradox. This is shown in [9] for system F and in [4] for the calculus of constructions

2.3 Sections in Coq

The calculus of inductive constructions is supported by a proof assistant named *Coq* [7]. In Coq proofs/functions can be developed in an incremental way using commands that transform the proof tree.

It is also possible in Coq to declare a common environment for several definitions using *sections*. For instance if we want to define several functions having some natural n as parameter, it is possible to declare n only once at the beginning of a section :

```
Section nat_functions.
  Variable n : nat.
  Definition dbl : nat := (plus n n).
  Definition square : nat := (mult n n).
  Definition pol1 : nat→nat→nat := [a,b:nat](plus (mult a n) b).
  Definition quad : nat := (plus dbl dbl).
End nat_functions.
```

After the end of this section the definition of `dbl` is actually `[n:nat](plus n n)`. The definition of `quad` becomes `[n:nat](plus (dbl n) (dbl n))`.

However this mechanism is not completely satisfactory if we want `dbl` to be just an intermediate definition for `quad`: we would prefer to get something like `[n:nat](let dbl=(plus n n) in (plus dbl dbl))`. In the following we suppose that this effect is obtained by using a *local* definition in the section :

```
Section nat_functions.
  Variable n : nat.
  Local dbl : nat= (plus n n).
  ...
End nat_functions.
```

This is not so far from the actual behavior of Coq, where these local definitions get expanded, at the price of potential replication of code.

In the general case common types, hypotheses, functions (like X, P and e below), are shared by several functions. Moreover P and e could depend on parameters. We would then use something similar to the functors of SML-NJ, i.e. modules parameterized by types and functions offering an interface consisting of several functions, while common auxilliary functions are hidden.

3 Continuations and Exceptions

When we develop a function f in continuation passing style, one always supposes that f is directly or indirectly called by some "main function" $\mathcal{M}$. Let X be the type of the result of $\mathcal{M}$.

If the "normal" type of the result of f is A, that is, if the type of the result of f is A when we express f in direct style, this type becomes $(A{\rightarrow}X){\rightarrow}X$ in continuation passing style. $A{\rightarrow}X$ is the type of the normal continuation.

In a first attempt for introducing an exception we can assume another continuation $e{:}B{\rightarrow}X$, where B is the type of the value carried by the exception. The type of the result becomes $(B{\rightarrow}X){\rightarrow}(A{\rightarrow}X){\rightarrow}X$, which is just an instance of the encoding of $B + A$ in system F: X is arbitrarily fixed instead of beeing universally quantified. Now there is no good reason to consider that the meaning of f should be tied to $\mathcal{M}$, since the same f could be used in completely different environments. Hence at some stage X will be an argument of f, i.e. will be universally quantified in the type of f. However if f has an argument using X we still cannot get exactly $B + A$.

In other respects we sometimes want several functions, say f and h, to share a common X and e. If f calls h, we prefer X and e not to be passed as parameters from f to h. A way to get this behaviour is to use the section mechanism of Coq and to declare X and e at the beginning of a section (however see the discussion above on this mechanism).

3.1 Simple Exceptions

Let us first consider the special case where e carries no value, i.e. $e{:}X$. (By the way it is enough for the first order unification algorithm studied below.) Even in this case an exception is raised for some reason, it implicitly carries some logical information. Let P be the weakest condition for raising the exception. We give e the type $P{\rightarrow}X$. Assuming e amounts to suppose that X is not empty if P is provable.

It is then possible to take $(C{\rightarrow}P){\rightarrow}(A{\rightarrow}X){\rightarrow}X$, where C is of kind Prop, as type of the result of f. In short the normal result of such a f has type A, but f may raise an exception if condition C is established. In this way anything about exceptions – excepted e itself – will be removed by program extraction. We call the whole type $(Nx\ C\ A)$, and use the infix notation C V+ A:

Section algo.
Variable X:Set.   Variable P:Prop.   Variable e:P→X.
Local Nx := [C:Prop][A:Set](C→P)→(A→X)→X.

Values of type C V+ A are constructed from either a value of type A or a proof of C:

Local Nx_unit : (C:Prop)(A:Set)A→(C V+ A) :=
   [C:Prop][A:Set][a:A] [i:C→P][k:A→X](k a).

Local Nx_raise : (C:Prop)(A:Set)C→(C V+ A) :=
   [C:Prop][A:Set][c:C] [i:C→P][k:A→X](e (i c)).

In the following we use the abbreviations[4] **Nxunit** v and **Nxraise** respectively for **Apply Nx_unit; Apply** v and **Apply Nx_raise.**

It is also possible to get an inhabitant of C' V+ A' from (i) an inhabitant of C V+ A, (ii) a function that yields an C' V+ A' from an A and (iii) a proof of C→C':

```
Local Nx_elim_Nx :
  (A,A':Set)(C,C':Prop)(A→(C' V+ A'))→(C→C')→(C V+ A)→(C' V+ A') :=
  [A,A':Set][C,C':Prop]
    [f:A→ C' V+ A'][j:C→C']
      [nx: C V+ A]
        [i:C'→P][k:A'→X](nx ([c:C](i (j c))) ([a:A](f a i k))).
```

Nx_elim_Nx is used when, at the direct style level, we call some function f yielding a useful value a of type **A** and we don't want to catch an exception possibly raised by f. Technically, when v:C V+ A is available, we use the tactic **Apply Nx_elim_Nx with** 3:=v (under the abbreviated form **Nxelim** v). This yields two subgoals corresponding respectively to **f** and **j** above. The second subgoal is purely logical and we generally manage to automatically discharge it using auxilliary lemmas. The first subgoal is handled by an introduction of a of type **A**, yielding the original goal (**Nx C' A'**). This is expressed at the direct style level by **let** $a=v$ **in** ...

Finally we need a connection between functions f developed in this section and external world (the "main" function $\mathcal{M}$ – actually any function calling f and catching the exception). **Nx_handle** builds a value of type X from a proposition P, an exceptional continuation e, a function whose result has type $(Nx\ X\ P\ e\ C\ A)$, a proof of $C{\to}P$ and a normal continuation of type $A{\to}X$.

```
Definition Nx_handle : (C:Prop)(A:Set)(Nx C A)→(C→P)→(A→X)→X :=
  [C:Prop][A:Set][nx:(Nx C A)]nx.
```

3.2 Dealing with several Exceptions Carrying a Value

In practice one needs to simultaneously handle several exceptions. Moreover they can carry a value, for instance a string to be printed. This is dealt with using a base type **Txlev** and a type **Txval** depending on **Txlev**. Intuitively, **Txlev** is the type of names of exceptions, and the type of values carried by an exception l, where l inhabits **Txlev**, is (Txval l). Possible definitions of **Txlev** and **Txval** are discussed in appendix A. We provide an exceptional continuation for each member of **Txlev**.

```
Section algo.
Variable X:Set.
Local Propx:=(l:Txlev)(Txval l)→Prop.
Variable P:Propx.
Variable e:(l:Txlev)(x:(Txval l))(P l x)→X.
```

The remaining definitions are straightforward generalisations of the ones given above, for instance:

---

[4] In Coq V5.10 user-defined notations and abbreviations are available.

```
Local Nx :=
  [C:Propx][A:Set]((1:Txlev)(x:(Txval 1))(C 1 x)→(P 1 x))→(A→X)→X.
```

```
Local Nx_elim_Nx :
  (A,A':Set)(C,C':Propx)
  (A→(C' V+ A'))→((1:Txlev)(x:(Txval 1))(C 1 x)→(C' 1 x))→
    (C V+ A)→(C' V+ A') :=
[A,A':Set][C,C':Propx]
  [f:A→(C' V+ A')]
    [j:(1:Txlev)(x:(Txval 1))(C 1 x)→(C' 1 x)]
      [nx:(C V+ A)]
        [i:(1:Txlev)(x:(Txval 1))(C' 1 x)→(P 1 x)][k:A'→X]
        (nx ([1:Txlev][x:(Txval 1)][c:(C 1 x)](i 1 x (j 1 x c)))
        ([a:A](f a i k))).
```

The second subgoal mentioned in the discussion about Nx_elim_Nx in 3.1 is here dealt with by case analysis on 1. That is, instead of just **Auto** we use a pattern like: **Intro 1; Elim 1; Simpl; Intros x Hx; ... Auto.**

3.3 Using Impredicativity

Suppose we are in the following common situation.

- The function $\mathcal{M}$ calls a function f which itself calls h.
- Both f and h use exceptions build upon a common pair ⟨Txlev, Txval⟩.
- But the exception systems e given to f and h are different. This typically arises when f filters some exceptions raised by h.

This leads to develop f and h in separate sections. Outside of its defining section h has type $\forall X \,\forall P\, (\forall l\, \forall x\, (P\, l\, x) \to X)(Nx\, X\, P\, D\, B)$ for some D and B. Inside the defining section of f the instance of Nx currently used is locally renamed as Nx_f. The type of f is then $(Nx_f\, C\, A)$ and a call to h in the body of f is represented by a call to **Nx_handle** with h as nx, and $(Nx_f\, C'\, A')$ as X, where $(Nx_f\, C'\, A')$ is the current subgoal.

Now if we examine the types involved in f after the end of the defining section of f, we see that $Nx = \forall X \ldots$ is sometimes used with $X = Nx$.

If we accept to loose the abstraction level provided by the primitives like **Nx_raise**, i.e. if we program directly at the level of continuations impredicativity is no longer needed. The example of 4.1 was earlier developed in this way. There are already similar phenomena with the representation of data structures in system F. For instance boolean negation can be encoded by $\lambda b^{\text{bool}} (b\ \textbf{bool}\ \textbf{f}\ \textbf{t})$, using impredicativity and the "primitive" constants **f** and **t**, or by $\lambda b^{\text{bool}} \lambda X \lambda x^X \lambda y^X\ (b\ X\ y\ x)$ in a simple typing-like fashion.

4 Two Case Studies

4.1 Computing the Weight of a Tree

Version with one Exception. In this example we want to compute a boolean which is **true** if the sum of the leaves of a binary tree is greater than or equal to a given threshold m, and false otherwise. These trees are built using leaf and node:

```
Inductive tree : Set :=
    leaf : nat→tree   |   node : tree→tree→tree.
```

We aim at the following algorithm, which travels the tree t from right to left while accumulating in a the sum of the encountered leaves; as soon as a exceeds m we know that the answer is true; if no exception has been raised the answer is false[5]. Notice that the result r is not compared to m – it is even not used at all. Therefore we must ensure that in the case where the answer is true an exception does have to be raised[6].

```
Function core (m:nat;t:tree):nat =
    letrec comprec(t:tree;a:nat):nat =
        match t with
            leaf(n) → (g a+n)
        | node(t1,t2) →
            let an2=(comprec t2 a) in let an=(comprec t1 an2) in an
    in (comprec t 0)
    where g (n:nat):nat =
        if n≤m then n else raise threshold.

Function F_overweight (m:nat;t:tree):bool =
    try let r = (core m t) in false
    with threshold→true.
```

The first thing to do is to state the specification of the final result.

Definition P_overweight := [m:nat][t:tree](le m (leaveplus t)).
Definition RESU :=
    [m:nat][t:tree]{(P_overweight m t)}+{¬(P_overweight m t)}.

$\{P\} + \{Q\}$ denotes a enumerated type with two values; the first (resp. second) value can be built if P (resp. Q) is provable. When $Q = \neg P$, $\{P\} + \{Q\}$ denotes the truth value of P.

For the development of the algorithm we need a more general form of P_overweight which takes an accumulator into account.

Definition P_overweight_accu :=
    [m,a:nat][t:tree](le m (plus a (leaveplus t))).

The result of core is *exception* if (leaveplus t) exceeds m and (leaveplus t) otherwise. We also want that if the function actually computes (leaveplus t) then this value does not exceed m. The internal function comprec has a similar specification taking the accumulator into account, hence we introduce:

---

[5] A first version of this development, without accumulator, came from [12]. Two calls to g were then needed, one for leaf and one for node. In the present version there is no real reason to keep g, except for showing how such a local function can be dealt with.

[6] This constraint is stronger than the one considered in the example of Castéran.

Inductive condsum_accu [m,a:nat;t:tree] : Set :=
  condsum_accu_intro : (n:nat)(n=(plus a (leaveplus t)))→
                       ¬(le m n)→(condsum_accu m a t).

Definition condsum_accu_cps :=
  [m,a:nat][t:tree] (P_overweight_accu m a t) V+ (condsum_accu m a t).

The specification of (g m n) is quite naturally (le m n) V+ (T_aux m n) where
T_aux is defined by:

Local T_aux := [m,n:nat]{n':nat|n=n'&¬(le m n')}.

The proof/function of **core** has exactly the same structure as the definition given
above, see appendix B. One proves the theorem:

Theorem core : (m:nat)(t:tree)(condsum_accu_cps m 0 t).

Finally the function F_overweight is specified by (m:nat)(t:tree)(RESU m
t) and is easily obtained using **Nx_handle** and **core**. In this process X is in-
stanciated to (RESU m t) and we prove (condsum_accu m 0 t)→(RESU m t)
and (P_overweight_accu m 0 t)→(RESU m t) using respectively the witnesses
false and **true**.

Version with Two Exceptions. The problem can be slightly complicated as
follows: *given a list l of trees and an integer* m, *compute a list of booleans such
that each boolean indicates whether the weight of the corresponding tree exceeds*
m, *but abort the whole execution if a zero is detected on one of the leaves of the
trees of* l.
  This leads to introduce two exception levels, **xl1** and **xl2**. The first carries
no value, the second carries a boolean (other choices are possible). Here is a way
for specifying this:

Inductive Txlev : Set := xl1 : Txlev | xl2 : Txlev.
Inductive Txval : Txlev → Set :=
  xv1 : (Txval xl1) | xv2 : bool→(Txval xl2).

We need to specify assertions about exceptions. The following definition of
(prop_exc Pz Pw) indicates that if **xl1** has been raised then **Pz** is provable,
and if **xl2** has been raised then the carried boolean cannot be **false** and **Pw** is
provable.

Definition prop_exc: (Pz,Pw:Prop)Propx.
  Unfold Propx; Intros Pz Pw l.
  Case 1.
    Intro zer; Exact Pz.   (*first kind of exception*)
    Intro b;   (*second kind of exception*)
      Exact (b=(xv2 true)→Pw) ∧ (b=(xv2 false)→False).
Defined.

In the specification of **core** we just replace P_w = (P_overweight_accu m a t)
by (prop_exc (Pposs_zer t) P_w).

Definition condsum2_accu_cps :=
  [m,a:nat][t:tree]
    (prop_exc (Pposs_zer t) (P_overweight_accu m a t)) V+
    (condsum_accu m a t).

The specification of **g** says that the first kind of exception cannot be raised.

(n:nat) (prop_exc False (le m n)) V+ (T_aux m n).

The function working on a list of trees is developed using similar techniques. This function calls **core** via **Nx_handle** using the impredicativity of **Nx** as described in 3.3.

4.2 First Order Unification

Attempting to unify two terms T and U roughly consists in a double induction over T and U taking care of propagation of substitutions. The result is either a most general unifier, in case of success, or an answer "T an U are not unifiable", i.e. a failure. The obvious choice for the type of the result is a sum like <mgu>+<failure>. In his original development [18] J. Rouyer chose:

Inductive Unification[t1,t2:quasiterm]:Set :=
  Unif_succeed:(f:quasisubst)(unif t1 t2)→
      further conditions for f to be an mgu
      →(Unification t1 t2)
  | Unif_fail:(∀f:quasisubst ¬(Subst f t1)=(Subst f t2))
      →(Unification t1 t2).

In the original development this type is also the type of the result of the function corresponding to the double induction, hence a failure is transmitted backwards step by step until the root.

With the definitions given above we can construct an algorithm that just tries to compute the mgu. As soon as an incompatibility is detected, e.g. between two constants, an exception is raised: this is the expected behavior of a real implementation.

We proceed from the original development as follows.

– Split the initial definition of Unification in two parts, Unification_s of kind Set and Unification_f of kind Prop:

  Inductive Unification_s[t1,t2:quasiterm]:Set :=
    Unif_succeed_def:(f:quasisubst)(unif t1 t2)→
        further conditions for f to be an mgu
        →(Unification_s t1 t2).
  Inductive Unification_f[t1,t2:quasiterm]:Prop :=
    Unif_fail_def:(∀f:quasisubst ¬(Subst f t1)=(Subst f t2))
        →(Unification_f t1 t2).

– ¿From Unification_s and Unification_f inductively define Unification_or_fail which is equivalent to the original definition of Unification (two obvious clauses).

- Redefine `Unification` with `Nx`:

  Definition `Unification` :=
      `[t1,t2:quasiterm] (Unification_f t1 t2) V+ (Unification_s t1 t2)`.

  Redefine `Unif_succeed` and `Unif_fail` using respectively `Nx_unit` and
  `Nx_raise`. Define `Unif_elim` with `Nx_elim_Nx`. The latter plays the rôle of
  `Unification_rec` although it is less general, see below.
- Adapt the script of the original development.

It turns out that the last step requires very few modifications, and that they
are systematic. They split into two classes.

1. Replacing **Elim** H by <u>Unifelim</u> H (an abbreviation for **Apply** `Unif_elim`
   with `3:=`H) when H has type (`Unification` t u). In this development the
   current subgoal is always of type (`Unification` t' u'), and this fits well the
   restriction on the use of `Unif_elim` mentioned above. Otherwise we should
   have used the more primitive `Nx_elim_Nx`.
2. Sometimes the current subgoal becomes (`Unification_f` t u) instead of
   (`Unification` t u).
   It is then necessary to replace `Unif_fail` by `Unif_fail_def`. Similarly the
   type of the result of two lemmas must be changed to (`Unification_f` t u).

There are 7 modifications of the first kind, and 3+2 of the second kind. About
100 lines have been added for the new definitions of `Unification`, `Unif_succeed`,
`Unif_fail` and `Unif_elim`. The original development takes about 2.800 lines.
This can be compared to the modifications needed for the same transformation
if the algorithm was expressed in a usual programming language: each statement
returning the value *failure* would be systematically replaced by a statement
raising an exception.

5 Concluding Remarks

We have shown that it is possible to add – or to simulate the addition of – control
operators to the programming language of extracted programs in the framework
of calculus of constructions. All the examples mentioned in this paper have been
completely and mechanically verified.

Writing a lambda-term using the introduced primitives is not to be recom-
mended, because explicit typing makes the terms quite heavy. However the tactics language of Coq can be seen as a programming language, via Curry-Howard
isomorphism. For instance **Intro a**; **Exact E** is just a peculiar syntax of $\lambda a. E$.

In this language types are most of the time inferred. This is an advantage
when using constructs with long types, like `Nx_xxx`. In other respects scripts can
be fully understood only when interactively input in the system.

Note that thanks to the tactic **Realizer** recently introduced in Coq one can
give the algorithmic structure of a proof using a more conventional syntax called
Real. Further work is needed to see how this tactic can be combined with our
primitives. Another approach would be to internalize these primitives in *Real*.

347

Acknowledgement

I wish to thank the members of the Coq Project, for their help on Coq, and Pierre Crégut and Chet Murthy for their explanations on continuations. Pierre Lescanne suggested the example of first order unification.

References

1. J-R. Abrial. The B-Book. Prentice Hall, 1994 (in preparation).
2. H.P. Barendregt. Lambda Calculi with Types. In S. Abramsky & al., editors, Handbook of Logic in Computer Science, vol 2, S. Abramsky & al. Eds. Clarendon Press, Oxford, 1992.
3. P. Castéran. Pro[gramm,v]ing with continuations: A development in Coq. Coq contribution, 1993 (available by FTP on ftp.inria.fr).
4. Th. Coquand and G. Huet. The calculus of constructions. Information and Computation, 76:95–120, 1988.
5. Th. Coquand and C. Paulin-Mohring. Inductively defined types. In P. Martin-Löf and G. Mints, editors, Proceedings of Colog'88. Springer Verlag, 1990. LNCS 417.
6. E.W. Dijkstra. A Discipline of Programming. Prentice-Hall, 1976.
7. G. Dowek & al. The Coq Proof Assistant User's Guide. version 5.8, INRIA-Rocquencourt et CNRS-ENS Lyon, fév. 1993.
8. J-Y. Girard. A new constructive logic: classical logic. Mathematical Structures in Computer Science, vol 1, pp. 225–296, 1991.
9. J-Y. Girard, Y. Lafont, P. Taylor. Proofs and Types. Cambridge Univ. Press, vol 7, 1990.
10. T. Griffin. A formulae-as-types notion of control. POPL, Orlando, 1990.
11. S. Hayashi, H. Nakano. PX, a Computational Logic. Foudations of Computing, MIT Press, 1988.
12. J.L. Lawall and O. Danvy. Separating Stages in Continuation-Passing Style Transformation. POPL, 1993.
13. C. Morgan. Programming form Specification. Prentice Hall International Series in Computer Science. Prentice Hall, 1990.
14. C. Murthy. An evaluation semantics for classical proofs. LICS, Amsterdam, 1991.
15. C. Paulin-Mohring. Extraction de programmes dans le calcul des constructions. thèse de doctorat de l'université Paris VII, 1989.
16. C. Paulin-Mohring. Inductive Definitions in the system Coq; Rules and Properties. In M. Bezem and J.F. Groote, editors, Proceedings of TLCA'93. Springer Verlag, 1993. LNCS 664.
17. C. Paulin-Mohring and B. Werner. Synthesis of ML Programs in the system Coq. *Journal of Symbolic Computation*, 15:607–640, 1993.
18. J. Rouyer. Développement de l'algorithme d'unification dans le calcul des constructions avec types inductifs. Research Report 1795, INRIA-Lorraine, nov. 1992.

A   Dependent Types for Exceptions

The base type Txlev for exceptions is generally a simple enumeration. It is unfortunately impossible in the calculus of constructions to define Txval: Txlev→Set by elimination on the argument. However we can obtain an isomorphic structure using an inductive definition. For instance in the example above we consider two exceptions xl1, which carries nothing, and xl2 which carries a boolean. Let us suppose here that xl1 and xl2 carry respectively a value of type A and B.

```
Inductive Txlev : Set :=  xl1 : Txlev  |   xl2 : Txlev.
Inductive Txval : Txlev→Set :=
     xv1 : A→(Txval xl1)  |  xv2 : B→(Txval xl2).
```

It is useful and easy (in goal mode) to define left inverses xl1_A and xl2_B of xv1_B and xv2_B (we consider only the latter in the sequel), at least when B is not empty. But this assumption gives a special rôle to a specific inhabitant of B. This can be avoided using an auxilliary function defined on (Txval l) with l=xl2

```
Definition xl2_B_eq : (l:Txlev)(Txval l) → l=xl2 →B.
   Destruct l; Intros v e; Discr e Orelse Exact v.
Defined.
Definition xl2_B : (Txval xl2)→B.
   Intro v2; Apply (xl2_B_eq xl2 v2); Auto.
Defined.
```

It is also useful to prove that xl2_B is really a left inverse.

```
Theorem left_inv_xv2 : ∀v:(Txval xl2) v=(xv2 (xl2_B v)).
```

A method is to define a conversion function

```
Definition l_xl2 : ∀l:Txlev (l=xl2)→(Txval l)→(Txval xl2).
```

by induction on l, and to prove

```
∀l:Txlev ∀v:(Txval l) ∀e:l=xl2 (l_xl2 l e v)=(xv2 (xl2_B (l_xl2 l e v))).
```

We get the desired theorem by using (l_xl2 xl2 e v)=v. As an interesting consequence, we get the induction principle :

```
Theorem xv2_rec :
   ∀P:(Txval xl2)→Set (∀b:B (P (xv2 b)))→ ∀v:(Txval xl2) (P v).
```

Reciprocally left_inv_xv2 is a special case of xv2_rec. Christine Paulin pointed out that theorems like xv2_rec have an independent proof to me. The trick is to define an alter ego of (eq_rec Txlev).

```
Definition eqTxlev_rec :
   ∀P:Txlev→Set ∀k,l:Txlev (eqTxlev k l)→(P k)→(P l).
   Destruct k; Destruct l; Simpl; Intros; Trivial Orelse Contradiction.
Defined.
```

where (eqTxlev) is a typical auxilliary function used in "inversion lemmas":

```
Definition eqTxlev : Txlev→Txlev→Prop :=
   xl1 xl1 => True  |  xl1 xl2 => False  |
   xl2 xl1 => False  |  xl2 xl2 => True.
Defined.
```

Of course dependent types like Txval are needed in other situations, such as the modelling of records.

B Constructive Proof of core

B.1 Coq Script

In the following script, Split_condsum n H1 H2 is an abbreviation for **Intro** s; **Elim** s; **Clear** s; **Intros** n H1 H2. Hence NxElim R; [Split_condsum an1 Han1t1 Hman1 | **Auto**] means that we compute R of type P V+ (consum_accu ...), and in case of success we decompose the result into an integer n and two hypotheses H1, H2 on n.

Section algo.

Variable X:Set.   Variable P:Prop.   Variable e:P→X.
Local Nx := [C:Prop][A:Set](C→P)→(A→X)→X.

Local Nx_unit : (C:Prop)(A:Set)A→(C V+ A).
. . .

Theorem core : (m:nat)(t:tree)(condsum_accu_cps m 0 t).
Intros m t.
Cut (n:nat)(le m n) V+ (T_aux m n).
  Intro g.
  Cut (a:nat)(condsum_accu_cps m a t);
      [Intro comprec; **Apply** comprec | **Idtac**].

  (* definition of comprec *)
  Unfold condsum_accu_cps; **Elim** t.
    Intros n a.
    Nxelim (g (plus a n)); [Intro sn'; Nxunit Realizer sn' | **Auto**].

    Intros t1 R1 t2 R2 a.
    NxElim (R1 a);   [Split_condsum an1 Han1t1 Hman1 | **Auto**].
    NxElim (R2 an1); [Split_condsum an Hant2 Hmn | **Rewrite** Han1t1; **Auto**].
  NxUnit Realizer an.
  Rewrite Hant2; **Rewrite** Han1t1; **Rewrite** plus_assoc_r; **Simpl**; **Auto**.

  (* definition of g *)
  Intro n; **Case** (le_dec m n).
    Intro Hlemn; Nxraise; **Assumption**.
    Intro Nlemn; Nxunit Realizer n.
Save.

End algo.

The proof is almost the same in the case with two exceptions. Nxraise must be used with an argument, for instance in the definition of g:

   Intro Hlemn; Nxraise (xv2 true); **Simpl**; **Auto**.

A few tactics must be added in order to automatically discharge the propositional subgoal of Nx_elim_Nx, by case on 1, for instance concerning (R2 a):

Nxelim (R1 a);
      [Split_condsum an1 Han1t1 Hman1 |
       Intro 1; Elim 1; Simpl; Intros v Hv; Elim Hv; Auto].

B.2 Extracted program

The program obtained with extract and conversion to Caml code, in Coq V5.8, is as follows (plus is expanded in the actual code):

```
let plus = fun n -> fun m ->
  let rec REC1 = function 0_C -> m | S_C VAR3 -> S_C ((REC1 VAR3)) in
  REC1 n;;
```

```
(* core : 'a -> nat -> tree -> (nat -> 'a) -> 'a *)
let core = fun e -> fun m -> fun t ->
  let rec REC1' = function
    leaf_C VAR3 ->
      (fun a -> fun k ->
        match le_dec m (plus VAR3 a) with
          true_C -> e
        | false_C -> k (plus VAR3 a))
  | node_C(VAR4,VAR5) ->
      (fun a -> fun k ->
        REC1' VAR4 a (fun a' -> REC1' VAR5 a' (fun a' -> k a')))
  in REC1' t (0_C);;
```

Replacing nat by int, plus by + and renaming bound variables gives :

```
type itree = ileaf_C of int | inode_C of itree * itree;;
```

```
let core e m t =
  let rec COMPREC = function
    ileaf_C n ->
      (fun a -> fun k ->  if m < n+a then e else k (n+a))
  | inode_C(t1,t2) ->
      (fun a -> fun k ->
        COMPREC t1 a (fun a' -> COMPREC t2 a' (fun a' -> k a')))
  in COMPREC t 0;;
```

We recognise the CPS translation of the intended function where g has been unfolded.

Synthesizing proofs from programs
in the Calculus of Inductive Constructions

Catherine Parent *

LIP, URA CNRS 1398, ENS Lyon
46 Allée d'Italie, 69364 Lyon cedex 07, France
e-mail : parent@lip.ens-lyon.fr

Abstract. We want to prove "automatically" that a program is correct
with respect to a set of given properties that is a specification. Proofs of
specifications contain logical parts and computational parts. Programs
can be seen as computational parts of proofs. They can then be extracted
from proofs and be certified to be correct. We focus on the inverse problem : is it possible to reconstruct proof obligations from a program and
its specification ? The framework is the type theory where a proof can
be represented as a typed λ-term [Con86, NPS90] and particularly the
Calculus of Inductive Constructions [Coq85]. A notion of coherence is introduced between a specification and a program containing annotations
as in the Hoare sense. This notion is based on the definition of an extraction function called the weak extraction. Such an annotated program can
give a method to reconstruct a set of proof obligations needed to have a
proof of the initial specification. This can be seen either as a method of
proving programs or as a method of synthetically describing proofs.

1 Introduction

This paper talks about proving correctness of functional programs and, in particular, how to prove "automatically" that a program is correct with respect to
a set of given properties that is a specification.

As an example, the specification of a division algorithm can then be expressed
by the logical formula $\forall a, b.(b > 0) \rightarrow \exists q, r.(a = b*q+r) \wedge (b > r)$. A constructive
proof of this specification describes a method that transforms a, b and a proof
of $b > 0$ into two objects q, r and a proof of $(a = b * q + r) \wedge (b > r)$. In such a
proof, two parts can be distinguished : a computational part (how to construct
q and r from a and b) and a logical part (why $a = b * q + r$ is true knowing
$b > 0$). The proof follows an induction scheme on a. The computational part of
the proof corresponds to the case analysis on a and to the construction of q and
r from a and b in the two cases, by recursion on $a - 1$ if it is not equal to 0. The
logical part of the proof corresponds to the justification that $a = b * q + r$ is true
in the two cases.

---

* This research was partly supported by ESPRIT Basic Research Action "Types for
Proofs and Programs" and by Programme de Recherche Coordonnées and CNRS
Groupement de Recherche "Programmation".

A proof then represents a functional program which validates the specification. However, in general, to have more efficient programs, all the logical parts of a term are suppressed. This is the principle of an extraction function [PM89b, PM89a] that suppresses some parts of proofs and that we call the strong extraction.

An extraction function forgets all the non-computational parts of a proof to give a program. Different proofs can then correspond to different programs. Indeed, there can be many different proofs for a specification of a sorting algorithm. Each different proof can give a different algorithm for sorting a list.

It is also important to note that an extracted program is a skeleton of its corresponding proof. For the example of the division, the ML program that could be extracted is :

```
let rec div a b = match a with
           0    -> (0,0)
         | n+1 -> let (q,r) = div n b in
                       if b<=(r+1) then (q+1,0)
                                   else (q,r+1) ;;
```

In this paper, we focus on the inverse problem. Given a specification and a description of an algorithm that solves the problem, is it possible to generate proofs obligations that allow to reconstruct the proof of the specification ? This approach has two applications : proof of functional programs and proofs description.

We choose a framework where proofs are seen as programs. This is the Curry-Howard isomorphism [How80]. Each proof is a priori seen as a program. Nevertheless, some propositions can be distinguished if their proofs are not interpreted as computational ones. Then, a program can be extracted from a proof.

The reconstruction of a proof from a program is then particularly natural. Control structures in the program naturally correspond to proofs methods (recursion corresponds to induction, pattern matching to case analysis ...). Reconstructing proof obligations then corresponds to retrieve more or less a weakest precondition (in the Hoare sense) and, so, subspecifications for subparts of the program. In the division example, the following can be found :

```
let rec div a b =
match a with
    0    -> { (0 = b * 0 + 0) ∧ (b > 0) }
            (0,0)
  | n+1 -> { ∃q, r(n = b * q + r) ∧ (b > r) → ∃q, r(n + 1 = b * q + r) ∧ (b > r) }
           let (q,r) = div n b in
                { (n + 1 = b * q + r) ∧ (b > r) }
                if b<=(r+1)
                then { (n + 1 = b * (q + 1) + 0) ∧ (b > 0) }
                     (q+1,0)
                else { (n + 1 = b * q + r + 1) ∧ (b > r + 1) }
                     (q,r+1);;
```

We choose a particular framework that is the Calculus of Inductive Constructions [Coq85, PM89b] which is a typed λ-calculus with polymorphism, higher-order and dependent types. We focus on the *Coq* [DFH+93, CCF+94] system which is an implementation of this calculus. It is a system for formalizing and checking the mathematical reasoning [Bar91, ML84]. It contains a specification language and a programming language. By the Curry-Howard isomorphism , a proof can be represented by a typed λ-term whose type is the proposition that it proves. In the Calculus of Inductive Constructions, the specification of a program is regarded as a proposition.

In [Par93], we described an implemented method that generates proof obligations from a program and a specification. Here, we give a theoretical description of this method. More precisely, a new extraction function called the weak extraction is defined. The strong extraction applies on terms and types. It suppresses in both of them all logical terms. The weak extraction applies only on terms and keeps all the informations in types. Then, a new notion of typing on weak extracted terms is necessary. It can be proved that a program, coherent with a given specification, can be transformed into a proof of an equivalent specification modulo some logical lemmas. This corresponds to invert the weak extraction.

This problem is not simple because the framework is very general. The Calculus of Inductive Constructions is a powerful language. Some restrictions on the proof system have to be made. Given a program p that is exactly a trace of a proof P, it can be proved that the generated logical lemmas have a proof in P. This method is the basis of an effective heuristic method corresponding to a tactic in the *Coq* system described in [Par93, Par95]. This heuristic method considers strong extracted programs and synthesizes types by unification from the initial specification.

The plan is in three main parts. First, we present the Calculus of Inductive Constructions and the extraction of [PM89b]. Secondly, we show the weak extraction, why and how it can be inverted. Thirdly, we explain a derived heuristic method as a consequence of the inversion. Finally, a non trivial example is developed in the appendix, for people familiar with a *Coq* syntax.

2 Extraction in the Calculus of Inductive Constructions

This section presents the framework. The proof language is the Calculus of Inductive Constructions. We first present the Pure Calculus of Constructions and how it can be extended with primitive inductive types. Then, we explain the motivations for extracting programs and present the extraction of [PM89a].

2.1 The Calculus of Constructions

We present a variant due to [PM89b] of the standard Calculus of Constructions [Coq85]. In this variant, two sorts are distinguished : *Set* : *TypeSet* and *Prop* : *Type*. These two sorts allow to separate computational terms and logical terms by marking them. Terms marked with *Set* are computational terms and terms marked with *Prop* are logical terms. The inference rules for the calculus are then the following (types are generally in upper case, terms in lower case).

Definition 1.

$$\overline{[] \ well \ formed}$$

$$\frac{\Gamma \vdash A : s}{\Gamma[x : A] \ well \ formed} \quad s \in \mathcal{S} = \{Set, Prop, TypeSet, Type\}$$

$$\frac{\Gamma \ well \ formed}{\Gamma \vdash Set : TypeSet} \quad \frac{\Gamma \ well \ formed}{\Gamma \vdash Prop : Type}$$

$$\frac{\Gamma \ well \ formed \quad x : A \in \Gamma}{\Gamma \vdash x : A}$$

$$\frac{\Gamma \vdash A : s \quad \Gamma[x : A] \vdash B : s'}{\Gamma \vdash (x : A)B : s'} \quad (s, s') \in \mathcal{R} = \mathcal{S} \times \mathcal{S}$$

$$\frac{\Gamma[x : A] \vdash t : B \quad \Gamma \vdash (x : A)B : s}{\Gamma \vdash [x : A]t : (x : A)B}$$

$$\frac{\Gamma \vdash t : (x : A)B \quad \Gamma \vdash t' : A}{\Gamma \vdash (t \ t') : B[x \leftarrow t']}$$

$$\frac{\Gamma \vdash A' : s \quad \Gamma \vdash t : A \quad A =_\beta A'}{\Gamma \vdash t : A'} \quad s \in \mathcal{S}$$

2.2 Inductive Types

We consider the Calculus of Constructions without universes. Since data types cannot be easily coded in this calculus, we consider the addition of primitive inductive types. This allows to define concrete data types in a more natural way. For example, natural numbers can be defined as an inductive structure with two constructors 0 and S (natural numbers are constructed from 0 with the successor). This section presents the syntax and rules for inductive types. Our presentation is much inspired by [PM93, PC89], but we treat explicitly the parameters of inductive types. In [PM93], inductive types are presented without parameters and these ones are treated as λ-abstractions.

Definition 2. Arity :
An arity is a term with the following syntax, where M is any term :

$$Ar ::= Set \mid Prop \mid (x : M)Ar$$

In the following, T is a generic term for the syntax of types and t for the syntax of terms.

Definition 3. Inductive Types :

$$T ::= Ind[p_1 : P_1| \ldots |p_n : P_n](X : Ar)\{c_1 : C_1| \ldots |c_m : C_m\}$$

Ar is an arity, p_i are the parameters of the inductive type, n the number of parameters and c_i the constructors of the inductive type.

Definition 4. Syntax for the constructors type :

$$Co ::= X \mid (Co\ m) \mid (P \to Co) \mid (x : M)Co$$

with X not appearing in m nor in M and P strictly positive w.r.t. X, where m and M are any terms.

Definition 5. A term is strictly positive with respect to X if it has the following syntax :

$$Pos ::= X \mid (Pos\ m) \mid (x : M)Pos \quad with\ X \notin FV(M, m)$$

Definition 6. Constructors :

$$t ::= \text{Constr}(i, T)$$

Example 1.

- The $\exists$ connective can be defined by :

$$sig := Ind[A : Set; P : A \to Prop](X : Set)\{exist : (x : A)(P\ x) \to X\}$$

- The $\vee$ connective can be defined by :

$$sumor := Ind[A : Set; B : Prop](X : Set)\{inleft : A \to X|inright : B \to X\}$$

The inductive type *sumor* is a simulation for exceptions. Indeed, this is a sum type. The first component has a computational sense (marked with *Set*) and the second a logical sense (marked with *Prop*). The first component contains the result if it exists, the second simulates raising an exception.

Notations :
We note *constructor(Co_i, X)* for Co_i is a *constructor type w.r.t.* X.
A vectorial notation is used for lists of variables. We note a for $a_1 \ldots a_n$ and $(a : A)t$ for $(a_1 : A_1) \ldots (a_n : A_n)t$.

Then, a notion of elimination can be defined.

Definition 7. Elimination :

$$t ::= \text{Elim}(t_0, T)\{t_1| \ldots |t_n\}$$

where t_0 is the term on which the elimination is done, T the type of the elimination term and t_i the different branches of the elimination.

There are two kinds of eliminations : the dependent elimination $(Dep(s, s'))$ and the non-dependent elimination $(Nodep(s, s'))$. The non-dependent one is a particular case of the dependent one. It corresponds to the situation where the proposition to be proved does not depend on the term on which the elimination is done. We present here only the dependent elimination. For this, an auxiliary definition is needed.

Definition 8. Given s and s' two sorts, $A \equiv (x : A)s$, X a variable of type A, Q a variable of type $(x : A)(X\ x) \to s'$, C a constructor type w.r.t. X and c a term of type C, we define a new type noted $C\{X, Q, c\}$ by induction on C :

$$(P \to C)\{X, Q, c\} = (p : P)P\{X, Q, p\} \to C\{X, Q, (c\ p)\}\ \ X \text{ strict. pos. in } P$$
$$(x : M)C\{X, Q, c\} = (x : M)C\{X, Q, (c\ x)\}\ \ X \text{ not in } M$$
$$(X\ a)\{X, Q, c\} = (Q\ a\ c)$$

Then, three new rules are defined for typing an inductive type, a constructor and an elimination.

Definition 9. Inductive Types in the Calculus of Constructions :

$$\frac{(\forall i = 1 \ldots m)}{\Gamma[p : P] \vdash A : s\ \ \Gamma[p : P; X : A] \vdash C_i : s'\ \ constructor(C_i, X)}{\Gamma \vdash \mathsf{Ind}[p : P](X : A)\{c : C\} : (p : P)A}$$

$$\frac{\Gamma \vdash I : (p : P)A\ \ 1 \leq i \leq m}{\Gamma \vdash \mathsf{Constr}(i, I) : (p : P)C_i[X \leftarrow (I\ p)]}$$

$$\frac{\forall i = 1 \ldots m, \Gamma \vdash f_i : C_i\{(I\ p), Q, (\mathsf{Constr}(i, I)\ p)\}}{\Gamma \vdash c : (I\ p\ a)\ \ \Gamma \vdash Q : (x : A)(I\ p\ x) \to s'}{\Gamma \vdash \mathsf{Elim}(c, Q)\{f_1 | \ldots | f_m\} : (Q\ a\ c)}\ \ Dep(s, s')$$

The rules of elimination are parametered by two sorts s and s'. s is the sort of the arity of the inductive type and s' the sort of the type of the elimination predicate.

There is a particular notion of reduction on inductive types called the ι-reduction that we do not detail here. A definition of this reduction can be found in [PM93].

Example 2.

Let us give an example on lists. We show an elimination to illustrate the definition 8 and an example of ι-reduction. The inductive type *list* has one parameter corresponding to the type of the elements. If $A : Set$ is this parameter, then an elimination predicate Q on lists is of type $(list\ A) \to Set$. The elimination has two cases f_1 and f_2 with the following types :

$$f_1 : (Q\ (nil\ A))$$
$$f_2 : (x : A)(l : (list\ A))(Q\ l) \to (Q\ (cons\ A\ x\ l))$$

The ι-reduction corresponds to the following reduction for the two cases *nil* and *cons* :

$$\mathsf{Elim}(nil\ A, Q)\{f_1|f_2\} \succ_\iota f_1$$
$$\mathsf{Elim}(cons\ A\ x\ l, Q)\{f_1|f_2\} \succ_\iota (f_2\ x\ l\ \mathsf{Elim}(l, Q)\{f_1|f_2\})$$

Coq notations :

We present here the *Coq* syntax for some particular inductive types and for eliminations. This syntax will be used in the following sections.

A+{B} is the syntax for $(sumor\ A\ B)$.

{x:A|P(x)} is the syntax for $(sig\ A\ [x : A](P\ x))$.

<P>Match c with f1...fn end is the syntax for $\mathsf{Elim}(c, P)\{f_1|\dots|f_n\}$.

2.3 The strong extraction function

A proof is a very inefficient program. For the division example, a program does not need to keep the proof of $a = b * q + r$. The extraction of [PM89b] consists in forgetting all the logical parts of the proof. These parts have been marked by the programmer initially with *Prop* for logical parts and *Set* for computational (or informative) parts. Moreover, dependent types are suppressed. Then, resulting terms are typable in the system $F_\omega{}^{Ind}$ (F_ω [Gir72, PM89b] plus inductive types). $F_\omega{}^{Ind}$ corresponds to the Calculus of Inductive Constructions with only *Set* : *TypeSet* and without the rule $(Set, TypeSet)$. This corresponds to a calculus without the possibility for types to depend on terms.

An auxiliary definition of level on terms is needed. Indeed, terms and types are nested in the Calculus of Constructions. Levels can be introduced and are given by the typing. Indeed, if $\Gamma \vdash M : N$ then either $N = Type(Set)$ or $\exists s$ s.t. $N : s$. Three levels can then be defined.

Definition 10. Levels of terms :

- *Type* and *TypeSet* have level -1.
- A term is of level 0 if it is an arity. This is the domain of propositional types.
- A term is of level 1 if its type is of level 0. This is the domain of propositional schemes or predicates.
- A term is of level 2 if its type is of level 1. This is the domain of proofs.

Remark.

- Each term has a unique level defined by its type.
- $(B\ A)$, $(x : A)B$ and $[x : A]B$ have the same level as B.
- In $(x : A)B$ and $[x : A]B$, A has necessarily level 0 or 1.
- In $(B\ A)$, A has level 1 or 2.

Example 3.

- Level 0 : if A is a type, $A \rightarrow Set$ has level 0.
- Level 1 : inductive types have level 1.

- Level 2 : constructors of inductive types and weak eliminations have level 2. The arithmetical variable $+ : nat \rightarrow nat \rightarrow nat$ has level 2 if one supposes that the type nat is an inductive type with two constructors 0 and S. Then, the term $[x : nat](+ x (S 0))$ has level 2.

The property for a term to be informative (computational) or logical can now be formally defined.

Definition 11. Informative arity :
An informative arity is a term with the following syntax :

$$InfAr ::= Set \mid (x : M)InfAr$$

Definition 12. Informative term, logical term :

- A term of level 0 is informative if it is an informative arity.
- A term of level 1 is informative if its type is an informative arity.
- A term of level 2 is informative if the type of its type is Set.

A term is logical if it is not informative.

The extraction function of [PM89b] can now be presented. In the following, we refer to this function as the strong extraction function. Intuitively, this function suppresses all the logical informations from a proof term. Moreover, it suppresses all the dependences of types with terms. This function can be applied only on informative terms.

Notation : The application of a constructor to its parameters is treated as a particular case. Indeed, in an application, all the informative arguments are kept (whatever their level is). For the parameters of a constructor, only the informative ones of level 1 have to be kept. Parameters of constructors are then not treated as usual arguments of an application. A constructor applied to its parameters is noted $\mathsf{Constr}(i, ind, p)$ where i is the number of the constructor, ind the corresponding inductive type and p the vector of parameters.

Definition 13. Strong extraction on terms :

$$\varepsilon_0(Set) = Set$$

$$\varepsilon_0((x : A)B) = \begin{cases} \varepsilon_0(A) \rightarrow \varepsilon_0(B) & \text{if A informative of level 0} \\ \varepsilon_0(B) & \text{otherwise} \end{cases}$$

$$\varepsilon_1(x) = \bar{x} \text{ where } \bar{x} : \varepsilon_0(T_x) \text{ if } x : T_x$$

$$\varepsilon_1((x : A)B) = \begin{cases} (\bar{x} : \varepsilon_i(A))\varepsilon_1(B) & \text{if A informative of level } i \leq 1 \\ \varepsilon_1(B) & \text{otherwise} \end{cases}$$

$$\varepsilon_1([x : A]B) = \begin{cases} [\bar{x} : \varepsilon_0(A)]\varepsilon_1(B) & \text{if A informative of level 0} \\ \varepsilon_1(B) & \text{otherwise} \end{cases}$$

$$\varepsilon_1(A\ B) = \begin{cases} (\varepsilon_1(A)\ \varepsilon_1(B)) & \text{if } B \text{ informative of level 1} \\ \varepsilon_1(A) & \text{otherwise} \end{cases}$$

$\varepsilon_1(\mathsf{Ind}[\boldsymbol{p} : \boldsymbol{P}](X : A)\{\boldsymbol{c} : \boldsymbol{C}\}) =$
$\mathsf{Ind}[\overline{\boldsymbol{p}} : \varepsilon_0(\boldsymbol{P})](\bar{X} : \varepsilon_1(A))\{\overline{\boldsymbol{c}} : \varepsilon_1(\boldsymbol{C})\}$ for informative P_i of level 0

$\varepsilon_2(x) = \bar{x}$ where $\bar{x} : \varepsilon_1(T_x)$ if $x : T_x$

$$\varepsilon_2([x : A]B) = \begin{cases} [\bar{x} : \varepsilon_i(A)]\varepsilon_2(B) & \text{if } A \text{ informative of level } i \leq 1 \\ \varepsilon_2(B) & \text{otherwise} \end{cases}$$

$$\varepsilon_2(A\ B) = \begin{cases} (\varepsilon_2(A)\ \varepsilon_i(B)) & \text{if } B \text{ informative of level } i \leq 2 \\ \varepsilon_2(A) & \text{otherwise} \end{cases}$$

$\varepsilon_2(\mathsf{Elim}(c, P)\{f_1|\ldots|f_n\}) = \mathsf{Elim}(\varepsilon_2(c), \varepsilon_1(P))\{\varepsilon_2(f_1)|\ldots|\varepsilon_2(f_n)\}$

$\varepsilon_2(\mathsf{Constr}(i, ind, \boldsymbol{p})) = \mathsf{Constr}(i, \varepsilon_1(ind), \varepsilon_1(\boldsymbol{p}))$

Remark. The extraction function corresponding to a term of level i is noted ε_i, since each term has a unique level.

Definition 14. Strong extraction on contexts :
  $\varepsilon_i(\Gamma)$ is the extracted context of Γ defined by induction on Γ :

- $\varepsilon_i([]) = []$
- $\varepsilon_i([\Gamma; x : A]) = \varepsilon_i(\Gamma)$ if A logical or if level of $A > i$.
- $\varepsilon_i([\Gamma; x : A]) = [\varepsilon_i(\Gamma); \bar{x} : \varepsilon_j(A)]$ otherwise.

Proposition 15. *If* $\Gamma \vdash t : P$ *then* $\varepsilon_i(\Gamma) \vdash \varepsilon_i(t) : \varepsilon_{i-1}(P)$.

Proof. By induction on the length of the derivation. $\qquad\qquad\square$

Example 4.
  Let us consider the case of the predecessor function which can be specified through the proposition : $(n : nat)\{m : nat|(S\ m) = n\} + \{0 = n\}$. The proof of this proposition proceeds by induction on n. If $n = 0$ then the right part of the specification is true. Otherwise, if $n = y+1$, then the left part of the specification is true and y is the witness. A proof term for this specification is then :

```
[n:nat]<[n0:nat]{m:nat|(S m)=n0}+{0=n0}>Match n with
            (inright {m:nat|(S m)=0} (0=0) (refl_equal nat 0))
            [y:nat][H:{m:nat|(S m)=y}+{0=y}]
                (inleft {m:nat|(S m)=(S y)} (0=(S y))
                    (exist nat [m:nat](S m)=(S y) y
                        (refl_equal nat (S y))))
        end
```

The extraction of this term is, if over-lines are forgotten :

```
[n:nat]<(sumor (sig nat))>Match n with
            (inright (sig nat))
            [y:nat][H:(sumor (sig nat))]
                (inleft (sig nat) (exist nat y))
        end
```

Since *sumor* is a simulation for exceptions, the extraction keeps only the argument of the first component (the witness y) and forgets the argument of the second component.

In an ML-like language, this term could be written :

```
let pred n = match n with
                0 -> raise except_pred
              | y+1 -> y ;;
```

2.4 Non-inversibility of the strong extraction

The extraction function allows to synthesize programs from proofs. However, a complementary idea could be to start from a program and its specification and try to retrieve the corresponding proof. A natural idea for this is to invert the extraction function. Unfortunately, the function of [PM89b] cannot be inverted. Indeed, not all the intelligence to prove properties is reflected by the program.

Example 5.

For a specification $\{x : A|(P\ x)\}$ and a program a, we need to reconstruct a proof of $(P\ a)$ for an arbitrary P. This is impossible. Indeed, this is an undecidable property. It is impossible to retrieve a proof only from its type.

There is another problem : intermediate specifications disappear. Let us take the case of a specification $(n : nat)\{p : nat|2*p = n\} \vee \{p : nat|2*p+1 = n\}$. In a proof, this specification can be enforced by a distinction between n even and n odd. The intermediate specification is then $(n : nat)((even\ n) \wedge \{p : nat|2*p = n\})\vee((odd\ n)\wedge\{p : nat|2*p+1 = n\})$. It is impossible to retrieve from a program such a specification because logical informations are not in the program.

Then, it seems natural not to be able to retrieve logical proofs. It corresponds to logical properties the programmer will have to prove on the program. However, one can hope to be able to retrieve intermediate specifications. That is why we introduce a new extraction function.

3 The weak extraction function

The aim of this new extraction function is to find a way of keeping a sufficient number of informations to be able to retrieve a proof term from a weak extracted term. Since we show the problem is to retrieve intermediate specifications, this new function keeps the specifications and no more suppresses them. Then, this function only suppresses logical proofs.

3.1 Definitions and properties

In this case, arguments of constructors are treated as usual arguments. Indeed, we now want to keep all the informative parameters of a constructor (whatever their level is). Then, we go back now to the notation $\text{Constr}(i, ind)$.

Definition 16. Weak extraction on terms :

$$\sigma_i([x:A]B) = \begin{cases} \sigma_i(B) & \text{if } A:Prop \\ [\bar{x}:\sigma_j(A)]\sigma_i(B) & \text{otherwise} \end{cases}$$

$$\sigma_i(A\ B) = \begin{cases} \sigma_i(A) & \text{if } B \text{ logical of level 2} \\ (\sigma_i(A)\ \sigma_j(B)) & \text{otherwise} \end{cases}$$

$$\sigma_i(\mathsf{Elim}(c,P)\{f_1|\ldots|f_n\}) = \mathsf{Elim}(\sigma_2(c),\sigma_{i-1}(P))\{\sigma_i(f_1)|\ldots|\sigma_i(f_n)\}$$

$$\sigma_i(x) = \bar{x} \ \text{ where } \bar{x}:\sigma_{i-1}(T_x) \text{ if } x:T_x$$

$$\sigma_2(\mathsf{Constr}(i,ind)) = \mathsf{Constr}(i,\sigma_1(ind))$$

$$\sigma_1((x:A)B) = (\bar{x}:\sigma_i(A))\sigma_1(B)$$

$$\sigma_1(\mathsf{Ind}[p:\boldsymbol{P}](X:A)\{c:\boldsymbol{C}\}) =$$

$$\mathsf{Ind}[\bar{\boldsymbol{p}}:\sigma_j(\boldsymbol{P})](\bar{X}:\sigma_0(A))\{\bar{\boldsymbol{c}}:\sigma_1(\boldsymbol{C})\} \ \text{ for } P_i \text{ not of type } Prop$$

$$\sigma_i(K) = K \ \text{ where } K \text{ is a sort}$$

$$\sigma_0((x:A)B) = \begin{cases} \sigma_0(B) & \text{if } A:Prop \\ (\bar{x}:\sigma_0(A))\sigma_0(B) & \text{otherwise} \end{cases}$$

All the dependences w.r.t. logical proofs are suppressed as in definition 13 but only these ones (in definition 13 for strong extraction, informative proofs and logical specifications are suppressed too). To keep a coherence, logical types of level 1 are suppressed in λ-expression (but not informative types of level 1 as in definition 13). Note the rule on product of level 1. Here, nothing is suppressed. This is the case of a specification. We said before we do not want to suppress specifications. So, we keep them all. Let us look at the example given to show the non-inversibility of the strong extraction. We wanted to keep the informations on *even* and *odd*. This is not possible with the strong extraction in definition 13 but possible with the weak extraction with the rule on product of level 1.

This is the main difference between the two definitions (13 and 16).

Definition 17. Weak extraction on contexts :
$\sigma_c(\Gamma)$ is the weak extracted context of Γ defined by induction on Γ :

- $\sigma_c([]) = []$
- $\sigma_c([\Gamma;x:A]) = \sigma_c(\Gamma)$ if $A:Prop$.
- $\sigma_c([\Gamma;x:A]) = [\sigma_c(\Gamma);\bar{x}:\sigma_i(A)]$ otherwise.

Example 6.
Let us show the weak extraction on the previous example of the predecessor. Note that the weak extraction does not change the inductive types *sig* and *sumor*. The weak extracted term is then the following :

```
[n:nat]<[n0:nat]{m:nat|(S m)=n0}+{0=n0}>Match n with
        (inright {m:nat|(S m)=0} (0=0))
        [y:nat][H:{m:nat|(S m)=y}+{0=y}]
          (inleft {m:nat|(S m)=(S y)} (0=(S y))
                  (exist nat [m:nat](S m)=(S y) y))
    end
```

Note that this program has the same computational contents than the strong extracted program. The only difference is that there are annotations corresponding to intermediate specifications.

The terms obtained by application of this function on terms of the Calculus of Inductive Constructions are $F_\omega{}^{Ind}$ programs annotated with specifications in the Calculus of Inductive Constructions. Such terms contain logical informations which allow the inversion of the weak extraction (the informations on *even* and *odd* in our previous example for non-inversibility). We need a new notion of typing for these particular terms since they are neither typable in the Calculus of Inductive Constructions nor in $F_\omega{}^{Ind}$.

Definition 18. Typing on weak extracted terms :

$$\frac{}{[]\ well\ formed}$$

$$\frac{\Gamma \vdash T : s}{\Gamma[x : T]\ well\ formed}\quad s \in \mathcal{S} = \{Prop, Set, Type, TypeSet\}$$

$$\frac{\Gamma\ well\ formed}{\Gamma \vdash Prop \in Type}$$

$$\frac{\Gamma\ well\ formed}{\Gamma \vdash Set \in TypeSet}$$

$$\frac{\Gamma\ well\ formed \quad x : T \in \Gamma}{\Gamma \vdash x \in T}$$

$$\frac{\Gamma \vdash T \in s \quad \Gamma[x : T] \vdash T' \in s'}{\Gamma \vdash (x : T)T' \in s'}\quad (s,s') \in \mathcal{R} = \mathcal{S} \times \mathcal{S} \setminus \left\{ \begin{array}{c} (Prop, Type) \\ (Prop, TypeSet) \end{array} \right\} \quad (1)$$

$$\frac{\Gamma \vdash (x : T)T' \in s \quad \Gamma[x : T] \vdash t \in T'}{\Gamma \vdash [x : T]t \in (x : T)T'}\quad s \in \mathcal{S}$$

$$\frac{\Gamma \vdash t \in (x : A)B \quad \Gamma \vdash t' \in A}{\Gamma \vdash (t\ t') \in B[x \leftarrow t']}\quad A\ of\ level\ 0\ or\ informative\ of\ level\ 1$$

$$\frac{\Gamma \vdash A \in Prop \quad \Gamma \vdash t \in A \to U}{\Gamma \vdash t \in U}\quad (2)$$

$$\frac{\Gamma \vdash t \in U \quad \Gamma \vdash A \in Prop}{\Gamma \vdash t \in A \to U}\quad (3)$$

$$\frac{\Gamma \vdash T' \in s \quad \Gamma \vdash t \in T \quad T =_{\beta\iota} T'}{\Gamma \vdash t \in T'}$$

$$\frac{(\forall i = 1\ldots m)}{\Gamma[p : P] \vdash A \in s \quad \Gamma[p : P; X : A] \vdash C_i \in s' \quad constructor(C_i, X)}{\Gamma \vdash \mathsf{Ind}[p : P](X : A)\{c : C\} \in (p : P)A}\quad \not\exists P_j : Prop$$

$$\frac{\Gamma \vdash Ind \equiv \mathsf{Ind}[p : P](X : A)\{c : C\} \in B \quad 1 \leq i \leq m}{\Gamma \vdash \mathsf{Constr}(i, Ind) \in (p : P)C_i[X \leftarrow (Ind\ p)]}$$

$$\frac{\forall i = 1\ldots m, \Gamma \vdash f_i \in C_i\{(I\ p), Q, (\mathsf{Constr}(i, I)\ p)\}_\sigma}{\Gamma \vdash c \in (I\ p\ a) \quad \Gamma \vdash Q \in (x : A)(I\ p\ x) \to s'}{\Gamma \vdash \mathsf{Elim}(c, Q)\{f_1|\ldots|f_m\} \in (Q\ a\ c)}$$

The definition of $C\{X,Q,c\}$ is modified into $C\{X,Q,c\}_\sigma$. Indeed, no proof variables have to appear in constructors. If a constructor is $c : (n : nat)(n > 0) \rightarrow C$, the elimination principle should be $(n : nat)(n > 0) \rightarrow (P\ (c\ n))$ and not $(n : nat)(h : n > 0) \rightarrow (P\ (c\ n\ h))$. The new definition of $C\{X,Q,c\}_\sigma$ allows to avoid this problem.

Definition 19. Given s and s' two sorts, $A \equiv (\boldsymbol{x} : \boldsymbol{A})s$, X a variable of type A, Q a variable of type $(\boldsymbol{x} : \boldsymbol{A})(X\ \boldsymbol{x}) \rightarrow s'$, C a constructor type w.r.t. X and c a term of type C, we define $C\{X,Q,c\}_\sigma$ by induction on C :

$$(P \rightarrow C)\{X,Q,c\}_\sigma = (p : P)P\{X,Q,p\}_\sigma \rightarrow C\{X,Q,(c\ p)\}_\sigma$$

$$(x : M)C\{X,Q,c\}_\sigma = \begin{cases} C\{X,Q,c\}_\sigma & \text{if } M : Prop \\ (x : M)C\{X,Q,(c\ x)\}_\sigma & \text{otherwise} \end{cases}$$

$$(X\ \boldsymbol{a})\{X,Q,c\}_\sigma = (Q\ \boldsymbol{a}\ c)$$

The above rules for typing are close to the ones of the Calculus of Inductive Constructions (see definition 1) but not exactly the same. The rules who are differing are the rules 1, 2, 3 and the application formation. The motivations for the rule 1 is given in the following remarks. The application formation is allowed only with arguments having a type of level 0 or informative of level 1 : this is due to the fact that we suppress only logical proofs in application. Finally, logical proofs are suppressed in applications but the corresponding logical specifications are not suppressed in types (due to the rule on the product of level 1). The rules 2 and 3 are direct consequences of this fact. Rules are needed to play with logical products in types that have no corresponding argument in an application. The rules 2 and 3 deal with this and allow to add or suppress any logical products in a type.

Remark.

1. In the first case of the precedent definition, P cannot have the type *Prop*. Indeed, an inductive type in an elimination is always informative. Moreover, P is strictly positive w.r.t. X. Then, $P : Set$.
2. In the rule 1, $(Prop, Type)$ and $(Prop, TypeSet)$ are not necessary because they allow the formation of dependent types on logical proofs and these have been suppressed.
3. In the following, σ applies to all terms except logical proofs. ε applies only on informative terms.

Definition 20. If $\Gamma \vdash t \in S$ then the program t is said to be coherent with the specification S.

We can now give a list of standard properties on this weak extraction and the corresponding new typing judgment.

Proposition 21. *Coherence of the new typing judgment w.r.t. the strong extraction :*
  If $\Gamma \vdash t \in P$ and P is informative then $\varepsilon_i(\Gamma) \vdash \varepsilon_i(t) : \varepsilon_{i-1}(P)$.

Proof. By induction on the length of the derivation of $\Gamma \vdash t \in P$. $\qquad\qquad$ □

Proposition 22. *First substitutivity lemma :*
  For all term t of level 0, 1 or informative of level 2 :

$$\sigma_i(T[x \leftarrow t]) = \sigma_i(T)[x \leftarrow \sigma_j(t)]$$

where i is the level of T and j the level of t and x. Moreover, informations of x and t have to be coherent (if one is logical, the other one too).

Proof. By induction on the structure of t. $\qquad\qquad$ □

Proposition 23. *Second substitutivity lemma :*
  For all logical term t of level 2 :

$$\sigma_i(T[x \leftarrow t]) = \sigma_i(T)$$

where i is the level of T with levels and informations of x and t coherent.

Proof. By induction on the structure of t. $\qquad\qquad$ □

Proposition 24. *Coherence of the weak extraction :*
  $\forall \Gamma, \forall t, \forall P,$ *such that P is not of type Prop,* $\Gamma \vdash t : P \Rightarrow \sigma(\Gamma) \vdash \sigma(t) \in \sigma(P).$

Proof. By induction on the length of the derivation of $\Gamma \vdash t : P$. $\qquad\qquad$ □

3.2 Inversion of the weak extraction

We now want to invert the weak extraction. Given a weak extracted program and a specification, we want to retrieve a proof term. We show that we can reconstruct a partial proof term with "holes" corresponding to logical proofs to be proved by the user. Then, all the logical proofs of one specification have to be identified. The proof of inversibility gives such an algorithm. Some restrictions on the model have to be stated in order to be able to invert the function.

1. We want to forbid some situations in which we do not know how to retrieve a proof term from a weak extracted term. Typically, let us take a term T whose type is $(x : nat)(P : (y : nat)(x > y) \rightarrow Set)(P\ 1\ h_1) \rightarrow (P\ 2\ h_2)$. Its weak extraction is $\bar{T} : (x : nat)(P : nat \rightarrow Set)(P\ 1) \rightarrow (P\ 2)$. The link between h_1 and h_2 is lost. Moreover, let us take a term $root$ of type $(x : nat)(x > 0) \rightarrow nat$. Its weak extraction is $\overline{root} : nat \rightarrow nat$. Suppose we consider a weak extracted proposition $(root\ x)$, then a proof term $(root\ x\ h_1)$ where h_1 is an existential variable of type $x > 0$ can be reconstructed.
   In fact, we want to be able to define types that depend on logical proofs (as for $root$) but no arities that depend on logical proofs (as the type of T). This implies we consider a PTS without the rules $(Prop, Type)$ and $(Prop, TypeSet)$.

Remark. In a PTS without $(Prop, Type)$ and $(Prop, TypeSet)$, the following points are always valid :

- $\sigma_i((x : A)B) = (x : \sigma_j(A))\sigma_i(B)$ whatever the level of B is (since this is always true for level 1 and the restrictions of the PTS implies it is true for level 0).
- if $\sigma_0(A) = s$ where s is a sort then $A = s$ (for the same reason).
- if $\sigma_i(A) = (x : B)C$ then $A = (x : B')C'$.
- if $\sigma_i(A) = [x : B]C$ and if A has level 1 then $A = [x : B']C'$.

2. Now, if we know how to generate a proof obligation h_1 for $x > 0$ in the example of *root*, there exist many possibilities for h_1. We want to identify all the proofs of a same logical proposition. We need a *proof-irrelevance* of logical proofs. For this, the conversion rule between two terms as to be extended to be a rule between typed terms.

Definition 25. Extended equality between typed terms (noted $=_e$) :
If $B =_{\beta\iota} B'$ and if l and l' are logical terms of level 2 then $B[x \leftarrow l] =_e B'[x \leftarrow l']$.

We can give a method to explicitly compare two typed terms without any problems (by comparing their normal form recursively).

Proposition 26. *Proof-irrelevance of logical proofs :*
If A and A' are two typed terms, equal modulo $=_e$, verifying the previous conditions 1 and 2 and that are not logical proofs, then $\sigma_i(A) = \sigma_i(A') \Rightarrow A = A'$.

Proof. We consider the terms in their η-long normal form and compare them. By induction on their shape, there is no problem. □

We can now state the theorem of inversibility. It corresponds to the following intuition. A program p is invertible if, given a context Γ and a specification S where S is provable and p coherent with S in Γ, a proof term for p can be reconstructed with holes corresponding to logical proofs. We place us in a model verifying the two precedent restrictions and all judgments are restricted to this model.

Notation : we note $\vdash_r$ for restricted judgments.

Theorem 27. *Inversibility of the weak extraction :*
If $\Delta \vdash t \in T$ and if Γ is a well formed environment such that $\sigma_c(\Gamma) = \Delta$ then $\exists t', \mathcal{L}$ well formed logical context and S' such that $\Gamma, \mathcal{L} \vdash_r t' : S'$ with $\sigma(t') = t$, $\sigma(S') = T$.

Proof. By induction on the derivation of $\in$. We do not detail the cases of context formation. Each step gives the construction of the proof term t. At each step, Γ is known such that $\sigma_c(\Gamma) = \Delta$. In all the proof, the L are logical terms of level 2, and $\mathcal{L}$ is a logical context.

- Variable :

$$\frac{\Delta \ well \ formed \quad x : T \in \Delta}{\Delta \vdash x \in T}$$

The proof term is the variable x of type Γ_x. As $\sigma_c(\Gamma) = \Delta$, $\sigma(\Gamma_x) = \Delta_x = T$.
Then, $\Gamma \vdash x : \Gamma_x$ with $\sigma(x) = x$ and $\sigma(\Gamma_x) = T$.
The searched environment is Γ, the proof term x and its type Γ_x.

- Application formation :

$$\frac{\Delta \vdash t \in (x : A)B \quad \Delta \vdash u \in A}{\Delta \vdash (t \ u) \in B[x \leftarrow u]} \quad \text{A of level 0 or informative of level 1}$$

By induction hypothesis, $\exists t'$, $\mathcal{L}$ and T' such that $\Gamma, \mathcal{L} \vdash_r t' : T'$ with $\sigma(t') = t$
and $\sigma(T') = (x : A)B$. Moreover, $\exists u'$, $\mathcal{L}'$ and A' such that $\Gamma, \mathcal{L}' \vdash_r u' : A'$
with $\sigma(u') = u$ and $\sigma(A') = A$.
Necessarily, $T' = (x : A'')B'$ with $\sigma(A'') = A$ and $\sigma(B') = B$. There are
no logical products at the head of T'. Indeed, the condition 1 imposes arities not depending on logical proofs. Then, $\Gamma, \mathcal{L} \vdash_r t' : (x : A'')B'$ and
$\sigma(A') = \sigma(A'') = A$. To apply the standard typing rule for application,
$A' = A''$ is needed. The irrelevance of logical proofs is then necessary (see
proposition 26. $A' = A''$ can be deduced from $\sigma(A') = \sigma(A'')$. Then, $\exists \mathcal{L}''$,
union of $\mathcal{L}$ and $\mathcal{L}'$, such that $\Gamma, \mathcal{L}'' \vdash_r (t' \ u') : B'[x \leftarrow u']$. $(t' \ u')$ is the proof
term with the following properties :

$$\sigma(t' \ u') = (\sigma(t') \ \sigma(u'))$$
$$= (t \ u)$$

$$\sigma(B'[x \leftarrow u']) = \sigma(B')[x \leftarrow \sigma(u')]$$
$$= B[x \leftarrow u]$$

- Product formation :

$$\frac{\Delta \vdash T_1 \in s_1 \quad \Delta[x : T_1] \vdash T_2 \in s_2}{\Delta \vdash (x : T_1)T_2 \in s_2} \quad (s_1, s_2) \in \mathcal{R} = \mathcal{S} \times \mathcal{S} \setminus \{ \begin{matrix} (Prop, Type) \\ (Prop, TypeSet) \end{matrix} \}$$

By induction hypothesis, $\exists t'$, $\mathcal{L}$ and S' such that $\Gamma[x : A], \mathcal{L} \vdash_r t' : S'$ with
$\sigma(t') = T'$, $\sigma(S') = s_2$ and $\sigma(A) = T$. As $s_2 \in \mathcal{S}$, $S' = s_2$. Indeed, the
condition 1 imposes arities not depending on proofs, then S' is necessarily a
sort. Then, $\Gamma[x : A], \mathcal{L} \vdash_r t' : s_2$.
To give a proof term, the logical variables of $\mathcal{L}$ have to be commuted in the
context. A vector $l' : L'$ is defined with $L'_i = (x : A)L_i$ if $\mathcal{L} = [l : L]$. In t', l_i
are substituted by $(l'_i \ x)$ and a term t'' is obtained. Then, $\Gamma[l' : L'; x : A] \vdash_r$
$t'' : s_2$.
The application of the standard typing rule for the product gives : $\Gamma[l' :$
$L'] \vdash_r (x : A)t'' : s_2$. The conditions are :

$$\sigma((x : A)t'') = (x : \sigma(A))\sigma(t'')$$
$$= (x : T_1)T_2$$
$$\sigma(s_2) = s_2$$

– Abstraction formation :

$$\frac{\Delta \vdash (x : T_1)T_2 \in s \quad \Delta[x : T_1] \vdash t \in T_2}{\Delta \vdash [x : T_1]t \in (x : T_1)T_2} \quad s \in \mathcal{S}$$

By induction hypothesis, $\exists t', \mathcal{L}$ and S' such that $\Gamma[x : A], \mathcal{L} \vdash_r t' : S'$ with $\sigma(t') = t$, $\sigma(S') = T_2$ and $\sigma(A) = T$.

To give a proof term, the logical variables of l have to be commuted in the context. A vector $l' : L'$ is defined with $L'_i = (x : A)L_i$ if $\mathcal{L} = [l : L]$. We note $(l' \ x)$ for the vector $((l'_1 \ x), \ldots, (l'_n \ x))$. The, $\Gamma[l' : L'; x : A] \vdash_r t'[l \leftarrow (l' \ x)] : S'[l \leftarrow (l' \ x)]$.

The application of the standard typing rule for the abstraction gives : $\Gamma[l' : L'] \vdash_r [x : A]t'[l \leftarrow (l' \ x)] : (x : A)S'[l \leftarrow (l' \ x)]$. The conditions are :

$$\sigma([x : A]t'[l \leftarrow (l' \ x)]) = [x : \sigma(A)]\sigma(t')$$
$$= [x : T_1]t$$

$$\sigma((x : A)S'[l \leftarrow (l' \ x)]) = (x : \sigma(A))\sigma(S'[l \leftarrow (l' \ x)])$$
$$= (x : T_1)T_2$$

– Rule 2 :

$$\frac{\Delta \vdash A \in Prop \quad \Delta \vdash t \in A \to U}{\Delta \vdash t \in U}$$

By induction hypothesis, $\exists t', \mathcal{L}$ and S' such that $\Gamma, \mathcal{L} \vdash_r t' : S'$ with $\sigma(t') = t$ and $\sigma(S') = A \to U$. Then, $S' = (x : A')B'$ with $\sigma(A') = A$ and $\sigma(B') = U$. Then, $\Gamma, \mathcal{L} \vdash_r t' : (x : A')B'$.

This is exactly the same case as application and the proof term can be reconstructed. $\exists \mathcal{L}', x'$ such that $\Gamma, \mathcal{L}' \vdash_r x' : A'$. Then, $\exists \mathcal{L}''$ union of $\mathcal{L}$ and $\mathcal{L}'$ such that $\Gamma, \mathcal{L}'' \vdash_r (t' \ x') : B'[x \leftarrow x']$ with $\sigma(t' \ x') = t$ and $\sigma(B'[x \leftarrow x']) = U$. B' can depend on x but the weak extraction suppresses this dependence. This is the only place where a logical lemma is introduced. In the other cases, the logical lemmas of the induction hypotheses have repercussions but no new one is introduced.

– Rule 3 :

$$\frac{\Delta \vdash t \in U \quad \Delta \vdash A \in Prop}{\Delta \vdash t \in A \to U}$$

By induction hypothesis, $\exists t', \mathcal{L}$ and S' such that $\Gamma, \mathcal{L} \vdash_r t' : S'$ with $\sigma(t') = t$ and $\sigma(S') = U$.

Then, $\mathcal{L} = [l_1 : L_1; \ldots; l_i : L_i; x : A'; l_{i+1} : L_{i+1}; \ldots; l_n : L_n]$ with $\sigma(A') = A$. Commutations are done in $\mathcal{L}$, to obtain $\mathcal{L}' = [l_1 : L_1; \ldots; l_i : L_i; l'_{i+1} : L'_{i+1}; \ldots; l'_n : L'_n; x : A']$ where $L'_i = (x : A')L_i$.

Then, $\Gamma', \mathcal{L}' \vdash_r t' : S'$.

Then, $\Gamma'[l_1 : L_1; \ldots; l_i : L_i; l'_{i+1} : L'_{i+1}; \ldots; l'_n : L'_n] \vdash_r [x : A']t' : A' \to S'$ with $\sigma([x : A']t') = \sigma(t') = t$ and $\sigma(A' \to S') = A \to U$.

- Inductive type formation :

$$\frac{(\forall i = 1 \ldots m)}{\Delta[\boldsymbol{p}:\boldsymbol{P}] \vdash A \in s_1 \quad \Delta[\boldsymbol{p}:\boldsymbol{P}; X:A] \vdash C_i \in s_2 \; constructor(C_i, X)}{\Delta \vdash \mathsf{Ind}[\boldsymbol{p}:\boldsymbol{P}](X:A)\{\boldsymbol{c}:\boldsymbol{C}\} \in (\boldsymbol{p}:\boldsymbol{P})A} \; \not\exists P_j : Prop$$

By induction hypothesis, $\exists \mathcal{L}, t_i'$ and S_i' such that $\Gamma[\boldsymbol{p}' : \boldsymbol{P}'; X' : A'], \mathcal{L} \vdash_r$ $t_i' : S_i'$ with $\sigma(t_i') = C_i$, $\sigma(S_i') = s_2$, $\sigma(P_j') = P_j$ and $\sigma(A') = A$. Moreover, $\exists \mathcal{L}', t''$ and S' such that $\Gamma, \mathcal{L}' \vdash_r t'' : S'$ with $\sigma(t') = A$ and $\sigma(S') = s_1$. Then, $\Gamma[\boldsymbol{p}' : \boldsymbol{P}'; X' : A'; l : \boldsymbol{L}] \vdash_r t_i' : S_i'$ where $[l : \boldsymbol{L}]$ is the union of $\mathcal{L}$ and $\mathcal{L}'$. As $\sigma(t'') = \sigma(A')$, thanks to the irrelevance of logical proofs, $t'' = A'$. Then, as for precedent cases, l have to be commuted and the standard typing rule for inductive types can be applied. A proof term is obtained and it verifies the good properties.
- Constructor formation :

$$\frac{\Delta \vdash Ind \equiv \mathsf{Ind}[\boldsymbol{p}:\boldsymbol{P}](X:A)\{\boldsymbol{c}:\boldsymbol{C}\} \in B \quad 1 \le i \le m}{\Delta \vdash \mathsf{Constr}(i, Ind) \in (\boldsymbol{p}:\boldsymbol{P})C_i[X \leftarrow (Ind \; \boldsymbol{p})]}$$

By induction hypothesis, $\exists ind', \mathcal{L}$ and S' such that $\Gamma, \mathcal{L} \vdash_r ind' : S'$ with $\sigma(ind') = Ind$ and $\sigma(S') = B$.
$B = (\boldsymbol{p} : \boldsymbol{P})A$, then $\sigma(S') = (\boldsymbol{p}' : \boldsymbol{P}')A'$ with $\sigma(p_i') = p_i$ and $\sigma(A') = A$.
Then, $\Gamma, \mathcal{L} \vdash_r ind' : (\boldsymbol{p}' : \boldsymbol{P}')A'$. Then, $ind' = \mathsf{Ind}[\boldsymbol{p} : \boldsymbol{P}](X : A')\{\boldsymbol{c}' : \boldsymbol{C}'\}$.
Then, $\Gamma, \mathcal{L} \vdash_r \mathsf{Constr}(i, ind') : (\boldsymbol{p}' : \boldsymbol{P}')C_i'[X \leftarrow (ind' \; \boldsymbol{p}')]$ with $\sigma(\mathsf{Constr}(i,-ind')) = \mathsf{Constr}(i, Ind)$ and $\sigma((\boldsymbol{p}' : \boldsymbol{P}')C_i'[X \leftarrow (ind' \; \boldsymbol{p}')]) = (\boldsymbol{p} : \boldsymbol{P})C_i[X \leftarrow (Ind \; \boldsymbol{p})]$.
- Elimination formation :

$$\frac{\forall i = 1 \ldots m, \Gamma \vdash f_i \in C_i\{(I \; p), Q, (\mathsf{Constr}(i, I) \; p)\}_\sigma}{\Gamma \vdash c \in (I \; p \; a) \quad \Gamma \vdash Q \in (x : A)(I \; p \; x) \to s'}{\Gamma \vdash \mathsf{Elim}(c, Q)\{f_1 | \ldots | f_m\} \in (Q \; a \; c)}$$

By induction hypothesis, $\exists c_1, \mathcal{L}_1$ and S_c such that $\Gamma, \mathcal{L}_1 \vdash_r c_1 : S_c$ with $\sigma(c_1) = c$ and $\sigma(S_c) = (I \; p \; a)$; $\exists Q_1, \mathcal{L}_2$ and S_Q such that $\Gamma, \mathcal{L}_2 \vdash_r Q_1 : S_Q$ with $\sigma(Q_1) = Q$ and $\sigma(S_Q) = (x : A)(I \; p \; x) \to s'$; $\exists f_i', \mathcal{L}^i$ and S_i such that $\Gamma, \mathcal{L}^i \vdash_r f_i' : S_i$ with $\sigma(f_i') = f_i$ and $\sigma(S_i) = C_i\{(I \; p), Q, (\mathsf{Constr}(i, I) \; p)\}_\sigma$.
Then, $S_Q = (\boldsymbol{x_1} : \boldsymbol{A'})(I_1 \; \boldsymbol{p_1} \; \boldsymbol{x_1}) \to s'$ with $\sigma(A_i') = A_i$, $\sigma(I_1) = I$, $\sigma(\boldsymbol{p_1}) = p$ and $\sigma(\boldsymbol{x_1}) = x$; $S_c = (I_2 \; \boldsymbol{p_2} \; \boldsymbol{a_1})$ with $\sigma(I_2) = I$, $\sigma(\boldsymbol{p_2}) = p$ and $\sigma(\boldsymbol{a_1}) = a$; $S_i = C_i'\{(I_3 \; \boldsymbol{p_3}), Q_2, (\mathsf{Constr}(i, I_4) \; \boldsymbol{p_4})\}_\sigma$ with $\sigma(C_i') = C_i$, $\sigma(I_3) = I$, $\sigma(\boldsymbol{p_3}) = p$, $\sigma(Q_2) = Q$, $\sigma(I_4) = I$ and $\sigma(\boldsymbol{p_4}) = p$.
Then, thanks to the proof irrelevance, $I_1 = I_2 = I_3 = I_4$, $\boldsymbol{p_1} = \boldsymbol{p_2} = \boldsymbol{p_3} = \boldsymbol{p_4}$ and $Q_1 = Q_2$.
Then, $\exists \mathcal{L}_3$, union of $\mathcal{L}_1$, $\mathcal{L}_2$ and $\mathcal{L}^i$, such that $\Gamma, \mathcal{L}_3 \vdash_r \mathsf{Elim}(c_1, Q_1)\{f_i'\}$: $(Q_1 \; \boldsymbol{a_1} \; c_1)$ with the good properties.

$\square$

This proof is constructive. It explicitly gives a method to construct a proof term from a weak extracted program and a specification. Note that the proof term is partial. Indeed, in practice, logical proofs cannot be retrieved (in the proof of inversibility, we identify all of them). However, this proof is based on an analysis of the typing of the program. This typing is not deterministic due to the two rules 2 and 3. We need to replace these two rules with a new one (4) to have a new equivalent typing system. This system will be deterministic. In fact, we say it is deterministic in the sense that the application of the rules 2 and 3 are postponed and used via an equivalence relation only when typing an application. The rules 2 and 3 can then no more be used whenever we want but only when absolutely necessary.

Definition 28. Logical equivalence :
Two types A and B are logically equivalent ($A \equiv_L B$) if and only if there exist L and M logical of level 1, and C such that $A = L \to C$ and $B = M \to C$.

Remark.

1. This property is decidable.
2. If $A \equiv_L B$ and $\Gamma \vdash M \in A$, then $\Gamma \vdash M \in B$. Trivial by a suit of applications of the rules 2 and 3.
3. $\equiv_L$ is reflexive, symmetric and transitive.
4. $L \to A \equiv_L A$ if L is logical of level 1.

We can now define a new typing system called $\in_2$. It is the same as $\in$ but 2 and 3 are replaced by the following 4.

Definition 29. Typing system $\in_2$:

$$\frac{\Gamma \vdash t \in_2 A \quad \Gamma \vdash u \in_2 B \quad A \equiv_L (x : M)N \quad B \equiv_L M}{\Gamma \vdash (t\ u) \in_2 N[x \leftarrow u]} \tag{4}$$

We can now prove the equivalence between $\in$ and $\in_2$. The proof deals with the fact that 4 can be deduced from 2 and 3 and conversely.

Proposition 30. Equivalence of $\in$ and $\in_2$:
$\Gamma \vdash t \in S$ if and only if $\exists S'$ such that $\Gamma \vdash t \in_2 S'$ with $S \equiv_L S'$.

Proof.

- Necessary condition : $\in \Rightarrow \in_2$.
  By induction on the typing $\in$. We consider only th rules 2 and 3.
  - Rule 2 :
    $$\frac{\Gamma \vdash A \in Prop \quad \Gamma \vdash t \in A \to U}{\Gamma \vdash t \in U}$$
    By induction hypothesis, $\exists T$ such that $\Gamma \vdash t \in_2 T$ and $T \equiv_L A \to U$. Remark 3 on $\equiv_L$ gives $A \to U \equiv_L U$. Transitivity of $\equiv_L$ gives $T \equiv_L U$. Then, we have what we are looking for.

- • Rule 3 : exactly the same principle.
- – Sufficient condition : $\in_2 \Rightarrow \in$.
  By induction on the typing $\in_2$. The problematic rule is the rule 4.

$$\frac{\Gamma \vdash t \in_2 A \quad \Gamma \vdash u \in_2 B \quad A \equiv_L (x : M)N \quad B \equiv_L M}{\Gamma \vdash (t\ u) \in_2 N[x \leftarrow u]}$$

By induction hypothesis, $\exists A_1, B_1$ such that $\Gamma \vdash t \in A_1$, $\Gamma \vdash u \in B_1$, $A_1 \equiv_L A$ and $B_1 \equiv_L B$. By transitivity of $\equiv_L$, $A_1 \equiv_L (x : M)N$ and $B_1 \equiv_L M$. Finally, remark 1 on $\equiv_L$ gives $\Gamma \vdash (t\ u) \in N[x \leftarrow u]$.

$\square$

By this proposition and the theorem 27, we have a deterministic method to reconstruct a partial proof term from a specification and a weak extracted program. Given a proof $t : S$, the proof synthesis method applied to $\sigma(t)$, by the theorem 27, gives $\Gamma', \mathcal{L} \vdash_r t' : S'$ with $\sigma(t) = \sigma(t')$, $\sigma(S) = \sigma(S')$ and $\mathcal{L}$ a well formed logical context. The proof term contents holes corresponding to logical proofs to be retrieved by hand. These holes are existential variables in the logical context.

We can give some results directly from this theorem. First of all, what happens if the proof synthesis method is applied to a term who is exactly the weak extraction of a proof ? It can be proved the logical generated lemmas are provable. This gives a weak completeness notion for the method.

Let us explain this result. The inversion method defined by the proof of the theorem 27 can be seen as a functor F which, from a derivation of $\Gamma \vdash t \in S$ builds Γ', t', S' such that $\Gamma' \vdash_r t' : S'$.

Notation : let φ be a derivation $\Gamma \vdash_r t : S$, we note $\sigma(\varphi)$ the corresponding derivation for σ, that is $\sigma(\Gamma) \vdash \sigma(t) \in \sigma(S)$. We consider $\in$ and not $\in_2$, because the proof of the theorem 27 uses the rules of $\in$ and the completeness proof will follow the same structure than this proof. Moreover, the two typing judgments are equivalent.

Proposition 31. *Weak completeness of the inversion of the weak extraction :*
If $\varphi \equiv \Gamma \vdash_r t : S$ then $F(\sigma(\varphi)) \equiv \Gamma', \mathcal{L} \vdash_r t' : S'$ with t and t', S and S' identical modulo the identification of all the logical proofs of a same proposition, Γ' provable in Γ and with $\mathcal{L}$ containing logical lemmas which have a proof in Γ.

Proof. The proof follows exactly the same structure as for the inversion theorem. Each step shows that the constructed logical lemmas are provable. $\square$

Then, let us see what happens if the method is applied to a provable specification and a term which is only coherent with it (it is not necessarily a trace of a proof). Naturally, if the program is not correct, the logical lemmas are not provable. But, it cannot be ensured that, if the program is correct, the logical lemmas are provable. We give examples where the program is correct w.r.t. to the specification but can generate non provable logical lemmas.

Example 7.

Let us take the specification $(x : nat)(x > 0) \rightarrow \{y : nat | y < x\}$ with a *Coq* syntax. An program coherent with this specification can be :

```
[x:nat]<{y:nat|y<x}>Match x with
            0
            [n:nat]n
     end
```

A non provable lemma is then generated : $(0 < 0)$.

A program that would generate only logical lemmas could be :

```
[x:nat]<(x>0)->{y:nat|y<x}>Match x with
            0
            [n:nat]n
     end
```

The method is then deterministic. It reconstructs a partial proof term from a weak extracted program and its specification. Proof obligations are left to the user. They represent logical properties that the program has to verify to valid its specification. This implies that we have a canonical representation for proofs. This approach is both a method of proving programs and a method of synthetically describing proofs.

4 A heuristic method

Weak extracted programs are not very natural. It would be nice to consider more natural programs, that is, programs with less specifications. In fact, we would like the programmer to write F_ω^{Ind} programs and the method to use unification to retrieve subspecifications. This is the goal of a tactic implemented in *Coq* and presented in [Par93, Par95].

This heuristic approach should follow the same method as the deterministic method, but the use of unification introduces non-determinism. Nevertheless, we introduce annotations in F_ω^{Ind} programs that the heuristic method could use and that allow to keep a certain notion of completeness. We briefly describe some heuristics and optimizations. We refer the reader to [Par93, Par95] for further details.

A notion of typing is always necessary. This typing is a little different from $\in$. We define $\in_3$ which replaces 2 and 3 by 5. Programs are now F_ω^{Ind} programs and this new rule only allows to go back to a typing corresponding to F_ω. It just introduces a notion of correction for programs.

Definition 32. Typing on natural programs :

$$\frac{\Gamma \vdash T' \in_3 s \quad \Gamma \vdash t \in_3 T \quad \varepsilon(T) = \varepsilon(T')}{\Gamma \vdash t \in_3 T'} \tag{5}$$

4.1 Heuristics

The problem is to retrieve specifications. For this, we use higher-order unification between the type of the program and the specification. Since unification is not deterministic, we have to make some choices. We prefer not to give all the details in this paper, but we can give an idea of where the problems are and how they can be solved. The main problematic cases are applications and eliminations. In an application, the problem is to retrieve all the logical arguments. Moreover, if one argument is a predicate, it is not deterministic to retrieve it by unification. For the elimination, the problem is to retrieve the elimination predicate. Heuristics deal with unification between the type of the program and the specification. The problem is to choose the good unifier. The choice is to always keep the most general unifier (in the sense of the one which bounds the biggest number of variables). In practice, it seems to be a good choice.

Example 8.
   Let us give an example for a heuristic in an application.
   Let us take the specification $\forall n.\exists m.(S\ m) = n \vee n = m = 0$. A strong extracted program coherent with this specification is :

```
[n:nat](nat_rec (sig nat) (exist nat 0)
                [y:nat][H:(sig nat)](exist nat y))
```

where **nat_rec** is the usual induction principle on natural numbers whose type is $(P : nat \to Set)(P\ 0) \to ((n : nat)(P\ n) \to (P\ (S\ n))) \to (n : nat)(P\ n)$. Note that in the previous program, **nat_rec** is a program variable and then its type is $(P : Set)P \to (nat \to P \to P) \to nat \to P$.
   The proof term to be retrieved is :

```
[n:nat](nat_rec [n0:nat]{m:nat|(S m)=n0 \/ n0=m=0}
                (exist nat [m:nat]((S m)=0 \/ 0=m=0) 0 P1)
                [y:nat][H:{m:nat|(S m)=y \/ y=m=0}]
                (exist nat [m:nat]((S m)=(S y) \/ (S y)=m=0)
                y P2))
```

where P1 and P2 are proofs for $((S\ 0) = 0) \vee (0 = 0 = 0)$ and $((Sy) = (Sy)) \vee ((Sy) = y = 0)$.
   Let us consider only the application case (the previous abstraction is trivial). We look for the predicate whose extraction is *nat*. **nat_rec** and its proof type are known. The searched predicate P has type $nat \to Set$. Let us use the specification to instantiate P. The head of the type of **nat_rec** (i.e. $(P\ n)$) can be unified with the specification (i.e. $\exists m.(S\ m) = n \vee n = m = 0$).
   This is non deterministic and there are many possible unifiers :

1. $P = [n0]\exists m.(S\ m) = n0 \vee n0 = m = 0$.
2. $P = [n0]\exists m.(S\ m) = n0 \vee n = m = 0$.
3. $P = [n0]\exists m.(S\ m) = n \vee n0 = m = 0$.
4. $P = [n0]\exists m.(S\ m) = n \vee n = m = 0$.

The heuristic consists in keeping the unifier which bounds the biggest number of variables, thus the first one in this case. Two subgoals are generated :

$$\begin{cases} \exists m.(S\ m) = 0 \vee 0 = m = 0 \\ \forall n.\exists m.((S\ m) = n \vee n = m = 0) \to \exists m.(S\ m) = (S\ n) \vee (S\ n) = m = 0 \end{cases}$$

associated to two subprograms (exist nat 0) and

```
[y:nat][H:{m:nat|(S m)=y\/y=m=0}]
  (exist nat [m:nat]((S m)=(S y)\/(S y)=m=0) y)
```

4.2 Annotations

The heuristic method deals with cases where the higher-order unification succeeds. In practice, this seems to be quite often the case. However, to ensure the determinism of this method, we must be able to direct the choices and then to allow the programmer to add logical informations in the program. These annotations have to be taken into account by the method to take good decisions.

Syntax : S is an annotation for the program p is noted $p :: S$.

Definition 33. Annotations :

$$\frac{\Gamma \vdash p \in_3 S \quad \varepsilon(S) = \varepsilon(S')}{\Gamma \vdash (p :: S) \in_3 S'}$$

The intuition is the following. S is an annotation for p if p is coherent with S. Moreover, if p is coherent with S' then $p :: S$ is coherent with S' and $\varepsilon(S) = \varepsilon(S')$. Annotations are logical specifications that mark programs and allow to precise their specification. The goal is to use them to give explicitly the specification of a program when the heuristic method fails.

An annotation can contain free variables. These variables can be program variables or logical variables. It is necessary to be able to refer to logical variables inside a program and then to authorize logical λ-abstractions. This corresponds to the already existing rule of $\in_3$:

$$\frac{\Gamma[x : L] \vdash p \in_3 S}{\Gamma \vdash [x : L]p \in_3 (x : L)S} \quad \text{if } L : Type$$

4.3 Validity and Completeness

The heuristic method can either succeed or fail. There are three possible behaviors.

1. The method fails. Then, either the program is false, or there are not enough logical informations in the program. It can be necessary to add annotations in the program.

2. The method generates a set of logical lemmas that are not provable. Then, either the program is false, or there are not enough logical informations in the program. It can be necessary to add annotations in the program.
3. The method generates a set of provable logical lemmas. The theorem 27 ensures that the inversion of the weak extraction generates a partial proof of the initial specification. Then, the validity of the method is ensured.

We come now to the problem of the completeness of the heuristic method. The heuristic method fails on a correct program when there are not enough logical informations. The method on weak extracted terms is deterministic. As a consequence, the heuristic method succeeds on sufficiently annotated programs that is if the annotated program is the weak extracted program. The completeness of the heuristic method can then be stated.

Proposition 34. *If S is provable and if the associated program p is sufficiently annotated to be a trace of a proof of S, then the logical lemmas generated by the heuristic method are provable.*

Proof. Comes directly from the proposition 31. □

Then, if programs are weak extracted programs, the heuristic method is complete. The notion of sufficiently annotated programs corresponds in the worst case to a weak extracted term. In practice, annotations are typically elimination predicates. It corresponds to recursive structures in a program. One retrieves the problem of loop invariants search in the Hoare's logic [Hoa69]. We discuss this comparison in the conclusion.

4.4 Optimizations

The strong extraction can be optimized in order to generate programs that are closer to a natural form. Such optimizations generate programs more and more far from the proof. Until this section, we never consider such an optimization. By now, if we consider it, the heuristics to retrieve a proof term in such a case are much more harder. Special heuristics have to been developed to deal with these cases. A possible optimization of the strong extraction consists in distinguishing particular types that we call singleton types. Such an optimization suppresses constructors on singleton types and eliminations on singleton types. Then, for instance, heuristics have to be found to retrieve an elimination on a singleton type which has disappeared by extraction or a constructor on a singleton type.

Other optimizations can be introduced to consider more natural programs. An operator of well-founded recursion can be introduced. It is based on a well-founded induction principle. Extracted programs often contain trivial expressions such as `if b then true else false`. A more natural program is b. This implies that heuristics have to deal with such situations. They have to be able to retrieve the underlying structure of proof even if this is not the same in the program.

We do not detail at all this part but one can refer to [Par93, Par95] for an explanation of such optimizations.

5 Conclusion

We have defined a new extraction function for the Calculus of Inductive Constructions called the weak extraction. Weak extracted terms are condensed forms of proofs. They are F_ω^{Ind} programs annotated with specifications. A new notion of typing has been defined for such terms. This weak extraction has an important property : it can be inverted. The proof of inversibility gives an algorithm to reconstruct a proof from a program and its specification. Given a weak extracted program and its specification, a partial proof term, with "holes" corresponding to logical lemmas to be proved, can be deterministically reconstructed. The method is complete in the sense that there exists a proof for these logical lemmas in the original proof term.

A heuristic method can be deduced based on the same idea. The considered programs are F_ω^{Ind} programs. Heuristics are needed to retrieve intermediate subspecifications by unification. Annotations can be added in F_ω^{Ind} programs to explicitly give subspecifications. Then, the heuristic method is complete for sufficiently annotated programs. Optimizations can be introduced to consider more natural programs. This method presents two different aspects : it is both a method of proving programs and a method of synthetically describing proofs. Indeed, weak extracted programs can be seen as proofs descriptions.

This method can be compared with the Hoare's logic. Indeed, Hoare's logic proves that programs meet specifications. The structure of the program is analyzed and subspecifications corresponding to subprograms are generated until arriving at axioms. Our idea is exactly the same. Hoare's axioms corresponds to our logical lemmas. A known problem of Hoare's logic is the problem of retrieving loop invariants. This can be compared to our problem of retrieving elimination predicates in the heuristic method. In Hoare's logic, the user has to explicitly give invariants. In our method, it is necessary to add annotations. The main difference between the two methods is that they are in different frameworks. Hoare's logic considers imperative programs and specifications in first order predicate calculus. We consider functional programs and specifications in the Calculus of Inductive Constructions. Moreover, this work can be compared with the problem of retrieving the weakest precondition in Hoare's Logic. This problem consists in looking for a minimal precondition. This can be done by analyzing the program and the postcondition and building step-by-step the weakest precondition. Our method is close to this one. Indeed, we can reconstruct a proof term for a specification logically equivalent to the initial one. In fact, this specification contains less logical informations than the initial one. It can be considered as a construction of the "weakest specification".

The motivations of this work were that the user knows in general the algorithm he wants to prove. The same motivations are the basis of two works [BM92, Pol94]. These works construct a proof and a program hand in hand. They are not the same method as ours but the motivations are the same : allowing the user to direct the proof with a program.

This method has been implemented as a tactic in the *Coq* system. As we already said, the description of this tactic can be found in [Par93, Par95]. A library of examples has been developed with optimizations on the input language for programs. These examples are non trivial : they consist in algorithms on graphs, trees, lists (different sorts)... We can use the ProPre tactic of [MS92] which has been integrated into *Coq* to define functions via equations. This definition is transformed into a primitive recursive definition which can be used as input for our tactic. This allows to write input programs for our tactic more easily. In the current state, this is possible but only for a restricted number of functions. We hope the number of functions easily expressible with ProPre will increase and then allow us to use it in a more general way. Moreover, we hope to be able to write programs in more natural form than F_ω^{Ind} programs.

Finally, other methods of proof synthesis from programs could perhaps be developed. It should be possible to work with the program f and with the proof to do of $\forall x.(P\,x) \to (Q\,x\,(f\,x))$. This formula express that f realizes $\forall x.(P\,x) \to \exists y.(Q\,x\,y)$. The developed technology should not be very different but one can hope to prove more things since a proof of "f realizes B" can sometimes be done when a proof of B does not exist.

Acknowledgments

I am grateful to Christine Paulin-Mohring for supervising this work and for many helpful discussions.

A   An example : a division algorithm

We detail here a complete example for a division algorithm. Some notions n the *Coq* syntax have to be known here. The **Program_all** tactic corresponds to the implementation of the proof synthesis method. It automatically generates a proof (with eventually holes corresponding to logical lemmas) from a program (in a *Coq* syntax) associated to a specification (in a *Coq* syntax too) by a command called **Realizer**.

Let us give the specification of the euclidean division algorithm. We want to prove that for a and b ($b > 0$), there exist q and r such that $a = b * q + r$ and $b > r$.

An ML program following this specification can be :

```
let div b a = divrec a where rec divrec = function
          if (b<=a) then let (q,r) = divrec (a-b) in (Sq,r)
                    else (0,a)
```

Suppose we give the following definition in *Coq* which describes what has to be proved, ie, $\exists q \exists r.\ (a = b * q + r \land b > r)$:

```
Coq < Inductive diveucl [a,b:nat] : Set :=
          divex : (q,r:nat)(a=(plus (mult q b) r))->
                    (gt b r)->(diveucl a b).
```

The decidability of the ordering relation has to be proved first, by giving the associated function of type **nat->nat->bool** :

```
Coq < Recursive Definition le_gt_dec_func : nat->nat->bool :=
Coq <    O m => true
Coq < | (S n) O => false
Coq < | (S n) (S m) => (le_gt_dec_func n m).
Coq <
Coq < Theorem le_gt_dec : (n,m:nat){(le n m)}+{(gt n m)}.
Coq < Realizer le_gt_dec_func.
Coq < Program_all.
Coq < Save.
```

Then the specification is (b:nat)(gt b O)->(a:nat)(diveucl a b). The associated program corresponding to the ML program will be :

```
Coq < Realizer [b:nat](<nat*nat>rec div :: :: { lt }
                  [a:nat]<nat*nat>if (le_gt_dec b a)
                     then <nat*nat>let (q,r:nat) = (div (minus a b))
                          in <nat,nat>((S q),r)
                     else <nat,nat>(O,a)).
```

Where lt is the well-founded ordering relation defined by :

```
Coq < Definition lt := [n,m:nat](gt m n).
```

Note the syntax for recursive programs. The rec construction needs 4 arguments : the type result of the function (nat*nat because it returns two natural numbers) between < and >, the name of the induction hypothesis (which can be used for recursive calls), the ordering relation lt (as an annotation because it is a specification), and the program itself which must begin with a λ-abstraction. The specification of le_gt_dec is known because it is a previous lemma. The term (le_gt_dec b a) is seen by the Program_all tactic as a term of type bool which satisfies the specification {(le a b)}+{(gt a b)}. The tactic Program_all can be used, and the following logical lemmas are obtained :

```
6 subgoals
  b : nat
  H : (gt b O)
  a : nat
  ============================
   (well_founded nat lt)
subgoal 2 is:
 x=(plus (mult (S q) b) r)
subgoal 3 is:
 (gt b r)
subgoal 4 is:
 (lt (minus x b) x)
subgoal 5 is:
 x=(plus (mult O b) x)
subgoal 6 is:
 (gt b x)
```

References

[Bar91]   H. Barendregt. Lambda Calculi with Types. Technical Report 91-19, Catholic University Nijmegen, September 1991.

[BM92]   R. Burstall and J. McKinna. Deliverables : a categorical approach to program development in type theory. Technical Report 92-242, LFCS, October 1992. Also in [NPP92].

[CCF+94] C. Cornes, J. Courant, J.C. Filliâtre, G. Huet, P. Manoury, C. Paulin-Mohring, C. Muñoz, C. Murthy, C. Parent, A. Saïbi, and B. Werner. Coq V5.10 Reference Manual. Technical report, 1994. Disponible en ftp anonyme sur ftp.inria.fr, à paraître.

[Con86]   R. L. Constable et al. Implementing Mathematics with the Nuprl Proof Development System. Prentice-Hall, 1986.

[Coq85]   T. Coquand. Une théorie des constructions. PhD thesis, Université Paris VII, 1985.

[DFH+93] G. Dowek, A. Felty, H. Herbelin, G. Huet, C. Murthy, C. Parent, C. Paulin-Mohring, and B. Werner. The Coq Proof Assistant User's Guide - Version 5.8. Technical Report 154, Projet Formel - INRIA-Rocquencourt-CNRS-ENS Lyon, May 1993.

[Gir72]   J.Y. Girard. Interprétation fonctionnelle et élimination des coupures de l'arithmétique d'ordre supérieur. PhD thesis, Université Paris 7, 1972.

[Hoa69]   C.A.R. Hoare. An Axiomatic Basis for Computer Programming. Communications of the ACM, 12(10), October 1969.

[How80]   W.A. Howard. The formulaes-as-types notion of construction. In J.R. Hindley, editor, To H.B.Curry : Essays on Combinatory Logic , lambda-calculus and formalism. Seldin, J.P., 1980.

[ML84]   P. Martin-Löf. Intuitionistic Type Theory. Studies in Proof Theory. Bibliopolis, 1984.

[MS92]   P. Manoury and M. Simonot. Des preuves de totalité de fonctions comme synthèse de programmes. PhD thesis, Université PARIS 7, December 1992.

[NPP92]   B. Nordström, K. Petersson, and G. Plotkin, editors. Proceedings of the 1992 workshop on types for proofs and programs, June 1992.

[NPS90]   B. Nordström, K. Petersson, and J. M. Smith. Programming in Martin-Löf's Type Theory : an introduction. Oxford Science Publications, 1990.

[Par93]   C. Parent. Developing certified programs in the system Coq - The Program tactic. In H. Barendregt and T. Nipkow, editors, Types For Proofs and Programs, volume 806 of LNCS, pages 291–312, May 1993.

[Par95]   C. Parent. Synthèse de preuves de programmes dans le Calcul des Constructions. PhD thesis, Ecole Normale Supérieure de Lyon, January 1995.

[PC89]   F. Pfenning and Paulin-Mohring C. Inductively Defined Types in the Calculus of Constructions. In 5th International Conference on Mathematical Foundations of Programming Semantics, volume 442 of LNCS, pages 209–228, 1989.

[PM89a]   C. Paulin-Mohring. Extracting F_ω's programs from proofs in the Calculus of Constructions. In Sixteenth Annual ACM Symposium on Principles of Programming Languages, Austin, January 1989.

[PM89b]   C. Paulin-Mohring. Extraction de programmes dans le Calcul des Constructions. PhD thesis, Université Paris VII, 1989.

[PM93]   C. Paulin-Mohring. Inductive Definitions in the System Coq - Rules and Properties. In *Typed Lambda Calculi and Applications*, volume 664 of *LNCS*, March 1993. Also in research report 92-49, LIP-ENS Lyon, December 1992.

[Pol94]   E. Poll. *A Programming Logic Based on Type Theory*. PhD thesis, Technische Universiteit Eindhoven, 1994.

A General Scheme for Breadth–First Graph Traversal

Martin Russling

Lehrstuhl für Informatik II, Universität Augsburg, D–86135 Augsburg, Germany,
FAX ++49/821/598–2274, e-mail: russling@uni-augsburg.de

Abstract. We survey an algebra of formal languages suitable to deal with graph algorithms. As an example of its use we derive a general scheme for breadth–first graph traversal. This general scheme is then applied to a reachability and a shortest path problem.

1 Introduction

In books about algorithmic graph theory algorithms are usually presented without formal specification and formal development. Some approaches, in contrast, provide a more precise treatment of graph algorithms, resulting in algorithms which are not only correct "in principle" but also in all details (see e.g. [Pair 70], [Backhouse, van Gasteren 92], [van den Eijnde 92], [Möller, Russling 92], [Gibbons 94] and [King, Launchbury 95]). In the present paper a uniform treatment of a class of graph algorithms is given using the algebra of formal languages and relations presented in [Möller, Russling 92], a straightened version of the framework introduced in [Möller 91]. The emphasis is not laid on the invention of new algorithms, but on a purely algebraic derivation of existing ones. In sum, the algebra allows derivations which are purely formal, concise and understandable at the same time.

2 An Algebra of Formal Languages

2.1 Formal Languages and Relations

We consider an alphabet A. In the context of graph algorithms the letters of A are interpreted as graph vertices. The cardinality of A is, as usual, denoted by $|A|$. By A^* we denote the set of all words over A. A **(formal) language** is a subset of A^*. Formal languages are used to describe sets of paths in a directed graph by listing the vertex sequences along the paths. We denote the number of letters of a word u by $\|u\|$ and call it the **length** of u. A **relation of arity** n is a language R over A such that all words in R have length n. Note that $\emptyset$ is a relation of any arity. For relation $R \neq \emptyset$ we denote the arity of R by $\text{ar } R$. Unary relations represent vertex sets, whereas binary relations represent edge sets. The only two nullary relations (the singleton relation ε, consisting just of the empty word, and the empty relation $\emptyset$) play the role of the Boolean values. This also allows easy definitions of assertions and conditional expressions.

All operations on words are extended pointwise to sets of words. By this convention, the extended operations distribute through union in all arguments and hence are monotonic w.r.t. inclusion and strict w.r.t. $\emptyset$. In particular, fixpoints of functions using these operations exist [Tarski 55] and may be computed using Kleene's approximation sequence [Kleene 52]. Moreover, linear equational laws, i.e., laws in which each side has exactly one occurrence of every variable, are preserved (see e.g. [Gautam 57]). We define that the set theoretic operations have lowest priority. Essential operations are (besides union, intersection and difference) concatenation, composition and join.

To save braces, we identify a singleton set with its only element; e.g., the empty word ε is not distinguished from the relation ε, consisting just of the empty word. And, as usual, a word of length 1 is not distinguished from the only letter it contains.

Concatenation is denoted by $\bullet$. It is associative, with ε, the empty word, as the neutral element:

$$u \bullet (v \bullet w) = (u \bullet v) \bullet w \; , \tag{1}$$

$$\varepsilon \bullet u \; = u = \; u \bullet \varepsilon \; . \tag{2}$$

Concatenation is extended pointwise to languages. Since the above laws are linear, they carry over to languages U, V, W over A:

$$U \bullet (V \bullet W) = (U \bullet V) \bullet W \; , \tag{3}$$

$$\varepsilon \bullet U \; = U = \; U \bullet \varepsilon \; . \tag{4}$$

2.2 Join and Composition

For words u and v over alphabet A we define their **join** $u \bowtie v$ and their **composition** $u \,; v$ by

$$\varepsilon \bowtie \varepsilon \stackrel{\text{def}}{=} \varepsilon \; , \tag{5}$$

$$\varepsilon \bowtie w \stackrel{\text{def}}{=} \emptyset \stackrel{\text{def}}{=} w \bowtie \varepsilon \; , \tag{6}$$

$$(u \bullet a) \bowtie (b \bullet v) \stackrel{\text{def}}{=} \begin{cases} u \bullet a \bullet v \text{ if } a = b \; , \\ \emptyset \qquad\quad \text{otherwise} \; , \end{cases} \tag{7}$$

$$\varepsilon \,; u \stackrel{\text{def}}{=} \emptyset \stackrel{\text{def}}{=} u \,; \varepsilon \; , \tag{8}$$

$$(u \bullet a) \,; (b \bullet v) \stackrel{\text{def}}{=} \begin{cases} u \bullet v \text{ if } a = b \; , \\ \emptyset \qquad \text{otherwise} \; , \end{cases} \tag{9}$$

where $u, v \in A^*$, $w \in A^* \setminus \varepsilon$ and $a, b \in A$. These operations provide two different ways of "glueing" two words together upon a one–letter overlap: join preserves one copy of the overlap, whereas composition erases it. Again, they are extended pointwise to languages. (The definition of the join operation differs slightly from former papers: Defining now $\varepsilon \bowtie \varepsilon \overset{\text{def}}{=} \varepsilon$ makes $(\mathcal{P}(A^*), \bowtie, \varepsilon \cup A)$ a monoid whereas with $\varepsilon \bowtie \varepsilon \overset{\text{def}}{=} \emptyset$ only the subset $(\mathcal{P}(A^*)\backslash\varepsilon, \bowtie, A)$ not containing the empty word is a monoid.) On relations, the join is a special case of the one used in database theory (see e.g. [Date 88]). Remember that set theoretic operations have lowest priority, i.e. join and composition bind stronger.

For binary relations $R \subseteq A \bullet A$ the relations

$$
\begin{array}{l}
\varepsilon\ , \\
A\ , \\
R\ , \\
R \bowtie R\ , \\
R \bowtie (R \bowtie R)\ , \\
\quad\vdots
\end{array}
\tag{10}
$$

consist of the words which are vertex sequences along paths of vertex lengths $0, 1, 2, 3, 4, \ldots$ in the directed graph associated with R.

The operations associate nicely:

$$
\left.
\begin{array}{ll}
U \bowtie (V \bowtie W) = (U \bowtie V) \bowtie W\ , & \\
U\, ;(V\, ; W) = (U\, ; V)\, ; W & \Leftarrow V \cap A = \emptyset\ , \\
U\, ;(V \bowtie W) = (U\, ; V) \bowtie W & \Leftarrow V \cap A = \emptyset\ , \\
(U \bowtie V)\, ; W = U \bowtie (V\, ; W) & \Leftarrow V \cap A = \emptyset\ .
\end{array}
\right\}
\tag{11}
$$

We shall omit parentheses whenever one of these laws applies.

If one operand, say S, of the join operation has arity 1, then $S \bowtie U$, viz. $U \bowtie S$, yields those words of language U the first, viz. last, letters of which are elements of S. In particular

$$
S \bowtie U \subseteq U \supseteq U \bowtie S \quad \Leftarrow S \subseteq A\ .
\tag{12}
$$

If both operands have arity 1 then join intersects the two sets $S, T \subseteq A$, i.e.,

$$
S \bowtie T = S \cap T\ ,
\tag{13}
$$

and composition tests whether the intersection is not empty:

$$
S\, ; T = \begin{cases} \varepsilon & \text{if } S \cap T \neq \emptyset\ , \\ \emptyset & \text{if } S \cap T = \emptyset\ , \end{cases}
\tag{14}
$$

$$
S\, ; S = \begin{cases} \varepsilon & \text{if } S \neq \emptyset\ , \\ \emptyset & \text{if } S = \emptyset\ , \end{cases}
\tag{15}
$$

$$
x\, ; S = S\, ; x = \begin{cases} \varepsilon & \text{if } x \in S\ , \\ \emptyset & \text{if } x \notin S\ , \end{cases}
\tag{16}
$$

$$
x\, ; y = y\, ; x = \begin{cases} \varepsilon & \text{if } x = y\ , \\ \emptyset & \text{if } x \neq y\ , \end{cases}
\tag{17}
$$

where $x, y \in A$. Because these "tests" will be used frequently, we introduce more readable notations for them by setting

$$S \neq \emptyset \stackrel{\text{def}}{=} S \,;\, S \,, \tag{18}$$

$$x \in S \stackrel{\text{def}}{=} x \,;\, S \,, \tag{19}$$

$$(x = y) \stackrel{\text{def}}{=} x \,;\, y \,, \tag{20}$$

$$S \subseteq T \stackrel{\text{def}}{=} (S \cup T = T) \,. \tag{21}$$

2.3 Assertions and Conditional Expressions

As we have just seen, the nullary relations ε and $\emptyset$ characterize the outcomes of certain tests. More generally, they can be used instead of Boolean values; therefore we call expressions yielding nullary relations **assertions**. Note that in this view "false" and "undefined" both are represented by $\emptyset$. Negation is defined by

$$\overline{\emptyset} \stackrel{\text{def}}{=} \varepsilon \,, \tag{22}$$

$$\overline{\varepsilon} \stackrel{\text{def}}{=} \emptyset \,. \tag{23}$$

Note that this operation is not $\subseteq$-monotonic.

Conjunction and disjunction of assertions are represented by their intersection and union. To improve readability, we write $B \wedge C$ for $B \cap C = B \bullet C$ and $B \vee C$ for $B \cup C$.

For assertion B and arbitrary language U we have

$$B \bullet U = U \bullet B = \begin{cases} U & \text{if } B = \varepsilon \,, \\ \emptyset & \text{if } B = \emptyset \,. \end{cases} \tag{24}$$

This shows how assertions can be used as restrictions.

Using assertions we can define a **conditional** by

$$\text{if } B \text{ then } U \text{ else } V \text{ fi} \stackrel{\text{def}}{=} B \bullet U \cup \overline{B} \bullet V \,, \tag{25}$$

for assertion B and languages U, V. Note that this operation is not $\subseteq$-monotonic in B.

It can easily be calculated that conditionals may be manipulated as usual, e.g.,

$$\text{if } B \text{ then } U \text{ else if } C \text{ then } U \text{ else } V \text{ fi fi } = \text{ if } B \vee C \text{ then } U \text{ else } V \text{ fi} \,, \tag{26}$$

for assertions B, C and languages U, V.

2.4 Path Closure

The **path closure** $R^\leadsto$ of a binary relation $R \subseteq A \bullet A$ is defined as the least fixpoint of a recursion equation:

$$R^\leadsto \stackrel{\text{def}}{=} \mu X \,.\, \varepsilon \cup A \cup R \bowtie X \,. \tag{27}$$

It consists of all words which are vertex sequences along finite paths in the directed graph associated with R (see (10)).

3 Graph Algorithms

In the context of graph algorithms the alphabet A is interpreted as a finite vertex set of a graph. The edges are represented by a binary edge relation $R \subseteq A \bullet A$.

For $Q, R \subseteq A \bullet A$ the definition of composition (see appendix) coincides with the usual definition of relational composition (see e.g. [Tarski 41] or [Schmidt, Ströhlein 93]):

$$Q \,;R = \bigcup_{x \in A} \bigcup_{y \in A} \bigcup_{z \in A} \{x \bullet y : x \bullet z \in Q \land z \bullet y \in R\} \,. \tag{28}$$

Thus $Q\,;R$ states the existence of a Q–edge followed by an R–edge between pairs of vertices abstracting over the intermediate vertices, while

$$Q \bowtie R = \bigcup_{x \in A} \bigcup_{y \in A} \bigcup_{z \in A} \{x \bullet z \bullet y : x \bullet z \in Q \land z \bullet y \in R\} \tag{29}$$

lists also the intermediate vertices.

Further interesting special cases of composition and join arise when one of the operands has arity 1 and the other has arity 2. Suppose $S \subseteq A$ and $R \subseteq A \bullet A$. Then

$$S\,;R = \bigcup_{y \in A} \bigcup_{z \in S} \{y : z \bullet y \in R\} \tag{30}$$

and hence gives the successor set of set S in the directed graph associated with R, whereas $R\,;S$ is the predecessor set. Supposing again $S \subseteq A$ and $R \subseteq A \bullet A$ then

$$S \bowtie R = \bigcup_{y \in A} \bigcup_{z \in S} \{z \bullet y : z \bullet y \in R\} \,. \tag{31}$$

This means that $S \bowtie R$ is the restriction of R to S, containing only those edges beginning in S. Likewise $R \bowtie S$ is the corestriction of R to S, i.e. the set of all edges ending in S. For a set of paths $P \subseteq R^\leadsto$, $S \bowtie P$ selects the paths in P that start in S while $P \bowtie S$ gives those paths that end in S. Hence, for $S, T \subseteq A$,

$$S \bowtie R^\leadsto \bowtie T \tag{32}$$

is the language of all paths between elements of S and T in this graph.

Successor and predecessor sets are closely related to restrictions and corestrictions. We have, for $R \subseteq A \bullet A$ and $S, T \subseteq A$,

$$S \,;R \subseteq T \Leftrightarrow S \bowtie R \bowtie T = S \bowtie R \,, \tag{33}$$

$$R \,;T \subseteq S \Leftrightarrow S \bowtie R \bowtie T = R \bowtie T \,. \tag{34}$$

4 A General Scheme for Breadth–First Graph Traversal

For certain graph problems one considers the set of all paths starting in a subset, say S, of the vertex set and ending in a subset T. An operation $f \colon A^* \to M$ is used to abstract over each path and is extended pointwise to set of paths. M is an arbitrary set depending on what we are actually interested in; e.g., if we are interested in the lengths of the paths we choose the set of natural numbers. Then, an operation $g \colon \mathcal{P}(M) \to \mathcal{P}(M)$ selects certain abstractions, e.g. the minimum w.r.t. some order on M. These motivating considerations will be made precise in postulates below.

4.1 Specification

We specify a graph traversal operation F by

$$F(f, g)(S, T) \stackrel{\text{def}}{=} g(f(S \bowtie R^{\curvearrowright} \bowtie T)) \,, \tag{35}$$

for $S, T \subseteq A$ and $R \subseteq A \bullet A$. We involve two operations instead of only one: The abstraction f is a pointwise extended operation, thus providing nice algebraic properties, i.e., distributivity, monotonicity and strictness, but the selection g isn't. However, we postulate a weak distributivity of g:

(i) $g(K \cup L) = g(g(K) \cup g(L))$,

for $K, L \subseteq M$. Note that by (i) g is idempotent and (i) is equivalent to

(i') $g(K \cup L) = g(K \cup g(L))$.

4.2 Examples of Application

Reachability. We consider the problem of computing the set of vertices reachable by paths starting in a subset $S \subseteq A$ of the vertex set.

Therefore we define

$$reach(S) \stackrel{\text{def}}{=} last(S \bowtie R^{\curvearrowright} \bowtie A) = F(last, id)(S, A) \,, \tag{36}$$

where $M = A$, id is the identity operation and *last* selects the last letter of a word where u_i $(1 \leq i \leq \|u\|)$ is the i-th letter of word u:

$$last(u) \stackrel{\text{def}}{=} (u \neq \varepsilon) \bullet u_{\|u\|} . \tag{37}$$

last is extended pointwise to set of paths. Note that by (35) in our calculations f and thus *last* is not applied to ε. Further, by the above definitions of abstraction and selection operation we are not allowed to choose $f = id$ and $g = last$.

By this definition the set of last vertices of all paths starting in S, i.e. the desired reachable vertices, is specified.

Length of a Shortest Connecting Path. Next, we consider the problem of finding the length of a shortest connecting path from a vertex x to a vertex y. Therefore we choose $M = \mathbb{N}$ and define

$$shortestpath(x, y) \stackrel{\text{def}}{=} min(edgelength(x \bowtie R^{\rightsquigarrow} \bowtie y)) = F(edgelength, min)(x, y) \tag{38}$$

where, for path p,

$$edgelength(p) \stackrel{\text{def}}{=} \text{if } u = \varepsilon \text{ then } 0 \text{ else } \|p\| - 1 \text{ fi} \tag{39}$$

gives the number of edges in path p, is extended pointwise to sets of paths, and, for a set N of natural numbers,

$$min(N) \stackrel{\text{def}}{=} \begin{cases} k \text{ if } k \in N \wedge N \subseteq k \,; \leq_{\mathbb{N}} \,, \\ \emptyset \text{ if } N = \emptyset \,. \end{cases} \tag{40}$$

4.3 Recursive Solution

For deriving a recursion we calculate:

$F(f, g)(S, T)$

$=$ $\{\!\!\{$ definition $\}\!\!\}$

$g(f(S \bowtie R^{\rightsquigarrow} \bowtie T))$

$=$ $\{\!\!\{$ by (27) $\}\!\!\}$

$g(f(S \bowtie (\varepsilon \cup A \cup R \bowtie R^{\rightsquigarrow}) \bowtie T))$

$=$ $\{\!\!\{$ distributivity $\}\!\!\}$

$g(f(S \bowtie \varepsilon \bowtie T) \cup f(S \bowtie A \bowtie T) \cup f(S \bowtie R \bowtie R^{\rightsquigarrow} \bowtie T))$

$=$ $\{\!\!\{$ by (6), (13) $\}\!\!\}$

$g(\emptyset \cup f(S \cap T) \cup f(S \bowtie R \bowtie R^{\rightsquigarrow} \bowtie T))$.

Here the direct attempt to derive a recursion fails, since we are not able to perform a fold–step. In the second application of f we need a vertex set instead of $S \bowtie R$. Thus we introduce an operation $v: M \to M$ being pointwise extended to $\mathcal{P}(M)$ and stating the difference of f being applied to joined and composed languages, i.e.,

(ii) $V \cap (\varepsilon \cup A) = \emptyset \Rightarrow f(U \bowtie V) = v(f(U \,;V))$

for $U \subseteq A$ and $V \subseteq A^*$. (ii) corresponds to a forward step within paths. Further, we postulate that "corrections" brought in by v are ignored by g and that g and v may be applied in arbitrary order:

(iii) $g(K) = g(K \cup v(K))$ and
(iv) $g(v(K)) = v(g(K))$,

for $K \subseteq M$. Condition (iii) will help accumulate the vertices already visited. We calculate

$$F(f,g)(S,T)$$
$$= \quad \{\!| \text{ definition }|\!\}$$
$$g(f(S \bowtie R^{\leftrightarrow} \bowtie T))$$
$$= \quad \{\!| \text{ by (iii) }|\!\}$$
$$g(f(S \bowtie R^{\leftrightarrow} \bowtie T) \cup v(f(S \bowtie R^{\leftrightarrow} \bowtie T)))$$
$$= \quad \{\!| \text{ by the above derivation }|\!\}$$
$$g(f(S \cap T) \cup f(S \bowtie R \bowtie R^{\leftrightarrow} \bowtie T) \cup v(f(S \bowtie R^{\leftrightarrow} \bowtie T)))$$
$$= \quad \{\!| \text{ by (ii) }|\!\}$$
$$g(f(S \cap T) \cup v(f(S \,;R \bowtie R^{\leftrightarrow} \bowtie T)) \cup v(f(S \bowtie R^{\leftrightarrow} \bowtie T)))$$
$$= \quad \{\!| \text{ distributivity }|\!\}$$
$$g(f(S \cap T) \cup v(f((S \cup S \,;R) \bowtie R^{\leftrightarrow} \bowtie T)))$$
$$= \quad \{\!| \text{ by (i') }|\!\}$$
$$g(f(S \cap T) \cup g(v(f((S \cup S \,;R) \bowtie R^{\leftrightarrow} \bowtie T))))$$
$$= \quad \{\!| \text{ by (iv) }|\!\}$$
$$g(f(S \cap T) \cup v(g(f((S \cup S \,;R) \bowtie R^{\leftrightarrow} \bowtie T))))$$
$$= \quad \{\!| \text{ definition }|\!\}$$
$$g(f(S \cap T) \cup v(F(f,g)(S \cup S \,;R \,,\, T))) \ .$$

For obtaining a termination case we deal now with two obvious special cases in which F can be simplified. For $T \subseteq S \subseteq A$ we have

$$F(f,g)(S,T)$$

$=$ 〚 definition 〛

$$g(f(S \bowtie R^{\leadsto} \bowtie T))$$

$=$ 〚 by (27) we have $A \subseteq R^{\leadsto}$, hence $R^{\leadsto} = A \cup R^{\leadsto}$, distributivity 〛

$$g(f(S \bowtie A \bowtie T) \cup f(S \bowtie R^{\leadsto} \bowtie T))$$

$=$ 〚 by (13) twice 〛

$$g(f(S \cap T) \cup f(S \bowtie R^{\leadsto} \bowtie T))$$

$=$ 〚 by $T \subseteq S$ 〛

$$g(f(T) \cup f(S \bowtie R^{\leadsto} \bowtie T)) \ .$$

Now, g selects from the union of the abstraction of a vertex set T and the abstraction of paths ending in T. For this case we suppose that the latter brings no new information and thus is ignored by operation g:

(v) $g(f(U)) = g(f(U) \cup f(V \bowtie U))$,

for $U \subseteq A$ and $V \subseteq A^*$. Note that (v) holds for both examples of section 4.2. We complete our calculation:

$$g(f(T) \cup f(S \bowtie R^{\leadsto} \bowtie T))$$

$=$ 〚 by (v) 〛

$$g(f(T)) \ .$$

Further, for $S \,;\, R \subseteq S$ each path in $S \bowtie R^{\leadsto} \bowtie T$ runs entirely inside S. In particular, each last vertex of a path is in S.

Before proving the latter fact we shall study the path closure more thoroughly: By its definition and using Kleene's approximation [Kleene 52] we get

$$R^{\leadsto} = \bigcup_{i \in \mathbb{N}} {}^{i}R \qquad (41)$$

where

$$ {}^{0}R \stackrel{\text{def}}{=} \varepsilon \cup A \ , \qquad (42)$$

$$ {}^{i+1}R \stackrel{\text{def}}{=} R \bowtie {}^{i}R \qquad (i \geq 0) \ . \qquad (43)$$

Note that

$$(\mathcal{P}(A^*), \bigcup, \bowtie, \emptyset, \varepsilon \cup A) \ , \qquad (44)$$

forms a Kleene algebra (see e.g. [Conway 71]). Now, we take from [Möller, Russling 92] an induction principle for closure operators of Kleene algebras, but here specialized to the above defined path closure. We call a predicate P over $(\mathcal{P}(A^*), \bigcup, \bowtie, \emptyset, \varepsilon \cup A)$ **continuous** if for all $T \subseteq \mathcal{P}(A^*)$

$$(\bigwedge_{X \in T} P[X]) \Rightarrow P[\bigcup_{X \in T} X] . \qquad (45)$$

Lemma 1.
Consider a fixed $R \subseteq A \bullet A \ (\subseteq \mathcal{P}(A^*))$ and let P be continuous. If $P[\varepsilon \cup A]$ and $P[X] \Rightarrow P[R \bowtie X]$ or $P[X] \Rightarrow P[X \bowtie R]$ then $P[R^{\leadsto}]$ holds as well.

Proof: A straightforward induction shows $P[{}^iR]$ for all $i \in \mathbb{N}$. Now Kleene's approximation (41) and continuity show the claim. ∎

Now we are able to show that for $S\,;R \subseteq S$ each last vertex of a path is in S.

Lemma 2.
For $S\,;R \subseteq S$ we have $S \bowtie R^{\leadsto} = S \bowtie R^{\leadsto} \bowtie S$.

Proof: ($\supseteq$) by (12).
($\subseteq$) We use the induction principle of Lemma 1 with the continuous predicate

$$P[X] \overset{\text{def}}{\Leftrightarrow} S \bowtie X \subseteq S \bowtie X \bowtie S .$$

To show $P[\varepsilon \cup A]$ we calculate
$S \bowtie (\varepsilon \cup A)$

$=\qquad \{\!\!\{ \text{ distributivity } \}\!\!\}$

$S \bowtie \varepsilon \cup S \bowtie A$

$=\qquad \{\!\!\{ \text{ by (6) and (13) } \}\!\!\}$

$\emptyset \cup S$

$=\qquad \{\!\!\{ \text{ by (6) and (13) } \}\!\!\}$

$S \bowtie \varepsilon \bowtie S \cup S \bowtie A \bowtie S$

$=\qquad \{\!\!\{ \text{ distributivity } \}\!\!\}$

$S \bowtie (\varepsilon \cup A) \bowtie S .$

Now assuming $P[X]$ we show $P[X \bowtie R]$.
$S \bowtie X \bowtie R$

$\subseteq\qquad \{\!\!\{ \text{ by } P[X] \text{ and monotonicity } \}\!\!\}$

$S \bowtie X \bowtie S \bowtie R$

$=\qquad \{\!\!\{ \text{ by } S\,;R \subseteq S \text{ and (33) } \}\!\!\}$

$$S \bowtie X \bowtie S \bowtie R \bowtie S$$

$$\subseteq \quad \{\!\!\{ \text{ by (12) and monotonicity } \}\!\!\}$$

$$S \bowtie X \bowtie R \bowtie S \;.$$

∎

Using the Lemma we may simplify F in the case where $S\,;R \subseteq S$:

$$F(f,g)(S,T)$$

$$= \quad \{\!\!\{ \text{ definition } \}\!\!\}$$

$$g(f(S \bowtie R^{\smile} \bowtie T))$$

$$= \quad \{\!\!\{ \text{ by Lemma 2 } \}\!\!\}$$

$$g(f(S \bowtie R^{\smile} \bowtie S \bowtie T))$$

$$= \quad \{\!\!\{ \text{ by (13) } \}\!\!\}$$

$$g(f(S \bowtie R^{\smile} \bowtie (S \cap T)))$$

$$= \quad \{\!\!\{ \text{ by (27) we have } A \subseteq R^{\smile}, \text{ hence } R^{\smile} = A \cup R^{\smile},$$
$$\text{distributivity and (13) twice } \}\!\!\}$$

$$g(f(S \cap T) \cup f(S \bowtie R^{\smile} \bowtie (S \cap T)))$$

$$= \quad \{\!\!\{ \text{ by (v) } \}\!\!\}$$

$$g(f(S \cap T)) \;.$$

Altogether we have derived, using (26),

$$F(f,g)(S,T) = \text{ if } T \subseteq S \lor S\,;R \subseteq S$$
$$\text{then } g(f(S \cap T))$$
$$\text{else } g(f(S \cap T) \cup v(F(f,g)(S \cup S\,;R\,,\,T))) \text{ fi } , \qquad (46)$$

where f, g, v are such that (for $K, L \subseteq M$, $U \subseteq A$ and $V \subseteq A^*$)

(o) f and v are pointwise extended to sets,
(i) $g(K \cup L) = g(g(K) \cup g(L))$,
(ii) $V \cap (\varepsilon \cup A) = \emptyset \Rightarrow f(U \bowtie V) = v(f(U\,;V))$,
(iii) $g(K) = g(K \cup v(K))$,
(iv) $g(v(K)) = v(g(K))$ and
(v) $g(f(U)) = g(f(U) \cup f(V \bowtie U))$.

Since a new operation v was introduced during the derivation, we define a graph traversal operation $F1$ having v as additional parameter:

$$
\begin{aligned}
F1(f,g,v)(S,T) \stackrel{\text{def}}{=} \ &\text{if } T \subseteq S \vee S\,;R \subseteq S \\
&\text{then } g(f(S \cap T)) \\
&\text{else } g(f(S \cap T) \cup v(F1(f,g,v)(S \cup S\,;R\,,\,T))) \text{ fi } .
\end{aligned}
$$

(47)

Trivially,

$$
F(f,g)(S,T) = F1(f,g,v)(S,T) \ ,
$$

(48)

again, under conditions (o)–(v).

Termination is guaranteed since parameter S increases properly in each recursive call and is bounded by the finite vertex set A.

5 Applications of $F1$

5.1 Reachability

We consider again the problem of computing the set of vertices reachable by paths starting in a subset $S \subseteq A$ of the vertex set and have now

$$
reach(S) \stackrel{\text{def}}{=} F1(last, id, id)(S, A) \ .
$$

(49)

where v was chosen such that the operation fulfill conditions (o)-(v).

So we may use the derived recursion for the reachability problem, and we simplify the result:

$reach(S)$

$=$ $\{\!|$ definition $|\!\}$

$F1(last, id, id)(S, A)$

$=$ $\{\!|$ by (47) $|\!\}$

if $A \subseteq S \vee S\,;R \subseteq S$ then $last(S \cap A)$
  else $last(S \cap A) \cup reach(S \cup S\,;R)$ fi

$=$ $\{\!|$ by set theory and definition of $last$ $|\!\}$

if $A \subseteq S \vee S\,;R \subseteq S$ then S
  else $S \cup reach(S \cup S\,;R)$ fi

$=$ $\{\!|$ $A \subseteq S$ implies $A = S$ implying $S\,;R \subseteq S$ $|\!\}$

if $S\,;R \subseteq S$ then S
  else $S \cup reach(S \cup S\,;R)$ fi .

5.2 Length of a Shortest Connecting Path

Next, we consider the problem of finding the length of a shortest connecting path from a vertex x to a vertex y. We have

$$shortestpath(x,y) \stackrel{\text{def}}{=} F1(edgelength, min, 1+)(x,y) , \qquad (50)$$

where $1+$, the successor function on natural numbers, had to be chosen for fulfilling condition (ii). Again, the definition meets the other conditions (o)–(v) as well. So we plug it into the general scheme (47) of $F1$ by allowing a set of vertices as first parameter:

$shortestpath(S,y)$

$=$ $\{\!\!\{$ definition $\}\!\!\}$

$F1(edgelength, min, 1+)(S,y)$

$=$ $\{\!\!\{$ by (47) $\}\!\!\}$

if $y \in S \vee S\,;R \subseteq S$ then $min(edgelength(S \cap y))$
else $min(edgelength(S \cap y) \cup$
$1 + shortestpath(S \cup S\,;R\,,\,y))$ fi

$=$ $\{\!\!\{$ by (26) $\}\!\!\}$

if $y \in S$ then $min(edgelength(S \cap y))$
else if $S\,;R \subseteq S$
then $min(edgelength(S \cap y))$
else $min(edgelength(S \cap y) \cup$
$1 + shortestpath(S \cup S\,;R\,,\,y))$ fi fi

$=$ $\{\!\!\{\, y \in S \Rightarrow S \cap y = y$ and $y \notin S \Rightarrow S \cap y = \emptyset \,\}\!\!\}$

if $y \in S$ then $min(edgelength(y))$
else if $S\,;R \subseteq S$
then $min(edgelength(\emptyset))$
else $min(edgelength(\emptyset) \cup$
$1 + shortestpath(S \cup S\,;R\,,\,y))$ fi fi

$=$ $\{\!\!\{$ by (39) and (40) $\}\!\!\}$

if $y \in S$ then 0
else if $S\,;R \subseteq S$ then $\emptyset$
else $1 + shortestpath(S \cup S\,;R\,,\,y)$ fi fi .

6 Improving Efficiency

The recursive version (47) of F is not efficient since it keeps all vertices already visited in parameter S and thus repeatedly calculates their successors. For gaining efficiency we introduce an additional parameter, say U, for accumulation of vertices already visited while S will keep only the not yet visited part of the successor set. Therefore we define

$$F2(f,g,v)(S,T,U) \stackrel{\text{def}}{=} (S \cap U = \emptyset) \bullet F1(f,g,v)(S \cup U, T) . \qquad (51)$$

The embedding

$$F1(f,g,v)(S,T) = F2(f,g,v)(S,T,\emptyset) \qquad (52)$$

is straightforward.

From (47) and (52) we obtain a special case:

$$F2(f,g,v)(S,T,U) = g(f((S \cup U) \cap T)) \quad \Leftarrow T \subseteq S \cup U \vee (S \cup U); R \subseteq (S \cup U) . \qquad (53)$$

For the recursion case we derive

$$\begin{aligned}
&F2(f,g,v)(S,T,U) \\
=\quad &\{\!\!\{ \text{ definition } \}\!\!\} \\
&F1(f,g,v)(S \cup U, T) \\
=\quad &\{\!\!\{ \text{ let } V \stackrel{\text{def}}{=} S \cup U \}\!\!\} \\
&F1(f,g,v)(V,T) \\
=\quad &\{\!\!\{ \text{ by } (47) \}\!\!\} \\
&g(f(V \cap T) \cup v(F1(f,g,v)(V \cup V ; R , T))) \\
=\quad &\{\!\!\{ \text{ set theory } \}\!\!\} \\
&g(f(V \cap T) \cup v(F1(f,g,v)(V ; R \setminus V \cup V , T))) \\
=\quad &\{\!\!\{ \text{ definition } \}\!\!\} \\
&g(f(V \cap T) \cup v(F2(f,g,v)(V ; R \setminus V , T , V))) .
\end{aligned}$$

Altogether,

$$\begin{aligned}
F2(f,g,v)(S,T,U) = (S \cap U = \emptyset) \bullet \\
\text{let } V \stackrel{\text{def}}{=} S \cup U \\
\text{in if } T \subseteq V \vee V ; R \subseteq V \\
\text{then } g(f(V \cap T)) \\
\text{else } g(f(V \cap T) \cup \\
v(F2(f,g,v)(V ; R \setminus V , T , V))) \text{ fi } .
\end{aligned}$$

$$(54)$$

Now S includes only the successors, but still the $V ; R$ has to be calculated expensively. However, the assertion of $F2$ can be strengthened by the conjunct

$U \,;\, R \subseteq S \cup U$, since it holds for the embedding (52) and the recursive call. Using $U \,;\, R \subseteq S \cup U$ we may simplify the algorithm to

$$
\begin{aligned}
F3(f,g,v)(S,T,U) = (S \cap U = \emptyset) \bullet (U \,;\, R \subseteq S \cup U) \bullet \\
\text{let } V \stackrel{\text{def}}{=} S \cup U \\
\text{in if } T \subseteq V \vee S \,;\, R \subseteq V \\
\text{then } g(f(V \cap T)) \\
\text{else } g(f(V \cap T) \cup \\
v(F3(f,g,v)(S \,;\, R \setminus V \,,\, T \,,\, V))) \text{ fi} \quad.
\end{aligned}
$$

$$(55)$$

Note that conditions (o)–(v) were not used in the derivations of $F2$ and $F3$.

Termination is guaranteed since U increases properly for each recursive call and is bounded by A.

The algorithm starts with a vertex subset S, calculates the successors of S, then the successors of the successors, and so on. So it covers the reachable part of the graph layer by layer like the cross–section of an onion (greek: κρόμμυον). Therefore, we called it a krommyomorphism, enriching the list of cata–, para–, hylo–, ana–, mutu– and zygomorphisms (see e.g. [Meertens 92]).

The algorithm scheme is similar to oil–spread algorithms (see e.g. [van de Snepscheut 93]).

7 Applications of $F3$

7.1 Reachability

Now, we apply $F3$ to the reachability problem. The simplification steps are similar to those in section 5.1 and hence we omit them. We obtain:

$$reach(S) = r3(S, \emptyset) \,,$$

$$
\begin{aligned}
r3(S,U) = (S \cap U = \emptyset) \bullet (U \,;\, R \subseteq S \cup U) \bullet \\
\text{let } V \stackrel{\text{def}}{=} S \cup U \\
\text{in if } S \,;\, R \subseteq V \\
\text{then } V \\
\text{else } V \cup r3(S \,;\, R \setminus V \,,\, V) \text{ fi} \quad.
\end{aligned}
$$

$$(56)$$

Since parameter U accumulates the result, the algorithm can be simplified further to

$$reach(S) = r4(S, \emptyset) \; ,$$

$$
\begin{aligned}
r4(S, U) = {} & (S \cap U = \emptyset) \bullet (U \,;\, R \subseteq S \cup U) \bullet \\
& \textsf{let } V \stackrel{\text{def}}{=} S \cup U \\
& \textsf{in if } S \,;\, R \subseteq V \\
& \quad \textsf{then } V \\
& \quad \textsf{else } r4(S \,;\, R \setminus V \,,\, V) \textsf{ fi} \; .
\end{aligned}
\tag{57}
$$

7.2 Length of a Shortest Connecting Path

Next, we apply $F3$ to the problem of finding the length of a shortest path. After some simplifications which are basically the same as in section 5.2 we get:

$$shortestpath(x, y) = s3(x, y, \emptyset) \; ,$$

$$
\begin{aligned}
s3(S, y, U) = {} & (S \cap U = \emptyset) \bullet (U \,;\, R \subseteq S \cup U) \bullet \\
& \textsf{let } V \stackrel{\text{def}}{=} S \cup U \\
& \textsf{in if } y \in V \\
& \quad \textsf{then } 0 \\
& \quad \textsf{else if } S \,;\, R \subseteq V \\
& \qquad \textsf{then } \emptyset \\
& \qquad \textsf{else } 1 + s3(S \,;\, R \setminus V \,,\, y \,,\, V) \textsf{ fi fi} \; .
\end{aligned}
\tag{58}
$$

Since the algorithms use some relatively abstract operations, further transformation steps have to be performed in order to obtain truly efficient programs. (E.g., instead of keeping various vertex sets one could state the membership of vertices by boolean arrays.) In [Möller, Russling 92] a cycle detection algorithm using an indegree vector instead of an abstract calculation of sources is derived, thus showing that such data refinement can nicely be performed at applicative level. For further standard techniques of transformation of data structures see [Partsch 90].

7.3 Further Applications

Of course, the derived algorithm scheme can be applied to related problems such as, e.g., testing the existence of a path between two subsets of the vertex set. Further, the algorithm also seems to be applicable to iteration paradigms for deductive databases (see e.g. [Güntzer et al. 86]).

The postulates (o)–(v) entail minimizing the path lengths involved. So, one could define a dual graph traversal operation which maximizes the path lengths. With it cycle detection could be expressed by checking if the length of a path involved is greater than the cardinality of the vertex set. (Note that this dual operation is not obtained immediately by taking the converse of an ordering on paths, since there is no such ordering defined so far.)

8 Conclusion

Our framework enables us to derive graph algorithms in a formal way from precise specifications while still in an understandable manner. The notations of specifications and algorithms are closely related. The algebraic laws ease concise derivations. The approach has also proved to be suitable for other areas such as pointer algorithms and stream processing problems (see [Möller 93] and [Möller 94]).

Transformational or calculational developments of single graph algorithms are already performed by various authors (see e.g. [Bird 84] for an early and beautiful example). In other approaches, i.e., in each [Pair 70] and [King, Launchbury 95], a class of graph algorithms with a surprising variety of applications is presented, but not derived.

We advocate combing these two aspects resulting in purely calculational derivations of entire graph algorithm classes. One of the most advanced papers in this sense is [Backhouse, van Gasteren 92], proposing a framework based on regular algebra. However, there some elementwise argumentation is still needed, the transitions to the algorithms level are performed by introducing loop invariants and the uniform treatment of different problems takes place more on the specification level than within the derivations. For an interesting comparision of this approach and ours see [Clenaghan 95]. In [Gibbons 94] an initial–algebra framework to model graphs is given and a graph homomorphism is defined. The graphs are modelled at a relatively low level of abstraction, thus restricting the scope of the approach. Further, in [Bird, de Moor 96] algorithms of various fields are treated in a schematic way.

Another example how different problems, i.e. hamiltonian paths and sorting problems, can be dealt by our framework in a unified view can be found in [Russling 94].

Acknowledgement

I gratefully acknowledge valuable remarks by B. Möller and the anonymous referees.

References

[Backhouse, van Gasteren 92] R.C. Backhouse, A.J.M. van Gasteren: Calculating a Path Algorithm. In R.S. Bird, C. Morgan, J. Woodcock (eds.): Proc. 2nd International Conference on the Mathematics of Program Construction, Oxford, UK, 29 June – 3 July 1992. Lecture Notes in Computer Science **669**. Berlin: Springer 1993. Extended version (together with J.P.H.W. van den Eijnde): Science of Computer Programming **22**, 3–19 (1994)

[Bird 84] R.S. Bird: The Promotion and Accumulation Strategies in Transformational Programming. ACM Transactions on Programming Languages and Systems **6**, 487–504 (1984)

[Bird, de Moor 96] R.S. Bird, O. de Moor: The Algebra of Programming (forthcoming book). Prentice Hall International 1996.

[Clenaghan 95] K. Clenaghan: Calculational graph algorithmics: reconciling two approaches with dynamic algebra. CWI Amsterdam, Report CS-R9518, 1995

[Conway 71] J.H. Conway: Regular algebra and finite machines. London: Chapman and Hall 1971

[Date 88] C.J. Date: An introduction to database systems. Vol. I, 4th edition. Reading, Mass.: Addison–Wesley 1988

[van den Eijnde 92] J.P.H.W. van den Eijnde: Conservative fixpoint functions on a graph. In R.S. Bird, C. Morgan, J. Woodcock (eds.): Proc. 2nd International Conference on the Mathematics of Program Construction, Oxford, UK, 29 June – 3 July 1992. Lecture Notes in Computer Science **669**. Berlin: Springer 1993.

[Gautam 57] N.D. Gautam: The validity of equations of complex algebras. Arch. Math. Logik Grundlag. **3**, 117–124 (1957)

[Gibbons 94] J. Gibbons: Algebraic Models of Graphs. 46th Meeting of IFIP TC2/WG 2.1, Renkum, The Netherlands, 10–13 January 1994, Document 722 REN-7

[Güntzer et al. 86] U. Güntzer, W. Kiessling, R. Bayer: Evaluation paradigms for deductive databases: from systolic to as–you–please. Institut für Informatik der Technischen Universität München, Report Nr. I8605, 1986

[King, Launchbury 95] D.J. King, J. Launchbury: Structuring Depth–First Search Algorithms in Haskell. Proc. 22nd ACM Symposium on Principles of Programming Languages, San Francisco, CA, USA, January 1995.

[Kleene 52] S.C. Kleene: Introduction to Metamathematics. New York: Van Nostrand 1952

[Meertens 92] L. Meertens: Paramorphisms. Formal Aspects of Computing 4, 413–424 (1992)

[Möller 91] B. Möller: Relations as a program development language. In B. Möller (ed.): Constructing programs from specifications. Proc. IFIP TC2/WG 2.1 Working Conference on Constructing Programs from Specifications, Pacific Grove, CA, USA, 13–16 May 1991. Amsterdam: North-Holland 1991, 373–397

[Möller 93] B. Möller: Towards pointer algebra. Institut für Mathematik der Universität Augsburg, Report No. 279, 1993. Also in Science of Computer Programming **21**, 57–90 (1993)

398

[Möller 94]   B. Möller: Ideal streams. In: E.-R. Olderog (ed.): Programming Con-
                 cepts, Methods and Calculi. IFIP Transaction A-56. Amsterdam: North-
                 Holland 1994, 39–58
[Möller, Russling 92] B. Möller, M. Russling: Shorter Paths to Graph Algorithms. In
                 R.S. Bird, C. Morgan, J. Woodcock (eds.): Proc. 2nd International Con-
                 ference on the Mathematics of Program Construction, Oxford, UK, 29
                 June – 3 July 1992. Lecture Notes in Computer Science **669**. Berlin:
                 Springer 1993. Extended version: Science of Computer Programming
                 22, 157–180 (1994)
[Pair 70]   C. Pair: Mille et un algorithmes pour les problème de cheminement
                 dans les graphes. Revue Française d'Informatique et de Recherche
                 opérationelle (R.I.R.O.) **B–3**, 125–143 (1970)
[Partsch 90]   H.A. Partsch: Specification and transformation of programs — A formal
                 approach to software development. Berlin: Springer 1990
[Russling 94]   M. Russling: An algebraic treatment of graph and sorting algorithms.
                 Proc. 14th Int. SCCC Conference, Concepción, Chile, 31 October – 4
                 November 1994. (Extended version: Institut für Mathematik der Uni-
                 versität Augsburg, Report Nr. 324, 1995)
[Schmidt, Ströhlein 93] G. Schmidt, T. Ströhlein: Relations and Graphs. Discrete
                 Mathematics for Computer Scientists, EATCS Monographs on Theo-
                 retical Computer Science. Berlin: Springer 1993.
[van de Snepscheut 93] J.L.A. van de Snepscheut: What Computing is all about. New
                 York: Springer 1993.
[Tarski 41]   A. Tarski: On the calculus of relations. J. Symbolic Logic **6**, 73–89 (1941)
[Tarski 55]   A. Tarski: A lattice theoretical fixpoint theorem and its applications.
                 Pacific J. Math. **5**, 285–310 (1955)

Specware:[*]
Formal Support for Composing Software

Yellamraju V. Srinivas and Richard Jüllig

Kestrel Institute, 3260 Hillview Avenue, Palo Alto, CA 94304, USA

Abstract. SPECWARE supports the systematic construction of formal specifications and their stepwise refinement into programs. The fundamental operations in SPECWARE are that of composing specifications (via colimits), the corresponding refinement by composing refinements (via sheaves), and the generation of programs by composing code modules (via colimits). The concept of diagram refinement is introduced as a practical realization of composing refinements via sheaves. Sequential and parallel composition of refinements satisfy a distributive law which is a generalization of similar compatibility laws in the literature. SPECWARE is based on a rich categorical framework with a small set of orthogonal concepts. We believe that this formal basis will enable the scaling to system-level software construction.

1 Introduction

SPECWARE[TM] supports the systematic construction of executable programs from axiomatic specifications via stepwise refinement. The immediate motivation for the the development of SPECWARE is the desire to integrate on a common conceptual basis the capabilities of several earlier systems developed at Kestrel Institute [14], including KIDS [23] and DTRE [6].

1.1 Reasoning about the Structure of Specifications, Refinements, and Code

The most important new aspect of the framework developed is the ability to represent explicitly the structure of specifications, refinements, and program modules. We believe that the explicit representation and manipulation of structure is crucial to scaling program construction techniques to system development.

The basis of SPECWARE is a category of axiomatic specifications and specification morphisms. Specification structure is expressed via specification diagrams, directed multi-graphs whose nodes are labeled with specifications and arcs with specification morphisms. Specification diagrams are useful both for composing specification from pieces and for inducing on a given specification a structure suitable for the design task at hand.

---

[*] SPECWARE is a trademark of Kestrel Development Corporation, Palo Alto, USA.

In SPECWARE the design process proceeds by stepwise refinement of an initial specification into executable code. The unit of refinement is an interpretation, a theorem-preserving translation of the vocabulary of a source specification into the terms of a target specification. Each interpretation reduces the problem of finding a realization for the source specification to finding a realization for the target specification. The overall result of the design process is to refine an initial specification into a program module.

Of course, it is desirable to structure the overall refinement. Progression through multiple stages requires sequential composability of refinements. Similarly, parallel composition lets us exploit the structure of specifications by putting refinements together from refinements between sub-specifications of the source and target specifications. It is for this purpose that we introduce the notion of diagram refinements in this paper: just as specification diagrams impose a component structure on specifications, so do diagram refinements make explicit the component structure of a specification refinement.

Specification refinement exploits specification structure; code generation, in turn, exploits the refinement structure. Given translations to code for the specifications that serve as the final refinement targets, SPECWARE generates a system of modules by induction on the refinement structure. Layered module construction mirrors sequential composition of refinements, and the "gluing together" of modules into larger modules reflects the (parallel) composition of specifications and refinements from components.

Our work combines ideas and notions from the fields of algebraic specifications, category theory, and sheaf theory. We believe that the use of such "heavy" formal machinery is well-justified. For instance, category theory seems ideally suited for describing the manipulation of richly detailed structures at various levels of granularity. Similarly, the sheaf-theoretic notion of compatible families seems fundamental to and pervasive in putting systems together from interdependent components.

The ideas and concepts presented in this paper have been implemented in the SPECWARE 1.0 system, which continues to be developed. It is interesting to note that the implementation efforts seem to fare the better the more closely the implementation reflects the underlying theoretical concepts. Conversely, experimentation with the SPECWARE system has had a significant impact on the theory of diagram refinement presented here.

1.2 Outline

We briefly present our specification language in Sect. 2 and in Appendix A. The focus of this paper is the sequential and parallel composition of refinements, as described in Sect. 4. Sect. 5 discusses how sufficiently refined specifications can be translated to programs. Sect. 6 describes related work. Finally, we offer some conclusions and an outlook on future work.

2 Putting Specifications Together

The primary component of the SPECWARE workspace is the category of specifications and specification morphisms. Diagrams in this category describe system structure. Specifications can be put together via colimits to obtain more complex specifications. We will only briefly describe these concepts because these ideas are well known; see, e.g., [7, 21].

2.1 Specifications

A *specification* is a finite presentation of a theory in higher-order logic. An uncommon feature of SPECWARE is that subsorts and quotient sorts can be defined using predicates and equivalence relations, respectively. For details of the particular logic used, see Appendix A.

Specification-Constructing Operations. Specifications can either be directly given (as a set of sorts, operations, axioms, etc.) or constructed from other specifications via the following operations (inspired by ASL [28, 21])

> **translate** ⟨spec⟩ **by** ⟨renaming-rules⟩
> **colimit of** ⟨diagram⟩
> **spec import** ⟨spec⟩ ⟨spec-elements⟩ **end-spec**

"Translate" creates a copy of a specification with some elements renamed according to the given renamings; an isomorphism is also created between the original and the translated specifications. "Colimit" is the standard operation from category theory (see, e.g., [18]); colimits are constructed using equivalence classes of sorts, operations, etc. "Import" places a copy of the imported specification[2] in the importing specification; an inclusion morphism is also generated.

2.2 Specification Morphisms

A *specification morphism* (or simply a *morphism*) translates the language of one specification into the language of another specification in a way that preserves theorems. Specification morphisms underlie almost all constructions in SPECWARE.

Flavors of Specification Morphisms. The set of sorts given in a specification generates a free algebra via sort-constructing operations such as product, coproduct, etc. A specification morphism is a map from the sorts[3] and operations of one specification to the sorts and operations of another such that (1) the map is a homomorphism on the sort algebras, (2) the ranks of operations are

---

[2] Only one specification can be imported. A colimit is necessary if multiple specifications are to be imported.

[3] Here, we take "sorts" to mean all the sorts in the sort algebra.

translated compatibly with the operations, and (3) axioms are translated to theorems.

A presentation of a specification morphism in SPECWARE is a finite map from the declared sorts in the source specification to the declared or constructed sorts in the target specification, and from source operations to target operations, such that the map generates a specification morphism as described above.

Many flavors of morphisms can be defined for specifications, ranging from axiom-preserving presentation morphisms to logical morphisms between the toposes (theories) generated by the source and target specifications. The choice made in SPECWARE (declared sorts mapping to constructed sorts) is a pragmatic one, a compromise between simplicity and flexibility—morphisms are simple enough for use in putting specifications together, while flexible enough to model refinement.

2.3 Specification Diagrams

A morphism from A to B may be construed as indicating how A is a "part of" B. Thus, we can use morphisms to express a system as an interconnection of its parts, i.e., as a diagram. Formally, a *diagram* is a directed multigraph in which the nodes are labeled by specifications, and the edges by specification morphisms (in a multigraph, there can be more than one edge between any two nodes).[4]

Composition (Putting Specifications Together). We can reduce a diagram of specifications to a single specification by taking the colimit of the diagram. The colimit of a diagram is constructed by first taking the disjoint union (coproduct) of all the specifications in the diagram and then the quotient of this coproduct via the equivalence relation generated by the morphisms in the diagram. The result will be a valid specification (i.e., the colimit exists) only if the sort algebra is free (this means that two structurally dissimilar sorts cannot be identified in a colimit).

Example 1. The specifications for topological sorting are shown in Fig. 1 (following Knuth [15, pp. 258–265]). The problem of topological sorting is specified as an input-output relation. To specify this relation, we need the concepts of partial order and total order on some set of elements; these specifications are first put together via a colimit and then imported. The specification for partial orders contains a membership predicate and a less-or-equal predicate with appropriate axioms. The specification for total orders renames the partial orders specification and extends it with a totality axiom and a less-than predicate.

In the figure, the arrow labeled "d" is a definitional extension and the arrows labeled "c" are part of a colimit cocone.

---

[4] When convenient, we will treat a diagram as a functor from the category freely generated by its underlying graph to the category of specifications and specification morphisms.

403

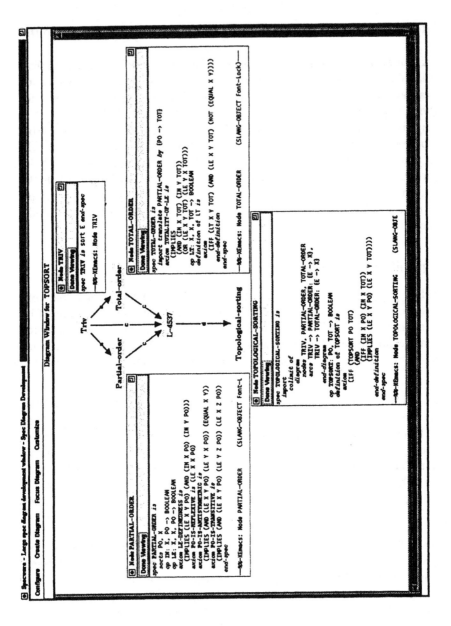

Fig. 1. Specification for topological sorting

3 Stepwise Refinement

The development process of SPECWARE is intended to support the refinement of a problem specification into a solution specification. Refinements introduce additional design detail, e.g., the transformation of definitions into constructive definitions, representation choices for data types, etc. SPECWARE's refinement constructs, introduced below, address three important aspects of refinement:

problem reduction: construction of a solution relative to some base;
stepwise refinement: sequential composition of refinements; and
putting refinements together: parallel composition of refinements.

3.1 Interpretations

The notion of refinement in SPECWARE is that a specification B refines a specification A if there is a construction which produces models of A from models of B [22]. Specification morphisms serve this purpose because associated with every morphism $\sigma : A \rightarrow B$ there is a reduct functor $\_|_\sigma$ which produces models of A from models of B. Morphisms, however, are too weak to represent refinements which normally occur during software development. So, we use a more general notion, *interpretations*, which are specification morphisms from the source specification to a definitional extension of the target specification.

Definition 1 (*Interpretation*). An *interpretation* $\rho : A \Rightarrow B$ from a specification A (called *domain* or *source*) to a specification B (called *codomain* or *target*) is a pair of morphisms $A \rightarrow A$-*as*-$B \leftarrow B$ with common codomain A-*as*-B (called *mediating* specification or simply *mediator*), such that the morphism from B to A-*as*-B is a definitional extension.

Definition 2 (*Definitional extension*). A morphism $S \rightarrow T$ is a *strict definitional extension* if it is injective and if every element of T which is outside the image of the morphism is either a defined sort or a defined operation. A *definitional extension* is a strict definitional extension optionally composed with a specification isomorphism.

In this case, we also sometimes say that T is a definitional extension of S. Definitional extensions are indicated in diagrams by $\xrightarrow{\ \ d\ \ }$.

A specification and any definitional extension of it generate the same topos (or theory). Hence, interpretations are generalized morphisms. Interpretations are a suitable notion of refinement because models of the source specification can be constructed from models of the target specification by first expanding them along the definitional extension and then taking reducts.

Example 2. We show in Fig. 2 an interpretation from total orders to sequences in which total orders are represented as a subsort of sequences: a sequence represents a total order if and only if it does not contain any duplicate elements.

This subsort is defined in the mediating specification. Total-order operations are then defined on this subsort in terms of the underlying sequence operations.

In general, a source sort may be represented by a more elaborately constructed sort. For example, partial orders can be represented as a quotient of a subsort of graphs: to qualify as a representative, a graph must be acyclic (this is the subsort predicate), and two acyclic graphs represent the same partial order if their transitive closure is the same (this is the equivalence relation for the quotient sort).

Interpretations encompass and generalize the data type refinement introduced in [12] and other similar schemes.

3.2 Sequential (Vertical) Composition of Interpretations

Given two interpretations $\rho_1 : A \Rightarrow B$ and $\rho_2 : B \Rightarrow C$ such that the codomain of the first is the domain of the second, their sequential composition $\rho_2 \circ \rho_1 : A \Rightarrow C$ is obtained as in the diagram below (the marking "po" indicates a pushout square).[5] We use the facts that definitional extensions are closed under composition and are preserved by pushouts.

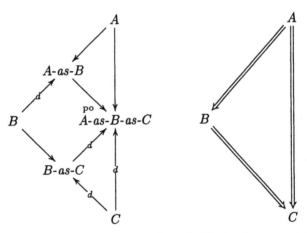

Sequential composition of interpretations facilitates incremental, layered refinement.

3.3 Algorithm Synthesis and Interpretation Construction

Algorithm synthesis plays two roles in the model of software development supported by SPECWARE:

- the creation of constructive definitions in interpretations, and
- the refinement of input-output relations sufficient to extract a constructively defined function.

---

[5] Diagrams are assumed to be commutative unless stated otherwise.

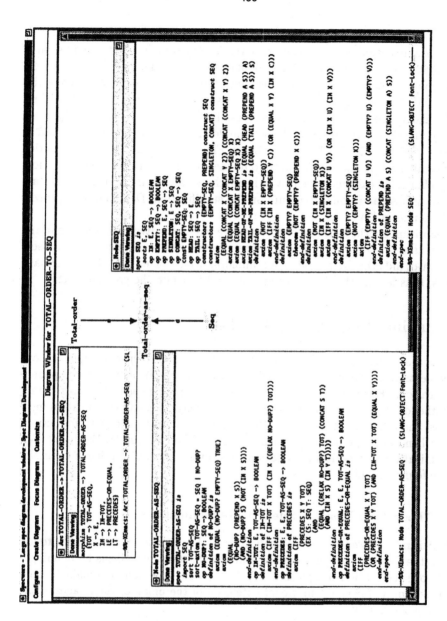

Fig. 2. An interpretation of total orders as a subset of sequences

Note that the definitions used in the mediating specification of an interpretation are not required to be constructive. As an example, see the definition of PRECEDES in the specification TOTAL-ORDER-AS-SEQ in Fig. 2. If we want to generate code corresponding to this operation, then we have to further refine this definition, with the goal of replacing the existential quantifier by an algorithm.

Similarly, the input-output relations used in a top-level specification are not usually functional. As an example, see the definition of the relation TOPSORT in the specification TOPOLOGICAL-SORTING in Fig. 1. If we want to find a function which satisfies this relation, we have to further refine the enclosing specification. This refinement can be guided by a hierarchy of algorithm theories which are used to impose additional structure on the specification. Details of this process can be found in [24, 25].

Algorithm synthesis is one of the creative parts of software development and can be used to construct basic interpretations which can then be composed. SPECWARE aids this by providing a scaffolding which takes care of the mundane details, thus letting the developer identify and focus on the creative part.

4 Putting Refinements Together

Just as a specification can be put together from smaller specifications, so can refinements of a specification be put together from refinements of component specifications. Formally, the various ways of constructing specifications generate a Grothendieck topology on the category of specifications and specification morphisms, and refinements form a sheaf with respect to this topology. Introductions to Grothendieck topologies and sheaves can be found in [19], [1, Exposés I–IV]; an application to algorithm derivation and several computer science examples can be found in [26].

4.1 Theoretical Basis: A Sheaf of Refinements

Definition 3 (*A Topology for Specifications*). We obtain a Grothendieck topology on the category of specifications and specification morphisms by defining a family of specification morphisms $\{ S_i \rightarrow S \}$ with common codomain to be a covering family if S is a definitional extension of the union of the images of the arrows in the family.

Definition 4 (*Image of a Specification Morphism*). The image of a specification morphism $\sigma : S \rightarrow T$ is the specification consisting of all elements $\sigma(x)$ where x is any element of the source specification, e.g., sort, operation, theorem, etc.

To see that the topology above encompasses the specification constructing operations of Section 2.1, observe that a translation generates an isomorphism (which is a singleton covering family), and that a colimit specification is covered by its family of cocone arrows. The case of import can be reduced to that of colimit. However, it is useful to distinguish the case when the import morphism is a definitional extension; it then forms a (singleton) covering family.

Given any cover for a specification, a refinement for the specification can be constructed from refinements for the elements of the cover, provided the refinements are "compatible". This observation leads to a sheaf.

Definition 5 (*A Sheaf of Refinements*). Assume a fixed specification B, the base specification. Define a functor $\mathcal{R} : \mathbf{Spec}^{\mathrm{op}} \to \mathbf{Set}$ by assiging to each specification S the set of all interpretations (refinements) from S to B, and to each specification morphism $m : S \to T$ the function which restricts an interpretation $\rho : T \Rightarrow B$ to an interpretation $\rho \circ m : S \Rightarrow B$. This functor is a sheaf with respect to the Grothendieck topology defined above.

The sheaf condition asserts that for every cover $\{\, f_i : S_i \to S \mid i \in I \,\}$, every compatible family of interpretations $\{\, \rho_i : S_i \Rightarrow B \mid i \in I \,\}$ can be uniquely extended to an interpretation $\rho : S \to B$ such that the restriction of ρ along any f_i is equal to ρ_i.

Informally, a family of interpretations $\{\, \rho_i : S_i \Rightarrow B \mid i \in I \,\}$ is compatible if the member interpretations agree wherever the pieces of the cover overlap. In this case, an interpretation $\rho : S \to B$ can be constructed as the shared union of the given family of interpretations. The details of this construction will be omitted here, because the construction is similar to the parallel composition of interpretations described below.

4.2 Practical Realization: Diagram Refinement

Three factors prevent a direct realization of the sheaf-theoretic view of putting interpretations together presented in the previous section: (1) The compatibility condition is hard to check because pullbacks do not exist in general in the category of specification morphisms; (2) Equality of interpretations is hard to check; (3) It is unrealistic to assume that a single base specification (the refinement target) is given. Typically, we would like to assemble a target specification as we refine pieces of the source specification.

We handle (1) by using only those covers which are directly given by specification construction operations. In particular, a (finite) colimit explicitly indicates the shared parts among the components of a specification. (2) is handled by introducing interpretation morphisms, which explicitly indicate how one interpretation specializes another. We also use a strong equality for morphisms which can be checked syntactically; see Definition 6 below. (3) is handled by using diagrams in the category of interpretations and interpretation morphisms. A preliminary target specification can be assembled from the codomains of the interpretations in a diagram. The target specification can be further modified by modifying the diagram of specifications that defines it.

We will describe these concepts below, finally obtaining a notion of refinement for diagrams.

Definition 6 (*Strong Morphism Equality*). Two specification morphisms $\sigma, \tau :$ $S \to T$ are equal if for each sort or operation $x \in S$, $\sigma(x) = \tau(x)$.

Definition 7 (*Interpretation Morphism*). An interpretation morphism from an interpretation $\rho_1 : S_1 \Rightarrow T_1$ to another interpretation $\rho_2 : S_2 \Rightarrow T_2$ is a triple of specification morphisms such that the diagram on the right below commutes.

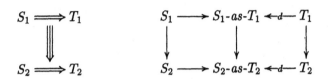

Interpretations and interpretation morphisms form a category **Interp**. Another view of this category is as (a sub-category of) the functor category of functors from $\bullet \to \bullet \leftarrow \bullet$ to the category **Spec** of specifications and specification morphisms. Hence, colimits in **Spec** lift to colimits in the category of interpretations.[6]

Specifications, interpretations, and interpretation morphisms for a double category. That is, in addition to the obvious sequential/vertical composition of interpretation morphisms, there is also a parallel/horizontal composition of interpretation morphisms. The two compositions satisfy an interchange law: given six interpretations and four interpretation morphisms as shown on the left below, the equation on the right is true.

$$(\beta_2 \bullet \alpha_2) \circ (\beta_1 \bullet \alpha_1) = (\beta_2 \circ \beta_1) \bullet (\alpha_2 \circ \alpha_1)$$

Now, given two specifications which are defined as colimits, a compatible family of interpretations can be given as a diagram of interpretations. It will be useful here to treat diagrams as functors.

Definition 8 (*Diagram Refinement*). Given two diagrams of specifications $d_1 :$ $I_1 \to$ **Spec** and $d_2 : I_2 \to$ **Spec**, a diagram refinement $\langle \delta, \sigma \rangle : d_1 \to d_2$ is a pair consisting of a diagram of interpretations $\delta : I_1 \to$ **Interp** with shape I_1 and a functor $\sigma : I_1 \to I_2$ between the two shapes such that the following diagram commutes (dom and cod are the obvious functors which maps interpretations and interpretation morphisms to their domains and codomains, respectively).

---

[6] Definitional extensions are preserved by colimits.

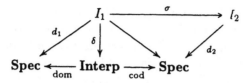

Example 3. In Fig. 3, we show a refinement of the specification for topological sorting (shown in Fig. 1): the partial orders are refined to pairs of sequences (one listing the elements and another listing the ordering relation), and the total orders are refined to sequences (as shown in Fig. 2).

The components of the colimit which defines the import into the specification for topological sorting are refined in parallel. The vertical interpretations emanating from this diagram form a diagram refinement. Note that the target diagram has a shape which is different from that of the source diagram: the extra arrow in the target diagram is used to identify the sequences which represent the elements of the partial orders and the total orders (remember that topological sorting takes as input a partial order and produces a total order on the *same* set of elements).

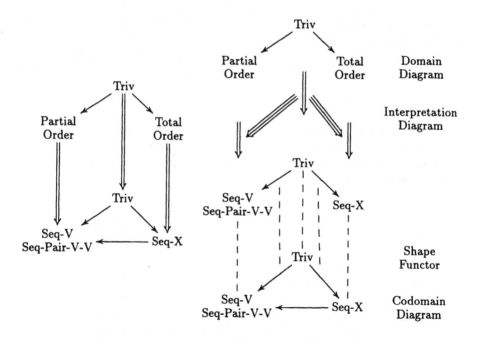

Fig. 3. Components of a diagram refinement

Parallel (Horizontal) Composition of Interpretations. As expected, a diagram refinement yields a refinement from the colimit of the source diagram to the colimit of the target diagram. Consider the diagram refinement $\langle \delta, \sigma \rangle : d_1 \to d_2$ above. Let S_1 and S_2 be the colimits of the two diagrams. The colimit of the interpretation diagram δ is an interpretation $\rho_1 : S_1 \Rightarrow S_2'$ from S_1 to the colimit (say S_2') of the diagram $d_2 \circ \sigma : I_1 \to \mathbf{Spec}$. The colimit cocone $d_2 \xrightarrow{\cdot} S_2$ when composed with the shape morphism σ gives a cocone $d_2 \circ \sigma \xrightarrow{\cdot} S_2$. From this, we obtain a witness arrow $\rho_2 : S_2' \to S_2$. The composition $\rho_2 \circ \rho_1$ is the desired parallel composition of the diagram refinement $\langle \delta, \sigma \rangle : d_1 \to d_2$.

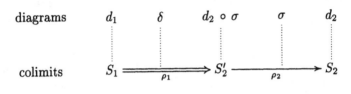

We will denote the parallel composition of a diagram refinement Δ by $|\Delta|$.

Example 4. In Fig. 4, we show details of the refinement of the specification for topological sorting. The figure illustrates both sequential and parallel composition of interpretations. As an example of sequential composition, partial orders are refined to pairs of sequences by representing them as graphs; the graphs are then represented as sets of nodes and sets of edges; then, these sets are represented as sequences. There are also several parallel compositions, e.g., the refinements of Set-of-Pair and TS-Import.

Composing Diagram Refinements. Diagram refinements can be composed by composing the individual interpretations which comprise them. Let $\langle \delta_1, \sigma_1 \rangle : d_1 \to d_2$ and $\langle \delta_2, \sigma_2 \rangle : d_2 \to d_3$ be two diagram refinements. We can juxtapose these as shown below.

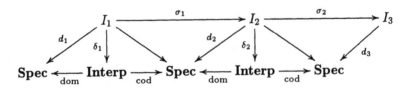

Now, as shown below, we get two diagrams of interpretations with shape I_1, namely δ_1 and $\delta_2 \circ \sigma_1$, such that the codomains of the interpretations in the first diagram match with the domains of the interpretations in the second diagram. By composing the individual interpretations, we get another interpretation diagram with shape I_1. We will denote this horizontally composed diagram of interpretations by $(\delta_2 \circ \sigma_1) \bullet \delta_1$. The shape morphism for the composed diagram refinement is obtained by composing the individual shape morphisms,

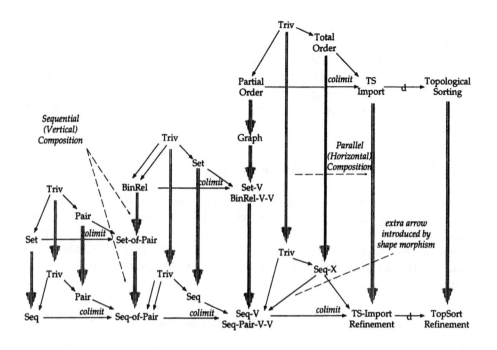

Fig. 4. Refinement of topological sorting

$\sigma_2 \circ \sigma_1 : I_1 \to I_2 \to I_3$. Thus, $\langle (\delta_2 \circ \sigma_1) \bullet \delta_1, \sigma_2 \circ \sigma_1 \rangle : d_1 \to d_3$ is the composition of the two diagram refinements we started with.

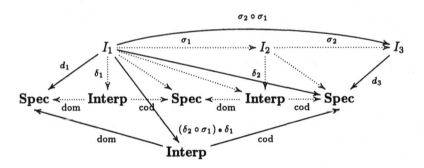

Compatibility of Vertical and Horizontal Interpretation Composition. If $\Delta_1 : d_1 \to d_2$ and $\Delta_2 : d_2 \to d_3$ are two diagram refinements which can be composed, then the distributive law satisfied by them is

$$|\Delta_2| \circ |\Delta_1| = |\Delta_2 \circ \Delta_1|.$$

This can be verified by straighforward diagram chasing (using the interchange law for interpretation morphisms). Thus, $|_-|$ is a functor from the category of diagrams and diagram refinements to the category of specifications and interpretations.

The distributive law above is a generalization of other such laws introduced in the literature. The law introduced by Goguen and Burstall [9] is too constraining to be practically useful. The law introduced by Sannella and Tarlecki [22] uses parameterization and does not handle colimits; moreover, it is semantically oriented.

5 Putting Code Fragments Together

When specifications are sufficiently refined, they can be converted into programs which realize them. This involves a switching of logics. We use the theory of logic morphisms described by Meseguer [20]. We will confine our attention to entailment systems and their morphisms, rather than logics (which include models and institutions). Entailment systems are sufficient for the purpose of code generation.

5.1 Entailment Systems and their Morphisms

Definition 9 (*Entailment System*). An entailment system is a triple $\langle \mathbf{Sig}, sen, \vdash \rangle$ consisting of

1. a category **Sig** of signatures and signature morphisms,
2. a functor $sen : \mathbf{Sig} \to \mathbf{Set}$ (where **Set** is the category of sets and functions) which assigns to each signature Σ the set of Σ-sentences, and to each signature morphism $\sigma : \Sigma \to \Sigma'$, the function which translates Σ-sentences to Σ'-sentences (this function will also be denoted by σ), and
3. a function $\vdash$ which associates to each signature Σ a binary relation $\vdash_\Sigma \subseteq \mathcal{P}(sen(\Sigma)) \times sen(\Sigma)$, called Σ-entailment,

such that the following properties are satisfied:

1. *reflexivity:* for any $\varphi \in sen(\Sigma)$, $\{\varphi\} \vdash_\Sigma \varphi$;
2. *monotonicity:* if $\Gamma \vdash_\Sigma \varphi$ and $\Gamma' \supseteq \Gamma$, then $\Gamma' \vdash_\Sigma \varphi$
3. *transitivity:* if $\Gamma \vdash_\Sigma \varphi_i$, for $i \in I$, and $\Gamma \cup \{\varphi_i \mid i \in I\} \vdash_\Sigma \psi$, then $\Gamma \vdash_\Sigma \psi$;
4. $\vdash$-*translation:* if $\Gamma \vdash_\Sigma \varphi$, then for any signature morphism $\sigma : \Sigma \to \Sigma'$, $\sigma(\Gamma) \vdash_{\Sigma'} \sigma(\varphi)$.

To map one entailment system into another, we map the syntax (i.e., signatures and sentences) while preserving entailment. Preservation of entailment represents the relevant correctness criterion for translating specifications from one logic to another. Note that this is similar to the correctness criterion for refinement within a single logic.

A simple way to map syntax is to map signatures to signatures, and sentences over a signature to sentences over the translated signature. If the former is a functor, the latter becomes a natural transformation.

Definition 10 (*Entailment system morphism—plain version*). A morphism between entailment systems $\langle \Phi, \alpha \rangle : \langle \mathbf{Sig}, sen, \vdash \rangle \to \langle \mathbf{Sig}', sen', \vdash' \rangle$ is a pair consisting of a functor $\Phi : \mathbf{Sig} \to \mathbf{Sig}'$ which maps signatures to signatures and a natural transformation $\alpha : sen \overset{\cdot}{\to} sen' \circ \Phi$ which maps sentences to sentences such that entailment is preserved:

$$\Gamma \vdash_\Sigma \varphi \Rightarrow \alpha_\Sigma(\Gamma) \vdash'_{\Phi(\Sigma)} \alpha_\Sigma(\varphi).$$

We can visualize α and the naturality condition in the following diagrams.

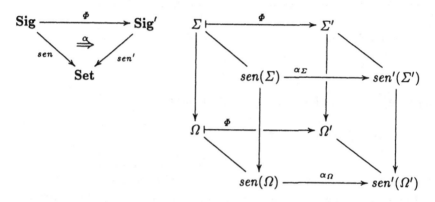

Morphisms which map signatures to signatures are not flexible enough, especially for code generation. In general, it may be necessary to map built-in elements of one logic into defined elements of another, and vice versa. This can be realized by mapping signatures to specifications, and vice versa, or, in general, specifications to specifications.

However, morphisms which map specifications to specifications are too unconstrained. So Meseguer [20] proposes a general version of entailment system morphisms which map specifications to specifications "sensibly". We will use these morphisms but omit the detailed definition here.

5.2 Translating from Slang to Lisp

The specification language used in SPECWARE is called SLANG. We distinguish SLANG because SPECWARE may have multiple back-ends, Lisp, C, Ada, etc., each with its own logic.

We consider a sub-logic of SLANG, called the *abstract target language* (for LISP); there is one sub-logic for each language into which SLANG specifications can be translated. We will denote this sub-logic by SLANG⁻⁻. The sub-logic SLANG⁻⁻ is defined by starting with a set of basic specifications, such as integers, sequences, etc., which have direct realizations in the target language. All specifications which can be constructed from the base specifications, with the following restrictions, are then included in the sub-logic:

– for colimit specifications, only injective morphisms are allowed in the diagram;[7]
– all definitions must be constructive, i.e., they must either be explicit definitions (e.g., (equal (square x) (times x x))), or, if they are recursive, they must be given as conditional equations using a constructor set.

The goal of the refinement process is to arrive at a sufficiently detailed specification which satisfies the restrictions above.

The sub-logic SLANG^{--} will be translated into a functional subset of LISP. To facilitate this translation, we couch this subset as an entailment system, denoted LISP^{--}. The signatures of this entailment system are finite sets of untyped operations and the sentences are function definitions of the form

```
(defun f (x)
  (cond ((p x) (g x))
   ...))
```

and generated conditional equations of the form

```
(if (p x) (equal (f x) (g x))).
```

The entailment relation is that of rewriting, since theories in LISP^{--} can be viewed as conditional-equational theories over the simply-typed λ-calculus.

In Fig. 5, we show a fragment of an entailment system morphism from SLANG^{--} to LISP^{--}. Note, in particular, the translations from and to empty specifications. The set of sentences in the SLANG specification INT translates to the empty set; this is because integers are primitive in LISP. Similarly, the empty SLANG specification translates to a non-empty LISP specification; this is because some built-in operations of SLANG are not primitive in LISP.

Translating Constructed Sorts. There are numerous details in entailment system morphisms such as that from SLANG^{--} to LISP^{--}. We will briefly consider the translation of constructed sorts. Subsorts can be handled by representing elements of a subsort by the corresponding elements of the supersort. Similarly, quotient sorts can be handled by representing their elements by the elements of the base sort. Sentences have to be translated consistently with such representation choices: e.g., injections associated with subsorts ((relax p)) and the surjections associated with quotient sorts ((quotient e)) must be dropped. Also, the equality on a quotient sort must be replaced by the equivalence relation defining the quotient sort.

In Fig. 6, we show the representation of coproduct sorts by variant records. This translation exploits the generality of entailment system morphisms: a signature is mapped into a theory.

---

[7] For colimit specifications which can be construed as "instantiations" of a "generic" specification, the morphisms from the formal to the actual may be non-injective.

SLANG⁻⁻	⟶ LISP⁻⁻

| EMPTY | ⟼ ```spec SLANG-BASE is```
```ops implies, iff```
```(defun implies (x y)```
```(or (not x) y))```
```(defun iff (x y)```
```(or (and x y)```
```(and (not x) (not y))))```
```end-spec``` |

| INT | ⟼ SLANG-BASE |

| ```spec FOO is```
```import INT```
```op abs : Int -> Int```
```definition of abs is```
```axiom```
```(implies (ge x zero)```
```(equal (abs x) x))```
```axiom```
```(implies (lt x zero)```
```(equal (abs x) (minus zero x)))```
```end-definition```
```end-spec``` | ⟼ ```spec FOO' is```
```import SLANG-BASE```
```op abs```
```(defun abs (x)```
```(cond ((>= x 0) x)```
```((< x 0) (- 0 x))))```
```end-spec``` |

Fig. 5. Fragment of entailment system morphism from SLANG⁻⁻ to LISP⁻⁻

```
spec STACK is                    ⟼    spec STACK' is
import INT                              import SLANG-BASE
...                                     op size, E-Stack?, NE-Stack?
sort-axiom                              (defun E-Stack? (s)
  Stack = E-Stack + NE-Stack             (= (car s) 1))
...                                     ...
op size  : Stack -> Int                 (defun size (s)
definition of size is                    (cond
 axiom                                     ((E-Stack? s) 0)
 (equal (size ((embed 1) s))               ((NE-Stack? s)
        zero)                               (1+ (size (pop (cdr s)))))
 axiom                                    ))
 (equal (size ((embed 2) s))            end-definition
        (succ (size (pop s))))          end-spec
end-definition
end-spec
```

Fig. 6. The representation of coproduct sorts as variant records

5.3 Translation of Colimits: Putting Code Fragments Together

If an entailment system morphism is defined in such a way that it is co-continuous, i.e., colimits are preserved, then we obtain a recursive procedure for translation, which is similar to that of refinement: the code for a specification can be obtained by assembling the code for smaller specifications which cover it.

The entailment system morphism from SLANG^{--} to LISP^{--} briefly described above does preserve colimits because of our restriction to injective morphisms. In general, this is true for most programming languages because they only allow imports, which are inclusion morphisms.

6 Related Work

SPECWARE builds upon a large body of work in formal specifications and program synthesis and transformation developed over the last two decades.

The design of SLANG, the specification language of SPECWARE, was inspired by Sanella and Tarlecki's [21] and Wirsing's work [28] on structured algebraic specifications. Putting theories together via colimits was first proposed by Burstall and Goguen as part of CLEAR [7]. SLANG was further influenced by CIP [2, 3] and OBJ [10].

SPECWARE adopts in a higher-order setting the notion of interpretations as refinements from Turski's and Maibaum's development in first-order logic [27]. SPECWARE could be construed as a realization of the design methodology espoused by Lehman, Stenning, and Turski, with the addition of parallel refinement composition [17]. The notion of parallel refinement composition described in this paper is different from the horizontal composition of parameterized specifications described by Sannella and Tarlecki [22].

The explicit use of subsort and quotient sort constructions in SPECWARE connects data type refinement in an algebraic setting with Hoare's abstraction/refinement functions [12] which also underlie the refinement found in VDM [13].

Our work is both similar and complementary to Bird's and Meertens' equational reasoning approach to program development [4, 5]. Reasoning about commuting specification diagrams is equational reasoning at the specification level; Bird's and Meertens' equations are at the axiom level. Of course the two can happily co-exist.

Our framework for structured code generation is adopted from Meseguer's work on logic morphisms [20].

The direct impetus to the development of SPECWARE came from the desire to integrate several systems developed at Kestrel Institute over the last ten years, and the realization that they shared a common conceptual basis. These include the algorithm design system KIDS [23], the data type refinement system DTRE [6], REACTO, a system for the development of reactive systems [8], and a synthesis system for visual presentations [11]. An overview is presented in [14].

7 Conclusions

7.1 Summary

We presented the specification and refinement concepts of SPECWARE, a system aimed at supporting the application of formal methods to system development. Specware draws on theoretical work in formal specification and program synthesis as well as on experience with experimental systems over the past two decades. The development of SPECWARE continues; however, all concepts introduced here have been implemented. We have found the co-development of theory and implementation mutually beneficial.

The basic specification concepts of SPECWARE are specifications, specification morphisms, and diagrams of specifications and specification morphisms. The colimit operation takes diagrams of specifications to specifications.

The basic refinement notion is an interpretation, a morphism from a source specification into a definitional extension of a target specification. Interpretations are closed under sequential composition. To arrive at a notion of parallel refinement composition, we first observed that colimits and definitional extensions generate a Grothendieck topology on the category of specifications and specification morphisms, and that refinements form a sheaf with respect to this topology. Essentially this means that that given a specification diagram and an assignment of an interpretation to each node in the diagram one can construct an interpretation for the colimit of the given specification diagram, provided the compatibility condition holds: the interpretations assigned to the nodes must agree on shared parts.

The difficulty of checking the compatibility condition, among other reasons, prevented the direct application of this theory in practice. We instead developed diagram refinements as a practical realization; in diagram refinements the compatibility of interpretations is explicit ensured by the presence of interpretation morphisms.

7.2 Future Work

Current work includes adding to SPECWARE parameterized specifications and interpretations of parameterized specifications. This will lead to a vertical composition similar to that of Sannella's and Tarlecki's [22] but to a different horizontal composition notion.

With the addition of parameterized specifications SPECWARE contains a set of primitives rich enough to allow for substantial experimentation. For this purpose we will recreate the algorithm design capabilities of KIDS in SPECWARE. We also expect the addition of code generation to other programming languages in addition to LISP.

A The Logic of Slang

The specification language used in SPECWARE is called SLANG. We distinguish SLANG because SPECWARE may have multiple back-ends, Lisp, C, Ada, etc., each with its own logic.

SLANG is based on higher-order logic, or higher-order type theory, as described in [16]. However, unlike Lambek and Scott, we use classical logic (rather than intuitionistic logic) because the theorem prover currently used in SPECWARE is a resolution prover based on classical first-order logic (with some higher-order facilities).

Logically speaking, a SLANG specification is a finite collection of sorts, operations, and theorems (some of which are axioms). For pragmatic reasons, we have added sort-axioms (which are currently used to name sort terms), constructor sets (which are equivalent to induction axioms), and definitions (which are sets of axioms characterizing new operation symbols).

Every SLANG specification can be freely completed to a topos (see [16, Section II.12] for a description of this construction). The objects in this topos are all sorts definable in the specification; the arrows are all definable operations (i.e., provably functional relations).

Built-in Constructs. The only sort which is built-in, i.e., is implicitly part of every specification, is Boolean. Along with this sort, the standard operations on it such as true, false, and, or, etc., and axioms characterizing them are built-in. The universal (fa) and existential (ex) quantifiers, and a polymorphic equality (equal) are also built-in.

Sort Constructors. Lambek and Scott adopt a minimal set of sort constructors. While this is theoretically economical, we have chosen a richer set of sort constructors which arise in practice, especially in interpretations. We will use the generated topos to characterize these sort constructors; it is straightforward to generate the corresponding axioms.

N-ary products and coproducts. Given a set of n sorts, their product and coproduct are sorts which come equipped with the normal projections and embeddings, and characterized by the usual universal property.

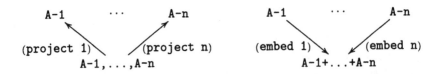

Function sorts. Given two sorts A and B, the function sort from A to B, written A -> B, satisfies the usual universal property and comes equipped with an evaluation operation, written (<rator> <ap>), and an abstraction operation, written (lambda (<args>) <body>).

Subsorts. Given a sort A and a predicate op p: A -> Boolean on this sort, the subsort of A consisting of those elements which satisfy the predicate, written A|p, and the induced injection are characterized by the following pullback diagram (1 is the terminal object, and ! denotes the unique arrow into it from A|p).

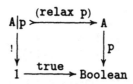

Quotient sorts. Given a sort A and an equivalence relation op e:A,A -> Boolean on this sort, the quotient sort consisting of equivalence classes of elements of A, written A/e, and the induced surjection are characterized by the following co-equalizer diagram ((A,A)|e is the equivalence relation as a subsort of A,A).

$$(A,A)|e \underset{\text{(project 2)}\circ\text{(relax e)}}{\overset{\text{(project 1)}\circ\text{(relax e)}}{\rightrightarrows}} A \xrightarrow{\text{(quotient e)}} A/e$$

Sort Axioms. Sort axioms are equations between sorts. Currently, these are restricted so that the left-hand side is a primitive sort (i.e., a sort which is not constructed using one of the sort constructors). Thus, in effect, sort axioms create new names for sorts. This keeps the sort algebra free, which is convenient for the type-checker. In the future, we may allow non-free sort algebras, and extend the type-checker to handle this.

Constructor Sets. A constructor set for a sort is a finite set of operations with that sort as the codomain. A constructor set is equivalent to an induction axiom. Here is an example.

```
constructors {zero, one, plus} construct NAT

axiom induction-for-NAT is
(fa (P) (implies
          (and (and (P zero) (P one))
               (fa (x y) (implies (and (P x) (P y))
                                  (P (plus x y)))))
          (fa (n) (P n))))
```

Note that a constructor set need not freely generate the constructed sort, i.e., the images of the constructors need not be disjoint. Additional axioms are necessary to force this.

Definitions. Definitions in SLANG are finite sets of axioms which completely characterize an operation. What this means is that to define a new operation f: A -> B in a specification S, there must be a formula phi with exactly two free variables x:A and y:B such that the relation specified by phi is provably functional in S:

```
(and (fa (x) (ex (y) (phi x y)))
     (fa (x) (implies (and (phi x y1) (phi x y2))
                      (equal y1 y2))))
```

Then S can be extended with the operation f together with the defining axiom

```
(iff (equal (f x) y) (phi x y)).
```

References

1. Artin, M., Grothendieck, A., And Verdier, J. L. *Théorie des Topos et Cohomologie Etale des Schémas, Lecture Notes in Mathematics*, Vol. 269. Springer-Verlag, 1972. SGA4, Séminaire de Géométrie Algébrique du Bois-Marie, 1963–1964.
2. Bauer, F. L., Et Al. *The Munich Project CIP, Volume I: The Wide Spectrum Language CIP-L, Lecture Notes in Computer Science*, Vol. 183. Springer-Verlag, Berlin, 1985.
3. Bauer, F. L., Ehler, H., Horsch, A., Möller, B., Partsch, H., Paukner, O., and Pepper, P. *The Munich Project CIP, Volume II: The Program Transformation System CIP-S, Lecture Notes in Computer Science*, Vol. 292. Springer-Verlag, Berlin, 1987.
4. Bird, R. S. Introduction to the theory of lists. Tech. Rep. PRG-56, Oxford University Computing Laboratory, Programming Research Group, October 1986. Appeared in Logic of Programming and Calculi of Discrete Design, M. Broy, Ed., Springer-Verlag, NATO ASI Series F: Computer and Systems Sciences, Vol. 36, 1987.
5. Bird, R. A calculus of functions for program derivation. Tech. Rep. PRG-64, Oxford University, Programming Research Group, December 1987.
6. Blaine, L., And Goldberg, A. DTRE – a semi-automatic transformation system. In *Constructing Programs from Specifications*, B. Möller, Ed. North-Holland, Amsterdam, 1991, pp. 165–204.
7. Burstall, R. M., And Goguen, J. A. Putting theories together to make specifications. In *Proceedings of the Fifth International Joint Conference on Artificial Intelligence* (Cambridge, MA, August 22–25, 1977), IJCAI, pp. 1045–1058.
8. Gilham, L.-M., Goldberg, A., And Wang, T. C. Toward reliable reactive systems. In *Proceedings of the 5th International Workshop on Software Specification and Design* (Pittsburgh, PA, May 1989).
9. Goguen, J. A., And Burstall, R. M. CAT, A system for the correct elaboration of correct programs from structured specifications. Tech. Rep. CSL-118, SRI International, Oct. 1980.
10. Goguen, J. A., And Winkler, T. Introducing OBJ3. Tech. Rep. SRI-CSL-88-09, SRI International, Menlo Park, California, 1988.
11. Green, C. Synthesis of graphical displays for tabular data. Tech. Rep. SBIR.FR.86.1, Kestrel Institute, October 1987. Final Report for Phase I; Note: accompanying videotape.

12. Hoare, C. A. R. Proof of correctness of data representation. *Acta Informatica 1* (1972), 271–281.

13. Jones, C. B. *Systematic Software Development Using VDM.* Prentice-Hall, Englewood Cliffs, NJ, 1986.

14. Jüllig, R. Applying formal software synthesis. *IEEE Software 10*, 3 (May 1993), 11–22. (also Technical Report KES.U.93.1, Kestrel Institute, May 1993).

15. Knuth, D. E. *The Art of Computer Programming, Volume 1: Fundamental Algorithms.* Addison-Wesley, Reading, Massachusetts, 1968.

16. Lambek, J., And Scott, P. J. *Introduction to Higher Order Categorical Logic.* Cambridge University Press, Cambridge, 1986.

17. Lehman, M. M., Stenning, V., And Turski, W. M. Another look at software design methodology. *ACM SIGSOFT Software Engineering Notes 9*, 2 (April 1984), 38–53.

18. Mac Lane, S. *Categories for the Working Mathematician.* Springer-Verlag, New York, 1971.

19. Mac Lane, S., And Moerdijk, I. *Sheaves in Geometry and Logic.* Springer-Verlag, New York, 1992.

20. Meseguer, J. General logics. In *Logic Colloquium'87*, H.-D. Ebbinghaus et al., Eds. North-Holland, 1989, pp. 275–329.

21. Sannella, D., And Tarlecki, A. Specifications in an arbitrary institution. *Inf. and Comput. 76* (1988), 165–210.

22. Sannella, D., And Tarlecki, A. Toward formal development of programs from algebraic specifications: Implementations revisited. *Acta Informatica 25*, 3 (1988), 233–281.

23. Smith, D. R. KIDS – a semi-automatic program development system. *IEEE Transactions on Software Engineering Special Issue on Formal Methods in Software Engineering 16*, 9 (September 1990), 1024–1043.

24. Smith, D. R. Constructing specification morphisms. *Journal of Symbolic Computation, Special Issue on Automatic Programming 15*, 5-6 (May-June 1993), 571–606.

25. Smith, D. R., And Lowry, M. R. Algorithm theories and design tactics. *Science of Computer Programming 14*, 2-3 (October 1990), 305–321.

26. Srinivas, Y. V. A sheaf-theoretic approach to pattern matching and related problems. *Theoretical Comput. Sci. 112* (1993), 53–97.

27. Turski, W. M., And Maibaum, T. E. *The Specification of Computer Programs.* Addison-Wesley, Wokingham, England, 1987.

28. Wirsing, M. Structured algebraic specifications: A kernel language. *Theoretical Comput. Sci. 42* (1986), 123–249. A slight revision of his Habilitationsschrift, Technische Universität München, 1983.

A Refinement Relation Supporting the Transition from Unbounded to Bounded Communication Buffers

Ketil Stølen

Fakultät für Informatik, TU München
Arcisstrasse 21, D-80290 München

Abstract. This paper proposes a refinement relation supporting the transition from unbounded to bounded communication buffers. Employing this refinement relation, a system specification based on purely asynchronous communication can for example be refined into a system specification where the components communicate purely in terms of handshakes. First a weak version called partial refinement is introduced. Partial refinement guarantees only the preservation of safety properties — preservation in the sense that any implementation of the more concrete specification can be understood as an implementation of the more abstract specification if the latter is a safety property. This refinement relation is then strengthened into total refinement which preserves both safety and liveness properties. Thus a total refinement is also a partial refinement. The suitability of this refinement relation for top-down design is discussed and some examples are given.

1 Introduction

During the final phases of a system development many implementation dependent constraints have to be taken into consideration. This is not a problem as long as the introduction of these constraints is supported by the refinement relation being used — supported in the sense that the specifications in which these constraints have been embedded can be understood as refinements of the earlier more abstract system specifications where these implementation dependent constraints did not occur. Unfortunately this is not always the case.

One important class of such implementation dependent constraints, which (in general) is not supported by standard refinement relations like behavioral refinement and interface refinement, is the class of requirements imposing upperbounds on the memory available for a communication channel. Such a requirement may for example characterize the maximum number of messages which at one point can be stored in a certain channel without risking malfunction because of channel overflow. Clearly this number may vary from one channel to another depending on the type of messages that are sent along the channel, and the way the channel is implemented.

Of course one way to treat such channel constraints is to introduce them already at the most abstract level. However, this solution is not very satisfactory because these rather trivial constraints may considerably complicate the specifications and the whole refinement process. The other alternative is to introduce them first in the final phases of a development. However, as already pointed out, this requires a refinement relation supporting the introduction of such constraints.

Consider a network consisting of two specifications S_1 and S_2 communicating purely asynchronously via an internal channel y, as indicated by Network 1 of Fig. 1.

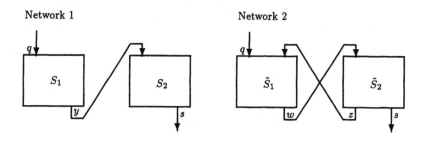

Fig. 1. Introducing Synchronization

We want to refine Network 1 into a network of two specifications $\tilde{S}_1$ and $\tilde{S}_2$ communicating in a synchronous manner — in other words into a network of the same form as Network 2 of Fig. 1.

That Network 2 is a refinement of Network 1 in the sense that any external behavior of Network 2 is also a behavior of Network 1 is only a necessary requirement, because we may still instantiate $\tilde{S}_1$ and $\tilde{S}_2$ in such a way that the communication via w is completely independent of the communication along z. Thus that Network 2 is a refinement of Network 1 does not necessarily mean that we have managed to synchronize the communication. It is still up to the developer to formulate $\tilde{S}_1$ and $\tilde{S}_2$ in such a way that they communicate in accordance with the synchronization protocol the developer prefers.

Nevertheless what is needed is a refinement relation supporting this way of introducing feedback loops. Clearly this refinement relation must allow for the formulation of rules which do not require the proof efforts already invested at the earlier abstraction levels to be repeated. For example, if it has already been proved that Network 1 has the desired overall effect, then it should not be necessary to repeat this proof when Network 1 is refined into Network 2. The formulation of such a refinement relation is the objective of this paper.

The close relationship between specification formalisms based on hand-shake communication and purely asynchronous communication is well-documented in the literature. For example [HJH90] shows how the process algebra of CSP can be extended to handle asynchronous communication by representing each asynchronous communication channel as a separate process. A similar technique allows different types of synchronous communication to be introduced in an asynchronous system specification: each asynchronous channel is refined into a network of two components which internally communicate in a synchronous manner, and which externally behave like the identity component.

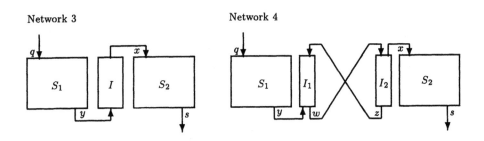

Fig. 2. Naive Transformation

In fact with respect to the two networks of Fig. 1, using this strategy, we may move from Network 1 to Network 2 in three steps, employing the usual relation of behavioral refinement, which basically says that a specification S' is a refinement of a specification S iff any behavior of S' is also a behavior of S:

- Step 1: Insert an identity specification I between S_1 and S_2 of Network 1, as indicated by Network 3 of Fig. 2. The soundness of this refinement step is obvious.
- Step 2: Refine the identity specification into two sub-specifications I_1 and I_2 which communicate in accordance with the desired protocol. We then get Network 4 of Fig. 2.
- Step 3: Refine the network consisting of S_1 and I_1 into $\tilde{S}_1$ and the network consisting of S_2 and I_2 into $\tilde{S}_2$, in which case we get Network 2 of Fig. 1.

Unfortunately, this strategy is rather tedious, and more importantly: it can only be employed to internal channels. To handle external channels accordingly, a more general refinement relation than behavioral refinement is needed — namely a refinement concept which allows the more concrete specifications to have additional input and output channels.

One might expect that some sort of interface refinement would be sufficient. However, the principles of interface refinement known to us either are not sufficiently general or do not have the desired compositionality properties. The principle of (interaction) interface refinement proposed in [Bro93] allows a channel to be refined into a pair of channels, but only as long as the channels are all of the same direction. Thus the refinement of a channel into two channels of opposite directions is not supported. On the other hand, refinement principles in the tradition of [Hoa72], [Jon87], [AL88], where the concrete state is related to the abstract state via a refinement function, do not seem to offer the required flexibility. (In our context the state can be understood as a mapping from channel identifiers to their communication histories.)

Below we attempt to deal with this problem by introducing two generalizations of behavioral refinement — one for partial correctness, and one for total correctness — referred to as partial and total refinement, respectively. Partial refinement is sufficient when only safety properties are considered. Total refinement preserves both safety and liveness properties (and also any conjunction of safety and liveness properties) — preserves in the sense that any implementation of the more concrete specification can be understood as an implementation of the more abstract specification. Thus a total refinement is also a partial refinement.

Total refinement allows for the introduction of both acknowledgment based and demand-driven synchronization. However, it is suited only for synchronization protocols which do not depend upon that acknowledgments (demands) sent along a channel are fairly distributed over sets of acknowledgments (demands).

Of course the use of hand-shake synchronization is not the only way to avoid buffer overflow — another alternative is to synchronize the computation by imposing real-time constraints on the behavior of processes and channels. However, this alternative can be used only if the programming language in which the specified system is to be implemented supports the realization of such constraints.

The investigations are conducted in the context of data-flow networks modeled by sets of continuous functions. The proposed relation can easily be restated in the context of other models for reactive systems.

The paper is organized as follows. Section 2 introduces the basic concepts. What we mean by specification and refinement is formalized in Sect. 3. Then partial and total refinement are the subjects of Sects. 4 and 5 Finally, Sect. 6 contains a summary and discusses a possible generalization.

2 Basic Notations

N denotes the set of natural numbers, and N_+ denotes $N \setminus \{0\}$. A stream is a finite or infinite sequence of actions. It models the communication history of a directed channel. Each action represents one message sent along the channel. Throughout the paper D denotes the set of all streams. We do not distinguish between different types of streams (streams of naturals etc.). However all our results can easily be generalized to such a setting (and this is exploited in Ex. 4).

Let d be an action, r and s be streams, and j be a natural number, then:

- ϵ denotes the empty stream;
- $\mathrm{ft}(r)$ denotes the first element of r if r is not empty;
- $\#r$ denotes the length of r;
- $r|_j$ denotes the prefix of r of length j if $j < \#r$, and r otherwise;
- $d \& s$ denotes the result of appending d to s;
- $r \frown s$ denotes r if r is infinite and the result of concatenating r to s, otherwise;
- $r \sqsubseteq s$ holds if r is a prefix of s.

A named stream tuple is a mapping from a finite set of identifiers to the set of streams. It can be thought of as an assignment of channel histories to channel identifiers. Given a set of identifiers I, then I^ω denotes the set of all named stream tuples of signature $I \rightarrow D$. Moreover, $I \mapsto \epsilon$ denotes the element of I^ω which for each identifier in I returns the empty stream; I^∞ denotes the subset of I^ω which maps every identifier to an infinite stream; I^* denotes the subset of I^ω which maps every identifier to a finite stream.

The prefix ordering $\sqsubseteq$ is also used to order named stream tuples. Given two named stream tuples $\alpha \in I^\omega$ and $\beta \in O^\omega$, then $\alpha \sqsubseteq \beta$ iff $I = O$ and for all $i \in I : \alpha(i) \sqsubseteq \beta(i)$. We also overload the concatenation and length operators. $\alpha \frown \beta$ denotes the named stream tuple in $(I \cup O)^\omega$ such that:

$$i \in I \setminus O \Rightarrow (\alpha \frown \beta)(i) = \alpha(i),$$
$$i \in O \setminus I \Rightarrow (\alpha \frown \beta)(i) = \beta(i),$$
$$i \in I \cap O \Rightarrow (\alpha \frown \beta)(i) = \alpha(i) \frown \beta(i).$$

$\#\alpha$ denotes $\min\{\#\alpha(i) \,|\, i \in I\}$. Finally, α/O denotes the projection of α on O, namely the named stream tuple $\alpha' \in (I \cap O)^\omega$ such that for all $i \in I \cap O$, $\alpha'(i) = \alpha(i)$.

By a chain of named stream tuples we mean an infinite sequence of named stream tuples ordered by $\sqsubseteq$. Since streams may be infinite any such chain δ has a least upper-bound denoted by $\sqcup\delta$.

When convenient named stream tuples are represented as sets of maplets. For example, the set

$$\{a \mapsto r, b \mapsto s\}$$

denotes the named stream tuple $\alpha \in \{a, b\}^\omega$, where $\alpha(a) = r$ and $\alpha(b) = s$.

Following [BD92] components are modeled by sets of functions mapping named stream tuples to named stream tuples. Each such function

$$f \in I^\omega \rightarrow O^\omega$$

is required to be monotonic:

for all named stream tuples $\alpha, \beta : \alpha \sqsubseteq \beta \Rightarrow f(\alpha) \sqsubseteq f(\beta)$,

and continuous:

for all chains δ of named stream tuples $: f(\sqcup\delta) = \sqcup\{f(\delta_j) \,|\, j \in \mathbb{N}_+\}$.

In the sequel we refer to such functions as stream processing functions.

To reduce the use of the projection operator and thereby simplify the presentation, each function $f \in I^\omega \rightarrow O^\omega$ is overloaded to any domain $Q^\omega \rightarrow O^\omega$ where $I \subseteq Q$, by requiring that for any $\alpha \in Q^\omega$, $f(\alpha) \stackrel{\text{def}}{=} f(\alpha/I)$.

Given two stream processing functions

$$f \in I^\omega \to O^\omega, \qquad \tilde{f} \in \tilde{I}^\omega \to \tilde{O}^\omega,$$

where $I \cap \tilde{I} = O \cap \tilde{O} = \emptyset$, then $f \parallel \tilde{f}$ is a function of signature

$$(I \cup \tilde{I})^\omega \to (O \cup \tilde{O})^\omega,$$

such that $(f \parallel \tilde{f})(\alpha) = f(\alpha) \frown \tilde{f}(\alpha)$. If in addition $I \cap O = \tilde{I} \cap \tilde{O} = \emptyset$, we define $f \otimes \tilde{f}$ and $f \hat{\otimes} \tilde{f}$ to be functions of signatures

$$((I \setminus \tilde{O}) \cup (\tilde{I} \setminus O))^\omega \to ((O \setminus \tilde{I}) \cup (\tilde{O} \setminus I))^\omega,$$
$$((I \setminus \tilde{O}) \cup (\tilde{I} \setminus O))^\omega \to (O \cup \tilde{O})^\omega,$$

respectively, such that

$$(f \otimes \tilde{f})(\alpha) = \beta / (O \setminus \tilde{I} \cup \tilde{O} \setminus I), \qquad (f \hat{\otimes} \tilde{f})(\alpha) = \beta,$$

where β is the least fix-point of $(f \parallel \tilde{f})(\alpha \frown \beta) = \beta$ with respect to $\sqsubseteq$.

It follows straightforwardly that $f \parallel \tilde{f}$, $f \otimes \tilde{f}$ and $f \hat{\otimes} \tilde{f}$ are stream processing functions.

In Fig. 3, Network 1 represents composition by $\otimes$, and Network 2 represents composition by $\hat{\otimes}$. Thus $\otimes$ differs from $\hat{\otimes}$ in that it hides the feedback channels.

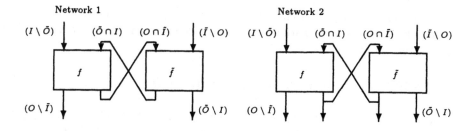

Fig. 3. Networks Relating the Operators $\otimes$ and $\hat{\otimes}$

Given $n > 1$ stream processing functions

$$f_j \in I_j^\omega \to O_j^\omega \qquad 1 \le j \le n,$$

such that $I_j \cap O_j = \emptyset$ and $l \ne k$ implies $I_l \cap I_k = O_l \cap O_k = \emptyset$, then $\otimes_{j=1}^n f_j$ is a short-hand for $f_1 \otimes \ldots \otimes f_n$. Note that the restrictions imposed on the identifier sets imply that $\otimes$ is associative — thus the bracketing is unimportant. $\hat{\otimes}$ and $\parallel$ are generalized accordingly.

3 Specification and Refinement

A specification is represented by a triple

$$(I, O, R),$$

where I and O are disjoint sets of identifiers, and R is a formula with the elements of I and O as its only free variables. The identifiers in I and O name the input channels and the output channels, respectively. We refer to these identifiers as the input and the output identifiers. Moreover, (I, O) is called the specification's interface. In R each such identifier is of type stream. Each input identifier models the communication history of an input channel, and each output identifier models the communication history of an output channel. R characterizes the allowed relation between the communication histories of the input channels and the communication histories of the output channels and is therefore called the input/output relation.

For example the specification

$$(\{a\}, \{c, d, e\}, \#c = \#a \land d = e = 0 \,\&\, a)$$

characterizes a component with one input channel a and three output channels c, d, e. Along the channel c this component outputs exactly one (arbitrary) message for each message it receives on a, and along the channels d and e the component first outputs a 0 and thereafter any message received on a.

The denotation of a specification $S \stackrel{\text{def}}{=} (I, O, R)$ is a set of stream processing functions mapping named stream tuples to named stream tuples, namely the set characterized by:

$$[\![S]\!] \stackrel{\text{def}}{=} \{f \in I^\omega \to O^\omega \mid \forall \alpha \in I^\omega : (\alpha \frown f(\alpha)) \models R\},$$

where for any named stream tuple $\beta \in Q^\omega$ and formula P whose free variables are contained in Q, $\beta \models P$ iff P evaluates to true when each identifier $i \in Q$ is interpreted as $\beta(i)$.

The basic refinement relation is represented by $\leadsto$. It holds only for specifications whose interfaces are identical. Given two specifications S_1 and S_2, then $S_1 \leadsto S_2$ iff $[\![S_2]\!] \subseteq [\![S_1]\!]$. Thus a specification S_2 refines a specification S_1 iff any function which satisfies S_2 also satisfies S_1. This corresponds to what is normally referred to as behavioral refinement.

Given two specifications $S_1 \stackrel{\text{def}}{=} (I_1, O_1, R_1)$ and $S_2 \stackrel{\text{def}}{=} (I_2, O_2, R_2)$, such that

$$I_1 \cap I_2 = O_1 \cap O_2 = \emptyset,$$

then $S_1 \otimes S_2$ represents the network pictured in Fig. 4. The channels modeled by $O_1 \cap I_2$ and $O_2 \cap I_1$ are internal. The external input channels are represented by $(I_1 \setminus O_2) \cup (I_2 \setminus O_1)$, and $(O_1 \setminus I_2) \cup (O_2 \setminus I_1)$ represents the external output channels. The denotation of this network is characterized by

$$[\![S_1 \otimes S_2]\!] \stackrel{\text{def}}{=} \{f_1 \otimes f_2 \mid f_1 \in [\![S_1]\!] \wedge f_2 \in [\![S_2]\!]\}.$$

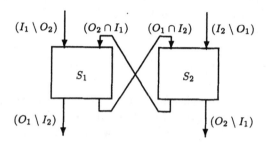

Fig. 4. $S_1 \otimes S_2$

The operator $\otimes_{j=1}^n$ is lifted from functions to specifications in a similar way.

The properties characterized by a specification can be split into several classes. For example, there is a long tradition for distinguishing between safety and liveness properties [AS85]. Informally speaking:

- a safety property characterizes what a correct implementation is not allowed to do,
- a liveness property characterizes what a correct implementation is required to do.

Given a specification $S \stackrel{\text{def}}{=} (I, O, R)$ then S characterizes a safety property iff

$$\forall \alpha \in I^\omega : \forall \beta \in O^\omega : (\alpha \frown \beta) \models R \Leftrightarrow \forall \beta' \in O^* : \beta' \sqsubseteq \beta \Rightarrow (\alpha \frown \beta') \models R,$$

and a liveness property iff

$$\forall \alpha \in I^\omega : \forall \beta \in O^* : \exists \beta' \in O^\omega : \beta \sqsubseteq \beta' \wedge (\alpha \frown \beta') \models R.$$

4 Partial Refinement

This section introduces a refinement relation, called partial refinement, which guarantees the preservation of safety properties. The suitability of this refinement relation for top-down system development is investigated.

Given two specifications

$$S \stackrel{\text{def}}{=} (Q, O, R), \qquad \tilde{S} \stackrel{\text{def}}{=} (\tilde{Q}, \tilde{O}, \tilde{R}),$$

where $Q \subseteq \tilde{Q}$ and $O \subseteq \tilde{O}$. We want to characterize what it means for $\tilde{S}$ to refine S. If only the "old" channels are considered one might expect this to be equivalent to insisting that for each function $\tilde{f} \in [\![\, \tilde{S}\,]\!]$ there is a function $f \in [\![\, S\,]\!]$ which behaves in the same way as $\tilde{f}$. Since by definition $f(\alpha)$ is equal to $f(\alpha/Q)$ this suggests:

$$\forall \tilde{f} \in [\![\, \tilde{S}\,]\!] : \exists f \in [\![\, S\,]\!] : \forall \alpha \in \tilde{Q}^{\omega} : \tilde{f}(\alpha)/O = f(\alpha).$$

However, due to the synchronization conducted via the new channels the output can be halted too early because the required acknowledgments have not been received. Thus, in the general case, unless we make certain assumptions about the environment's behavior, the insistence upon equality is too strong. On the other hand, if only safety properties are considered, the following constraint is sufficient:

$$\forall \tilde{f} \in [\![\, \tilde{S}\,]\!] : \exists f \in [\![\, S\,]\!] : \forall \alpha \in \tilde{Q}^{\omega} : \tilde{f}(\alpha)/O \sqsubseteq f(\alpha).$$

If $\tilde{S}$ and S are related in this way, we say that $\tilde{S}$ is a partial refinement of S, and we write $S \stackrel{p}{\leadsto} \tilde{S}$. Thus $\tilde{S}$ is a partial refinement of S iff for any function $\tilde{f}$ which satisfies $\tilde{S}$, there is a function f which satisfies S, such that for any input history α for the channels represented by $\tilde{Q}$, the projection of $\tilde{f}(\alpha)$ on O is a prefix of $f(\alpha)$.

The rest of this section is devoted to partial refinement. In the next section, we will introduce a more general refinement relation which guarantees equality under the assumption that sufficiently many acknowledgments are received.

Clearly, if S is a safety property and $S \stackrel{p}{\leadsto} \tilde{S}$ then $\tilde{S}$ behaves in accordance with S with respect to the interface of S. Thus $\stackrel{p}{\leadsto}$ preserves safety properties in the sense that $\tilde{S}$ does not falsify S. Note that this does not mean that $\tilde{S}$ has to be a safety property. On the other hand, if S is a liveness property then there is no guarantee that $\tilde{S}$ behaves in accordance with S. Thus $\stackrel{p}{\leadsto}$ preserves safety properties but not liveness properties.

It is straightforward to prove that partial refinement is reflexive and transitive, and below we show that it is also a congruence with respect to $\otimes$. This implies that whenever we have refined a specification S into a network of specifications $\otimes_{j=1}^{n} S_j$ such that

$$S \stackrel{p}{\leadsto} \otimes_{j=1}^{n} S_j, \qquad (*)$$

and there is a network of specifications $\otimes_{j=1}^{n} S_j'$ such that

$$S_j \overset{p}{\leadsto} S'_j \qquad 1 \le j \le n,$$

then it also holds that

$$S \overset{p}{\leadsto} \otimes_{j=1}^n S'_j.$$

Thus the workload invested in establishing (*) does not have to be repeated when the refinement of the component specifications of $\otimes_{j=1}^n S_j$ is continued. This implies that the principle of partial refinement is well-suited for top-down system development.

Before stating the general congruence property for partial refinement, we prove an intermediate result, whose conclusion (3) is visualized by Fig. 5. Thus we have four specifications $S_1, S_2, \tilde{S}_1, \tilde{S}_2$. Their interfaces are characterized by $(Q \cup X, O \cup Y)$, $(Y \cup Z, X \cup K)$, $(\tilde{Q} \cup \tilde{X}, \tilde{O} \cup \tilde{Y})$, $(\tilde{Y} \cup \tilde{Z}, \tilde{X} \cup \tilde{K})$, respectively. It is assumed that the sets of identifiers $\tilde{Q}, \tilde{X}, \tilde{O}, \tilde{Y}, \tilde{Z}, \tilde{K}$ are all disjoint, and that $Q \subseteq \tilde{Q}, X \subseteq \tilde{X}, O \subseteq \tilde{O}, Y \subseteq \tilde{Y}, Z \subseteq \tilde{Z}, K \subseteq \tilde{K}$.

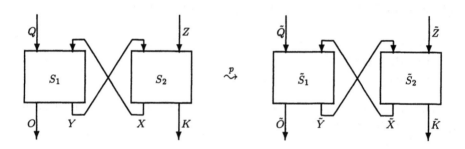

Fig. 5. Partial Refinement

Proposition 1. *If*

(1) : $S_1 \overset{p}{\leadsto} \tilde{S}_1$,
(2) : $S_2 \overset{p}{\leadsto} \tilde{S}_2$

then

(3) : $S_1 \otimes S_2 \overset{p}{\leadsto} \tilde{S}_1 \otimes \tilde{S}_2$.

Proof. Let $\tilde{f}_1$ and $\tilde{f}_2$ be such that

(4) : $\tilde{f}_1 \in [\tilde{S}_1]$,
(5) : $\tilde{f}_2 \in [\tilde{S}_2]$.

(1), (2), (4), (5) imply there are f_1 and f_2 such that

(6) : $f_1 \in [S_1]$,
(7) : $f_2 \in [S_2]$,
(8) : $\forall \alpha \in (\tilde{Q} \cup \tilde{X})^\omega : \tilde{f}_1(\alpha)/(O \cup Y) \sqsubseteq f_1(\alpha)$,
(9) : $\forall \alpha \in (\tilde{Y} \cup \tilde{Z})^\omega : \tilde{f}_2(\alpha)/(X \cup K) \sqsubseteq f_2(\alpha)$.

(3) follows if it can be shown that

(10) : $\forall \alpha \in (\tilde{Q} \cup \tilde{Z})^\omega : (\tilde{f}_1 \otimes \tilde{f}_2)(\alpha)/(O \cup K) \sqsubseteq (f_1 \otimes f_2)(\alpha)$.

Given some $\alpha \in (\tilde{Q} \cup \tilde{Z})^\omega$ and let $\beta \in (O \cup Y \cup X \cup K)^\omega$ be defined by

(11) : $(f_1 \hat{\otimes} f_2)(\alpha) = \beta$.

The monotonicity of $\tilde{f}_1$ and $\tilde{f}_2$ implies there are chains $\tilde{\alpha}, \tilde{\beta}$ such that

(12) : $\tilde{\alpha}_1 = \alpha \frown (\tilde{X} \cup \tilde{Y} \mapsto \epsilon)$,
(13) : $\tilde{\beta}_j = (\tilde{f}_1 \| \tilde{f}_2)(\tilde{\alpha}_j)$,
(14) : $\tilde{\alpha}_{j+1} = \alpha \frown \tilde{\beta}_j$.

(Remember that any stream processing function $f \in I^\omega \to O^\omega$ is overloaded to any domain $Q^\omega \to O^\omega$ where $I \subseteq Q$.)
(12), (13), (14) imply

(15) : $(\tilde{f}_1 \hat{\otimes} \tilde{f}_2)(\alpha) = \sqcup \tilde{\beta}$.

We want to prove that

(16) : $\tilde{\beta}_j/(O \cup Y \cup X \cup K) \sqsubseteq \beta$.

The base-case follows trivially from (8), (9), (11), (12), (13) and the monotonicity of f_1 and f_2. Assume for some $k \geq 1$

(17) : $\tilde{\beta}_k/(O \cup Y \cup X \cup K) \sqsubseteq \beta$.

We show that

(18) : $\tilde{\beta}_{k+1}/(O \cup Y \cup X \cup K) \sqsubseteq \beta$.

(13) implies that

$(19): \tilde{\beta}_{k+1}/(O \cup Y \cup X \cup K) = (\tilde{f}_1 \parallel \tilde{f}_2)(\tilde{\alpha}_{k+1})/(O \cup Y \cup X \cup K).$

(19) and the definition of $\parallel$ imply that

$(20): \tilde{\beta}_{k+1}/(O \cup Y \cup X \cup K) = \tilde{f}_1(\tilde{\alpha}_{k+1})/(O \cup Y) \frown \tilde{f}_2(\tilde{\alpha}_{k+1})/(X \cup K).$

(8), (9), (20) imply

$(21): \tilde{\beta}_{k+1}/(O \cup Y \cup X \cup K) \sqsubseteq f_1(\tilde{\alpha}_{k+1}) \frown f_2(\tilde{\alpha}_{k+1}).$

(14), (21) imply

$(22): \tilde{\beta}_{k+1}/(O \cup Y \cup X \cup K) \sqsubseteq f_1(\alpha \frown \tilde{\beta}_k) \frown f_2(\alpha \frown \tilde{\beta}_k).$

(17), (22) and the monotonicity of f_1 and f_2 imply

$(23): \tilde{\beta}_{k+1}/(O \cup Y \cup X \cup K) \sqsubseteq f_1(\alpha \frown \beta) \frown f_2(\alpha \frown \beta).$

(11), (23) imply (18). This ends the proof of (16).
(16) and the definition of $\sqcup$ imply

$(24): \sqcup\tilde{\beta}/(O \cup Y \cup X \cup K) \sqsubseteq \beta.$

(11), (15), (24) and the fact that $\otimes$ is equal to $\hat{\otimes}$ plus hiding imply (10).

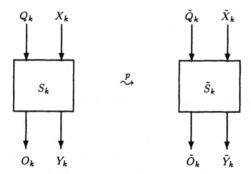

Fig. 6. Partial Refinement of the k'th Component Specification

We now extend Prop. 1 to finite networks of n specifications. Each of the n component specifications S_k is partially refined into a component specification $\tilde{S}_k$ in accordance with Fig. 6. $\tilde{Q}_k$ represents the external input channels, $\tilde{X}_k$ represents the internal input channels, $\tilde{O}_k$ represents the external output channels, and $\tilde{Y}_k$ represents the internal output channels. This means that $\cup_{j=1}^n \tilde{X}_j = \cup_{j=1}^n \tilde{Y}_j$. It is assumed that the $3 \times n$ sets $\tilde{Q}_k, \tilde{X}_k, \tilde{O}_k$ are all disjoint, that the n sets $\tilde{Y}_k$ are all disjoint, that $\cup_{j=1}^n X_j = \cup_{j=1}^n Y_j$, and that $Q_k \subseteq \tilde{Q}_k$, $X_k \subseteq \tilde{X}_k$ etc. .

Proposition 2. *If*

$$(1) : S_j \overset{p}{\leadsto} \tilde{S}_j \qquad 1 \le j \le n,$$

then

$$(2) : \otimes_{j=1}^n S_j \overset{p}{\leadsto} \otimes_{j=1}^n \tilde{S}_j.$$

Proof. Follows from Prop. 1 by induction on n.

5 Total Refinement

In the previous section a refinement relation called partial refinement was introduced. It was shown that this relation is reflexive, transitive and a congruence with respect to $\otimes$. Thus partial refinement is well-suited as a principle for top-down design. Unfortunately, partial refinement only preserves safety properties. To ensure the preservation of both safety and liveness properties a stronger refinement relation is needed — namely what we refer to as total refinement.

Given two specifications

$$S \overset{\text{def}}{=} (Q, O, R), \qquad\qquad \tilde{S} \overset{\text{def}}{=} (\tilde{Q}, \tilde{O}, \tilde{R}),$$

where $Q \subseteq \tilde{Q}$ and $O \subseteq \tilde{O}$, then $\tilde{S}$ is a total refinement of S, written $S \overset{t}{\leadsto} \tilde{S}$, iff

$$\forall \tilde{f} \in [\![\tilde{S}]\!] : \exists f \in [\![S]\!] : \forall \alpha \in \tilde{Q}^\omega : \#\alpha/(\tilde{Q} \setminus Q) = \infty \Rightarrow \tilde{f}(\alpha)/O = f(\alpha).$$

Thus $\tilde{S}$ is a total refinement of S iff for any function $\tilde{f}$ which satisfies $\tilde{S}$, there is a function f which satisfies S, such that for any input history α, whose projection on $\tilde{Q} \setminus Q$ is infinite, the projection of $\tilde{f}(\alpha)$ on O is equal to $f(\alpha)$.

The antecedent "projection on $\tilde{Q} \setminus Q$ is infinite" may seem too strong. However, since we in this paper restrict ourselves to synchronization protocols whose behavior depend only upon whether an acknowledgment (demand) is received or not, and not upon what sort of acknowledgment (demand) is received, this is exactly what is needed. Note that this antecedent can be thought of as an environment assumption. We will later discuss the generality of total refinement in more detail.

We first prove that total refinement degenerates to behavioral refinement if the interface is not extended, and that total refinement implies partial refinement.

Proposition 3. *Given two specifications S and $\tilde{S}$ whose interfaces are characterized by (Q, O) and $(\tilde{Q}, \tilde{O})$, respectively. Then:*

$(1) : Q = \tilde{Q} \wedge O = \tilde{O} \Rightarrow (S \stackrel{t}{\rightsquigarrow} \tilde{S} \Leftrightarrow S \rightsquigarrow \tilde{S}),$
$(2) : S \stackrel{t}{\rightsquigarrow} \tilde{S} \Rightarrow S \stackrel{p}{\rightsquigarrow} \tilde{S}.$

Proof. (1) follows trivially. To prove (2), assume

$(3) : S \stackrel{t}{\rightsquigarrow} \tilde{S}.$

It must be shown that

$(4) : S \stackrel{p}{\rightsquigarrow} \tilde{S}.$

Let

$(5) : \tilde{f} \in [\![\, \tilde{S} \,]\!].$

(3), (5) imply there is an f such that

$(6) : f \in [\![\, S \,]\!],$
$(7) : \forall \alpha \in \tilde{Q}^{\omega} : \#\alpha/(\tilde{Q} \setminus Q) = \infty \Rightarrow \tilde{f}(\alpha)/O = f(\alpha).$

Given some arbitrary $\alpha \in \tilde{Q}^{\omega}$. (4) follows if it can be shown that

$(8) : \tilde{f}(\alpha)/O \sqsubseteq f(\alpha).$

If $\#\alpha/(\tilde{Q} \setminus Q) = \infty$ then (8) follows trivially from (7). Otherwise, there is an $\alpha' \in \tilde{Q}^{\omega}$ such that

$(9) : \alpha'/Q = \alpha/Q,$
$(10) : \alpha \sqsubseteq \alpha',$
$(11) : \#\alpha'/(\tilde{Q} \setminus Q) = \infty.$

(7), (9), (11) imply

$(12) : \tilde{f}(\alpha')/O = f(\alpha'/Q) = f(\alpha/Q) = f(\alpha).$

(10), (12) and the monotonicity of $\tilde{f}$ imply (8).

The next step is to prove that $\overset{t}{\rightsquigarrow}$ is reflexive and transitive.

Proposition 4. *Given three specifications S_1, S_2, S_3 whose interfaces are characterized by $(Q_1, O_1), (Q_2, O_2), (Q_3, O_3)$, respectively. Assume that $Q_1 \subseteq Q_2 \subseteq Q_3$ and $O_1 \subseteq O_2 \subseteq O_3$. Then*

$(1) : S_1 \overset{t}{\rightsquigarrow} S_1,$
$(2) : S_1 \overset{t}{\rightsquigarrow} S_2 \wedge S_2 \overset{t}{\rightsquigarrow} S_3 \Rightarrow S_1 \overset{t}{\rightsquigarrow} S_3.$

Proof. (1) follows trivially. To prove (2), assume

$(3) : S_1 \overset{t}{\rightsquigarrow} S_2,$
$(4) : S_2 \overset{t}{\rightsquigarrow} S_3.$

Let f_3 be such that

$(5) : f_3 \in [\![S_3]\!].$

(4), (5) imply there is an f_2 such that

$(6) : f_2 \in [\![S_2]\!],$
$(7) : \forall \alpha \in (Q_3)^\omega : \#\alpha/(Q_3 \setminus Q_2) = \infty \Rightarrow f_3(\alpha)/O_2 = f_2(\alpha).$

(3), (6) imply there is an f_1 such that

$(8) : f_1 \in [\![S_1]\!],$
$(9) : \forall \alpha \in (Q_2)^\omega : \#\alpha/(Q_2 \setminus Q_1) = \infty \Rightarrow f_2(\alpha)/O_1 = f_1(\alpha).$

Given an $\alpha \in (Q_3)^\omega$ such that

$(10) : \#\alpha/(Q_3 \setminus Q_1) = \infty.$

(10) and $Q_1 \subseteq Q_2$ imply

$(11) : \#\alpha(Q_3 \setminus Q_2) = \infty.$

(7), (11) imply

$(12) : f_3(\alpha)/O_2 = f_2(\alpha) = f_2(\alpha/Q_2).$

(10) and $Q_2 \subseteq Q_3$ imply

$(13) : \#(\alpha/Q_2)/(Q_2 \setminus Q_1) = \infty.$

(9), (13) and $Q_1 \subseteq Q_2$ imply

$(14) : f_2(\alpha/Q_2)/O_1 = f_1(\alpha/Q_2) = f_1(\alpha)$.

(12) and $O_1 \subseteq O_2$ imply

$(15) : f_2(\alpha/Q_2)/O_1 = f_3(\alpha)/O_2/O_1 = f_3(\alpha)/O_1$.

(14), (15) imply

$(16) : f_3(\alpha)/O_1 = f_1(\alpha)$.

The way (16) was deduced from (10) implies

$(17) : \forall \alpha \in (Q_3)^\omega : \#\alpha/(Q_3 \setminus Q_1) = \infty \Rightarrow f_3(\alpha)/O_1 = f_1(\alpha)$.

The way (17) was deduced from (3), (4) implies (2).

It has been proved that partial refinement is a congruence with respect to the composition operator $\otimes$. The same does not hold for total refinement.

Example 1. To see that total refinement does not have this property, let

$S_1 \stackrel{\text{def}}{=} (\{q\}, \{y\}, y = q),$
$S_2 \stackrel{\text{def}}{=} (\{y\}, \{k\}, k = y),$
$\tilde{S}_1 \stackrel{\text{def}}{=} (\{q, x\}, \{y\}, y \sqsubseteq q \wedge \#y = \min\{\#x + 1, \#q\}),$
$\tilde{S}_2 \stackrel{\text{def}}{=} (\{y\}, \{x, k\}, k = y \wedge \#x = \max\{\#y - 1, 0\}).$

Clearly $S_1 \stackrel{t}{\leadsto} \tilde{S}_1$ and $S_2 \stackrel{t}{\leadsto} \tilde{S}_2$. Unfortunately, for all $f \in [\![\, S_1 \hat{\otimes} S_2 \,]\!]$ and $\tilde{f} \in [\![\, \tilde{S}_1 \hat{\otimes} \tilde{S}_2 \,]\!]$, and any nonempty stream s, it holds that

$f(\{q \mapsto s\}) = \{y \mapsto s, k \mapsto s\},$
$\tilde{f}(\{q \mapsto s\}) = \{y \mapsto \text{ft}(s) \& \epsilon, x \mapsto \epsilon, k \mapsto \text{ft}(s) \& \epsilon\}.$

Thus

$f \in [\![\, S_1 \otimes S_2 \,]\!] \Rightarrow f(\{q \to s\}) = \{k \mapsto s\}$
$\tilde{f} \in [\![\, \tilde{S}_1 \otimes \tilde{S}_2 \,]\!] \Rightarrow f(\{q \to s\}) = \{k \mapsto \text{ft}(s) \& \epsilon\}.$

Since $s \neq \text{ft}(s) \& \epsilon$ if $\#s > 1$ it follows that

$S_1 \otimes S_2 \not\stackrel{t}{\leadsto} \tilde{S}_1 \otimes \tilde{S}_2.$

What is required is some additional proof obligation characterizing under what conditions total refinement is a "congruence" with respect to $\otimes$. To allow systems to be developed in a top-down style this proof obligation must be checkable based on the information available at the point in time where the refinement step is carried out — for example this proof obligation should not require knowledge about how $\tilde{S}_1$ and $\tilde{S}_2$ are implemented. With respect to Ex. 1 the following condition is obviously sufficient:

$$\forall \tilde{f} \in [\![\tilde{S}_1 \otimes \tilde{S}_2]\!] : \exists f \in [\![S_1 \otimes S_2]\!] : \tilde{f}(\alpha) = f(\alpha). \qquad (**)$$

If $(**)$ holds there is no need to require that $S_1 \overset{t}{\rightsquigarrow} \tilde{S}_1$ and $S_2 \overset{t}{\rightsquigarrow} \tilde{S}_2$. This fact also characterizes the weakness of $(**)$. If we later decide to compose $\tilde{S}_1 \otimes \tilde{S}_2$ with another network $\tilde{S}_3$ such that $S_3 \overset{t}{\rightsquigarrow} \tilde{S}_3$, then it is not easy to exploit the fact that we have already proved $(**)$ when we now decide to prove that

$$\otimes_{j=1}^3 S_j \overset{t}{\rightsquigarrow} \otimes_{j=1}^3 \tilde{S}_j.$$

What we want is a proof obligation which takes advantage of the fact that $S_1 \overset{t}{\rightsquigarrow} \tilde{S}_1$ and $S_2 \overset{t}{\rightsquigarrow} \tilde{S}_2$ in the sense that the formulation of this additional obligation is independent of S_1 and S_2.

The problem observed in Ex. 1 is that total refinement may lead to premature termination when the specifications are composed into networks with feedback loops. This phenomenon can be understood as deadlock caused by an erroneous synchronization protocol.

With respect to the given semantics this problem occurs only when the refinement step introduces a new least fix-point — new in the sense that the least fix-point is reached too early. For the refinement step conducted in Ex. 1, it therefore seems sensible to require that for any $\alpha \in \{q\}^\omega$, $\tilde{f}_1 \in [\![\tilde{S}_1]\!]$, $\tilde{f}_2 \in [\![\tilde{S}_2]\!]$:

$$(\tilde{f}_1 \hat{\otimes} \tilde{f}_2)(\alpha) = \beta \wedge \alpha' \in \{x\}^\infty \Rightarrow \tilde{f}_1(\alpha \frown \beta \frown \alpha') = \beta/\{y\}. \qquad (***)$$

This condition states that when the least fix-point has been reached then the output along y will not be extended if additional input is received along the feedback channel x. It makes sure that no new least fix-point has been introduced as a result of the synchronization.

In some sense the proof obligation corresponds to the freedom from deadlock tests in more traditional proof systems [OG76], [Stø91] and [PJ91]. In Ex. 1 this proof obligation is not fulfilled. However, if $\tilde{S}_2$'s input/output relation is replaced by

$$k = y \wedge \#x = \#y$$

then $(***)$ holds. Thus in the case of Ex. 1, $(***)$ seems to be a reasonable proof obligation. The next step is to figure out how this obligation should look in the general case.

Example 2. Let S_1, S_2 and $\tilde{S}_1$ be as in Ex. 1, and let

$$\tilde{S}_2 \stackrel{\text{def}}{=} (\{y, z\}, \{x, k\}, k \sqsubseteq y \wedge \#k = \#x = \min\{\#y, \#z\}).$$

We then have that

$$S_1 \otimes S_2 \stackrel{t}{\leadsto} \tilde{S}_1 \otimes \tilde{S}_2.$$

Unfortunately, (***) does not hold. To see that, let $\tilde{f}_1 \in [\![\tilde{S}_1]\!]$, $\tilde{f}_2 \in [\![\tilde{S}_2]\!]$, and assume that s is a stream such that $\#s > 1$. Clearly

$$(\tilde{f}_1 \hat{\otimes} \tilde{f}_2)(\{q \mapsto s, z \mapsto \epsilon\}) = \{y \mapsto \text{ft}(s) \,\&\, \epsilon, x \mapsto \epsilon, k \mapsto \epsilon\}.$$

Moreover

$$\tilde{f}_1(\{q \mapsto s, x \mapsto s\}) = \{y \mapsto s\}.$$

Thus (***) is not satisfied.

In fact (***) must be weakened by adding assumptions about the environment's behavior. In the case of Ex. 2 it seems sensible to require that for any $\alpha \in \{q, z\}^\omega$:

$$\tilde{f}_1 \in [\![\tilde{S}_1]\!] \wedge \tilde{f}_2 \in [\![\tilde{S}_2]\!] \wedge (\tilde{f}_1 \hat{\otimes} \tilde{f}_2)(\alpha) = \beta \wedge \#(\alpha/\{z\}) = \infty \wedge \alpha' \in \{x\}^\infty$$
$$\Rightarrow$$
$$\tilde{f}_1(\alpha \frown \beta \frown \alpha') = \beta/\{y\}.$$

This motivates the next proposition, which characterizes a condition under which a total refinement corresponding to Fig. 5 is valid. It is assumed that $\tilde{Q}$, $\tilde{X}$, $\tilde{O}$, $\tilde{Y}$, $\tilde{Z}$, $\tilde{K}$ are disjoint sets of identifiers with corresponding subsets Q, $\hat{Q}$, X, $\hat{X}$, etc. such that $\hat{Q} = \tilde{Q} \setminus Q$, $\hat{X} = \tilde{X} \setminus X$, etc.

Proposition 5. *If for any* $\alpha \in (\tilde{Q} \cup \tilde{Z})^\omega$, $\beta \in (\tilde{O} \cup \tilde{Y} \cup \tilde{X} \cup \tilde{K})^\omega$, $\alpha' \in (\hat{X} \cup \hat{Y})^\infty$

(1) : $S_1 \stackrel{t}{\leadsto} \tilde{S}_1$,
(2) : $S_2 \stackrel{t}{\leadsto} \tilde{S}_2$,
(3) : $\tilde{f}_1 \in [\![\tilde{S}_1]\!] \wedge \tilde{f}_2 \in [\![\tilde{S}_2]\!] \wedge (\tilde{f}_1 \hat{\otimes} \tilde{f}_2)(\alpha) = \beta \wedge \#\alpha/(\hat{Q} \cup \hat{Z}) = \infty$
$$\Rightarrow$$
$$(\tilde{f}_1 \| \tilde{f}_2)(\alpha \frown \beta \frown \alpha')/(O \cup Y \cup X \cup K) = \beta/(O \cup Y \cup X \cup K)$$

then

(4) : $S_1 \otimes S_2 \stackrel{t}{\leadsto} \tilde{S}_1 \otimes \tilde{S}_2.$

Proof. Assume (1), (2), (3). Let $\tilde{f}_1$ and $\tilde{f}_2$ be such that

(5) : $\tilde{f}_1 \in [\![\, \tilde{S}_1 \,]\!]$,
(6) : $\tilde{f}_2 \in [\![\, \tilde{S}_2 \,]\!]$.

(1), (2), (5), (6) imply there are f_1 and f_2 such that

(7) : $f_1 \in [\![\, S_1 \,]\!]$,
(8) : $f_2 \in [\![\, S_2 \,]\!]$,
(9) : $\forall \alpha \in (\tilde{Q} \cup \tilde{X})^\omega : \#\alpha/(\hat{Q} \cup \hat{X}) = \infty \Rightarrow \tilde{f}_1(\alpha)/(O \cup Y) = f_1(\alpha)$,
(10) : $\forall \alpha \in (\tilde{Y} \cup \tilde{Z})^\omega : \#\alpha/(\hat{Y} \cup \hat{Z}) = \infty \Rightarrow \tilde{f}_2(\alpha)/(X \cup K) = f_2(\alpha)$.

It is enough to show that

(11) : $\forall \alpha \in (\tilde{Q} \cup \tilde{Z})^\omega : \#\alpha/(\hat{Q} \cup \hat{Z}) = \infty \Rightarrow$
$\quad\quad (\tilde{f}_1 \otimes \tilde{f}_2)(\alpha)/(O \cup K) = (f_1 \otimes f_2)(\alpha)$.

Given some $\alpha \in (\tilde{Q} \cup \tilde{Z})^\omega$ such that

(12) : $\#\alpha/(\hat{Q} \cup \hat{Z}) = \infty$.

Let $\beta \in (O \cup Y \cup X \cup K)^\omega$ be such that

(13) : $(f_1 \hat{\otimes} f_2)(\alpha) = \beta$.

The monotonicity of $\tilde{f}_1$ and $\tilde{f}_2$ implies there are chains $\tilde{\alpha}, \tilde{\beta}$ such that

(14) : $\tilde{\alpha}_1 = \alpha \frown (\tilde{X} \cup \tilde{Y} \mapsto \epsilon)$,
(15) : $\tilde{\alpha}_{j+1} = \alpha \frown \tilde{\beta}_j$,
(16) : $\tilde{\beta}_j = (\tilde{f}_1 \,\|\, \tilde{f}_2)(\tilde{\alpha}_j)$.

As in the proof of Prop. 1 it follows straightforwardly by induction on j that

(17) : $\tilde{\beta}_j/(O \cup Y \cup X \cup K) \sqsubseteq \beta$.

(17) and the definition of $\sqcup$ imply

(18) : $\sqcup \tilde{\beta}/(O \cup Y \cup X \cup K) \sqsubseteq \beta$.

Since $\tilde{\beta}$ characterizes the Kleene-chain, it also holds that

(19) : $(\tilde{f}_1 \hat{\otimes} \tilde{f}_2)(\alpha) = \sqcup \tilde{\beta}$.

Assume

$(20) : \alpha' \in (\hat{X} \cup \hat{Y})^{\infty}$.

(3), (5), (6), (12), (19), (20) imply

$(21) : (\tilde{f_1} \parallel \tilde{f_2})(\alpha \frown (\sqcup \tilde{\beta}) \frown \alpha')/(O \cup Y \cup X \cup K) = \sqcup \tilde{\beta}/(O \cup Y \cup X \cup K)$.

(9), (10), (12), (20) imply

$(22) : (\tilde{f_1} \parallel \tilde{f_2})(\alpha \frown (\sqcup \tilde{\beta}) \frown \alpha')/(O \cup Y \cup X \cup K) = (f_1 \parallel f_2)(\alpha \frown (\sqcup \tilde{\beta}) \frown \alpha')$.

(20), (21), (22) imply

$(23) : (f_1 \parallel f_2)(\alpha \frown (\sqcup \tilde{\beta}) \frown \alpha') = (f_1 \parallel f_2)(\alpha \frown (\sqcup \tilde{\beta})) = \sqcup \tilde{\beta}/(O \cup Y \cup X \cup K)$.

(13), (18), (23) imply

$(24) : (f_1 \parallel f_2)(\alpha \frown (\sqcup \tilde{\beta})) = (f_1 \hat{\otimes} f_2)(\alpha)$.

(23), (24) imply

$(25) : \sqcup \tilde{\beta}/(O \cup Y \cup X \cup K) = (f_1 \hat{\otimes} f_2)(\alpha)$.

(19), (25) imply

$(26) : (\tilde{f_1} \hat{\otimes} \tilde{f_2})(\alpha)/(O \cup Y \cup X \cup K) = (f_1 \hat{\otimes} f_2)(\alpha)$.

(26) and the fact that $\otimes$ is equal to $\hat{\otimes}$ plus hiding imply (11).

It can be argued that the freedom from deadlock test (3) of Prop. 5 is too strong, because we may find specifications S_1, S_2, $\tilde{S}_1$ and $\tilde{S}_2$ which satisfy (1), (2) and (4), but not (3). For example this is the case if:

$S_1 \stackrel{\text{def}}{=} (\{q\}, \{y\}, y = q)$,
$S_2 \stackrel{\text{def}}{=} (\{y\}, \{k\}, k = y|_{10})$,
$\tilde{S}_1 \stackrel{\text{def}}{=} (\{q, x\}, \{y\}, y \sqsubseteq q \wedge \#y = \min\{\#q, \#x + 1\})$,
$\tilde{S}_2 \stackrel{\text{def}}{=} (\{y\}, \{k, x\}, x = k = y|_{10})$.

However, whenever we run into such a problem, which seems to be a rather artificial one, there are specifications S_1', S_2', $\tilde{S}_1'$, $\tilde{S}_2'$ such that

$$S_1 \otimes S_2 \rightsquigarrow S_1' \otimes S_2', \qquad \tilde{S}_1' \otimes \tilde{S}_2' \rightsquigarrow \tilde{S}_1 \otimes \tilde{S}_2,$$

holds, and

$$S_1' \otimes S_2' \overset{t}{\leadsto} \tilde{S}_1' \otimes \tilde{S}_2'$$

follows by Prop. 5. For example, with respect to our example, this is the case if

$$S_1' \overset{\text{def}}{=} (\{q\}, \{y\}, y = q|_{10}),$$
$$S_2' \overset{\text{def}}{=} S_2,$$
$$\tilde{S}_1' \overset{\text{def}}{=} (\{q, x\}, \{y\}, y \sqsubseteq q \wedge \#y = \min\{\#q|_{10}, \#x + 1\}),$$
$$\tilde{S}_2' \overset{\text{def}}{=} \tilde{S}_2.$$

Thus it is enough to strengthen the specifications in such a way that the communication along the internal channels is halted as soon as the external channels have reached their final value.

Since $\leadsto$ is a special case of $\overset{t}{\leadsto}$ it follows that Prop. 5 is (relative, semantic) complete modulo a (relative, semantic) complete set of rules for behavioral refinement.

Another point to note is that in practice it is normally so that whenever (3) holds we also have that

$$\tilde{f}_1 \in [\![\, \tilde{S}_1 \,]\!] \wedge \tilde{f}_2 \in [\![\, \tilde{S}_2 \,]\!] \wedge (\tilde{f}_1 \,\|\, \tilde{f}_2)(\alpha \frown \beta) = \beta \wedge \alpha/(\hat{Q} \cup \hat{Z}) = \infty$$
$$\Rightarrow$$
$$(\tilde{f}_1 \,\|\, \tilde{f}_2)(\alpha \frown \beta \frown \alpha')/(O \cup Y \cup X \cup K) = \beta/(O \cup Y \cup X \cup K).$$

Thus in order to use Prop. 5 it is in most cases not necessary to characterize the least fix-point solution.

We now generalize Prop. 5 in the same way as Prop. 1 was generalized above. Thus we have a network of n component specifications S_k which are totally refined into n component specifications $\tilde{S}_k$ in accordance with Fig. 6. As before $\tilde{Q}_k$ represents the external input channels, $\tilde{X}_k$ represents the internal input channels, $\tilde{O}_k$ represents the external output channels, and $\tilde{Y}_k$ represents the internal output channels. Moreover, we also have the same constraints as earlier, namely that $\cup_{j=1}^{n} X_j = \cup_{j=1}^{n} Y_j$, that $\cup_{j=1}^{n} \tilde{X}_j = \cup_{j=1}^{n} \tilde{Y}_j$, that the $3 \times n$ sets $\tilde{Q}_k, \tilde{X}_k, \tilde{O}_k$ are all disjoint, that the n sets Y_k are all disjoint, and that $Q_k \subseteq \tilde{Q}_k$, $X_k \subseteq \tilde{X}_k$ etc. In addition, let $\tilde{Q} = \cup_{j=1}^{n} \tilde{Q}_j$, $\tilde{O} = \cup_{j=1}^{n} \tilde{O}_j$, $\tilde{Y} = \cup_{j=1}^{n} \tilde{Y}_j$, $O = \cup_{j=1}^{n} O_j$, $Y = \cup_{j=1}^{n} Y_j$, $\hat{Q} = \cup_{j=1}^{n}(\tilde{Q}_j \setminus Q_j)$, $\hat{X} = \cup_{j=1}^{n}(\tilde{X}_j \setminus X_j)$, $\hat{Y}_k = \tilde{Y}_k \setminus Y_k$.

Proposition 6. *If for any $\alpha \in \tilde{Q}^{\omega}$, $\beta \in (\tilde{O} \cup \tilde{Y})^{\omega}$, $\alpha' \in \hat{X}^{\infty}$*

$$(1): S_j \overset{t}{\leadsto} \tilde{S}_j \qquad 1 \le j \le n,$$

$$(2): \wedge_{j=1}^{n} \tilde{f}_j \in [\![\, \tilde{S}_j \,]\!] \wedge (\hat{\otimes}_{j=1}^{n} \tilde{f}_j)(\alpha) = \beta \wedge \#\alpha/\hat{Q} = \infty$$
$$\Rightarrow$$
$$(\|_{j=1}^{n} \tilde{f}_j)(\alpha \frown \beta \frown \alpha')/(O \cup Y) = \beta/(O \cup Y)$$

then

$$(3) : \otimes_{j=1}^{n} S_j \overset{t}{\leadsto} \otimes_{j=1}^{n} \tilde{S}_j.$$

Proof. Assume (1), (2). Let

$$(4) : \tilde{f}_j \in [\,\tilde{S}_j\,] \qquad 1 \le j \le n.$$

(1), (4) imply there are functions $f_1, \ldots, f_n$ such that

$$(5) : f_j \in [\,S_j\,] \qquad 1 \le j \le n,$$
$$(6) : \forall \alpha \in (\hat{Q}_j \cup \hat{X}_j)^{\omega} :$$
$$\#\alpha/(\hat{Q}_j \cup \hat{X}_j) = \infty \Rightarrow \tilde{f}_j(\alpha)/(O_j \cup Y_j) = f_j(\alpha) \qquad 1 \le j \le n.$$

It is enough to show that

$$(7) : \forall \alpha \in \tilde{Q}^{\omega} : \#\alpha/\hat{Q} = \infty \Rightarrow (\otimes_{j=1}^{n} \tilde{f}_j)(\alpha)/O = (\otimes_{j=1}^{n} f_j)(\alpha).$$

Given some $\alpha \in \tilde{Q}^{\omega}$ such that

$$(8) : \#\alpha/\hat{Q} = \infty.$$

Let $\beta \in (O \cup Y)^{\omega}$ be such that

$$(9) : (\hat{\otimes}_{j=1}^{n} f_j)(\alpha) = \beta.$$

The monotonicity of the functions $\tilde{f}_1, \ldots \tilde{f}_n$ implies there are chains $\tilde{\alpha}, \tilde{\beta}$ such that

$$(10) : \tilde{\alpha}_1 = \alpha \frown (\tilde{Y} \mapsto \epsilon),$$
$$(11) : \tilde{\alpha}_{j+1} = \alpha \frown \tilde{\beta}_j,$$
$$(12) : \tilde{\beta}_j = (\|_{l=1}^{n} \tilde{f}_l)(\tilde{\alpha}_j).$$

As in the proof of Prop. 1 it follows straightforwardly by induction on j that

$$(13) : \tilde{\beta}_j/(O \cup Y) \sqsubseteq \beta.$$

(13) and the definition of $\sqcup$ imply

$$(14) : \sqcup \tilde{\beta}/(O \cup Y) \sqsubseteq \beta.$$

Since $\tilde{\beta}$ characterizes the Kleene-chain, it also holds that

$(15): (\hat{\otimes}_{j=1}^{n} \tilde{f}_j)(\alpha) = \sqcup \tilde{\beta}.$

Assume

$(16): \alpha' \in \hat{X}^{\infty}.$

(2), (4), (8), (15), (16) imply

$(17): (\|_{j=1}^{n} \tilde{f}_j)(\alpha \frown (\sqcup \tilde{\beta}) \frown \alpha')/(O \cup Y) = \sqcup \tilde{\beta}/(O \cup Y).$

(6), (8), (16) imply

$(18): (\|_{j=1}^{n} \tilde{f}_j)(\alpha \frown (\sqcup \tilde{\beta}) \frown \alpha')/(O \cup Y) = (\|_{j=1}^{n} f_j)(\alpha \frown (\sqcup \tilde{\beta}) \frown \alpha').$

(16), (17), (18) imply

$(19): (\|_{j=1}^{n} f_j)(\alpha \frown (\sqcup \tilde{\beta}) \frown \alpha') = (\|_{j=1}^{n} f_j)(\alpha \frown (\sqcup \tilde{\beta})) = \sqcup \tilde{\beta}/(O \cup Y).$

(9), (14), (19) imply

$(20): (\|_{j=1}^{n} f_j)(\alpha \frown (\sqcup \tilde{\beta})) = (\hat{\otimes}_{j=1}^{n} f_j)(\alpha).$

(19), (20) imply

$(21): \sqcup \tilde{\beta}/(O \cup Y) = (\hat{\otimes}_{j=1}^{n} f_j)(\alpha).$

(15), (21) imply

$(22): (\hat{\otimes}_{j=1}^{n} \tilde{f}_j)(\alpha)/(O \cup Y) = (\hat{\otimes}_{j=1}^{n} f_j)(\alpha)$

(22) and the fact that $\otimes$ is equal to $\hat{\otimes}$ plus hiding imply (7).

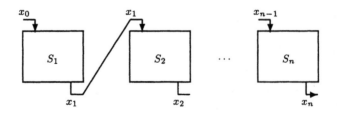

Fig. 7. Asynchronous Network

Example 3. To see how Prop. 6 can be employed in practice, assume we have a network consisting of n specifications composed in sequence as indicated by Fig. 7. The network communicates with its environment via x_0 and x_n. Each specification S_j characterizes a component which applies an operation represented by the function g_j to each message received on x_{j-1} and outputs the result along x_j. This means that the j'th component is required to satisfy the specification

$$S_j \stackrel{\text{def}}{=} (\{x_{j-1}\}, \{x_j\}, x_j = map(x_{j-1}, g_j)),$$

where $map(s, f)$ is equal to the stream we get by applying the function f to each element of the stream s.

Assume we want to implement this network employing some architecture based on hand-shake communication. We then get the network pictured in Fig. 8.

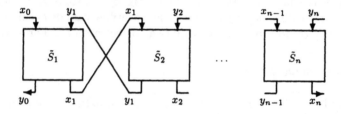

Fig. 8. Synchronous Network

Each of these new components is characterized by

$$\tilde{S}_j \stackrel{\text{def}}{=} (\{x_{j-1}, y_j\}, \{x_j, y_{j-1}\}, \tilde{R}_j),$$

where

$$\tilde{R}_j \stackrel{\text{def}}{=} x_j \sqsubseteq map(x_{j-1}, g_j) \wedge \#x_j = \min\{\#x_{j-1}, \#y_j + 1\} \wedge y_{j-1} = x_j.$$

Clearly

$$S_j \stackrel{t}{\leadsto} \tilde{S}_j \qquad 1 \le j \le n.$$

Since each $\tilde{R}_j$ is deterministic in the sense that for any (x_{j-1}, y_j) there is a unique pair (x_j, y_{j-1}) such that $\tilde{R}_j$ holds, and we have that

$$\#y_n = \infty \wedge (\wedge_{j=1}^n \tilde{R}_j) \Rightarrow \wedge_{j=1}^{n-1} \tilde{R}_j [^{y_j}_{y_j} \frown y_j'] \wedge \tilde{R}_n,$$

where $\tilde{R}_j[^{y_j}_{y_j} \frown y'_j]$ denotes that each occurrence of y_j in $\tilde{R}_j$ is replaced by the expression $y_j \frown y'_j$, it follows by Prop. 6 that

$$\otimes_{j=1}^n S_j \overset{t}{\leadsto} \otimes_{j=1}^n \tilde{S}_j. \qquad (\dagger)$$

This is of course not the only way to synchronize the network pictured in Fig. 7. Assume the architecture chosen for the implementation offers channels which can store up to 100 messages. Given that $//$ is the operator for integer division, we may then redefine the input/output relation of $\tilde{S}_j$ as below:

$$\tilde{R}_j \overset{\text{def}}{=} x_j \sqsubseteq map(x_{j-1}, g_j) \wedge$$
$$\#x_j = \min\{\#x_{j-1}, (\#y_j + 1) \times 100\} \wedge \#y_{j-1} = (\#x_j)//100.$$

Again it follows straightforwardly by Prop. 6 that this is a correct total refinement.

Of course the fact that the network in Fig. 8 is a total refinement of the network in Fig. 7 does not mean that buffer overflow cannot occur. It remains the developer's responsibility to formulate a correct protocol. For example if

$$\tilde{R}_j \overset{\text{def}}{=} x_j = map(x_{j-1}, g_j)$$

then $(\dagger)$ holds although there is no synchronization between the components in $\otimes_{j=1}^n \tilde{S}_j$ — the output along x_j is completely independent of the input along y_j. On the other hand, if

$$\tilde{R}_j \overset{\text{def}}{=} x_j \sqsubseteq map(x_{j-1}, g_j) \wedge \#x_j = \min\{\#x_{j-1}, \#y_j + 1\} \wedge y_{j-1} = x_{j-1},$$

then $(\dagger)$ holds, and buffer overflow cannot occur. However, there is no correct implementation of $\tilde{S}_j$ which requires only a bounded amount of local memory. Thus in this case the buffer overflow problem has been transferred from the channels to the components.

As already pointed out in the introduction, the use of hand-shake communication is not the only way to avoid buffer overflow — another alternative is to synchronize the computation by imposing real-time constraints on the behavior of processes and channels. Since in this paper we use a semantic model without any notation of time, we can obviously not handle this kind of refinement. However, by adding ticks to the streams along the lines of [Par83], [BS94], we believe this type of refinement can be dealt with using ordinary behavioral refinement.

In the untimed case some sort of hand-shake algorithm must be used. As mentioned in the introduction total refinement is not sufficiently general to deal with all sorts of hand-shake protocols. To clearly see the limit of our approach, consider the following example.

Example 4. So far in this paper we have worked in an untyped setting. However, our approach can of course be generalized straightforwardly to handle typed channels, and this will be exploited here. Thus assume each channel is assigned a type, and moreover that the definition of $\overset{t}{\leadsto}$ is modified in the obvious way to take typed channels into account.

In this example, for any set M, we use $M^{\overline{\infty}}$ to denote the set of all infinite streams over M. For any infinite stream s and $k \in \mathsf{N}_+$, we use $s(k)$ to denote the k'th element of s. Finally, the concatenation operator $\frown$ is overloaded to pairs of streams in the obvious point-wise way.

Given the specifications S_1 and S_2 of Ex. 1. Moreover, let $\tilde{S}_1$ and $\tilde{S}_2$ be specifications with the same interfaces as in Ex. 1. Assume $\tilde{S}_1$ and $\tilde{S}_2$ work in a demand-driven fashion, in the sense that whenever $\tilde{S}_2$ is ready to receive a (positive) number of data elements along y it informs $\tilde{S}_1$ about this by sending the corresponding number along x. Thus we assume that the channel x is of type N_+ — the set of positive natural numbers. After having sent a demand $\tilde{S}_2$ waits until the requested number of data elements have been received before it sends a new demand along x. $\tilde{S}_1$, on the other hand, waits until it receives a demand along x, and then outputs the requested number of data elements along y. If the number of data elements demanded by $\tilde{S}_2$ exceeds the number of data elements that is forwarded to $\tilde{S}_1$ by the environment, it outputs what it has received. The input/output relations $\tilde{R}_1$ (of $\tilde{S}_1$) and $\tilde{R}_2$ (of $\tilde{S}_2$) are characterized as below:

$$\tilde{R}_1 \overset{\text{def}}{=} y = g(0)(q, x)$$

where

$n = 0 \Rightarrow$

$\quad g(n)(q, \epsilon) = \epsilon$

$\quad g(n)(q, m \mathbin{\&} x) = g(m)(q, x)$

$n > 0 \Rightarrow$

$\quad g(n)(\epsilon, x) = \epsilon$

$\quad g(n)(a \mathbin{\&} q, x) = a \mathbin{\&} g(n - 1)(q, x)$

$$\tilde{R}_2 \overset{\text{def}}{=} \exists p \in (\mathsf{N}_+)^{\overline{\infty}} : (x, k) = f(0)(p, y)$$

where

$n = 0 \Rightarrow$

$\quad f(n)(\epsilon, y) = (\epsilon, \epsilon)$

$\quad f(n)(m \mathbin{\&} p, y) = (m \mathbin{\&} \epsilon, \epsilon) \frown f(m)(p, y)$

$n > 0 \Rightarrow$

$\quad f(n)(p, \epsilon) = (\epsilon, \epsilon)$

$\quad f(n)(p, a \mathbin{\&} y) = (\epsilon, a \mathbin{\&} \epsilon) \frown f(n - 1)(p, y)$

It follows straightforwardly that $S_1 \overset{t}{\leadsto} \tilde{S}_1$, $S_2 \overset{t}{\leadsto} \tilde{S}_2$. Moreover, it is also clear that

$$S_1 \otimes S_2 \overset{t}{\leadsto} \tilde{S}_1 \otimes \tilde{S}_2. \qquad (\ddagger)$$

If we change the type of the channel x from N_+ to N and also replace N_+ by N in the definition of $\tilde{R}_2$ then $(\ddagger)$ does not hold anymore. For example, p in the definition of $\tilde{R}_2$ may consist of only 0's in which case nothing will be output along k. However, if we add the liveness constraint

$$\forall j \in N_+ : \exists k \in N_+ : k \geq j \wedge p(k) \neq 0,$$

to the definition of $\tilde{R}_2$ then $(\ddagger)$ is valid. Unfortunately,

$$S_1 \overset{t}{\leadsto} \tilde{S}_1.$$

does not hold, because our definition of total refinement does not allow the liveness constraint guaranteed by $\tilde{S}_2$ to be exploited. This clearly points out the limit of our approach: synchronization protocols whose correctness depend upon that the demands (acknowledgments) sent along a channel are fairly distributed over sets of demands (acknowledgments) cannot be handled.

6 Conclusions

Since Kahn's influential paper on the modeling of deterministic data-flow networks was published in 1974 [Kah74], a number of authors have proposed formalisms for the representation of reactive systems based on asynchronous communication via unbounded, directed channels (see for example [Kel78], [BA81], [Par83], [Kok87], [Jon87], [LT87], [BDD+93]). The unboundedness assumption is very useful when specifying and reasoning about systems at an abstract level. However, at some point in a development this assumption must be discharged in the sense that the communication is synchronized in order to avoid channel overflow. The contribution of this paper is the formulation of a refinement relation allowing the transition from unbounded to bounded communication to be conducted in a natural way.

We first proposed a relation for partial correctness — called partial refinement, which then was generalized into a refinement relation for total correctness — called total refinement. Partial refinement guarantees only the preservation of safety properties. To be sure that both safety and liveness properties are preserved, the principle of total refinement is required.

Partial refinement was proved to be reflexive, transitive and a congruence with respect to the composition operator on specifications. It was shown that total refinement characterizes a reflexive and transitive relation, but does not satisfy the congruence property. The problem was found to be that deadlocks can be introduced when feedback loops are added — deadlock in the sense that the least fix-point is reached too early. Nevertheless, we have shown that rules can be formulated which allow for top-down system development in a modular style — modular in the sense that design decisions can be checked at the point in a development where they are made, i.e., on the basis of the component specifications alone, without knowing how they are finally implemented. In addition to the obvious premise that each (concrete) component specification is a total refinement of the corresponding (abstract) component specification, a freedom from deadlock test must be fulfilled.

As already explained (see Ex. 4) the proposed refinement relation is not suited for synchronization protocols whose correctness depend upon that the demands (acknowledgments) sent along a channel are fairly distributed over sets of demands (acknowledgments). Such a protocol is for example proposed in [AvT87].

However, there are several ways of generalizing total refinement. For example, let A be a formula whose free variables are contained in $\tilde{Q} \setminus Q$, we may then define $\overset{A}{\leadsto}$ to be the refinement relation characterized by

$$\forall \tilde{f} \in [\![\ \tilde{S}\ ]\!] : \exists f \in [\![\ S\ ]\!] : \forall \alpha \in \tilde{Q}^\omega : (\alpha/(\tilde{Q} \setminus Q)) \models A \Rightarrow \tilde{f}(\alpha)/O = f(\alpha).$$

This refinement relation seems to be sufficiently general, but leads to more complicated proof obligations based on an assumption/commitment style of reasoning [AL90], [SDW93].

Another approach is to try to combine the ideas of this paper with what [Bro93] calls interface interaction refinement, which can be understood as behavioral refinement modulo two representation specifications allowing also the input and the output histories (including the number of channels and their types) to be refined. When the representation specifications are sufficiently constrained interface interaction refinement is a congruence with respect to the composition operator on specifications [Bro92].

7 Acknowledgments

The author has benefited from discussions with Manfred Broy and Bernhard Schätz. Pierre Collette read an earlier version of this paper and provided valuable comments. The recommendations of the referees led to several improvements.

References

[AL88]   M. Abadi and L. Lamport. The existence of refinement mappings. Technical Report 29, Digital, SRC, Palo Alto, 1988.

[AL90]   M. Abadi and L. Lamport. Composing specifications. Technical Report 66, Digital, SRC, Palo Alto, 1990.

[AS85]   B. Alpern and F. B. Schneider. Defining liveness. *Information Processing Letters*, 21:181–185, 1985.

[AvT87] J. K. Annot and R. A. H. van Twist. A novel deadlock free and starvation free packet switching communication processor. In *Proc. PARLE'87, Lecture Notes in Computer Science 258*, pages 68–85, 1987.

[BA81] J. D. Brock and W. B. Ackermann. Scenarios: A model of non-determinate computation. In *Proc. Formalization of Programming Concepts, Lecture Notes in Computer Science 107*, pages 252–259, 1981.

[BD92] M. Broy and C. Dendorfer. Modelling operating system structures by timed stream processing functions. *Journal of Functional Programming*, 2:1–21, 1992.

[BDD⁺93] M. Broy, F. Dederichs, C. Dendorfer, M. Fuchs, T. F. Gritzner, and R. Weber. The design of distributed systems — an introduction to Focus (revised version). Technical Report SFB 342/2/92 A, Technische Universität München, 1993.

[Bro92] M. Broy. Compositional refinement of interactive systems. Technical Report 89, Digital, SRC, Palo Alto, 1992.

[Bro93] M. Broy. (Inter-) Action refinement: The easy way. In *Proc. Program Design Calculi, Summerschool, Marktoberdorf*, pages 121–158. Springer, 1993.

[BS94] M. Broy and K. Stølen. Specification and refinement of finite dataflow networks — a relational approach. In *Proc. FTRTFT'94, Lecture Notes in Computer Science 863*, pages 247–267, 1994.

[HJH90] J. He, M. Josephs, and C. A. R Hoare. A theory of synchrony and asynchrony. In *Proc. IFIP WG 2.2/2.3 Working Conference on Programming Concepts and Methods*, pages 459–478, 1990.

[Hoa72] C. A. R. Hoare. Proof of correctness of data representations. *Acta Informatica*, 1:271–282, 1972.

[Jon87] B. Jonsson. *Compositional Verification of Distributed Systems*. PhD thesis, Uppsala University, 1987.

[Kah74] G. Kahn. The semantics of a simple language for parallel programming. In *Proc. Information Processing 74*, pages 471–475. North-Holland, 1974.

[Kel78] R. M. Keller. Denotational models for parallel programs with indeterminate operators. In *Proc. Formal Description of Programming Concepts*, pages 337–366. North-Holland, 1978.

[Kok87] J. N. Kok. A fully abstract semantics for data flow nets. In *Proc. PARLE'87, Lecture Notes in Computer Science 259*, pages 351–368, 1987.

[LT87] N. Lynch and M. R. Tuttle. Hierarchical correctness proofs for distributed algorithms. In *Proc. 6th Annual ACM Symposium on Principles of Distributed Computing*, pages 137–151, 1987.

[OG76] S. Owicki and D. Gries. An axiomatic proof technique for parallel programs. *Acta Informatica*, 6:319–340, 1976.

[Par83] D. Park. The "fairness" problem and nondeterministic computing networks. In *Proc. 4th Foundations of Computer Science, Mathematical Centre Tracts 159*, pages 133–161. Mathematisch Centrum Amsterdam, 1983.

[PJ91] P. K. Pandya and M. Joseph. P-A logic — a compositional proof system for distributed programs. *Distributed Computing*, 5:37–54, 1991.

[SDW93] K. Stølen, F. Dederichs, and R. Weber. Assumption/commitment rules for networks of asynchronously communicating agents. Technical Report SFB 342/2/93 A, Technische Universität München, 1993. To appear in Formal Aspects of Computing.

[Stø91] K. Stølen. A method for the development of totally correct shared-state parallel programs. In *Proc. CONCUR'91, Lecture Notes in Computer Science 527*, pages 510–525, 1991.

ImpUNITY:
UNITY with procedures and local variables

Rob T. Udink * & Joost N. Kok

Department of Computer Science, Utrecht University,
P.O. Box 80089, 3508 TB Utrecht, The Netherlands.
Email rob@cs.ruu.nl.

Abstract. In this paper we present the ImpUNITY framework, a framework that supports the development of parallel and distributed programs from specification to implementation in a stepwise manner. The ImpUNITY framework is an extension of UNITY, as introduced by Chandy and Misra, with features of the Action System formalism of Back and Kurki-Suonio. Due to this extension, the ImpUNITY framework is more suitable for the *implementation* phase of the develop process. It supports local variables and (remote) procedure calls. has a UNITY like temporal logic.

1 Introduction

The UNITY framework, as introduced by Chandy and Misra [CM88], supports the idea of stepwise refinement of specifications. The framework consists of a programming language and a programming logic. The logic is based on a small set of temporal properties for describing specifications. The UNITY approach is to refine specifications towards a specific architecture until a program can be derived easily. Case studies show that the method is useful for deriving parallel and distributed algorithms [CM88]. However, it is not always easy to deal with low-level implementation details at the level of specifications. In this stage of the development process, program refinement seems to be preferable to refinement of specifications. Program refinement consists of program transformations that preserve semantic properties of the programs. The standard UNITY framework does not support program refinement, but several proposals have been put forward. Sanders [San90] defines program refinement as a syntactic notion on programs and identifies the (adjusted) UNITY properties that are preserved by a specific refinement. Singh [Sin93] defines program refinement as the preservation of unless, leadsto and fixed-point properties of a program and gives a number of program transformation rules that satisfy this criterion. In [UHK94], the latter approach is modified to obtain a compositional notion of program refinement that can handle local variables. In this paper, we propose an extension

---

* This research has been supported by the Foundation for Computer Science in the Netherlands SION under project 612-317-107.

of this approach that deals with different kinds of variables and with procedures. We also present a number of refinement rules.

The Action System framework [BKS83, Bac90] supports the refinement of parallel and distributed programs. It is based on Back's Refinement Calculus [Bac93], which was originally built for the preservation of total correctness. By modeling reactive systems as sequential programs and by using data refinement, the Refinement Calculus can be used for the refinement of reactive systems [Bac90]. In [BS94], (remote) procedures are added to this framework to model synchronous communication. Refinement corresponds to the reduction of behaviors of a program and preserves all temporal properties. However, the framework does not support temporal reasoning about programs.

The ImpUNITY framework combines UNITY and Action Systems in such a way that it supports a modular way of program design. Like UNITY, it consists of a programming language and a programming logic. ImpUNITY programs are similar to Action Systems: a program can have local variables, and statements in a program may be nondeterministic and may contain (remote) procedure calls. The notion of fairness of a program execution is taken from UNITY. The ImpUNITY logic is a generalization of the UNITY logic to support the extra features of ImpUNITY programs. It is an extension of the compositional logic presented in [UHK94], which, as a generalization of the logic of Sanders [San91], takes invariant of programs in a context into account. In this way, the UNITY union theorem (giving a way to derive properties of a composed program from properties of its components) is still valid. In this paper, we define program refinement as preservation of all properties in any context. By definition, this results in a compositional notion of refinement. This notion is supported by a small set of transformation rules that are flexible enough to do interesting program refinements, and we show their power by a small case study. This case study deals with the implementation of a buffer program by two buffers. It shows that atomicity of statements can be refined as long as it deals with progress on local variables. A more complex case study is given in [UK94]. This paper extends the work of [UHK94] in two ways. We deal with more kinds of variables, and we introduce procedure calls in the programming language and we give a number of refinement rules.

Section 2 defines some domains and gives an overview of the command language that we use for statement and data refinement. In section 3 we give the ImpUNITY programming language for which the ImpUNITY logic is given in section 4. Section 5 deals with the notion of program refinement. Section 6 gives some program transformation rules, which are used to refine a buffer program in section 7.

2 Command Language

In this section, we give a language for monotonic predicate as presented by Back [Bac93]. We first introduce some semantic domains. Let Var be a set of program variables with typical elements x, y, z and let $X, Y, Z \subseteq Var$ be typical sets of variables. We choose a special subset V of Var from which we choose the variables in UNITY programs. A state on X is a function in $X \to Vals$ where $Vals$ is a fixed domain of values, assigning a value to each variable in X. A state space (typical elements σ, τ) is a set of states, and the state space on X, denoted by σ_X, is the set of all functions in $X \to Vals$. For defining predicate transformers, we need the domain $Bool$ of Boolean values. Then, state predicates on σ are elements in the domain $Pred_\sigma = \sigma \to Bool$ and are denoted by p, q, r. State transformers from σ to τ are functions in $(f \in) Oper_{\sigma,\tau} = \sigma \to \tau$. The domain of predicate transformers is $Ptrans_{\sigma,\tau} = Pred_\sigma \to Pred_\tau$, and the monotonic predicate transformers $Mtrans_{\sigma,\tau} = Pred_\sigma \to_m Pred_\tau$.

Back gives a language for describing monotonic predicate transformers, also called commands. A subset of this language is used to denote statements in UNITY programs and another subset for stating data refinement. The syntax of the language is as follows; its semantics in terms of predicate transformers is explained below.

$$A ::= \langle f \rangle \mid [p] \mid \{p\} \mid \bigwedge_{i \in I} A_i \mid \bigvee_{i \in I} A_i \mid A_1; A_2.$$

The language is typed, but we omit the details about the typing. It can be shown [BvW90] that all commands are monotonic predicate transformers and that all monotonic predicate transformers can be generated by this language. A state transformer $f \in \sigma \to \tau$ can be lifted to the update command $\langle f \rangle \in Ptrans_{\tau,\sigma}$ by

$$\langle f \rangle(q)(u) = q(f(u)).$$

So, the update command $\langle f \rangle$ establishes postcondition q for a state u if and only if q holds in $f(u)$. A state predicate p can be lifted to a command as a guard command defined by

$$[p](q) = (p \Rightarrow q),$$

or to an assert command defined by

$$\{p\}(q) = (p \wedge q).$$

From predicate transformers we can build new predicate transformers using demonic composition $\bigwedge$, angelic composition $\bigvee$, and sequential composition ; as follows. For some set I,

$$(\bigwedge_{i \in I} A_i)(q) = \langle \forall i : i \in I : A_i(q) \rangle,$$
$$(\bigvee_{i \in I} A_i)(q) = \langle \exists i : i \in I : A_i(q) \rangle,$$
$$(A_1; A_2)(q) = A_1(A_2(q)).$$

Refinement of commands in the refinement calculus is a direct consequence of the lattice properties of the domains. Domain $Bool$ of boolean values forms a complete boolean lattice which is ordered by the implication ordering. This ordering can be extended pointwise to the domain of predicates. So, for predicates $p, q \in Pred_\sigma$,

$$p \leq q = \langle \forall u : u \in \sigma : p(u) \Rightarrow q(u) \rangle.$$

The ordering on predicate transformers, which is called the refinement ordering, is the pointwise extension of the ordering on predicates: for predicate transformers S and S';

$$S \leq S' = \langle \forall p : p \in Pred_\sigma : S(p) \leq S'(p) \rangle.$$

This notion of refinement corresponds to the reduction of demonic nondeterminism and the increase of termination of commands.

Data refinement is a tool for changing the state space of a program. In its most general form, data refinement is refinement through a command B in the following way:

$$A \leq_B A' = B; A \leq A'; B.$$

In the ImpUNITY framework, we use only a subset of the language for statements. A statement A is a command that is

- terminating: $A(true) = true$,
- non-miraculous: $A(false) = false$, and
- conjunctive: $A\langle \forall i : i \in I : p_i \rangle = \langle \forall i : i \in I : A(p_i) \rangle$.

In the sequel, we use S to denote a typical UNITY statement. In the book [CM88], Chandy and Misra require statements to be deterministic, but we do not impose this restriction.

Although the language of Back is complete, it is convenient to introduce some shorthands.

1. The commands skip, magic, and abort are defined by

$$
\begin{aligned}
skip(p) &= p, \\
magic(p) &= true, \\
abort(p) &= false.
\end{aligned}
$$

Hence, the guard command behaves as *skip* if p holds; otherwise as *magic*. The assert command behaves as *skip* if p holds; otherwise as *abort*.

2. A binary relation on states $R \in \sigma \times \tau \to Bool$ can be lifted to an angelic update command:

$$\{R\}(p)(u) = \langle \exists u' : R(u, u') : p(u') \rangle,$$

or to a demonic update command:

$$[R](p)(u) = \langle \forall u' : R(u, u') : p(u') \rangle.$$

3. The multiple assignment is a special case of the update command. For example, for variables x, y and expressions e_1, e_2 (functions from states to values) the multiple assignment $x, y := e_1, e_2$ is equivalent to $\langle f \rangle$, where f assigns the value of expression e_1 to variables x and the value of e_2 to y.

4. For a command A, command $A^* = \bigwedge_{i \in Nat} A^i$ where $A^0 = skip$, and for $i \in Nat$, $A^{i+1} = A; A^i$.

5. For a command A, and $x \in V$, hiding x in a block construct

$$[\mathbf{v}\,ar\; x := e.\; A]\!]$$

is modeled by $\langle f \rangle; A; \langle g \rangle$ where f introduces variable x in the state space and assigns to it its initial value: $f(u)(x) = e(u)$ and $f(u)(y) = u(y)$ for all other variables y in X. After execution of A, $\langle g \rangle$ removes variable x from the state space.

6. If demonic composition has only two elements, say A_1 and A_2, then it is often written as $A_1 \wedge A_2$.

7. The **if**-statement

$$
\begin{aligned}
&\mathbf{if}\; p_1 \rightarrow s_1 \\
&\;\|\; p_2 \rightarrow s_2 \\
&\;\|\; \cdots \\
&\mathbf{fi}
\end{aligned}
$$

is an abbreviation for

$$(\bigwedge_{i \in \{1,2,\ldots\}} ([p_i]; s_i)) \wedge [\langle \forall i : i \in \{1, 2, \ldots\} : \neg p_i \rangle].$$

The **if**-statement chooses nondeterministicly one of the branches whose guard evaluates to *true*. If all the guards are *false*, then the statement skips. This is different than the normal **if**-statement, which aborts if no guard is *true*. The **if**-statement is terminating, non miraculous and conjunctive.

8. We use $p \rightarrow S$ as an abbreviation of **if** $p \rightarrow S$ **fi**.

9. For sets of variables X, Y such that $Y \subseteq X$, and for a predicate p on σ_X, the predicate transformer $\downarrow_Y$ is defined by

$$\downarrow_Y = [R],$$

where

$$R(u, v) = \langle \forall y : y \in Y : u(y) = v(y) \rangle.$$

Hence

$$\downarrow_Y (p)(u) = \langle \forall u' : \langle \forall y : y \in Y : u(y) = u'(y) \rangle : p(u') \rangle.$$

So, $\downarrow_Y$ is the predicate transformer that can change the values of all variables outside Y to arbitrary values, and $\downarrow_Y (p)$ is the weakest predicate that implies p and that depends only on variables in Y. The expression $p = \downarrow_Y (p)$ states that p depends only on variables in Y. Universal quantification over the UNITY state space is expressed by $\downarrow_\emptyset (p)$.

3 The ImpUNITY programming language

In this section, we introduce ImpUNITY programs. First, we give an overview of the programming language. Then, we show how programs can be composed by the union operator, which models parallel composition by interleaving of actions. Finally, a subset of the programs is examined that corresponds to closed systems. This subset corresponds to normal UNITY programs.

The ImpUNITY programming language is an extension of the standard UNITY programming language with new sections for hiding parts of the state space and sections for (remote) procedure calls (like Action Systems [BS94]). An ImpUNITY program F consists of the following sections:

- A *shared*-section declaring the set of *shared* variables of the program, i.e., the variables that can be read and written by both the program and its environment. The set is denoted by $shared(F)$ and is a subset of V.
- A *local*-section declaring the set of *local* variables of the program, i.e., the variables that can be read and written by the program itself, but not by the environment. The set is denoted by $local(F)$ and is a subset of V.
- An *output*-section declaring variables that are read and written by the program, but can only be read by the environment. The set is denoted by $output(F)$ and is a subset of V.
- A *read*-section declaring variables that are read and written by the environment, but can only be read by the program. The set is denoted by $read(F)$ and is a subset of V.
- An *import*-section declaring procedures that are imported by the program. Definitions of these procedures must be provided by an environment. A procedure declaration consists of the name of the procedure and the type of its argument. For example,

$$proc \ name(int).$$

  The set of procedure declarations in this section is denoted by $import(F)$.
- An *export*-section defining procedures that are exported by the program. They can be called by both the environment and the program. A procedure definition consists of a procedure declaration, where a name is given to the parameter, and a (terminating, non-miraculous, and conjunctive) statement on the state space of the program extended with the parameter variable. These statements may refer to all these variables, but they cannot change the values of the read variables of the program. For example,

$$proc \ name(a : int) \ = \ x := 3; a := a + 1; y := 3 * a.$$

The *import*-section and the *export*-section are disjoint, i.e., they do not declare procedures with the same name. The set of procedure definitions in this section is denoted by $export(F)$. The set of procedure declarations in this section is denoted by $headers(F)$. For the moment we do not allow recursion in procedures.

458

- A *procs*-section, defining procedures that can be called only by the program itself, not by its environment. This section is only used for abbreviation and does not play a significant role in program refinement. All programs can be written without using local procedures. The set of procedure definitions in this section is denoted by *procs(F)*. The names of the procedures declared in this section must be different from the names of the procedures declared in the *import*-section and the *export*-section.
- An *initially*-section containing a state predicate giving the set of initial states. When no *initially*-section is mentioned, *init(F) = true* is assumed.
- An *assign*-section containing a finite set of statements on the program variables. These statements may contain procedures calls to procedures mentioned in the *export, import,* and *procs*-sections. A call consists of the name of the procedure and an expression (a function on the state space) of the proper type. For a procedure

$$proc \ d(a : int) \ = \ S,$$

a call $d(e)$ is equivalent to execution of the statement

$$[\textbf{var} \ a = e. \ S].$$

So, if the procedure definition is known, a call to the procedure can be resolved by substituting the call by its corresponding statement. In a program, this can be done for all calls to procedures defined in the *export* and *procs*-sections. Calls to procedures in the *import*-section can be resolved only by composing the program with an environment that exports the procedure. Statements in the *assign*-section must be terminating, non-miraculous, and conjunctive. For statements containing calls to import-procedures this can be derived from the fact that bodies of procedures are terminating, non-miraculous, and conjunctive.

Statements are separated by a ⟦, and a UNITY way of quantification is sometimes used. The set of statements in the *assign*-section is denoted by *assign(F)*.

If a section of a ImpUNITY program is empty, then the program section is not mentioned explicitly. ImpUNITY programs are meant to be composed with an environment, i.e., other ImpUNITY programs. The environment provides imported procedures, calls exported procedures, and changes shared and input variables. Together with an environment, a program can form a closed system that can be seen as a standard UNITY program (see section 3.2). Execution of a program F in a context starts in a state satisfying the *initially*-sections of F and its environment. In each step, either the environment performs an action (which may call procedures of F) or an arbitrary statement of F is executed. An execution may reach a fixed point, but it never terminates. There is a fairness constraint that every statement of F is executed infinitely often. An example of a ImpUNITY program is the following buffer program:

```
Program Buf
  local in, b
  output out
  export
    proc put(a : int)  =  in := in ++[a]
  ▯ proc get()  =  out, b := b, ⊥
    init in = [ ], b = ⊥, out = ⊥
    assign b = ⊥ ∧ in ≠ [ ] → b, in := hd(in), tl(in)
end{Buf}
```

The environment communicates with the program by calling procedure *put* when it wants to put an item into the buffer or by calling procedure *get* when it wants to read an item from the buffer. On a *get*, the value is shown in output variables *out*. The buffer acts rather slowly in the sense that items in the buffer are not ready for output immediately. If no item is available, *out* is set to ⊥. It can take some time before items become available, which is taken care of by the statement in the *assign*-section of the program. Due to the fairness constraint, every item in the buffer becomes available if it is requested.

3.1   Program Union

The ImpUNITY extensions deals composition of programs. When we compose programs, we have to take these concepts into account. Therefore, we redefine the notion of program composition. First, we define when two programs can be composed.

Definition 1. Let F, H be ImpUNITY programs. Program H is an environment of F iff

$$local(F) \cap variables(H)\ = \emptyset,$$
$$output(F) \cap variables(H) \subseteq read(H).$$

The first item in the definition says that H does not refer to the local variables of F. The second item states that H may only read the output variables of F. Note that this definition is not symmetric.

Now we can define program union.

Definition 2. For ImpUNITY programs F, H that are environments of each other, the union of F and H, denoted by $F\,\|\,H$, consists of the following sections:

$$
\begin{aligned}
shared(F\|G) &= (shared(F) \cup shared(G)),\\
output(F\|G) &= (output(F) \cup output(G)),\\
local(F\|G) &= (local(F) \cup local(G)),\\
read(F\|G) &= (read(F) \cup read(G))\backslash(shared(F\|G) \cup output(F\|G)),\\
export(F\|G) &= export(F) \cup export(G),\\
import(F\|G) &= (import(F) \cup import(G))\backslash(headers(F) \cup headers(G)),\\
init(F\|G) &= init(F) \wedge init(G),\\
assign(F\|G) &= assign(F) \cup assign(G).
\end{aligned}
$$

As in the definition of the union of normal UNITY programs, the *assign*-section of a union consists of the union of the *assign*-sections of both components, which models parallelism as interleaving of actions, and the *initially*-section is the conjunction of the *initially*-sections of both components. The *export*-section of the union consists of procedures that are exported by one of the programs. The *import*-section gives the set of procedures that need to be imported from the environment, so for the union this is the set of procedures that are imported by one of the components minus the procedures exported by the other component. The *shared*, *output*, and *local*-section of the composition are the union of the corresponding sections of the components. The *read*-section consists of the read variables of both programs, minus the variables written by one of the programs.

3.2 Closed ImpUNITY programs are UNITY programs

Above, we have given an extension of the standard UNITY framework. The extension gives more structure to program composition. However, these extensions are only important when programs are viewed as open systems that must be composed with other programs.

A closed system runs in isolation and does not communicate with an environment; it can only be observed. This means that the program does not have shared variables, it does not call external procedures and its exported procedures are not called an environment.

Definition 3. ImpUNITY program F is a closed program iff $shared(F) = \emptyset$, $read(F) = \emptyset$, $export(F) = \emptyset$, and $import(F) = \emptyset$.

When the *import*-section of a program is empty, the program can be transformed to a closed program in the following way.

Definition 4. For a ImpUNITY program F with $import(F) = \emptyset$, the closed program $\widehat{F}$ is defined by

$$
\begin{aligned}
output(\widehat{F}) &= shared(F) \cup output(F) \cup read(F), \\
local(\widehat{F}) &= local(F), \\
procs(\widehat{F}) &= ext(F) \cup procs(F), \\
init(\widehat{F}) &= init(F), \\
assign(\widehat{F}) &= assign(F).
\end{aligned}
$$

The *procs*-section can be removed resolving all procedures calls to procedures in this section. In that case, a normal UNITY program is obtained with the only difference that a part of the state space is invisible. This fact will play an important role in section 5, which deals with refinement.

4 The ImpUNITY logic

For reasoning about UNITY programs and for the formulation of specifications, Chandy and Misra gave a nice and simple (temporal) logic [CM88] based on three temporal properties: unless, ensures and leadsto. First, we give an overview of this logic. Then, we give a modified logic of Sanders in which properties are modified for reasoning about programs as closed systems. The ImpUNITY logic is a logic between these two alternatives. We will introduce this logic in two steps. First, Sanders's logic is generalized; then, a new progress property is introduced.

The UNITY properties are attached to an entire program and are defined in terms of the *assign*-section of the program. In contrast to UNITY programs, the statements in the *assign*-section of an ImpUNITY program may contain procedure calls. Since the bodies of the procedures in the *procs*-section are known, these calls cause no problem. However, bodies of imported procedures are not known, but due to the way programs are composed, an upper bound of a call can be given. A call $d(e)$ to a procedure of $import(F)$ does not change the local variables and the output variables of F. So, letting Z be the complement of $local(F) \cup output(F)$ in the set of variables, we know that $\downarrow_Z$ is refined by $d(e)$. So, if we replace procedure calls by $\downarrow_Z$, we can check whether properties hold. Because we introduce more logics later, we subscript the properties by CM.

Definition 5. (Chandy-Misra Logic) Let p, q be arbitrary state predicates and F an ImpUNITY program. Define the following properties of F by

1. unless property:

$$p \; unless_{CM} \; q \; \textbf{in} \; F \; = \; \langle \forall S : S \in F : \downarrow_\emptyset ((p \wedge \neg q) \Rightarrow S(p \vee q)) \rangle.$$

2. ensures property:

$$p \; ensures_{CM} \; q \; \textbf{in} \; F \; = \; \begin{array}{l} p \; unless_{CM} \; q \; \textbf{in} \; F \\ \wedge \; \langle \exists S : S \in F : \downarrow_\emptyset ((p \wedge \neg q) \Rightarrow S(q)) \rangle. \end{array}$$

3. leadsto property: $\mapsto$ is defined as the smallest binary relation *Prop* between predicates satisfying the following conditions:
   (a) $p \; Prop \; q \; \textbf{in} \; F \supseteq p \; ensures_{CM} \; q \; \textbf{in} \; F$,
   (b) *Prop* is transitive,
   (c) if, for any set W, $\langle \forall m : m \in W : p_m \; Prop \; q \; \textbf{in} \; F \rangle$
       then $\langle \exists m : m \in W : p_m \rangle \; Prop \; q \; \textbf{in} \; F$.

Using these properties other properties can be defined, for example,

$$
\begin{array}{ll}
stable_{CM} \; p \; \textbf{in} \; F & = \; p \; unless_{CM} \; false \; \textbf{in} \; F, \\
invariant_{CM} \; p \; \textbf{in} \; F & = \; ((init(F) \Rightarrow p) \wedge stable_{CM} \; p \; \textbf{in} \; F), \\
p \; until_{CM} \; q \; \textbf{in} \; F & = \; (p \; unless_{CM} \; q \; \textbf{in} \; F \wedge p \mapsto_{CM} q \; \textbf{in} \; F).
\end{array}
$$

Sanders [San91] gave a modification of the UNITY logic for reasoning about programs as closed systems. For closed systems, some states are not reachable by the program, and this can be coded into the properties by taking the invariants of the program into account. A characterization of this logic is given by the following definition. We use the subscript S for properties in this logic.

Definition 6. For an ImpUNITY program F and predicates p, q, properties of F are defined by

$$p \; unless_S \; q \; \textbf{in} \; F \; = \; \langle \exists r : invariant_{CM} \; r \; \textbf{in} \; F : (r \wedge p) \; unless_{CM} \; q \; \textbf{in} \; F \rangle,$$
$$p \; ensures_S \; q \; \textbf{in} \; F \; = \; \langle \exists r : invariant_{CM} \; r \; \textbf{in} \; F : (r \wedge p) \; ensures_{CM} \; q \; \textbf{in} \; F \rangle,$$
$$p \mapsto_S q \; \textbf{in} \; F \; = \; \langle \exists r : invariant_{CM} \; r \; \textbf{in} \; F : (r \wedge p) \mapsto_{CM} q \; \textbf{in} \; F \rangle.$$

Properties $stable_S$, $invariant_S$ and $until_S$ can be defined in a similar way using the new properties.

In Sanders's logic, properties are restricted to the reachable states of the program, since the set of reachable states of a program is its strongest invariant. This restriction has three important consequences. Firstly, the properties are weaker than the Chandy and Misra properties. Secondly, the substitution principle holds: if $invariant_S$ ($e_1 = e_2$), then e_1 may be substituted for e_2 in every property of the program. Thirdly, as shown in [Pac92], for the Sanders logic the interpretation of the properties can be given in terms of stutter-free execution sequences:

1. $p \; unless_S \; q$ **in** F holds if and only if for every state in every execution sequence of $\widehat{F}$, if $p \wedge \neg q$ holds then $p \vee q$ holds in the next state.
2. $p \mapsto_S q$ **in** F holds if and only if whenever p holds, q will hold later on in every execution sequence of $\widehat{F}$.

The original logic of Chandy and Misra can be used to reason about open systems. The modified logic of Sanders is meant for reasoning about closed programs. ImpUNITY programs are intended to be open systems. Program composition has more structure than in the standard framework: parts of ImpUNITY programs are local and cannot interfere with an environment. We follow the ideas of [UHK94], but we are now in a more complicated situation because ImpUNITY programs support more kinds of variables and also a procedure mechanism. We generalize properties using the localities of variables. Instead of using invariants of the program itself, we use invariants of programs in a context. Such invariants are called local invariants.

Definition 7. For ImpUNITY program F, the local invariant is defined by

$$linvariant_* \; r \; \textbf{in} \; F \; = \; \langle \forall H :: invariant_{CM} \; r \; \textbf{in} \; F [\![H \rangle.$$

For normal UNITY programs, $true$ is the only local invariant, since H can make any transition. However, in the ImpUNITY framework, programs and program union have more structure. The environment can interfere by executing its actions, which may call exported procedures. We can estimate this behavior in the following way. The environment can call all procedures of F with any parameter. Therefore, let $\bigwedge export(F)$ be the nondeterministic choice between all possible calls: $\bigwedge export(F) = \bigwedge_{d \in export(F)}(\bigwedge_e d(e))$. Moreover, the environment respects the *local* and *output*-section of F but can change all other variables (Z is the complement of $output(F) \cup local(F))$ in any way. Then, $ext(F)$ is a demonic choice of all finite sequences of possible steps of the environment:

$$ext(F) = (\downarrow_Z \wedge (\bigwedge export(F)))^*.$$

So, $ext(F)$ is the transitive closure of all steps of the environment and is defined in such a way that every statement of the environment is a refinement of $ext(F)$. This is exploited in the following lemma for the calculation of local invariants.

Lemma 8. *For ImpUNITY program F and predicate r,*

$$linvariant_* \ r \ \textbf{in} \ F \Leftarrow invariant_{CM} \ r \ \textbf{in} \ F \wedge \downarrow_\emptyset \ (r \Rightarrow ext(F)(r)).$$

By using local invariants instead of normal invariants, properties can be defined without losing compositionality. This is done in the next definition where we subscript these new properties by $*$.

Definition 9. For ImpUNITY program F, properties of F are defined by

$$
\begin{aligned}
p \ unless_* \ q \ \textbf{in} \ F &= \langle \exists r : linvariant_* \ r \ \textbf{in} \ F : (p \wedge r) \ unless_{CM} \ q \ \textbf{in} \ F \rangle, \\
p \ ensures_* \ q \ \textbf{in} \ F &= \langle \exists r : linvariant_* \ r \ \textbf{in} \ F : (p \wedge r) \ ensures_{CM} \ q \ \textbf{in} \ F \rangle, \\
p \mapsto_* q \ \textbf{in} \ F &= \langle \exists r : linvariant_* \ r \ \textbf{in} \ F : (p \wedge r) \mapsto_{CM} q \ \textbf{in} \ F \rangle.
\end{aligned}
$$

Again, properties $stable_*$, $invariant_*$ and $until_*$ can be defined using the new properties.

For a closed program, the definition gives the logic of Sanders. If the environment may interfere freely, i.e., if all variables of the program are shared variables, no local invariant can be obtained, and definition 9 yields the standard UNITY logic.

The properties defined above are UNITY-like properties in the way that they can be used in a similar way as the standard UNITY properties. All theorems derived in [CM88] for properties of a single program also hold for subscripted properties. However, the union theorem is slightly weaker:

Lemma 10. *For ImpUNITY programs F, H, and predicates p, q,*

$$
\begin{aligned}
p \ unless_* \ q \ \textbf{in} \ F[\![H \Leftarrow p \ unless_* \ q \ \textbf{in} \ F \wedge p \ unless_* \ q \ \textbf{in} \ H, \\
p \ ensures_* \ q \ \textbf{in} \ F[\![H \Leftarrow p \ ensures_* \ q \ \textbf{in} \ F \wedge p \ unless_* \ q \ \textbf{in} \ H.
\end{aligned}
$$

To get a feeling for the new properties, consider the following program.

```
Program F
  shared x
  local y
  init x = 0, y = 0
  assign y := y + 1
      [] y < 0 → x := -1
      [] x < 0 → x := 1
end{F}
```

When F runs in isolation, it does not change the value of x. This is expressed in Sanders's logic by $stable_S \, x \geq 0$ **in** F and $stable_S \, x \leq 0$ **in** F. These properties can be proven using the invariant: $invariant_{CM} \, y > 0 \wedge x = 0$ **in** F. In the standard logic, which assumes that the environment can interfere freely, neither $stable_{CM} \, x \geq 0$ **in** F nor $stable_{CM} \, x \leq 0$ **in** F hold, since F can set x to both 1 and -1 in a context that can change y. Taking into account the restriction of the environment, y will always be at least zero. Consequently, property $linvariant_* \, y \geq 0$ **in** F holds and F cannot set x to -1, but it can set x to 1. So, $stable_* \, x \geq 0$ **in** F holds, but $stable_* \, x \leq 0$ **in** F does not hold.

The logics defined above consist of three properties: the unless property for expressing safety properties and two properties for expressing progress, ensures and leadsto. Let us examine the progress properties more closely. As we have seen before, properties of closed programs in Sanders's logic can be interpreted as temporal properties. In that case, leadsto has a nice temporal interpretation, while ensures is used only for defining leadsto. In the UNITY logic, ensures is more important, since it can be exploited to reason about progress of programs in a composition. This is done by using a union theorem like lemma 10. Now, we defined progress property $\dashrightarrow_*$ for ImpUNITY programs. It is a property between $ensures_*$ and $\mapsto_*$ and can be used for reasoning about progress of components. Like the leadsto property, it is defined as a closure of ensures properties, however, by being more careful in taking the closure, a compositional progress property is obtained. First, we give the definition of $\dashrightarrow_*$. Then, we give a lemma expressing the compositionality of property $\dashrightarrow_*$ and by giving a sketch of the proof of this lemma we motivate and illustrate the definition of $\dashrightarrow_*$.

Definition 11. Let F be an ImpUNITY program. Property $\dashrightarrow_*$ is the smallest relation defined by

1. If $p \, ensures_* \, q$ **in** F, then $p \dashrightarrow_* q$ **in** F.
2. If $p \dashrightarrow_* r \vee q$ **in** F, $r \dashrightarrow_* q$ **in** F and $\Downarrow_\emptyset ((r \wedge \neg q) \Rightarrow ext(F)(\neg p \vee r \vee q))$, then $(p \vee r) \dashrightarrow_* q$ **in** F.
3. If (for any set W) $\langle \forall w : w \in W : p_w \dashrightarrow_* q$ **in** $F \rangle$ and

$$\langle \forall i : i \in W : \Downarrow_\emptyset (p_i \wedge \neg q \Rightarrow ext(F)(\langle \forall w : w \in W : \neg p_w \rangle \vee p_i \vee q)) \rangle,$$

then $\langle \exists w : w \in W : p_w \rangle \dashrightarrow_* q$ **in** F.

At first sight this definition looks complicated, however the complication is not so difficult to deal with. Firstly, in special cases the definition simplifies. Secondly, the property is similar to $ensures_*$, in that all theorems derived in [CM88] for $ensures$ also hold for $\dashrightarrow_*$.

Now examine the extra conditions in the second and third item (or inference rules) of the definition more closely. Recall that the conditions are posed in order to preserve compositionality. In fact, the definition is constructed such that the following lemma holds (compare with lemma 10).

Lemma 12. *For ImpUNITY programs F, G and predicates p, q*

$$p \rightarrow_* q \text{ in } F \| G \Leftarrow p \rightarrow_* q \text{ in } F \wedge p \text{ unless}_* q \text{ in } G.$$

To show the role of the extra conditions, we sketch the inductive proof of this lemma. The base step corresponds to the first item of the definition and follows directly from lemma 10. For the step, we have to examine the last two items of the definition. The second rule is a weak form of transitivity: in some sense it keeps track of the intermediate state, and there is the condition $\downarrow_\emptyset ((r \wedge \neg q) \Rightarrow ext(F)(\neg p \vee r \vee q))$. This condition says that $r \wedge \neg q$ cannot be falsified by the environment, without establishing $\neg(p \wedge r) \vee q$. This implies the following property of the environment: r *unless*$_*$ $\neg(p \vee r) \vee q$ **in** G. Assume $(p \vee r)$ *unless*$_*$ p **in** G. Then we can derive p *unless*$_*$ $(r \vee q)$ **in** G and (by conjunction) p *unless*$_*$ q **in** G. So, by the induction hypothesis and the definition of $\rightarrow_*$, we derive $(p \vee r) \rightarrow_* q$ **in** $F \| G$.

In other words, an environment program for which $(p \vee r)$ *unless*$_*$ q holds cannot disturb the progress expressed by $\rightarrow_*$. This is illustrated by program F given below. Program F, sets x to 0 in two steps. First it sets b to *true* and second it does the job. An environment could prevent F from setting x to 0 by resetting b to *false*. However, since this behavior is forbidden since b is local to F, we can derive: $\neg b$ *ensures*$_*$ $(b \vee x = 0)$, p *ensures*$_*$ $x = 0$ and $\downarrow_\emptyset ((b \wedge x \neq 0) \Rightarrow \downarrow_{\overline{\{b\}}} (b \vee x = 0))$, and consequently *true* $\rightarrow_{\{b\}} x = 0$ **in** F.

The third item gives an inference rule which we call disjunctivity. The condition here, $\langle \forall i : i \in W : \downarrow_\emptyset (p_i \wedge \neg q \Rightarrow ext(F)(\langle \forall w : w \in W : \neg p_w \rangle \vee p_i \vee \neg q))\rangle$, says that $p_i \wedge \neg q$ cannot be falsified by an environment without establishing predicate $\langle \forall w : w \in W : \neg p_w \rangle \vee q$. This corresponds to the property p_i *unless* $\langle \forall w : w \in W : \neg(p_w \vee p_i) \rangle \vee q$ **in** G. Again, by conjunction with $\langle \exists w : w \in W : p_w \rangle$ *unless* q **in** G and the induction hypothesis, we derive $\langle \exists w : w \in W : p_w \rangle \rightarrow_* q$ **in** $F \| G$. This reflects the idea that an environment for which $\langle \exists w : w \in W : p_w \rangle$ *unless*$_*$ q holds cannot disturb progress by flipping between predicates p_i. This is illustrated by program G given below. Since the environment cannot change the value of b, it cannot prevent F from setting x to 0, so *true* $\rightarrow_* x = 0$ **in** G.

Program F	Program G
shared x	**shared** x
local b	**local** b
assign $b := true$	**assign**
$\quad \| \ b \to b, x := false, 0$	$\quad \| \ b \to b, x := false, 0$
end$\{F\}$	$\quad \| \ b \to b, x := true, 0$
	end$\{G\}$

Let us examine our new property more closely. First, property $\rightarrow_*$ is a property between *ensures*$_*$ and *until*$_*$, i.e., $(p$ *ensures*$_*$ q **in** $F) \Rightarrow (p \rightarrow_* q$ **in** $F)$ and $(p \rightarrow_* q$ **in** $F) \Rightarrow (p \mapsto_* q$ **in** $F \wedge p$ *unless*$_*$ q **in** $F)$. Therefore, it can serve as a base for $\mapsto_*$; property $\mapsto_*$ can be defined as a closure of $\rightarrow_*$ properties similar to the definition of $\mapsto_{CM}$ in definition 5. Furthermore, we do not get unexpected results for the well-known cases. For Chandy and Misra's programs, no invariants are taken into account, the condition for transitivity reduces to $\downarrow_{\emptyset} (r \Rightarrow q) \vee \downarrow_{\emptyset} ((p \wedge \neg r) \Rightarrow q)$, and the condition for disjunctivity reduces to (if we take $W = \{1, 2\}$) $\downarrow_{\emptyset} (p_1 \Rightarrow q) \vee \downarrow_{\emptyset} (p_2 \Rightarrow q)$. Then, it can be shown that $\rightarrow_*$ reduces to $ensures_{CM}$, which is the (best) compositional base for leadsto [UK93]. For Sanders's logic, the conditions for transitivity and disjunctivity are always satisfied. Therefore, property $until_S$ is obtained, which is the largest base for $\mapsto_S$ that implies $unless_S$.

5 Program Refinement

In the UNITY framework, a natural notion of program refinement is preservation of properties [Sin93, UK93, UHK94]. We take this notion here with two modifications. Firstly, since we want to have a compositional notion, we define program refinement as preservation of all $unless_S$ and $\mapsto_S$ properties in any context. Secondly, we take into account that part of the state space is not observable. We incorporate this idea in the following definition. We subscript the properties with O (Observable).

Definition 13. For a closed ImpUNITY program F, we define observable properties of F by

$$p \; unless_O \; q \; \textbf{in} \; F \; = \; (\downarrow_{\overline{local(F)}} p) \; unless_S \; (\downarrow_{\overline{local(F)}} q) \; \textbf{in} \; F,$$
$$p \mapsto_O q \; \textbf{in} \; F \; = \; (\downarrow_{\overline{local(F)}} p) \mapsto_S (\downarrow_{\overline{local(F)}} q) \; \textbf{in} \; F.$$

The original UNITY framework was developed for refinement of specifications, that is, a specification of a program is given by a set of properties. This specification is refined by a new specification, using the theorems given in [CM88]. This process is repeated until a program can be derived easily. Like [San90, Sin93, UHK94], we take a different approach, since we are interested in notion of program refinement: program F is refined by G if and only if G satisfies every specification that F satisfies. Since specifications are ImpUNITY properties, program refinement corresponds to preservation of properties. Furthermore, we want to have a compositional notion of refinement, i.c., if F is refined by G, then G behaves the same in any context. We also take observability into account. This results in the following notion of program refinement:

Definition 14. ImpUNITY program F is refined by ImpUNITY program G, denoted $F \sqsubseteq G$, iff for every ImpUNITY program H and all state predicates p, q,

$$p \; unless_O \; q \; \textbf{in} \; F[\![H \Rightarrow p \; unless_O \; q \; \textbf{in} \; G[\![H,$$
$$p \mapsto_O q \; \textbf{in} \; F[\![H \;\; \Rightarrow p \mapsto_O \; q \; \textbf{in} \; G[\![H.$$

This notion of program refinement allows the change of the local state space, if the result is not observable. This change, called data refinement, can be modeled by abstraction commands as in [Wri94].

Definition 15. We say that command A is an $Y \sim Z$ abstraction iff

$$
\begin{aligned}
A(true) &= true, \\
A(\langle \exists w : w \in W : p_w \rangle) &= \langle \exists w : w \in W : A(p_w) \rangle, \\
A(p \wedge \downarrow_{\overline{(Y/Z)}} q) &= A(p) \wedge \downarrow_{\overline{(Y/Z)}} q, \\
A(\downarrow_Y p) &\Rightarrow \downarrow_Z (A(p)).
\end{aligned}
$$

We use $Y \sim Z$ abstraction to replace variables Y/Z by variables Z/Y in an environment that cannot change variables $Y \cap Z$. We require abstraction commands to be disjunctive and terminating and, therefore, only examine forward data refinement [Wri94]. The third requirement states that the abstraction only effects predicates on variables in Y/Z. The last requirement states that the abstraction transformers predicates on the local variables Y to predicates on the new local variables Z.

The following lemma expresses that data refinement is a special case of refinement.

Lemma 16. *Let F, G be ImpUNITY programs without procedures with the same output variables (output$(F) =$ output(G)). Let A be a conjunctive (output$(F) \cup$ local(F)) $\sim$ (output$(F) \cup$ local(G)) abstraction. If*

$$
\begin{aligned}
p \text{ unless}_* \ q \ \textbf{in} \ F &\Rightarrow Ap \text{ unless}_* \ Aq \ \textbf{in} \ G, \\
p \rightarrow_* q \ \textbf{in} \ F &\Rightarrow Ap \rightarrow_* Aq \ \textbf{in} \ G,
\end{aligned}
$$

then $F \sqsubseteq G$.

6   Refinement Rules

In the previous section, we defined refinement as preservation of all observable properties in any context. Often it is difficult and tedious to prove refinement using this definition. In this section, we provide program transformation rules that respect this notion of refinement. With this set of rules it is possible to prove interesting refinements, as shown in the next section. For a Dagstuhl seminar on reactive systems, this framework was used to specify and refine a memory component [UK94].

As shown in the previous section, data refinement is a tool for refinement of programs. In the previous section it was used on the level of properties. Now, we use it on the level of programs. We want to refine statements that may contain calls to procedures of other components. So, the definition of the procedure is unknown. For a component, we do know that an import procedure does not refer to the local variables of the component. The following lemma can be used to refine these procedure calls.

Lemma 17. *For a $Y \sim Z$ abstraction $\langle f \rangle$ and a procedure d not referring to variables in Y, Z,*

$$
d(e) \leq_{\langle f \rangle} d(e \circ f).
$$

Data refinement concerns the modification of local data structures. In an ImpUNITY program, these are referenced only only by statements in the *assign*-section and bodies of procedures in the *export*-section. These sections are modified by the following rule. To preserve fairness properties, statements are refinement independently. The local invariant r is used to

Transformation 18 (Data refinement) *Let F, G be the following programs*

Program F	**Program G**
shared *shared*	**shared** *shared*
output *out*	**output** *out*
read *read*	**read** *read*
local *locF*	**local** *locG*
export	**export**
$\langle i : i \in Exp : exp_i(x_i : T_i) = defF_i \rangle$	$\langle i : i \in Exp : exp_i(x_i : T_i) = defG_i \rangle$
import *imp*	**import** *imp*
init *initF*	**init** *initG*
assign $\langle [\![i : i \in Stats : statF_i \rangle$	**assign** $\langle [\![i : i \in Stats : statG_i \rangle$
end$\{F\}$	$[\![S$
	end$\{G\}$

and let A be a $(out \cup locF) \sim (out \cup locG)$ abstraction such that

- $(A(initF)) \Leftarrow initG$,
- $defF_i \leq_A defG_i$, *for all $i \in Exp$,*
- $statF_i \leq_A statG_i$, *for all $i \in Stat$, and*
- $((\bigwedge_{i \in Stats} statF_i) \wedge skip) \leq_A S$.

Then, F is refined by G.

Proof. Let H be an arbitrary environment solving all import procedures of F. From the first requirement and the fact that α does not change variables of H, we can derive that $\alpha.init(F [\![H) \Leftarrow init(G [\![H)$. Furthermore, for all statements of $F [\![H$ are refined by a corresponding statement of $G [\![H$. The addition of skip-statements preserves all properties. So, all properties are preserved.

A special case of this transformation rule ($A = skip$) is that we may refine statements of the program as long as we do not introduce angelic nondeterminism or miraculous termination.

The structure of the set of statements in the *assign*-section of a program determines the fairness properties of the program. The following rules can be used to change this structure without losing the relevant fairness. The first rule gives a method for combining statements.

Transformation 19 (Combining statements) *Let F be a program such that $\{(p \wedge q_j) \rightarrow S | j \in Statsj\} \subseteq assign(F)$. Let F' be program for which this set of statement is replaced by the statement $(p \wedge \langle \exists j : j \in Statsj : q_j \rangle) \rightarrow S$. Then, $F \sqsubseteq F'$.*

From this rule and the (simple) data refinement rule, we can derive that statements with disjoint guards can replaced by a single if statement. Under certain conditions, a statement can be split into more statements using the following rule.

Transformation 20 (Splitting a statements) *Let the program F such that $p \to S \in assign(F)$. Let F' be like program F except that $\langle [\![j : j \in J : (p \wedge q_j) \to S \rangle$ is substituted for $p \to S$ in the assign section. If*

- $linvariant_* (p \Rightarrow \langle \exists j : j \in J : q_j \rangle)$, *and*
- $q_j \; unless_* \; \neg p$ **in** F, *for* $j \in J$,

then, $F \sqsubseteq F'$.

The last rule gives a way to strengthen the guard of a statement, i.e. the domain on which the statement stutters.

Transformation 21 (Strengthening a guard) *Let the program F such that $p \to S \in assign(F)$. Program F' is the program F with $(p \wedge q) \to S$ substituted for $p \to S$ in the assign section. If*

- $q \; unless_* \; \neg p$ **in** F', *and*
- $p \to_* (q \vee \neg p)$ **in** F',

then, $F \sqsubseteq F'$.

For the rules above it follows that a guard of a statement can also be strengthened with a state predicate q' if a stronger state predicate q exists for which the conditions of the last rule hold.

7 Refining a buffer

In this section, we show how the ImpUNITY framework can be used to refine the buffer program of section 3. By a number of applications of the transformation rules given in the previous section, we transform the buffer program into a program consisting of two buffers. The first step in the process applies data refinement rule 18. We introduce the data structure of a buffer program by splitting input buffer b_i. This variable is implemented by 3 new variables in_2, b_2, in_1:

$$in := in_2 +\!\!+[b_1] +\!\!+ in_1.$$

(we use $in +\!\!+[\bot] = in$) We rename variables b to b_2 and introduce a new variable $nout$ that, for the moment, does not play any role. This results in the following program.

Program *Buf*
  local $in_1, b_1, in_2, b_2, nout$
  output *out*
  export
    proc $put(a : int) = in_1 := in_1 \mathbin{+\!\!+} [a]$
    $\|$ **proc** $get() = out, b_2 := b_2, \bot$
  init $in_1 = [\,], b_1 = \bot, out = \bot, in_2 = [\,], b_2 = \bot, nout = \bot$
  assign $b_1 = \bot \wedge in_1 \neq [\,] \rightarrow b_1, in_1 := hd(in_1), tl(in_1)$
    $\|$ $b_1, nout, in_2 := \bot, b_1, in_2 \mathbin{+\!\!+} [b_1]$
    $\|$ $b_2 = \bot \rightarrow$ **if** $in_2 \neq [\,]$ $\rightarrow b_2, in_2 := hd(in_2), tl(in_2)$
        $\|$ $in_2 = [\,] \wedge b_1 \neq \bot$ $\rightarrow b_2, b_1 := b_1, \bot$
        $\|$ $in_2 = [\,] \wedge b_1 = \bot \wedge in_1 \neq [\,] \rightarrow b_2, in_1 := hd(in_1), tl(in_1)$
      fi

end$\{Buf\}$

The first two statements correspond two *skip* statements under the under our abstraction relation. The last statement of this program takes care of filling variable b_2 with the first value in the input buffer (which is now divided over three variables). We can delay this action until a message is stored in in_2. This is done by strengthening the guard of this statement using transformation 21. This results in the following program, for which the condition

$$b_2 = \bot \wedge in_2 \mathbin{+\!\!+} [b_1] \mathbin{+\!\!+} in_2 \neq [\,] \rightarrow_* b_2 = \bot \wedge in_2 \neq [\,]$$

for strengthening guards holds.

    Program *Buf*
      local $in_1, b_1, in_2, b_2, nout$
      output *out*
      export
        proc $put(a : int) = in_1 := in_1 \mathbin{+\!\!+} [a]$
        $\|$ **proc** $get() = out, b_1 := b_1, \bot$
      init $in_1 = [\,], b_1 = \bot, out = \bot, in_2 = [\,], b_2 = \bot, nout = \bot$
      assign $b_1 = \bot \wedge in_1 \neq [\,] \rightarrow b_1, in_1 := hd(in_1), tl(in_1)$
        $\|$ $b_1, nout, in_2 := \bot, b_1, in_2 \mathbin{+\!\!+} b_1$
        $\|$ $b_2 = \bot \wedge in_2 \neq [\,] \rightarrow b_2, in_2 := hd(in_2), tl(in_2)$
    end$\{Buf\}$

By standard refinement calculus, the body of the second statement can be rewritten to the statement

$$nout, b_1 := b_1, \bot; in_2 := in_2 \mathbin{+\!\!+} nout.$$

Furthermore, we introduce two new procedures:

$$\text{proc } nget() = nout, b_1 := b_1, \bot, \text{ and}$$
$$\text{proc } nput(a : int) = in_2 := in_2 \mathbin{+\!\!+} [a].$$

Then, the second statement can be rewritten as a sequential composition of call to this procedures. This result in the following program.

> **Program** *Buf*
>   **local** in_1, b_1, in_2, b_2, $nout$
>   **output** out
>   **export**
>   **proc** $put(a : int) = in_1 := in_1 \mathbin{+\!\!+} [a]$
> $[\!]$ **proc** $get() = out, b_1 := b_1, \perp$
>   **procs**
>   **proc** $nput(a : int) = in_2 := in_2 \mathbin{+\!\!+} [a]$
> $[\!]$ **proc** $nget() = nout, b_2 := b_2, \perp$
>   **init** $in_1 = [\,], b_1 = \perp, out = \perp, in_2 = [\,], b_2 = \perp, nout = \perp$
>   **assign** $b_1 = \perp \wedge in_1 \neq [\,] \rightarrow b_1, in_1 := hd(in_1), tl(in_1)$
> $[\!]$ $nget(); nput(nout)$
> $[\!]$ $b_2 = \perp \wedge in_2 \neq [\,] \rightarrow b_2, in_2 := hd(in_2), tl(in_2)$
> **end**$\{Buf\}$

Now we can restructure the program *Buf* into three components, $Buf = Buf_1 [\!] Int [\!] Buf_2$, where Buf_1 and Buf_2 are similar (up to renaming of variables) to the buffer program we started with and program *Int* is the program following programs.

> **Program** *Int*
>   **read** $nout$
>   **import**
>   **proc** $nput(a : int)$
> $[\!]$ **proc** $nget()$
>   **assign** $get(); nput(nout)$
> **end**$\{Int\}$

This finishes the derivation that shows ImpUNITY program *Buf* can be implemented as a concatenation of two buffers.

Acknowledgement We would like to thank the anonymous referees for their useful suggestions and numerous comments.

References

[Bac90] R.-J.R. Back. Refinement calculus, part II: Parallel and reactive programs. In J.W. de Bakker, W.-P. de Roever, and G. Rozenberg, editors, *Stepwise Refinement of Distributed Systems: Models, Formalisms, Correctness*, volume 430 of *Lecture Notes in Computer Science*, pages 42–66. Springer-Verlag, 1990.

[Bac93] R.J.R. Back. Refinement calculus, lattices and higher order logic. In M. Broy, editor, *Program Design Calculi*, volume 118 of *Nato ASI Series, Series F*, pages 53–72. Springer-Verlag, 1993.

[BKS83] R.J.R. Back and R. Kurki-Suonio. Decentralization of process nets with centralized control. In *2nd ACM SIGACT-SIGOPS Symp. on Distributed Computing*, pages 131–142. ACM, 1983.

[BS94] R.J.R. Back and K. Sere. Action systems with synchronous communication. In E.-R. Olderog, editor, *Programming Concepts, Methods and Calculi*, volume A-56 of *IFIP Transactions*, pages 107–126. IFIP, Elsevier Science Publishers B.V. (North Holland), June 1994.

[BvW90] R.J.R. Back and J. van Wright. Duality in specification languages: A lattice-theoretical approach. *Acta Informatica*, 27:583–625, 1990.

[CM88] K.M. Chandy and J. Misra. *Parallel Program Design - A Foundation*. Addison-Wesley Publishing Company, Inc., 1988.

[Pac92] J. Pachl. A simple proof of a completeness result for *leads-to* in the UNITY logic. *Information Processing Letters*, 41:35–38, 1992.

[San90] B.A. Sanders. Stepwise refinement of mixed specifications of concurrent programs. In M. Broy and Jones C.B., editors, *Proceedings of the IFIP Working Conference on Programming and Methods*, pages 1–25. Elsevier Science Publishers B.V. (North Holland), May 1990.

[San91] B.A. Sanders. Eliminating the substitution axiom from UNITY logic. *Formal Aspects of Computing*, 3(2):189–205, 1991.

[Sin93] Ambuj K. Singh. Program refinement in fair transition systems. *Acta Informatica*, 30(6):503–535, 1993.

[UHK94] R.T. Udink, T. Herman, and J.N. Kok. Progress for local variables in UNITY. In E.-R. Olderog, editor, *Programming Concepts, Methods and Calculi*, volume A-56 of *IFIP Transactions*, pages 127–146. IFIP, Elseviers Science Publishers B.V. (North Holland), June 1994.

[UK93] R.T. Udink and J.N. Kok. Two fully abstract models for UNITY. In Eike Best, editor, *CONCUR'93, Proceedings of the 4th International Conference on Concurrency Theory*, volume 715 of *Lecture Notes in Computer Science*, pages 339–352. Springer-Verlag, August 1993.

[UK94] R.T. Udink and J.N. Kok. The Dagstuhl specification problem, UNITY-Refinement Calculus. Presentation at the Dagstuhl Seminar on Reactive Systems, September 1994.
http://www.research.digital.com/SRC/personal/Leslie_Lamport/dagstuhl/all.html

[Wri94] J. von Wright. The lattice of data refinement. *Acta Informatica*, 31(2):105–135, 1994.

Springer-Verlag
and the Environment

$\mathbf{W}$e at Springer-Verlag firmly believe that an international science publisher has a special obligation to the environment, and our corporate policies consistently reflect this conviction.

$\mathbf{W}$e also expect our business partners – paper mills, printers, packaging manufacturers, etc. – to commit themselves to using environmentally friendly materials and production processes.

$\mathbf{T}$he paper in this book is made from low- or no-chlorine pulp and is acid free, in conformance with international standards for paper permanency.

Lecture Notes in Computer Science

For information about Vols. 1–871
please contact your bookseller or Springer-Verlag

Vol. 907: T. Ito, A. Yonezawa (Eds.), Theory and Practice of Parallel Programming. Proceedings, 1995. VIII, 485 pages. 1995.

Vol. 908: J. R. Rao Extensions of the UNITY Methodology: Compositionality, Fairness and Probability in Parallelism. XI, 178 pages. 1995.

Vol. 909: H. Comon, J.-P. Jouannaud (Eds.), Term Rewriting. Proceedings, 1993. VIII, 221 pages. 1995.

Vol. 910: A. Podelski (Ed.), Constraint Programming: Basics and Trends. Proceedings, 1995. XI, 315 pages. 1995.

Vol. 911: R. Baeza-Yates, E. Goles, P. V. Poblete (Eds.), LATIN '95: Theoretical Informatics. Proceedings, 1995. IX, 525 pages. 1995.

Vol. 912: N. Lavrac, S. Wrobel (Eds.), Machine Learning: ECML – 95. Proceedings, 1995. XI, 370 pages. 1995. (Subseries LNAI).

Vol. 913: W. Schäfer (Ed.), Software Process Technology. Proceedings, 1995. IX, 261 pages. 1995.

Vol. 914: J. Hsiang (Ed.), Rewriting Techniques and Applications. Proceedings, 1995. XII, 473 pages. 1995.

Vol. 915: P. D. Mosses, M. Nielsen, M. I. Schwartzbach (Eds.), TAPSOFT '95: Theory and Practice of Software Development. Proceedings, 1995. XV, 810 pages. 1995.

Vol. 916: N. R. Adam, B. K. Bhargava, Y. Yesha (Eds.), Digital Libraries. Proceedings, 1994. XIII, 321 pages. 1995.

Vol. 917: J. Pieprzyk, R. Safavi-Naini (Eds.), Advances in Cryptology - ASIACRYPT '94. Proceedings, 1994. XII, 431 pages. 1995.

Vol. 918: P. Baumgartner, R. Hähnle, J. Posegga (Eds.), Theorem Proving with Analytic Tableaux and Related Methods. Proceedings, 1995. X, 352 pages. 1995. (Subseries LNAI).

Vol. 919: B. Hertzberger, G. Serazzi (Eds.), High-Performance Computing and Networking. Proceedings, 1995. XXIV, 957 pages. 1995.

Vol. 920: E. Balas, J. Clausen (Eds.), Integer Programming and Combinatorial Optimization. Proceedings, 1995. IX, 436 pages. 1995.

Vol. 921: L. C. Guillou, J.-J. Quisquater (Eds.), Advances in Cryptology – EUROCRYPT '95. Proceedings, 1995. XIV, 417 pages. 1995.

Vol. 922: H. Dörr, Efficient Graph Rewriting and Its Implementation. IX, 266 pages. 1995.

Vol. 923: M. Meyer (Ed.), Constraint Processing. IV, 289 pages. 1995.

Vol. 924: P. Ciancarini, O. Nierstrasz, A. Yonezawa (Eds.), Object-Based Models and Languages for Concurrent Systems. Proceedings, 1994. VII, 193 pages. 1995.

Vol. 925: J. Jeuring, E. Meijer (Eds.), Advanced Functional Programming. Proceedings, 1995. VII, 331 pages. 1995.

Vol. 926: P. Nesi (Ed.), Objective Software Quality. Proceedings, 1995. VIII, 249 pages. 1995.

Vol. 927: J. Dix, L. Moniz Pereira, T. C. Przymusinski (Eds.), Non-Monotonic Extensions of Logic Programming. Proceedings, 1994. IX, 229 pages. 1995. (Subseries LNAI).

Vol. 928: V.W. Marek, A. Nerode, M. Truszczynski (Eds.), Logic Programming and Nonmonotonic Reasoning. Proceedings, 1995. VIII, 417 pages. 1995. (Subseries LNAI).

Vol. 929: F. Morán, A. Moreno, J.J. Merelo, P. Chacón (Eds.), Advances in Artificial Life. Proceedings, 1995. XIII, 960 pages. 1995 (Subseries LNAI).

Vol. 930: J. Mira, F. Sandoval (Eds.), From Natural to Artificial Neural Computation. Proceedings, 1995. XVIII, 1150 pages. 1995.

Vol. 931: P.J. Braspenning, F. Thuijsman, A.J.M.M. Weijters (Eds.), Artificial Neural Networks. IX, 295 pages. 1995.

Vol. 932: J. Iivari, K. Lyytinen, M. Rossi (Eds.), Advanced Information Systems Engineering. Proceedings, 1995. XI, 388 pages. 1995.

Vol. 933: L. Pacholski, J. Tiuryn (Eds.), Computer Science Logic. Proceedings, 1994. IX, 543 pages. 1995.

Vol. 934: P. Barahona, M. Stefanelli, J. Wyatt (Eds.), Artificial Intelligence in Medicine. Proceedings, 1995. XI, 449 pages. 1995. (Subseries LNAI).

Vol. 935: G. De Michelis, M. Diaz (Eds.), Application and Theory of Petri Nets 1995. Proceedings, 1995. VIII, 511 pages. 1995.

Vol. 936: V.S. Alagar, M. Nivat (Eds.), Algebraic Methodology and Software Technology. Proceedings, 1995. XIV, 591 pages. 1995.

Vol. 937: Z. Galil, E. Ukkonen (Eds.), Combinatorial Pattern Matching. Proceedings, 1995. VIII, 409 pages. 1995.

Vol. 938: K.P. Birman, F. Mattern, A. Schiper (Eds.), Theory and Practice in Distributed Systems. Proceedings,1994. X, 263 pages. 1995.

Vol. 939: P. Wolper (Ed.), Computer Aided Verification. Proceedings, 1995. X, 451 pages. 1995.

Vol. 940: C. Goble, J. Keane (Eds.), Advances in Databases. Proceedings, 1995. X, 277 pages. 1995.

Vol. 941: M. Cadoli, Tractable Reasoning in Artificial Intelligence. XVII, 247 pages. 1995. (Subseries LNAI).

Vol. 942: G. Böckle, Exploitation of Fine-Grain Parallelism. IX, 188 pages. 1995.

Vol. 943: W. Klas, M. Schrefl, Metaclasses and Their Application. IX, 201 pages. 1995.

Vol. 944: Z. Fülöp, F. Gécseg (Eds.), Automata, Languages and Programming. Proceedings, 1995. XIII, 686 pages. 1995.

Vol. 945: B. Bouchon-Meunier, R.R. Yager, L.A. Zadeh (Eds.), Advances in Intelligent Computing - IPMU '94. Proceedings, 1994. XII, 628 pages.1995.

Vol. 946: C. Froidevaux, J. Kohlas (Eds.), Symbolic and Quantitative Approaches to Reasoning and Uncertainty. Proceedings, 1995. X, 420 pages. 1995. (Subseries LNAI).

Vol. 947: B. Möller (Ed.), Mathematics of Program Construction. Proceedings, 1995. VIII, 472 pages. 1995.

Vol. 948: G. Cohen, M. Giusti, T. Mora (Eds.), Applied Algebra, Algebraic Algorithms and Error-Correcting Codes. Proceedings, 1995. XI, 485 pages. 1995.